The Lawyer's Guide to Relocation

FROM FILE TO TRIAL

LINDA D. ELROD

AMERICAN BAR ASSOCIATION
Family Law Section

Cover design by Amanda Fry/ABA Design

The materials contained herein represent the opinions of the authors and/or the editors and should not be construed to be the views or opinions of the law firms or companies that such persons are in partnership with, associated with, or employed by, nor of the American Bar Association or the Family Law Section, unless adopted pursuant to the bylaws of the Association.

Nothing contained in this book is to be considered as the rendering of legal advice for specific cases, and readers are responsible for obtaining such advice from their own legal counsel. This book is intended for educational and informational purposes only.

Printed in the United States of America.

29 28 27 26 25 5 4 3 2 1

A catalog record for this book is available from the Library of Congress.

CONTENTS

PREFACE

The Road Map

The prospective relocation of a parent with a child is a difficult case for the judge, lawyer, and the parties involved. This book provides a guide to lawyers who have clients who anticipate a possible future relocation or who are presently involved in trying to move from a jurisdiction with a minor child. This book explores all aspects of a relocation case from interviewing the client to negotiating long-distance parenting plans and appeals. It includes a discussion of jurisdictional issues, the constitutional right to travel, notice requirements in state statutes, and whether and when a contemplated move is a change of circumstances. If the proposed move is a change of circumstances, then the parties will either mediate or negotiate a revised parenting plan or prepare for the hearing or trial. If the case goes to trial, there are recommendations to focus the court on the most relevant factors for an individual child's relocation and how parenting time, child support and travel costs will change. The book also explores expert testimony on "the best interests" of the child, hearing the voice of a child, parenting plans and social science research of the effects of relocation on children, appeals, and post-relocation parenting. The book also contains a chapter on additional considerations for international relocations and the enforcement of judgments.

Relocation disputes, often perceived to be no-win situations, require careful planning and drafting from the first decisions on parenting time. Family lawyers can help clients prepare to present the best possible relocation case that will ensure that the parents keep in mind their child's best interests.

ACKNOWLEDGMENTS

The Family Law Section publication board asked me to write this book years ago. The book I started back then is not the book I finished. Almost every state, either by statute or appellate case, has changed some aspect of its relocation laws. Changes in what used to be called "custody" and "visitation" have occurred as states have adopted new terminology like "parenting time" and "access." Most states now require the parties to submit parenting plans. Additionally, the increase in the number of mediated agreements with parents choosing joint physical or shared custody has changed the views about one parent being able to change the child's residence. In the past decade, there have been at least four international conferences, including one involving the Hague Conference on Private International Law, because of the Convention on Civil Aspects of International Child Abduction. Many abductions arise after a failed attempt to relocate. There have also been four national attempts to provide more predictability through some type of uniformity of standards. I kept thinking I would finish the book with the "new" standards. None, however, have been successful. At some point, the book just had to get done.

Patience has been a virtue. A special acknowledgment goes to Gail Baker, former and longtime chair of the ABA Family Law Publications Board, who was my original editor and convinced me to write the book. She has supported my efforts, had faith that I would eventually finish the book, and, ironically, was able to edit the last chapter. I also thank Lynne Ustach, former Publications Board member and chair, who read at least two early versions of the incomplete book. I also thank the current Publication's Board chair Joe Booth for his patience and support both with the book and with the Children and Family Law Center at Washburn. I also need to thank my secretary Shirley Jacobson who has been with me since I started the book project. I also need to thank numerous research assistants, including Elizabeth "Liz" Myers '04, Richard Budden '12, Jordan Blair '14, Ashley Green '15, and Kelli Trujillo '21. I thank Kay Rute, who helped edit the final version and Larry Rute and Dr. Bud Dale who gave me notes on a couple of chapters. I also thank the many lawyers, professors, and judges all over the world who work on children's issues and are trying to get children's voices heard, especially in relocation cases.

ABOUT THE AUTHOR

Linda D. Elrod is the Richard S. Righter Distinguished Professor of Law Emerita and former director of the Children and Family Law Center at Washburn University School of Law. Linda retired in June 2024 after 50 years. She was the first woman to receive the William O. Douglas Outstanding Professor Award at Washburn Law School. in 1979. In 2015, Washburn University awarded her the A. Roy Myers Excellence in Research award. In 2025, Linda became the first woman to receive the Kansas Supreme Court Justice Award for "individuals . . . who have contributed significantly to the improvement of justice in Kansas." The award was last given in 2014; Linda was the 18th recipient since it started in 1989.

She has been a Supreme Court certified mediator since 1999, has served as an expert witness in divorce cases, has written amicus briefs in Kansas and U.S. Supreme Court cases, and has served as a consultant for lawyers and judges. She has been a member of the U.S. Secretary of State Legal Adviser's Advisory Committee on Private International Law since 2009. She was an official observer for the International Society of Family Law at the Hague Conference on Private International Law's drafting of the Hague Convention on International Enforcement of Child Support and Other Forms of Family Maintenance in 2007. She served on the governor's and then the Kansas Supreme Court Child Support Advisory Committee from 1984 to 2016.

She is the author of *Kansas Law and Practice: Family Law* (Thomson Reuters 2024) and *Child Custody Practice and Procedure* (Thomson Reuters 2024), and co-author of a textbook *Principles of Family Law* (9th ed. West 2023). She is past chair of the ABA Family Law Section (2000–2001), served on the Family Law Council from

1988 to 2016, was editor in chief of the *Family Law Quarterly* 1992–2016, and remains as editor emeritus on the *FLQ* editorial board. For the Uniform Law Commission, she was reporter for the Uniform Family Law Arbitration Act (2016) and the Uniform Child Abduction Prevention Act (2007); and has been the reporter for the Joint Editorial Board for Uniform Family Law since 2016. She co-chaired the ABA Child Custody & Adoption Pro Bono Project from 2001 to 2008, and served on the ABA Steering Committee on the Unmet Legal Needs of Children from 2002 to 2005. She served as the founder and first president of the Family Law Section of the Kansas Bar Association, as editor of its newsletter, and as secretary-treasurer of the Kansas Bar Association. She was the first female president of the Topeka Bar Association in 1986–1987. In 2021, the Kansas Bar Association gave her its Distinguished Service Award for her 50 years of dedication to educating Kansas lawyers. She received the Chief Justice Kay McFarland Attorney of Achievement Award. She has received Outstanding and Distinguished Service awards from the ABA Family Law Section, Topeka Bar Association, the Kansas Child Support Enforcement Association, the Washburn Law School Association, Washburn Alumni Association, the YWCA Woman of Distinction, and the American Business Women's Woman of Distinction. In 2018, she received a Lifetime Achievement Award from the Washburn Law School Alumni Association.

CHAPTER 1

Relocation: An Overview

> *Relocation cases . . . present some of the knottiest and most disturbing problems that our courts are called upon to resolve. . . . [T]he court must weigh the paramount interests of the child, which may or may not be in irreconcilable conflict with those of one or both of the parents.*[1]

Relocation or "move away" disputes arise when a parent who has primary or shared residency wants to move to a new location, often geographically far away from the other parent. The other parent opposes relocation, not wanting the child, and maybe the other parent, to leave the area. Relocations alter the family dynamics; they can diminish the role of one parent, or force a parent to choose between retaining custody or seeking the benefits of relocation, perhaps with a new spouse or for a new job or family.

The definition of what constitutes a relocation varies. Some states use a geographical distance, or a move to another state or country. Other states consider relocation to be a move of the parent with primary residence of the child, and Florida considers the move of either parent to be a relocation case. The facts determine. Realistically, any move of a substantial distance by either parent, which makes it significantly more difficult for active, involved parents to remain connected to their children and maintain a parenting plan, is a relocation.

Prior to 2010, mothers had sole legal and physical custody close to 90 percent of the time. Courts often allowed a mother to move, presuming what was best for the primary parent was best for the child. The burden was on the nonmoving parent to challenge the move by seeking a change of custody. Even with shared legal decision-making (joint legal custody), parents retained responsibility for the child regardless of the physical custody schedule.

By 2020, however, nearly half of couples negotiated or sought significant shared physical custody time, often up to 50 percent. Many judges now start with shared physical custody as a preference or presumption. These cases pit two competing principles against each other. First, a child has a right to maintain a continuing relationship with both fit parents. Second, when relationships end, especially post-divorce, there should be a clean break. Each parent should be free to begin a new life without unnecessary restrictions, even if the parent is the custodial or residential parent. Absent some agreement by the parties, or the law in a state, generally the nonresidential parent's life choices are not restricted.[2] Recent research highlights that relocation can be difficult and potentially harmful for a child. Residential mobility is a general risk factor for negative long-term adjustment, development, and well-being for children, especially after divorce.[3]

The competing principles for and against relocation and potential harm to a child make it particularly difficult to predict accurately how judges will decide. Relocation cases are also unpredictable because of differences in applicable state statutes, burdens of proof, local rules, and the factors considered. There is literally no limit to the facts that bear on the best interests of the child. Studies reveal that judicial decisions denying or approving relocation are about equal. Attempts to create uniform standards for relocation have been unsuccessful so far.[4]

Historically, American families often moved from one city to another for educational or work opportunities, to be closer to family and support networks, or for new adventures. Over 60 percent of those who move are under age 40, often with young children. One estimate is that within four years of parental separation or divorce, 75 percent of parents with physical residency of children will relocate at least once. Half of them will then move again.[5]

The recession of 2008 caused many to relocate for economic support. In 2010, the five-year move rate was 35.4 percent, with 61 percent staying in the same county.[6] The 2015–16 Census revealed a large decline in relocations, to about 11 percent.[7] COVID-19, however, changed the relocation rate again. About one-fifth of the population relocated, either to move back in with family or to move to less expensive housing due to loss of employment and income.[8] COVID-19 also made it difficult to comply with many parenting plans due to restrictions on travel, quarantine periods, and remote education and working for children and parents. By 2024, life had returned to a new normal, with parents and children resuming their work and school routines and COVID-19 being treated much like the flu, with updated vaccinations.

Moving can be traumatic for adults and children, even when an entire family relocates intact. When the proposed move, however, involves only one parent and child, the potential move can generate conflict where there had been none before or can exacerbate an existing high-conflict situation. Relocation, or move-away, cases present complex, confusing, and sometimes heartbreaking issues. As one court noted, "Parental relocation cases are often wrenching, with weighty competing considerations and a profound impact on both parents and children."[9]

Initial relocation issues can arise between unmarried parents in a parentage action who have a dispute arising over parenting time. When married parents separate or file for divorce, issues often arise because one parent wants to move back to be near family. Because the relocation issue is so intertwined with the residential placement determination, each parent wants to convince the judge that placement with that parent is in the best interests of the child. (See Chapter 4.)

The most common relocation scenario arises post-separation or post-divorce, when there is already a parenting plan or custody order in place. The parent with primary residential placement or joint custody announces an intent to move to a new location that is out of state or a significant distance from the other parent's residence. The parent may have told the other parent informally, given notice as required under state law or the parties' parenting agreement (see Chapter 6), or asked a lawyer to file a motion to modify a parenting plan or custody order. Under most statutes and recent cases, if the parent has a good reason for the move, the question becomes whether the child will be better off remaining with the moving parent in the proposed new geographical location or staying with the nonmoving parent, which may require a legal change of residency. The move of one parent, whether the residential or nonresidential parent, will have a significant impact on the child in most instances. If the moving parent is the parent with whom the child has lived primarily, the move can have a long-term traumatic impact, whether the child moves with the parent or changes residences to the other parent.

Terminology matters and differs from state to state. The definition of what constitutes a "relocation" varies—some states (Michigan) define it by a certain number of miles, others (Wisconsin) by whether it impairs the current parenting schedule, and others (Kansas) just say "any" move.

Terminology also differs as to whether a parent has sole or joint legal custody, parenting time, primary residency, joint physical custody or shared residency, or is a joint managing conservator. The relocating parent is the one who wants to move away with the child. The other parent, called the nonmoving or left-behind parent, wants to prevent the move or, if the move cannot be prevented, change residential custody of the child. The type of parenting time—"sole residency" in one parent with other exercising parenting time or "joint or shared physical residency"—makes a difference in how courts view a relocation request. There are four usual alternative outcomes:

1. The court allows a parent to relocate with the child and a new parenting plan is put in place.
2. The court may disallow the child's relocation; the parent decides not to move without the child and the status quo is preserved.
3. The court may disallow the child's relocation, but the parent decides to move without the child, resulting in primary residency being transferred to the nonmoving parent.
4. The court may allow relocation, the parent moves with the child, and the other parent chooses to also move to the new community.

A fifth possibility, unfortunately, is that one parent retains the child after a visit, or worse unilaterally takes the child to another state or country, which may result in loss of contact between the other parent and child for a long time.

Whereas predicting results in general custody cases is difficult, it is nearly impossible in relocation cases. So much depends upon the judge hearing the case, the perception of the motives of the parents, and the complex relationships of the parents with each other and their child. In addition, more states are recognizing children's rights to have their wishes heard in relocation cases. and in some instances a lawyer or a guardian ad litem may be appointed to the child. (See Chapter 14.) Therefore, the lawyer must begin preparing for the possibility of relocation during initial custody discussions and parenting plan drafting. Relocation cases also require extensive preparation for mediation or negotiation and often result in litigation because a win/win is not always possible.

State Laws Differ

Family law is primarily the law of the 50 individual states and the District of Columbia. The Constitution leaves most domestic relations matters to the states under the Tenth Amendment. With the exception of actions under the International Child Abduction Remedies Act, which implements the Hague Convention on the Civil Aspects of International Child Abduction (see Chapter 15) and federal criminal parental kidnapping statutes, the federal courts do not hear custody and relocation actions. The Parental Kidnapping Prevention Act, 28 U.S.C.A. section 1738A, requires states to give full faith and credit to sister state custody decrees that are made in conformity with its provisions, which are the same principles in the Uniform Child Custody Jurisdiction and Enforcement Act that 49 states use. (See Chapter 3.)

The law in the United States is complex and confusing because the 50 states have taken different, often conflicting, approaches to relocation issues. Thirty-seven states have relocation statutes, but they vary considerably on requirements of notice, burdens of proof,[10] and factors for or against relocation. Some states have a large body of case law; others do not. Within the past decade, several states have amended their statutes or abolished prior precedent in favor of a different approach.[11]

What rules should apply to relocation cases continues to evolve.[12] At one time, several states discouraged relocation by using a rebuttable presumption against relocation. Another group of states favored relocation if the custodial parent demonstrated by a preponderance of the evidence that the move would substantially improve the child's quality of life. The burden then shifted to the nonrelocating parent to establish why relocation would not be in the child's best interests. A few states required the nonrelocating parent to demonstrate harm to the child that outweighs the harm that would be caused by a change in custody. As more states have moved toward a preference for joint physical custody or shared parenting time, the issue of relocation has become even more complex.[13] A few states apply different standards for relocation when there is shared residential custody.[14]

Most recently, the trending view abandons presumptions and requires that each case be analyzed individually, and at great length, to determine what is in the best interest of the child.[15] While at one time courts presumed that the interests of the moving parent and the child were identical, that is no longer the case. As a result, predictions are rarely possible, making it difficult to advise a client as to the outcome of a request to relocate.[16]

While legal standards change and confuse, the mental health community has also failed to reach consensus on what is in the best interests of the child. There is still little empirical social science research to guide judges as to whether relocating or staying is in the best interests of children.[17] There is, however, a growing number of articles by mental health professionals about child custody evaluations in relocation cases.

Public policy considerations in most states include that both parents should share in the rights and duties respecting their children, even after separation.[18] Lawyers must keep current on changes in both statutes and cases in their jurisdictions. In states with no recent relocation cases, case law from other states can provide guidance and persuasive authority, either to fill a void in state law or to help persuade the jurisdiction to change its position, as the New Jersey Supreme Court did in 2017.[19]

Cases Are Fact Specific

Relocation cases are intensely fact-driven and do not lend themselves to comparison. No two cases are the same. Each parent's relationship with the child and with the other parent differs. Parents' reasons for wanting to move or opposing the move are as different as the parties and the relationships involved. One thing is clear, a parent trying to relocate should have a good reason for moving. The moving parent should have thought through the proposed move enough to be able to present specific plans about work, housing, schools, activities, travel, and budgeting. Additionally, the moving parent should have a good track record of cooperating and not thwarting the other parent's relationship with the child.

The nonmoving parent, upset at the change in the status quo and the possibility of losing contact with the child, will try to show that the move is a change of circumstances that requires the court to reconsider physical placement of the child. In some states, any proposed move is a change in circumstances; in others, only a proposed move when parents share custody is a change. (See Chapter 8.) If a change of circumstances is shown, the court will hold a hearing, but even then, states differ on the burden of proof. The nonmoving parent may have the burden of showing that the move is not in the child's best interests. Some courts require the moving party to demonstrate that the move is in the child's best interests or that there is a "real advantage" to the move.[20] The clear trend in the last decade has been for courts to adopt a neutral "best interests" of the child test placing the burden equally on both parents to show that the child's best interests are being served.[21] (See Chapter 9.)

If the court allows a reexamination based on an evaluation of the child's best interests, then the parties can become involved in expensive, emotionally charged and time-consuming litigation. While the goal of family court is to resolve disputes in a just and fair manner with a minimum of cost and delay, relocation cases take up considerable time, and both parties often incur overwhelming financial burdens. The custodial/residential parent's freedom of movement bumps against the nonresidential parent's interest in a continuing relationship with the child. The child also has an interest in a continuing and healthy relationship with both parents. Relocation also affects grandparents, stepparents, stepsiblings, de facto parents, foster parents, friends, and others. The question becomes how to create a workable new arrangement to maintain contact with the important people in a child's life while allowing the adults the freedom to move.

Outcomes of parental relocation requests are difficult to predict. The law of a particular jurisdiction, the unique facts of the case, the way parents present to the court, and the judge's views are key factors. One empirical survey in the United States showed that permissions to relocate were granted in 41 percent of cases and denied in 43 percent of cases, and the issue remanded to the trial court in 16 percent of cases.[22] An Australian survey revealed comparable percentages—about half of removal petitions were granted and about half denied. The outcome of any given case will depend upon the existence of a statute or case precedent making it easy or difficult for a parent to relocate with a child, the type of parenting arrangement that currently exists, and the attitudes of the judge who will be hearing the motion. There are few bright line uniform rules. As the Pennsylvania court stated in 1990:

> Our research has failed to reveal a consistent, universally accepted approach to the question of when a custodial parent may relocate out-of-state over the objection of the non-custodial parent. . . . Across the country, applicable standards remain distressingly disparate.[23]

Even though Pennsylvania has changed its relocation laws since 1990, the court's statement is still true today. The law is still in a state of flux and results are still unpredictable.

Many parents do not seek a judicial resolution because it is too expensive and time-consuming. The children may grow up amid continual litigation. One California relocation case took nine years to resolve.[24] To reduce the uncertainty, lawyers should encourage clients to think about the possibility of relocation at the time of the initial parenting plan. (See Chapter 4.)

Assessing the Chances of Winning a Relocation Case—Questions

The first step in any relocation case is to make a realistic assessment of the case and the client's chances of winning it. The lawyer will need to consider the following:

- Is the request being made at the time of the initial decree? If so, what standard is to be applied?
- Is there an order in place, either temporary or permanent?
- If a permanent order is in place, was it made by agreement or stipulation, after a hearing at which evidence was presented, or by default?
- Are any restrictions on domicile contained in the initial custody order?
    - If so, what does the order or parenting plan require?
    - Notice? How much? How?
    - Alternative dispute resolution mandated? Mediation? Parent coordination?
- How old is the child involved?
    - What year in school?
    - How is the child currently doing with the existing parenting arrangements?
    - Does the child have many friends? Where do they live?
    - In what activities does the child participate?
- How is parenting time designated? Sole or primary residency? Joint legal custody? Joint legal and physical or shared residency? Divided or split custody?
- Regardless of label, what type of parenting is going on? Are the parents engaged in active co-parenting or does one parent have most of the time and responsibility? What is the actual time share? Who shoulders what responsibility?
- Does the state have a statute on relocation?
- Does the statute require notice of intent to move? How much? (See Chapter 6.)

- Is a proposed move a change of circumstances that is sufficient to reopen the custody and residency issues to a de novo determination? (See Chapter 8.)
- Is there a presumption for or against allowing a move? (See Chapter 9.)
- Who has the initial burden of proof?
- What standard will be applied? Best interests of the child or endangerment?
- Is there an emergency justifying a relocation? Drug, alcohol abuse? Domestic or intimate partner violence?
- Is the proposed move within the state? To another state?
- Is the proposed move to another country? If so, has the country adopted the Hague Convention on the Civil Aspects of International Child Abduction? If not, what protections are in place to ensure the child returns to the United States? (See Chapter 15.)
- Why does the parent want to move?
    - o Moving back to family?
    - o Military transfer?
    - o New job?
    - o New spouse or fiancée?
    - o New prospective partner?
    - o Educational opportunities?
    - o Other
- What advantages is the child likely to incur from the move?
- Is it possible to move and maintain the same parenting arrangements?
- Is it likely the court will seek an expert? If a new custody evaluation or parenting assessment is ordered, how will your client fare?
- Is there any history of abuse of either the moving parent or child?
- How close is the relationship between the nonmoving parent and the child?
    - o How important is that relationship developmentally to the child?
    - o Is there extended family in the area?

- If the relocation is to be permitted, how viable are the proposals for contact with the nonmoving parent?
  - o What are the work responsibilities of the nonmoving parent?
  - o Are more summer or vacation times realistic?
  - o What technologies can help?
- Are there viable alternatives to the parents living a long distance apart?
- Can the nonmoving parent also move to the new location?[25]
- Is a move with the primary caregiver the least detrimental alternative?
- Is the moving parent likely to comply with the new arrangements for contact with the nonmoving parent?[26]
  - o Past history of cooperation?
  - o Evidence of willingness to foster relationship with the other parent?
- What are the anticipated living arrangements, including the physical setting, schools, day care?
  - o Will a new stepparent or other parent figure be in the home?
  - o What is the child's relationship with that person?
- What impact will the relocation have on child support?
  - o Can the parties afford the new access arrangements?
  - o Will the moving parent be willing or able to accept less child support to help defray transportation costs?
- What are going to be the likely costs of litigation—both financial and emotional?

The answers to these questions will determine the potential for a successful relocation strategy. To complicate matters further, relocation cases have become part of the "gender" wars as fathers' and mothers' groups, social scientists, mental health professionals, and others weigh in on the topic. See the Bibliography of Relocation Articles at the end of the book. Judges have difficulty deciding these cases because so little is known about what is good for children generally, how to assess the strengths and weaknesses of parent–child relationships in a particular family, and how to predict what impact any decision will have on each member of the family.

The lawyer who represents either a parent who wants to relocate or one who wants to prevent relocation can do much to prepare and educate the client to prevent costly and lengthy litigation. For example, all parenting plans and mediated or negotiated agreements should include provisions as to how the parties wish to address relocation. The lawyer who is appointed to represent a child can help focus the parents on the child's needs and wishes as parents draft new parenting plans.

Endnotes

1. Tropea v. Tropea, 665 N.E.2d 145, 148 (N.Y. 1996).
2. *But see* Brooks v. Brooks, 164 So. 3d 162, 165 (Fla. Dist. Ct. App. 2015) (interpreting the relocation statute to require even a nonresidential parent to seek court permission before changing his residence).
3. Patrick Parkinson, Nicola Taylor, et al., Relocation, Research and Child Custody Disputes in Parenting Plan Evaluations 431, 432 (Leslie Drozd, Michael Saini & Nancy Olesen eds., 2d ed. 2016) (citing studies).
4. The AAML Proposed Model Relocation Act has served as a model for about three or four state statutes; the ABA's Model Standards for Relocation have not been enacted, and the Uniform Law Commission gave up on drafting a Uniform Act on Relocation after one meeting.
5. Sarah L. Gottfried, Note, *Virtual Visitation: The New Wave of Communication Between Children and Noncustodial Parents in Relocation Cases*, 9 Cardozo L.J. 567, 568 (2003).
6. U.S. Census Bureau, Geographical Mobility: 2005 to 2010, Current Population Reports (Dec. 2012).
7. U.S. Census Bureau, Geographical Mobility: 2015 to 2016, Current Population Reports (Nov. 2016) (showing 11.2 percent of the population moved in 2016). The 11 percent is down from 16 percent in earlier years.
8. D'vera Cohn, *About a Fifth of U.S. Adults Moved Due to COVID-19 or Know Someone Who Did*, Pew Rsch. Ctr. (July 6, 2020).
9. Aragon v. Aragon, 511 S.W. 3d 447 (Tenn. 2017).
10. *See* Baxter v. Baxter, 171 So. 3d 1159 (La. App. 4th Cir. 2015) (noting that statute places the burden on the relocating parent to prove that the relocation is made in good faith and in the best interest of the child).
11. Bisbing v. Bisbing, 166 A.3d 1155 (N.J. 2017); Arnott v. Arnott, 293 P.3d 440 (Wyo. 2012) (overruling long-standing precedent).
12. Linda D. Elrod, *National and International Momentum Builds for More Child Focus in Relocation Disputes*, 44 Fam. L.Q. 341 (2010).
13. Brooks v. Brooks, 164 So. 3d 162 (Fla. Dist. Ct. App. 2015).

14. *See* Baird v. Baird, 654 S.W.3d 367 (Ark. Ct. App. 2022) (the presumption in favor of relocation does not apply when parents are sharing equal time); Aragon v. Aragon, 513 S.W.3d 447 (Tenn. 2017) (relocation act applied because father had 80 percent of time with child); *In re* Marriage of Ruff & Worthley, 393 P.3d 859 (Wash. Ct. App. 2017) (Child Relocation Act does not apply where parents had substantially equal parenting time; the modification statute applies.).

15. *See* Tropea v. Tropea, 665 N.E.2d 145, 151 (N.Y. 1996) ("courts should be free to consider and give appropriate weight to all of the factors that may be relevant to" determination of whether the proposed relocation would be in the best interests of the children).

16. *See* Rollie Thompson, *Presumptions, Burdens and Best Interests of the Child in Relocation Law*, 53 Fam. Ct. Rev. 40 (2015) (arguing that presumptions should still apply in some cases to enhance predictability and reduce litigation).

17. *See* Nicola Taylor & Marilyn Freeman, *International Research Evidence on Relocation: Past, Present and Future*, 44 Fam. L.Q. 3317 (2010) (summarizing existing research). For a study on what happens to parents who are not allowed to move, see Patrick Parkinson & Judith Cashmore, *When Mothers Stay: Adjusting to Loss After Relocation Disputes*, 47 Fam. L.Q. 65 (2013).

18. *See* Tex. Fam. Code § 153.001(a): "The public policy of this state is to: assure that children will have frequent and continuing contact with parents who have shown the ability to act in the best interest of the child; provide a safe, stable and nonviolent environment for the child; and encourage parents to share in the rights and duties of raising their child after the parents have separated or dissolved their marriage."

19. Bisbing v. Bisbing, 166 A.3d 1155 (N.J. 2017).

20. There is a lack of consensus about who bears the burden of proof. *See* American Academy of Matrimonial Lawyers, Proposed Model Relocation Act, 15 J. Amer. Acad. of Matrimonial L. 1 (1998) (set out three proposals for burdens).

21. *See* DePrete v. DePrete, 44 A.3d 1260 (R.I. 2012) (best interest paramount; children should stay in Rhode Island). *See also* Linda D. Elrod, *A Move in the Right Direction? Best Interests of the Child Emerging as the Standard in the Relocation Cases*, 3 J. Child Custody 29 (2006). See Chapter 9.

22. Theresa Glennon, *Still Partners? Examining the Consequences of Post-Dissolution Parenting*, 41 Fam. L.Q. 101, 119 (2007).

23. Gruber v. Gruber, 583 A.2d 434, 437 (Pa. Super. Ct. 1990).

24. *In re* Marriage of LaMusga, 88 P.3d 81 (Cal. 2004). *See also* Keven McK. v. Elizabeth A.E., 972 N.Y.S.2d 25 (App. Div. 2013) (reversing trial court's denial of mother's move to Mississippi for job in her field of horse training but the custody and relocation trial was conducted on 13 days over two and a half years).

25. Merle H. Weiner, *Inertia and Inequality: Reconceptualizing Disputes over Parental Relocation*, 40 U.C. Davis L. Rev. 1747 (2007) (suggesting that more courts should look at this factor).

26. Zepeta v. Zepeta, 2001 S.D. 101, 632 N.W.2d 48 (2001).

CHAPTER 2

Opening the File and Ethical Issues

Relocation cases raise both general issues which pertain to any custody representation and specific issues that relate only to the relocation.[1]

A relocation case may start as any other case. Although the lawyer uses the same interviewing and assessment skills,[2] relocation cases are often more complex, expensive, and time-consuming than other cases. The extremely volatile emotions that surround relocation disputes can create ongoing tensions for both parents and children because of the "all or nothing, win or lose" results. Whether the court allows or denies a parent's request to relocate with their child, one parent may be emotionally devastated, and the child may be emotionally harmed. One parent may move with their child, leaving the other parent with less contact; one parent may move without their child, which may emotionally harm the child if the primary relationship is with the moving parent; or a parent may decide not move to try to maintain the status quo and give up on the advantages of a move. One of the lawyer's tasks is to keep the client focused on the child to ensure that whatever the decision, the child suffers the least harm possible.

A relocation case can arise at any time—before a custody order is in place, during a paternity or divorce case, or after the initial custody determination in a modification proceeding. Before a custody order is issued, both parents have equal rights to custody, unless there has been a finding of unfitness. Whether one parent can move with the child before there is a custody order without the other parent's permission depends upon state law.[3]

There is a caveat. If one parent takes the child from the state in which the child has been living for the past six months (the home state), often in an attempt to "relocate" before there is any custody order, the left behind parent has six months to file an action to keep home state jurisdiction. If, however, a parent takes a child out of state with the permission of the other parent and has resided there for longer than six months, the new state may have become the child's home state, unless the absence was a temporary one (see Chapter 3). Also, the court cannot prevent either parent from relocating without taking the child because of the constitutional right to travel.[4] (See Chapter 5.)

If the parents are unmarried and paternity has not been established or is not presumed, there will be no custody order in place and some courts may allow the mother and child to move. If paternity is presumed or has been established by acknowledgment or otherwise, some states give unmarried parents equal custody rights to their child absent a court order to the contrary. Nevada, therefore, found that one parent may not relocate with the child out of state over the other parent's objection without a judicial order authorizing the move. The proper procedure is to file a motion for primary physical custody with a request to relocate.[5] In some states, the mother has sole legal and physical custody, until the father brings an action to establish parentage and parenting time.

If the relocation issue arises at the time of separation, divorce, or original paternity action, most courts use a straight best-interest-of-the-child analysis (see Chapter 4). In more than half the cases, however, the relocation issue arises post-divorce or post initial custody order. In that case, courts may treat the request to relocate as a motion to modify an existing order and parenting plan, which requires a showing of a material and substantial change in circumstances. The case can arise in a couple of ways. The primary residential parent may file a motion with the court that issued the custody determination to allow the relocation and modify the existing parenting plan. Another possibility is the nonrelocating parent, who has just received notice that the other parent wants to move away with the child, may file a motion to modify the existing order, which can include a request for residential restrictions if there are none, a request for an injunction to block the relocation, or a motion to modify the original order to grant primary residency to the nonmoving parent. The allegation in either case is that the relocation is a material or substantial change in circumstances. Whether the proposed relocation constitutes a change may depend on the state statute and whether the parties share legal and physical custody.[6] (See Chapter 8.)

If the court finds the relocation is a change of circumstances, the court will hold a hearing. The parties can present their cases as to why the relocation is in the child's best interests or why a transfer of physical residence to the other parent is in the child's best interests (see Chapter 9). The party must follow the proper procedure, however. An Alaska court found that although the father filed a motion for a preliminary injunction, he did not file a motion to modify custody, which should have accompanied the motion.[7] In a Florida case, where the nonresidential father's relocation with the children was disapproved and he unilaterally moved to Oregon anyway, the statute did not provide for modification of parenting time. The court noted that having chosen to relocate prior to trial and without court permission, the father essentially did so at his own peril as to the impact on his ability to easily exercise his agreed upon time-sharing with the children.[8]

If the person seeking to block the relocation is not covered by the relocation statute, such as a grandparent who has visitation rights, the person may lack standing to bring an action in court. For example, an Arizona court found that its relocation statute was unambiguous and did not apply to grandparent visitation. The mother had relocated to Indiana. The court dismissed the grandmother's action, finding she had no standing to bring an action to prohibit the mother's relocation.[9] The lawyer may suggest that the grandparent try mediation or direct negotiation with the moving parent. If, however, the grandparent has specific visitation rights and times that the relocating parent refuses to honor, the parent can be found in contempt for violating the court order.[10]

Ethical Considerations

Lawyers are bound by the professional ethical rules adopted by the jurisdictions in which they are licensed. Most jurisdictions have adopted rules that are based on the American Bar Association Model Rules of Professional Conduct (ABA Model Rules (2023). The ABA issues Formal Ethics Opinions interpreting the Model Rules and has adopted the ABA Family Law Section's Civility Standards. The American Academy of Matrimonial Lawyers (AAML) has written *Bounds of Advocacy—Goals for Family Lawyers*, which provides specific aspirational rules for family law cases. While only members of the AAML are bound by the *Bounds of Advocacy*, these rules are immensely helpful because they are more tailored to family law situations than the ABA Model Rules. The ABA has adopted more specific standards for lawyers who represent children in abuse and neglect cases or in custody cases and for lawyers who mediate. Each state also has additional ethical rules.

The ABA Model Rules include provisions for competence, diligence, confidentiality, honesty, and fair dealing. Model Rule 2.1 requires a lawyer to exercise independent professional judgment and render candid advice. The lawyer may refer not only to the law but also to other considerations such as moral, economic, social, and political factors.[11] During the course of litigation the lawyer's role may change depending on whether the lawyer is being an advisor, an advocate, a negotiator, an evaluator, an educator, or a communicator.

Establish Relationship

From the first meeting with a potential client, the lawyer tries to create a trust relationship so the client and lawyer can work together. The lawyer should screen for domestic violence as part of the first interview. The lawyer needs to inform the client of the lawyer's philosophy of handling the case (negotiation, settlement if possible) and that other lawyers may have different philosophies. This provides the client with the choice of hiring a lawyer with a compatible philosophy. It also gives the lawyer the chance to weed out a high demand client who may be difficult to work with. The lawyer will have difficulty with the client who wants everything done yesterday, thinks they know as much as the lawyer, has a scorched earth mentality, and lacks empathy. Clients with personality disorders, such as narcissism, paranoid, avoidant, antisocial, and others, can be problem clients, which can lead to burnout.[12] The lawyer can also inform the client that this will be a shared project and the client's input is valued and necessary.

The lawyer must try to discover the relocating client's goals, motivations (reasons for the move), and timelines (school, new job, military transfer). Clients sometimes arrive with preconceived ideas of what they can and cannot do and how fast they can do it. One of the lawyer's first tasks is to demystify the law and educate the client. The person who appears a week before planning to move faces numerous legal and practical obstacles, such as notice to the other parent and time for a response and to schedule a hearing, which often takes a minimum of several months. As a general rule, judges are not sympathetic to emergency motions to relocate, especially if the parent knew about the proposed relocation for a long time. By the same token, many judges have ordered the child back to the jurisdiction if the parent moved without consent of the other parent or court permission.

The lawyer will need to advise the client on what is possible and what is not. The lawyer needs to understand the client's reasons for seeking a relocation, which may range from moving home to getting a new job to a hidden attempt to put miles between the other parent and the child. The lawyer informs the client about the relevant statutes, which may include a specific relocation statute, as well as additional procedures and factors. The lawyer should explain the landmark cases in the jurisdiction that have looked at the types of reasons for relocation the courts have considered valid. The lawyer can also advise the client about the procedural steps that need to be met, such as giving notice of the relocation, filing the proper paperwork, and adhering to the timeline.

The lawyer must candidly advise the client of the law in the jurisdiction and not build up unrealistic expectations for a relocating parent, especially in states with restrictive statutes or cases. Even in states with fairly liberal relocation policies, the judges may not allow *this* move. The lawyer should honestly evaluate the likelihood of success. In most states, outcomes of relocation cases are extremely difficult to predict. Relocation disputes can be expensive, emotionally challenging, and take months, if not years, to resolve. A client needs to know this from the beginning. If simple negotiations do not resolve the issue, the lawyer may want to recommend the parties try mediation as the next step before litigation (see Chapter 10).

Competence

ABA Model Rule 1.1 requires a lawyer to provide competent representation. Competent representation requires the legal knowledge, skill, thoroughness, and preparation *reasonably* necessary for the representation. In all family law cases, the lawyer must know the state's basic family law and procedure. This means statutes, cases, and court rules applicable to temporary orders, custody, and parenting plans. Lawyers need to know the requirements of Uniform Child Custody Jurisdiction and Enforcement Act (UCCJEA) and Parental Kidnapping Prevention Act (PKPA) (see Chapter 3). With a relocation case, the lawyer must know the factors for awarding child custody and residency, creating parenting plans, and understanding standards for modification generally.[13]

Lawyers also must know any additional specific laws applicable in relocation cases. Three-fourths of the states have a separate relocation statute with procedures for notice and objections and factors to judge a child's best interests in evaluating a move. In several states, the judge has to review the general custody factors, as well as additional factors pertaining to the relocation (see Chapter 9). In a modification case, the lawyer may be required to figure out if the general modification of custody judgments, the relocation statutes, or both apply. In several states, different rules apply if there is a primary residential parent than if there is shared physical residency.

Family lawyers should be familiar with the literature on domestic or intimate partner violence—its prevalence, as well as its use as a tool by abusers in custody disputes.[14] There are also brain studies on the harm to children, not only from witnessing domestic violence but also by being in the same place where the violence occurs.[15]

Lawyers need to know about child development and the impact of relocation on children at various ages. For example, relocation of a young child may create a high risk of potential disruption of the attachment relationship.[16] Additionally, very young children are less able than older children to use Zoom, Skype, and other electronic means to maintain contact. Older school-age children can better cope with physical and psychological distance from a parent but may have other adjustment issues. Often relocation cases involve siblings who are at differing stages of development.

Competency, according to Comment 8 to Rule 1.1 also requires that lawyers must stay abreast of the "benefits and risks associated with relevant technology." Additionally, confidentiality issues arise more frequently with some of the new technologies. Competently using technology also means keeping client information confidential. ABA Model Rule 1.6(c) requires a lawyer to make reasonable efforts to ensure that communications with their clients are secure and not subject to inadvertent or unauthorized cybersecurity breaches.

Diligence

ABA Model Rule 1.3 requires a lawyer to act with reasonable diligence and promptness in representing the client. As one court noted, "clients in contested divorce proceedings, especially involving child custody disputes, need expeditious resolution of the issues . . . so they can get on with their lives."[17] In a relocation case, often time is of the essence. A spouse or partner may have already moved, a new job is waiting, or there was a last-minute acceptance to a school or program. Whatever the motivation, usually the relocating parent wants to go as soon as possible. In states with notice statutes, the parent must give 30 to 90 days' written notice of the intent to move. Then there is a reply time before a hearing can even be set (see Chapter 6). The lawyer may try to get an interim order to allow the move on a temporary basis.

The nonrelocating parent, however, may wish to delay so as to keep the child in the current location as long as possible. In some states, the parent may have the benefit of a presumption against allowing relocation on an interim basis. This is because a temporary move interrupts the child's stability, maybe forcing a school change. If the move is not allowed, the child will again be interrupted as the child is transferred back to the original state to live with the other parent. An interim order may be allowed if there is a strong probability that the relocation would be allowed at trial.

Advising the Client

ABA Model Rule 1.4(b) requires the lawyer to explain a matter to the extent reasonably necessary to permit the client to make informed decisions regarding the representation. In addition to advising the client on the law and procedure, the lawyer will advocate for the client's position, negotiate with the other side to try to accomplish the client's result, and continue to evaluate the client's position as the case progresses.[18]

Prior to the 1990s, caregiver mothers who had what was called "sole custody" had an easier time getting permission to relocate. Fathers, as providers, had "visitation." The demise of the tender-years doctrine and the rise in joint legal and physical custody and shared parenting has changed the dynamics of relocation cases considerably. It may be the father who is seeking to relocate with the child. Stability and physical caretaking time remain important considerations regardless of the label, sole or joint custody. The lawyer needs to discover and present evidence of the parent being loving, warm, affectionate, and nurturing. The type of parenting skills and caregiving that can be emphasized are things like sitting up at night with a sick child or leaving work to take the child to the doctor or lessons. In some states, it still may be more difficult to represent the father seeking to block a relocation, than a mother seeking to move. If this is the situation, the lawyer should advise the client of the uphill road.

The lawyer cannot counsel a client to engage, or assist a client to engage, in conduct that the lawyer knows is criminal or fraudulent.[19] The lawyer must advise the client against any course of conduct contravening existing court orders, such as leaving the state without permission. Lawyers have been found liable in tort actions if they have helped a client abduct a child. Even if joint custody exists, a parent may be prosecuted under statutes for interfering with parental custody.[20] A Colorado lawyer was disbarred when she helped her client flee, after the attorney learned that a custody evaluator was going to recommend that the father have custody of the son and yet-to-be-born baby. The mother had temporary custody, but she could not take the child out of Colorado without permission.[21]

The lawyer should advise the client against making a unilateral move without the permission of the other parent or the court. The only exception might be if the client is escaping imminent harm from an abuse situation. The parent who makes a unilateral move prima facie demonstrates a lack of concern for the child's relationship with the other parent. A unilateral move could jeopardize the entire case by upsetting the judge as well as the other parent. In one case, the appellate court reversed the trial court and found a mother in contempt for unilaterally moving the child to another city in a new school district four hours away from the father who had joint legal custody.[22] In another case, a mother who shared joint legal and physical custody with the father remarried and moved with their toddler from Carthage, Missouri, to Red Bud, Arkansas, without approval or court permission. The court sustained the father's objection to relocation, adopted his parenting plan retaining custody, and designated father's address as child's for mailing and educational purposes.[23]

Fair Dealing

The lawyer has an ethical duty of fair dealing with other attorneys and of candor to the court. Rule 4.1 provides that in the course of representing a client, the lawyer shall not (1) make a false statement of a material fact or law to a third person; or (2) fail to disclose a material fact when disclosure is necessary to avoid assisting in a criminal or fraudulent act. A Kentucky lawyer was publicly reprimanded for falsely telling the court that he was unaware of the divorce client's relocation with the child outside of the state.[24] The lawyer must advise the client to be honest about their motives for the move, new partners, and other facts that might influence the negotiations and the judge's view of the credibility of the parties.

Model Rule 8.4(c) provides that it is professional misconduct for a lawyer to engage in conduct involving dishonesty, fraud, deceit, or misrepresentation. Rule 1.2(d) provides that a lawyer may not counsel a client to engage in, or assist a client in, conduct the lawyer knows is criminal or fraudulent, but may discuss the legal consequences of such proposed conduct.

The AAML Bounds of Advocacy Rule 6.1 states that while a lawyer must competently represent the interests of the client, it cannot be at the expense of the children. Bounds of Advocacy Rule 6.2 says that an attorney should not permit a client to contest child custody, contact, or access for either financial advantage or vindictiveness. Therefore, the lawyer should be confident that the parents are thinking of their child more than just vengeance or their pocketbook. A lawyer can advise the client about the hurt that children may suffer from bad-faith custody claims, and about the "immorality of a terroristic threat directed to an area of especial vulnerability."[25]

Communication

ABA Model Rule 1.4, Comment 1, indicates the lawyer must keep the client informed and respond to reasonable requests for information. ABA Model Rule 1.2 requires a lawyer to abide by the client's decisions concerning the objectives to be achieved and consult with the client about the means to pursue those objectives. A client who comes for advice about moving with the child first and seeking "permission" later is likely to make the other parent furious. Additionally, the conduct may lead a judge to look unfavorably on the move. Judges have little sympathy with a parent who makes a unilateral move without the consent of the other parent, especially if there is a restriction on relocation.

If the client knows about the relocation at the time of negotiating the initial agreement, the lawyer should advise the client to reveal this information at the time. Otherwise, the parties may negotiate an agreement that will have to be modified within a very short time, and the client will appear in a bad light. In an Oklahoma case, the court terminated joint legal custody, awarded the father sole legal custody, and transferred residential custody to him where the facts showed the mother wishing to relocate knew before the initial decree that her future husband had already taken a job in another state. The appellate judge affirmed denial of relocation and opined, "if this is not bad faith, I don't know what is."[26]

ABA Model Rule 1.6(a) states that a lawyer shall not reveal information relating to the representation, unless the client gives informed consent, the disclosure is impliedly authorized to carry out the representation, or the disclosure is permitted by (b). The permissible exceptions to revealing a confidence under Rule 1.6(b) include to prevent death or substantial bodily harm, prevent specific crimes or frauds, or to comply with a court order. A tough question arises when the client does not want information revealed, but it may be in the best interests of the child to reveal that information. For example, the client-wife asks her lawyer to negotiate a divorce settlement agreement that includes a parenting plan for seven-year-old Carol. Carol is close to both parents and has been having emotional problems because of the divorce and parental conflict. The draft agreement gives the mother and father joint legal custody and decision-making, with the mother having primary residential custody. In the state, the parent with primary residential custody may move if the reason is valid, unless there is a provision against relocation, or the other parent shows it is contrary to the best interests of the child. A couple of days after the draft agreement has been circulated, the mother tells the lawyer she has been offered a fantastic job opportunity in another state that would start soon after the divorce is final. The client has not mentioned her intent to relocate to anyone and does not want her lawyer to tell father's lawyer because it might scuttle the agreement. The client has not told Carol either, because she might tell her father. In this situation, the lawyer should counsel the client about the child's best interests and encourage the client to either tell the father directly or authorize the lawyer to let the opposing counsel know of the proposed relocation.

However, the lawyer may not reveal this information without the client's informed consent. No exceptions under either Rule 1.6(a) or (b) are presented by these facts. Although Model Rule 4.1 prohibits lawyers from making "a false statement of material fact or law to a third person" or "fail[ing] to disclose a material fact when disclosure is necessary to avoid assisting a criminal or fraudulent act by a client," it does not directly apply to this situation because there have been no false statements made to the father or his attorney. No one has asked about relocation. Relocation is not a criminal or fraudulent act by the client. The Model Rules still contemplate adversary proceedings and do not specifically address the duty of a parent's lawyer to avoid harm to the child.

There are a couple of reasons the lawyer should encourage the client to reveal the relocation even though the Model Rules do not directly mandate it. Rule 2.1 requires the lawyer to exercise independent professional judgment and render candid advice, and the rule allows a lawyer to refer to not only the law but also other factors that may be relevant to the client's situation.

ABA Model Rule 1.4(b) suggests that the lawyer explain to the extent reasonably necessary to permit the client to make informed decisions regarding the representation. The lawyer does have a duty to inform the client as to why the course of conduct might not be in the client's best interests. There is no duty on the lawyer, however, to consider the child's interests and potential threat to her well-being from the proposed relocation.[27] Carol most likely will not be separately represented by her own lawyer because the parents are settling by agreement, not going to trial.

The AAML Bounds of Advocacy supports the concept that the divorce lawyer should serve as counselor and would, under these facts, encourage the mother to think about the consequences of not revealing her intent to relocate and the potential harm not revealing could cause. The lawyer should use the counseling role to advise the client of the possible practical and moral repercussions of the proposed relocation. The father is likely to feel blindsided. The relocation would have a major impact on the father's relationship with his daughter. He also may become hostile or antagonistic and claim either fraud in not disclosing the potential relocation during the drafting of the agreement, or he may try to modify the parenting plan based on a material change of circumstances. Carol is fragile emotionally. The relocation would take her away from her father with whom she is close and from her familiar surroundings, her school and her friends. Not dealing with the relocation issue in the original divorce in this case would be a mistake. The AAML Bounds of Advocacy identifies aspirational duties that a divorce lawyer owes to the children of clients, including the duty to "consider the welfare of, and seek to minimize the adverse impact of the divorce on, the minor children."[28]

Technology

ABA Model Rule 1.6(c) requires a lawyer to make reasonable efforts to prevent the inadvertent or unauthorized disclosure of, or access to, information relating to the representation of a client. The ABA Standing Committee on Ethics and Professional Responsibility Formal Op. 477 indicates that the lawyer must make reasonable efforts to ensure that communications with their clients are secure and not subject to inadvertent or unauthorized cybersecurity breaches.

Technology has transformed the practice of law. Lawyers must be competent and ethical in the use of technology, and clients must be advised of the hazards of technology, especially social media.[29] Lawyers advertise on the Internet, use email, and store documents in the cloud. Lawyers and clients use social media such as Facebook, Snapchat, and Instagram. Technology may help or harm the client's case. Because of this, the lawyer needs to add questions to the traditional client questionnaire, such as the following:

1. What social media accounts do you have? Facebook, Instagram, Snapchat, YouTube, TikTok, LinkedIn, Pinterest, Reddit, Hootsuite, Tinder, Grindr, X, or other.
2. How often do you post? To which accounts and what kinds of things do you post?
3. Do you ever post about your children?

4. Do you ever post about partying or drinking to excess?
5. Have you ever sent risqué pictures of yourself or anyone else over the Internet?
6. Have you ever hit the "post" button in anger or while under the influence of drugs or alcohol?
7. Are you aware that private posts are never totally private?
8. Have you ever been the victim of a cyberbully? Have you ever been the bully?

The lawyer must advise the client not to destroy any of the social media posts because spoliation is actionable. If there is a shared computer, tablet, or phone, there may be shared passwords. The client should back up what the client wants to preserve. The factory can reset the computer if one parent is keeping it. The lawyer should advise clients about the use (and abuse) of social media, including the following:

1. The partner probably knows all the important passwords used on a daily basis for online banking, Netflix, and so on. The client should make a list of all shared passwords and change to strong passwords on all the accounts the client is planning to keep.
2. If possible, the lawyer can advise the client to take down social media sites, like Facebook and X, until the relocation case is over. The client can create their own private profile or, at the least, adjust the privacy profile.[30] The material must remain available if sought by the other side, but there is no need to keep it public.
3. The client should not post anything denigrating the other parent.[31]
4. The client should not post their travel pictures if they have been away from home the majority of the year and the other parent has been the primary caregiver.
5. The client should not post any pictures that show the client violating a court order, such as drinking or doing drugs while the child is present.

6. The client should not try to "friend" the judge, the spouse's attorney, or any person who is working for the other party.
7. The client should not "hack" into the other parent's computer.
8. The client should not cyberstalk the other parent, the new partner, the other attorney, or the judge.

Fact Gathering

Relocation cases are fact specific. The basic interview information remains much the same as any divorce case, but with more emphasis on the relocation aspects. The client interview and information sheet are the places to start. The information will include the name of the client, any last names previously used (including the maiden name of women), addresses, social security numbers, date of marriage, names and birthdates of children, and the home addresses of the parties. Additionally, the lawyer will want to get a picture of the history leading up to the current conflict. This includes any existing informal custody arrangement, any court orders or prior parenting plans, and any litigation or motions to enforce existing plans.

Because most courts require a good faith reason for the relocation, the first questions are "why?" and "why now?" The general reasons are for emotional and financial support from family; following a new spouse or partner; wanting a fresh start; finding a better job to have a better quality of life; or escaping intimate partner violence. (See Chapter 9.)

Relevant factors will be the distance of the proposed move, the relationship of the parties prior to the proposed move, and the potential for a continuing relationship if the move is allowed. As a general rule, the lesser the distance, say 150 miles or less, the more likely it is that a court will approve the relocation of the children. On the other hand, courts have refused to allow parents to move less than 27 miles away.[32]

Because of the uncertainty as to how a court will treat a relocation request, the lawyer will want to get as much information as early as possible. If the parties are divorced, there should be a current parenting plan. The lawyer must discover its contents and how it is working. Part of fact finding will be to get a detailed history of the parents' relationship with each other and with the child. In addition, the lawyer will need all relevant legal documents. In any event, the lawyer must ascertain the historical and present family situation. At the initial meeting, the lawyer will also need to evaluate the possible need for any temporary or emergency orders because of domestic violence or another emergency situation. If there is a fear of abduction, the lawyer may want to seek an emergency order or other protections to prevent that possibility (see Chapter 4).

Whether proposing or opposing a relocation, there must be adequate research about the proposed place of relocation. For the lawyer representing the client wanting to relocate, the more knowledge about the future residence, the more reasonable and sensible the relocation will appear. Likewise, when opposing a relocation, the lawyer must have a basic knowledge about comparisons between the current place and the proposed place to successfully challenge the move.

If the relocation is being made as part of the original divorce or separation proceeding, that is, establishing the initial order, refer to Chapter 4. If the interview is post-judgment or a modification of an existing parenting plan or court decree, the lawyer needs an extensive amount of information about reasons for the relocation to determine if the proposed move will be a material change of circumstances that will justify a hearing on revising the parenting plan (see Chapter 8).

Researching the Case

The first issue may be which statute to apply—the factors included in the initial custody/residency determination, the modification of custody statute, or a specific relocation statute with additional factors. If a state treats a relocation as any other modification of a custody order, the moving party must show a material or substantial change of circumstances since the last order. If shown, a hearing is held on the child's best interests. In some states, there is a special statute governing relocation. The lawyer starts with the statutes involved, the burden of proof, and the case law in the jurisdiction. (See Chapters 8 and 9.)

Custody and Relocation Law in the State

The relevant statutes and case law determine what is considered a relocation. Every relocation or move away case implicates many of the same factors used in any custody case. Therefore, the lawyer should start with the relevant custody statute and be prepared to argue best interest under the custody statute as well as adding the relocation criteria. For example, New Jersey Statutes Annotated, section 9:2-4, sets out the following 14 specific factors:

A. The parents' ability to agree, communicate and cooperate in matters relating to the child.
B. The parents' willingness to accept custody and any history of unwillingness to allow parenting time not based on substantiated abuse.
C. The interaction and relationship of the child with its parents and siblings.
D. The history of domestic violence, if any.
E. The safety of the child and the safety of either parent from physical abuse by the other parent.
F. The preference of the child when of sufficient age and capacity to reason so as to form an intelligent decision.
G. The needs of the child.
H. The stability of the home environment offered.
I. The quality and continuity of the child's education.
J. The fitness of the parents.
K. The geographical proximity of the parents' homes.
L. The extent and quality of the time spent with the child prior to or subsequent to the separation.
M. The parents' employment responsibility.
N. The age and number of children.

The New Jersey statute requires a showing of "cause" before a court will authorize the permanent removal of a child to another state without the consent of both parents or, if the child is of "suitable age" to decide, the consent of the child.[33] There is not a separate relocation statute.[34] Every relocation case involves the same issues that are likely to arise in a modification of child custody action. In fact, a few states decide relocation cases using the modification of custody approach.[35] (See Chapter 8.)

Thirty-seven states have a specific removal statute. The first step in the process is to examine and analyze the controlling statute carefully. In some states, "any" move, even across the street, is a "relocation."[36] In other states, only a move out of state is considered a relocation. In still others, only a move over a certain number of miles is considered a relocation. For example, several states have statutes that allow parents to move up to a certain distance without seeking court approval, ranging from 75 to 150 miles.[37] Some states only consider if the parent with primary residential custody is relocating; other states require parents to have permission of the other parent or the court for any relocation.[38]

Many states use both the relocation statute and the modification statute—requiring a showing of a change of circumstances. Therefore, the lawyer needs to know the relevant custody and relocation statutes. Colorado and Pennsylvania have a list of factors, both in the basic custody statute and in the removal statute. For example, Colorado's relocation statute has nine factors; its custody statute has 11.[39] Pennsylvania has ten additional factors for a relocation.[40] Washington's Child Relocation Act includes 11 factors to determine if the detrimental effects of relocation outweigh the benefits to the child and the parent seeking to relocate.[41]

Relevant Case Law

Every jurisdiction has some cases on relocation. These cases address the burden of proof,[42] relevant factors if there is not a specific statute, and appellate standards of review. As a general rule, the beginning point is an understanding of the leading cases that interpret the statute. For example, the New Jersey Supreme Court found that the legislature required a showing of "cause" for an out-of-state relocation in order "to preserve the rights of the noncustodial parent and the child to maintain and develop their familial relationship."[43] Michigan held that its 100-mile rule is to be measured not by actual road miles but by radial miles, that is, in a straight line or as the crow flies.[44] Another state might find that miles should be measured by road miles because the parties had to go by car.[45] Generally, the reported cases focus on the best interests of the child, viewed against the background of the parents' reasons for advocating or opposing the removal. (See Chapter 9.)

The Procedural Considerations

No removal case can be brought or begun without a fundamental understanding of the potential for litigation. If the parties are unable to resolve the issue through negotiation or mediation, the great majority of such cases will require a trial or plenary hearing. This is because the issues in controversy are highly fact sensitive. While much discovery can be informal, there may be a need for formal discovery. The lawyer needs to analyze what discovery will be needed in the particular case. Will depositions be needed or permitted? What is the procedure for deposing an out of state party or witness? (See Chapter 7.)

Interviewing the Relocating Client

In the interview with the client wishing to relocate, the lawyer will be seeking the answers to two basic questions: Why does the client want to relocate? Will the other parent object? This will require answers to specific questions such as:

1. What type of custodial/parenting arrangement do you currently have? Sole, joint legal, primary, or shared residency?
2. What is the history of the parenting schedule?
    a. Have there been prior motions and proceedings pertaining to parenting disputes?
    b. To what extent do the parents have a present and past relationship that is otherwise reasonable or amicable?
3. How much residential time does the child spend with the other parent?
4. Describe a typical week in your household as to how you spend time with your child.

5. What are the child's educational needs and interests?
   a. What are the child's academic performance records?
   b. What is your child's favorite subject?
   c. Do you attend parent/teacher conferences?
   d. Who are your child's teachers? Please provide email, address, and phone numbers.
   e. What would the child's teacher likely say about the proposed move?
6. What are the child's after-school activities and interests, such as teams, sports, clubs, hobbies, and scouting?
   a. Who takes the child to these activities?
   b. Who are the coaches/leaders? Please provide email, address, and phone numbers.
   c. What might the coach or leader say about the child's proposed move?
   d. To what extent can these activities be continued in the state of relocation?
7. Who takes your child to medical and dental appointments? Day care?
8. To what extent does the child have relationships with playmates, friends, and neighbors?
   a. Who is your child's best friend?
   b. To what extent can these relationships be continued or replicated in the event of relocation?
9. Does the child have extended family here? Describe the nature of the child's relationship with the extended family.
10. Is there a sincere, good faith reason for the parent's relocation?
    a. Is a new spouse or partner involved? If yes, what is the child's relationship with the new spouse or partner?
    b. Have there been problems with the other parent?
    c. Is this a work-related move?
    d. Is an employer offering a transfer or forcing a reassignment, such as the military? If the attorney, a guardian ad litem, or even the judge calls the human resources department to ask if the move is a

mandatory move for the employee, will the answer be yes?

e. Is interpersonal violence or child abuse involved? Who was the victim? Have there been any police reports filed? Are there any protection orders? Describe the type of violence.
f. Are there family members, relatives, or other close friends at the proposed location?
g. Are there health considerations of either parent or the child that need to be considered?
h. Is there more than one such reason?

11. How would the existing parenting schedule be changed if the relocation were allowed?
12. What is the distance between the home state and the removal state?
    a. How long will it take to travel from one parent's home to the proposed location?
    b. What means of transportation will most likely be used?
    c. Is the new residence near a major airport, train, or bus route?
        i. Do airlines or other carriers give discounts for advance travel or Internet bookings?
        ii. At what age can a child travel unaccompanied? What type of adult supervision is offered and what does it cost?
        iii. Are there reasonably priced hotels, motels, or guesthouses in a safe neighborhood near the new residence?
        iv. What is the average cost of car rental in the area? Are infant or toddler seats available, if necessary?
13. What are the economic circumstances of the parties?
    a. Would financial considerations affect your ability to send the child for visitation at the nonrelocating parent's residence?
    b. Would additional child support payments enable you to stay in the current location?

   c. Would you be open to reducing child support if the costs of transporting the child to the new location make it too difficult for the child to visit the other parent?
14. How have holidays, vacations, and school recesses been handled in the past?
   a. Can the present contact plan continue without major inconvenience to the other parent or disruption to the child's schedule?
   b. If the move were granted, to what extent could additional parenting time be structured in favor of the parent opposing the move?
   c. Do religious, health, or other considerations affect the child's visiting or traveling during certain periods?
   d. Have special holiday or vacation traditions been enjoyed by either parent, and can they continue after the relocation?
15. Why the decision to move now? Why not earlier or why not wait until a later time when the child is older?
16. What has been the historical relationship with the other parent? Current?
17. Has there been a guardian ad litem or a child's attorney involved? Name?
18. Does the child have a therapist? Would he or she be able to testify if needed?
19. Who might be prospective witnesses if we go to trial? Please provide email, address, and phone numbers.
   a. Who knows the child well enough to talk authoritatively about the child's relationships?
   b. List family and extended family members who can address issues related to the move.
20. Have you looked at housing in the new location?
   a. Will housing be better or the same as current location?
   b. Is the cost of housing higher or lower in new location?

   c. Will the child's room be the same size, larger, or smaller than what the child has now?
   d. Does the child currently have a room alone or share with a sibling? What will be the situation in the new location?
   e. If the child will be sharing, will it be with a sibling, half-sibling, or step sibling of the same sex?
21. Where will the child attend school?
   a. How far is the school from the child's proposed new residence?
   b. Can the child walk or will the child have to take a bus?
   c. Will the school be able to meet the child's educational needs?
   d. If the child has special needs, does the school or outside agency have a program that is comparable or better than the current one?
   e. What is the school's policy on allowing out of town parents to visit school, teachers, and counselors other than on scheduled "parents" nights?
   f. Will school be able to provide a calendar designating holidays, teacher workdays, and vacations in advance of the next school year?
   g. Does the school offer remote learning possibilities? Online?
   h. What are the safety policies at the school for health? Vaccinations? Masks?
22. What is the other parent's motive for resisting relocation?
   a. Does the other parent exercise parenting time regularly?
   b. What is the extent of the other parent's involvement in extracurricular activities for the child, doctor visits, school activities, PTA, etc.?
23. Is there extended family in the area? How often does the other parent take the child to visit extended family?

24. Have you discussed the possibility of a move with the other parent?
25. Have you discussed the possibility of a move with your child(ren)?
    a. Do you think your child is old enough to express a preference?
    b. Do you think the child has a preference? If yes, what do you think that preference is? Why?
    c. Do you think the child needs a guardian ad litem or child's attorney?
26. If the child is in counseling, are there mental-health professionals in the new location who are willing to consult with current caregivers and continue therapy?
27. Will existing health insurance cover the child in the new location? If a new policy must be obtained, what will it cost? When will it be effective?
28. Is a hospital or emergency care center nearby the proposed residence?
29. If supervised visitation has been ordered, are there supervised visitation centers in the new location? If not, will friends, relatives, or other suitable third parties be available to supervise visitation in the new location?
30. What types of computer equipment do you have?
    a. Will a computer with a camera be available to the child in the new location for emailing, FaceTiming, and Skyping the nonrelocating parent?
    b. Will a telephone be available to the child for calling the nonrelocating parent? Is the phone a landline? The parent's phone? Child's cell phone?
31. Are you able to delay your move until the child is of sufficient age to travel as an unaccompanied minor? Are you willing to travel with the child and serve as the escort?
32. What will you do if the court determines you cannot relocate with your child?
33. What kind of contact and time-sharing will you require if you must relocate without your child?

34. How would your economic circumstances be impacted in the event of removal?
35. What is the cost of living in the home state compared with the relocation state?
36. What are the increased travel costs (if any) compared to the (presumed) decreased weekly parenting expenses to the nonrelocating parent?
37. To what extent has the nonrelocating parent fulfilled or failed to fulfill their child's support or alimony obligations?
38. Are there any recommendations of a court-appointed or privately retained mental health expert?
39. What are the tangible and intangible factors (such as lifestyle, climate, standard of living, environmental congestion, crime, etc.) that make up the "quality of life" in the home state as compared with the proposed relocation state?
40. Would it be feasible or practical for the nonrelocating parent to also move to the intended relocation state?

Questions for the Nonrelocating Party Client

1. What type of custody/parenting arrangement do you currently have? Sole, joint legal, primary, or shared residency?
2. How much residential time does the child spend with you? How often do you see your child? What do you do when the child is with you?
3. How often do you talk or text with your child on the phone?
4. Who is your child's best friend?
5. What are the names of your child's teachers? Coaches? Do you go to parents' night, games, etc.?
6. How many miles away does the other parent want to move?
7. Can the present contact plan continue without major inconvenience to you or disruption to the child's schedule?

8. Do business, health, or religious considerations limit your ability or the child's ability to travel or visit during certain periods?
9. Do financial considerations affect your ability to visit the child or have the child visit in your residence?
10. Do you and the child participate in any special activities or responsibilities that would be affected by the child's relocation?
11. Are you able to provide appropriate day care and babysitting for the child during prolonged periods of parenting time?
12. Are you able to provide for the child's special health or other needs in your residence during prolonged periods of parenting time?
13. Are you able to visit for periods of time at the child's new location?
14. Do you have a computer with a camera that you can use to exchange email with the child? Is high-speed Internet access available? Is Skype an option? Instant messaging with Google? Zoom? FaceTime?
15. Will your existing health plan cover the child in the new location?
16. Have special holiday or vacation traditions been enjoyed by you or the other parent? Can they continue after the relocation?
17. Are you willing to increase your support payments in exchange for the custodial parent's agreement to remain in the jurisdiction?
18. Are you (and your new partner) prepared to undertake primary residential responsibility if it is determined that the other parent cannot relocate with the child?
19. How would you arrange the long-distance plan if the other parent moves but the child stays with you?
20. What kind of arrangements will you need to make in accepting primary residential responsibility?
    a. Are your present living accommodations suitable for your child?

b. Are your present living accommodations in the child's school district?
c. Can the child remain at the same school and continue present activities while residing with you?
d. Is there appropriate transportation to school?
e. Do your work hours permit you to care for the child during nonschool hours and on weekends? If the answer is no, who will be watching the child?

Documents to Be Obtained

If the relocation request is being made as part of the original divorce or custody action, then the documents needed and evidence to be presented will be the same as for any custody case. Each state has certain requirements for procedure, discovery, and the creation of parenting plans. See Chapters 7 and 13. The parties may have equal burdens to show it is in the best interests of the child to live with them in their chosen location.

If the parent is seeking to relocate after an initial custody order, the action may be a modification proceeding. Modification proceedings often require more preparation than the initial action. In most states, the moving party must show that there has been a material and substantial change in circumstances since the last custody order (see Chapter 8). The attorney must review the court file from the divorce case with the original decree, any subsequent modifications, any enforcement orders, and any separation agreement. If the first decree did not involve a full court hearing, there may be much evidence to be gathered from the pre-decree, as well as the current living situation. Even if there was a trial, new discovery may be required. For example, if the custodial parent is contemplating a move from the jurisdiction, there may be a need to present evidence as to why the quality of life in the client's state is superior to the state of the prospective move. Statistics on crime, pollution, school quality, and so on may be relevant. As with the initial determination, thorough preparation and mastery of the facts are the keys to successfully obtaining permission to move or change the residential placement or develop new parenting plans.

The lawyer will also need to assemble a number of existing documents:

1. Motions, notice of intent to move, or other document that has been filed with a court;
2. Preliminary or temporary orders that are in effect;
3. Separation or property settlement agreement or existing parenting plan to determine:
   a. Existing arrangement;
   b. Presence or absence of geographical restrictions (see Chapter 4);
   c. Presence or absence of provision setting jurisdiction;[46]
   e. Financial terms that may affect parenting time issues.
4. An underlying agreement, statute, or court directive that requires notice of the move;
5. Court judgments of original orders that may include a court-imposed radius restriction;
6. Any prior proceedings relating to parenting time issues.

If the parties have an agreement that does not limit or restrict relocation, the court may allow the move. In one case, where the parties' agreement inferentially recognized the right to move when some property was sold and did not in any way restrict a move to another county in the state, the court allowed the move.[47]

Temporary or Extraordinary Relief

Based on the facts, such as the start of a new job or beginning of school classes, the lawyer will want to seek a temporary order allowing the parent and child to move. Some judges are reluctant to grant temporary relocation because of the fear the parent will use the child's adapting well, if that is the case, to bolster the case for a more permanent move.

If asking for extreme ex parte relief, as in the case of domestic violence, this needs to be supported by an affidavit of facts directly observed. The applicant client should be present in case the judge has some questions, which will be on the record. If there is advance notice from respondent's counsel asking to be present at presentation of an ex parte application, the judge will notify counsel so they can attend. The judge may ask applicant if it is possible to agree on some kind of interim supervision while awaiting a hearing for temporary orders. Louisiana has a specific statute that allows the court to grant a temporary order allowing relocation, if the moving party has requested an expedited preliminary hearing. The court will not allow the parent to relocate the child on an ex parte basis. If the court authorizes relocation, the court may require the person relocating to provide reasonable security guaranteeing that the court-ordered physical custody or visitation with the child will not be interrupted or interfered with or that the relocating person will return the child if court authorization for the relocation is denied at trial. The court shall not give undue weight to the temporary relocation as a factor in reaching its final determination.[48]

Attorney Fees

The trial court has discretion to award attorney's fees as justice and equity require.[49] States have rules for how to apply. Several states allow for an award of legal fees caused by one party's intransigence. A Washington court awarded the father attorney's fees of $10,000 and assessed $500 in costs, where the mother violated the parenting plan by failing to provide father with 60 days' notice of intent to relocate more than a 30-minute drive.[50]

Endnotes

1. Lewis Becker, *Ethical Responsibilities of a Lawyer for a Parent in Custody and Relocation Cases: Duties Respecting the Child and Other Conundrums*, 15 J. Am. Acad. Matrim. Law. 33 (1998).

2. *See* Mark Chinn, How to Build and Manage a Family Law Practice (ABA rev. 2018); Sanford M. Portnoy, The Family Lawyer's Guide to Building Successful Client Relationships (ABA 2000).

3. Merrells v. Dotray, 299 So. 3d 208 (La. Ct. App. 2020) (mother did not need to give notice under relocation and was allowed to move children to Arizona when there was no custody order in place).

4. Allbright v. Allbright, 215 P.3d 472, 475 (Idaho 2009) ("[C]ourt presiding over a child custody matter does not become a family czar with unlimited authority to order the parents to do anything that the court believes is in the best interest of the child.").

5. *See* Druckman v. Ruscitti, 327 P.3d 511 (Nev. 2014). *See also* Gutierrez v. Fox, 394 P.3d 1096 (Ariz. Ct. App. 2017) (because unwed father's paternity established, mother was required to get his permission or court approval before moving to Wisconsin; court had authority to enter temporary orders requiring mother and child to return to Arizona).

6. In most states, the type of custody is sole or joint legal custody and sole or joint physical custody. Many states, however, have different designations. For example, Pennsylvania lists the types of custody as (1) shared physical custody, (2) primary physical custody, (3) partial physical custody, (4) sole physical custody, (5) supervised physical custody, (6) shared legal custody, (7) and sole legal custody. 23 PA. CON. STAT. ANN. § 5328(b).

7. Misyura v. Misyura, 244 P.3d 519 (Alaska 2010).

8. Hull v. Hull, 273 So. 3d 1135 (Fla. Dist. Ct. App. 2019).

9. Sheehan v. Flower, 170 P.3d 288 (Ariz. Ct. App. 2007), *rev. denied*.

10. Munari v. Hotham, 177 P.3d 860 (Ariz. Ct. App. 2008).

11. MODEL RULES OF PRO. CONDUCT r. 2.1 (AM. BAR ASS'N). *See also* LOUIS PARLEY, THE ETHICAL FAMILY LAWYER (1995).

12. SANFORD PORTNOY, THE FAMILY LAWYER'S GUIDE TO BUILDING SUCCESSFUL RELATIONSHIPS (ABA 2000). *See also* AMIRAM ELWORK, STRESS MANAGEMENT FOR LAWYERS (3d ed 2007).

13. *See generally* Lewis Becker, *Ethical Responsibilities of a Lawyer for a Parent in Custody and Relocation Cases: Duties Respecting the Child and Other Conundrums*, 15 J. AM. ACAD. MATRIM. LAW. 33 (1998).

14. Peter G. Jaffe, et al., *Custody Disputes Involving Allegations of Domestic Violence: Toward a Differentiated Approach to Parenting Plans*, 46(3) FAM. CT. REV. 500 (July 2008).

15. *See* Lynn Hecht Schafran, *Domestic Violence, Developing Brains, and the Lifespan: New Knowledge from Neuroscience*, 53(3) JUDGES' J. 32 (2014). *See also* Allen M. Bailey, *Prioritizing Child Safety as the Prime Best Interest Factor*, 47 FAM. L.Q. 35 (2013).

16. Joan B. Kelly & Michael E. Lamb, *Developmental Issues in Relocation Cases Involving Young Children: When, Whether, and How?*, 17 J. FAM. PSYCH. 193 (2003); Pamela Ludolph & Milfred D. Dale, *Attachment in Child Custody: An Additive Factor, Not a Determinative One*, 46 FAM. L.Q. 1 (2012).

17. *In re* Daugherty, 83 P.3d 789, 793 (Kan. 2004).

18. MODEL RULES OF PRO. CONDUCT, Preamble (AM. BAR ASS'N 2025).

19. *Id.* at r. 1.2(d). *See also* Becker, *supra* note 13.

20. State v. West, 688 P.2d 406 (Or. Ct. App. 1984).

21. People v. Chappell, 927 P.3d 829 (Colo. 1996).

22. Vyhlidal v. Vyhlidal, 973 N.W.2d 171 (Neb. 2022) (mother ordered to return child to previous school district and pay father's attorney fees).

23. Allen v. Seely, 64 S.W.3d 236 (Mo. Ct. App. 2021).

24. Ky. Bar Ass'n v. Rye, 336 S.W.3d 462 (Ky. 2011).

25. Lewis Becker, *Ethical Concerns in Negotiating Family Law Agreements*, 30 FAM. L.Q. 587, 628–29 (1996).

26. Galarza v. Galarza, 231 P.3d 694, 697 (Okla. Civ. App. 2009).

27. Linda D. Elrod, *Reforming the System to Protect Children in High Custody Cases*, 28 WM. MITCHELL L. REV. 495, 539 (2001).

28. AM. ACAD. OF MATRIM. LAWYERS, BOUNDS OF ADVOCACY: GOALS FOR FAMILY LAWYERS, r. 6.1. (2000).

29. *See* MODEL RULES OF PRO. CONDUCT, r. 1.1 cmt. 8 (AM. BAR ASS'N 2025).

30. *See* FLA. ADV. OP. 14-1 states that a lawyer can advise client to adjust privacy settings to conceal content from the public eye and remove information from social media as long as appropriate record is maintained.

31. *See In re* Rutland v. O'Brien, 41 N.Y.S.3d 292 (App. Div. 2016) (sole legal custody to father where mother's numerous Facebook communications with daughter denigrating father were admitted).

32. Mantonya v. Mantonya, 311 S.W.3d 392 (Mo. Ct. App. D. 2010); Petroski v. Petroski, 808 N.Y.S.2d 852 (App. Div. 2005) (denying mother's request to relocate 27 miles away).

33. N.J. STAT. ANN. § 9:2-2.

34. Bisbing v. Bisbing, 166 A.3d 1155 (N.J. 2017).

35. ALASKA STAT. ANN. § 25.24.150 (c); IND. STAT. ANN. § 31-17-2-2.

36. KAN. STAT. ANN. § 23-3222.

37. MICH. REV. STAT. § 722.31 (100 miles); UTAH CODE ANN. § 30-3-37(1) (150 miles).

38. *See* Hull v. Hull, 273 So. 3d 1135 (Fla. Dist. Ct. App. 2019) (finding Florida statute applies to either parent relocating).

39. COLO. REV. STAT. § 14-10-129(2)(c).

40. D.K. v. S.P.K., 102 A.3d 467 (Pa. Super. Ct. 2014) (applying factors in § 5337(h) and allowing the move).

41. WASH. REV. STAT. § 26.09.520.

42. McCay v. McCay, 9 N.W.3d 687 (N.D. 2024) (parent moving for permission to relocate has burden of providing by preponderance of the evidence that the move is in the child's best interests).

43. Bisbing v. Bisbing, 166 A.3d 1155 (N.J. 2017).

44. Bowers v. Vandermeulen-Bowers, 750 N.W.2d 597 (Mich. Ct. App. 2008). *See also* Holley v. Holley, 232 So. 3d 717 (La. Ct. App. 2017); Barrett v. Killings, 700 S.W.3d 399 (Tenn. Ct. App. 2023).

45. State v. Titus, 274 So. 3d 591 (La. Ct. App. 2019).

46. Friedman v. Eighth Judicial Dist. Court of State, *ex rel.* Cnty. of Clark, 264 P.3d 1161 (Nev. 2011).

47. Schulze v. Morris, 825 A.2d 1173 (N.J. Super. Ct. App. Div. 2003) (finding a move by residential custodial parent to another county in the state was not a statutory removal).

48. La. Rev. Stat. § 9:355.12.

49. *In re* Marriage of Laidlaw, 409 P.3d 1184 (Wash. Ct. App. 2018). *See also* Brosnan v. Brosnan, 840 N.W.2d 240 (S.D. 2013) (allowing attorney fees on appeal).

50. *In re* Marriage of Raskob, 334 P.3d 30 (Wash. Ct. App. 2014) (mother's failure to comply was consistent with her rigidity in parenting and not communicating with the father).

CHAPTER 3

Jurisdictional Issues: PKPA and UCCJEA

The UCCJEA is designed to avoid jurisdictional competition between states over child custody in an increasingly mobile society.[1]

Relocation cases, unless they are within the same state, almost always involve more than one jurisdiction. Therefore, one of the first considerations in any case involving the custody of a child is which court has the jurisdiction to hear the case. Jurisdiction is foundational. Before filing an action involving the custody of a minor child, a lawyer must determine which court has jurisdiction to hear the case so that the custody determination is entitled to full faith and credit by other states. Generally, there are three jurisdictional elements: (1) over the subject matter, (2) over the person, and (3) power to render the particular relief requested. If a judgment is rendered by a court of competent jurisdiction, it is not void merely because there are irregularities or errors of law, unless an appellate court voids it.[2]

Prior to 1968 when states began adopting the Uniform Child Custody and Jurisdiction Act (UCCJA), a state could assert jurisdiction over child custody if it had a "substantial interest" in a case based on the residence of either parent, the child, or marital domicile.[3] The U.S. Supreme Court in *May v. Anderson* in 1953 indicated that personal jurisdiction over the parties was needed for a court to determine custody. Justice Frankfurter's concurrence, however, noted that even though full faith and credit did not require Ohio to recognize Wisconsin's custody decree (because custody decrees are modifiable throughout a child's minority), Ohio could recognize it.[4]

Today, three main jurisdictional statutes govern: the Parental Kidnapping Prevention Act (PKPA) (federal law); the Uniform Child Custody Jurisdiction and Enforcement Act (UCCJEA) and the Uniform Child Abduction Prevention Act (UCAPA), which is in 20 states. If a parent is on active duty in the military, the Servicemembers' Civil Relief Act also may apply.[5] In addition, the Hague Convention on the Civil Aspects of International Child Abduction (103 countries) may be relevant in cases in which the child is abducted to a foreign country.[6] (See Chapter 15.)

Child Custody Jurisdiction Is Subject Matter Jurisdiction

The relocation case must be heard in the state that has jurisdiction to adjudicate the child custody issues. Most states use the terminology that child custody determinations require "subject matter" jurisdiction—the threshold requirement for a court to hear a case or controversy before it.[7] The court must have jurisdiction over the child based on sufficient contacts as of the date of filing the action.[8] Even if the parents leave the state after filing the action, the court can hear the case if it had jurisdiction on the date the case was filed.[9]

The parents cannot consent to subject matter jurisdiction; it either exists or it does not.[10] So where the mother and children had lived in Oregon for two years before the father filed for divorce and custody in Kentucky, Oregon was the children's home state. Oregon was the only place that could determine custody even though the mother had answered the Kentucky action and agreed in a separation agreement to Kentucky's jurisdiction.[11] If the state does not have subject matter jurisdiction, the state's order is not valid and the order is not entitled to full faith and credit, nor is it enforceable in other states.[12] A defect in subject matter jurisdiction can be raised at any time, even years later.[13] Subject matter jurisdiction is a question of law subject to de novo review.[14]

Brief History: UCCJA and Parental Kidnapping Prevention Act

Prior to 1968, child custody cases were marked by forum shopping, repetitive custody litigation, and inconsistent judgments. Although states did not have to give full faith and credit to sister states' custody decrees because they were modifiable throughout a child's minority, some gave comity. The Uniform Child Custody Jurisdiction Act (UCCJA) set out four alternative, but co-equal jurisdictional bases: (1) home state where the child had lived for the six months preceding the custody filing; (2) significant connection of the child and contestant and substantial evidence exists in the state about the child's future care, custody, and control; (3) emergency; or (4) default because no state has jurisdiction under the first three. The UCCJA set out reasons for a state to decline jurisdiction due to pending litigation in another state, inconvenient forum, or unclean hands.[15] The UCCJA was enacted in all 50 states but there were still some issues with more than one court exercising jurisdiction.

In 1980, because of the potential for simultaneous jurisdiction in two states under the UCCJA, Congress enacted the Parental Kidnapping Prevention Act (PKPA), 28 U.S.C. § 1738A(a). The PKPA requires that a state court must enforce an order from another state if the first state exercised jurisdiction in substantial conformity with or under factual circumstances that meet the jurisdictional standards of the PKPA. A custody order is made consistently with the PKPA if the court issuing the order had jurisdiction under its own laws, and one of five conditions enumerated in § 1738A(c)(2) is met. The PKPA sets out the following bases for jurisdiction:

> (A) Such state (i) is the home State of the child on the date of the commencement of the proceeding, or (ii) had been the child's home State within six months before the date of the commencement of the proceeding and the child is absent from such State because of his removal or retention by a contestant or for other reasons, and a contestant continues to live in such State;

> (B) (i) *it appears that no other State would have jurisdiction under subparagraph (A)*, and (ii) it is in the best interest of the child that a court of such State assume jurisdiction because (I) the child and his parents, or the child and at least one contestant, have a significant connection with such State other than mere physical presence in such State, and (II) there is available in such State substantial evidence concerning the child's present or future care, protection, training, and personal relationships [emphasis added];
>
> (C) the child is physically present in such State and (i) the child has been abandoned, or (ii) it is necessary in an emergency to protect the child because he has been subjected to or threatened with mistreatment or abuse;
>
> (D) (i) it appears that no other State would have jurisdiction under subparagraph (A), (B), (C), or (E) or another State has declined to exercise jurisdiction on the ground that the State whose jurisdiction is in issue is the more appropriate forum to determine the custody of the child, and (ii) it is in the best interest of the child that such court assume jurisdiction; or
>
> (E) the court has continuing jurisdiction pursuant to subsection (d) of this section.

The PKPA prioritized home state jurisdiction in section (B)(i) by allowing the use of significant connection jurisdiction *only* if there is no home state and it is in the child's best interests because substantial evidence exists as to the child's future care and welfare.[16] The PKPA also set out the concept of "exclusive continuing jurisdiction." Once a state has exercised jurisdiction properly, the initial decree-granting state has "exclusive continuing jurisdiction" so long as it remains the residence of a child or any contestant.[17] The state with continuing jurisdiction is the only state that can make an enforceable order until all parties have left the state or the state with continuing jurisdiction declines jurisdiction.[18]

The PKPA requires that one state give full faith and credit to a sister state decree if that state used PKPA criteria. In the event of a conflict between the states, the PKPA controls.[19] The PKPA preempts state law.[20] The result is that courts will decline jurisdiction to hear an initial case if another state has initial jurisdiction. So where a putative father filed a paternity and custody action in Texas where he lived and the baby had been born, the Alabama court refused to hear the adoptive parents' attempt to adopt the child in Alabama.[21] Courts decline to hear a modification of a child custody determination if the order was made in a state that has continuing jurisdiction.[22]

There is no private right of action under PKPA.[23] Only Massachusetts still uses the UCCJA but, because of the PKPA, its jurisdictional rules are basically the same as the other 49 states.

Uniform Child Custody Jurisdiction and Enforcement Act (UCCJEA)

In 1998, the Uniform Child Custody Jurisdiction and Enforcement Act (UCCJEA)[24] replaced the UCCJA and follows the language of the PKPA. The UCCJEA now sets out the bases for subject matter jurisdiction in custody cases.[25] A few courts have noted that subject matter jurisdiction is granted by the state constitution, and legislation cannot limit that jurisdiction.[26] The vast majority of courts, however, speak of the UCCJEA as subject matter jurisdiction.[27]

Courts must follow the UCCJEA when they are deciding whether:

1. to make an initial custody order;
2. to exercise jurisdiction even though there is a custody proceeding already pending in another jurisdiction;
3. to modify an existing custody or visitation order from another jurisdiction;
4. to decline jurisdiction because another state is a more convenient forum; or
5. to register and enforce a custody determination made by a court in another state, country, or tribe because UCCJEA § 105 treats a tribe and foreign countries the same as a state.[28]

The United States may someday enact the 1996 Hague Convention on Jurisdiction, Applicable Law, Recognition, Enforcement and Co-operation in Respect of Parental Responsibility and Measures for the Protection of Children (the Protection of Children Convention).[29] The Protection of Children Convention contains applicable law with respect to measures of protection for a child. It uses the term "habitual residence" rather than "home state" language and uses the term "measures of protection" instead of "custody" orders. It does not contain the concept of continuing exclusive jurisdiction. The Uniform Law Commission revised the UCCJEA in 2013 to provide additional definitions for a "measure of protection" if the United States ratifies the Convention. At this time, no state has enacted the 2013 amendments to the UCCJEA.

Definitions

The definitions in UCCJEA Section 102 are important. The UCCJEA consistently uses the singular word "child" and never uses the plural word "children." Jurisdiction is child specific, not "family specific." Because it is possible for a court to have jurisdiction over one child and not another, custody jurisdiction must be determined individually for each child. If the parents have split custody that results in all parties (mom and child, dad and child) leaving the original decree state, jurisdiction will be determined for each child.

A "child custody determination" is any judgment, decree, or other order of a court providing for legal custody, physical custody, placement, or visitation of any child. The term includes permanent, temporary, initial, and modification orders. A temporary custody order entered in a mother's Maryland domestic violence protection action against her child's father was considered an initial custody determination, so Maryland had exclusive continuing jurisdiction even though the mother had fled with the child to Puerto Rico.[30] On the other hand, a temporary order of custody that was dismissed without entry of a permanent decree did not qualify as an "initial" child custody determination to give an Iowa court subject matter jurisdiction over an unwed father's pending application for modification of child custody after Texas had become the child's home state.[31] A Michigan case found that an Acknowledgment of Parentage is not an "initial custody determination" because it is not issued or entered by any court, nor is it in the form of a "judgment, decree, or other court order." The consent to personal jurisdiction required by the Acknowledgment does not provide the basis for custody jurisdiction.[32]

A "child custody proceeding" refers to any proceeding in which child custody, placement, or visitation are at issue. Any action for relocation or modification of a custody order falls under the jurisdictional provisions of the UCCJEA. A California judgment establishing the parental relationship of a nonbiological father, who had been a same-sex partner of the biological father of a child born to a surrogate, was a child custody determination and subject to registration in Texas.[33]

The "home state" is the state in which a child lived with a parent or person acting as a parent[34] for at least six consecutive months immediately before the commencement of a child custody proceeding.[35] In the case of a child less than six months, the term means the state in which the child lived from birth with a parent or person acting as a parent. Temporary absences do not count.

UCCJEA Pleadings Affidavit

The pleadings must contain specific information. The UCCJEA requires a detailed affidavit as to the child's whereabouts and to pending custody actions. If the state requires a verified petition, the information can be placed in the petition. In the first pleading or in an affidavit attached to the pleading that involves child custody, the party must give information under oath as to:

1. the child's present address or whereabouts, the places where the child has lived during the last five years, and the names and present addresses of the persons with whom the child has lived during that period;
2. whether the party has participated as a party or witness or in any other capacity in any other proceeding concerning the custody of or visitation with the child and, if so, identify the court, the case number, and the date of the child custody determination, if any;

3. whether the party knows of any proceeding that could affect the current proceeding, including proceedings for enforcement and proceedings relating to domestic violence, protective orders, termination of parental rights, and adoption, and if so, identify the court, the case number and the nature of the proceeding; and
4. whether the party knows the names and addresses of any person not a party to the proceeding who has physical custody of the child or claims rights of legal custody or physical custody of, or visitation with, the child, and if so, the names and addresses of those persons.

The court can stay the proceedings until the information is furnished. Each party has a continuing duty to inform the court of any proceeding in the state or in another state that could affect the current proceeding.[36] Note, "any other proceedings" includes a proceeding in a Tribal Court.

Initial Jurisdiction and Home State

UCCJEA section 201 establishes a hierarchy for initial jurisdiction purposes, giving "home state" jurisdiction the priority over any other basis for jurisdiction.[37] The home state is the state that has been the home of the child and the child's parent or someone acting as a parent for six months before commencing the child custody proceeding. If the relocation is sought at the time of the initial custody action, then the child's "home state" will be the proper forum to decide the issue. The important date is that the state has been the child's place of residence (absent temporary absences) for the six months before the action is filed.[38] The six-month rule is strictly applied.[39] So where a child had never been in Montana for the requisite six months, Montana was not the home state, even though the father was there and parties had intended to move there.[40] A foreign country is included in the definition of "state."[41]

The home state of the child, not the domicile or legal residency of the parents, is the consideration for jurisdiction.[42] Parents cannot consent to jurisdiction in a state other than the child's home state.[43] Where a child had only lived in Guatemala, Maine lacked jurisdiction to adjudicate custody.[44]

Infants

The UCCJEA section 102(7) defines the home state as "the state in which the child lived from birth with a parent or person acting as a parent for six months immediately before filing." It is not the state where the mother lived during the pregnancy. The UCCJEA does not apply to unborn children who do not yet have a home state.[45] Even if another state has been the marital residence and one party files for divorce there, the place where the child is born and lives with the parent is the home state.[46] A Colorado case found that while the court had personal jurisdiction over the father to adjudicate parentage, its court lacked jurisdiction to determine custody of the unborn child where the mother gave birth in New Hampshire.[47]

A putative father cannot keep a pregnant woman from exercising her constitutionally protected right to travel to another state.[48] A pregnant woman does not need to file for relocation to move to another state.[49] Only Indiana and Kentucky appear to have allowed courts to issue orders for a child prior to birth.[50] Louisiana recently found that the UCCJEA does not apply to preembryos or unborn children.[51]

While a pregnant woman may move without court permission, it may be too late after the child's birth for the mother to try to relocate without the father's permission or court order.[52] An Arizona court found that Arizona was the home state of a child who was born and lived there two months, and father's paternity was established by acknowledgment before the mother moved with the child to Wisconsin. The mother had to secure father's agreement or a court order to permanently relocate with the child. The temporary order required the mother to return the child to Arizona.[53]

A state can become the newborn child's home as soon as the child is born. Where a child lived in the state with her parents for the first eight days of her life at the time the action was filed, Kentucky was the home state.[54] New Jersey was the home state of a child who was born and lived there before mother took the child to New York and filed for custody. At the time the petition was filed, the child's home state was New Jersey. The fact that the child was physically present in New York or had lived there with mother for several years did not give New York jurisdiction.[55] In another case in which the mother tried to move to New York, the court found that from birth to mother's relocation, the child, who was less than six months old, had lived in Florida with both parents. Father's filing a custody action in Florida precluded New York from taking jurisdiction.[56] Texas was the home state and had proper jurisdiction where the mother had filed a parentage action because she had lived with the child there exclusively for the first five weeks after birth, after which she took him back and forth to Louisiana when she visited her other son.[57] In another case, however, the mother gave birth in Texas, but actually had her residence in Louisiana and lived there with the infant 51 of 61 days.[58]

Six Month Extension of Home State

The home state continues for six months after the child is removed from the state. If one parent takes a child to another state or country, the left-behind parent can, and should, file for custody in the home state within six months, especially if it appears the other parent is not returning. The six-month period within which the parent in the original state could file a custody action within the state does not begin to run until that parent had reason to recognize the permanency of the out-of-state absence. Therefore, when a father gave permission for the mother to take the children to Japan to visit her family for the summer, the six-month period started in October when it became apparent that the mother was not returning.[59]

While a child's home state can continue for six months following the child leaving a state (allowing a left-behind parent to file and keep the home state), if the child is in another state for six months and one day, the latter state becomes the home state unless the absence was a temporary absence. In one case, the mother took the children to South Dakota where she filed for custody before they had lived there six months. The father, however, did not file his petition for residential custody in North Dakota until the children had been living in South Dakota for over a year. The date the father filed petition was important. If he had filed within six months of the children leaving the state, North Dakota would have been the home state and the only state to hear the custody issue. The North Dakota court, however, would not hear the case unless the South Dakota court determined that it was not the home state or that North Dakota was a more appropriate forum.[60]

Temporary Absences

Temporary absences from the home state do not count in the six-month time period.[61] Unfortunately, the UCCJEA does not define what a "temporary absence" is. The results in cases have been far from uniform.[62] A temporary absence occurs when the child leaves the state and both parents intend to return. If both parents intend to leave the state permanently, the absence is not temporary.[63] The most typical situation is when a child leaves the home state to spend time with the other parent in another state.[64] There have also been cases where one parent takes the child with the permission of the other parent to visit relatives; does not return when expected, like at the end of summer; waits six months and files in the new state. The other parent did not file during the six months the child was gone because that parent thought the other was coming back. A court may find the absence "temporary" and allow the parent in the former home state to file. Outcomes are heavily dependent on the particular facts actually adduced as evidence in each specific case.

If a parent wrongfully removes a child from the state, the time following the removal is considered a temporary absence for purposes of establishing home state jurisdiction. The court may need to hold a hearing to determine whether a child's stay in another state is a temporary absence, especially if one parent withheld the child from the other parent in an attempt to establish the home state elsewhere.[65]

Some courts have looked at the duration such that short trips with an out-of-state parent or grandparent that last weeks to even months could be considered temporary. The focus on duration fails to recognize that some short absences may be the start of a parent's intended relocation. Other courts have considered the intention of a child's parent(s), grandparents, or other caregivers.[66] The problem, however, is that parties' intentions may change over time.

In the past ten years, the trend has been for courts to adopt a totality of the circumstances test to determine what a temporary absence is.[67] Among the factors are:

- the physical presence of the child;
- the parent's purpose in removing the child from the state;
- the actual duration of the absence;
- any agreement between the parents;
- the parents' intent regarding the nature of the child's out-of-state absence;
- the child's living arrangements; and
- any other relevant factors.[68]

Kentucky found that the parent's purpose in removing the child was one of the most important factors. Where the children went to Kentucky for the summer so the mother would not have to find day care, the absence from Colorado was temporary.[69] Some of the other factors may be the parties' living arrangement, the location of the child's doctor and medical care, receipt of public benefits, and frequency of relocation.[70]

UCCJEA's bright-line rules can be undermined when subjective considerations, like intent, are permitted into the analysis. On the other hand, intent can be important. A Montana court found that the eight- to nine-month period the child and mother spent residing in Minnesota was a temporary absence, so Montana remained the home state. The court looked at the physical presence of the child, the integration of the child into the Montana community, the duration of the absence, the parties' living arrangements, the location of other family members, the frequency of relocation, and the parties' intentions.[71]

A Nevada court used the totality of circumstances test when a mother unilaterally took the children to California four days before they would have resided in Nevada for six consecutive months. Among the factors the court used to find the absence was temporary was that the father believed the mother would return with the children; she did not inform him she was taking them to California nor get permission to leave. She and the father started marriage counseling after she went to California.

The children remained enrolled in their private school in Nevada about a month after removal; the Nevada school was superior to the school in California. The mother's writ of mandamus or prohibition challenging the Nevada court's finding of home state jurisdiction was denied.[72]

Military custody cases often include relocation of the military family to several states preceding or during the custody case. Military parents may be "deployed" or "stationed." Those terms have meaning in the context of their military service. But, for purposes of the UCCJEA, children "live" or "reside" in the state in which their parent is "deployed" or "stationed." One court distinguished military absences from other types of "temporary" absences indicating that logic supports the conclusion that a military absence is a temporary absence.[73]

A father who moved his family from Nebraska to Japan when his son was ten weeks old due to a permanent military duty assignment could not successfully claim that the two and one-half years in Japan constituted a temporary absence from Nebraska. Time spent living in another state or country because of military duty is not "temporary."[74]

In another case, a Navy father who was currently stationed in Washington, D.C., could not commence a custody action in Louisiana where the parties had their matrimonial domicile. Although the Canadian mother had lived there during the father's four deployments overseas, she and the child had moved to Canada in August 2012. Since 2012, the father had been in Afghanistan and Washington, D.C., not Louisiana. Canada was the child's home state at the time the father filed for divorce in 2014. The absence from Louisiana was not "temporary."[75] In cases dealing with modification, however, the courts are likely to find that the military parent's decree state continues to have jurisdiction if the servicemember intends to return, even if deployed elsewhere.[76]

The six-month extension of time can be important. If one parent removes the child from the home state, the left-behind parent has up to six months from the date of removal, a "window of opportunity," to petition for relief. In a Minnesota case, the mother took the children to Japan for a visit in July 2014, at first with father's permission. When the father visited at the end of October 2014, the mother evidenced her intent to not return the children. Father filed for divorce on April 27, 2015. The court found that the children who had lived their entire lives in Minnesota were temporarily absent as of October 27, 2014, six months preceding the filing of the petition. A period of temporary absence is part of the time period. Minnesota would be their home state if they were temporarily absent on October 27, 2014.[77]

Initial Jurisdiction: Significant Connection and Substantial Evidence

If there is no home state, or a court of the home state has declined to exercise jurisdiction on the ground that another state is the more appropriate forum, then the petitioned court may be able to assume significant connection jurisdiction under section 201(a)(2). A significant connection is more than mere physical presence and can be demonstrated by substantial evidence concerning the child's care, protection, training, and personal relationships in that state.

The requirement is that the child and the child's parents, or the child and at least one parent (or a person acting as a parent), have a significant connection with the state and substantial evidence is available there concerning the child's care, protection, training, and personal relationships.[78] In one case, the child was born in Idaho but all parties left the state. They moved to Colorado but six weeks later, the mother and child moved to Massachusetts. Father filed for custody in Colorado; mother in Massachusetts. The court found that the child had no home state—all parties had left Idaho, child and a parent had not been in either Colorado or Massachusetts for 182 days preceding the filing of the petition. Using the significant connection provision, the Colorado court found the child had a more significant connection and there was more evidence in Massachusetts; mother had been the child's primary caregiver and mother's extended family was in Massachusetts.[79]

Significant connection jurisdiction applies to the state that has the most information about the child's present and future care, protection, training, and personal relationships. Usually the second basis will apply if the child and a parent have moved from the home state, and the other parent has also moved to another state.[80] The court can balance the evidence to determine which state has the closest connection to the child. Oklahoma decided that children who were only in the state for three weeks did not have a significant connection with Oklahoma, nor was there substantial evidence concerning the children's past, present, and future care.[81] Indiana, however, decided it did have significant connection jurisdiction where the child did not have a home state. Even though the parents lived in Indiana, the child had spent large amounts of time with the paternal grandparents in Oklahoma while the parents were working on their marriage. Mother filed for divorce in Indiana before father moved to Oklahoma and filed.[82]

Initial Jurisdiction: Default

Section 201(a)(4) provides for default jurisdiction where no state in which a parent and child had lived could properly exercise jurisdiction under the other bases for jurisdiction.[83] This basis is also known as "no other state has jurisdiction." In a multistate case, the mother had hidden the child from the father, ending up in North Carolina with a new husband and baby at the time she died. The grandmother from Michigan, with whom the mother had lived some of the time, took the child to her home and filed for custody. Michigan declined jurisdiction. Father, who now lived in South Carolina, learned of mother's death and came to North Carolina to file a custody action. The stepfather was not making a claim. The appellate court allowed North Carolina to take jurisdiction because no other state had jurisdiction under UCCJEA.[84]

Temporary Emergency Jurisdiction

Section 204 of the UCCJEA allows a court to exercise temporary emergency jurisdiction in cases where the child is present in the state and the child, or a parent or sibling of the child, has been abused or is threatened with abuse by the other parent.[85] The question is whether the child will be in immediate risk of harm upon return to the parent if the court does not take jurisdiction.[86] If the state has enacted the Uniform Child Abduction Prevention Act, the threat of abduction may also be an emergency basis.[87] The parent using UCAPA must be prepared to show a "credible risk" of abduction.[88]

Emergency jurisdiction is temporary.[89] A temporary emergency jurisdiction order is subject to a custody order from the state that has proper initial or continuing jurisdiction of the child, either the home state or the decree state if continuing. A court taking emergency jurisdiction must communicate with the court that has proper jurisdiction.[90] A court that has taken emergency jurisdiction must contact the court where a custody determination has been made to set a limit on the emergency and determine whether the original court will relinquish its exclusive continuing jurisdiction.[91] Failure to communicate with the court in the state with appropriate jurisdiction can result in reversal.[92] On the other hand, if there is judicial communication between the courts, it may be harmless error to not allow the counsel for a party to participate.[93]

The UCCJEA encourages states to decline jurisdiction if invoking jurisdiction may compromise the safety of a parent or the children. The Violence Against Women Act of 2000 (VAWA II) broadened the PKPA definition of emergency jurisdiction to cover domestic violence cases in a manner consistent with the UCCJEA.[94] Where a child was with her father in Massachusetts when he was arrested, Massachusetts had temporary emergency jurisdiction. New York, the child's home state, had jurisdiction to determine permanent custody issues or termination of parental rights.[95]

Emergency jurisdiction, however, should not be used when there is no emergency.[96] The Texas court could not exercise temporary emergency jurisdiction over a child with dual citizenship who had lived most of her life in Finland when there was no real emergency.[97] In appropriate cases, a court may impose sanctions.[98] A court may not enter permanent orders without following the procedures set forth in the UCCJEA.[99]

Being temporary, an order expires at the time stated in the order. If a state makes a six-month temporary emergency order, the parent should return to the state with continuing exclusive jurisdiction to modify the order or ask the state to decline jurisdiction.[100] If, however, the state that has jurisdiction does not act, the emergency jurisdiction state may become the home state.[101] So where a child had been residing in New York for more than 17 months under father's temporary order, the court made legal custody permanent.[102]

Declining Jurisdiction

A court that has jurisdiction may decline to exercise it if there is a pending action in another state acting with jurisdiction, if the state is an inconvenient forum, or if the parent has been guilty of unjustifiable conduct. The UCCJEA section 110 provides for communication between courts. When a trial court declines jurisdiction under the UCCJEA, the "objecting party is entitled to know that the trial court has engaged in a proper consideration of 'all relevant factors' and to a record that allows for meaningful appellate review."[103]

Pending Action

A court is prohibited from exercising jurisdiction over child custody questions when at the time of the filing of the petition, a proceeding concerning the custody of the child is pending in a court of another state exercising jurisdiction in conformity with that state's law.[104] A proceeding is only pending in another state, however, if that state is exercising jurisdiction in substantial conformity with the UCCJEA, which requires that the other parent has been given notice of the proceeding.

One case involved a mother who as a tennis player traveled internationally with her husband and baby. She filed for custody in Belarus while the family was living in Paris. Belarus found itself to be baby's place of residence. The parents separated later and the father, unaware of the Belarus filing, filed in California where the baby had been born and where the mother came to train for the U.S. Open. Because the father had not been given notice, which a Belarus expert testified would have been by registered mail, return receipt requested, its action was not a pending action such that a California court could not assume jurisdiction.[105]

Inconvenient Forum

UCCJEA section 201(a)(3) provides for jurisdiction when all courts, otherwise having jurisdiction under home state or significant connection, have declined to exercise jurisdiction on the ground that another state is the more appropriate forum to determine custody of the child. UCCJEA section 207(a) provides that a court may decline jurisdiction on the basis that the state is an inconvenient forum to hear a matter and that another more appropriate forum exists. If a court in the home state determines it is an inconvenient forum, a temporary emergency order can become permanent.

The factors of an "inconvenient forum" analysis are

1. whether domestic violence or mistreatment or abuse of a child or sibling has occurred and is likely to continue in the future and which state could best protect the parties and the child;[106]
2. the length of time the child has resided outside this state;
3. the distance between the court in this state and the court in the state that would assume jurisdiction;[107]
4. the relative financial circumstances of the parties;
5. any agreement of the parties as to which state should assume jurisdiction;
6. the nature and location of the evidence required to resolve the pending litigation, including testimony of the child;
7. the ability of the court of each state to decide the issue expeditiously and the procedures necessary to present the evidence;[108] and
8. the familiarity of the court of each state with the facts and issues in the pending litigation.[109]

The inconvenient forum is most often raised when one state has continuing jurisdiction, and one parent and the child have moved to another state. For example, New York made initial decree. Father sought to modify a custody order that granted mother sole legal and primary physical custody. The mother moved to dismiss on the basis that New York was an inconvenient forum. The New York Family Court properly considered the length of time the children had resided in New Jersey with the mother, the nature and location of the evidence required to resolve the litigation, and the familiarity of the court of each state with the facts and issues in the pending litigation.[110]

One of the factors used to determine if a state is an inconvenient forum is whether the parties had an agreement as to which state should assume jurisdiction. While the parents cannot give a court subject matter jurisdiction by agreement, the parties' determination as to which state should hear modifications can factor into the inconvenient forum analysis. In one case, the parties originally agreed that New Hampshire would retain jurisdiction even though there was an anticipated relocation of the child to California. The mother then moved to Indiana. The trial court failed to consider whether the move from California to Indiana made New Hampshire a more or less convenient forum, considering Indiana was closer than California. The court should give meaningful consideration to all relevant factors.[111]

Parties sometimes want to include a provision in the settlement agreement that the state in which the initial custody order is made shall continue to have future jurisdiction, including the right to hear future relocation cases. The provision could reserve jurisdiction during the child's minority so long as the nonresidential parent continues to live in the decree state. Because child custody jurisdiction is subject matter jurisdiction, this type of provision probably would not be enforced if all parties left the forum state.[112] An agreement as to future jurisdiction, however, may be relevant if there is an inconvenient forum determination. For example, in a Rhode Island case, the couple were dual citizens of Ireland and the United States. Following a 2008 divorce, they shared joint custody of their three children, with the mother having physical placement. The parties entered into an agreement that mother and children could return to Ireland in 2009 but that all future child custody disputes would remain under the jurisdiction of the PKPA, UCCJEA, and Rhode Island family court. The father visited the children regularly in Ireland; the children spent two weeks in the summer with him in Rhode Island. During the summer visit in 2014, the two oldest children expressed a desire not to return to the mother who had allegedly abused one of them. When the father filed an emergency petition, the mother filed for custody in Ireland. The Irish court said it would take jurisdiction if Rhode Island declined. The trial court declined. The father, who is a doctor, contended the clause relating to retention of jurisdiction in Rhode Island was vital to his decision to allow the children to relocate to Ireland. The appellate court found that the trial judge gave too little consideration to the parties' agreement. Where the court is vested with subject matter jurisdiction, an enforceable forum selection clause can settle the proper venue and prevent a party who has agreed to be bound from asserting forum non conveniens. The parties' final judgment entered by stipulation or consent cannot be set aside simply because one litigant no longer wants to be bound.[113]

Unjustifiable Conduct: Clean Hands

A court may decline to exercise its jurisdiction if a parent is guilty of bad faith. A Texas court declined jurisdiction when it became the home state only because of the mother's unjustifiable conduct in hiding the child by moving constantly between 36 states and two foreign countries.[114] A mother could not use her unauthorized conduct in removing the child from the state two years earlier and defying court's order to defeat the Arizona court's jurisdiction. The father continued to reside in the state and there was still substantial evidence.[115]

While "unjustifiable conduct" is not affirmatively defined, it does not include instances where a parent left the jurisdiction with a child because of domestic violence:

> a court shall not consider as a factor weighing against the petitioner any taking . . . or retention of the child . . . from the person who has legal custody, if there is evidence that the taking or retention of the child was to protect the petitioner from domestic violence or the child or sibling from mistreatment or abuse.[116]

Modification of Decrees and Exclusive Continuing Jurisdiction

Section 202 of the UCCJEA gives the decree state "exclusive continuing jurisdiction" until a court in the decree state determines that neither the child, the child's parents, nor any person acting as a parent have a significant connection with the decree state and substantial evidence concerning the child's care, protection, training, and personal relationships is no longer available[117] or a court of this state or another state determines that all parties have left the decree state. If a previous child custody order is in effect from a court that properly exercised initial jurisdiction, the petitioned court must determine whether the decree state continues to have jurisdiction to consider any modifications that may be requested, including a relocation request.

The PKPA recognizes continuing jurisdiction in the state that issued the initial custody determination. A court may modify a custody or visitation order from another state if it has jurisdiction to do so, and the court of the initial state no longer has, or has declined to exercise, jurisdiction over the custody matter. If a state has entered a temporary order or an interim parenting plan, that state retains jurisdiction.[118]

Continues as Long as One Party Remains in State

If the decree state properly had jurisdiction to make the initial custody determination, it retains jurisdiction generally as long as one party remains in the state and the child has some connection with that party in the state.[119] So even if one parent and child move out of the state and live in another state for years, the decree state retains jurisdiction if one party remains and the child visits the parent in that state.[120] North Dakota retained jurisdiction over custody even though the child has been out of the state for two years where the child had spent a great deal of time visiting his mother, had medical treatments, and had extended family in North Dakota.[121] Note that the registration of an out-of-state decree does not confer jurisdiction to modify, just to enforce.[122]

ECJ Ceases When All Parties Leave the Decree State

If, and only if, the decree state has lost jurisdiction because all parties have left the state or the state has given up jurisdiction may another state's court consider modification of the decree state's initial custody order. In the relocation context, this means that following a custody order, even if a parent and child move to a new state, the decree state retains jurisdiction to modify as long as the other parent remains in the decree state and the child retains contact with the parent and state. For example, in one case the mother had relocated the child to Wyoming where they had lived for several years. The New York Court of Appeals upheld the exclusive continuing jurisdiction of the New York courts to hear a modification of custody where the father remained in New York, the child visited, and had relatives there.[123] In another case, Virginia retained jurisdiction as the decree state because the mother continued to live there although the child alternated between the mother and father in California who worked for the state department.[124] Only if the decree state declines jurisdiction can the child's new "home state" assume jurisdiction.

New York lacked exclusive continuing jurisdiction over father's petition to enforce visitation where he lived in New Jersey and the mother and children lived in North Carolina.[125] A Kentucky family court was divested of jurisdiction to hear a mother's motion to relocate to Texas because the mother, the child, and the father all had relocated to Ohio before the mother filed her motion.[126] Parties by agreement cannot keep jurisdiction in the decree state if all parties leave the state. Even though the parties' divorce decree provided for Nevada to retain exclusive continuing jurisdiction, Nevada lost jurisdiction when all parties moved to Colorado.[127]

Whether all parties have left the state depends upon whether the parties have relinquished residency in the decree state.[128] In cases involving a military parent, the court may find that the parent has retained residency in the decree state, even if absent due to service.[129] Alaska determined that the term "presently resides" should be interpreted consistently with "residency" under Alaska law. A father in the military was stationed in South Carolina. Because of the shared parenting order, the mother and children also moved to South Carolina. Even though all parties had "left the state," the court determined the father at all times intended to return to Alaska. Thus, his residency remained in

Alaska, and Alaska retained exclusive continuing jurisdiction.[130] If a state has too tenuous of a relationship over the custody issues, the state can decline to exercise jurisdiction in favor of a more convenient forum.

Notice/Service

Before a custody determination is made, the UCCJEA requires notice and an opportunity to be heard be given to all persons entitled to notice. A parent is certainly a person entitled to notice. Adequate notice is a factor fundamental to jurisdiction. Notice must be given in a manner reasonably calculated to give actual notice.

Where an unwed California father filed an ex parte request for temporary emergency orders on child custody and visitation with a baby, the California court found it had jurisdiction because mother's notice to the father of her action filed in Belarus was insufficient under the UCCJEA. Belarus did not have jurisdiction in conformity with UCCJEA standards.[131]

A trial court's failure to specify the purpose of a UCCJEA hearing provided the parties with inadequate notice of hearing and violated the provision governing communication between courts.[132] In another case, a father was denied procedural due process to have the opportunity to prove that Japan declined to exercise jurisdiction.[133]

The UCCJEA requires service by certified/registered mail *or* such service as the judge may direct, which *may* be by publication. It is best to send by registered mail *and* publication right at the beginning. Then, the next time the case has to be in court, the lawyer can file a motion asking the judge to allow the service requirement to be satisfied by the publication. It is preferable to file a motion requesting an order of publication, even though the publication may be issued without such a motion.

Registration and Recognition of Sister State Decrees

The UCCJEA section 303 mandates recognition and enforcement of child custody determinations if the decree court made the orders in substantial conformity with the UCCJEA.[134] If a proceeding in another country did not give notice to a parent, the country is not exercising jurisdiction in conformity with the UCCJEA, and a state does not have to defer to that proceeding.[135] The person seeking the registration has the burden of producing evidence that the custody determination was made in accordance with the UCCJEA.[136]

Any relocation order should require registration of the decree in the new state. The lawyer may decide which party should file the registration. In many instances, it will be better for the non-relocating parent to have local counsel in the other state register the order. The left-behind parent will feel more at ease, knowing there is an enforcement mechanism, and he or she already has contact with a lawyer if the need arises. Either parent could be required to pay the expense, if any, of registration.

The orders entitled to enforcement include temporary emergency orders, foreign custody orders, tribal custody orders, registered orders, and the custody and visitation provisions of a domestic violence civil order. Registration of a child custody determination can be done with or without a simultaneous request for enforcement. The proceedings are generally ministerial.[137] The lawyer representing a person wishing to register should consult the procedures in the new state and seek co-counsel in the state in which registration is sought. Seeking co-counsel avoids practicing law without a license and builds relationships that may be needed for an enforcement action later. A court did not lose jurisdiction under the UCCJEA when the parent registered its custody order in another state.[138]

Registration Requirements

The UCCJEA requires that the person seeking to register an order send:

1. a letter requesting registration;
2. two copies, including one certified copy, of the custody order to be registered;
3. an affidavit (or "statement under penalty of perjury") that the order has not been modified; and
4. the name and address of the person seeking registration and any parent or person who has been awarded custody or visitation in the determination sought to be registered.

If the applicant claims that their health, safety, or liberty or that of the child would be jeopardized by openly disclosing such information, there is a special procedure for separately furnishing information confidentially.

The court shall file the custody determination as a foreign judgment and give notice to the persons named in the request, so they have an opportunity to contest by filing notice of contest within 20 days of service. All states require a cover sheet from the new jurisdiction or a local form over the certified copy. A copy of the entire packet is then served on the other parent.

Once registration is requested and attachments delivered, the clerk must:

1. File the custody order as a "foreign judgment" along with one copy of the registration request and all accompanying information—regardless of their form.
2. Serve all persons who have been awarded custody, visitation, or placement rights with a notice of the registration. The notice itself must state that:
   a. the out of state custody order has been registered and is immediately enforceable just as a custody order of the registering state,
   b. a hearing to contest the order's validity must be requested within 20 days, and
   c. if the registration is not contested, the order will be confirmed and further contest precluded.
3. Serve copies of the order and application. Especially where there are Internet accessible UCCJEA registration forms, clerks should include copies (uncertified) of the order being registered and its accompanying documents along with the notice.

While the statute refers to the "clerk," these duties usually fall on the registering party. Sometimes the clerk will have a "service packet" that one can pick up to make service. In some states, a court administrator may send out the notice of registration letter.

If the parent requests a hearing, UCCJEA section 310(a) provides only three bases for contesting a registration:

1. That the issuing court did not have subject-matter jurisdiction;[139] or
2. A court of competent jurisdiction has stayed or vacated the child custody determination; or
3. The person contesting was entitled to notice in the proceeding but did not receive it.[140]

A court is not required to register an order that was ineffective or issued without jurisdiction. Vermont was not required to register an Alabama custody order obtained by the father because Alabama lacked subject matter jurisdiction. At the time father commenced the Alabama proceeding, Vermont was already exercising jurisdiction in conformity with the UCCJEA.[141]

A North Carolina Court of Appeals found that the trial court lacked subject matter jurisdiction over father's petition to register provisional and final custody determinations by a Shar'ia court in Jerusalem where he failed to provide certified copies of the orders. The stamp on the order was not sufficient to render either document a certified copy.[142] A party seeking to enforce a foreign custody order must show not only factual circumstances in substantial conformity with the initial jurisdictional requirements of the UCCJEA but also show that the foreign order substantially conforms to the UCCJEA's policies of enforcing prior decrees and avoiding conflicting jurisdiction.[143]

The court shall recognize and enforce (but not modify, except in accordance with other provisions) a registered child custody determination. As soon as the registration request is initially filed with the clerk, the out-of-state custody order is fully enforceable, as any state custody order is, unless and until it is challenged successfully. Once the order is confirmed, whether because there is no contest within the time period or after a hearing, any further contest is precluded for any matter that could have been asserted at registration.

Registering in Relocation Cases

Prior registration is not essential to getting expedited enforcement of a sister state's custody order. However, there are benefits to getting a custody determination registered and confirmed before the children leave the "home" or "judgment decree" state to spend time or live with the other parent. Once the custody order is confirmed and registered, the only defense to expedited enforcement is that the order has been modified, vacated, or stayed. The registration process eliminates the defenses that the court lacked jurisdiction or the respondent did not get proper notice. It is a good idea to put the federal statutes for interstate recognition of custody orders by sister states (PKPA) and the C.F.R. cite in the text of the order.

Jurisdiction Checklist[144]

- [ ] Initial order of custody—jurisdiction to determine child custody
  - [ ] child is American citizen and lives in the United States
  - [ ] child is foreign citizen
    - [ ] Hague Child Abduction Convention does not apply because
      - [ ] child is here with permission of both parents,
      - [ ] United States is habitual residence, or
      - [ ] other country is not a signatory to the convention
      - [ ] other parent did not have or was not exercising rights of custody
    - [ ] Hague Child Abduction Convention may apply but there is defense because
      - [ ] the child has been here more than a year and the child is settled in environment
    - [ ] Hague Child Abduction Convention applies but
      - [ ] there is a grave risk of harm if the child is returned
      - [ ] the child is "mature" and wishes to remain
  - [ ] the child is not of Native American origin
  - [ ] the child is Native American—check applicability of Indian Child Welfare Act
    - [ ] divorce context—Indian Child Welfare Act not applicable in this state
    - [ ] ICWA applies
    - [ ] notice to tribe required

- [ ] no existing ties to tribe or reservation
- [ ] unsure if applies but notify tribe anyway

[ ] Home state jurisdiction

- [ ] child and parent or person acting as parent have been residents of this state for six consecutive months preceding the filing of the petition
  - [ ] any absence has been temporary
- [ ] addresses of child for last five years
- [ ] child living with parent(s)
- [ ] child living with person acting as parent
- [ ] child not wrongfully brought into state or retained from foreign country
- [ ] no other pending actions regarding custody

[ ] There is no home state, and the child and the contestant have significant connections and there is substantial evidence in this state about child's welfare and care

[ ] Emergency—

- [ ] child has been abandoned, neglected, abused, or is otherwise in need of temporary emergency protection by court
- [ ] one parent has threatened to abduct the child [UCAPA]

[ ] no other state has jurisdiction

- [ ] no home state
- [ ] other

[ ] declining jurisdiction

- [ ] unjustifiable conduct
- [ ] pending action in another state that is properly exercising jurisdiction

[ ] forum is inconvenient—relevant factors:

- [ ] whether domestic violence has occurred and is likely to continue in the future and which state could best protect the parties and the child
- [ ] the length of time the child has resided outside this state
- [ ] the distance between the court in this state and the court in the state that would assume jurisdiction

        [ ] the relative financial circumstances of the parties
        [ ] any agreement of the parties as to which state should assume jurisdiction
        [ ] the nature and location of the evidence required to resolve the pending litigation, including testimony of the child
        [ ] the ability of the court of each state to decide the issue expeditiously and the procedures necessary to present the evidence
        [ ] the familiarity of the court of each state with the facts and issues in the pending litigation
    [ ] no other reason to decline jurisdiction
[ ] Jurisdiction of parents or other party
    [ ] other party is resident of or domiciled in this state
    [ ] other party will consent to jurisdiction
    [ ] other party will voluntarily enter general appearance
    [ ] personal service of process within state, "tag" jurisdiction, possible
    [ ] long-arm jurisdiction possible
        [ ] does business in this state
        [ ] child conceived in state and child remained here
        [ ] parties had marital domicile in state and one spouse continued to reside here
        [ ] child was conceived in state and one party continues to reside with child here
        [ ] other activity in state to support minimum contacts
        [ ] notice sent pursuant to UCCJEA but no personal jurisdiction
    [ ] Notice given
        [ ] personal
        [ ] mail, receipt requested, certified, other
        [ ] publication
    [ ] Modification
        [ ] state of original decree with continuing jurisdiction because all parties are still in state
        [ ] state of original decree and parent and child still live here, although one parent has moved

[ ] state of original decree; parent and child have moved from the state but one contestant remains in state and child has significant connection with state

[ ] not state of original decree but both parents and child have moved from that state; this is child's new home state

Endnotes

1. Brandt v. Brandt, 268 P.3d 406 (Colo. 2012). *See also* Mouritsen v. Mouritsen, 459 P.3d 476 (Alaska 2020).

2. *In re* Marriage of Orate, 455 P.3d 1158 (Wash. Ct. App. 2020).

3. Restatement, Conflict of Law § 117 (1934).

4. May v. Anderson, 345 U.S. 528, 535–36 (1953) (Ohio was not required to give full faith and credit to father's ex parte divorce granting custody in Wisconsin where family had lived until mother's move to Ohio). The long-arm statute of most states would have extended personal jurisdiction over the mother under the facts of the case.

5. Servicemembers Civil Relief Act, 50 U.S.C. App. §§ 501 *et seq*. *See* Sara Estrin, *The Servicemembers Civil Relief Act: Why and How This Act Applies to Child Custody Proceedings*, 27 Law & Ineq. 211 (2009). *See also* Mark Sullivan, The Military Divorce Handbook ch. 3 (ABA 3d ed 2019).

6. *See In re* Marriage of Rostrom, 339 P.3d 185 (Wash. Ct. App. 2014).

7. *In re* M.B., 635 S.E.2d 810 (N.C. Ct. App. 2006). *See also In re* N.U., 369 P.3d 984 (Kan. Ct. App. 2016) (noting the UCCJEA is a limitation provided by law on the subject matter jurisdiction of the Kansas courts).

8. Bowman v. Bowman, 811 S.E.2d 103 (Ga. Ct. App. 2018) (Georgia was not the home state when children had only been there 30 days and there was no emergency.). *See In re* Marriage of Fontenot, 77 P.3d 206 (Mont. 2003); *In re* J.B., 595 S.E.2d 794 (N.C. Ct. App. 2004).

9. Plummer v. Plummer, 823 S.E.2d 258 (Ga. 2019) (trial court had continuing jurisdiction over father's petition to modify custody even though after filing mother, child and father all moved out of state).

10. M.H. v. D.E.H., 376 So. 3d 536 (Ala. Civ. App. 2022); Kubal v. Anderson, 8 N.W.3d 811 (N.D. 2024); *In re* Jones, 430 P.3d 544 (Okla. Civ. App. 2018); *In re* Ruff, 275 P.3d 1175 (Wash. Ct. App. 2012). *See* Linda D. Elrod, Child Custody Practice and Procedure § 3:1 (Thomson Reuters 2024).

11. Officer v. Blankenship, 555 S.W.3d 449 (Ky. Ct. App. 2018).

12. *In re* A.G.M., 773 S.E.2d 123, 129 (N.C. Ct. App. 2015). *See also* Greenhough v. Goforth, 126 S.W.3d 345 (Ark. 2003) (Arkansas lacked subject matter jurisdiction over custody and paternity case of child who lived in Philippines, Australia, and South Carolina.).

13. Cook v. Arimitsu, 907 N.W.2d 233 (Minn. Ct. App. 2018). *See also* DeLima v. Tsevi, 921 N.W.2d 89 (Neb. 2018) (vacating years of custody orders where the child's home state was Togo; Nebraska lacked subject matter jurisdiction).

14. Kragen v. Eighth Jud. Dist. Ct. 555 P.3d 1218 (Nev. Ct. App. 2024).

15. UCCJA § 3, 9 UNIF. L. ANN. (Part IA) 261 (1999). *See* Brigitte Bodenheimer, *The Uniform Child Custody Jurisdiction Act: A Legislative Remedy for Children Caught in the Conflict of Laws*, 22 VAND. L. REV. 1207 (1969).

16. *See* Ramirez v. Barnet, 384 P.3d 828 (Ariz. Ct. App. 2016) (PKPA prohibited New York from granting adoption of child where Arizona was the home state and a paternity action had been filed there first).

17. 28 U.S.C. § 1738A(d)(f); Parisi v. Niblett, 238 A.3d 740 (Conn. App. Ct. 2020). *See* MARIE FAHNERT & MELYSE MPIRANYA, CHILD-CUSTODY JURISDICTION: THE UCCJEA & PKPA (ABA 2015).

18. Guardianship of a Minor, 1542 N.E.3d 772 (Mass. App. Ct. 2020) (Massachusetts as child's home state and mother's residence had jurisdiction to terminate guardianship even though Michigan court purported to issue a permanent guardianship).

19. Ramirez v. Barnet, 384 P.3d 828 (Ariz. Ct. App. 2016). *See also* Miller-Jenkins v. Miller-Jenkins, 637 S.E.2d 330 (Va. Ct. App. 2006); Miller-Jenkins v. Miller-Jenkins, 912 A.2d 951 (Vt. 2006).

20. Ledoux-Nottingham v. Downs, 210 So. 3d 1217 (Fla. 2017); Fitzpatrick v. McCrary, 183 A.3d 737 (Me. 2018).

21. *See* B.M. v. J.M., 306 So. 3d 38 (Ala. Civ. App. 2020).

22. *In re* M.R.F.-C., 158 N.E.3d 688 (Ohio Ct. App. 2020) (family's long-time residence in Michigan was appropriate in determining whether Michigan court retained continuing exclusive jurisdiction and was more appropriate forum).

23. *See* Thompson v. Thompson, 484 U.S. 174 (1988).

24. 9 UNIF. L. ANN. Part IA 649 (1999). For a discussion of the UCCJEA, *see* Patricia M. Hoff, *The ABC's of the UCCJEA: Interstate Child-Custody Practice Under the New Act*, 32 FAM. L.Q. 267 (1998); *Uniform Child Custody Jurisdiction and Enforcement Act (with Prefatory Note and Comments by Robert G. Spector)*, 32 FAM. L.Q. 301 (1998).

25. *See* Patricia Hoff, *The Uniform Child Custody Jurisdiction and Enforcement Act* 4 (OJJDP 2001).

26. McCormick v. Robertson, 28 N.E.3d 795 (Ill. 2015) (2010 consent custody order was not void for lack of subject-matter jurisdiction where mother had submitted to the jurisdiction of Illinois, the parentage decision was valid).

27. *See generally* LINDA D. ELROD, CHILD CUSTODY PRACTICE AND PROCEDURE, Ch. 3 (Thomson Reuters 2024).

28. *See, e.g.*, *In re* T.L.B., 272 P.3d 1148 (Colo. App. 2012) (Canada is treated as a state under the UCCJEA); Atkinson v. Atkinson, 664 N.W.2d 249 (Mich. Ct. App. 2003); *In re* Y.M.A., 111 S.W.3d 790 (Tex. App. 2003).

29. Convention of 19 October 1996 on Jurisdiction, Applicable Law, Recognition, Enforcement and Co-operation in Respect of Parental Responsibility and Measures for the Protection of Children (Hague Protection Convention).

30. Cabrera v. Mercado, 146 A.3d 567 (Md. Spec. Ct. App. 2016). *See also In re* Marriage of Fernandez-Abin, 120 Cal. Rptr. 3d 227 (Ct. App. 2011) (trial court's determination to include parties' children within the scope of the protective order for wife in a Domestic Violence Protection Act action was a child custody determination).

31. Stauffer v. Temperle, 794 N.W.2d 317 (Iowa Ct. App. 2010).

32. Foster v. Wolkowitz, 785 N.W.2d 59 (Mich. 2010). *See also* Powers v. Wagner, 716 S.E.2d 354 (N.C. Ct. App. 2011) (finding Florida paternity and support order not to be a custody determination).

33. Berwick v. Wagner, 336 S.W.3d 805 (Tex. App. 2011).

34. UCCJEA § 102(14) describes a person acting as a parent as one who has physical custody of the child and has been awarded legal custody by a court or claims a right to legal custody under the law of the state.

35. UCCJEA § 102(7). *See* Duckett v. Goforth, 649 S.E.2d 72 (S.C. Ct. App. 2007); Rhoads v. Rhoads, 209 S.W.3d 24 (Mo. Ct. App. 2006) ("lived" means physically present, not legal residence). Bowman v. Bowman, 811 S.E.2d 103 (Ga. Ct. App. 2018) (Georgia lacked jurisdiction to make custody order where Michigan was home state and there was no emergency); Chamberlin v. Chamberlin, 176 So. 3d 1118 (La. Ct. App. 2015).

36. *See* Rosen v. Celebreeze, 83 N.E.3d 420 (Ohio 2008).

37. *See* N.M.C. v. J.L.W. *ex rel.* N.A.W., 90 P.3d 93 (Wyo. 2004) (home state jurisdiction trumps the forum state's significant connection jurisdiction).

38. Plummer v. Plummer, 823 S.E.2d 258 (Ga. 2019) (date of filing controls).

39. *See* Reisinger v. Reisinger, 125 S.W.3d 879 (Mo. Ct. App. 2004) (a child's being in a state based upon a court's invalid order that mother reside with her there, gave the court home-state jurisdiction). *See also* Baxter v. Baxter, 171 So. 3d 1159 (La. Ct. App. 2015) (Louisiana was not the home state when no one currently lived there: mother and child in Canada since 2012 and Navy father had lived in Afghanistan and D.C.); Chamberlin v. Chamberlin, 176 So. 3d 1118 (La. Ct. App. 2015).

40. *In re* Marriage of Sampley, 347 P.3d 1281 (Mont. 2015) (parties moved from Alaska to Montana but the next month, the mother and child went to Canada to visit her parents and stayed when her father had cancer diagnosis).

41. Fitzgerald v. Jackson, 307 A.3d 1283 (R.I. 2024) (Rhode Island where children had been living for four years was home state; Australia declined to exercise jurisdiction and dismissed the father's case there.).

42. Seligman-Hargis v. Hargis, 186 S.W.3d 582 (Tex. App. 2006) (fact that Texas was military father's domicile did not give it custody jurisdiction when children had lived in Germany).

43. Officer v. Blankenship, 555 S.W.3d 449 (Ky. App. 2018) (even though mother consented to Kentucky's jurisdiction, the Kentucky custody order was invalid because the children had been living with the mother in Oregon for two years prior to the filing of the petition).

44. Seekins v. Hamm, 129 A.3d 940 (Me. 2015).

45. Gray v. Gray, 139 So. 3d 802, 806 (Ala. Civ. App. 2013): *In re* McK v. Bode, 974 N.Y.S.3d 434 (App. Div. 2013); Mireles v. Veronie, 154 N.E.3d 727 (Ohio Ct. App. 2020); Arnold v. Price, 365 S.W.3d 455 (Tex. App. 2011).

46. *See* B.B. v. A.B., 916 N.Y.S.2d 920 (Sup. 2011) (Minnesota where mother had gone while pregnant and gave birth was the home state, not New York, which had been marital residence); *In re* Custody of Kalbes, 733 N.W.2d 648, 650 (Wis. Ct. App. 2007) (Wisconsin was home state of child born there even though there was a pending divorce action in Idaho). *See also* Castro v. Castro, 818 N.W.2d 753 (N.D. 2012).

47. In Interest of G.C.M.M., 477 P.3d 792 (Colo. App. 2020).

48. *In re* Wilner v. Prowda, 601 N.Y.S.2d 518 (Sup. 1993); Waltenberg v. Waltenberg, 270 S.W.3d 308, 316–17 (Tex. App. 2008) (pregnant mother allowed to relocate to New York).

49. Sara Ashton McK. v. Samuel Bode M., 974 N.Y.S.2d 434 (App. Div. 2013) (New York was the home state because child was born and lived there for two days when the mother filed for custody); Fleckles v. Diamond, 35 N.E.3d 176 (Ill. App. Ct. 2015) (Illinois lacked jurisdiction where pregnant mother had moved to Colorado, had baby and remained there). *See also* Ocegueda v. Perreira, 181 Cal. Rptr. 3d 845 (Ct. App. 2015) (Hawaii was home state where child was born there and lived six weeks before going to California where father immediately filed action).

50. Barwich v. Ceruti, 31 N.E.3d 1008 (Ind. Ct. App. 2015).

51. Loeb v. Vergara, 313 So. 3d 346 (La. Ct. App. 2021) (recognizing human ovum as a juridical person but not a natural person; UCCJEA provides no definitions for embryos or unborn children and an unborn child cannot have a home state).

52. Swanson v. Swanson, 503 P.3d 982 (Idaho 2022) (Utah where child was born had jurisdiction to determine custody issues, not Idaho where mother had brought infant).

53. Gutierrez v. Fox, 394 P.3d 109 (Ariz. Ct. App. 2017).

54. Mauldin v. Bearden, 293 S.W.3d 392 (Ky. 2009) (home state court, however, deferred to Alabama where child and prospective adoptive parents had lived for over a year).

55. Nemes v. Tutino, 101 N.Y.S.3d 538 (App. Div. 2019).

56. Baker v. Tunney, 201 So. 3d 1235 (Fla. Dist. Ct. App. 2016). *See also* Ramirez v. Barnet, 384 P.3d 828 (Ariz. Ct. App. 2016).

57. *In re* C.J.S., 702 S.W.3d 573 (Tex. App.-Houston 2024).

58. McNeil v. Stern, 370 So. 3d 1187 (La. Ct. App. 2023), *writ denied* 376 So. 3d 847 (La. 2024).

59. Cook v. Arimitsu, 907 N.W.2d 233 (Minn. Ct. App. 2018).

60. Kubal v. Anderson, 8 N.W.3d 811 (N.D. 2024).

61. Bata v. Konanm, 217 A.3d 774 (N.J. Super. Ct. Chancery Div. 2019). *See also* Adams v. Adams, 432 S.W.3d 49 (Ark. Ct. App. 2014); Shao v. Ma, 861 N.E.2d 788 (Mass. App. Ct. 2007). *See* Andrea Charlow, *There's No Place Like Home: Temporary Absences in the UCCJEA Home State*, 28 J. AMER. ACAD. MATRIM. LAWYERS 25 (2015).

62. *See, e.g.*, Norris v. Norris, 345 P.3d 924, 928–29 n.22 (Alaska 2015); *In re* Marriage of Sampley, 347 P.3d 1281 (Mont. 2015) (Montana was not the child's home state because there was no six-month period that child lived there).

63. *In re* Marsalis, 338 S.W.3d 131 (Tex. App. 2011).

64. Felty v. Felty, 882 N.Y.S.2d 504, 505–09 (App. Div. 2009).

65. Dean v. Sherron, 91 N.Y.S.3d 639 (App. Div. 2018).

66. *See, e.g.*, Ogawa v. Ogawa, 221 P.3d 699, 704 (Nev. 2009) (absence was temporary because parents intended it to be a three-month vacation).

67. Antonetti v. Westerhausen in and for Cnty. of Maricopa, 523 P.3d 969 (Ariz. Ct. App. 2023) (mother and child born in Tunisia came to Arizona during COVID-19 shut down during vacation in Italy); Garba v. Ndiaye, 143 A.3d 908 (Md. Spec. Ct. App. 2016); Sajjad v. Cheema, 51 A.3d 146 (N.J. Super. Ct. App. Div. 2012); *In re* Marriage of Margain and Ruiz-Bours, 372 P.3d 313 (Ariz. Ct. App. 2016); Chick v. Chick, 596 S.E.2d 303 (N.C. Ct. App. 2004); *In re* Marriage of Schwartz and Battini, 410 P.3d 319 (Or. Ct. App. 2017).

68. Bata v. Konan, 217 A.3d 774 (N.J. Super. Ct. Ch. Div. 2019) (time spent with mother in New Jersey was temporary absence from New York). *See also* Ogawa v. Ogawa, 221 P.3d 699, 704–05 (Nev. 2009).

69. Dellapenta v. Goldy, 575 S.W.3d 697 (Ky. Ct. App. 2018).

70. Norris v. Norris, 345 P.3d 924, 928–29 (Alaska 2015); *In re* A.W., 94 A.3d 1161, 1167–68 (Vt. 2014); Carter v. Carter, 758 N.W.2d 1, 8–9 (Neb. 2008); Chick v. Chick, 596 S.E.2d 303, 308 (N.C. Ct. App. 2004).

71. *In re* B.K., 425 P.3d 703 (Mont. 2018) (intent was to move to Minnesota temporarily to increase father's employment opportunities but mother had agreement with father of her other child that she would stay less than a year).

72. Kragen v. Eighth Jud. Dist. Ct., 555 P.3d 1218 (Nev. Ct. App. 2024).

73. *In re* Brilliant, 86 S.W.3d 680 (Tex. App. 2002). *See* Mouritzen v. Mouritzen, 459 P.3d 476 (Alaska 2020).

74. Carter v. Carter, 958 N.W.2d 1 (Neb. 2008). *See also* Consford v. Consford, 711 N.Y.S.2d 199 (Sup. 2000) (time spent in Arizona was not a temporary absence from Texas where child had lived in Texas only two months and in Arizona five).

75. Baxter v. Baxter, 171 So. 3d 1159 (La. Ct. App. 2015).

76. Brandt v. Brandt, 268 P.3d 406 (Colo. 2012) (Maryland retained continuing jurisdiction even though child was living with father in Colorado during mother's deployment); *Mouritsen*, 459 P.3d 476 (Alaska retained

continuing jurisdiction even though father deployed to South Carolina and mother and children followed to continue shared parenting plan.).

77. Cook v. Arimitsu, 907 N.W.3d 233 (Minn. Ct. App. 2018). *See also* Ogawa v. Ogawa, 221 P.3d 699 (Nev. 2009).

78. *In re* Marriage of Hamilton, 84 P.3d 259 (Wash. Ct. App. 2004).

79. *In re* B.C.B., 411 P.3d 926 (Colo. Ct. App. 2015).

80. *See In re* Diaz, 845 N.E.2d 935 (Ill. App. Ct. 2006) (significant connection appropriate where child had no home state, child was born in Illinois; maternal grandmother lived there; mother had returned often during marriage; and Illinois had substantial evidence).

81. *In re* Marriage of Jones & White, 430 P.3d 544 (Okla. Civ. App. 2018). *See also* Wolter v. Fortuna, 928 N.W.2d 416 (Neb. Ct. App. 2019) (Florida did not have significant connection jurisdiction based on mother living there four months).

82. Hays v. Hockett, 94 N.E.3d 300 (Ind. Ct. App. 2018).

83. *See also* Wolter v. Fortuna, 928 N.W.2d 416 (Neb. Ct. App. 2019) (finding Florida did not have significant connection jurisdiction based on mother living there four months and that Nebraska had "last resort" jurisdiction).

84. Sulier v. Veneskey, 878 S.E.2d 633 (N.C. Ct. App. 2022).

85. UCCJEA § 204; 28 U.S.C. 1738A(c)(2)(C)(ii). *See* Schultz v. Schultz, 187 P.3d 1234 (Idaho 2008).

86. Dept of Hum. Servs. v. T.G., 425 P.3d 480 (Or. Ct. App. 2018).

87. *See* UCAPA § 5b (2007). *See* Linda D. Elrod, *The Uniform Child Abduction Prevention Act: A New Tool to Prevent Child Abduction, in* 2009 FAMILY LAW UPDATE 187 (Ronald L. Brown & Laura W. Morgan, eds. 2009).

88. *In re* Marriage of Badawiyeh, 528 P.3d 194 (Colo. App. 2023) (citing COLO. REV. STAT. § 14-13.5-108(2)).

89. *In re* D.N.H.W., 955 So. 2d 1236 (Fla. Dist. Ct. App. 2007).

90. Melgar v. Campo, 161 P.3d 1269 (Ariz. Ct. App. 2007).

91. R.B. v. S.M., 570 S.W.3d 9 (Ky. Ct. App. 2019).

92. McAbee v. McAbee, 259 So. 3d 134 (Fla. Dist. Ct. App. 2018). *See also* Interest of D.L., 928 N.W.2d 133 (Iowa Ct. App. 2019) (juvenile case remanded for the trial court to communicate with Texas and determine if Texas had closed its prior-in-time juvenile case).

93. Lunsford v. Engle, 312 So. 3d 904 (Fla. Dist. Ct. App. 2021).

94. *See* Deborah Goelman, *Shelter from the Storm: Using Jurisdictional Statutes to Protect Victims of Domestic Violence After the Violence Against Women Act of 2000,* 13 COLUM. J. GENDER & L. 101 (2004).

95. Adoption of Twila, 240 N.E.3d 233 (Mass. App. Ct. 2024).

96. Bowman v. Bowman, 811 S.W.2d 103 (Ga. Ct. App. 2018) (Georgia lacked jurisdiction when mother filed custody action less than 30 days after children were in state and there was no emergency). *See also* Prabnarong v. Oudomhack, 780 S.E.2d 393 (Ga. Ct. App. 2015) (trial court erred in exercising emergency jurisdiction after mother's death where there was no emergency and Washington court had custody jurisdiction).

97. *In re* Salminen, 492 S.W.3d 31 (Tex. App. 2016).

98. LaCroix v. Verdoorn, 2016 WL 4384429 (Iowa Ct. App. 2016) (unpublished) (imposing sanctions on both a mother and her attorney for abusing the emergency jurisdiction process by repeatedly filing emergency petitions when there was no emergency).

99. *In re* Marriage of Ruff, 275 P.3d 1175 (Wash. Ct. App. 2012); S.C. v. J.T.C., 47 So. 3d 1253, 1257–58 (Ala. Civ. App. 2010); *In re* Maxwell T., 721 N.W.2d 676 (Neb. Ct. App. 2006).

100. *In re* N.U., 369 P.3d 984 (Kan. Ct. App. 2016).

101. *In re* K.L.B., 431 P.3d 883 (Kan. Ct. App. 2018). *See also* W.H. v. Dep't for Children & Fam., 2020 WL 6822505 (Vt. Nov. 20, 2020).

102. People v. N.N., 197 N.Y.S.3d 671 (Sup. Ct. 2023).

103. *In re* Matter of McAndrews, 193 A.3d 834 (N.H. 2018) (reversing court for not examining the inconvenient forum factors because New Hampshire had continuing exclusive jurisdiction and father still resided there at the time mother filed for modification in Indiana).

104. Jones v. Whimper, 727 S.E.2d 700 (N.C. Ct. App. 2012) (trial court properly declined jurisdiction where there was a pending action in New Jersey which had home state jurisdiction). *See also* Cox v. Cantrell, 866 N.E.2d 798 (Ind. Ct. App. 2007).

105. W.M. v. V.A., 241 Cal. Rptr. 3d 170 (Ct. App. 2018).

106. Rice v. McDonald, 390 P.3d 1133 (Alaska 2017); Stoneman v. Drollinger, 64 P.3d 997 (Mont. 2003); *In re* T.R., 792 S.E.2d 197 (N.C. Ct. App. 2016).

107. Symington v. Symington, 167 P.3d 658 (Wyo. 2007).

108. Kevin McK., v. Elizabeth A.E., 54 N.Y.S.3d 17 (App. Div. 2017) (finding Mississippi was more convenient forum after mother and child relocated there).

109. *See* Hogan v. McAndrew, 131 A.3d 717 (R.I. 2016); Duckett v. Goforth, 649 S.E.2d 72 (S.C. Ct. App. 2007); Griffith v. Tressel, 925 A.2d 702 (N.J. Super. Ct. App. Div. 2007).

110. Feltz v. Yanucil, 182 N.Y.S.3d 836 (App. Div. 2023).

111. *In re* Matter of McAndrews, 193 A.3d 834 (N.H. 2018) (reversing trial court for not examining the inconvenient forum factors when New Hampshire had exclusive continuing jurisdiction and father continued to reside there at the time mother filed for modification in Indiana).

112. Friedman v. Eighth Jud. Dist. Ct. of Nev., 264 P.3d 1161 (Nev. 2011) (parties agreement to keep Nevada jurisdiction invalid where all parties had lived in California for years).

113. Hogan v. McAndrew, 141 A.3d 717 (R.I. 2016) (appellate court also noted that there was a lack of evidence presented and findings about whether Irish law would recognize joint custody awards and would consider the wishes of the children).

114. *In re* S.L.P., 123 S.W.3d 685 (Tex. Ct. App. 2003). *See also In re* Lewin, 149 S.W.3d 727 (Tex. App. 2004).

115. *In re* Marriage of Mangan, 258 P.3d 164 (Ariz. Ct. App. 2011).

116. UCCJEA § 208. *See* Hector G. v. Josefina P., 771 N.Y.S.2d 316, 331 (2003).

117. *In re* Sheys, 120 A.3d 150 (N.H. 2015). *See* Billhime v. Billhime, 952 A.2d 1174 (Pa. Super. Ct. 2008); Wallace v. Wallace, 224 S.W.3d 587 (Ky. Ct. App. 2007).

118. *In re* Ruff, 275 P.3d 1175 (Wash. Ct. App. 2012) (Montana which entered interim order retained jurisdiction because father still lived there even though mother and child had left the state).

119. *In re* Marriage of Kent, 247 Cal. Rptr. 3d 466 (Ct. App. 2019) (father still lived in North Carolina, which retained ECJ); Harvey v. Harvey, 303 So. 3d 357 (La. Ct. App. 2020) (Louisiana court lacked jurisdiction to modify order where mother and children still lived in decree state of Florida); Shelstad v. Shelstad, 927 N.W.2d 129 (S.D. 2019) (South Dakota as decree state where father continued to live had jurisdiction).

120. *In re* Marriage of Lloyd, 255 P.3d 166 (Mont. 2011) (Montana retained ECJ because father and extended family remained there even though child lived in Kentucky). *See also In re* Sheys, 120 A.3d 150 (N.H. 2015); Roach v. Breeden, 777 S.E.2d 689 (Ga. Ct. App. 2015); Wallace v. Wallace, 224 S.W.3d 587 (Ky. Ct. App. 2007); Rennie v. Rosenthal, 995 A.2d 1217 (Pa. Super. Ct. 2010).

121. State *ex rel.* Klein v. Winegar, 893 N.W.2d 741 (N.D. 2017).

122. Schroeder v. Schroeder, 658 N.W.2d 909 (Minn. Ct. App. 2003) (Minnesota lacked jurisdiction to modify custody where father still lived in decree state).

123. Vernon v. Vernon, 800 N.E.2d 1085 (N.Y. 2003) (child still had significant connection to New York where she was born and her father, half-sister, and other relatives live, and where substantial evidence regarding the child's present and future welfare exists). *See also* Swanson v. Perez-Swanson, 259 A.3d 39 (Conn. App. Ct. 2021) (Connecticut retained jurisdiction even though father and children had moved to North Carolina for more than six months).

124. Segal v. Fishbein, 306 Cal. Rptr. 3d 241 (Ct. App. 2023).

125. Joshua A. v. Shaquanda T., 200 N.Y.S.3d 347 (App. Div. 2023).

126. Wahlke v. Pierce, 392 S.W.3d 426 (Ky. Ct. App. 2013).

127. Friedman v. Eighth Jud. Dist. *Ex rel.* Cnty of Clark, 264 P.3d 1161 (Nev. 2011).

128. Hogan v. Hogan, 954 N.W.2d 868 (Neb. 2021) (Nebraska lost jurisdiction when both parties moved to Arizona, even though mother went back later); Russell v. Cox, 678 S.E.2d 460 (S.C. App. 2009).

129. Brandt v. Brandt, 268 P.3d 406 (Colo. 2012) (Maryland retained continuing jurisdiction even though child lived with father while mother was deployed).

130. Mouritsen v. Mouritsen, 459 P.3d 476 (Alaska 2020).

131. W.M. v. V.A., 241 Cal. Rptr. 3d 170 (Ct. App. 2018).

132. Winters v. Ingersoll, 456 P.3d 862 (Wash. Ct. App. 2020).

133. Stone v. Suzuki, 308 So. 3d 1100 (Fla. Dist. Ct. App. 2020).

134. Francois B. v. Fatoumata L., 97 N.Y.S.3d 83 (App. Div. 2019) (enforcing a French order changing custody from mother to father). *See also* People in Interest of A.B.-A., 451 P.3d 1278 (Colo. Ct. App 2019) (recognizing Iranian order made in substantial conformity with UCCJEA).

135. W.M. v. V.A. 241 Cal. Rptr. 3d 170 (Ct. App. 2018); Maria G. v. Comm'r, 202 A.3d 1100 (Conn. App. Ct. 2019) (Guatemalan guardianship order was obtained with false birth certificate and no notice to the respondent).

136. Qaisi v. Aleddin, 580 S.W.3d 891 (Ky. Ct. App. 2019).

137. Hollomon v. Taylor, 926 N.W.2d 670 (Neb. 2019).

138. North v. North, 2008 WL 5159844 (Ohio Ct. App. Dec. 10, 2008) (unpublished).

139. Lindmeier v. Lindmeier, 867 So. 2d 165 (La. Ct. App. 2003) (Louisiana court did not have to enforce an invalid Canadian custody decree where the mother was denied basic due process and the information presented to Canadian court was incorrect).

140. Chick v. Chick, 596 S.E.2d 303 (N.C. Ct. App. 2004) (actual notice was fine, even if the notice did not technically comply with UCCJEA; mother did not object to lack of notice).

141. W.H. v. Dep't of Children and Families, 251 A.3d 41 (Vt. 2020).

142. Hamdan v. Freitekh, 844 S.E.2d 338 (N.C. Ct. App. 2020).

143. *In re* Marriage of Nurie, 98 Cal. Rptr. 3d 200 (Ct. App. 2009).

144. Linda Elrod, Child Custody Practice and Procedure § 3.2 (Thomson Reuter, 2024).

CHAPTER 4

Initial Custody Order: Travel Restrictions in Parenting Plans

If no prior custody order, relocation should be considered as one factor in determining the child's best interests.[1]

The goal of facilitating the child's best interest is certainly a noble one, but the notion that courts can even know with any certainty what will truly be in a given child's best future interest is perhaps unrealistic.[2]

Move at Time of Initial Custody Proceeding

If a parent plans to relocate at the time of the initial custody order, most courts use the state's general custody factors to determine the best interest of the child.[3] Although the impact and effect of a parent's relocation can be part of the best-interest analysis, relocation is but one factor among many in the custody determination.[4] The lawyer prepares for relocation the same as any child custody dispute between two fit parents.[5] In the absence of an existing order, both parents generally stand on equal footing, sharing the burden of proof and persuasion.[6] So where a father was stationed in California and the mother and child were living in Nebraska, the court did not have to do a relocation analysis; the court had merely to decide whether it was in the child's best interest to live with the mother in Nebraska or with the father in California.[7]

During an initial decision, many states find that the relocation statute or a state relocation case that applies when modifying an existing order is not implicated. The court does not need to add the relocation analysis because the child never relocated. The trial court is deciding, as an initial matter, where the child would live.[8] The trial court must scrutinize the two possible custodial living environments offered by each parent, without favoring one over the other, as part of the best interest analysis.[9] Note, however, Indiana has a statute that provides if the party gives notice of relocation at an initial hearing to determine custody, the court may consider the statutory relocation factors.[10]

A New York court noted that when both a residential schedule and a petition to relocate are contested issues, the court must first determine whether one parent is entitled to a majority of residential time using the Parenting Act. Then the court can apply the relocation factors under the Child Relocation Act.[11]

When a parent has given notice of the intent to move at the time of the divorce, the trial court has no authority to order a party to live in a specific location.[12] While the court cannot prevent either party from relocating without the child,[13] the court can award custody and residency based on the child's best interests. Some courts do require that the moving parent show a "sensitive good faith reason for the move."[14] When a father proposed to move 100 miles from the child's legal residence, the court found the parent must seek court approval or the mother's consent.[15]

Even if the state has a presumption for or against allowing a custodial parent to relocate, the presumption does not apply to an initial determination.[16] In many states, only the general custody factors, not the statutory relocation factors, apply.[17] In Florida, a mother met the burden to show that her move with the two children to Virginia was in their best interests because the mother's work was there and commute time would be reduced. The father, who had mental health and compulsive gambling issues, could not overcome his burden by showing he would change his future behavior.[18]

Because both parents have equal rights to custody, the parent wishing to relocate must ask the court for permission if the other parent objects. Relocation is just one factor in the court's best-interest determination.[19] The main issue is whether it is in the best interests of the child to go with the moving parent or to remain with the other parent in the same location.[20] Child custody cases involving the relocation of a parent with a minor child bring into direct conflict a parent's freedom to move to another state without permission from the court and the other parent's right to continue their relationship with the child as established before the relocation. It should not be assumed that merely relocating and potentially burdening one parent's parenting time always negatively affects the children. The South Carolina court granted the divorce, granting the mother primary residency and her request to relocate to Louisiana where she had job prospects. The court found that the mother had been the primary caregiver and noted some concern over the father's alcohol use and harsh disciplinary style.[21]

A Pennsylvania court noted that when the court fashions an initial custody order, the relocating parent does not have a greater burden of proof with regard to establishing the best interests of the child than the parent who does not intend to move. The focus is the best interests of the child—which parent and which living situation provides a family setting that better serves the child's best interests.[22] The court will look at the child's relationship with each parent.[23]

This is especially true if the parties are living in different states at the time of the divorce. In one case, the mother and child were living with the mother's parents in Nebraska and the father was stationed in California. The court was not required to conduct a relocation analysis, nor did the father have to prove a legitimate reason for moving to California.[24]

In one case the parents had ties with London; they annually visited the mother's extended family there, and the father's employer had an office there. The father had told mother if she were able to get a job at a certain salary, the family would all move there, but he changed his mind. The divorce court allowed the primary caregiver mother, who already had an apartment and job, to take the children to London for a year partly because father gave no reason why he could not work there too.[25]

Temporary Orders

If the parents are in the process of divorce, one parent may apply for temporary orders allowing them to leave the state with the children. The court may grant a temporary relocation order pending a final hearing if the court finds, from an examination of the evidence presented at a preliminary hearing, that there is a likelihood that on final hearing, the court will approve the relocation of the child.[26]

Any temporary order requires a finding that such an order would be in the children's best interests.[27] One Louisiana case allowed the mother to move with the children from Shreveport to Houston where her parents lived. The court found she was unable to support herself in Shreveport; the father could fly free because of his airline job; and she was more likely to promote a continuing relationship with the father.[28]

An Arkansas court, however, denied a mother's motion to relocate to Virginia during the pendency of the divorce proceeding. The court found that the fact that a final custody determination had not been entered made it premature to decide the relocation issue. It was not in the child's best interests to disrupt his life and move him away from half of his support system in the interim.[29] In another case, the New York court denied a mother's request for a temporary order to relocate, indicating that no move should be made until the court makes its final decision at trial.[30]

There are also some situations in which the court will allow a move that is to be a time-limited or temporary move. For example, a trial court allowed a mother to relocate to London for one year for employment. The father had indicated that if mother found a job at a certain salary the family would move. Mother's family lived there, and the children had spent a significant amount of time there every year.[31]

Already Moved

When one parent has already moved to a new location before the separation or divorce is filed,[32] timing may be important. If the parent and the child have lived in the new location for more than six months, absent a parent's unjustifiable conduct, the new state will have jurisdiction to determine custody. (See Chapter 3.)

If the parent who has taken the child to another state files for divorce and custody, the moving parent may not have to file a motion to relocate. The court will do a best-interest-of-the-child analysis based on one parent living in the new state and the stay-behind parent in the other.[33] The same is true if the parent did not take the child and the stay-behind parent files an action for custody. The custody determination will be viewed as whether it is in the best interests of the child to live with parent A in one state or parent B in the other state.[34]

If the parent and child are already living in another city or state at the initial hearing, most courts find that the relocation statute factors do not apply.[35] A father had already moved to California for employment opportunities and extended family before the initial custody determination, so the Indiana court used the general best interest factors and awarded father primary physical custody.[36]

Even though a mother had relocated to Maine without the father's consent, the court awarded her primary residency where she had been the children's primary caretaker and was more involved in the children's lives. The court found that mother's relocation was not a proper basis upon which to award primary physical custody to the father because the children were going to have to travel between the parties' two residences regardless of which parent was awarded primary physical residency.[37]

In another case, the family had gone to Sweden for the mother's fourth surgery; she and the three children stayed for health reasons. The appellate court found that the trial judge erred in granting the father, who had returned to the United States, primary physical custody if the mother chose to remain in Sweden. The court should have allowed testimony on the children's emotional, educational, and social roots in Sweden, which had developed during the two years in Sweden, for the most part with father's consent.[38] Stability is a factor not only of physical structures but also with regard to continuity of caregiver and patterns of care.[39]

On the other hand, the Maine Supreme Court upheld a trial judge's decision to award primary residence to a mother only if she remained in the country. If she returned to Italy, the residency would change to the father because it was in the best interest of the eight-year-old child to remain in Maine.[40] Where the parties had shared physical custody equally, a New York court awarded primary physical custody to the father where the mother proposed to relocate 25 miles from father's residence once the parties divorced.[41]

Florida, however, has applied its relocation statute's factors[42] even if the request is made as part of the initial marriage dissolution.[43] A few other states require the courts to use the relocation factors.[44]

Travel Restrictions Generally

As a general rule, the court cannot prevent either parent from relocating without the child.[45] Courts, however, may have the power to place reasonable travel restrictions upon a parent, including geographical limitations, as long as the limitations are supported by the record and are reasonable.[46] A New York appellate court found that a trial judge properly awarded the unwed mother who had moved to Binghamton sole legal and physical custody of the child. The court erred, however, in imposing the condition that she relocate to New York City and enroll the child in a school in Brooklyn within a 20-minute commute of the father's residence. The placement with mother was in the child's best interests because of mother's past performance in caring for the child, the child's academic performance and making friends in the new location, the child's need for stability, and the child's stated wishes. The requirement to move to New York City lacked a sound basis in the record so the case was remitted to develop a parenting plan with mother and child in her present location and father in Brooklyn.[47]

Travel restrictions are not always the same as relocation restrictions. A travel restriction may limit the places a parent may take the child during parenting time. A travel restriction may be imposed if there is a fear of abduction.

Relocation restrictions may determine the geographical area in which a parent with primary residency may live. For example, the parties may agree that if either party moves beyond a certain distance, say 75 miles, from the residence of the other parent, the party must have consent of the other parent or a court order.[48]

Whether to ask for travel restrictions depends upon a variety of factors. A restriction on a parent relocating with the child implicates the parent's right to travel and should be imposed cautiously and only when there is sufficient proof that the restriction is in the best interests of the child.[49] The other issue is whether the parents should agree or ask the court to impose relocation restrictions in a parenting plan or court decree of custody. The court may be more likely to continue restrictions the parties agreed to as opposed to those ordered by the court.

A court can or should insert or approve an agreement with restrictions on parental travel with the children if there is a fear of abduction (a type of unilateral relocation) of the children.[50] Where a mother had taken the children to Puerto Rico without father's knowledge and attempted to start custody proceedings there, the New York court was justified in imposing travel restrictions.[51] Courts are more likely to impose travel restrictions to prevent a parent from taking a child outside of the United States where the parent has substantial ties, family and otherwise, in another country.[52] (See Chapter 15.)

Courts generally uphold relocation restrictions that are in the best interests of the child. A court's temporary award of sole physical custody to the mother, contingent upon her remaining in Minnesota, was part of the oral stipulation to a negotiated settlement. If the mother violated the restriction, the court would award sole custody to the father. Four years after the divorce, the mother sought to remove the restriction and relocate to New York City, where more Orthodox Jews lived. The court found that the residency restriction was an integral part of the prior custody order. Where the mother did not make a prima facie case that there was a change of circumstances or endangerment and that the benefit of the move outweighed its detriments, the court could deny mother's requests without holding an evidentiary hearing.[53]

In another case, the trial court granted the mother primary physical custody of the children but found it in the best interests of the children to order her to live within 25 miles of the father's residence in Virginia. The custody evaluator had recommended that both parents and children live in Virginia and that the parents reside no more than a 45-minute drive from each other.[54] A

Texas court upheld a trial judge's residency restriction to Bowie County, Texas, where the child had been attending school.[55] Florida, however, found that the court should not have included a geographical restriction to prohibit relocation outside of Miami-Dade county because it was contrary to the provisions of the Florida statute.[56]

On the other hand, a South Carolina court reversed a family court's award of primary custody of the eight-year-old to the father if the mother should relocate to Florida. The court found that the court erred in ordering joint custody and creating a custody arrangement that penalized the mother if she moved with her new husband (and baby). The son's best interests was for mother to have sole custody even if she did choose to relocate.[57]

If the state allows relocation within a certain geographical area, the court may not be able to impose tighter geographical restrictions unless there is a proven threat of abduction.[58] The parties, however, may agree to a more limited area. In states without a permissible geographical radius, one party may seek to have the judge impose restrictions. Although a trial judge can properly deny a relocation petition based on application of statutory factors and articulated findings of fact, a judge may not prospectively restrict any relocation of the minor child outside of the county in which the child currently resided.[59]

Some abductions are failed relocations. It is crucial that the court's custody order contain sufficient information to ensure its enforcement in other states and countries. The Uniform Child Abduction Prevention Act, section 8, recommends that to ensure the custody determination is clear and enforceable, any child custody determination should include:

1. the basis for the court's exercise of jurisdiction;
2. the manner in which notice and the opportunity to be heard were given to the persons entitled to notice of the proceedings;
3. a detailed description of each party's custody and visitation rights and residential arrangements for the child;

4. a provision stating that a violation of the order may subject the party in violation to civil and criminal penalties; and
5. identification of the child's country of habitual residence at the time of the issuance of the order.[60]

These provisions should be in every custody order as a matter of good drafting because they cannot only help to prevent abductions but also can facilitate enforcement of custody determinations.[61]

Relocation Restrictions

Many relocation issues can be avoided by anticipating them at the time of the initial custody action, and by providing specific provisions in the parenting plan or court order. Even if the client is not currently planning to relocate, the lawyer should get the client to think ahead. Many of the provisions in the agreement, including division of assets and child support, will be premised on the existing geography. Even a shared residential custody order will be premised on the parties living in relatively close proximity. Negotiated provisions that anticipate relocation can prevent litigation and encourage resolution. If a negotiated agreement does not include restrictions on relocation, a parent will not be in violation of the agreement.[62]

Because parties, with lawyers or mediators, settle close to 85 percent of all cases, the parties can make provisions in parenting plans that are mediated or negotiated for how future relocations should be handled. Several states presume that the parents' agreement is in the best interests of the child because negotiated agreements mean that parents intend to live by them and support them.[63] The presence of relocation provisions, however, can make it more difficult for a parent to relocate. For example, a New Jersey agreement provided for joint legal custody with primary residency with the mother, and did anticipate relocation:

> Relocation. The parties agree that each shall inform the other with respect to any change of residence concerning himself

> or herself or the said minor Children for the period of time wherein any provision contained in this Agreement remains unfulfilled. The parties represent that they both will make every effort to remain in close proximity, within a fifteen (15) minute drive from the other. Neither party shall permanently relocate with the Children from the State of New Jersey without the prior written consent of the other. Neither parent shall relocate intrastate further than 20 miles from the other party. In the event either party relocates more than 20 miles from the other party, the parties agree to return to mediation to review the custody arrangement. In the event a job would necessitate a move, the parties agree to discuss this together and neither will make a unilateral decision. Neither party shall travel with the minor Children out of the United States without the prior written consent of the other party.
>
> The parties hereby acknowledge that the Children's quality of life and style of life are provided equally by Husband and Wife. The parties hereby acknowledge a direct causal connection between the frequency and duration of the Children's contact with both parties and the quality of the relationship of the Children and each party.
>
> The parties hereby acknowledge that any proposed move that relocates the Children further away from either party may have a detrimental impact upon the frequency and duration of the contact between the Children and the non-moving party.

Under prior New Jersey law, the primary residential custodian could relocate if there was a good faith reason, and the move would not be inimical to the children's interests. Just four months after the agreement, the mother proposed to move to Utah with a new love interest. The father argued mother had entered the agreement in bad faith. The New Jersey court changed its relocation standard to require a best-interest analysis in all contested relocation disputes in which the parents share legal custody, whether the arrangement is denoted a primary residence or provides for equally shared custody.[64]

Some state statutes recognize that parents should be able to include the possibility of a relocation in their parenting plans. For example, the Arizona statute provides:

> The court shall not deviate from a provision of any parenting plan or other written agreement by which the parents specifically have agreed to allow or prohibit relocation of the child unless the court finds that the provision is no longer in the child's best interests. There is a rebuttable presumption that a provision from any parenting plan or other written agreement is in the child's best interests.[65]

Some states require the lawyer to look not only at the statute but also at relevant court rules. The Michigan statute indicates that if the parents include a provision on relocation, it governs, rather than the statute restricting relocation to 100 miles of the place at the time of the original order. Presumably that applies in the state. However, Michigan Court Rule 3.211(C)(1) provides that the parties cannot agree to move the domicile or residence of the minor from Michigan without the approval of the trial court.[66]

A restriction can be as simple as:

> We agree that any move more than 100 miles away from __________ will make the parenting plan impracticable and unworkable. The parties agree to create a new plan or obtain a court order to move.[67]

Where the parties include a geographical restriction, the parent seeking to relocate must seek mediation or a court order before moving. If there is a restriction, courts are generally not sympathetic to a parent who moves in violation of the restriction. For example, the parties lived in New York. The parenting plan provided that the mother could have sole legal and physical custody. If either parent moved the residence of either child beyond a radius of 75 miles from the current residence, the parents were to confer and enter into "fair and equitable" revision of parental access. The mother moved to Georgia without telling the father because she felt it was her right and father was "no good." The court modified the plan to give the father sole legal and physical custody in New York.[68]

On the other hand, a New York court noted that a court is not bound by the parties' agreement. The existence of a provision in the agreement allowing a parent to relocate within a "fifty five mile radius" was not dispositive of the father's petition to modify a prior custody order and keep mother from relocating out of state with the children. The agreement was one factor to consider in the best-interest analysis.[69]

Joint Physical Custody or Shared Residency as Bar to Relocation

More states have moved toward a preference for joint physical custody or shared parenting time. If a parent intends to move, this can make the issue even more complex.[70] Imposing an equal time parenting schedule makes relocation nearly impossible. A Colorado magistrate judge erred in forcing a mother, who planned to move to California, to stay in Colorado by ordering a 5-2-2-5 parenting schedule.[71]

A few states, such as New Jersey and Washington, apply different standards for relocation when there is shared residential custody.[72] If the parents have shared physical custody, the relocation might be a change of circumstances allowing a hearing on modification of the existing parenting arrangement. (See Chapter 8.)

The Oklahoma statute allows the person with primary physical custody, the "custodial parent," to change their residence, which can be limited by a court if it finds the relocation would prejudice the rights or welfare of the child. Where the mother and father were designated as equal custodians with equal rights and time, there was no designation of the child's primary residence.[73] (See Chapter 9.)

Shared parenting can create issues. In one case, a mother did not have to file a petition to relocate 49 miles when the statute only required approval if the change of location was 50 miles. The mother, however, could not enroll the child in a different school in the new location over the father's objection because the parties had shared parental responsibilities.[74]

The lawyer should consider planning ahead on the relocation issue, especially if the parenting is shared physical custody. The lawyers should list fundamental issues, such is how far is too far to keep the joint physical custody. How much travel is acceptable for a child? What age should a child be able to travel alone? Would schools that provide certain things be a reason to relocate? For example, not all schools provide international baccalaureate. Another consideration should be whether the child has a good peer group in their current state and is actively involved in school and community activities. Other considerations may be communication tools available to the parties, transportation costs, and costs of living in both states. The lawyer can reduce the risk for the long-distance parent by setting out a schedule presuming the move but not presuming whether the child will move. In some cases, a long-distance plan might improve communication and parenting schedules. If parties have been alternating weekly, having the child the whole summer and school holidays might not be so bad.

Judge Decides Best Interest

The judge or the parties can include a geographical restriction. There may be two caveats, however. If a state statute allows a parent to move up to 150 miles, the trial court may err in restricting the parent to a smaller geographical area.[75] The parties themselves, however, could agree to a smaller geographical area.

There is a second overall caveat. While geographical restrictions may indicate the intent of the parties, the judge retains authority to determine what is in the best interests of the child at the time the issue is raised.[76] In a Utah case, the parties had stipulated in the original decree that if the mother relocated out of state, the change of custody to the father would be automatic. The Utah court found that despite the parties' agreement, the judge still has to make a finding on best interests of the child.[77] In a Wyoming case, the court determined that the parties' agreement that a parent's move out of state was a change of circumstances sufficient to seek modification of custody was speculative and unenforceable.[78] A New York court, however, upheld a trial judge who awarded primary physical custody to the mother with the condition that if she relocated to a different county, primary physical custody would be awarded to the father.[79]

To best protect clients, the separation agreement should contain provisions as to how the parties intend to handle a future relocation issue. Any clauses used must be tailored to meet the specific requirements of the parties' situation.

Some attorneys think that geographical issues should be addressed in every decree. For example, if the parent intends to move and it is provided for in the decree or agreement, then the objecting party will not be able to show a material change of circumstances—because it was contemplated in the original decree. This may prevent a hearing on the issue of the move and its effects. For example, in a Florida case, the court found that mother's and father's relocations to different cities within the county did not constitute a change of circumstances because the agreement indicated the possibility of relocation was expressly contemplated.[80]

If, however, the anticipated move is to a different location than originally planned, or the cost factors are substantially different, there still may be a question raised. The parties should state the basis for financial arrangements. For example, if the noncustodial parent moves, there may be increased costs and expenses. The parties may want to allow return to mediation or the negotiation table to contemplate new expenses. Does the agreement or the financial arrangements need to be revisited based on the new known circumstances?

Clauses If Parent Plans to Move at Time of Initial Order

As noted at the beginning of the chapter, if a parent is planning to move at the time of the initial custody proceeding, most courts use the same best-interest-of-the-child standard used in any custody dispute between fit parents.[81] The proposed relocation will be viewed as part of the best-interest analysis with one parent living in another jurisdiction.[82] The trial court must scrutinize the custodial environment offered by each parent, without favoring one over the other, as part of the requisite best interest analysis; both parents stand on equal footing, sharing the burden of production and persuasion.[83]

Even if the state has a presumption for or against allowing a custodial parent to relocate, the presumption does not apply to an initial determination.[84] If the parents agree and want to ensure that the court and others know that the parties have contemplated the move, there are several things to do.

When negotiating the custodial arrangement during the pendency of the case, one of the parents may try to draft a blanket consent to be used if and when the parent decides to move. For example:

> The father [mother] will raise no objection in the event that the mother [father] chooses to move out of the state of [____________] and relocate with the child to another state at any time. The parents agree that this is in the best interest of the child to continue to live with [____________].

This is an extremely broad provision and may be subject to the same objections that the self-executing change of custody provisions are because they are speculative. The judge wants to address the best interests of the child in the immediate situation when the issue arises because circumstances may have changed considerably since the restriction was put in the agreement. Even with such a provision, a judge may refuse to enforce it if it is not in the child's best interests.[85]

Judges sometimes make the initial custody order conditional upon a parent not relocating. For example, in one case, the district court awarded unwed parents joint legal and physical custody, with the mother having primary residential custody if she, who had moved 300 miles from the father, would return to live within 20 miles. Otherwise, the father would have primary residential custody, and the mother would have two evenings per week and every other weekend in the county where the father resided. The appellate court, in an unpublished opinion, upheld the award, finding that the trial judge relied on evidence that the mother and father shared all parenting duties and that residing in the community where both parents had lived close to extended family was in the children's best interests.[86]

Many courts, however, disapprove of automatic transfer of custody provisions.[87] New York found that a court's direction that in the event the mother relocated to Connecticut, physical custody of the parties' child would belong with the father, was an impermissible attempt to alter the custodial arrangement automatically without considering the child's best interests at the time.[88]

In one case, the 2004 stipulated order provided the mother with primary legal and physical custody with alternate weekend visitation and permitted the mother to move to any county contiguous to Ulster County, or a county that would be contiguous if not separated by the Hudson River. In 2010, the mother filed for "full custody" and a request to move to Cranberry Township, Pennsylvania, with her current husband. Appellate court upheld trial court's denial of the move, noting that there was a lack of evidence the current community was unsatisfactory or that the school would not meet the child's needs.[89]

A 2008 Connecticut parenting plan awarded joint legal custody with primary residence to the mother and provided:

> that for as long as the parties continue to live within twenty miles of Fairfield and any of the children was a minor, the parent having physical custody of any minor children could not relocate to a residence more than twenty driving miles from the primary residence of the other party without there first having been a determination of the issue of relocation either by written agreement between the parties or by order of a court.

After the father filed to reduce his child support, the mother filed to relocate with the child to Maine. The court ordered primary residential custody of the two oldest boys (18 and 17) to the father but allowed the mother to move with the three youngest children.[90]

Parent Knows of Imminent Transfer or Remarriage

If one of the parties is remarrying and planning on a move to another state or knows of a job transfer or military assignment during the divorce, the parties may want to insert a specific clause that acknowledges that both parties are aware of the proposed move and consent to it.

A specific provision that states the intended location and reason for the move is more likely to be upheld than a blanket consent to move:

> The parties anticipate that the mother (father) will move to [name of state] within [time period] after the divorce for [purpose]. Both parties agree that this is in the best interests of the child and that the father (mother) will not seek a redetermination of the custodial arrangements based on this move.
>
> [The parenting plan was devised with the relocation in mind and no further changes need to be made]
>
> or
>
> [The parties agree that when the relocation occurs, in order to ensure reasonable parenting time for the father (mother), the following schedule will go into place: [list particulars]
>
> The parties agree to allocate between themselves the additional expenses of travel and lodging for the children during parenting time following the relocation.

Parties Not in Same State at Time of Initial Order

If the parents are not living in the same state at the time of the initial custody order, it may be helpful in the future to have that information reflected in the agreement of the parties:

> The parents currently do not live in the same state. Mother lives in [state name] and Father in [state name]. The current parenting plan contemplates long distance parenting and should not need revision if one of the parents moves to another state. Neither shall object if either wants to relocate and will not seek a redetermination of custody solely because of such a relocation, unless the relocation is to a country outside of the United States [or to a distance greater than ________ miles from the other parent].

Notice Provisions

Several states require notice of a move (see Chapter 6). Even without a statute, the parties may want to include a notice provision in a negotiated or mediated agreement. The provision could provide for more or less notice than the statute requires.

> Neither party shall change the principal place of residence of the child[ren] from the State of [______] without [30/45/60] days written notice.
>
> or
>
> The parent wishing to relocate the residence of the child must give notice to the other parent in writing by [certified mail, return receipt requested] at least [30/45/60] days in advance of the proposed relocation [or as soon as practicable]. The notice of the proposed relocation shall include the following information:
>
> > (1) The intended new residence, including the specific address and mailing address, if known, and if not known, the city;
> >
> > (2) the home telephone number of the new residence if known;
> >
> > (3) the date of the intended move or proposed relocation;
> >
> > (4) a brief statement of the specific reasons for the proposed relocation of a child, if applicable; and
> >
> > (5) a proposal for a revised [parenting plan] [schedule of custody or visitation with the child].
>
> Upon receipt of such notice, the parties agree to attempt to renegotiate a new parenting plan [through mediation, attorneys, other]. If the parties are unable to come to a mutual agreement within thirty (30) days after the receipt by the father (mother) of the notice to move, the parties will ask the Court to set the new parenting plan and adjust and allocate the child support and expenses of the new plan.

Geographical or Mileage Restrictions

One parent may agree to the other parent having sole physical custody or residency in exchange for a provision that precludes that parent from moving more than a certain number of miles (50/100/350) from the child's existing home without the other's explicit consent. A few states, however, have indicated that an agreement containing a provision to remain in one community is contrary to the best interest of a child.[91] The presence of a geographical restriction, however, may help the left-behind parent if the other violates it. For example, the New York parties stipulated: "if either party moved the residence of either child beyond a radius of 75 miles from their present residence, the parties had to confer and enter into . . . fair and equitable revisions" of parental access. The mother unilaterally moved to Georgia without telling the father. The court changed sole legal and primary physical to the father.[92]

Some state statutes do not find that a move is a change of circumstances unless the move will be beyond a certain number of miles or distance. For example, Iowa uses 150 miles. The parties could agree to a lesser or greater number of miles.

> The mother (father) agrees not to establish a residence for the child(ren) beyond a distance of [50/100/150] miles from [name of city] as measured by automobile travel over public roads, without the prior written consent of the other parent. This provision shall not be applicable to any temporary residence (less than two weeks) that the mother (father) may establish for the children. If ____________________ [name of parent] does not permit such a proposed relocation, either party may apply to a court of competent jurisdiction for a determination of whether relocation is in the best interest of the child(ren).
>
> or
>
> If the (mother) (father) want to move one or more of the children to a permanent residence to be located more than [___] miles from her (his) present home at (street address/city/state), she (he) shall notify the other in writing ____ days in advance of the proposed move, giving the intended place of the new home for the child(ren). The term "permanent residence" shall be deemed to mean any residence where the children are to reside for a period of more than two weeks unless such residence shall be at a boarding school, college, or university

Detailed Restrictions

1. It is the intention of the parties to live in relatively close proximity to one another in ______________ County, ______________ (State) so as to facilitate frequent and regular contact between the child and each parent.
2. It is not presently anticipated that either party will wish to relocate the residence he or she maintains with the minor child. However, in the event that either party proposes such a relocation in the future, prior to the time the child reaches majority, the following procedures and requirements shall apply:
   a. The relocating parent shall give the other parent written notice, by certified mail, at least ____ [30, 45, 60] days in advance of any proposed relocation. The written notice shall include, at a minimum:
      i. the date and reason of the intended move
      ii. the proposed state and city to which relocation is planned;
      iii. the proposed street address for the child, and
      iv. the name and address of the child's proposed school.
   b. In the event the nonrelocating parent objects to the proposed relocation, he or she shall notify the relocating parent of the objection in writing by certified mail within [14] days of his or her receipt of the notice of proposed relocation.
   c. If the nonrelocating parent objects to a proposed relocation, the relocating parent shall file a motion to modify the [parenting plan] before the ______________ Court for the Judicial District of ______________ for determination within [14] days of receipt of the objection if he or she wishes to pursue the issue of relocation of the residence he or she maintains for the minor child.
   d. In the event that the parent proposing relocation fails to file an appropriate motion to bring the matter before the court within [14] days, as set

forth above, he or she shall be deemed to have abandoned the proposed relocation, and the initial notice requirements shall again apply to any future proposed relocation.

or

3. The nonrelocating parent who objects must file a motion to modify the existing parenting plan within [14] days of receiving the notice to move.
4. In the event that the issue of a proposed relocation of the residence of the minor child is placed before the court, the party proposing the relocation shall pay all incidental costs, fees, and expenses incurred in connection with the psychological evaluation of the child and the parties, and shall pay the fees of any attorney appointed to represent the minor child.

Provisions for Allowing Move If Other Parent Moves from Jurisdiction

All agreements should include a provision that allows the residential parent to move with the child if the nonresidential parent has moved from the decree jurisdiction. The agreement may include a provision that waives notice and consent of the nonresidential parent or the court if the nonresidential parent has left the state. The only restriction might be if there are third-party access rights that might be affected.

Provisions for Handling Relocation

The parties' agreement concerning a proposed relocation of a child with one parent is not dispositive but, rather, is a factor to be considered along with all of the other factors a judge should consider when determining whether the relocation is in the best interests of the child.[93] The parties, however, may want to think through and include provisions as to how they want to handle a proposed relocation. The parties can prioritize the factors for a court to consider in making future relocation determinations. The nonresidential parent will want the court to consider as a priority the history of access between the child and the nonresidential parent and the frequency, regularity, and quality of the relationship. The nonresidential parent will want to allow a move only for "economic necessity." The residential parent will prioritize the child's best interest and emotional stability and the parent's fresh start. The residential parent will want to have the option to move for "economic opportunity."

The agreement may also provide for a contemplated move in the future by spelling out the details of the parenting time schedule, telephone contact with the children, the cost of transportation, and an abatement of support during extended parenting time. Although an agreement for the change of custody in the future is probably not enforceable, the intent of the parties may be honored by the court if the provisions of the agreement seem to be consistent with the best interests of the children. For example:

> The parties agree that in any proceeding relating to a proposed relocation of the residence of the minor child, the following terms shall govern:
>
> 1. There shall be a psychological evaluation of the child and of each of the parties;
> 2. The relocation shall not be allowed unless the move is determined by the court to be in the best interests of the minor child;
> 3. The party proposing the relocation shall have the burden of establishing that the move is in the best interests of the child; and,
> 4. No interim or temporary relocation shall be allowed prior to a final determination of the relocation issue on the merits by the court.

If Either Parent Plans to Move

Some parents want to renegotiate if either parent intends to move, not just the one with primary residential custody. One example:

> In the event either party changes their residence to a location outside the State of ____________, he or she shall not similarly change the residence of the child(ren) without first providing the other party with (60 days) advance written notice and obtaining the written permission of the other parent or the approval of the [____________ Court] after a full hearing on the

matter. It shall be the obligation of the parent seeking to make such change of residence to obtain the approval of the other party or to petition the court for a final determination.

Another example:

The parties anticipate that the child will reside primarily with the mother (father). However, they recognize that changes in circumstances and educational opportunities may make it desirable, at some time in the future, for the child to reside with the father (mother) or at an educational institution. Any changes in the child's residence will be made only after full discussion and consultation among the mother, father and the child.

[Any change will be made only with the child's consent]

or

[The final decision will be left to the [mother/father] [the parties jointly] or to the [____________ Court]

The parties may want to contemplate subsequent moves. For example, if a nonresidential parent moves the family to a new location for his job and the move was part of what killed the marriage, there is an argument that the other parent should not be stuck in that new state. The parties may want to include a provision that if the father is transferred again, then the mother can return home.

The parties may not be able to agree on the move being a change of circumstances. A provision of a Wyoming custody decree stating that parties agreed that an out-of-state move was a material change of circumstances sufficient to seek modification of custody was treated as speculative and unenforceable because no material change in circumstances had occurred, as required to modify a custody decree.[94]

Transportation Costs

If the distance requires a long drive, generally over 100 miles, or an airplane or train ride, there may need to be provisions included for how the transportation costs will be divided. In some places, the parent relocating bears all the costs. In other states, the parties may split the costs. Because of uncertainty, the parties should specify how they want those costs apportioned.

> It is contemplated that the mother (father) shall be moving with the minor children of the parties to [location]. With respect to transportation expenses of the children for purposes of visitation with the father (mother), mother (father) shall be responsible for the costs of said transportation. The foregoing transportation expenses have been taken into consideration in agreeing to the amount of child support payments.
>
> or
>
> The parties agree to allocate the costs of transportation between themselves [in proportion to income] [equally].

Sanctions

An agreement may include provisions similar to Federal Rule 11. If a parent objects to a relocation and is subsequently found by a court to have interposed a meritless or frivolous objection, that parent shall bear the responsibility of paying the relocating parent's attorney's fees. Another type of sanction could be to place the costs and attorney's fees on a parent who makes a frivolous relocation request or one that the court finds to be malicious and intended to deprive a parent of contact with the child. If a parent relocates in violation of the court order or marital agreement, that parent may have to pay the expenses of the other parent in litigating.[95]

Automatic Change of Custody Provisions

Sometimes one of the parties wants to include a provision that if the residential parent moves so many miles from the jurisdiction, custody will automatically change to the other parent. Most courts find automatic change of custody provisions are unenforceable as inconsistent with modification statutes that require a contemporary look at best interests.[96] A Georgia court noted that a trial court erred in including a self-executing change of custody in favor of the mother after 18 months because the Georgia statute required the trial court to use discretion at the time of proposed change.[97]

Even if the parties agree, the court may find that a stipulated judgment precluding modification of primary [residential] responsibility may violate public policy.[98] In North Dakota, a stipulated divorce provision for an automatic change in residential responsibility on the occurrence of a future event is unenforceable. The district court retains control over the rights of children, regardless of a contrary agreement.[99]

Courts across the country have stated that changes in custody must be based on "real-time determinations" of best interest, not some future speculation.[100] Even though one parent may want a provision in the agreement to provide that the parent who moves will relinquish custody to the other parent who will assume sole physical custody, courts just do not like these provisions. Several courts have either stricken or ignored the provisions and gone on to a best-interest-of-the-child analysis.[101]

Some courts have found that these restrictions amount to improper speculation concerning the possibility of future changed circumstances and are unenforceable.[102] These cases follow the majority view that the judge must look at the relocation issue when it arises and is not bound by the parties' agreement. As with other provisions relating to children in agreements, the judge has the authority to act in the best interests of the child, irrespective of what the parties have stipulated as to a geographical restriction. Based on the circumstances, a court may find that an agreement containing a provision to remain in one community is contrary to the best interest of a particular child.[103]

A self-executing change of custody provision might be justified when the child is 14 or older and can decide with which parent he or she wants to live.[104]

Judicial Restrictions

Even if the parties cannot reach an agreement, one of the parties may persuade the court to place some type of geographical restriction in the custody order. A court may condition a present award of custody on the continuation of the child's residence, if it is in the best interests of the child. The court cannot, however, order an automatic modification upon the move.[105] The restriction must be reasonable. For example, an appellate court found that the family court could not place a restriction that the mother would continue to live in the same apartment building, unless the father approved, but the court could have imposed a reasonable radius restriction.[106] Some courts will place geographical restrictions in the decrees.[107] Other courts do not like them.[108] If there is a fear of abduction, as when a parent has already taken the children without permission and attempted to start custody proceedings, the court will generally approve the restriction.[109]

Risks of Abduction: UCAPA

There is a link between relocation and abduction. A parent, whose relocation request was denied or fears that it may be denied, may unilaterally "kidnap" their own child. In 1999, the Office of Juvenile Justice and Delinquency Prevention estimated of the 262,100 children abducted, 78 percent were taken by a parent or family member. From 2008 to 2017, the National Center for Missing and Exploited Children reported that from 16,264 child abduction cases, 71 percent were taken by a parent or family member.[110] If the abduction is domestic and the child can be found, the courts can generally deal with the interstate issues using the UCCJEA Article 3 enforcement provisions (see Chapter 3), contempt, and, in 20 states, the Uniform Child Abduction Prevention Act (UCAPA). If the child is abducted internationally, the Hague Convention on the Civil Aspects of International Child Abduction may apply to seek the return of the child, if the other country is a party and the child can be located. (See Chapter 15.)

UCAPA is not meant to prevent a parent's legitimate relocation request, nor to prevent a victim of intimate partner violence from escaping abuse. UCAPA's sole purpose is to prevent the wrongful removal and retention of a child, whether it occurs pre- or post-decree, and whether it is domestic or international. The taking must be wrongful and the person seeking imposition of an abduction prevention remedy must prove a credible risk of abduction.[111] A credible risk of abduction is more than just the parent wants to take the child to a country that is not a signatory to the Hague Abduction Convention. For example, where the father and children had Jordanian and U.S. passports and had often traveled to visit relatives in the UAE, the appellate court found the trial court erred in ordering surrender of the minor children's passports and posting of a $50,000 bond. There was no showing of a credible risk of abduction under UCAPA.[112]

Preventing an abduction is important. Research over the years has shown that children are generally harmed, at the least emotionally, by an abduction.[113] Parenting plans and court orders that contain child custody determinations must be drafted with the idea that they may have to be enforced in other states or countries. UCAPA authorizes several ways to prevent the abduction of children, including travel restrictions. Twenty states have enacted it; a few other states have statutes allowing for travel restrictions.[114]

The National Center for Missing and Exploited Children and other researchers have identified several risk factors for abduction.[115] UCAPA provides a list of risk factors that incorporate the known red flags and profiles for potential intrastate, interstate, and international abductions. The number one predictor of a future abduction is a history of abduction, attempted abduction, and threats to abduct.[116] Another key risk factor is a parent who engages in abduction planning activities such as (1) abandoning employment; (2) selling a primary residence; (3) terminating a lease; (4) closing bank or other financial management accounts, liquidating assets, hiding or destroying financial documents, or conducting any unusual financial activities; (5) applying for a passport or visa or obtaining travel documents for the respondent, a family member, or the child; and (6) seeking to obtain the child's birth certificate or school or medical records.[117] These planning activities imply premeditation. The parent has been thinking about abducting the child and is preparing. Some of these activities may be normal day-to-day activities for some people. It is the combination of these activities in conjunction with an ongoing contentious custody dispute and other actions that may warrant the imposition of some abduction prevention measures.

Another risk category to consider is whether the person has engaged in domestic violence, stalking, or child abuse or neglect; or has refused to follow an existing child custody determination.[118] Half of abducting parents have a history of violent behavior, a criminal record, or a substance abuse problem.[119] These threats are often particularly prevalent in cases involving domestic violence; three-fourths of family abduction cases involve allegations of domestic violence. An abduction may be committed as an act of revenge to provoke, agitate, control, or psychologically torture the other parent.[120] While in a few instances, a parent is protecting a child from real or imagined abuse,[121] the primary motives appear to be to force a reconciliation with the other parent, to blame or punish the other parent, or to reduce the fear of losing custody or visitation.[122]

Social scientists Janet Johnston and Linda Girdner have suggested that more restrictive measures are warranted in three situations:

1. when the risks for abduction are particularly high, as indicated by prior custody violations, clear evidence of plans to abduct, and overt threats to take the child;
2. when obstacles to locating and recovering an abducted child would be particularly great, as they would be in uncooperative jurisdictions in some states and abroad—especially in countries that are not parties to the Hague Convention; and
3. when the child faces substantial potential harm from an abducting parent, such as a parent who has a serious mental or personality disorder, a history of abuse or violence, or little or no prior relationship with the child.[123]

These situations may require an order for supervised visitation or require the respondent to post a bond or other security.[124]

The trial court's finding that the father posed a risk of absconding with the children to India justified the imposition of passport and travel restrictions in the parenting plan. The mother testified that the father had made numerous threats to take the children to India, the threats were corroborated by other witnesses, and the father had engaged in a pattern of "abusive controlling, punishing behavior" that put the children at "risk of being used as the tools to continue this conduct."[125] The restrictions should be sufficient to deter an abduction, but not so onerous as to prevent the parent and child's relationship. Imposing permanent restrictions on a parent's right to travel, however, may be overbroad.[126] (See Chapter 15.)

Endnotes

1. Matter of Michael B., 42 N.Y.S.3d 141 (App. Div. 2016).

2. Taylor v. Taylor, 849 S.W.2d 319, 326 (Tenn. 1993).

3. Taylor-Couchman v. Dewitt-Couchman, 964 N.W.2d 320 (Neb. Ct. App. 2021) (awarding joint custody and allowing father to relocate out of state); Lynch v. Gillogly, 920 N.Y.S.2d 437 (App. Div. 2011) (awarding mother sole custody and allowing her to move two and a half hours away). *See also* Dillon v. Dillon, 42 N.E.3d 165 (Ind. Ct. App. 2015); Varner v. Glass, 13 N.Y.S.3d 671 (App. Div. 2015).

4. Wright v. Burke, 209 N.Y.S.3d 67 (App. Div. 2024) (finding sole legal and physical custody to mother but denying relocation to Brooklyn); Johnson v. Johnson, 145 N.Y.S.3d 262 (App. Div. 2021). *See also* Brown v. Brown, 84 A.3d 905 (Conn. App. Ct. 2014) (allowing young child to relocate to Canada where parties had already agreed older child could live with mother there).

5. *See* Spahmer v. Gullette, 113 P.3d 158 (Colo. 2005); Barney v. Barney, 754 N.Y.S.2d 108 (App. Div. 2003); *In re* Marriage of Kim, 317 P.3d 555 (Wash. Ct. App. 2014) (mother who had closer relationship with children allowed to move to California). *See* Linda D. Elrod, Child Custody Practice and Procedure § 4:35 (Thomson Reuters, 2024).

6. Collins v. Collins, 897 A.2d 466 (Pa. Super. Ct. 2006).

7. Taylor-Couchman v. DeWitt-Couchman, 964 N.W.2d 320, 336 (Neb. Ct. App. 2021) (mother had taken children to Nebraska and tried to thwart father's relationship).

8. Brandon v. Coffey, 886 S.E.2d 780 (Va. Ct. App. 2023). *See also* Miller v. Miller, 88 N.E.3d 843 (Mass. 2018) ("real advantage test" rather than relocation factors used to allow mother to move to Germany with child); Wright v. Burke, 209 N.Y.S.3d 67 (App. Div. 2024) (strict application of relocation factors not required for initial custody determination; awarding mother custody where she had been primary caregiver).

9. Morelli v. Morelli, 226 N.Y.S.3d 559 (App. Div. 2025) (where mother had been primary caretaker of two special needs children, court allowed her to relocate to Virginia where she would have financial and family support). *But see* Tuel v. Tuel, 840 S.E.2d 917 (N.C. Ct. App. 2020) (reversing trial court's award of physical custody to the mother who was moving to Indiana without comparing child's interests in both locations).

10. Pilkington v. Pilkington, 227 N.E.3d 885 (Ind. Ct. App. 2024) (court denied mother's move to Utah for better employment and to live closer to her family and significant other because of the distance and fear that mother's gatekeeping would interfere with father's relationship).

11. *In re* Thomas SS. v. Alicia TT., 170 N.Y.S.3d 389 (Fam. Ct. 2022) (mother could not move to Oregon until family court made decision at trial).

12. *See In re* Marriage of Morgan, 428 P.3d 550 (Colo. App. 2018) (trial court erred in creating parenting plan that effectively coerced mother into abandoning her plan to move to California).

13. Allbright v. Allbright, 215 P.3d 472 (Idaho 2009) (trial court lacked authority to order the mother to live within a specific geographical location).

14. *See* Druckman v. Ruscitt, 327 P.3d 511 (Nev. 2014) (finding mother's increased economic prospects justified relocation to California). *But see* Mark T. v. Jamie Z., 124 Cal. Rptr. 3d 200 (Ct. App. 2011) (even if a parent is partly motivated by a desire to frustrate contact, the court must still consider the child's best interests).

15. Eickelberg v. Eickelberg, 871 N.W.2d 561 (Mich. Ct. App. 2015).

16. LaChapelle v. Mitten, 607 N.W.2d 151 (Minn. Ct. App. 2000), *review denied.*

17. Alvarado v. Cordova, 71 N.Y.S.3d 566 (App. Div. 2018) (mother's request in initial proceeding to relocate to Florida was governed by best interest factors). *See also* Fisher v. Fisher, 50 N.Y.S.3d 773 (App. Div. 2017) (awarding father primary residency and denying mother's request to move to Texas because it would adversely affect the child's relationship with the father due to the distance); Wright v. Stewart, 16 N.Y.S.3d 860 (App. Div. 2015) (strict application to relocation petitions are not required in initial action).

18. Solomon v. Solomon, 221 So. 3d 652 (Fla. Dist. Ct. App. 2017).

19. Druckman v. Ruscitti, 327 P.3d 511 (Nev. 2014) (allowing unwed mother to move to California); McDonald v. Thomas, 62 N.Y.S.3d 148 (App. Div. 2017) (finding it in children's best interest to allow father to relocate to Las Vegas with sole custody of children when paternal grandmother no longer able to care for them).

20. Lynch v. Gillogly, 920 N.Y.S.2d 437 (App. Div. 2011) (awarding mother sole custody and allowing her to move two and a half hours back to her hometown; child had always lived with mother and older sisters; father had reduced support and had deceived mother). Mark T. v. Jamie Z., 124 Cal. Rptr. 3d 200 (Ct. App. 2011) (mother wanted to move to Minnesota to live with her mother and stepfather where cost of living was less; maintaining status quo or coercing mother to abandon her move were not proper reasons to deny relocation).

21. Gandy v. Gandy, 898 S.E.2d 208 (S.C. Ct. App. 2024), *reh'g denied.*

22. Collins v. Collins, 897 A.2d 466 (Pa. Super. Ct. 2006). *See In re* Marriage of Burgess, 51 Cal. Rptr. 2d 444 (Ct. App. 1996) (considering all the circumstances affecting best interests, including the proposed relocation; allowing mother to relocate 40 miles with children for a career advancing job).

23. *See* Kolbach v. Kolbach, 877 N.W.2d 822 (S.D. 2016) (allowing mother who had moved during divorce with two children to Sioux Falls to remain where she had better employment opportunities and father exercised alternating weekends with his 11-year-old from a prior marriage there); *In re* Marriage of Kim, 317 P.3d 555 (Wash. Ct. App. 2014).

24. Taylor-Couchman v. DeWitt-Couchman, 964 N.W.2d 320, 326 (Neb. Ct. App. 2021) (father granted custody in California where mother tried to thwart relationship between him and child).

25. Mathiew v. Michels, 118 N.Y.S.3d 581 (App. Div. 2020).

26. Alinat v. Curtis, 86 So. 3d 552 (Fla. Dist. Ct. App. 2012) (court erred in granting wife's request for a three-year temporary order, which was the duration of her work contract, allowing her and children to live in Australia).

27. Albanese v. Albanese, 135 So. 3d 532 (Fla. Dist. Ct. App. 2014) (reversing trial court's temporary order allowing father to take children to New York where there was no evidence to support it was in the children's best interests and they had bond with mother).

28. Moore v. Moore, 111 So. 3d 1120 (La. Ct. App. 2013).

29. Zihala v. Staley, 689 S.W.3d 82 (Ark. Ct. App. 2024) (court's order denying mother's motion to relocate was intermediate order that could be raised on appeal of final divorce decree).

30. *In re* Thomas SS v. Alicia TT., 170 N.Y.S.3d 389 (Fam. Ct. 2022).

31. Mathiew v. Michels, 118 N.Y.S.3d 581 (App. Div. 2020).

32. Dillon v. Dillon, 42 N.E.3d 165 (Ind. Ct. App. 2015) (relocation statute did not apply because court did not have to modify an existing order).

33. Sayler v. Sayler, 994 N.W.2d 351 (N.D. 2023) (court awarded primary residential responsibility to mother who had moved to Minnesota with children).

34. *See In re* Marriage of Guthrie, 915 N.E.2d 43 (Ill. App. Ct. 2009) (mother allowed to move with 11-month-old child to Arizona where her relations were). *See also* Ragghanti v. Reyes, 20 Cal. Rptr. 3d 522 (Ct. App. 2004); Potter v. Potter, 119 P.3d 1246, 1250 (Nev. 2005); Jelsing v. Peterson, 729 N.W.2d 157 (N.D. 2007) (where both parents were good, children had strongest bond with mother who was nurturing parent); Davis v. Davis, 588 S.E.2d 102 (S.C. 2003).

35. Rolison v. Rolison, 144 So. 3d 610 (Fla. Dist. Ct. App. 2014) (the mother and children were already living in Georgia at the time the father filed petition for dissolution in Florida).

36. Dillon v. Dillon, 42 N.E.3d 165 (Ind. Ct. App. 2015).

37. Sitts v. Sitts, 902 N.Y.S.2d 274 (App. Div. 2010), *lv. Dismissed*, 935 N.E.2d 799 (2010).

38. B.K.M. v. J.A.M., 50 A.3d 168 (Pa. Super. Ct. 2012).

39. *Id.* (finding that the trial court erred in not giving sufficient weight to mother's primary caregiving role of children ages 16, 13, and 5 where father had provided little help over the years).

40. Light v. d'Amato, 105 A.3d 447 (Me. 2014).

41. Petroski v. Petroski, 808 N.Y.S.2d 852 (App. Div. 2005).

42. Fla. Stat. Ann. § 61.13001 (defining relocation as a change of location that is at least 50 miles from the location of the principal residence of a parent at the time of the last order establishing or modifying time-sharing).

43. *See* Cecemski v. Cecemski, 954 So. 2d 1227 (Fla. Dist. Ct. App. 2007) (no competent evidence to support finding that two year old child's quality of life would be improved by moving with mother to Louisiana); *In re* Marriage of Muller, 964 So. 2d 732 (Fla. Dist. Ct. App. 2007) (reversing order in divorce allowing mother to relocate to Colorado where she had no prospects for higher income or education and the long distance would harm the child's relationship with the father).

44. *See* Ind. Code § 31-17-2.2-2 (if a party provides notice at initial hearing, court may consider the factors in the relocation statute); Bailey v. Bailey,

196 So. 3d 96 (La. Ct. App. 2016) (trial court erred in giving mother permission to move without using statutory factors to determine if relocation was in children's best interest even in initial action).

45. Allbright v. Allbright, 215 P.3d 472 (Idaho 2009).

46. *See* James U. v. Catalina V., 56 N.Y.S.3d 642 (App. Div. 2017). *In re* Marriage of Christensen, 570 S.W.3d 933 (Tex. App. 2019) (upholding trial court's sua sponte requirement that child to reside in county in which parties currently resided, and granting mother exclusive right to designate child's primary residence in county).

47. Wright v. Burke, 209 N.Y.S.3d 67 (App. Div. 2024).

48. *See* Sukul v. Sukul, 151 N.Y.S.3d 684 (App. Div. 2021) (changing New York father custody after mother violated 75-mile restriction and unilaterally moved to Georgia).

49. *In re* M.C., 343 P.3d 569 (Mont. 2015) (allowing court to impose restriction that mother would remain residential parent only if she lived in Montana after she interfered with father's involvement and moved to Ohio); Goldman v. Greenwood, 748 N.W.2d 279 (Minn. 2008) (finding locale restriction valid); Light v. D'Amato, 105 A.3d 447 (Me. 2014). *But see* Davis v. Ewalefo, 352 P.3d 1139 (Nev. 2015) (reversing travel restrictions on father exercising visitation in a non-Hague signatory country in Africa where he lives and works).

50. Katare v. Katare, 283 P.3d 546 (Wash. 2012), *cert. denied*, 133 S. Ct. 889 (2013) (upholding travel and passport restrictions in parenting plan based on a serious risk of rather absconding with the children to India; father has a pattern of controlling, abusive behavior).

51. James U. v. Catalina V., 56 N.Y.S.3d 642 (App. Div. 2017).

52. *See* Lehn v. Al-Thanayyan, 438 P.3d 646 (Ariz. Ct. App. 2019); Sahibzada v. Sahibzada, 757 S.E.2d 51 (Ga. 2014) (upholding restriction on father's international travel without mother's consent until sons were age 16).

53. Goldman v. Greenwood, 748 N.W.2d 279 (Minn. 2008).

54. Vanderzon v. Vanderzon, 402 P.3d 219 (Utah Ct. App. 2017).

55. *In re* Marriage of Christensen, 570 S.W.3d 933 (Tex. App. 2019).

56. Naime v. Corzo, 208 So. 3d 296 (Fla. Dist. Ct. App. 2016) (trial court could not prospectively restrict any relocation where Florida statute defined relocation as a change that is 50 miles from the location of child's principal residence).

57. Burgess v. Arnold, 810 S.E.2d 255 (S.C. Ct. App. 2018).

58. Allbright v. Allbright, 215 P.3d 472 (Idaho 2009) (trial court lacked authority to order mother to live in specific geographical area so that both parents could have frequent contact and physical custody of the child).

59. Naime v. Corzo, 208 So. 3d 296 (Fla. Dist. Ct. App. 2016).

60. Uniform Child Abduction Prevention Act (UCAPA) § 8(a)(1)–(5). Although only 18 states have enacted UCAPA, all custody orders will be more enforceable if they include the Section 8 requirements.

61. *The Uniform Child Abduction Prevention Act (Statutory Text, Comments and Unofficial Comments by Linda D. Elrod, Reporter)*, 41 FAM. L.Q. 23 (2007).

62. Dickson v. Dickson, 169 So. 3d 287 (Fla. Dist. Ct. App. 2015).

63. *See* KAN. STAT. ANN. § 23-3222; MINN. STAT. ANN. § 518.1705, subdiv. 7; OHIO REV. CODE ANN. § 3109.04(D)(1)(a)(i) (parents can agree on the legal standard to govern the decision concerning removal of a child's residence if both were represented by counsel and parents were fully informed, the agreement was voluntary) *See also* LINDA D. ELROD, CHILD CUSTODY PRACTICE AND PROCEDURE § 4.07 (Thomson Reuters, 2024).

64. Bisbing v. Bisbing, 166 A.3d 1155 (N.J. 2017).

65. ARIZ. REV. STAT. ANN. § 25-408 (A), (G) (if both parents reside in the state and are entitled to joint decision making, a relocation requires 45 days' notice and court shall determine whether to allow relocation in best interest of the child).

66. *See* Brausch v. Brausch, 770 N.W.2d 77 (Mich. Ct. App. 2009).

67. Suter v. Biggers, 337 P.3d 1271 (Idaho 2014) (changing primary residency of two boys to the father who remained in Emmett when mother moved more than 100 miles away).

68. Sukul v. Sukul, 151 N.Y.S.3d 684 (App. Div. 2021).

69. Jaimes v. Gyerko, 87 N.Y.S.3d 53 (App. Div. 2018).

70. Brooks v. Brooks, 164 So. 3d 162 (Fla. Dist. Ct. App. 2015).

71. *In re* Marriage of Morgan, 428 P.3d 550 (Colo. Ct. App. 2018).

72. Aragon v. Aragon, 513 S.W.3d 447 (Tenn. 2017) (relocation act applied because father had 80 percent of time with child); *In re* Marriage of Ruff and Worthley, 393 P.3d 859 (Wash. Ct. App. 2017) (modification statute, not Child Relocation Act, applies where parents had substantially equal parenting time).

73. Boatman v. Boatman, 404 P.3d 822 (Okla. 2017) (remanding for a determination of which parent was primary physical custodian).

74. Dickson v. Dickson, 169 So. 3d 287 (Fla. Dist. Ct. App. 2015).

75. Derleth v. Cordova, 841 N.W.2d 552 (Wis. Ct. App. 2013) (finding judge could not restrict mother to a 45-mile area when the statute allowed 150).

76. *See* Woelfel v. Gifford, 948 N.W.2d 814. 815 (N.D. 2020); Taylor v. Elison, 263 P.3d 448 (Utah Ct. App. 2011) (trial court still needs to make a determination that a modification of custody is in the best interest of the child).

77. Taylor v. Elison, 263 P.3d 448 (Utah Ct. App. 2011) (reversing trial court which changed custody to father upon mother's move to Arizona).

78. Hanson v. Belveal, 280 P.3d 1186 (Wyo. 2012) (finding that a provision in agreement saying an out of state move is a change in circumstances was unenforceable).

79. O'Hara v. DeMarsh, 75 N.Y.S.3d 673 (App. Div. 2018).

80. Moore v. McIntosh, 128 So. 3d 985 (Fla. Dist. Ct. App. 2014).

81. LINDA D. ELROD, CHILD CUSTODY PRACTICE AND PROCEDURE § 4:35 (Thomson Reuters, 2024). *See* Spahmer v. Gullette, 113 P.3d 158 (Colo. 2005); Ford v. Ford, 789 A.2d 1104, *cert. denied*, 796 A.2d 556 (Conn. 2002).

82. *See* Ragghanti v. Reyes, 20 Cal. Rptr. 3d 522 (Ct. App. 2004); Davis v. Davis, 588 S.E.2d 102 (S.C. 2003); Pahl v. Pahl, 87 P.3d 1250 (Wyo. 2004).

83. Collins v. Collins, 897 A.2d 466 (Pa. Super. Ct. 2006).

84. LaChapelle v. Mitten, 607 N.W.2d 151 (Minn. Ct. App. 2000), *rev. denied*, Mitten v. LaChapelle, 121 S. Ct. 565 (2000).

85. Savage v. Morrison, 691 N.Y.S.2d 842 (App. Div. 1999) (stating that provision in agreement was relevant as to best interests, but not dispositive). Goldman v. Greenwood, 748 N.W.2d 279 (Minn. 2008).

86. *In re* Custody of S.S.E, 2004 WL 1327808 (Minn. App. June 15, 2004) (unpublished).

87. Malenko v. Handrahan, 979 A.2d 1269 (Me. 2009) (striking clause awarding primary residence to be transferred to the father if the mother relocated out of state).

88. Bzozowski v. Bzozowski, 817 N.Y.S.2d 127 (App. Div. 2006).

89. Kishy-Stallworth v. Chapman, 934 N.Y.S.2d 592 (App. Div. 2011).

90. Emrich v. Emrich, 15 A.3d 1104 (Conn. App. 2011).

91. *See* Godwin v. Balderamos, 876 So. 2d 1169 (Ala. Civ. App. 2003) (agreement only valid as long as best interests have not changed). Zeller v. Zeller, 640 N.W.2d 53 (N.D. 2002); *In re* Duckett, 905 P.2d 1170 (Or. App. 1995) (orders prohibiting party from removing a child from the state are disfavored; mother allowed to move to Kansas City with her new husband).

92. Sukul v. Sukul, 151 N.Y.S.3d 684, 686 (App. Div. 2021).

93. Schwartz v. Schwartz, 132 N.Y.S.3d 34 (App. Div. 2020).

94. Hanson v. Belveal, 280 P.3d 1186 (Wyo. 2012).

95. State v. Titus, 274 S.3d 591 (La. Ct. App. 2019).

96. Oxford v. Fuller, 790 S.E.2d 303 (Ga. App. 2016) (court must look to child's best interest). *See also* Zeller v. Zeller, 640 N.W.2d 53 (N.D. 2002) (court was not bound by stipulated divorce provision for an automatic change in custody from mother to father upon the mother moving from jurisdiction); Myers v. Myers, 13 N.E.3d 478 (Ind. Ct. App. 2014); Knutsen v. Cegalis, 989 A.2d 1010 (Vt. 2009) (collecting cases).

97. *See* Bankston v. Warbington, 771 S.E.2d 726 (Ga. App. 2015).

98. Hageman v. Hageman, 827 N.W.2d 23 (N.D. 2013).

99. Woelfel v. Gifford, 948 N.W.2d 814 (N.D. 2020).

100. Knutsen v. Cegalis, 989 A.2d 1010 (Vt. 2009). Arthur v. Arthur, 54 So. 3d 454 (Fla. 2010), *as revised on denial of reh'g* (Feb. 10, 2011).

101. *See* Scott v. Scott, 578 S.E.2d 876, 879 (Ga. 2003); *In re* Marriage of Seitzinger, 775 N.E.2d 282 (Ill. App. Ct. 2002); *In re* Marriage of Thielges, 623 N.W.2d 232 (Iowa Ct. App. 2000).

102. *See* Scott v. Scott, 578 S.E.2d 876, 879 (Ga. 2003) (effect of provision is fatally inflexible and "altogether ignores the best interests of the child at the time of the triggering event"); *In re* Marriage of Pape, 989 P.2d 1120 (Wash. 2000) (allowing move even though restriction in parties' agreement because move was in child's best interests); Savage v. Morrison, 691 N.Y.S.2d 842 (App. Div. 1999); Grathwol v. Grathwol, 727 N.Y.S.2d 825 (App. Div. 2001).

103. *See* Godwin v. Balderamos, 876 So. 2d 1169 (Ala. Civ. App. 2003); Bell v. Bell, 572 So. 2d 841 (Miss. 1990); Zeller v. Zeller, 640 N.W.2d 53 (N.D. 2002); *In re* Duckett, 905 P.2d 1170 (Or. App. 1995).

104. Bankston v. Warbington, 771 S.E.2d 726 (Ga. Ct. App. 2018) (ordering primary residence to the father if the mother relocated to Italy).

105. *In re* Paternity of C.J.A., 3 N.E.3d 1020 (Ind. Ct. App. 2014); *In re* M.C., 343 P.3d 569 (Mont. 2015).

106. Ece D. v. Sreeram M., 114 N.Y.S.3d 287 (App. Div. 2019) (modifying to get father's consent or court order if mother wished to move more than ten miles from current residence).

107. *See* Leeds v. Adamse, 832 So. 2d 125 (Fla. Dist. Ct. App. 2002), *aff'd*, 840 So. 2d 253 (2003); Carlson v. Carlson, 661 P.2d 833 (Kan. Ct. App. 1983); Ziegler v. Ziegler, 691 P.2d 773 (Idaho 1985); Lozinak v. Lozinak, 569 A.2d 353 (Pa. Super. Ct. 1990); Pointer v. Bell, 719 So. 2d. 222 (Ala. Civ. App. 1998).

108. *See* Moeller-Prokosch v. Prokosch, 27 P.3d 314 (Alaska 2001); *In re* Marriage of Thielges, 623 N.W.2d 232 (Iowa Ct. App. 2000); *In re* Marriage of Pape, 989 P.2d 1120 (Wash. 2000).

109. James U. v. Catalina V., 56 N.Y.S.3d 642 (App. Div. 2017) (upholding restriction on mother's travel outside of the continental United States where she had already unilaterally taken the children to Puerto Rico where she had ties).

110. Nat'l Ctr. for Missing & Exploited Children, Family Abductions: What We've Learned 1 (2018).

111. Kostreva v. Kostreva, 976 N.W.2d 889 (Mich. Ct. App. 2021) (no abduction prevention measures needed when mother was taking child to Poland for grandmother's funeral).

112. *In re* Marriage of Badawiyeh, 528 P.3d 194 (Colo. Ct. App. 2023). *But see* Shady v. Shady, 858 N.E.2d 128 (Ind. Ct. App. 2006) (transfer denied Mar. 8, 2007) (Egypt was not a signatory at the time so supervised visitation ordered for father who had threatened to take child to Egypt).

113. *See* Geoffrey L. Greif, *The Long-Term Impact of Parental Abduction on Children: Implications for Treatment*, 26 J. Psych. & L. 45 (1998); Marilyn Freeman, *Parental Child Abduction: The Long-Term Effects*, Int'l Centre for Fam. Law, Pol'y & Practice (2014) (study showed that 91.17 percent of previously abducted children had some negative effects but 73.53 percent suffered significant mental health problems). *See also* Janet R. Johnston, *Parental Abduction of Children: Identifying Families at Risk: Prevention and Early Intervention*, AFCC 43rd Annual Conference Materials 80 (2006) (noting long-term effects may include indoctrinated beliefs, poor reality testing, behavioral problems (aggression, depression, and regression), and school learning problems).

114. Tex. Fam. Code § 153.501–.503. *See* Matter of O'Neil v. O'Neil, 17 N.Y.S.3d 187 (App. Div. 2015) (family court has discretion to place reasonable travel restrictions on a parent, including geographical restrictions).

115. *See* Janet R. Johnston & Linda K. Girdner, Family Abductors: Descriptive Profiles and Preventive Interventions (2001); Family Resource Guide on International Parental Kidnapping 4–5 (2007 ed.) (noting several "red flags" or warning signs that a parent intends to abduct his or her child).

116. Uniform Child Abduction Prevention Act (UCAPA) § 7(a)(1)–(2). *See, e.g.*, Katare v. Katare, 283 P.3d 546 (Wash. 2012) (upholding travel restrictions for Indian father who made threats of abduction); Al-Silham v. Al-Silham, No. 94-A-0048, 1995 WL 803808 (Ohio Ct. App. Nov. 24, 1995) (upholding supervised visitation for Saudi Arabian father who, among other things, threatened that mother would never see child again if she divorced him and the child was better off dead if not raised in his culture).

117. UCAPA § 7(A)(3)(a)–(f).

118. *Id.* § 7(A)(4)–(5). *In re* A.R., 236 S.W.3d 460 (Tex. App. 2007) (finding mother violated possession order more than once and had been found in contempt).

119. *What Is Family Abduction?*, StopFamilyAbductionsNow.org, http://www.stopfamilyabductionsnow.org/about_abduction.html (last visited May 4, 2024).

120. D.C. Rand, *The Spectrum of the Parental Alienation Syndrome*, 15 Am. J. Forensics Psych. 4 (1997).

121. *In re* A.R., 236 S.W.3d 460 (Tex. App. 2007) (even after mother had father's visits supervised, she alleged abuse—even though he was never alone with child).

122. Janet Chiancone, *Parental Abduction: A Review of the Literature*, U.S. Dep't of Just., OJJDP (2002). *See also In re* A.R., 236 S.W.3d 460 (Tex. App. 2007) (mother filed several unsubstantiated allegations of sexual abuse by father).

123. Johnston & Girdner, *supra* note 115.

124. Many reported prevention cases involve bonds, supervised visitation, and passport controls. *See In re* A.R., 236 S.W.3d 460 (Tex. App. 2007) (posting of bond and supervised visitation not arbitrary or unreasonable where mother refused to follow court orders and made false allegations of abuse).

125. Katare v. Katare, 283 P.3d 546 (Wash. 2012). *See also* Messier v. Messier, 389 S.W.3d 904 (Tex. App. 2012) (placing restrictions on mother's international travel due to her irrational and threatening behavior).

126. Arredondo v. Betancourt, 383 S.W.3d 730 (Tex. App. 2012).

CHAPTER 5

Constitutional Rights and Relocation

Decisions as to the custody of children always involve a balance between competing, legitimate parental interests, some of which are constitutional in magnitude.[1]

The constitutional right to travel from one State to another . . . occupies a position fundamental to the concept of our Federal Union. It is a right that has been firmly established and repeatedly recognized.[2]

Relocation cases can implicate constitutional rights. Constitutional issues can arise under the federal or state constitutions. A statute is presumed to be constitutional; the party asserting the unconstitutionality must persuade the court that there is no reasonable doubt the statute violates the constitution.[3] Challenges may be made based upon the constitutional rights of parents to the care, custody, and control of their children; on the right to privacy; the right to travel; or on due process and equal protection grounds.[4] An allegation that the statute is unconstitutional as applied must be raised at the trial level.[5] Facial unconstitutionality of a statute may be raised for the first time on appeal if the error is fundamental.[6]

The U.S. Supreme Court has recognized several fundamental rights that may compete in a relocation case.[7] First, parents have a fundamental right to the care, custody, and control of their children.[8] Custody orders should protect both parents' constitutional rights to the care, custody, and control of their children. The second fundamental right is that of citizens of the United States to travel freely between the states, which includes "the right to migrate, resettle, find a new job, and start a new life."[9] Therefore, a custody order should not be a sentence of immobilization.[10]

Constitutional rights can only be restricted in furtherance of a compelling state interest. State judges, however, are charged with the responsibility of protecting the best interests of a child.[11] Research supports that generally it is in the child's best interest to know and love both parents. Therefore, some courts have found that the state's compelling interest in protecting the child's best interests as well as protecting the child's frequent and continuing contact with both parents, can justify restrictions on the parents' right to travel.[12]

The child arguably may also have a constitutional right to maintain relationships with both parents that can be asserted in a relocation case. An Indiana court noted that the child's interests are powerful countervailing considerations that cannot be swept aside as irrelevant in the face of a parent's claimed right to relocate.[13] While the U.S. Supreme Court has not yet recognized a child's liberty interests in preserving established familial bonds, Justice Stevens mentioned the possibility in his dissent in *Troxel v. Granville*:

> [I]t seems to me extremely likely that, to the extent parents and families have fundamental liberty interests in preserving . . . intimate relationships, so, too, do children have these interests, and so, too, must their interests be balanced in the equation.[14]

Though consideration of the parents' competing constitutional interests is important in relocation cases, the real challenge for courts is how to best promote the welfare of the child. In most circumstances, the welfare of the child requires looking at the stability and continuity of relationships while affording protection equally between the relocating parent's right to travel and the nonrelocating parent's right to maintain a relationship with the child.[15] A Montana court noted that although the mother had a constitutional right to travel and to relocate, this right did not outweigh the father's right to have regular and ongoing parental contact with his daughter and the child's right to a relationship with her father.[16]

Parents' Rights to Privacy and to Rear Children

Although not specifically mentioned in the Constitution, the U.S. Supreme Court has recognized that certain parental rights are fundamental,[17] such as the fundamental right to personal choice regarding private family matters.[18] The fundamental right of parents to choose how to raise their children is grounded in the Fifth and Fourteenth Amendments[19] and in the individual right to privacy.[20] It is presumed that fit parents, married or divorced, act with the best interests of their children at heart. "The Due Process Clause does not permit a State to infringe on the fundamental right of parents to make child rearing decisions simply because a state judge believes a better decision could be made."[21]

The family privacy argument works best if the relocating parent has sole legal and residential custody because a judge has made a determination that only one parent should have ultimate decision-making power over the child's education, religion, health, and residence.[22] While a parent has a right to the care, custody, and control of their children over a third party, a parent's right is not absolute against the other parent. If one parent has sole custody and decision-making authority over the child, the parent may have a stronger expectation of privacy than if the parents are sharing custody. Even with sole custody or primary residency situations, however, some argue that the nonresidential parent has a fundamental right to parent.[23]

If the award is of joint legal custody, then neither parent makes childrearing decisions unilaterally. Where parents share parental responsibility, even when one is designated as the "primary residential" parent, neither has exclusive privacy rights to make decisions for the child to the exclusion of the other.[24] The parent with less parenting time also has an equally important fundamental right of familial association.[25] The parent, however, does not have any constitutional right in any particular schedule of parenting time.[26] Courts have found the decision to relocate justifies the exercise of *parens patriae*, allowing the state to intrude upon the family because the decision could conflict with the physical or mental health of the child.[27] Where parents share not only legal custody but also physical residency, the parenting plan must be modified if one relocates and the existing plan is unworkable due to distance.

Right to Travel

> A restriction on a parent's fundamental right to travel must be imposed cautiously and only when there is sufficient [legitimate, case-specific] proof that the restriction is in the best interest of the . . . particular child, rather than general discussion about the effects of relocation on children.[28]

The right to travel exists under state and federal law. Some states have determined there is a right to intrastate travel within their own states under their own constitutions.[29] Whether based on the Fourteenth Amendment or the Commerce Clause, the right to travel is rooted in our nation's history and culture.[30] The right to travel includes many aspects,[31] but certainly encompasses the right to migrate, resettle, find a new job, and start a new life. A statute that attempts to limit the fundamental right to travel is subject to "strict scrutiny" and can only be valid upon a showing of a compelling state interest.[32] The right to travel is intrastate, interstate, and to another country. The U.S. Supreme Court has explicitly stated foreign travel can be constitutionally limited.[33] A court may place travel and passport restrictions on a parent's travel with the child, especially if there is a threat of abduction.[34] (See Chapter 15.)

There is no restriction on a pregnant woman's right to travel. A husband or putative father cannot force a pregnant woman to remain in the same state.[35] A court cannot force one parent to stay in close proximity to the other parent.[36] In a Montana case, an unwed father, who had only seen the child once in the last 15 months and had not provided financial assistance, failed to show that mother's relocation with the child to Vermont for a job was not in the best interests of the child. The court looked at the specific facts and allowed the move.[37]

A court, however, may keep a child from moving with a parent if the judge finds that it is in the best interest of the child. While any person, including a parent, is free to move to another state and become a citizen of that state, that does not mean the parent has the right to take a child with them. As the New Jersey Supreme Court recently stated:

> The statute places no constraint on a plaintiff's right to travel. It does, however, place a limitation on her claimed right to permanently relocate her children from our State without the court's approval when another parent's rights and the child's best interests are at stake.[38]

Alabama courts have found that the noncustodial parent and child have a compelling interest in assuring that their fundamental constitutional rights are not unduly impaired by the custodial parent's choice of residence. If the state has any compelling interest, it is in preserving the familial relationship between parent and child.[39]

Changing a child's custody and residency, however, solely because the residential parent attempts to relocate, would appear to infringe on the residential parent's right to travel.[40] A parent should raise the constitutional argument at the trial court level. The New Mexico court noted that

> it makes no difference that the parent who wishes to relocate is not prohibited outright from doing so; a legal rule that operates to chill the exercise of the rights, absent a sufficient state interest to do so, is as impermissible as one that bans exercise of the right altogether.[41]

Prior to 2012, the Wyoming Supreme Court had held that the rights of a parent to the care and custody of a child and the duty of state courts to adjudicate custody do not themselves justify restricting the custodial parent's right to travel under the U.S. and Wyoming Constitutions.[42] In 2012, however, the Wyoming Supreme Court found that a relocation by a primary physical custodian, as well as factors that are derivative of the relocation, may constitute a change of circumstances sufficient to warrant consideration of the best interests of the children in a proceeding to modify child custody.[43]

International travel restrictions that keep a parent from removing the child from the United States generate a different discussion and are generally permissible.[44] The court, however, may strike a restriction which requires the parent to get approval for any travel, even if the child is not traveling with the parent.[45] (See Chapter 15.)

A parent may waive the constitutional right to travel by not raising the issue in the trial court.[46] A parent may also waive the argument by agreeing to a restriction on geographic mobility.[47] (See Chapter 4.) Other courts, however, have found that this is not the case. The furtherance of the child's best interests *may* constitute a compelling state interest worthy of reasonable interference with the right to travel interstate.

Parent Can Move, Child Cannot

Several courts have determined that a parent is free to travel but just cannot take the child with them.[48] The Washington Court of Appeals found that the relocation statute that prevented the divorced father from relocating to another state with his child did not violate his right to travel, but rather served a valid exercise of state power to protect the child. Moreover, the father was not required to refrain from moving, unless he elected to remain the custodial parent.[49] The statute listed 11 specific factors for the court to consider in balancing the many and competing interests at stake. The father was afforded an evidentiary hearing and had the benefit of the presumption that relocation was proper. The constitutional rights of children could be treated differently than those of adults because of the particular vulnerability of children, their inability to make informed, mature, and critical decisions, and the importance of the parental role in child rearing.[50]

These jurisdictions minimize the parent's constitutional right to travel.[51] The Maine Supreme Court upheld a trial court's award of minor child's primary residence to the mother, only if she remained in the country. If she relocated to Italy, the child's primary residence changed to the father. The court found the mother was free to travel or relocate permanently in Italy, but it was in the child's best interests to retain primary residence in Maine.[52]

The reality is that the threat of losing custody makes the right to travel meaningless for many custodial parents, who will not leave even though they have few job prospects or career potential in the current location or have a spouse living elsewhere.[53] At least one scholar has asserted that punitive orders that require a parent to give up the primary residency of their child to exercise their right to travel could be argued to be an unconstitutional penalty and unenforceable.[54] A basic fairness problem exists. In most states, the nonresidential parent retains full right to travel because, in most states, they do not need to give notice or obtain court approval.[55]

Balancing Test: Qualified Right to Travel

Several states find that the right to travel is not absolute but qualified by the state's compelling interest in protecting the best interests of the child. Courts in Colorado, Florida, Indiana, Maryland, Missouri, Montana, and New Mexico use a balancing test between the majority parent's right to travel and the minority parent's constitutional right to care and control of the child.[56]

> There is no constitutional infirmity in giving equal status, in determining the child's best interests, to the custodial parent's right to travel, and the benefit to be given the child from remaining with the custodial parent; and (2) the benefit from the noncustodial parent's exercise of his right to maintain close association and frequent contact with the child.[57]

The court must promote the best interests of the child, while affording protection equally between the primary residential parent's right to travel and the other parent's right to parent.[58] While the parents have a liberty interest in the care of their children, the state has a competing interest in the welfare of children within its jurisdiction, and may, as *parens patriae*, intervene in the family milieu if a child's welfare is at stake. Parental rights are subordinate to the State's *parens patriae* power and must yield to the welfare of the child.[59] The "best interests of the child" then is a competing, intertwined interest.[60] The Montana Supreme Court affirmed that the right to travel throughout the United States is a fundamental constitutional right that can be restricted only by a compelling state interest. A compelling state interest could be found in "furtherance of the best interests of the child, by assuring the maximum opportunities for the love, guidance and support of both natural parents." Therefore, the mother's right to travel with the child to Ohio was less important than the child's best interests.[61]

New Jersey courts noted that a court that has determined custody on the assumption of residence within the state of New Jersey so as to protect the visitation rights of the noncustodial parent and the interests of the child in maintaining a close relationship has the authority to constrain a parent from altering custody without violating the parent's due process right to travel.[62] Several states—Alabama, Arizona, Idaho, Kansas, Massachusetts,[63] Minnesota,[64] Montana, Nevada, Rhode Island, and Washington—have found that the "best interests" of the child is a compelling state interest that can trump a parent's right to travel.[65]

The Colorado Supreme Court explicitly rejected this view, finding that "in the absence of demonstrated harm to the child, the best interests of the child standard is insufficient to serve as a compelling state interest overruling the parents' fundamental rights."[66] The court noted:

> This is because a parent's ability to relocate would become subject to the changing views of social scientists and other experts who hold strong, but conflicting, philosophical positions as to the theoretical "best interests of the child."[67]

Although the Florida court also determined that the best interests of the child is not a compelling state interest, it found the Florida statute constitutional. It did not provide a presumption allowing the majority time parent's right to travel because it was important to equally balance the rights of the minority time parent's ability to parent.[68] The mother claimed the law offended equal protection rights as well as rights of privacy and travel.[69]

Nonresidential Parent's Right to Visitation

Illinois[70] and North Dakota[71] have found that the noncustodial parent's right to visitation is a sufficient compelling governmental interest to restrict the custodial parent's right to travel. A restriction on a parent's right to travel for as long as the court order of supervised visitation with the father was in existence, became moot when the supervision ended and the restriction was no longer in effect.[72]

Child's Right(s)

Although not fully developed yet in American law, there may also be a right of children to maintain relationships with parents and to have their voices heard.[73] The child should be recognized as an individual with legal interests separate and apart from the parents and any other adults involved in the dispute.[74] This would require recognizing that the child has a constitutional right to standing to file their own action.[75] At the very least, the judge should ascertain the child's perspective. (See Chapter 14, Hearing Children's Voices in Relocation.)

Endnotes

1. *In re* Ba.S., 911 N.E.2d 1252, 1257 (Ind. Ct. App. 2009).
2. United States v. Guest, 383 U.S.745, 757–58 (1966) (Stewart, J.) (right to travel is a right that is firmly established and repeatedly recognized). *See also In re* Sigmar, 270 S.W.3d 289 (Tex. App. 2008) (imposing restrictions because parental rights bow to the best interests of the child).
3. *In re* Marriage of Momb, 130 P.3d 406 (Wash. Ct. App. 2006).
4. Equal protection analysis is only appropriate if similarly situated individuals are treated differently. Equal protection is not violated because some persons are treated differently from others. Custodial and noncustodial parents are not similarly situated. *See* Reel v. Harrison, 60 P.3d 480, 483 (Nev. 2002).
5. *See* Vanderzon v. Vanderzon, 402 P.3d 219 (Utah Ct. App. 2017); Kulstad v. Maniaci, 244 P.3d 722 (Mont. 2010); *In re* Marriage of Cooksey, 125 P.3d 57 (Or. Ct. App. 2005); B.C. v. Dep't of Children & Families, 864 So. 2d 486, 491 (Fla. Dist. Ct. App. 2004).
6. Fredman v. Fredman, 960 So. 2d 52, 55 (Fla. Dist. Ct. App. 2007) (challenging the prior Florida statute in mother's appeal from trial court finding that relocation was not in the best interests of the child).
7. *See* David B. Chipman & Mindy M. Rush, *The Necessity of "Right to Travel" Analysis in Custodial Parent Relocation Cases*, 10 Wyo. L. Rev. 267 (2010). In addition to the right to travel and rights of parents to their children, there are other rights that could be argued, including the right to personhood, right to privacy, autonomy, right to home and family, and right of association. *See* Gary A. Debele, *A Children's Rights Approach to Relocation: A Meaningful Best Interests Standard*, 15 Am. Acad. Matrim. L.J. 75 (1998).
8. Troxel v. Granville, 530 U.S. 57, 66 (2000) (citing Meyer v. Nebraska, 262 U.S. 390, 399 (1923)); Santosky v. Kramer, 455 U.S. 745 (1982). *See also In re* Paternity of Ba.S., 911 N.E.2d 1252 (Ind. Ct. App. 2009) (change of physical custody to father affirming his constitutional right to parent children when mother wanted to relocate to Virginia with her new husband).

9. Shapiro v. Thompson, 394 U.S. 618, 629 (1969); United States v. Guest, 383 U.S. 745 (1966); Jones v. Helms, 452 U.S. 412 (1981) (noting, "It is, of course, well settled that the right of a United States Citizen to travel from one State to another and to take up residence in the State of his choice is protected by the Federal Constitution"); Saenz v. Roe, 526 U.S. 489 (1999).

10. Korth v. Korth, 958 N.W.2d 683 (Neb. 2021).

11. Bisbing v. Bisbing, 166 A.3d 1155 (N.J. 2017).

12. *In re* M.C., 343 P.3d 569 (Mont. 2015).

13. Baxendale v. Raich, 878 N.E.2d 1252, 1259 (Ind. 2008).

14. Troxel v. Granville, 530 U.S. 57, 88–89 (2000). Justice Stevens dissent:

> The constitutional protection against arbitrary state interference with parental rights should not be extended to prevent the States from protecting children against the arbitrary exercise of parental authority that is not in fact motivated by an interest in the welfare of the child.

15. Korth v. Korth, 958 N.W.2d 683 (Neb. 2021); Arnott v. Arnott, 293 P.3d 440, 457 (Wyo. 2012). *See also In re* Paternity of Ba.S., 911 N.E.2d 1252 (Ind. Ct. App. 2009).

16. *In re* M.C., 343 P.3d 569 (Mont. 2015). *See also In re* G.M.N, 433 P.3d 715 (Mont. 2019) (denying move).

17. Meyer v. Nebraska, 262 U.S. 390 (1923); Pierce v. Society of Sisters, 268 U.S. 510 (1925).

18. Moore v. City of East Cleveland, 431 U.S. 494 (1977).

19. Troxel v. Granville, 530 U.S. 57, 66 (2000) (it cannot now be doubted that the Due Process Clause of the Fourteenth Amendment protects the fundamental right of parents to make decisions concerning the care, custody, and control of their children).

20. Planned Parenthood v. Casey, 505 U.S. 833, 851 (1992) (stating Fourteenth Amendment affords constitutional protection to personal decisions, including marriage, family relationships, child rearing, and education); Prince v. Massachusetts, 321 U.S. 158, 166 (1944).

21. Troxel v. Granville, 530 U.S. 57, 68 (2000).

22. *See* Salichs v. James, 708 N.Y.S.2d 385 (App. Div. 2000) (denying attorney mother's move to Puerto Rico where child had relationship with both parents). *See* Carol Bruch & Janet Bowermaster, *The Relocation of Children and Custodial Parents: Public Policy, Past and Present*, 30 FAM. L.Q. 245, 251 (1996); Judith S. Wallerstein & Tony J. Tanke, *To Move or Not to Move—Psychological and Legal Considerations in the Relocation of Children Following Divorce*, 30 FAM. L.Q. 305 (1996).

23. David D. Meyer, *The Constitutional Rights of Non-Custodial Parents*, 34 HOFSTRA L. REV. 1461, 1474–84 (2006).

24. Fredman v. Fredman, 960 So. 2d 52, 56–57 (Fla. Dist. Ct. App. 2007).

25. Michael v. Hertzler, 900 P.2d 1144, 1147 (Wyo. 1995).

26. Arnold v. Arnold, 679 N.W.2d 296, 298 (Wis. Ct. App. 2004) (father was not constitutionally entitled to 182 days of physical custody).

27. Weaver v. Kelly, 18 S.W.3d 525, 528 (Mo. Ct. App. 2005); *In re* Marriage of Momb, 130 P.3d 406 (Wash. Ct. App. 2006). *See* Carlson v. Carlson, 661 P.2d 833, 836 (Kan. Ct. App. 1983).

28. *In re* C.J., 369 P.3d 1028 (Mont. 2016).

29. *See In re* White, 158 Cal. Rptr. 562, 567 (Ct. App. 1979); *In re* Marriage of Seitzinger, 775 N.E.2d 282 (Ill. App. Ct. 2002) (trial court erred in conditioning mother's primary physical custody on her remaining in Sangamon or Cass County; parent can move within the state with impunity); *In re* Marriage of Griffin, 209 P.3d 255 (Mont. 2009).

30. Laurence H. Tribe, American Constitutional Law 1379 (2d ed. 1998).

31. Saenz v. Roe, 526 U.S. 489 (1999) (identifying the right of interstate travel guaranteed by the Privileges and Immunities clause).

32. Jones v. Helms, 452 U.S. 412, 415–16 (1981).

33. Califano v. Aznavorian, 439 U.S. 170, 176 (1978).

34. Katare v. Katare, 283 P.3d 546 (Wash. 2012) (placing restrictions on father's travel to India with children); Messier v. Messier, 389 S.W.3d 904 (Tex. App. 2012) (placing restrictions on mother's international travel due to her irrational and threatening behavior).

35. *In re* Sara Ashton McK v. Samuel Bode M, 974 N.Y.S.2d 434 (App. Div. 2013) (putative father's prebirth petition in California did not give the court jurisdiction where mother had moved to New York).

36. Allbright v. Allbright, 215 P.3d 472, 474–46 (Idaho 2009) (court has no authority to dictate geographic area; cannot order mother not to move even if she does not take the child).

37. *In re* C.J., 369 P.3d 1028 (Mont. 2016).

38. Bisbing v. Bisbing, 166 A.3d 1155, 1171 (N.J. 2017). *See also In re* M.C., 343 P.3d 569 (Mont. 2015); Light v. D'Amato, 105 A.3d 447 (Me. 2014).

39. Boyd v. Boyd, 291 So. 3d 488 (Ala. Civ. App. 2019). *See also* Soohoo v. Johnson, 731 N.W.2d 815 (Minn. 2007).

40. *See* Arthur B. La France, *Child Custody and Relocation: A Constitutional Perspective*, 34 U. Louisville J. Fam. L. (1995–96).

41. Jaramillo v. Jaramillo, 823 P.2d 299, 306 (1991); *In re* Marriage of Ciesluk, 113 P.3d 135, 142 (Colo. 2005) (finding that the Colorado statute ". . . chills the exercise of [the majority time] parent's right to travel because, in seeking to relocate, that parent risks losing majority parent").

42. Watt v. Watt, 971 P.2d 608, 615–16 (Wyo. 1999) (overruled by Arnott v. Arnott, 293 P.3d 440 (Wyo. 2012)).

43. Arnott v. Arnott, 293 P.3d 440 (Wyo. 2012) (mother's attempt to relocate daughters to Virginia was a material change of circumstances).

44. Light v. D'Amato, 105 A.3d 447 (Me. 2014) (refusing to allow mother to relocate to her native Italy).

45. Arredondo v. Betancourt, 383 S.W.3d 730, 744 (Tex. App. 2012) (vacating an order that required the mother to seek approval from her ex-husband for any travel outside of the United States, whether or not their child was with her).

46. Hull v. Hull, 273 So. 3d 1135 (Fla. Dist. Ct. App. 2019).

47. Tomasko v. DuBuc, 761 A.2d 407 (N.H. 2000).

48. *In re* Marriage of Ciesluk, 113 P.3d 135, 143 (Colo. 2005); Fredman v. Fredman, 960 So. 2d 52, 58 (Fla. Dist. Ct. App. 2007); *In re* C.R.O., 96 S.W.3d 442 (Tex. App. 2002) (mother could relocate without the children).

49. Momb v. Ragone, 130 P.3d 406 (Wash. Ct. App. 2006), *rev. denied* (denied primary residential custody father's relocation with child from Spokane where mother, who had been primary residential parent for ten years, lives, to South Dakota where his new wife lives).

50. *Id.* at 412–13 (child's relationship with mother was equal to or better than with father and relationship with stepmother was not good).

51. *See In re* M.C., 343 P.3d 569 (Mont. 2015) (mother was primary caregiver if she remained in Montana).

52. Light v. D'Amato, 105 A.3d 447 (Me. 2014).

53. *See* Leslie Eaton, *Divorced Parents Move, and Custody Gets Trickier*, LAW WISE 5 (Feb. 2005) (discussing Colorado case in which judge denied mother's move to Arizona for a job and another case of a mother who shuttles between her husband and son in California and her daughter from a first marriage who judge made stay in New York).

54. Brigitte Bodenheimer, *Progress Under the UCCJA and Remaining Problems, Punitive Decrees, Joint Custody and Excessive Modifications*, 65 CAL. L. REV. 978, 1008–09 (1977) (imposing the condition of leaving the children behind places the most direct and oppressive burden on the exercise of constitutional freedom one can imagine).

55. Theresa Glennon, *Still Partners? Examining the Consequences of Post-Dissolution Partnering*, 41 FAM. L.Q. 105, 106 (Spring 2007) (noting no restrictions placed on noncustodial parents or minority residential parents). *But see* FLA. STAT. § 61.13001 (defining relocation as a change in the location of the principal residence of either parent at least 50 miles away from his or her place of residence at the time of the last order). *See also* Merle Hope Weiner, *Inertia and Inequality: Reconceptualizing Disputes over Parental Relocation*, 40 U.C. DAVIS L. REV. 1747 (2007) (arguing nonresidential parent's mobility should be factored into the equation).

56. *In re* Marriage of Ciesluk, 113 P.3d 135, 148 (Colo. 2005); Fredman v. Fredman, 960 So. 2d 52 (Fla. Dist. Ct. App. 2007); Jaramillo v. Jaramillo, 823 P.2d 299, 309 (N.M. 1991); *In re* C.H., 412 S.W.3d 375 (Mo. Ct. App. 2013), *reh'g and transfer denied* (upholding geographic restrictions as child's best interest took precedence over mother's right to travel). *See also In re* Custody of D.M.G. & T.J.G., 951 P.2d 1377 (Mont. 1998) (discussing constitutional aspects).

57. Braun v. Headley, 750 A.2d 624, 635 (Md. Ct. Spec. App. 2000), *cert. denied*, 755 A.2d 1139 (Md. 2000), *cert. denied*, 531 U.S. 1191 (2001);

58. *In re* Marriage of Ciesluk, 113 P.3d 135, 142 (Colo. 2005).

59. Preston v. Mercieri, 573 A.2d 128 (N.H. 1990). *See also* Weiland v. Ruppel, 75 P.3d 176 (Idaho 2003); LaChappelle v. Mitten, 607 N.W.2d 151, 163 (Minn. Ct. App.), *cert. denied*, Mitten v. LaChappelle, 531 U.S. 1011 (2000).

60. *In re* Marriage of Ciesluk, 113 P.3d at 142.

61. *In re* Parenting of M.C. (Collie and Pirkle), 343 P.3d 569 (Mont. 2015). *See also In re* G.M.N., 433 P.3d 715 (Mont. 2019) (upholding lower court decision that it was in the daughter's best interest to remain in the home community rather than move to Boston).

62. Bisbing v. Bisbing, 166 A.3d 1155 (N.J. 2017).

63. Mason v. Coleman, 850 N.E.2d 513 (Mass. 2006).

64. *See* Goldman v. Greenwood, 748 N.W.2d 279 (Minn. 2008); Weiland v. Ruppel, 75 P.3d 176 (Idaho 2003).

65. *See generally* Linda D. Elrod, *A Move in the Right Direction? Best Interests of the Child Emerging as Standard in Relocation Cases*, 3 J. Child Custody 29 (2006).

66. *In re* Marriage of Ciesluk, 113 P.3d 135, 144–45 (Colo. 2005).

67. *Id.*

68. Fredman v. Fredman, 960 So. 2d 52, 58 (Fla. Dist. Ct. App. 2007).

69. *Id.* at 52.

70. *See In re* Marriage of Seitzinger, 775 N.E.2d 282 (Ill. App. Ct. 2002) (trial court erred in conditioning mother's primary physical custody on her remaining in Sangamon or Cass County).

71. Stout v. Stout, 560 N.W.2d 903 (N.D. 1997) (noting importance of noncustodial parent's right to maintain and develop relationship but finding it could be satisfied by modifying visitation schedule to include less frequent but more extended periods of time).

72. CL v. ML, 351 P.3d 272 (Wyo. 2015).

73. *See* U.N. Convention on the Rights of the Child, art. 12 (right of child to be heard in all judicial or administrative proceedings determining their custody). *See also* James G. Dwyer, The Relationship Rights of Children (2006); David D. Meyer, *The Modest Promise of Children's Relationship Rights*, 11 Wm. & Mary L. Bill Rts. J. 1117 (2003).

74. *See* Gary A. Debele, *A Children's Rights Approach to Relocation: A Meaningful Best Interests Standard*, 10 Am. Acad. Matrim. L. 75, 78 (1998).

75. *Id.* at 95 (citing Gregory K. v. Ralph K., Nos. CI92-5127 & JU90-5245 (Fla. Orange Cnty. Cir. Ct. 1992). *See* George H. Russ, *Through the Eyes of a Child, "Gregory K.": A Child's Right to Be Heard*, 27 Fam. L.Q. 365 (1993). *See also* Linda D. Elrod, *Client-Directed Lawyers for Children: It's the "Right" Thing to Do*, 27 Pace L. Rev. 869 (2007) (noting that child should have counsel when parents are in high conflict situation, such as a relocation).

CHAPTER 6

Notice of Intent to Move

The notice provision . . . is designed to allow consideration of the likely impact of a move before it occurs, thereby minimizing disruptions in the child's life.[1]

As a general rule, a parent who has legal and physical custody of a child has a continuing duty to notify the other parent or a party who has parenting time or visitation of any change of the child's telephone number and address. If a parent intends to relocate the child's principal residence, courts may require additional information. In the past 30 years, the majority of states have enacted relocation statutes that provide for notice and factors for the court to consider in determining whether a parent can move with a child.

If there is no custody order in place, the decision is for an initial custody order using the general best-interest statute rather than the more specialized relocation statute.[2] So the notice requirement of the relocation statute generally does not apply if the petition to relocate is included as part of the original custody order.[3] Additionally, if the parties' parenting plan expressly provides for relocation, the relocating parent may not have to comply with statutory relocation procedures.[4] (See Chapter 4.) If, however, a parent relocates without obtaining the other parent's approval or the court's permission to relocate, the parent risks being found in contempt of court.[5] In addition, a parent may end up with the children ordered to return and an award of attorney's fees against the parent moving.[6]

A relocation statute may dictate who gets notice, how much notice is required, the form it should take, and what it should contain. Over half of the states now have specific notice requirements.

In Washington state, the notice statute is triggered by an intended relocation of the person with whom the child resides a majority of the time.[7] Some states, like Florida, require notice to be given if either parent wants to move, not just the one who has legal or physical custody of the child. The ABA Model Relocation Act provides the following:

> Sec. 4. Individuals Entitled to Notice; Time of Notice
>
> (a) Unless excused by an emergency, other exigent circumstances, or section 5(b), if either parent plans to relocate or to relocate with the child, the parent planning to relocate shall notify the other parent and any other individual with rights of custody, visitation, or parenting time at least [45] days before the proposed relocation.
>
> (b) Notice under this section may be excused or modified by the court for good cause. Good cause includes a finding by the court that the safety of the child or party will be endangered by notice.

State relocation statutes vary considerably. Some states require notice of any move, in state or out of state and any distance.[8] Others require notice of an intent to move only if the move is a certain distance away or if the nonresidential parent does not consent.[9] For example, Utah only requires notice if the intended move is "150 miles or more" from the other party's residence.[10] Louisiana requires notice if the intended move is more than 75 miles from the principal residence of the child.[11] Oklahoma's relocation act requires that either the other parent or court approve a move that is more than 75 miles away from the principal residence for more than 60 days.[12] Michigan requires a parent to get court approval or the other parent's consent if the move is 100 miles away.[13] States also vary on whether the miles are radial miles or driving miles.[14]

Some statutes prescribe the form of the notice; in others, a simple letter notice is enough. State law determines whether a party can mail the notice by regular mail or if certified mail is required. Some prescribe what is to be in the notice and what is to happen if no notice is given. The lawyer drafting the parenting plan should include specific notice requirements about a parent's intent to relocate, even if there is a statute requiring notice. The parties may want to include a provision specifying how far a parent can move without giving notice and how much notice will be given. The provision could require parties to comply with existing statutes or could allow more or less time or variations in distance. The agreement can define how the parties want notice and require more notice than the statute if they wish. In one case, the parties put in their parenting plan that the mother would provide father with 60 days' notice of her intent to relocate more than a 30-minute drive away from father's home by personal service or by mail with return receipt. When the mother unilaterally moved to Seattle, more than 30 minutes away, the court found her in violation of the parenting plan, awarded the father 24 more days of parenting time, and awarded him attorney's fees and costs.[15]

The presence of a relocation restriction in a journal entry and decree means that notice must be given to the other parent, even in the absence of a statute. In one case, the parenting plan provided that the parties would live within a 75-mile radius of their current residence in New York. The mother moved the children to Georgia without notifying the father. The New York court changed the parenting plan to give the father sole legal and physical custody.[16]

Even if there is no statute or relocation provision in the parenting agreement, the best practice is for the lawyer for the moving party to prepare a letter to the opposing counsel, or the other parent if there is no counsel, informing the lawyer of the client's intent to move. The letter should be sent at least 30 days (or more if required by statute or agreement) in advance of the move. The letter with proof of service will form the basis for the application, motion, or petition for the client's permission to move or for a modification of the existing parenting arrangements.

If the relocation request is being made after the initial order, the client is seeking to modify an existing order. In most states, the motion to modify is filed in the court that issued the initial decree as long as one party remains in the state (see Chapter 3). It is filed in the original case using the same caption and same docket number. Some jurisdictions require no additional filing fee; others require a post-judgment fee. Proper service must be obtained. In most states the motion may be filed at any time, if it is in the child's best interests and there has been the requisite finding of a change in circumstances.[17]

Who Gets Notice?

In most states, only the parent or other person exercising parental rights is entitled to receive notice. In a few states, the AAML Relocation standards and the ABA Model Relocation Act require notice to be given not only to parents but also to others with court-ordered access, such as grandparents. For example, in Alabama, a person entitled to custody of or visitation with a child shall provide notice to every other person entitled to custody of or visitation with a child of an intended change in their principal residence.[18] Pennsylvania requires notice to every individual who has custody rights to the child.[19] This could include a non-biological, nonmarital partner of the parent. Arkansas courts found, however, that a paternal grandmother, who was listed as the minor child's babysitter, did not have any rights to object to mother's relocation.[20]

How Much Notice Is Required?

A few state statutes list no specific time requirement in advance of the move.[21] Most statutes, however, require that the parent wishing to relocate must give notice a certain number of days in advance of the move. Although Colorado requires written notice of intent to relocate "as soon as practicable,"[22] most states have notice periods ranging from 30,[23] 45,[24] to 60 days.[25] The ABA Model Relocation Act uses a bracketed [45] days, which means that a state can choose the number of days but 45 is the default. The AAML Relocation Standards[26] and the American Law Institute Principles of the Law of Dissolution[27] require a 60-day notice. Indiana and Maryland require 90 days.[28]

The parent planning to move must comply with the time periods. A Missouri mother's email stating that she was moving in 20 days was not sufficient notice when the statute required 60 days.[29]

Contents of the Notice

Many states have no specified contents for the notice. The ABA Model Relocation of Children Act section 5(a) requires the following to be included, when available, in a written document or petition:

> (1) The intended new residence, including street address;
> (2) The telephone numbers, if any, of the parent and child who are relocating;
> (3) The intended date of the relocation;
> (4) A statement of the specific reasons for the relocation; and
> (5) A proposed revised schedule for parenting time or visitation with the child.[30]

If there is a fear of violence against the parent or child, section 5(b) of the ABA Model Relocation of Children Act states that

> If a party alleges in an affidavit or a pleading under oath that the health, safety, or liberty of a party or child would be jeopardized by disclosure of identifying information, the information must be sealed and may not be disclosed to the other party or the public unless the court orders the disclosure to be made after a hearing in which the court takes into consideration the health, safety or liberty of the party or child and determines that the disclosure is in the interest of justice.

The AAML Relocation Act requires the proposed change of address, including reasons for the move and a proposed revised visitation schedule.[31]

Sometimes a parent does not have all of the information 45 to 60 days in advance. The ABA Model Relocation of Children Act section 5(c) requires that if any information is not known at the time notice is given or if the information changes after the notice is given, the new information shall be provided not later than 72 hours after receipt of the information. Generally, substantial compliance with the information known is sufficient.[32] The Oklahoma statute requires that a party has a continuing obligation to keep the information regarding the proposed relocation current as information changes. In one case, the mother's initial notice to move to a city 138 miles away started in good faith, but she failed to update the information. She did not move to the rental house, but in with her boyfriend's parents, and she did not enroll in nursing school. The court found the notice to not be in good faith and changed custody to the father.[33]

Several states have more detailed provisions.[34] Some statutes require an acknowledgment of the other parent's right to object and the procedure to follow if there is an objection.[35] For example, the Florida statute requires the following statement in all capital letters:

> A RESPONSE TO THE PETITION OBJECTING TO RELOCATION MUST BE MADE IN WRITING, FILED WITH THE COURT, AND SERVED ON THE PARENT OR OTHER PERSON SEEKING TO RELOCATE WITHIN 20 DAYS AFTER SERVICE OF THIS PETITION TO RELOCATE. IF YOU FAIL TO TIMELY OBJECT TO THE RELOCATION, THE RELOCATION WILL BE ALLOWED, UNLESS IT IS NOT IN THE BEST INTERESTS OF THE CHILD, WITHOUT FURTHER NOTICE AND WITHOUT A HEARING.[36]

Because the goal for the moving parent is to be able to move as expeditiously as possible without going back to court, the notice sets the stage for later litigation. The notice can provide a brief history of the case, the actual time share (which can be very important if the other parent is not following the time share or not cooperating with parenting), the reason for the move, and a proposal for new parenting time arrangements. The easier the moving parent makes it for the nonmoving parent to say "yes," or at least not object, and file to change physical custody, the easier the case will be. If there is a "clear" local or state rule, the notice could provide citations that will point the opposing counsel in the right direction and help evaluate the likelihood of success if there is an objection.

How Notice Is Given

The majority of states require notice to be given in writing by certified mail, return receipt requested.[37] The ABA Model Relocation of Children Act section 6 provides the following alternative options:

> (a) (1) certified mail, return-receipt requested and first class mail to the last known address of the individual entitled to notice;
> (2) hand delivery, but there must be a signed receipt for delivery;
> (3) service of process;
> (4) commercially reasonable delivery services such as Federal Express, UPS, DHL; or
> (5) electronic means, such as e-mail or fax, reasonably calculated to provide actual notice.
>
> (b) The parties may agree in writing to a means of notice to be used in lieu of or in addition to the methods of notice specified in section (a).

Some statutes require that notice be given by mail but may be silent as to how to give notice. The best protection is to use certified mail.[38] In one case, even though the father's roommate refused the mother's certified mailing of notice of intent to relocate, the Oklahoma court found that the notice was effective to trigger the 30-day period within which the father was statutorily required to file his objection.[39]

As a general rule, neither an email notification nor a text notification of intent to move will be sufficient to comply with the notice requirements of statutes.[40] As electronic filings have gained respect, it is possible that states may allow other types of notice.

If the parent does not file an objection within the required time period, it is presumed that relocation is in the best interests of the child. In some states, this means an order can be entered in an expedited manner without an evidentiary hearing. In others, however, it does not. If the parent does respond, the moving parent may not relocate and must proceed to a temporary hearing. There may be extenuating circumstances that may justify a court remanding for a best interests hearing, even if the response was untimely.[41]

Notice Not Required

There are a few instances when notice may not be required. The first is if the state statute does not consider the move to be a "relocation," either because the decision is being made as part of the initial custody determination or because the move is not far enough away under the geographical restriction in a statute, court order, or parties' agreement. The second is when giving notice might endanger the parent or child, such as when there is an order of protection in place. A third situation might be where both parties are fine with one parent going to another state and are not planning on a relocation at the time.

Not Far Enough to Be "Relocation"

Some states do not require notice if the move is less than a certain distance away or within a state.[42] The Wisconsin statute provides that a court cannot restrict a parent wanting to move less than 150 miles away.[43] Tennessee uses radial miles to judge the distance. Because mother's proposed relocation was less than 50 radial miles, the parent relocation statute did not apply to require notice to the father or provide a basis for modification of the parenting plan.[44] Louisiana provides that the relocation statute applies requiring notice only if the parent moves a distance of more than 75 radial miles from the principal residence of the child at the time the most recent custody decree was rendered. In one case, the Court of Appeals found that the 75 miles is measured as the crow flies rather than in road miles.[45] In another case, however, the court upheld the family court, which found the distance to be 75.8 miles using Google Maps and 76 miles using Apple Maps. The family court stated:

> The mode of transportation in the modem world is by automobile, not boat, plane, helicopter, or some sort of aerocar reminiscent of The Jetsons' television show. The only practical and economical way of traveling between places is in an automobile and by using surface roads. Using any other method to calculate the distance would lead to absurd consequences.[46]

Abuse or Fear of Harm

Following the pattern of the Uniform Interstate Family Support Act, some states do not require notice of a move or identifying information if the reason for the move is fear of domestic violence,[47] especially if there is a valid protection order.[48] In some states, notice may not be required when a parent has been convicted of a crime that involves the child.[49] For example, South Dakota provides that no notice need be provided if (1) the relocation results in the child moving closer to the noncustodial parent; (2) the location is within the boundaries of the child's current school district; (3) there is an existing valid protection order in favor of the child or the custodial parent against the noncustodial parent; or (4) if within the preceding 12 months, the nonrelocating parent has been convicted of violation of a protection order, criminal assault, child abuse, or other domestic violence and either the child or the custodial parent was the victim of the crime or violation.

Relocation Not Contemplated at Time of Original Move

In one case, parties had lived in both Illinois (first 18 months of children's lives) and Colorado (last few years). Father was doing construction on a house and was fine with mother, who was primary caretaker, taking children to Colorado. When relationship broke down later, he tried to argue that mother's failure to follow the notice requirements should be an automatic denial of her petition to relocate to Colorado. The court disagreed, noting that there was no bad faith and the move was not originally planned as a relocation.[50]

Effect of Notice Statute

Once the moving parent gives notice of the intent to relocate, generally the nonrelocating parent has a certain number of days to decide what to do. There are several options:

Parent Agrees to the Relocation

The nonmoving parent can agree to the moving parent's request to move. The parents can negotiate or mediate a new parenting plan themselves or with the help of lawyers or mediators to accommodate the child's and parents' new living arrangements. Another way to agree is for the nonmoving parent to change their mind and decide to move to the new location to continue the existing parenting plan.

Parent Objects to the Move

The nonmoving parent can object to the move and follow the state procedure to object. In some states, the nonrelocating parent has a certain number of days, generally 30,[51] to object in writing to the move.[52] In Louisiana, the person proposing relocation shall initiate a summary proceeding to obtain court approval to relocate and has the burden of proof that proposed relocation is in good faith and in the best interest of the child.[53]

In some states, the filing of an objection may trigger a hearing on the objection. In other states, the nonmoving parent may file an action to prohibit the children from leaving the jurisdiction. In Missouri, if the parent files a timely objection, the other party cannot relocate until 60 days after notice is given pending judicial permission.[54] If the parent objects, a hearing may be held on any timely filed objection.[55] Florida has found that if the nonmoving party files an objection to relocation, the court must hold a temporary hearing or trial. The failure of the objector to include verified facts in their objection is not a basis to ignore the timely objection.[56] If a hearing is held, however, the failure of the nonmoving parent to show up may result in the court approving the relocation.[57]

Parent Files a Motion to Modify the Prior Order

The nonmoving parent can object and file a motion to change physical residence based upon a material change in circumstances. While a proposed change of residence may be a material change of circumstances, it is not always. In a modification proceeding when neither party is attempting to change their geographical location, the parent did not have to comply with the relocation notice provisions of the Child Custody Act.[58] An

Indiana case also indicated that a requirement for notice does not necessarily mean there is a change in circumstances.[59] A notice statute may mean, however, that the court will allow a hearing if the nonrelocating parent objects to the move.[60] (See Chapter 8.)

Parent Ignores the Notice and Fails to Respond

The nonmoving parent can choose not to respond at all. The ABA Model Relocation of Children Act section 7(d) states that if the nonrelocating parent does not file a petition objecting to relocation with the court or initiate an alternative dispute resolution process within 30 days of receipt of notice, the parent who gave notice may relocate with the child without permission of the other parent or the court. Some states take this approach.[61]

Under the AAML Standards section 405 and the laws of several states, if the other parent does not object within 30 days of notice, the court permits relocation without a return to the court.[62] If the notice was not properly given, a nonrelocating parent may get additional time to object.[63] If the nonrelocating parent has a good reason for not responding on time, the court may refuse to enter the relocation order without a hearing.

In Indiana, a nonrelocating parent may object to relocation of the other parent in either of two ways: (1) by filing a motion to modify the custody order, or (2) by filing, within 60 days of receipt of the notice, a motion to prevent relocation of the child. If the nonrelocating parent does not file a timely objection, there is a statutory presumption that relocation is in the best interests of the child. If there is good cause for the failure to file, the court will hold an evidentiary hearing to determine best interests.[64] On the other hand, an Indiana father's technical compliance with the statute governing response when objecting to a relocation petition did not entitle the mother to relocate with the children.[65]

In one Florida case, the mother missed the 20-day deadline to reply but she had hired a lawyer who failed to file due to circumstances beyond his control and it was apparent the mother intended to participate in the hearing.[66] An Alabama case, however, found that the left-behind parent's failure to object to the relocation did not constitute a defense for a relocating parent who moved in defiance of an existing order disallowing relocation.[67]

Effect of Noncompliance with Notice Statute

The effect of noncompliance may depend on the facts and circumstances. A court may consider that a parent relocated without the required notice.[68] A Florida appellate court found the trial court correctly ordered the children returned to Florida where the mother moved to Baltimore without following the notice statute.[69] A Louisiana court found a custodial parent's failure to file a timely notice of an intent to relocate before relocating was not fatal to her request, but it could result in consequences.[70] What consequences may depend on the reason for noncompliance and if the other party was prejudiced.

In Oklahoma, there is a continuing obligation to keep information about a proposed relocation updated as information changes. The court modified the custody order to make the father the primary custodial parent where the mother had given a rental address for a home she never occupied and moved in with the boyfriend's parents. She also did not enroll in nursing school as she had stated.[71]

If the nonmoving parent had actual notice, the court may excuse lack of statutory written notice.[72] In one case, a mother's failure to provide notice before actual in-state relocation did not outweigh the other factors favoring naming mother as domiciliary parent and allowing her relocation with the ten-month old child.[73]

Most courts are pretty strict about the notice requirement. Because Florida law requires a parent wishing to move to file a sworn petition with the trial court, the mother's hand delivery to father of her "Notice of Intent to Relocate" did not comply and the trial court erred in granting mother's relocation request.[74]

Missouri courts have been particularly strict about compliance.[75] A mother's email to father, stating she intended to relocate in 20 days, did not comply with Missouri's statutory requirements for notice of proposed relocation.[76] A mother's intent to move to "Orlando" was not specific enough of an address, when she knew where she would be living.[77] A mother's failure to include a proposed revised schedule for custody meant her notice was defective and father's failure to object within

30 days of receiving the notice did not give mother an absolute right to relocate.[78] On the other hand, a father objected after the mother and child moved to Tennessee on the basis that the mother's notice had been defective because it did not state the exact address and date for relocation. A Missouri court found the notice sufficient.[79]

A Utah court found that the ex-wife's failure to include her address and the name of her new husband in her initial relocation notice did not prejudice the ex-husband because he obtained the information prior to the evidentiary hearing.[80] Likewise, Oklahoma found that the mother's service of notice of relocation was sufficient, despite the fact she did not inform him in writing that he had to make an objection within 30 days to avoid an order permitting relocation. The father did file an objection and fully litigated the issue.[81]

Some courts have found that failure to give the statutorily required notice constitutes a change of circumstances that justifies a reevaluation of the custody arrangements.[82] A mother failed to give written notice of her intent to locate with her new husband but moved in June. The father filed a motion to be named domiciliary custodian in August, but did not object to the lack of notice, so waived that issue.[83] In a Maine case, the father filed a motion to enforce, and the mother filed a motion to modify. Even though the mother did not give written notice of her potential relocation abroad, the issue of relocation was tried by implicit agreement of the parties.[84]

Where the moving party fails to give the proper statutory notice and the other party raises that failure as an issue in the ensuing litigation, the trial court may consider a failure to provide notice of a proposed relocation of a child as:

1. A factor in making its determination regarding the relocation of a child.
2. A basis for ordering the return of the child if the relocation has taken place without notice or court authorization.
3. Sufficient cause to order the person proposing relocation to pay reasonable expenses incurred by the person objecting to the relocation.[85]

The failure to give notice can also result in a change in the parenting arrangements. In Illinois, the mother's failing to file a motion and give proper notice and relocating unilaterally resulted in a change in primary residency to the father.[86] In a Kansas case, the court found that a change in residential placement was not a permissible sanction for the mother's failure to provide father with the required 30-day notice of intent to relocate.[87]

The nonmoving parent's failure to object to the relocation, however, does not constitute a defense for the relocating parent who has moved in defiance of a court order disallowing relocation. Because the 2012 court order prohibited relocation, the mother was required to obtain father's permission or request to modify the prior order.[88]

The failure to comply with the notice statute and moving anyway may be contempt.[89] Failure of a party to notify of a relocation of the child may be taken into account in a modification of custody, visitation, or access to a child.[90] At the very least, when a parent moves without complying with the notice statute, the court may order return of the children to the other parent's residence and order the violating parent to pay the other party's expenses.[91]

Award of Attorney Fees

A court may consider a failure to comply with the notice requirements without good cause as a factor in determining whether the relocation is in good faith and as a basis for awarding reasonable expenses and attorney's fees attributable to such failure. The Washington Court of Appeals upheld an award of attorney's fees to the father of $10,000 and costs, where the mother moved a 30-minute drive away without giving the father the 60-day notice by personal service or mail with return receipt provided in the parenting plan.[92] Where a mother relocated with the children without court approval and refused to honor the father's visitation rights, the court found the mother in contempt, ordered her to pay attorney's fees and changed physical custody to the father.[93]

Endnotes

1. *In re* Marriage of Grippin, 186 P.3d 852, 856 (Kan. Ct. App. 2008) (where a mother did not give proper notice, the court observed that to allow her to argue that a child has adjusted to a new environment would effectively reward her for ignoring the notice provision).

2. Merrells v. Dotray, 299 So. 3d 208 (La. Ct. App. 2020).

3. Kenny v. Strang, 249 N.E.3d 427 (Ill. App. Ct. 2023) (where mother, children, and father had lived in both Colorado and Illinois throughout the marriage, case was not typical relocation).

4. *In re* Marriage of Coulter & Trinidad, 976 N.E.2d 337 (Ill. 2012).

5. *See* Boyd v. Boyd, 291 So. 3d 488 (Ala. Civ. App. 2019).

6. State v. Titus, 274 So. 3d 591 (La. Ct. App. 2019).

7. Wash. Stat. Ann. § 26.094.30. *See In re* Marriage of Fahey, 262 P.3d 128 (Wash. Ct. App. 2011).

8. Kan. Stat. Ann. § 23-2332. *See also* Fla. Stat. § 61-13001 (if either parent moves 50 miles away).

9. La. Rev. Stat. § 9:355.2(b)(3), (4) (75 miles); Thompson v. Thompson, 176 P.3d 722 (Ariz. Ct. App. 2008).

10. Utah Code Ann. § 30-3-37(1)–(2) (60 days written notice but no other requirements).

11. La. Rev. Stat. § 9:355.4. *See* Holley v. Holley, 232 So. 3d 717 (La. Ct. App. 2017) (mother not required to give notice when moving less than 75 radial miles, even though actual road travel miles would exceed 75). *But see* Thibodaux v. Thibodaux, ___ So. 3d ___, 2025 WL 655793 (La. Ct. App. 2025) (the difference in radial miles was 63.6 and 58.98 in radial miles but road miles were 91.8 and 117 if using automobile).

12. Okla. Stat. Ann. 43 § 112.3.

13. Mich. C. L. Ann. § 722.31(2, 4).

14. *See* Bowers v. Vanderneulen-Bowers, 750 N.W.2d 597 (Mich. Ct. App. 2008) (finding radial, not road miles, should be used to measure distance).

15. *In re* Marriage of Raskob, 334 P.3d 30 (Wash. Ct. App. 2014) (mother's failure to comply was consistent with her rigidity in parenting and not communicating with the father).

16. Sukul v. Sukul, 151 N.Y.S.3d 684 (App. Div. 2021).

17. Alaska Stat. § 25.20.110; Hawaii Rev. Stat. § 571-46(6); Kan. Stat. Ann. § 23-2332.

18. Ala. Code § 30-3-164.

19. Pa. Consol. Stat. Ann. § 5337(b).

20. Hurtt v. Hurtt, 216 S.W.3d 604 (Ark. Ct. App. 2005).

21. States with no time limit specified are Alaska, Arkansas, Colorado, Connecticut, Delaware, District of Columbia, Florida, Hawaii, Idaho, Iowa, Kentucky, Massachusetts, Michigan, Minnesota, Mississippi, Nebraska,

Nevada, New Jersey, North Carolina, North Dakota, Ohio, Rhode Island, Texas, Vermont, and Wyoming.

22. Colo. Rev. Code § 14-10-129 (1)(a)(II) (also requiring location, reason for relocation, and a proposed revised parenting plan).

23. Ga. Code Ann. § 19-9-3(f); Kan. Stat. Ann. § 23-2332; Mont. Code Ann. § 40-4-217; N.M. Stat. Ann. § 40-4-9.1(4)(a); Va. Code Ann. § 20-124.5.

24. Ala. Code § 30-3-165; Cal. Fam. Code § 3024 (unless prior agreement to move); S.D. Codified Laws § 25-4A-17 (shorter if reasonable under the specific facts).

25. Ariz. Rev. Stat. § 25-408(C)(1)7(H); La. Rev. Stat. Ann. § 9.355.5; Mo. Rev. Stat. § 452.377; N.H. Rev. Stat. Ann. § 461-A:12(III); Okla. Stat. Ann. tit. 43 § 112.3; Pa. Consol. Stat. Ann. § 5337 (c)(2)(I) (or ten days after person knows of relocation if they did not know in time to comply); Tenn. Code Ann. § 36-6-108(a); Utah Code Ann. § 30-3-37(2); W. Va. Code § 48-11-403; Wis. Stat. Ann. § 767.481.

26. *Perspectives on the Relocation of Children*, 15 J. Am. Acad. Matrim. L. § 202 (1998) [AAML Relocation Act].

27. Am. Law Inst., Principles of the Law of Family Dissolution § 2.17(2) & cmt. c.

28. Ind. Code § 31-17-2.2-3; Md. Code Ann. Family Law § 9-106.

29. Ashton v. Ashton, 511 S.W.3d 473 (Mo. Ct. App. 2017) (Mo. Rev. Stat. § 452.377.2 requires 60-day notice).

30. Mo. Rev. Stat. § 452.377.2. *See also* Ala. Code § 30-3-166.

31. AAML Relocation Act, § 203(b)(5)–(6).

32. Amick v. Smart, 535 S.W.3d 368 (Mo. Ct. App. 2017) (mother's notice complied even though she did not have the street address at the time of the initial notice).

33. Richards v. Richards, 401 P.3d 1175 (Okla. Civ. App. 2017).

34. Pa. Consol. Stat. Ann. § 5337(c)(3) adds

(ix) Any other information which the party proposing the relocation deems appropriate.

(x) A counteraffidavit as provided under subsection (d)(1) which can be used to object to the proposed relocation and the modification of a custody order.

(xi) A warning to the nonrelocating party that if the nonrelocating party does not file with the court an objection to the proposed relocation within 30 days after receipt of the notice, that party shall be foreclosed from objecting to the relocation.

See also Ind. Code § 31-17-2.2-3(2)(A)–(H). *See* Rogers v. Rogers, 876 N.E.2d 1121 (Ind. Ct. App. 2007) (rejecting father's argument that mother did not comply with notice statute when she filed pro se notice in December 2006 and amended her notice of intent upon getting counsel).

35. Ala. Code § 30-3-165; Fla. Stat. Ann. § 61-13001(3); Wash. Code § 26.09.440.

36. Fla. Stat. Ann. § 61.13001 (a)(7).

37. *See, e.g.*, Ala. Code § 30-3-166; Mo. Rev. Stat. § 452.377.2.

38. Ind. Code § 31-17-2.2-1(a) (requires the notice to be filed with the clerk of the court that issued the parenting time order and the notice be sent by registered or certified mail).

39. Plumlee v. Plumlee, 271 P.3d 807 (Okla. Civ. App. 2011).

40. *See* Ashton v. Ashton, 511 S.W.3d 473 (Mo. Ct. App. 2017) (email notice); State v. Titus, 274 So. 3d 591 (La. Ct. App. 2019) (text message of move).

41. Vaelizadeh v. Hossaini, 174 So. 3d 579 (Fla. Dist. Ct. App. 2015) (father's untimely response eight days after deadline was due to prior attorney having ill family member; mother had violated a prior order by taking child to Nebraska when child was supposed to be with father).

42. Tenn. Code Ann. § 36-6-108(a) (outside the state or if move is over 100 miles from other parent in state). *See also* Ariz. Rev. Stat. § 25-408 (relocation is out of state move or over 100 miles in the state).

43. Derleth v. Cordova, 841 N.W.2d 552 (Wis. Ct. App. 2013) (trial court erred in restricting the mother to a 45-mile geographical area).

44. Barrett v. Killings, 700 S.W.3d 399 (Tenn. Ct. App. 2023).

45. Holley v. Holley, 232 So. 3d 717 (La. Ct. App. 2017) (reversing interim joint custody and dissolving preliminary injunction which prohibited mother from moving).

46. State v. Titus, 274 So. 3d 591, 598–99 (La. Ct. App. 2019) (denied mother's relocation with child).

47. Ala. Code § 31-17-2-4 (notice requirements may be waived to the extent necessary to protect confidentiality and the health, safety, or liberty of a person or a child).

48. S.D. Codified Laws § 25-5-13.

49. Kan. Stat. Ann. § 23-2332.

50. Kenney v. Strang, 249 N.E.3d 427 (Ill. App. Ct. 2023).

51. La. Rev. Stat. § 9:355.7; Okla. Stat. 43 § 112.3; AAML Relocation Act § 301. *But see* Ind. Code § 31-17-2.2-5(a) (allows 60 days).

52. The ABA Model Relocation of Children Act § 7(a) uses a bracketed 30 days so states could choose another amount, 45, 60, or 90. The petition must specify the reasons for the objection and the relief sought. Sec. 7(c).

53. La. Rev. Stat. § 9:355.10.

54. Courtney v. Courtney, 458 S.W.3d 462 (Mo. Ct. App. 2015) (court erred as a matter of law finding father's objection untimely but it was harmless as father presented evidence at a hearing; court allowed mother to move with children to Michigan given her relative stability and her financial situation caused by father's failure to pay maintenance and support).

55. Pa. Consol. Stat. Ann. 23 § 5337(g) (requiring an expedited full hearing when an objection is filed unless there are exigent circumstances).

56. Pearce v. Boudreaux, 265 So. 3d 712 (Fla. Dist. Ct. App. 2019).

57. Allen v. Allen, 2018 WL 4677619 (Tenn. Ct. App. 2018) (allowing mother to relocate to California when father's attorney failed to appear at hearing).

58. D.K. v. S.P.K., 102 A.3d 467 (Pa. Super. Ct. 2014).

59. Lamb v. Wenning, 583 N.W.2d 745 (Ind. Ct. App. 1991).

60. Ind. Code § 31-17-2.2-1(b) (upon motion of a party, the court shall set the matter for a hearing to review and modify, if appropriate, a custody order).

61. Dent v. Dent, 248 S.W.3d 646, 648 (Mo. App. 2008). *See also* Rutherford v. Rutherford, 416 S.W.3d 845 (Tenn. Ct. App. 2013) (finding father's filing three days late barred his objection and mother allowed to move to Nebraska).

62. Ala. Code § 30-3-166 (failure to commence action to prevent relocation within 30 days after receipt can result in change being authorized); La. Rev. Stat. § 9:355.9. *See* Plumlee v. Plumlee, 281 P.3d 807 (Okla. Civ. App. 2011) (finding father not entitled to a hearing on mother's relocation where his roommate refused the certified mailing of notice and father did not request a hearing within the required 30 days).

63. Allen *ex rel.* Allen v. Gatewood, 390 S.W.3d 245 (Mo. Ct. App. 2013) (finding mother's failure to strictly comply with the notice statute allowed father more time to object).

64. *In re* Paternity of BaS., 911 N.E.2d 1252 (Ind. Ct. App. 2009).

65. Emslander v. Baine, 247 N.E.3d 1246 (Ind. Ct. App. 2024) (trial court should have held a hearing on the relocation factors).

66. Ryan v. Ryan, 252 So. 3d 272 (Fla. Dist. Ct. App. 2018). *See also* Sanabria v. Sanabria, 271 So. 3d 1101 (Fla. Dist. Ct. App. 2019) (father's attorney had filed a motion for additional time rather than the required objection within 20 days).

67. *Ex parte* Crum, 161 So. 3d 1212 (Ala. Civ. App. 2014) (where the court order prohibited mother's relocation to Wisconsin, father's failure to object to 2012 notice did not mean mother could move in 2013).

68. Ovide v. Rivers, 2024 WL 4499462 (La. Ct. App. 2024) (ordering mother to return children immediately finding relocation six hours away not in children's best interest).

69. Blatt v. Blatt, 394 So. 3d 1240 (Fla. Dist. Ct. App. 2024).

70. Langston v. Langston, 340 S. 3d 1272 (La. Ct. App. 2022) (where both parties participated in a hearing at which hearing officer evaluated both the statutory and relocation factors and allowed the move, the issue of relocation was properly before the court).

71. Richards v. Richards, 401 P.3d 1175 (Okla. Ct. App. 2017).

72. *See* Henry v. Henry, 353 S.W.3d 368 (Mo. Ct. App. 2011) (father was not prejudiced by mother's failure to give proper notice; he was fully prepared to and did litigate on the merits). *See also* Weaver v. Kelling, 53 S.W.3d 610 (Mo. Ct. App. 2001) (one having actual notice is not generally prejudiced by and may not complain of the failure to receive statutory notice).

73. Murray v. Murray, 398 So. 3d 688 (La. Ct. App. 2024).

74. Raulerson v. Wright, 60 So. 3d 487 (Fla. Dist. Ct. App. 2011).

75. Allen *ex rel.* Allen v. Gatewood, 390 S.W.3d 245 (Mo. Ct. App. 2013) (finding mother's notice failed to comply with statute where the address given was a field, not a house, so excused unwed father's failure to object in timely manner (two days late)).

76. Ashton v. Ashton, 511 S.W.3d 473 (Mo. Ct. App. 2017) (statute required 60 days' notice).

77. Abraham v. Abraham, 352 S.W.3d 617, 621 (Mo. Ct. App. 2011).

78. Cortez v. Cortez, 317 S.W.3d 630 (Mo. Ct. App. 2010). *See also* Wright *ex rel.* McBath v. Wright 129 S.W.3d 882 (Mo. Ct. App. 2004) (mother's failure to provide the required notice prior to relocating was a change of circumstances allowing modification to joint physical custody; mother's oral statement and note with her new address and telephone number were insufficient).

79. Amick v. Smart, 535 S.W.3d 368 (Mo. Ct. App. 2017).

80. Robertson v. Robertson, 370 P.3d 569 (Utah Ct. App. 2016) (allowing mother to move to Colorado with new husband).

81. *In re* Marriage of King, 371 P.3d 1139 (Okla. Civ. App. 2015).

82. *See In re* Marriage of Raskob, 334 P.3d 30 (Wash. Ct. App. 2014) (where mother failed to give notice as provided in the parenting plan, court awarded father an additional 24 days of parenting time); Melton v. Collins, 134 S.W.3d 749 (Mo. Ct. App. 2004) (mother's unilateral decision to homeschool son, along with her failure to provide father with required statutory notice of her relocation, constituted changed circumstances warranting change of primary physical custody to father); Johnston v. Dunham, 172 S.W.3d 442 (Mo. Ct. App. 2005) (mother's relocation with children over father's objections and without court's permission constituted violation of custody statute constituting a change in circumstances and evidence supported modifying custody of children).

83. Melvin v. Miller, 181 So. 3d 826 (La. Ct. App. 2015).

84. Verite v. Verite, 151 A.3d 1 (Me. 2016).

85. La. Rev. Stat. § 9:355.6.

86. *See In re* Marriage of Adams, 92 N.E.3d 962 (Ill. App. Ct. 2017).

87. *In re* Marriage of Grippin, 186 P.3d 852 (Kan. Ct. App. 2008).

88. *Ex parte* Crum, 161 So. 3d 1212 (Ala. Civ. App. 2014) (mother required to return children from Wisconsin or father would have residential custody even though he did not object to notice).

89. *See* Kan. Stat. Ann. § 23-3222(b). Failure to give notice as required by subsection (a) is an indirect civil contempt. In addition, the court may assess, against the parent required to give notice, reasonable attorney fees and any other expenses incurred by the other parent by reason of the failure to give notice.

90. Ala. Code § 30-3-166. *See* Boyd v. Boyd, 291 So. 3d 488 (Ala. Civ. App. 2019) (changing custody to the father where mother unilaterally moved child

to Texas); Richards v. Richards, 401 P.3d 1175 (Okla. Civ. App. 2017) (modifying residential custody to father where mother failed to include terms and factors involved in relocation and proper address).

91. State v. Titus, 274 So. 3d 591 (La. Ct. App. 2019) (mother moved 76 road miles from father without proper notice so father designated domiciliary parent).

92. *In re* Marriage of Raskob, 334 P.3d 30 (Wash. Ct. App. 2014) (violation was consistent with mother's rigid attitude toward parenting difficulty in reasonably communicating with father). *See also* Langston v. Langston, 340 So. 3d 1272 (La. Ct. App. 2022) (trial court may have erred in awarding $12,000 attorney fees because of statute but mother had not appealed so order stood).

93. Boyd v. Boyd, 291 So. 3d 488 (Ala. Civ. App. 2019) (mother had already relocated and was refusing to honor father's visitation).

CHAPTER 7

Gathering Information: Discovery

Written discovery should be precise rather than generic. Seek only information you need rather than serving thoughtless boilerplate forms on your opponents.[1]

Discovery is an essential part of any case, especially when one parent wants to relocate to another city or town. The purpose of discovery is to obtain information, shorten or reduce the need for a trial, and encourage settlement. Discovery provides advance notice of facts, documents, and names of witnesses. In addition, discovery can limit the disputed issues, lay the foundation for negotiating a parenting plan, determine the fitness of the parties, and ascertain the amount needed by both parties for support. On the other hand, discovery can be expensive and harm the client if the evidence discovered contradicts the client's version of events. Good discovery provides enough information to enable the parties to try to settle the case through negotiation. Discovery can be informal, that is, asking the client for information or the other counsel, or it can be more formal using the state's civil procedure rules. If the lawyer is needing discovery of documents in another country, special rules and conventions apply. (See Chapter 15.)

The type of discovery needed depends on whether the relocation is contemplated prejudgment, at the time of the initial custody determination, or post-judgment, after the original custody order. The lawyer starts with the relevant statutes, the code of civil procedure, and any local practice rules to determine what needs to be proved, what information will be necessary to prove those facts, and who has the burden of proof on any given issue. Civil procedure rules and scheduling orders of the local court may govern the dates by which lawyers must complete the discovery process, disclose witnesses, and exchange exhibits. As noted, the rules will vary depending on whether the case will be the initial custody determination (see Chapter 4) or a modification of an existing order (see Chapter 8).

Once the lawyer figures out what information will be necessary to prove the case for or against the relocation, the lawyer must determine who has that information and the easiest, least expensive way to obtain it. The basic options to obtain information are informal or formal discovery tools. The informal option starts with the domestic relations affidavit if a divorce case, the existing parenting plan if there is one, and any court orders or other documents filed in the case. Sometimes a simple phone call or letter to the other counsel may elicit this information. The client may be able to get copies of additional information in their possession.[2] The lawyer can also send requests to the opposing counsel for information.

More formal discovery tools include motions for production of documents, interrogatories, third-party subpoenas, and depositions. While thorough discovery is essential to preparing a relocation case, the lawyer should try to keep discovery costs to a minimum. The extent of discovery and preparation are determined by the facts of each case, the issues in dispute, the client's financial resources, and, sometimes, the lawyer for the opposing party.

The lawyer must discover as much as possible about the client, the client's relationship with the child and with the opposing party as well as the child's relationship with friends and family in the area. Before negotiations begin, the lawyer will need information about the child's past and present living conditions, the school or day care arrangements, the child's medical providers, whether the child has any unique medical or educational needs, and other relevant factors. (See Chapter 2.) Through formal or informal means, the lawyer needs to identify the following:

1. All persons with relevant knowledge about the parties or the child;
2. The main factual disputes;

3. The existing parenting arrangements, whether informal, by parenting plan, or court order;
4. The opponent's legal theories of the case;
5. The evidence supporting or contradicting the opponent's theory;
6. The proposed alternative parenting plan, including plans for transportation costs and expenses;
7. Issues that might require expert evaluation and names of experts;
8. The names of persons having knowledge of the parent or child;
9. The existence of real, documentary, or demonstrative evidence;
10. The existence of written statements, agency reports, or expert reports; and
11. Any interstate or jurisdictional problems.[3]

Discovery can help the parent who wants to relocate flesh out the principal reasons for the other parent's opposition and help create options to meet those objections. Discovery can help the parent opposing relocation develop information that will show the substance of the move-away plan and reasons for the move. Suppose the relocating parent's answer to interrogatory or deposition questions about schools, recreational activities, and other things in new location is, "I will not know until I move there." That answer demonstrates the parent just wants to move and has not fully thought out the logistics of the move for the child.[4]

Discovery can reveal the actual amount of parenting time each parent is exercising. A custody order may designate joint legal and physical custody but what is happening may actually be a 70/30 or different parenting time arrangement. For example, in one case the parents had a "50–50" residential parenting order. The mother's job, however, took her away, often out of the country, so that in actuality, the father had the children with him 80 percent of the time. This fact can be important in both application of presumptions for or against moving in some states and as a factor favoring the majority time parent.[5]

What Can Be Discovered?

Discovery is broad in family law cases. The trial judge has broad discretion regarding the scope of discovery, which an appellate court will only overturn for an abuse of discretion.[6] The lawyer will need to determine what discovery should be conducted. Sometimes interrogatories will be sufficient; but sometimes depositions will be necessary. The lawyer needs to know how the child's views may be presented—if the court will interview the child, and how, and whether an attorney or guardian ad litem should be appointed. (See Chapter 14.)

Many states pattern their discovery rules after the Federal Rules of Civil Procedure. The most commonly used rules are Rule 16: Pretrial Conferences, Rule 26: Disclosures, Rule 34: Production of Documents, and Rule 37: Disclosures and Cooperation in Discovery. Others that may be used are Rule 30: Depositions, Rule 33: Interrogatories, and Rule 35: Physical and Mental Examinations.

Parties can discover any nonprivileged relevant information. An item is relevant if it is reasonably calculated to lead to admissible evidence. The matter sought to be discovered need not be admissible in evidence at the trial, if it may lead to admissible evidence. Other states have particular rules that relate to civil cases that can aid discovery. For example, many states require a party seeking a divorce and custody of a child to file financial affidavits as well as a proposed parenting plan. The proposed parenting plan of the relocating parent can be a starting point for informal discovery.

In addition to traditional documents in paper form, there is digital evidence that can be easily deleted or destroyed. The American Academy of Matrimonial Lawyers in 2024 reported that 81 percent of divorce lawyers have seen an increase in the use of social media evidence. The lawyer will want to discover social media sites and keep the client or the other party from destroying what might be important evidence. (See Chapter 2 discussion.)

The lawyer should develop a discovery outline that identifies the possible witnesses and exhibits as well as other subject matters that will need additional testimony. The lawyer will investigate who the anticipated witnesses might be for the other party and what discovery might be necessary to rebut. The lawyer needs to know whether the court will interview the child, and how, and whether an attorney or guardian ad litem will or should be appointed. The lawyer can plan to present the type of evidence that will make the case clear to the judge. The planned strategy for discovery will include the type of evidence that will be needed for negotiation or to put into a trial "notebook" (electronic or old-school paper) if the case goes to trial. A discovery chart can map the possible types of discovery, the date a request is filed, the date it is served on the other side, and the response.[7]

The initial questions the lawyer needs to answer are:

1. How much discovery can be done informally?
   a. Client questionnaires and affidavits
   b. Internet—daily emails, stored data on computers, Google search on both parents, LinkedIn, Amazon Prime, Facebook, Instagram, Snapchat, Grindr, TindR, YouTube videos, Apple downloads, emails, Amazon sales
2. What formal discovery needs to be conducted?
   a. Interrogatories? What questions need to be answered under oath?
   b. Deposition? Any out of state or out of country witnesses to depose?
   c. Requests for Admission (a cheap way to get information without a lot of work).
   d. Requests for Production of Documents
3. How quickly is the case likely to reach a hearing or trial?
4. What is the deadline for concluding discovery?
5. Is the child's preference a factor based on age and maturity or statute?
   a. Does the client believe the child has a preference? Strong?
   b. Will the court appoint a child's attorney, best-interest attorney, or guardian ad litem?
   c. How will the judge obtain the child's preference?
      i. Judicial interview—in court or in chambers? If the latter, will counsel be there? Will the

interview be recorded? Who will have access to the transcript?
    ii. Attorney for the child or guardian ad litem?
    iii. Mental health professional in a custody evaluation?
    iv. Court service officer?
6. Will the case need experts? If so, what type? Mental health? Therapists? School professionals? Medical—child's doctor? What is the timeline for getting experts? When will experts' written reports be received? Will the expert testify? If so, what needs to be done to obtain the testimony? Should the expert be deposed? Will a custody evaluation be done? Who is likely to do the evaluation? (See Chapter 11.)
7. Does the child have special or extraordinary medical or physical needs? If so, information is needed on the extent to which those needs can be met and accommodated in the event of relocation. Are services available in both locations?
8. Attorney fees—should there be an application for an award of *pendente lite* counsel fees and costs? Will counsel fees and costs be assessed and awarded upon completion of the proceeding?
9. Are interlocutory appeals going to be necessary? Will you be able to accelerate or expedite an interim resolution?

The lawyer needs to plan for the possibility of litigation. If negotiation or mediation fails to resolve the issue, the case will require, at the least, a plenary hearing, possibly a multiday trial. The issues in controversy are highly fact sensitive. Rarely will a court grant a summary judgment in a relocation case. [8]

Informal Discovery

Much fact gathering can be done from the affidavits and pleadings filed in the case. Sometimes a phone call to opposing counsel will get the information and documents needed. Sometimes the

Internet provides a valuable tool. Information from social networking sites may be readily obtained through informal means of investigation rather than formal ones. Any person can obtain information from the "public" portions of a social media pages. Spouses may also have each other's passwords or permission to access the private portions of each other's social media accounts as well. The lawyer should advise the divorcing or separating client to restrict the other spouse's access to the private portions of the client's social media accounts. From that point forward, formal discovery will be necessary to access that electronic information.

Internet Research

The Internet can be a valuable research tool, both on the conduct and activity of the parties, and about the proposed new location. Social networking sites, like Facebook and MySpace, can provide valuable information that can help the parties settle a case or provide some damaging evidence during the trial. There may be evidence available to impeach the character of the opposing party. If someone is posting about themselves on the Internet, which is largely a public forum, there is no reasonable expectation of privacy.[9] If, however, the user has set the profile as "private," the issue is more complex. The terms and conditions of many Internet sites require users to provide their real names and information, which will prevent the lawyer or the client from creating a fictitious profile to try to find information on the spouse that is private. Much of this information may be only the beginning to obtaining admissible evidence.

The social media information may not be admissible because it is hearsay; however, it may be useful in attacking credibility. For example, the relocating mother may say, or even testify, that she has always been cooperative, carries no grudge about the separation, and is not relocating to get away from the father. The lawyer or client discovers that the relocating parent is a member of a Facebook group, "I Hate My Ex???" and posted the following, "I hate my ex-husband. I wish he wasn't the father of my kid so he could be out of my life for good." The post seems to contradict the statement about being cooperative.

In a South Carolina case, the trial court admitted posts from the father's MySpace page, which evidenced hostility, animosity, and anger toward the mother, and awarded her sole custody.[10] Pictures of the opposing party violating a court order (drinking alcohol or using drugs), engaging in sexually explicit conduct, or otherwise acting badly in a public forum may harm credibility. Posting pictures of the children can be even more problematic. If the other parent has posted travel pictures from 15 different pleasure trips, the lawyer can argue that their client is the primary parent.[11]

The Internet provides immediate, convenient, and relatively inexpensive access to useful information about the proposed place of relocation. The Chamber of Commerce in the new location, as well as the school district, may have extensive websites. The lawyer will have to check local rules to see if the Internet information is inadmissible hearsay and, if so, how it can be made admissible. Even materials from an official website of the Department of Defense regarding its schools, like teacher/student ratios and such, may need authentication. For example, in one case, the mother offered a printout of the neighborhood crime statistic website that purported to reflect FBI crime-rate-specific statistics for different areas. The trial court found it was inadmissible hearsay.[12] The lawyer can submit everything to opposing counsel several weeks before and ask for stipulations to the exhibits. If the opposing party will not stipulate and objects at trial, the judge decides whether to take judicial notice.

The only exhibits that may be admissible may be photographs taken by a witness and official [paper] publications of an agency. The only testimony that may be allowed is firsthand experience, or the exception of information from personal conversations with school personnel. If the client takes the pictures, then the client can testify.

If the child has special health needs or special educational needs, the relocating parent may be able to demonstrate more support for the child in the new location. The relocating parent may need to show that moving to another school within the region or state would not accomplish the same purpose.

As to quality of life issues, the Internet has made it easier for the lawyer to explore the advantages available to the child in the new community. Things that make the new city a more desirable place to live may be a high-quality public library, an outstanding educational system, or the quality and number of parks and recreational activities. If the child is in the arts, dance, or sports, the new location may have more opportunities for the child. The lawyer can also find out what type of homes are presently available in the relocating parent's price range. Courts want evidence, not just the testimony of the relocating party, as to why the child's quality of life will be better. A mother who testified she wanted to leave New Orleans because it was not a good place to live and Jacksonville, Florida, was better, needed something more than her testimony.[13]

Weather and air quality information is also available and may be relevant if the child has a chronic medical condition such as asthma. If the child has special health needs or special educational needs, then the relocating parent may be able to demonstrate more support for the child in the new location. On the other hand, the new location may have fewer supports. The relocating parent may need to show that moving to another school within the region or state would not accomplish the same purpose.

The Department of Labor traditionally has provided the cost-of-living information in different cities on its website. Suppose a mother who is a realtor earning $45,000 wants to move with her child from Topeka, Kansas, to Chicago, Illinois. Moving from Kansas to Illinois will probably require a substantial increase in pay to offset the higher cost of living. If the parent wants to move to Louisiana, the cost of living may be lower. Using the Internet, a lawyer can determine how much a parent needs to gross in order to maintain the parent's current standard of living.[14] On the realtor's website will be information on how much additional education the mother may need to have, what tests she must take, and the procedure and costs of getting a real estate license. The lawyer can research the real estate industry in the new location and can find information about specific real estate agents and agencies that the mother might consider joining. The Internet is also a resource for searching for an expert in the real estate market who can discuss the viability and likelihood of success of mother's potential relocation of her career. For example, there may be data on how many people make over $45,000 a year selling real estate in the new city. The Internet can also provide job data, poverty data, and crime rate information.

Requests for Production (RFP)

Federal Rules of Civil Procedure, Rule 34, governs requests for the production of documents. Most states have similar provisions. A document request can be directed only to a party to the lawsuit. Documents from third parties can be obtained by subpoena. The same basic discovery rules that relate to the scope of what can be requested and the proper bases for noncompliance apply to RFPs just the same as they do to interrogatories.

The lawyer should draft their RFPs clearly and precisely. Requests that are too narrow may miss important documents, while requests that are too broad may engender a voluminous response. Generally, an RFP starts with instructions and definitions and provides how the recipient can comply with the request. A recipient may choose to provide the requesting party with photocopies of the relevant documents but is not required to do so. The recipient does have to make the documents available for inspection but can require the requesting party to make and pay for any necessary copies.

Electronic Documents

Documents in an electronic form are now the predominant form of documents provided pursuant to an RFP. If the party cannot get them through informal discovery, an RFP may get them. Many forms of electronically stored information (ESI) may be relevant to the relocation dispute beyond electronic versions of documents that were formerly stored in paper format and would traditionally be considered to be relevant, such as letters, financial records, and so on. For example, postings on social media sites such as Facebook and Instagram may become critically important in the context of a relocation dispute. Electronic documents include email, voice mail, instant messages, chat room logs, blog postings, and text messaging. Rule 34 includes electronic evidence:

> Any designated documents or electronically stored information—including writings, drawings, graphs, charts, photographs, sound recordings, images, and other data or data compilations—stored in any medium from which information can be obtained either directly or, if necessary, after translation by the responding party into a reasonably usable form[.]

Document requests should seek printouts of all postings a party has made on the Internet, including but not limited to online personal ads, blogs, vlogs, and message board posts, photographs, and so on. Well-crafted requests for admissions can be used to authenticate Internet and electronic evidence.[15]

Spoliation

Spoliation is the destruction or the significant meaningful alteration of a document or other evidence. Parties generally have a duty to preserve evidence that might be utilized in a lawsuit in its original form, even in the absence of such a request, once it is clear that litigation is likely to ensue. Failure to do so, or allowing the evidence to "spoil," may subject the party, and potentially their lawyer to the extent the lawyer was aware of and failed to prevent or actively encouraged the spoliation, to a variety of sanctions from the court. The sanctions vary and may depend on whether the spoliation was and can be deliberate, negligent, or innocent. To avoid sanctions, the lawyer should take reasonable steps to prevent spoliation from happening and to set up procedures designed to preserve digital evidence. Lawyers should advise clients to retain records and not to destroy evidence, although privacy settings on media can be adjusted. (See Chapter 2.)

Not all of the information that might be sought through electronic discovery is likely to fall under the scope of the automatic restraining orders that go into effect at the beginning of the case. In order to prevent the opposing party from deleting or otherwise tampering with potentially useful evidence, a spoliation letter, or in some jurisdictions a "litigation hold" notice, should be sent to the opposing party. A litigation hold is simply a written notice to a prospective party to a lawsuit that certain information is potentially relevant to ongoing or planned litigation, and instructing that party to preserve such evidence for the duration of the lawsuit. The law generally supports such litigation hold requests, and concealing, destroying, or otherwise tampering with evidence that is subject to a litigation hold may subject the offending party to a variety of sanctions, similar to those that will be discussed later in the chapter in regard to a failure to comply properly with the discovery process.

Responding to Requests for Production

In addition to providing the requested documents, a party must also provide a written response to the RFP. The response must address each specific request, and state if the requested documents are being provided or not. If the requested documents are not being provided, the lawyer should note the grounds for any objection or the lack of existence of such documents in the response. If providing the documents, the responding party does not have to organize them in a manner that will make it easiest for the requesting party to review them. It is permissible to provide the documents in the way that the responding party found them when they endeavored to locate them. On the other hand, there are prohibitions on evidence concealment or tampering. A party may not take steps to organize or arrange the documents in a way that will make it more difficult for the requesting party to find the particular documents or information that they are seeking.

Discovery of Expert

If an expert has submitted a custody evaluation report (see Chapter 11), the lawyer will want to analyze the report, which can provide the blueprint for direct and cross-examination if the parties go to trial.[16] Among the questions the lawyer should look at are:

1. Does the psychologist who conducted the evaluation have specialized training in addition to experience in custody evaluation?
2. Is the psychologist a clinical or forensic psychologist?
3. Were the psychologist's procedures standardized or flawed?
    a. Did expert conduct a home visit?
    b. Did expert meet longer with one party than the other?
    c. Did the expert fail to observe interactions between one of the parents and the child?
4. Did the psychologist rely on biased or erroneous information or on objective data?
    a. Did the expert rely too heavily on unsubstantiated reports from one party?
    b. Did the expert use unreliable, invalid, irrelevant, or obsolete tests?
5. Did the psychologist make errors in their factual findings?
6. Do the psychologist's opinions follow from the factual findings?
7. Do the psychologist's recommendations follow from the factual findings?
8. Are the psychologist's opinions and recommendations supported by clinical consensus or widely accepted reviews of research?
    a. What does psychological research say about primary versus shared custody arrangements long distance? Has the psychologist read them?
    b. Do age and gender matter?
9. Does the psychologist have the raw data used to make the report?

If an expert has conducted testing, such as the SASSI-4 assessments (Substance Abuse Subtle Screening Inventory, Fourth Edition), Sexual Adjustment Inventory (SAI), Parenting Stress Index, Fourth Edition (PSI-4), or the Wechsler Abbreviated Scale of Intelligence, Second Edition (WASI-II), the lawyer may want to seek to discover the raw data. Some jurisdictions, but not all, allow discovery of the psychologist's raw data, including test results, interview notes, and all materials reviewed by the expert where it would aid the court in determining the child's best interests.[17]

Discovery of the raw data may be helpful in direct examination and may be essential for effective cross-examination. Errors can be found in the administration, scoring, and interpretation of test results. A mistake in addition can affect the scoring and interpretation test results. Sometimes interview notes conflict with the expert's report. A parent may have supplied inaccurate materials to the expert upon which they relied. Sometimes the expert may have ignored any materials supplied by a parent, even if they were relevant.

Request for Documents

To discover the basis for the testimony a mental health professional may give, the lawyer may ask for documents. If the mental health professional is treating the child, Dr. Milfred Dale, a clinical psychologist who is also a lawyer, suggests that the requests start with:

1. All completed intake/registration forms documenting demographic information about the patient and the patient's guardian(s) or custodial parents and information necessary for billing of services;
2. Information related to the patient/guardian's signed Informed Consent Agreement and their agreement regarding the Health Information Portability and Accountability Act (HIPAA);
3. Information regarding the billing of services to any third-party insurance policy (name of policy, insurance company, and insurance number) and any payments made by the insurance company (including the date and amount billed as well as the date and amount of any payment);

4. Information regarding the billing of services to any individual and any payments made by that individual or any other individual (including the date and amount billed as well as the date and amount of any payments);
5. Notes, documents, and/or detailed computer entries reflecting the patient's problems or symptoms and any and all diagnoses given to child #1, as well as any other professional consulted in connection with the provision of any medical, psychological, or psychiatric diagnosis or diagnoses;
6. Notes, documents, and/or detailed computer entries reflecting the following for each therapeutic contact or session with child #1:
   a. date of session;
   b. length of session;
   c. who was present for the session and the involvement of each person present;
   d. content of session including issues raised and interventions on these issues; and
   e. how these processes related to the treatment goals for the process;
7. Notes, documents, and/or detailed computer entries regarding the treatment plan for child #1, including any and all identified treatment goals and objectives, as well as planned interventions for achieving treatment goals and objectives;
8. Any correspondence by letter, email, or text messages with the patient, the patient's guardian or parent, regarding child #1, including but not limited to collecting information necessary to provide treatment or to coordinate treatment with other aspects of the child's life at home, at school, or in the community;
9. Copies of all releases signed by the guardian or parent allowing information about child #1 to be shared with other professionals, entities, or nonfamily persons, including the identity of such person(s)/entity and the date and content of the information that was shared;

10. Efforts to coordinate treatment with both guardians/custodial parents, including dates of contact, the content of these contacts, and notes related to these contacts.

Interrogatories

In relocation cases, one way to get information is through well-drafted interrogatories—written questions to be answered by the other party under oath. Interrogatories ask the opposing party to identify people and documents that are relevant to the issues in dispute. Once answers are obtained, the proponent can then follow up with investigation techniques directed at those people or documents (such as witness interviews, depositions, or requests for production).

State or local court rules will likely place a limit on the number of interrogatories a party can ask. Under the Federal Rules of Civil Procedure 26(a)(1), a party can ask no more than 25 interrogatories. In some states, it may be 30. Most courts will count subparts as separate interrogatories, except those seeking names and locations of witnesses or location and custodian of documents. A party should generally try to avoid using up all of their allowed interrogatories at once and instead save some questions in case issues come up during the course of the litigation that one may want to ask about.

A party can obtain a stipulation from the opposing side or seek leave of court to ask additional interrogatories beyond the allowable number if good cause for doing so can be shown. To exceed the number, counsel may have to show that counsel attempts to resolve the issue have been unavailing; show good cause for their use; and set forth the proposed additional interrogatories.

Interrogatories should be tailored to the case, rather than using a standard set. Today, interrogatories should ask the party to identify all social networking sites they have used over the past 12 months (or other relevant period of time). Questions should request all email addresses, usernames, screen names, avatars, and other forms of online identities the person has used.

The challenge in drafting interrogatories is to determine the appropriate breadth of questions. A common interrogatory in a relocation case might seek more detailed information than the petition provided. It is common to ask the opposing party to identify people and documents relevant to the issues in dispute. Interrogatories should be targeted to yield the particular information being sought without being too convoluted or complex. An overly broad question may draw an objection from the opposing party or bring a response that provides more information than is wanted. A common type of interrogatory seeks more detailed information regarding an allegation in a petition.

If a promotion, new job, or transfer is the reason, the follow-up questions can seek information about whether the parent looked for a job in the current state, the projected new salary, and the cost of living in the new location.

1. State with specificity the reasons you feel you should be allowed to relocate to __________ with [child's name].
2. Indicate the locale, with specific address, if known, to which you anticipate relocating [if not in the notice to relocate].
3. State what you perceive to be the advantages to you of moving from __________ to __________ [place of intended relocation].
4. State what you perceive to be the advantages to the child of this marriage of moving to ________________.
5. Describe the new job, its description, compensation package, duties, and hours.
6. What efforts, if any, did you make to find employment at a comparable salary with comparable hours in the current location?
7. State what arrangements you have made, if any, or will make for the care of your child in the event of an emergency, illness, or work, if you relocate.
8. What is the child's current school like?
   a. Size? Student/teacher ratio? Rural or urban school?
   b. Does the child have any extraordinary school needs? Gifted? Special education?
   c. What types of extracurricular activities is your child involved in now?

   d. How does your child get to and from school now? [bus, train (subway), car, walk]
   e. Where is the school located? [rural, city, high crime, low crime]
9. State how the local schools' ratings (rankings) in the locale to which you would like to relocate compare to the schools that the child currently attends (or would attend) if you do not relocate, if you know.
   a. How will the child get to school in the new location? How long will it take? [can the child walk to school or have to take a bus]
   b. What types of academic programs are available for special needs or gifted students? [specialty programs in language or the arts] [does the child have an IEP? If so, what is the current IEP?]
   c. What type of extracurricular programs are available in new location?
   d. What type of educational testing does the school do?
   e. What are graduation rates?
10. Medical
   a. What is the present and past mental and physical health of the child?
   b. Who is the child's current doctor? Psychologist?
   c. What would present healthcare providers testify about the proposed move?
   d. If the child needs services, are they available in both locations?
   e. State what doctors you would utilize in ____________ (the place of relocation), if you know.
11. State how the crime rates differ in the locale where you would like to relocate compared to the town in which you and the child presently reside, if you know.
12. In the event of your relocation, state what schedule of parenting time you would suggest be afforded to the respondent if you were to be awarded primary physical custody of the child.
13. In the event of your relocation, state what suggestions you have for transporting the child to and from your home for parenting time with the respondent.

A common way to approach interrogatories is to ask relatively broad questions first and follow up with more specific questions.

Interrogatories for Expert

If information about the expert is available through a request for production (RFP), interrogatories will be unnecessary. Interrogatories may be made to the party who may call an expert, though the requesting party may have to pay a reasonable expert fee for the answers. Specific statutes on expert testimony should be consulted in the specific jurisdiction. For example, in Oklahoma, the law allows to be treated as a single Interrogatory the following expert information:

1. State the subject matter on which the expert witness is expected to testify;
2. The substance of the facts and opinions to which the expert is expected to testify and a summary of the grounds for each opinion;
3. The qualifications of each expert witness, including a list of all publications authored by the expert within the last ten years;
4. The compensation to be paid the expert witness for the testimony and preparation for the testimony; and,
5. A listing of any other cases in which the expert has testified as an expert at trial or by deposition within the preceding four years.[18]

Responding to Interrogatories

If a question is non-objectionable, the shortest truthful response will suffice. The other side is seeking information to help them to make their case. The client need only answer the question *actually* asked by the other side, not the question the other side *should* have asked, or would have asked if they knew the case better, nor even the question the other side *meant* to ask but did not because of poor drafting.

The lawyer should make appropriate objections to improper interrogatories. The reasons for the objection should be stated with specificity. Any ground not stated in a timely objection is waived, unless the party's failure to object is excused by the court for good cause shown. If an interrogatory seeks privileged information, the burden is on the responding party to assert claims of privilege. Inadmissible evidence can be objected to at the time of the trial, but if privileged information is turned over to the opposing party, the privilege may be waived.

Proper objections to discovery include:

- the information sought is irrelevant (note, however, that most discovery rules have a broad definition of relevance);
- the request is overly broad;
- request is unduly burdensome to comply with; or
- the responding party lacks the knowledge or information necessary to respond to the inquiry.

To the extent that the answer to an interrogatory appears in a document, rather than answering the interrogatory, the responding party can generally provide the document that contains the information, if it would be equally burdensome to both parties to cull the answer from the document itself.

Deposition

In some areas, the deposition is still one of the most widely used, and one of the most expensive, discovery tools for ascertaining the testimony of opposing parties and witnesses. A deposition usually involves obtaining oral testimony under oath in the presence of a court reporter. Recent changes in some states allow depositions to be taken by phone in some instances or by written questions. The deposition can be directed not only to the adverse party but also to any third party who may have relevant information.

The deposition may be used under certain conditions at the trial or upon the hearing of a motion as if the witness were present and testifying if it is admissible under the rules of evidence. The deposition can be used against any party who was present or represented at the taking of the deposition or who had reasonable notice for the purpose of contradicting or impeaching testimony if the court finds the witness is dead; is at a distance greater than 100 miles from the place of trial or is outside the state; or the witness is unable to attend to testify because of age, illness, infirmity, or imprisonment; or otherwise could not be served. A court found that a father was not entitled to get a deposition of his 16-year-old daughter who alleged sexual abuse.[19]

To depose a party, notice alone may be sufficient. It is best, however, to subpoena either a party or a nonparty to appear at a designated time and place to answer oral questions under oath in the presence of a court reporter. Reasonable notice of the deposition (as defined by local court rules, usually five days) must be given so there is an opportunity to cross-examine the witness. For a nonparty witness, there must be notice and a subpoena. If the lawyer wants the witness to bring relevant books or documents to be examined, a subpoena *duces tecum* may be served with the notice and subpoena.

Video recorded evidentiary depositions are sometimes used for expert witnesses unavailable or too expensive to call at trial. Video recorded testimony is not a good substitute for live witnesses. If a video is to be used, it should be edited to eliminate objections as to quality and to eliminate long pauses so the presentation will be as tight as possible. Another reason to video record is if there is a fear that the opposing party or counsel will try to disrupt the deposition. The video can capture demeanor, behavior, and sarcasm lost in the court reporter's transcription. The camera has a deterrent effect on behavior. If the opposing counsel or deponent misbehave, replaying the deposition for the judge will support a request for sanctions. Any camera or sound recording devices may not distort or alter the appearance of the deponent or counsel. Depositions are usually conducted in the office of the lawyer who issued the notice, but local practice rules vary. The deposition can take place in the office of the opposing attorney or in a neutral location like a courthouse or bar association conference room.

Failure to Respond

If a party has served discovery upon the opposing party and believes that the opposing party has unreasonably failed to respond to the discovery entirely or has failed to respond in a complete and accurate manner, that party may file a motion with the court seeking an order compelling the party to provide the requested discovery.[20] A California court found that before filing a motion to compel responses to a deposition subpoena, the court must look at the history of litigation, the nature of the interaction between counsel, the nature of the issues, the type and scope of the discovery requested, and the prospects for success to determine whether the parties engaged in a reasonable good faith attempt to resolve the discovery dispute informally.[21]

If a party continues to fail to provide discovery after a motion compelling them to do so has been granted, the court can impose a variety of sanctions for noncompliance. Some of these sanctions are set forth specifically in Rule 37(b)(2):

(i) Directing that the matters embraced in the order or other designated facts be taken as established for purposes of the action, as the prevailing party claims;
(ii) Prohibiting the disobedient party from supporting or opposing designated claims or defenses, or from introducing designated matters in evidence;
(iii) Striking pleadings in whole or in part;
(iv) Staying further proceedings until the order is obeyed;
(v) Dismissing the action or proceeding in whole or in part;
(vi) Rendering a default judgment against the disobedient party; or
(vii) Treating as contempt of court the failure to obey any order except an order to submit to a physical or mental examination.

As a general rule the court may not grant a default judgment as a discovery sanction.[22]

Endnotes

1. Steven N. Peskind, One Hundred Days Before Trial 23 (ABA 2015).

2. Terrance Kapp, *Put Your Client to Work, in* 101+ Practical Solutions for the Family Lawyer: Sensible Answers to Common Problems (Herman ed., 3d ed 2009).

3. Linda D. Elrod, Child Custody Practice and Procedure, Ch. 9 (Thomson Reuters, 2024).

4. *In re* Marriage of Weaver, 505 P.3d 560 (Wash. Ct. App. 2022) (mother's vague plans for job and children' schools were a factor in court denying relocation and making father primary custodian).

5. Aragon v. Aragon, 513 S.W.3d 447 (Tenn. 2017).

6. Lessard v. Johnson, 970 N.W.2d 160 (N.D. 2022) (upheld trial court's grant of protective order limiting father's discovery of mother's earlier tax returns).

7. Lynne Z. Gold-Bikin & Stephen Kolodny, The Divorce Trial Manual: From Initial Interview to Closing Arguments (ABA 2003).

8. *See* Barblock v. Barblock, 890 A.2d 1005 (N.J. Super. Ct. App. Div. 2006), *cert. denied*, 899 A.2d 304 (2006) (court did not require a plenary hearing where the parent objecting to the move failed to offer any evidence at oral argument as to why the child should not move to Buffalo).

9. Dexter v. Dexter, No. 2006-P-0051, 2007 WL 1532084 (Ohio. App. Ct. May 25, 2007) (finding postings not private where mother in both in her testimony and through her writings in online blogs, stated she practiced sadomasochism, was a bisexual, a pagan, and used illicit drugs).

10. High v. High, 389 S.E.2d 690, 697 (S.C. Ct. App. 2010). *See In re* Rutland v. O'Brien, 41 N.Y.S.3d 292 (App. Div. 2016) (sole legal custody to father where court admitted mother's numerous Facebook communications with daughter denigrating father).

11. *See* A.D. v. C.A., 16 N.Y.S.3d 126 (Misc. 2015).

12. Madrigal v. Madrigal, 399 So. 3d 258 (Ala. Civ. App. 2023) (the printout was an out of court statement offered to prove that the crime rate was lower in the intended location than where mother and child currently resided).

13. Narcisse-Thomas v. Thomas, 390 So. 3d 890 (La. Ct. App. 2024) (mom in contempt for not bringing children back from Jacksonville to Louisiana for father's two-weekend-a-month visitation where relocation was denied but delayed return until end of school year).

14. The "Salary Calculator" is useful for determining whether the moving parent understands the impact that the move will have on the family's standard of living.

15. *See* Kathrine Minotti, *The Advent of Digital Diaries: Implication of Social Networking Web Sites for the Legal Profession*, 60 S.C. L. Rev. 1057 (2009).

16. *See* Milfred D. Dale, Jonathan Gould & Alyssa Levine, *Cross-Examining Experts in Child Custody: The Necessary Theories and Models . . . with Instructions*, 33 J. Am. Acad. Matrim. Law. 327 (2021) (outlines how to develop a theory of the case, how to use practice guidelines and ethical principles to evaluate the methodologies of court-appointed experts, and how to use traditional and contemporary cross-examination approaches to effectively support and/or challenge experts).

17. K.C. v. J.C., 25 N.Y.S.3d 798 (Misc. 2015) (forensic evaluator's entire file was subject to discovery).

18. Okla. Stat. tit. 12 § 3226.

19. *In re* Marriage of Doe, 250 N.E.3d 283 (Ill. App. Ct. 2024).

20. *See* Fed. R. Civ. P. 37.

21. *In re* Marriage of Moore, 322 Cal. Rptr. 3d 249 (Ct. App. 2024).

22. Blanco v. Blanco, 311 P.3d 1170 (Nev. 2013).

CHAPTER 8

Modifying Orders: Change of Circumstances

A relocation by the primary physical custodian . . . including the inherent difficulties that the increase in geographical distance between the parents imposes—may constitute a material change in circumstances.[1]

A material change of circumstances does not always warrant a change in custody.[2]

Modification Procedures: The Two-Part Test

Many, if not most, relocation cases involve an attempt to modify an existing custody order. Therefore, the lawyer must review the relevant state statutes to see (1) whether the court retains continuing exclusive jurisdiction to modify the custody order, and (2) what the standard is for seeking a modification of an existing order. Because of the interest in stability of custody arrangements, the majority of states require the petitioner to demonstrate that there has been a material or substantial change of circumstances since the original order before even holding a hearing or looking to see if a modification of the existing parenting arrangement is necessary. A couple of states have adopted the Uniform Marriage and Divorce Act (UMDA) two-year rule that does not allow for modification within the first two years absent extraordinary circumstances.[3] If the action is brought more than two years after the original decree, the best-interest standard is used.[4] Minnesota does not allow modifications of a parenting plan earlier than one year after the date of the custody order unless there is a denial of parenting time or endangerment.[5]

Some states find that a petition for relocation by a custodial parent, by itself and without a showing of how the move impedes the parenting plan, does not constitute a substantial and material change of circumstances.[6] Others find that a petition to relocate is a material change of circumstances.[7] While the mere desire to relocate may not be a change, an actual relocation is such a change. Some states have a specific statute with requirements for notice and specific factors that apply in relocation cases. (See Chapters 6 and 9.) A few states find that a request to move more than a certain number of miles is a change of circumstances.

What standard is used may depend upon whether the original custody order was made by mediated agreement,[8] stipulation, default, or by a judge after hearing all of the evidence. In other jurisdictions, the same standard applies whether the order was consensual or nonconsensual.[9] It may also depend on whether a statute allows parents to move a certain distance without permission or if there is a locale restriction in the initial custody order or parenting plan.[10] Even if the judge finds there is a change in circumstances in a custody case, the judge may find that it is in the child's best interests to continue the current parenting plan.[11]

Material Change of Circumstances Generally

To further the goal of "finality" in custody litigation, the motion for modification of parenting time, custody, or visitation must allege that a substantial or material change of circumstances has occurred since the entry of the original, or most recent, parenting time order that makes modification in the child's best interests.[12] The party seeking modification must prove the material change in circumstances by a preponderance of the evidence before a hearing will be held to determine if the custody or residency should be modified. A party seeking to modify a judgment denying a request to change the principal residence of a child must demonstrate a material change in circumstances since the entry of the most recent order.[13] An Idaho court found that the parent seeking to relocate with the child, which would explicitly violate or effectively frustrate the purpose of an existing custody order, bears the burden of proof of showing the child's best interests rather than the person seeking modification of the custody order.[14] While definitions vary as to what constitutes a "material" change in circumstances, the change generally must be of a substantial and continuing nature to make the terms of the initial decree unreasonable or unfair. There may not be a real, substantial, and unanticipated change in circumstances if the trial judge contemplated the potential relocation at the time of the original order.[15] The change must be significant and not a continuation of conditions existing prior to the existing order. Therefore, a mother's military deployment was not a change in circumstances when she was on full-time duty in the Naval Reserve at the time of the prior order.[16]

Generally, the mere improvement in the position of one party does not establish a substantial change. A relocation coupled with additional factors, such as remarriage of one or both parents, a strained relationship between the parent and child, or the preference of the children can be a change.[17] In one case, the father's relocation to be geographically closer to the children and his becoming self-employed were considered a sufficient change of circumstances.[18] Additionally, a deterioration in the primary custodial parent's circumstances may be a material change. The North Dakota court found a material change of circumstances when the custodial mother had moved several times and had been in "long-term" relationships with five different men who had moved in and out of the home, causing disorder in the children's lives.[19]

The standard required to obtain a hearing on whether a modification of the parenting plan is in the child's best interests may be different if the current custody arrangement was a result of the parties' agreement or was rendered by default because a judge did not review the evidence. Assuming that the parents know better what is in their child's best interest, judges usually approve or incorporate the parties' agreement as to custody without holding a fact-finding hearing as to the best interests of the child. Indeed, some state statutes provide that an agreement of the parties is presumed to be in the child's best interests, so the judge must have specific findings to not approve it. If the parenting plan was approved by default, an agreement of the parties, or a stipulation, some courts may not require a parent to show a change of circumstances but only that the change is in the child's best interests. If there is a valid custody stipulation or agreement between the parents, some courts will not even hold a hearing on an application to relocate unless there has been a substantial change in circumstances. Moreover, where there is a specific geographical relocation restriction agreed to by the parties included in their agreement, a court may consider the restriction as a factor in making its determination as to whether relocation was in the child's best interest.[20] An agreement providing for a self-executing change of custody upon relocation generally violates public policy. It may, however, constitute a material change of circumstances.[21]

Relocation, by itself and without any showing of how the move impeded the existing time-sharing plan, may not constitute changed circumstances.[22] If the proposed change would not modify the established custodial environment of the child, from the child's perspective, then it may not be a change of circumstances.[23] If the parties can continue with the existing schedule, even though one of the parents has moved, the court may find an insufficient change in circumstances to warrant modification of the parenting plan.[24]

If the parents are already living a couple of hours away from each other, it may not matter if one parent moves to another state as long as the travel time does not change. A Georgia court found a father's relocation with the child to Michigan was not a material change of circumstances where the parties had lived two hours from each other at the time of the divorce. The flight to Georgia and travel time were about the same, the child's grades had not suffered, and the child communicated regularly with the Georgia family.[25]

Relocation, however, coupled with communication difficulties making co-parenting difficult, may constitute a material change in circumstances.[26] A mother's relocation to Texas without notice to the father was one factor in finding a change of circumstances but also the child had attended seven school districts and had multiple unexcused absences while with mother and poor grades while mother was residential parent.[27] A father who had moved from Tennessee where he lived at the time of the custody order to Florida where the mother and child lived sought to modify the time-sharing. Mother had increasingly interfered with father's visitation and communications with the child, which caused the child stress. The trial court erred in granting mother's motion for summary judgment and remanded for a hearing on a change of circumstances.[28]

Unilateral relocation in violation of an existing custody order may be a sufficient change of circumstances to warrant a hearing with evidence.[29] A parent's unilateral act in taking the children from the jurisdiction may result in a change of custody.[30] Even if the relocation is a change of circumstances, however, the court is not required to modify custody.[31] Courts do not like to punish a child for the parent's actions.

Relocation as a Change in Circumstances

The initial question becomes if the proposed relocation of a parent constitutes a sufficient change in circumstances to warrant a hearing on modification of custody of a child. Jurisdictions are split on whether the custodial parent's relocation automatically constitutes a material change in circumstances. Alaska finds relocation out of state is a change of circumstances as a matter of law.[32] New York courts have also found that the proposed relocation of the custodial parent provides the requisite change of circumstances required for a court to determine if modification is in the best interests of the child.[33] Increased distance and travel time may necessitate modification of a prior order including custodial exchange times and who should bear the responsibility for increased transportation.[34] The court may not find a change of circumstances where a parent's new location is a shorter distance than the other parent had agreed to travel.[35]

Other jurisdictions have found that the proposed relocation of the residential parent does not necessarily constitute a change in circumstances.[36] It depends on the circumstances. As a

Mississippi court noted, it is the effect of the move on the child on the existing custody arrangement that may be the change of circumstances.[37] If the parents already live at a distance at the time of divorce, the relocation may not increase the travel time, and the court may not find a material change of circumstances.[38]

Depending on the facts, a relocation of the custodial parent to a different city or county may constitute a material change.[39] When the distance is great, the court is more likely to find a change of circumstances because the existing parenting plan may be unfeasible. Even a short move, however, may be a change of circumstances if it causes the existing parenting agreement to become impractical. A Wyoming mother's move to New Mexico was a material change in circumstances because the nine-hour distance created difficulties for visitation with the father and negatively impacted the father's relationship with the children. The mother's lack of cooperation was also a factor in changing primary residential custody to the father. The Wyoming Supreme Court listed the following factors to consider in determining if there has been a material change of circumstances:

1. A change in the ability of the parties to maintain the existing parenting agreement;
2. A change in the ability of the children to maintain a close relationship with the remaining parent;
3. Factors affecting quality of life in the new location;
4. The child's geographic preference; and
5. The relative merits of available social and educational opportunities in the new location.[40]

A mother's proposed out-of-state relocation from Buffalo, Wyoming, to Plains, Montana, 600 miles away, was a material change of circumstances because it rendered alternate weekend visitation unworkable.[41] Where a father with primary physical custody planned to move from New York to Florida, the court found the requisite change of circumstances.[42] Even if the move is not across the country, but merely to a different county two hours away, the court may find a real, substantial, and unanticipated change of circumstances.[43] In an Indiana case, the court found that the move of an 11-year-old one and a half hours away from the father caused a substantial change of circumstances in the interaction and relationship of the child and the father as well as the extended family.[44] In another case, the custody order provided that mother could not move more than 25 miles from the Bronx without the written consent of the father. When she lost her housing and could not afford the city, she petitioned to move to Rochester, New York. The court found a material change in circumstances.[45] In another case, however, a mother's intent to move 70 miles from the father in Iowa was not a substantial change justifying modification.[46]

Just because there is a statutory requirement to give notice of a proposed move does not mean that the move will be considered a change of circumstances that requires a full court hearing.[47] In Louisiana, if the custodial parent provides the required statutory notice, their attempt to relocate would not constitute a change of circumstances warranting a change of custody. On the other hand, relocating without prior notice in violation of a court order *may* constitute a change of circumstances warranting a full evidentiary hearing on modification of custody.[48]

In New York, a planned move with a request for relocation is a change in circumstances.[49] Washington also finds that a parent does not have to show a change of circumstances other than the other parent's intended relocation.[50] On the other hand, if a court refuses to allow a relocation, the fact that one parent proposed it does not constitute a change of circumstances.[51] If the distance is such that only minor alterations to the parenting schedule will be needed, the court may find no substantial change of circumstances.[52]

Relocation by a residential parent can be a change in circumstances if a real, substantial, and unanticipated change of circumstances would significantly impair the other parent's ability to continue exercising the rights and responsibilities that they had been exercising.[53] Therefore, the court must consider the nature and extent of the nonmoving parent and child's relationship and how the move would affect it. Florida found that a relocation did not amount to a substantial change warranting modification if the relocation is not distant from the child's current location. Where the father moved 47 miles away, the trial court erred in modifying the time-share. Even though the parties' communication was strained, the father was still able to comply with the existing order, and the move was not impacting the children's day-to-day routine.[54]

Courts have found a material and substantial change in circumstances when a parent wanted to relocate with a child from Georgia to New York,[55] from Texas to Mexico,[56] and from Wyoming to West Virginia.[57] A Vermont case found that a mother's relocation to a different county over two hours away and purchase of a home with a plan to open a business presented a real, substantial, and unanticipated change of circumstances that warranted modification of parent–child contact schedule. The move made it impossible for the father to exercise mid-week contact.[58] In another case, the mother relocated out of state 400 miles away to live with her fiancé and his two children, leaving the older child in the father's custody. The court found a change of circumstances.[59] Where a mother was uncooperative and attempted to cut the father out of the child's life, the Arkansas court found a change of circumstances, denied her request to move to Seattle, and changed the child's custody to the unwed father.[60]

If there is a material change in circumstances, the court will hold a hearing to determine the child's best interests. The court may find it in the best interests to go with the relocating parent or to stay with the nonrelocating.[61] One court has indicated that when a noncustodial parent seeks a change in custody based solely on the custodial parent's decision to relocate, the moving party faces a high hurdle to justify the violent dislocation caused by a change in custody from one parent to the other.[62] On the other hand, when child rearing and decision-making are shared, one parent's move to a remote location at the least requires a reassessment of the custodial and residential arrangements and, because of the practicalities of shared parenting, may require a change in custody.[63] As a matter of law, an Alaska court found that both the occurrence of a crime involving domestic violence and one parent's relocation out of state constituted a significant change of circumstances.[64]

Even if the relocation is determined to be a change of circumstances and the court denies the relocation, the parent who was planning to relocate may abandon the plan to move. The court may allow the parent to retain custody, because there is no change of circumstances.[65]

Specific Number of Miles Not a Change

Several states have statutes that allow a relocation move up to a certain number of miles from the existing location. In Florida, the relocation of either parent requires court approval because the statute says "a change in the location of the principal residence of a parent to a new location at least fifty miles away from his or her principal place of residence at the time of the last order establishing time-sharing."[66] If the relocation is approved, the trial court can modify the time-sharing to ensure frequent, continuing, and meaningful contact with the nonrelocating parent.

If both parents reside in the state, Arizona law requires notice if the parent wants to relocate out of state or more than 100 miles from the other parent in the state.[67]

The Florida court uses a straight line—or as the crow flies—test to find the mother had only moved 49 miles away.[68] A Louisiana court, however, rejected the "crow test" to find that actual driving time was the key. Mother moved more than 75 miles, so it was change of circumstances.[69] In a Tennessee case, the mother moved 44.45 radial miles, but 52 driving miles. The court found that radial miles should be used so the relocation statute was not applicable.[70]

Utah's statute allows a move of up to 150 miles. In one case, the father claimed that mother's relocation to a neighboring county within the state was a "clear and uncontroverted" change in circumstances. The court found that the mother's move was within the 150-mile threshold and the father was enjoying just as much parenting time after the mother's move as he had before. The children's change of schools was not necessarily something that constituted a substantial change in circumstances.[71]

American Law Institute Standard

The *ALI Principles of the Law of Family Dissolution* section 2.17(1), (3), and (4) makes a relocation a substantial change in circumstances only when the relocation "significantly impairs either parent's ability to exercise responsibilities the parent has been exercising or attempting to exercise under the parenting plan." Comment B explains that because relevant factors are too numerous and varied, there is no precise formula for determining when a parent's ability to exercise their responsibilities has been substantially impaired. The trial court must consider, among other factors, "the amount of custodial responsibility each parent has been exercising and for how long, the distance of the move and its duration, and the availability of alternate visitation arrangements." In addition, the court should consider the amount of parental responsibility the parent has actually been exercising, not what they were awarded. The court should revise the parenting plan to accommodate relocation without changing the proportion of each parent's custodial responsibilities. If that is not possible, the best interests govern.

Even if the relocation constitutes a change of circumstances, the ALI would allow the parent who has been exercising the clear majority of custodial responsibility to relocate with the child if that parent shows that the relocation is for a valid purpose, in good faith, and to a location that is reasonable in light of the purpose. Connecticut and Vermont have expressly adopted the ALI position.[72]

Sole Custody: Relocation Alone Not a Change of Circumstances

When one parent has parental rights and responsibilities for a significant majority of the time, the court may be more likely to find that a proposed relocation is not a change of circumstances.[73] Until 2000, the majority of courts did not find the fact that the custodial parent's wish to move was a sufficient change of circumstances by itself to revisit the custody issue.[74] The parent with primary residential custody could choose the place of where the child would live.[75] The Oklahoma Supreme Court cited a California case and stated:

> Ours is an increasingly mobile society . . . approximately one American in five changes residences each year. Economic

> necessity and remarriage account for the bulk of relocations. Because of the ordinary needs for both parents after a marital dissolution to secure or retain employment, pursue educational or career opportunities, or reside in the same location as a new spouse or other family or friends, it is unrealistic to assume that divorced parents will permanently remain in the same location after dissolution or to exert pressure on them to do so.[76]

The parent challenging relocation bears the heavy burden of demonstrating that the severe measure of transferring primary rights and responsibilities from one parent to the other is necessary to serve the child's best interests.[77] Several courts have found that the relocation of the primary residential parent does not necessarily constitute a change in circumstances.[78] Even so, however, the court may have to modify the parenting plan to reflect the parties in their new locations. For example, mother with 57 percent of child's time had presumption in her favor. Court could modify to reflect that mother and child would be in Utah and father in Washington.[79]

The South Carolina Court found that a father's relocation was not a change in circumstances:

> We decline to hold relocation in itself is a substantial change in circumstance affecting the welfare of a child. Relocation is one factor in considering a change in circumstances, but is not alone a sufficient change in circumstances. One location may not necessarily affect the best interest of the child as would another. The effect of relocation on the child's best interest is highly fact specific. It should not be assumed that merely relocating and potentially burdening the noncustodial parent's visitation rights always negatively affects the child's best interests.[80]

Some of these cases favor the child's stability (emotional as opposed to geographical) in the primary custodial relationship.[81] For example, the Oklahoma Supreme Court stated:

> In a relocation case the noncustodial parent seeking to restrain the custodial parent from moving must meet the heavy burden to show that circumstances justify reopening the question of "custody."[82]

Most courts that do not find the proposed relocation itself to be a change of circumstances have a presumption that favors the moving parent. These courts give the primary residential parent the right to make decisions as to residence and put the burden on the nonmoving parent to show harm.[83] For example, in 2003, the Arkansas Supreme Court stated:

> [T]oday, we hold that relocation alone is not a material change in circumstance. We pronounce a presumption in favor of relocation for custodial parents with primary custody. The noncustodial parent should have the burden to rebut the relocation presumption. The custodial parent no longer has the obligation to prove a real advantage to herself or himself and to the children in relocating.[84]

Arkansas courts, however, found that the presumption does not apply when parents share equal joint physical custody.[85] Additionally, even if the court has a presumption in favor of the relocating parent, it is not a given that the parent can relocate. A parent should not rely on the presumption to relocate before obtaining court permission because it gives the appearance of attempting to thwart the other parent's time with the child, and trial courts do not like it.[86]

If the distance from the other parent is not great, the court may find that it is inconvenient, but not a change of circumstances. If the distance is not too great, the court may allow the move. In one case in which the mother moved 70 miles away, the court found it was inconvenient for the father but not that difficult because he had a flexible schedule and was able to meet the existing parenting time schedule.[87]

In a Mississippi case the court found that a relocation of the custodial parent may not be a change of circumstances by itself. If, however, the effect of the move is to make the existing parenting plan unworkable, it is a change of circumstances.[88]

Relocation Alone Is a Change of Circumstances

If a parent relocates without court permission or the other parent's consent, it is a change of circumstances and the court may modify the existing custody order.[89] In a few states like Iowa,

Maine, and Missouri, statutes provide that a proposed relocation is a change of circumstances.[90] In other states, appellate decisions have found a proposed relocation to be a material change in circumstances.[91] For example, a New Mexico court indicated that in almost every case in which the change in circumstances is occasioned by one parent's proposed relocation, the move will establish the substantiality and materiality of the change.[92] Illinois has found that a parent's relocation constitutes a substantial change in circumstances.[93] Alaska has found that as a matter of law, relocation is a change of circumstances.[94] A California case indicated that while the move itself may not be a change of circumstances, under some circumstances, it may be treated as such.

> [T]he likely consequences of a proposed change in the residence of a child, when considered in the light of all the relevant factors, may constitute a change of circumstances that warrants a change in custody, and the detriment to the child's relationship with the noncustodial parent that will be caused by the proposed move, when considered in light of all the relevant factors, may warrant denying a request to change the child's residence or changing custody.[95]

A father's relocation to Arizona constituted a substantial change in circumstances, warranting a best interest hearing, even though the parties already had been living 600 miles apart in Alaska.[96]

Agreement of Parties Makes Relocation a Change of Circumstances

If parents contemplated relocation, the agreement may determine if the move is a change of circumstances. For example, where the parties agreed to remain in the same school district, the fact that both parents moved was not a change of circumstances because they remained in the same school district.[97] Just because parents, by agreement, stipulate to a change of custody upon the happening of a stated event, this does not require enforcement if there is no finding that it is in the child's best interest.[98] Changed circumstances should be viewed at the time of hearing, not based on projections of changes that may occur. So automatic changes of custody based on triggering events are generally not permitted.[99] If the triggering event is to occur in the near future, such an older preschooler going to kindergarten, the court may allow it.[100]

In other states, the parents' agreement or parenting plan provision may make the move a change of circumstances or allow reexamination of the existing custody arrangement.[101] If the parties' agreement expressly prohibits a move, the party who seeks to relocate must show a substantial change in circumstances to justify the relocation. The presence of a nonrelocation provision should at least entitle the nonmoving parent to a hearing. In one case the father argued the mother had not negotiated in good faith.[102]

Even if the parties have entered into an agreement, the judge has the power to inquire into what custody arrangement is in the best interest of the child at the time the issue arises. The presumption that the parents' agreement is in a child's best interests does not preclude the judge from looking at the child's best interests. Some courts look at the circumstances surrounding execution of the agreement. When the mother who signed the agreement was unmarried, newly pregnant, and threatened by the child's father, the court discounted the presence of an agreement.[103]

Sometimes the court will have to interpret what the agreement means. In a Louisiana case, the court found that a stipulated judgment permitting the mother to "move in and out of the state of Louisiana" with the children was not intended to permit her to permanently relocate, but rather to allow her to take children to visit her family in Florida.[104]

Joint Legal or Shared Custody

Joint legal custody does not require close proximity. Parents can communicate about the important decisions that need to be made for the child whether they are next door or across the country. To the extent, however, that the parenting plan is affected, there may be a change of circumstances. Parents in Mississippi had legal custody of three children with mother having primary residency. A court found that it was not in the best interests of three children to move with the mother when they had lived their entire lives with family and friends in Mississippi.[105] In a Connecticut case, the parties' parenting plan provided for joint legal custody of five children with primary residency with the mother. The parent having physical custody could not move more than 20 driving miles from Fairfield without an agreement of the parties or a court order. Although the court allowed the mother to relocate to Portland, Maine, the two oldest children were placed with the father and the three youngest went with the mother.[106]

States sometimes use a different analysis in considering petitions involving relocation if the parents share custody rather than where one parent has the majority of custody time. In an Arkansas case, the parties had a 60/40 school year and 50/50 summer and holiday split and both parents were active in the four children's lives and activities. The appellate court reversed the trial judge who allowed the mother to relocate to Texas, finding the court used the wrong standard. With shared and nearly equal custody, neither parent takes precedence over the other.[107]

There are multiple definitions of shared parenting, however. One court noted that "tethering the relocation standard to one party's status as the parent of primary residence . . . may generate unnecessary disputes regarding that designation, resulting in additional litigation."[108] Indeed, courts are more likely to find that a proposed relocation is a material change of circumstances in a true shared physical custody situation.[109] Arkansas courts found that a presumption favoring the move of a custodial parent does not apply when parents share equal joint physical custody.[110] The standards favoring a primary residential parent's desire to move will only be applied when the parent is not just labeled the primary custody but also spends significantly more time with the child than the other parent.[111]

A Louisiana court found that neither bickering between mother and father, their acrimonious relationship with a lack of effective communication, nor the fact that mother and her ill grandmother would benefit from the move were a material change in circumstances sufficient to support modification of the rotating custody arrangement.[112] If both parents are involved in the day-to-day care of the child, either the parents or the court will need to fashion a new parenting schedule.[113]

If true joint legal and physical custody exists, a few states have indicated that a motion to relocate requires a determination of primary custody before a parent can seek to relocate.[114] On the other hand, where a father who had joint legal and physical custody waited for two years after the mother moved 180 miles away to object, the court found he had acquiesced and changed the order to sole physical residency with the mother.[115]

In North Dakota, when the parents have joint custody, two motions must be made: one for a change of custody and one to relocate with the child.[116] Utah also requires a party wishing to relocate to file a petition to modify the custody order. The court cannot order a change in custody in favor of a relocating parent in the absence of such a petition.[117] In Washington, the Child Relocation Act was found not to apply when a child's time is designated equal or substantially equal in a parenting plan and the proposed relocation would result in modification. The parent whose desired relocation would terminate the existing arrangement had to show adequate cause under the modification statute.[118] While the court may modify the physical custody arrangement to allow a parent to move, it may retain a joint legal custody arrangement.[119]

When the court denied the child's relocation, the mother abandoned her plan to move. Therefore, the court found there was no change of circumstances.[120] If the parent will move without the child, then the court must decide the best interests between the parents in different locations.[121] In one case, the parties had abided by a custody stipulation that gave the father about 35 percent of time for four years, until the mother notified him that she and her fiancé were moving to Maryland because she had lost her teaching job. The move would substantially reduce the father's nearly equal time until school started and at least one-third of the time after that.[122]

Other courts, however, do not care. The same standard is applied—substantial a material change of circumstances. A parent's good and legitimate reason to leave the state, taken together with an express intent to do so, may constitute a material change of circumstances sufficient to require an examination of the child's best interests. A North Dakota court noted that with joint custody, both parents are custodial parents, so the children's lives are inextricably interwoven with the quality of life of both parents, not just one. Allowing one parent to relocate will disrupt the stability of the relationship between the other custodial parent and their family, which includes the child.[123] The distance between parents' homes may make shared residential time logistically a problem which may negatively impact the child's best interests.[124]

Preference of Child as a Change of Circumstances

As a general rule, the child's preference to move or not to move, standing alone, may not be a sufficient change in circumstances. The fact that a 12-year-old child wished to move to Nashville to attend a private school was not in and of itself a material and substantial change of circumstance to warrant the drastic action of a change of custody.[125] In one case, the court did listen to children who testified that their social, school, and sports schedules were negatively impacted by the parents' visitation schedule and was causing a strained relationship with the mother.[126]

On the other hand, the passage of time and the desires of a child not to move may constitute a change of circumstances sufficient for the court to hold a hearing and change custody.[127] Likewise, the testimony of children favoring the relocation and move away from one parent may be compelling. The court found a sufficient change in circumstances in that the mother had remarried, her husband had a good job and had bought a home in Michigan, the house the mother was renting was being sold, and the children testified they wanted to stay with the mother because of continued conflict with their father who had not tried to see them in a year.[128]

Some state statutes provide that the wishes of a child of a certain age can justify modification of a parenting plan if there is a change of circumstances. For example, the Montana statute indicates the court should listen to the child who is over 14 and desires an amendment.[129] (See Chapter 14.)

Hearing

If a material change of circumstances is found, the court must hold a hearing to determine whether the child should be allowed to relocate with the moving parent or stay with the nonrelocating parent. Summary judgment is not appropriate.[130] That may require a change of primary residency or, in some cases, a change of custody. A trial court abused its discretion when determining that the out-of-state relocation was in the child's best interests without a full evidentiary hearing.[131]

Just because the court finds that there has been a material change in circumstances does not mean that the child's custody and residency arrangements must change. In one study, the cases seem to indicate that just a few more than half of cases changed custody.[132] It does mean that the court must hold a full evidentiary hearing to determine if the proposed relocation is in the best interests of the child or whether the proposed relocation may justify a change in custody.[133] Some states use a version of the UMDA "endangerment" standard, which requires a showing that "the child's present environment may endanger seriously his physical, mental, moral, or emotional health" before custody may be modified.[134] The parent requesting the change may be required to show not only that there has been a change of circumstance but also that a change of custody or residency would materially promote the welfare and the best interests of child.[135]

The parent must show that the transfer of custody is in the child's best interests.[136] If there is no proof that the child's best interest would be served by a change, the original order will not be disturbed.[137] If the move does not impact the children's routine, the court should probably not modify the time-share arrangement.[138]

Montana found that while mother's out of state move 600 miles away was a change of circumstances, it did not warrant a change of primary physical custody to the father because the child would be separated from a half-sister.[139] A mother's relocation to New York, however, did warrant a change of custody in child's best interests.[140]

Some jurisdictions may require a showing that a change of custody is necessary to prevent injury to the child.[141] The party seeking the change bears a heavy burden of showing that continuation of the present custody is so detrimental to the child as to justify a modification of the custody decree, or bears the burden of proving by clear and convincing evidence that the harm likely to be caused by the child's change of environment is substantially outweighed by its advantages to the child. A father who had primary physical custody, but the parents split time with the children equally, petitioned to relocate from Georgia to Alabama because he wanted to start a new chapter. The Georgia Supreme Court upheld the trial court's finding of a change of circumstances and a transfer of physical custody to the mother because the father was putting his interests above those of the mother and the children, negatively affecting the mother's ability to be involved in the children's lives. The court noted that the evidence presented at trial clearly demonstrated that "the children would suffer irreparable harm in being denied regular contact with their mother."[142]

Military Deployments

When one or both parents are in the military, deployments may be common. Competing policies emerge with one being to maintain stability for the children and the other being to prevent the servicemember from being disadvantaged by virtue of their service.[143] Career servicemembers execute a military family care plan, which includes guardianship and power of attorney for care of children during deployment. If the primary residential parent is deployed, the issue becomes whether the other parent becomes primary residential custodian or if the deploying parent can designate a spouse, relative, or someone else to continue their residential custody. The court may be asked to deal with a change in custody, as least temporarily.

A proposed relocation out of state, especially overseas deployments, due to a military career may be a material change in circumstances,[144] but it is not always sufficient to modify "permanent" custody.[145] A couple of courts have found that a residential parent cannot delegate their right to custody to a spouse or friends if the other parent is fit.[146] Other courts have held the opposite.[147] A Kansas court found there was not a material change of circumstances to warrant a change in residential custody of the parties' two children during the father's one-year military tour abroad.[148]

Within the past ten years, several states have enacted statutes to specifically deal with military deployments and to provide more guidance for courts that a temporary deployment should not serve as a basis for a permanent change in custody.[149] In July 2012, the Uniform Law Commission approved the Uniform Deployed Parents Custody and Visitation Act (UDPCVA).[150] Seventeen states have enacted it; two more are considering it. The UDPCVA provides that the absence of a military parent from a state will not be used to deprive the state of jurisdiction over the custody or visitation proceeding. It requires the deploying parent to give seven days' notice, if possible, of deployment. Each parent shall provide the other parent with a plan for fulfilling the parent's share of custodial responsibility during deployment. The parents may enter into a temporary agreement specifying care arrangements with a parent or nonparent during deployment. The agreement terminates after the deploying parent returns. Note there is a distinction between a military assignment and a deployment. The special custody and military statutes apply to deployment.[151]

Endnotes

1. Cook v. Moore, 357 P.3d 749 (Wyo. 2015) (finding mother's intent to move 1,400 miles from father's residence was a material change in circumstances and in child's best interest to change custody to the father).
2. Ianelli v. Camino, 444 P.3d 61 (Wyo. 2019).
3. Uniform Marriage and Divorce Act (ULA) § 409(a) bars a motion to modify for two years except in an emergency. After that the court may modify based upon a change of circumstances if custodian agrees; the custodian has consented to child's integration into noncustodial parent's family; or child's present environment endangers the child's physical, mental, moral, or emotional health and the harm out to child from relocation outweighs its advantages. *Id.* § 409(b).
4. Arizona, Colorado, Illinois, Kentucky, Minnesota, Missouri, Montana, and Washington adopted variations of the UMDA. Baxendale v. Raich, 878 N.E.2d 1252 (Ind. 2008).
5. Minn. Stat. § 518.18(a)(c).
6. Bryan v. Wheels, 295 So. 3d 889 (Fla. Dist. Ct. App. 2020).
7. Julie E. v. David E., 1 N.Y.S.3d 431 (App. Div. 2015).

8. *In re* Marriage of Jennings, 50 P.3d 506 (Kan. App. 2002) (mediated agreement—no need to show change of circumstances).

9. *See* Linda D. Elrod, Child Custody Practice and Procedure, Ch. 17 (Thomson-Reuters, 2024).

10. Goldman v. Greenwood, 748 N.W.2d 279 (Minn. 2008).

11. Porter-Spaulding v. Spaulding, 83 N.Y.S.3d 350 (App. Div. 2018).

12. *In re* Marriage of Schilling, 414 P.3d 775 (Mont. 2018) (father's relocation to a different city 300 miles away from mother's place of residence was a substantial change of circumstances and required hearing to determine if parenting plan needed amendments).

13. Baird v. Hubbart, 98 So. 3d 1158 (Ala. Civ. App. 2012) (finding mother failed to show a change of circumstances since the trial court's un-appealed denial of her proposed relocation).

14. Gary v. Gray, 518 P.3d 1185 (Idaho 2022) (mother unilaterally took child to Costa Rica).

15. LaFlam v. LaFlam, 295 A.3d 406 (Vt. 2021) (mother had planned to move to Florida to live with her parents and had been applying for jobs there at time of divorce).

16. Spanier v. Spanier, 852 N.W.2d 284, 288 (Minn. Ct. App. 2014).

17. McCoy v. Kincade, 448 S.W.3d 740 (Ark. Ct. App. 2014).

18. Landwehr v. Landwehr, 715 N.W.2d 180 (Wis. 2006) (being closer with self-employment that allowed for more flexible hours).

19. State v. Neustel, 790 N.W.2d 476 (N.D. 2010).

20. Myers v. McCall, 334 S.W.3d 878 (Ark. Ct. App. 2009) (trial court changed custody to father where mother remarried and moved children to Missouri without notice required by agreement). *See also* Bisbing v. Bisbing, 166 A.3d 1155 (N.J. 2017) (parties' parenting plan had residency restrictions).

21. Jones v. Ahmad, 818 S.E.2d 263 (Ga. Ct. App. 2012).

22. Bryan v. Wheels, 295 So. 3d 889 (Fla. Dist. Ct. App. 2020).

23. Pierron v. Pierron, 782 N.W.2d 480 (Mich. 2010) (short distance move 60 miles was not a change of circumstances).

24. Hollis v. Hollis, 276 So. 3d 77 (Fla. Dist. Ct. App. 2019) (father's move 47 miles away was not a material change in circumstance where it did not impact the children's routine); H.K. v. R.C., 151 N.Y.S.3d 836 (Misc. 2021) (mother's move twenty miles away was not enough to warrant a hearing and it was in child's best interest).

25. Brazil v. Williams, 859 S.E.2d 490 (Ga. Ct. App. 2021).

26. Janda v. Janda, 9 N.W.3d 212 (Neb. Ct. App. 2023) (mother moved without notice to father and refused to promote relationship with children and father); Smith v. Smith, 661 S.W.3d 273 (Ark. Ct. App. 2023) (finding it best interest to allow mother to move with children from Lake City to Bentonville).

27. Jourdan v. Jourdan, 216 N.E.3d 42 (Ohio App. Ct. 2023).

28. Heath v. Lee, 372 So. 3d 283 (Fla. Dist. Ct. App. 2023).

29. Michael B. v. LaTisha T.M., 89 N.Y.S.3d 83 (App. Div. 2018).

30. Dymitro v. Dymitro, 927 P.2d 917 (Idaho Ct. App. 1996) (mother's actions in unilaterally removing the child from Idaho demonstrated that the father may be more suited to have primary residential custody); State v. Titus, 274 So. 3d 591 (La. Ct. App. 2019) (mother moved without notice and court changed primary residency to the father).

31. Baxendale v. Raich, 878 N.E.2d 1252 (Ind. 2008).

32. *See* Bagby v. Bagby, 250 P.3d 1127 (Alaska 2011) (even though parents lived 600 miles away from each other in Alaska, father's move to Arizona was a substantial change in circumstances); Williams v. Barbee, 243 P.3d 995 (Alaska 2010).

33. Megan NN v. Michael NN., 178 N.Y.S.3d 805 (App. Div. 2022) (allowing father to relocate to Portland, Oregon); James TT v. Shermaqiae UU, 126 N.Y.S.3d 224 (App. Div. 2020).

34. Mary N. v. Scott N., 193 N.Y.S.3d 344 (App. Div. 2023) (change of circumstances where prior to father's move, mother's time to exchange children had been 40 minutes; after move, it was one hour 15 minutes); Matter of Shayne FF. v. Julie GG., 200 N.Y.S.3d 163 (App. Div. 2023).

35. Mildred J. v. Joseph K., 213 N.Y.S.3d 484 (App. Div. 2024).

36. *See* Kan. Stat. Ann. § 23-3222(c) (move may be a change in circumstances). *See* Hollandsworth v. Knyzewski, 109 S.W.3d 653, 657 (Ark. 2003); Ragle v. Ragle, 82 So. 3d 109 (Fla. Dist. Ct. App. 2011) (28-mile move was minor); *In re* Marriage of Hoffman, 867 N.W.2d 26 (Iowa 2015); Robertson v. Roberts, 95 So. 3d 727 (Miss. Ct. App. 2012); Williamson v. Williamson, 87 N.E.3d 676 (Ohio App. 2017); Dailey v. Dailey, 854 S.E.2d 856 (S.C. Ct. App. 2021).

37. Domke v. Domke, 305 So. 3d 1233 (Miss. Ct. App. 2021).

38. Brazil v. Williams 859 S.E.2d 490 (Ga. Ct. App. 2021) (father's move to Michigan not a change where the flight to Georgia was about the same travel time, the child's grades had not suffered, and the child communicated regularly with the Georgia family).

39. State v. Titus, 274 So. 3d 591 (La. Ct. App. 2019) (relocation distance was 76 road, not radial, miles, because automobile would be means of transportation).

40. Gutierrez v. Bradley, 500 P.3d 984, 988–89 (Wyo. 2021). *See also* Walsh v. Smith, 458 P.3d 58 (Wyo. 2020) (mother's move to Idaho was sufficient change of circumstances and court changed physical residency to the unwed father).

41. Ianelli v. Camino, 444 P.3d 61 (Wyo. 2019). *See also In re* Marriage of Schilling, 414 P.3d 775 (Mont. 2018) (father's move 300 miles away was change of circumstances).

42. *In re* Matter of Anthony F. v. Kayla E, 141 N.Y.S.3d 782 (App. Div. 2021), *lv denied*, 37 N.Y.3d 901 (2021).

43. Bonk v. Bonk, 183 A.3d 600 (Vt. 2018) (where mother had moved, purchased a home with a plan to open a business; court modified the contact schedule because the move made it impossible for father to exercise mid-week contact).

44. McDaniel v. McDaniel, 150 N.E.3d 282 (Ind. Ct. App. 2020) (court found mother's contempt motions unsubstantiated and modified primary physical custody in mother to sole custody in father where mother had remarried an individual with significant involvement with the legal system).

45. Erica B. v. Louis M., 194 N.Y.S.3d 5 (App. Div. 2023) (mother failed to make prima facie case that move was in four-year-old son's best interest as it would reduce father's time substantially).

46. *In re* Marriage of Hoffman, 867 N.W.2d 26 (Iowa 2015) (father was emergency room doctor who works 12 hour shifts four nights and eight days a month and enjoyed an extraordinary amount of flexibility).

47. Barblock v. Barblock, 890 A.2d 1005, 1009 (N.J. Super. Ct. App. Div. 2006) (finding hearing not necessary where father did not seek to become primary custodial parent if mother relocated without the children; noting hearings costs, financially, personally, and in length of time).

48. La. Rev. Stat. § 9:355.17. *See* Michael B. v. Latasha T.M., 89 N.Y.S.3d 83 (App. Div. 2018).

49. Julie E. v. David E., 1 N.Y.S.3d 131 (App. Div. 2015) (mother's intended relocation to Texas was change of circumstances, but not in best interests of two children where father was unable to pay to get to Texas and move would limit or destroy relationships with extended family); *In re* Adams v. Bracci, 936 N.Y.S.2d 738 (App. Div. 2012), *lv. denied*, 18 N.Y.3d 809 (2012); Lauzonis v. Lauzonis, 993 N.Y.S.2d 586 (App. Div. 2014).

50. *In re* Marriage of Raskob, 334 P.3d 30 (Wash. Ct. App. 2014).

51. *In re* Marriage of Sconce and Sweet, 274 P.3d 303 (Or. App. 2012) (mother abandoned her plan to move when court would not let children go so no change of circumstances existed).

52. Pierron v. Pierron, 782 N.W.2d 480 (Mich. 2010) (finding mother's 60-mile move would require only minor adjustments to father's actual parenting time). *See also* Hollis v. Hollis, 276 So. 3d 77 (Fla. Dist. Ct. App. 2019).

53. Bonk v. Bonk, 183 A.3d 600 (Vt. 2018). *See also* Munday v. McLendon, 287 So. 3d 303, 310 (Miss. Ct. App. 2019) (mother's remarriage and relocation out of state made custodial schedule unworkable).

54. Hollis v. Hollis, 276 So. 3d 77 (Fla. Dist. Ct. App. 2019).

55. Gallo v. Kofler, 711 S.E.2d 687 (Ga. 2011). *See also* Frey v. Frey, 831 N.W.2d 753 (N.D. 2013) (mother's move about 400 miles away to be with fiancé, leaving oldest child with father was change of circumstances).

56. Arredondo v. Betancourt, 383 S.W.3d 730 (Tex. Ct. App. 2012).

57. Arnott v. Arnott, 293 P.3d 440 (Wyo. 2012) (overturning prior case law). *See also In re* Marriage of Schilling, 414 P.3d 775 (Mont. 2018) (father's

relocation to a different city 300 miles away from mother's place of residence was a substantial change of circumstances and required hearing to determine if parenting plan needed amendments).

58. Bonk v. Bonk, 183 A.3d 600 (Vt. 2018). *See also In re* Marriage of Schilling, 414 P.3d 775 (Mont. 2018) (father's relocation to a different city 300 miles away was a substantial change of circumstances).

59. Frey v. Frey, 831 N.W.2d 753 (N.D. 2013). *See also* Ianelli v. Camino, 444 P.3d 61 (Wyo. 2019) (mother's move 600 miles away was a change in circumstances).

60. Alsina v. Hicks, 678 S.W.3d 449 (Ark. Ct. App. 2023).

61. Arnott v. Arnott, 293 P.3d 440 (Wyo. 2012) (finding mother's relocation to Virginia was a material change of circumstances warranting a hearing on the child's best interests); Baxendale v. Raich, 866 N.E.2d 333 (Ind. Ct. App. 2007) (finding mother's move from Valparaiso to Minneapolis to not be a substantial change where mother had tried to make the move as seamless as possible with activities, apartment, and school).

62. Hoover v. Hoover, 764 A.2d 1192, 1194 (Vt. 2000).

63. Dunn v. Dunn, 775 N.W.2d 486 (N.D. 2009) (father's move to Wyoming to be a significant change in circumstances where he and mother had joint custody; changing custody to him and allowing the move).

64. Williams v. Barbee, 243 P.3d 995 (Alaska 2010) (reversing court order maintaining shared custody but awarding physical custody to mother if she relocated out of state based on father's act of domestic violence).

65. *In re* Marriage of Sconce and Sweet, 274 P.3d 303 (Or. Ct. App. 2012).

66. Fla. Stat. Ann. § 61.13001(1)(e). *See* Hull v. Hull, 273 So. 3d 1135 (Fla. Dist. Ct. App. 2019).

67. Ariz. Rev. Stat. § 25-308(A).

68. Tucker v. Liebknecht, 86 So. 3d 1240, 1242 (Fla. Dist. Ct. App. 2012).

69. State v. Titus, 274 So. 3d. 591 (La. Ct. App. 2019).

70. Barrett v. Killings, 700 S.W.3d 399 (Tenn. Ct. App. 2023).

71. Martinez v. Sanchez-Garcia, 532 P.3d 105 (Utah Ct. App. 2023).

72. *See* Conn. Gen. Stat. § 46b-56d; Hawkes v. Spence, 878 A.2d 273 (Vt. 2005).

73. *See* Wells v. Wells, 691 S.W.3d 269 (Ark. Ct. App. 2024) (even though decree said parties would have joint physical custody, mother was undisputedly the primary caregiver and her relocation to another state was not a material change in circumstances); Allen v. Allen, 2018 WL 4677619 (Tenn. App. Sept. 28, 2018) (mother who had 225 days of co-parenting time annually and most of decision-making was allowed to move to California); Parker v. Parker, 45 A.3d 48 (Vt. 2012) (mother who was sole custodian wanted to move three children to Buffalo).

74. *See* Linda D. Elrod, *National and International Momentum Builds for More Child Focus in Relocation Disputes*, 44 Fam. L.Q. 341 (2010) (discussing changes in the law).

75. *See* Carol Bruch & Janet M. Bowermaster, *The Relocation of Children and Custodial Parents: Public Policy, Past and Present*, 30 FAM. L.Q. 245 (1996).

76. Kaiser v. Kaiser, 23 P.3d 278, 284 (Okla. 2001).

77. Hawkes.v. Spence, 878 A.2d 273 (Vt. 2005).

78. *See* Hollandsworth v. Knyzewski, 109 S.W.3d 653, 657 (Ark. 2003); Evans v. Evans, 530 S.E.2d 576 (N.C. 2000). *See also* KAN. STAT. ANN. § 23-3222(c) (stating a proposed move *may* be change).

79. Cowan v. Cowan, 540 P.3d 158 (Wash. Ct. App. 2023) (court erred in modifying parenting plan beyond what is permitted pursuant to a relocation).

80. Latimer v. Farmer, 602 S.E.2d 32, 35 (S.C. 2004) (mother failed to bear burden of showing change of circumstances when father announced intention to move to Michigan for new job).

81. *See* Judith S. Wallerstein & Tony J. Tanke, *To Move or Not to Move—Psychological and Legal Considerations in the Relocation of Children Following Divorce*, 30 FAM. L.Q. 305 (1996); *but see* Richard Warshak, *Social Science and Children's Interest in Relocation Cases: Burgess Revisited*, 34 FAM. L.Q. 83 (2000).

82. Kaiser v. Kaiser, 23 P.3d 278, 284 (Okla. 2001) (citing *In re* Marriage of Burgess, 51 Cal. Rptr. 2d 444. 913 P.2d at 480).

83. Godwin v. Balderamos, 876 So. 2d 1169 (Ala. Civ. App. 2003).

84. Hollandsworth v. Knyzewski, 109 S.W.3d 653, 657, 663 (Ark. 2003).

85. Singletary v. Singletary, 431 S.W.3d 234 (Ark. 2013); Tidwell v. Rosenbaum, 545 S.W.3d 228 (Ark. Ct. App. 2018) (remanding for determination if true joint custody or if one parent spent significantly more time with the child); Wells v. Wells, 691 S.W.3d 269 (Ark. Ct. App. 2024).

86. Sill v. Sill, 228 S.W.3d 538 (Ark. Ct. App. 2006) (mother filed petition to relocate but moved to Oklahoma before the court ruled; court denied move finding sole reason was to make visitation more difficult for father); *In re* Marriage of Adams, 92 N.E.3d 962 (Ill. App. Ct. 2017) (mother's relocation 324 miles away without first obtaining leave of court or father's consent resulted in change of primary residency to the father).

87. *In re* Marriage of Hoffman, 867 N.W.2d 26 (Iowa 2015).

88. Scott v. Boudreau, 375 So. 3d 688 (Miss. Ct. App. 2023) (citing Munday v. McLendon, 287 So. 3d 3030, 310 (Miss. Ct. App. 2019)).

89. Kelly v. Kelly, 529 P.3d 494 (Wyo. 2023) (mother unilaterally moved to Tennessee, court modified custody during school year to the father in Wyoming).

90. *See* IOWA CODE ANN. § 598.21(8A); ME. REV. STAT. ANN. tit. 19-A, § 1657; MO. ANN. STAT. § 452.411.

91. Fortune v. Jasmin, 220 N.Y.S.3d 821 (App. Div. 2024) (a request to relocate a child constitutes a change of circumstances; parent seeking to move must demonstrate relocating is in the child's best interests); Rebekah R. v. Richard R., 112 N.Y.S.3d 291 (App. Div. 2019).

92. Jaramillo v. Jaramillo, 823 P.2d 299 (N.M. 1991).

93. *See In re* Marriage of Adams, 92 N.E.3d 962 (Ill. App. Ct. 2017) (court changed primary residency to father when mother moved the children 324 miles away without consent of father or following the law on filing a petition and notice motion and notice).

94. Williams v. Barbee, 243 P.3d 995 (Alaska 2010) (reversing court order maintaining shared custody; awarding physical custody to mother if she relocated out of state based on father's act of domestic violence).

95. *In re* Marriage of LaMusga, 88 P.3d 81, 97 (Cal. 2004).

96. Bagby v. Bagby, 250 P.3d 1127 (Alaska 2011).

97. Moore v. McIntosh, 128 So. 3d 985 (Fla. Dist. Ct. App. 2014) (requiring 90 days' notice if either moved outside the school district).

98. Jacobson v. Jacobson, 735 P.2d 627 (Or. Ct. App. 1987). *See also* Taylor v. Elison, 263 P.3d 448 (Utah Ct. App. 2011) (agreement providing automatic change of residence if mother moved out of state still required judicial finding of best interests of the child).

99. Arthur v. Arthur, 54 So. 3d 454 (Fla. 2010) *as revised on denial of reh'g* (Feb. 10, 2011); Knutsen v. Cegalis, 989 A.2d 1010, 1014 (Vt. 2009).

100. Durden v. Anderson, 790 S.E.2d 818, 820–21 (Ga. App. 2016).

101. *In re* Marriage of Pape, 989 P.2d 1120 (Wash. 2000) (agreement provided neither would move more than ten miles from county). *But see* Hanson v. Belveal, 280 P.3d 1186 (Wyo. 2012) (provision stating that parties agreed that an out of state move was a material change of circumstances sufficient to seek modification of custody was speculative and unenforceable; no material change in circumstances had occurred).

102. Bisbing v. Bisbing, 137 A.3d 535 (N.J. Super. Ct. App. Div. 2016) (father entitled to hearing on whether mother negotiated in good faith and required her to show substantial unanticipated change in circumstances).

103. Lorenz v. Lorenz, 788 P2d 328 (Mont. 1990).

104. Hulshoff v. Hulshoff, 81 So. 3d 57 (La. Ct. App. 2011).

105. Culver v. Culver, 371 So. 3d 726 (Miss. Ct. App. 2023).

106. Emrich v. Emrich, 15 A.3d 1104 (Conn. App. Ct. 2011).

107. Baird v. Baird, 654 S.W.3d 367 (Ark. Ct. App. 2022)

108. Bisbing v. Bisbing, 166 A.3d 1155, 1169 (N.J. 2017) (applying best interest standard in all cases).

109. *See* Ayers v. Ayers, 508 N.W.2d 515 (Minn. 1993); Brody v. Kroll, 53 Cal. Rptr. 2d 280 (Ct. App. 1996), *rev. denied* (father saw child four to five days a week so court needed to reconsider the custody arrangement).

110. Singletary v. Singletary, 431 S.W.3d 234 (Ark. 2013).

111. Cooper v. Kalkwarf, 532 S.W.3d 58, 67 (Ark. 2017). *See also* Aragon v. Aragon, 513 S.W.3d 447 (Tenn. 2017) (even though parents shared custody, father had 80 percent of time because of mother's job).

112. *See* Melvin v. Miller, 181 So. 3d 826 (La. Ct. App. 2015) (father had burden to show change of circumstances when mother moved from Beauregard Parish). *See also* Bazan v. Gambone, 924 So. 2d 952 (Fla. Dist. Ct. App.

2006) (bickering was not a substantial change in circumstances not reasonably contemplated at time of original judgment).

113. *See* O'Connor v. O'Connor, 793 A.2d 810 (N.J. Super. Ct. App. Div. 2002).

114. Maynard v. McNett, 710 N.W.2d 369 (N.D. 2006) (parent with joint physical custody who wishes to relocate with the child must make two motions: one for a change of custody and one to relocate).

115. Jarrell v. Jarrell, 5 N.E.3d 1186 (Ind. Ct. App. 2014).

116. Dunn v. Dunn, 775 N.W.2d 486 (N.D. 2009) (finding father's move to Wyoming to be a significant change in circumstances where he and mother had joint custody; changing custody to him and allowing the move).

117. Ross v. Ross, 447 P.3d 104 (Utah Ct. App. 2019) (citing Pingree v. Pingree, 365 P.3d 713 (Utah Ct. App. 2015) the court can change custody only in two circumstances: (1) the court "determines that relocation is not in the best interest of the child," thus denying the relocating parent's request for the children to relocate; and (2) the custodial parent decides to relocate—alone—in spite of the court's ruling).

118. *In re* Marriage of Ruff and Worthley, 393 P.3d 859 (Wash. Ct. App. 2017) (courts must look at actual parenting plan designation, not an actual number of overnights to consider with whom child resides a majority of the time). *See also* Bergerson v. Zurbano, 432 P.3d 850 (Wash. App. 2018).

119. Hopkins v. Wollaber, 458 P.3d 583 (N.M. Ct. App. 2018).

120. *In re* Marriage of Sconce and Sweet, 274 P.3d 303 (Or. App. 2012).

121. Wright v. Wright, 431 N.W.2d 301, 304 (N.D. 1988).

122. Hawkes v. Spence, 878 A.2d 273 (Vt. 2005).

123. Maynard v. McNett, 710 N.W.2d 369 (N.D. 2006) (mother wanted to move from Fargo, North Dakota, to Branson, Missouri, with nine-year-old daughter; while less frequent, extended visitation will preserve a noncustodial parent's ability to foster and develop a relationship with a child).

124. L.C. v. T.M., 996 N.E.2d 403 (Ind. Ct. App. 2013) (parents lived one hour apart, which interfered with children's friends and activities; coupled with different parenting styles, court modified shared custody).

125. Pippin v. Pippin, 277 S.W.3d 398 (Tenn. Ct. App. 2008) (noting that but for the oldest child's preference to attend a private school in Nashville, Tennessee, all other elements of the father's case had been litigated in a prior petition in 2005). *See also see* Melvin v. Miller, 181 So. 3d 826 (La. Ct. App. 2015).

126. McCoy v. Kincade, 473 S.W.3d 8, 11 (Ark. 2015).

127. Myers v. McCall, 334 S.W.3d 878 (Ark. Ct. App. 2009) (passage of ten years, mother's remarriage, relocation to Missouri, and intended move to Wisconsin coupled with children's religious preferences and wishes not to move were sufficient change of circumstances justifying change of custody to father).

128. Cappelluzzo v. Cole, 680 S.W.3d 754 (Ark. Ct. App. 2023).

129. Mont. Stat. Ann. § 40-4-219.

130. Heath v. Lee, 372 So. 3d 283 (Fla. Dist. Ct. App. 2023) (father had moved to Florida where the child lived and wanted to modify the time sharing because mother was interfering with this visitation; he was entitled to a hearing).

131. Michael B. v. Latasha T.M., 89 N.Y.S.3d 83 (App. Div. 2018).

132. Theresa Glennon, *Still Partners? Examining the Consequences of Pot-Dissolution Parenting*, 41(1) Fam. L.Q. 105, 138 (2007) (showing number of cases changing custody to other parent: Iowa 16/26; Mississippi 5/9; Ohio 18/46).

133. *See In re* Marriage of Matchen, 866 N.E.2d 683 (Ill. App. 2007); Jacob v. Schultz-Jacob, 923 A.2d 473 (Pa. Super. Ct. 2007); Jelsing v. Peterson, 729 N.W.2d 157 (N.D. 2007).

134. Ky. Rev. Stat. Ann. § 403.340(2)(a).

135. Robinson v. Brown, 58 So. 3d 38 (Miss. Ct. App. 2011) (testimony of daughters that they had strong bond with father; older daughter worried about sister who did not have good relationship with mother even before she moved to live with new husband). *See* Linda D. Elrod, Child Custody Law and Practice, ch. 17 (Thomson Reuters, 2024).

136. Hissam v. Mackin, 837 N.Y.S.2d 756 (App. Div. 2007) (family court changed custody to actively involved father where mother moved 400 miles from father without good cause and engaged in alienating conduct).

137. Weaver v. Kelling, 53 S.W.3d 610 (Mo. Ct. App. 2001) (mother's out-of-state relocation was a change in circumstances but father failed to show how children's best interest would be served by transfer of custody); *In re* Marriage of Colson, 51 P.3d 607 (Or. App. Ct. 2002) (father's petition to transfer custody was properly denied where he failed to establish that the change of custody was in the child's best interests).

138. Hollis v. Hollis, 276 So. 3d 77 (Fla. Dist. Ct. App. 2019) (court erred in modifying time share where husband moved 47 miles away but was able to comply with the existing order). *See also* Pierron v. Pierron, 782 N.W.2d 480 (Mich. 2010) (60-mile move would only require minor adjustments to father's actual parenting time so no need to change residency).

139. Ianelli v. Camino, 444 P.3d 61 (Wyo. 2019).

140. Gallo v. Kofler, 711 S.E.2d 687 (Ga. 2011).

141. Delaware, Illinois, Kentucky, Minnesota.

142. Bodne v. Bodne, 588 S.E.2d 728 (Ga. 2003) (father's motive for relocation was his desire to improve his economic circumstances by establishing a new medical practice and "to leave behind the predivorce chapter of his life"). *See also* Scott v. Scott, 578 S.E.2d 876 (Ga. 2003) (an initial custodial award will not always control after any "new and material change in circumstances that affects the child" is considered).

143. Servicemembers' Civil Relief Act, 50 U.S.C. §§ 501–596. *See* Lauren S. Douglass, *Avoiding Conflict at Home When There Is Conflict Abroad: Military Child Custody and Visitation*, 43(2) Fam. L.Q. 349 (2009).

144. Nelson v. Nelson, 263 P.3d 49 (Alaska 2011) (father's proposed relocation out of state due to his military career was a material change in circumstances that warranted modification of the existing custody order). *See also* Faucett v. Vasquez, 984 A.2d 460 (N.J. Super. Ct. App. Div. 2009), *cert. denied,* 3 A.3d (2010) (finding father's one-year deployment a prima facie change of circumstances warranting a hearing on mother's petition for a change of custody).

145. *In re* Marriage of Rayman, 47 P.3d 413 (Kan. 2002) (upholding court's continuing residential custody in father during his one-year deployment to Korea).

146. *See* Fischer v. Fischer, 157 P.3d 683 (Mont. 2007); Lubinski v. Lubinski, 761 N.W.2d 676 (Wis. Ct. App. 2008).

147. *In re* Marriage of DePalma, 176 P.3d 829 (Colo. App. 2007), *cert. denied* (allowing stepmother to act as children's caregiver during father's parenting time while he was deployed); Webb v. Webb, 148 P.3d 1267 (Idaho 2006).

148. *In re* Marriage of Rayman, 47 P.3d 413 (Kan. 2002).

149. *See e.g.* Ariz. Rev. Stat. § 25-411; Cal. Fam. Code § 3047; Ind. Code Ann. § 31-17-2-21.3(a); Kan. Stat. Ann. § 23-3217; Ky. Rev. Stat. § 403.340; Mich. Comp. L. Ann. § 722.27(7)(1); Tex. Fam. Code § 156.105.

150. http://www.uniformlaws.org/home. *See* Mark Sullivan, *Introduction to the Uniform Deployed Parents Custody and Visitation Act*, 47 Fam. L.Q. 97 (2013).

151. Rubino v. Rubino, 767 S.E.2d 260 (Va. Ct. App. 2015) (finding Virginia Military Parents Equal Protection Act did not apply where father was assigned to Virginia and family could accompany him).

CHAPTER 9

Using Best Interest Factors to Evaluate the Move

There is one common analytical thread in virtually every case involving relocation: the best interest of the child is paramount in any award of custody and visitation, and the trial court has a large measure of discretion in making that award.[1]

A decision in a child relocation case cannot be reduced to a simple tally of which party won a majority of the enumerated factors; . . . because some factors . . . may weigh more heavily than others, the trial court must consider all factors and evidence touching on the issue and must arrive at a reasonable result.[2]

Judges use the "best-interests-of-the-child" standard to determine child custody when parents cannot create their own parenting plans. The best interest requires an individualized decision regarding the needs of each unique child. Trial judges for decades had nearly unfettered discretion to determine the child's best interest under a vague, "indeterminate" and "amorphous" concept.[3] In 1973, the National Conference of Commissioners on Uniform State Laws, now the Uniform Law Commission, promulgated a Uniform Marriage and Divorce Act (UMDA) that contained five specific factors for judges to review in making the custody decision. While only a few states enacted the UMDA, many state legislatures began to add specific best-interest factors to limit unbridled judicial discretion and, hopefully, make custody decisions more predictable.

All states use the best-interest or welfare of the child standard. Some states have lists of up to 25 specific factors.[4] Most states do not require the trial judge to make a specific finding on each factor as long as the appellate court can tell that the factors were used.[5] A few states do require a judge to make a finding on each factor listed.[6] An Idaho judge noted, "A court presiding over a child custody matter does not become a family czar with unlimited authority to order the parents to do anything that the court believes is in the best interests of the child[.]"[7]

Many states have enacted an additional relocation statute that adds specific factors for a court to consider in a relocation case. In some states, the court either can, or must, use both sets of factors. Generally no single factor is dominant. What may be a minor factor in one case may have a greater impact on the court's decision on a motion to relocate.[8]

The history of relocation disputes has been like a pendulum, swinging between presumptions for and against relocation. Today, most courts have moved away from these presumptions in favor of statutory or court-created factors to analyze the best interest of an individual child under the circumstances. The development of factors for courts to consider in relocation cases has followed somewhat the same path as legislation for the general factors for child custody in divorce and paternity cases. The result is that in some states, courts must review not only the specific relocation factors but also the general custody factors. If the state has additional best-interest factors to consider in a relocation case, judges are not free to ignore those factors.[9] Most lawyers would probably say the additional factors have not made custody or relocation disputes any more predictable.

History of Presumptions in Relocation Cases

When the law awarded sole custody to mothers until about the 1980s, judges found that the custodial parent had the right to determine the child's residence. The California Supreme Court, as late as 2004, noted that "the paramount need for continuity and stability in custody arrangement and the harm that may result from disruption of the established pattern of care and emotional bonds with the primary caretaker weigh heavily in favor of maintaining ongoing custody arrangements."[10] This often meant there was a presumption that the child could move with the primary custodian or residential parent.[11] In 2002, the Arkansas Court of Appeals noted, "A rule of law that effectively requires custodial parents to gamble custody of their children before they can live with their children and new spouse . . . seems the very antithesis of domestic stability."[12] The state of Washington uses the Child Relocation Act, which has a rebuttable presumption that if there is a primary custodian the move should be allowed unless the nonresidential parent proves that the detrimental effect of relocation outweighs the benefit of change to the relocating parent.[13] Oklahoma, South Dakota, and Tennessee[14] have also been considered "pro move" states. California, Montana, and Wyoming put the burden of proof on the party opposing relocation. The American Law Institute Principles in 2002 contain a presumption for allowing relocation for the parent who was exercising the majority of the time with the child, that is, the primary caregiver. If neither parent is exercising a clear majority of custodial responsibility, the best-interest analysis is used.[15]

A few states, however, have used a rebuttable presumption that a change of the child's principal residence is not in the child's best interest.[16] The presumption against relocation had to be overcome by showing that the new community could provide more opportunities for the child and for the residential parent (as in job prospects, family support).[17] While some scholars have suggested a presumption based on the wishes of the child should be used, that has never been seriously considered.[18]

Presumptions were intended to make relocation decisions more predictable, but they can have unintended consequences. The New York Court of Appeals noted that children's interests were not served by viewing relocation cases through "prisms of presumptions and threshold tests that artificially skew the analysis in favor of one outcome or another"; rather, "courts should be free to consider and give appropriate weight to all of the factors that may be relevant to" a determination of whether a proposed relocation would be in the best interests of the children involved.[19]

As more states moved to joint legal and, often, physical custody, states began to move away from strict presumptions.[20] An award of joint custody, however, is not equivalent to a presumption against relocation by a custodial parent.[21] Parents who have joint legal custody share decision-making about where the child will live, but even if a relocation is allowed, parents could continue making other decisions even over a long distance. On the other hand, if the parents are sharing equal time, the parenting plan must be redone and there may not be a presumption in favor of one parent moving.

Even in states with presumptions in favor of the relocating custodial parent, have found that the presumptions do not apply when the parents are exercising about 50/50 parenting time, no matter what the label of the arrangement is.[22] For example, in Washington state, the Child Relocation Act factors do not apply to a proposed relocation where there is a schedule providing equal residential time with each parent.[23] Where the parents have substantially equal residential time, "both parents are equally entrusted to act in the child's best interests" and "the court presumes both parents act in the child's best interests."[24] The court must evaluate the child's welfare using various factors set out in statute or cases. In these states, there is no presumption in favor of or against a parent's request, even when the move would materially affect the current schedule of contact, access, and time-sharing.[25] The trend is toward a more fluid balancing test that allows, or requires, the trial court to take into account a greater number of relevant factors.[26] When both parents are actively involved in a child's life and share parenting, it is more difficult for judges to find it in the child's best interest to allow a relocation.[27]

The 2010 ABA Model Relocation of Children Act section 8 provides that there is no presumption in favor of or against relocation of the child. The court shall determine whether relocation is in the best interests of the child. Although the Uniform Law Commission considered drafting a uniform relocation act, the project was dropped because of the lack of consensus on presumptions and factors. As one court noted, however, "The difficulty is establishing standards that are flexible enough to allow trial courts to weigh the complex variables that come into play in relocation cases, and yet not so flexible that they fail to provide guidance to the trial courts and predictability to the litigants and lawyers involved."[28]

Although the primary factor is the best interests of the child, as in other custody decisions, the best interests is an amorphous concept.[29] While some states consider only the child's best interests,[30] many courts require sensitive case-by-case balancing to ensure both parents' and child's interests are treated as equitably as possible.[31] Courts are finding equal or shifting burdens with the relocating parent having to show, usually by a preponderance of evidence, that it is in the child's best interest to relocate.[32] If the moving parent meets that burden, the nonmoving parent must prove, by a preponderance of the evidence, that the proposed relocation is not in the best interests of the child or would harm the child.[33]

Several states now have specific factors, either by statute or court decision, addressing the relocation determination. Most factors parallel the general custody factors, but have a special emphasis on the logistical arrangements and economic circumstances associated with a relocation, especially out of state.[34] In some states, only the relocation factors are relevant; in others, judges must examine both the general custody and the specific relocation factors.[35] For example, Colorado's statute specifically addresses relocation factors and incorporates by reference the general best interest custody factors.[36] Florida's relocation statute also incorporates the general best interest custody factors.[37] A Pennsylvania court noted, when the proposed relocation of a child's residence necessarily involves a modification of the parents' child custody arrangement, courts must consider both the statutory child custody factors and the statutory relocation factors.[38] Indiana courts have found that under the statute governing a proposed relocation, the "other factors affecting the best interest of the child" include, by implication, the factors set forth for custody determinations and modifications.[39]

The trial judge is generally free to give whatever weight the judge deems appropriate to each factor listed in a relocation statute.[40] A Louisiana court, however, found that the trial judge was not required to analyze each best interest factor in the oral or written reasons for the decision in the custodial parent's relocation.[41] Unless required by statute, court rule, or one party makes a request for findings, the trial court does not have to make explicit findings on each factor.[42]

A trial judge abuses its discretion only by failing to consider and balance the statutory factors.[43] An Arizona appellate court vacated a decision because the trial judge failed to state the reasons for designating the father as primary residential parent after finding both parents equal on the factors.[44] The Indiana appellate court reversed a trial judge who appeared to have not considered all the factors and based its custody determination almost entirely on the fact that the unwed mother was no longer in Indiana (which she was) and awarded primary residency of a two-year-old to the unwed father.[45]

If the trial judge finds that relocation is a change of circumstances (Chapter 8), if relocation arises in an initial custody contest (Chapter 4), or if a parent was living or had moved with a child to another state long before the custody litigation, the court must determine what is in the best interests of the child given the relevant facts and circumstances.[46] Which factors are given the most weight may depend on whether one parent has primary custody or if the parents share joint physical and legal custody.[47] As one court noted, when physical custody is shared and neither parent has a clear majority of parental responsibility, the child's interests will favor protection of the child's relationship with both parents because both are, in a real sense, primary to the child's development.[48]

Although some scholars have found that "pure, unguided 'best interests' approach to relocation law is a failure,"[49] professional groups, states, and courts continue to promulgate lists of unweighted factors. The American Academy of Matrimonial Lawyers (AAML)'s Model Relocation section 405 lists eight factors:

(1) the nature, quality, extent of involvement, and duration of the child's relationship with the parents and other significant persons;
(2) the age, developmental stage, and needs of the child, and the likely impact the relocation will have on the child's physical, educational, and emotional development;

(3) the feasibility of preserving the relationship between the nonrelocating person and the child through suitable visitation arrangements, including logistics and finances;
(4) the child's preference, taking into consideration age and maturity;
(5) whether the relocating parent has an established pattern of conduct, either to promote or thwart the relationship with the nonrelocating parent;
(6) whether the relocation of the child will enhance the general quality of life for both the relocating parent and the child;
(7) the reasons of each person for seeking or opposing the relocation, and
(8) any other factor affecting the best interest of the child.[50]

Florida, Louisiana, and Oklahoma have adopted the basic AAML factors. Florida adds a few additional factors.[51] Oklahoma adds to the feasibility factor by "considering the logistics and financial circumstances of the parties" and adds to the quality-of-life factor "including but not limited to financial or emotional benefit or educational opportunity."[52]

The ABA Model Relocation Act incorporates most of the AAML factors but substitutes the child's "views" instead of "preference" and includes consideration of domestic violence and child abuse and neglect, reflecting the current view that the safety of the child should be the most important factor.[53] Relocation controversies pose risks for victims of domestic violence.[54]

Statutory and Judge-Created Relocation Factors

Several state statutes list specific factors to be considered in a relocation case to determine the child's best interest.[55] Other states may list a few factors but do not have an "approved laundry list."[56] Illinois codified factors established in prior cases in its relocation statute.[57] Several courts have developed factors for relocation in the absence of a specific statute. For example, the District of Columbia Court of Appeals listed the following factors:

(1) strength of the child's relationship with each parent;
(2) individual temperament, and special developmental needs of the child;
(3) psychological stability of relocating parent and parenting effectiveness of both parents;
(4) success of current custody arrangement;
(5) advantages and disadvantages of proposed relocation;
(6) any benefits for the child likely to be derived from a parent's improved circumstances;
(7) feasibility of alternative visitation and access schedule;
(8) motivations of the parents in proposing or opposing the move; and
(9) effect the move will have on the child's relationship with the noncustodial parent; the extent of any conflict between the parents and the recentness of separation.[58]

The Massachusetts court highlighted three criteria of the child's best interests that have emerged from the major precedents on removal and custody: (1) the objective of stability and continuity in a child's life; (2) the maximum involvement and participation of both parents in a joint custody arrangement in the children's lives; and (3) the reduction of disruptive shuttle transportation of children between custodial parents.[59]

One journal article listed 36 factors that have been used by various courts in determining relocation cases:

1. Distance of move
2. Length of the parent–child relationship
3. Were the parents married?
4. Parents' time-sharing agreement
5. Quality of parenting time
6. Quantity of parenting time
7. Age, maturity, and special needs of the child
8. Reason for the move
9. Reason the staying parent objects to the move
10. The advantages of the move to the moving parent
11. Advantages of the move to the child
12. Disadvantages of the move to the staying parent

13. Disadvantages of the move to the child
14. Travel time and cost of travel
15. The demands or benefits of the moving parent's second marriage/relationship
16. Feasibility of a parallel move by the staying parent
17. Feasibility of a move by the moving parent's new husband or significant other
18. Does the staying parent really want custody?
19. Is a change of custody practical?
20. Can meaningful child access for the staying parent be provided if the move is allowed?
21. Will the moving parent comply with the access order?
22. The effect of the move on extended family on both sides
23. Personal misconduct by either parent
24. The preference of a mature child
25. Any agreement between the parents about relocations
26. The child's adjustment to home, school, and community
27. The length of time the child has lived in a stable environment
28. The financial resources of the two-family units
29. The expected permanence of the new custodial environment
30. The mental and physical health of all persons in the two-family units
31. Continuation of the child's cultural and religious heritage
32. Ability of the parents to cooperate with each other
33. Ability of the moving parent to foster the child's relationship with the staying parent
34. The effect on the child of any domestic violence
35. Any false allegations of sex abuse
36. The citizenship status of the parents and the child[60]

Additional factors may also be relevant. For example, the judge may need to ensure the nonmoving parent is fit to have physical residency. If the court denies relocation of the child but the primary caregiver moves anyway, the child may be traumatized from the lack of the contact with that parent. Louisiana does not allow a judge to consider whether a parent seeking relocation will relocate without the child if relocation is not allowed.[61]

In most instances, there is not one determinative factor. For example, an Illinois court denied a move where the father had a significant visitation schedule with the children prior to the relocation, the new distance between residences creating difficulty in transportation on a routine basis, educational opportunities for the children, and the children's close relationships with extended family in the father's location and none in the mother's location.[62]

Starting Point: Good Faith, Legitimate Reason for the Move

Most states, even those with a presumption in favor of a relocating custodial parent,[63] require that the moving parent have a sound, good faith, or legitimate reason for relocation.[64] The move of a child has the potential to fundamentally alter the relationship between the child and nonmoving parent. Examining the reasons for the move may provide insights into the parent's credibility, how well thought out the move is, and the parent's willingness and ability to cooperate with the nonmoving parent if a relocation is allowed. The lawyer's job is to make it apparent to the court that the parent has a good faith reason to relocate; that the parent is offering a reasonable plan for ensuring and continuing the contact with the nonmoving parent (absent abusive situations); and the benefits of the move for the child outweigh the loss of frequent, significant contact with the other parent.

The American Law Institute proposes that the court should allow a parent who has been exercising the clear majority of custodial responsibility to relocate with the child if that parent shows that the relocation is for a valid purpose, in good faith, and to a location that is reasonable in light of the purpose.[65] The ALI Principles, used in a few states, lists the following as valid purposes:

- to be close to family or other sources of support;
- to address significant health problems;

- to protect the safety of the child or another member of child's household;
- to pursue significant employment or educational opportunities for the parent or parent's new partner; or
- to significantly improve the family's quality of life.[66]

The ALI puts the burden on the relocating parent to prove the validity of any other purpose.

The Oklahoma statute defines "good faith" as an honest intention to abstain from taking any unconscientious advantage of another. Personal happiness of the relocating parent cannot be the only factor, because the best interest of the child is more important.[67] Unfortunately, there are no explicit criteria for determining whether a request is made in good faith.[68] There may be stated and unstated reasons for the move. Because a move will reduce the checks and balances that exist in normal parenting, there should be some good reason.

Most courts do not require the parent to show that a move is a "necessity," although sometimes that is influential, as in the case of military transfers. Some courts require that the moving parent demonstrate an objective basis—that is, "more than a pretext" for relocating.[69] In most cases, there are multiple reasons for the move.[70] A mother was unable to get a job in the New York area but was able to find one in North Carolina where her new husband lived. The court found that even though the father was involved in child's activities, the parents had a poor relationship and were unable to communicate and the child had expressed a desire to move. The proposed parenting time for father included extended time in summer and vacations and he could go to North Carolina each month if he wished.[71]

Courts have approved a number of reasons as valid for moving, with most relating to starting a new life, better family support, and improving the overall economic condition of the custodial parent and the child.[72] The important thing is that the move is good for the child, not just the parent.[73] The more clearly the evidence shows a better life for the child in the new location, the more likely the court will find the relocation in the child's best interests.

Employment and Educational Opportunities

Employment opportunities and financial considerations are legitimate reasons to support relocation.[74] The custodial parent's employment opportunities or those of the spouse have been considered legitimate reasons to move with the child.[75] This factor may be most important when the other parent has failed to pay child support,[76] interfered with the relocating parent's work opportunities in the state,[77] or had little participation in the child's life.[78]

If the custodial parent has better career opportunities with higher pay, advancement options, or fewer hours, the court may find a sufficient reason for the move.[79] This is especially true when the parent did not create the circumstances for the new employment—such as when a corporation moves to another state. A court allowed a mother's relocation when her options were to take a promotion in Georgia with additional salary and benefits or be forced to leave the company.[80] Where a mother lacked employment opportunities in the current town, the court looked at testimony that the mother's current position was an "excessive" one that was identified for reduction, and mother's income from new job would be above anything she could get in current location.[81] A New York court allowed a mother's relocation over father's objection where she would earn twice as much, have more time to spend with a child who had been diagnosed with attention deficit disorder, and was willing to maintain the same visitation schedule that was in place and agreed to "creative extended visitation scheduling."[82]

Where there are no available jobs in a parent's field in the state, the court is likely to find the reason legitimate.[83] A parent who is moving to take a new job may be required to show that they, at the very least, applied for a job or seriously looked for one in the area.[84] On the other hand, the parent is not required to apply for every job that might be available in the state if the parent has made a reasonable search in the area.[85] A mother who had finished nursing school was seeking a position with a facility in the Indian healthcare network to help pay off her scholarship. She applied in Nebraska and South Dakota, but the only jobs she was offered were in New Mexico and Alaska. The court found she had a legitimate reason for leaving the state.[86]

If the job is speculative, the court may discount the reason.[87] A mother wanted to move to Boston claiming she believed there were better opportunities for her as an ER nurse, but she did not have a job. She had only looked at three places in her current location and had declined a phone interview with a potential employer to go to lunch with girlfriends.[88] A Florida appellate court reversed a trial judge's decision to let a mother move to Colorado with the two-year-old child partly because there was no substantial competent evidence that she had a greater chance to obtain better employment there or that she had applied or registered in nursing school.[89]

The lawyer for the nonmoving parent may want to show that the relocating parent can achieve the same purpose without moving or by moving to a location that is less disruptive of the other parent's relationship with the child.[90] The court denied a mother's request to relocate, even though she had stable employment out of state with increased salary and job security because the removal of the child from the other parent and extended family would not have increased the child's educational opportunities.[91]

A good faith reason may be to advance one's education.[92] A mother's move to another state to pursue a postdoctoral fellowship at a university in Nashville was a good reason.[93] A mother who was the primary custodial parent was allowed to move from New York to North Carolina where she had been matched to pursue postgraduate medical clinical training that would ensure she could earn a living wage to help support the child.[94] A Washington court allowed a mother of three to relocate to California to retrain as a pathologist after being out of her profession for 16-plus years where there was no training option in the state.[95]

Just because a parent wants to pursue higher education, however, does not mean that the court will allow the child to move.[96] If the educational program will not improve the parent's economic status or there are similar programs in the area, the court may not allow the move.[97]

Remarriage/New Partner

A common reason for relocation is that a parent has remarried or found a new partner. A move to be with a new spouse or for a new spouse's job may be a sufficient good faith reason for relocation.[98] A mother's remarriage to husband who lived out of state and subsequent pregnancy were legitimate reasons to move with the child.[99] A mother's desire to move to Canada to marry a fighter pilot in the Canadian Armed Forces was a reasonable purpose. The man could not get a similar job in the United States.[100] The court found that the mother's reason was valid, and she was allowed to relocate with the child to Mexico to rejoin her recently deported husband.[101] When the moving parent seeks to relocate to live with a new spouse, North Dakota makes that a dominant factor in favor of allowing the move.[102] The lawyer for the moving party may want to ask questions about the new spouse to verify the stability of the new relationship and ensure that there are no domestic violence reports in police or court records.

Most courts have been sympathetic when a primary residential parent wants to move because a new spouse is being transferred or getting a promotion.[103] A Pennsylvania court allowed a mother to relocate to Virginia with her new husband whose income was double that of mother and father combined. The child would benefit from the higher standard of living, and the mother's proposed custody schedule offered father alternating weekends and seven weeks in the summer.[104] A mother who had not worked for 11 years and had two additional children with her new husband was allowed to move the 11-year-old to Georgia because her husband had a new job with an increase in pay and career advancement possibilities.[105] A mother was allowed to move where her fiancé had purchased a home in Arizona. Mother would have more economic security and would benefit emotionally and socially by a fresh start away from extended family. There was no indication she sought to deprive father of reasonable visitation.[106]

An appellate court overturned the trial judge and allowed a mother's relocation to North Carolina, where the move would substantially increase the husband's income so the mother could stay home with the child, provide a supportive extended family, and permit the child to live in a spacious home in a rural setting.[107] In one case, the court found a real advantage existed for mother to move with children to California where she had married a man who was unable to move because of his parenting responsibilities of a disabled daughter. The mother and children would benefit from the increased standard of living.[108]

While most courts consider that the desire to move with a spouse is a good faith reason for the move, these cases are complicated and often create considerable anxiety. The nonmoving parent fears not only loss of the existing relationship with the children but also replacement by another parent figure. If the parent wishes to relocate due to a remarriage, the fact inquiry will include an analysis of the relationship between the new spouse and the child; the relationship between the new spouse and the other parent of the child; and the circumstances surrounding courtship and marriage, that is, was this person seen by the other parent as the "cause" of the breakup of the marriage or is this someone met post-divorce? Another question can be to explore the relationship between the new spouse and the new spouse's children and the new spouse's children and the parent's children.

Just because a move would benefit a parent and new spouse, however, does not mean that the child would benefit.[109] Not every request to move because of a new marriage will be honored.[110] A few states have found the mother's reason to move out of state to have a "fresh start" with her new husband was not enough.[111] An Indiana court found that while mother's reason to relocate with husband was proper, it was not in the child's best interests to live in New Mexico, 1,000 miles away from the father, making it difficult for him to maintain a relationship with the child who was only four.[112]

A North Carolina court denied mother's request to modify the parenting plan so she could take the children to Texas for her new husband's job because it found it unlikely that a "realistic visitation schedule could be arranged which would preserve and foster the children's relationship with the father who attended sporting events, saw the children weekly and provided horseback riding lessons."[113] A mother wanted to move with her military husband and new baby to Cape Canaveral, Florida. She showed that her home life would improve but failed to show that the proposed relocation, three hours away by car from the father and extended family, was in the other three children's best interests. Mother did not know what school the children would attend, had not prepared a post-relocation plan for timesharing, and so on.[114]

While a fiancé may be treated like a new spouse,[115] mere cohabitation may not be treated the same. Mother's desire to continue living with current boyfriend was not a legitimate reason to move the child 20 miles away, even though father's visitation would have remained the same.[116] In Utah, the court found that stability of parent's romantic relationships could affect the best interest of the child. Mother's remarriage was more stable than father's cohabitation.[117] A Louisiana court found that mother's proposed relocation with out-of-wedlock child to Texas was in good faith because her fiancé and her extended family lived there, and she was enrolling in a nurse anesthetist program.[118]

Family Support

Some courts have found a valid reason in the custodial parent's desire to move to an area in closer proximity to relatives.[119] The lawyer needs to demonstrate how the family support system will serve the child's best interests, for example, provide childcare, allow parent and child to live with them, or help with finances or transportation. This can be especially important if the child has frequently visited the family and is familiar with the location.

Family played a large role in the court's supporting a mother's request to move with her child from Massachusetts to Germany. The child would have support from a loving extended family with whom she had frequent and extensive contact since birth, was fluent in German, had already attended German schools, and had kept in touch with her friends in Germany. She would be attending better schools, would again be treated by her long-time pediatrician, and her quality of life would be particularly improved through the impact of the improvement in mother's quality of life in Germany. In Massachusetts, mother could not meet her expenses and lived in poverty.[120]

The court found father's reason to move to be valid. He had graduated from nursing school and secured a good job in Tucson,

Arizona. The child would live near his extended family and some of mother's extended family. Because the mother worked as a contractor, and was often overseas, the father spent more residential time with the daughter and cared for the mother's child from a previous relationship.[121]

A mother sought to move to be closer to family to take care of an ailing parent.[122] In another case, the mother was diagnosed with multiple sclerosis and moved to South Carolina to be near extended family who could help her. She had a good job and was living with grandparents, reducing costs. The appellate court reversed the trial court's changing custody to the father, finding that mother had been primary caretaker throughout the children's lives and the children wanted to move with her.[123]

Many courts look at the presence of extended family both in denying relocation or changing custody if a parent relocates. In a Connecticut case, the mother planned to relocate with her husband and their twin daughters to North Carolina. The father lived in Rhode Island in a city bordering Connecticut. Although the court twice had orally instructed her not to move without permission, the mother moved anyway. The father filed an ex parte emergency motion for modification of mother's sole legal and physical custody to joint legal custody with him having the primary residence. Father received an order for temporary custody, which mother did not appeal. After the hearing, the court granted father primary residency because both sets of grandparents lived near the father; the child had lived in the father's home for eight or nine months at the time of the modification hearing, was familiar with and happy there, and expressed a desire to live with the father.[124]

The presence of relatives made a difference in another case. The Nevada mother earned $19,000 in 1999 as a craps dealer and lived in a 900-square-foot trailer in Nevada. She wanted to move the child to New Jersey where she could earn at least $35,000 working for her sister and brother-in-law's company and live with them in their 3,000-square-foot, four-bedroom house. She planned to rent a home and enroll the child in a school dedicated to gifted and talented students, which was superior to any of the gifted programs in Carson City. She had extended family in New

Jersey, and no relatives in Carson City.[125] The Nevada legislature had removed a specific reference to joint custody in its child relocation statute, so the Nevada modification of custody statute applied.[126]

A Missouri court denied a mother's request to move from Clinton, Missouri, to Urich, Missouri, 15 miles away to live with her new husband and his children. Court found it not in the children's best interests to change schools.[127]

Insufficient Reasons

Courts have found the relocating parent's reasons inadequate when they appear to be in bad faith, disingenuous, or are an attempt to frustrate the nonresidential parent's visitation.[128] A history of post-dissolution litigation or an ongoing acrimonious relationship between the parents may undermine the moving parent's reasons, as the motivating factor may appear to be to put miles between the other parent and child. If the parents have had a poor relationship, the lawyer for the moving parent will want to show the parent has tried to repair the rift either through mediation, joint counseling, therapy, or some other means.

Another red flag for a judge may be if the parent seeking to relocate has already taken steps in furtherance of the move before letting the other parent know about the move or giving required statutory notice. A parent who has already enrolled the child in a new school in the new location, given up a lease, or sold a house in the present location may appear to be trying to move without permission of the other parent or court.

A judge can look at the past conduct of the parties to see if the motive actually is to defeat or deter the other parent's visitation with the child. The mother alleged she had a job opportunity, but the court noted that she had interfered with phone visitation and been held in contempt for failure to communicate. The court found her real motive was to thwart the father's visitation and denied the child's relocation.[129] A Nebraska court found that none of the custodial mother's reasons constituted a legitimate one to leave the state. Although the military base was closing, mother had quit her job earlier and the father was an involved noncustodial parent who regularly exercised visitation.[130]

The court denied a mother's request to relocate out of state where her primary motive was to avoid ongoing interaction with the father and she had no job out of state.[131] In the absence of abuse, the desire of one parent to distance the child from the other parent certainly will not be a sufficient reason.[132] For example, when a mother wanted to move from California to Florida to explore the possibility of a job as a parapsychologist, the court found the reason really to be to thwart the father's visitation.[133] A party's fault during the marriage, however, is not an appropriate consideration in determining whether relocation with a parent is in the child's best interest.[134]

The court could reject the request of a parent who "thinks" that the environment in another location may be better for their health.[135] The court may look as to whether there has been an established pattern of conduct by either party to promote or thwart the relationship of the child and the other party. If parents have never agreed on anything, a judge may be more suspicious when the relocating parent promises to be more agreeable if the relocation is allowed. In a relocation proceeding, the court may consider the custodial parent's interference with the noncustodial parent's visitation when determining the best interests of the child.[136] A Louisiana court denied a military father's relocation with the child where the evaluator noted that the father disregarded the mother's parental role and consistently withheld information about the child. He considered himself the primary parent, took her to California, enrolled her in school, and refused to return her even when ordered by the Louisiana court.[137] In another case, the trial court erred in allowing a mother to move to Florida with the child where she had a history of thwarting father's relationship with child.[138]

In one case, the mother claimed she was experiencing "intolerable conditions" and wanted to move 12.5 miles away. The court denied the move, finding the mother had not tried to move within the area to alleviate the alleged intolerable conditions.[139] On the other hand, getting away from an abusive, manipulative, and controlling parent may be a legitimate reason. In one case, the court allowed the move where the father went into mother's house, checked her messages, and tried to control her.[140] The court can look at the likelihood that allowing or denying the move would antagonize hostilities between the two parties.[141] The fact that a noncustodial parent had a problem with alcohol abuse, an inability to control his anger, and had violated past orders of protection also may be good reason for the move.[142] Sometimes the reasons for the move have not been well thought out or the parent's motives for moving are suspect.[143]

Using the Best-Interest Factors

Once the relocating parent has demonstrated a legitimate reason to relocate, the judge must review the relevant state factors to determine if the relocation is in the child's best interests. Although numerous factors are found in the statutes and cases, no one factor is determinative.[144] If there is a good reason for the move, trial judges seem to concentrate on the child's relationships with both parents, siblings, extended family, and friends and whether the move will enhance the child's quality of life. The courts also look at the reasons one parent opposes the move and the possibilities for alternative visitation to maintain a relationship with the nonmoving parent.[145]

There must be a comprehensive review of all possible factors impacting on a child's best interests.[146] The trial court's factual finding need not be extensive, but must be sufficient to understand which factor influenced the judge and how the factors were weighed against each other.[147] Indeed, the court must at least show use of some of the factors to determine the best interests of the child. A Virginia trial judge was reversed where there was only one brief paragraph regarding the children's best interests in the court's denial of mother's relocation request.[148]

Merely having good reasons for the move does not guarantee, however, that a judge will find the move in the best interest of the children. A Florida appellate court reversed a trial court's temporary order allowing the mother to relocate a three-hour drive away from the father. The mother had remarried a man in the military who was transferred to Cape Canaveral and had a new baby (good reason) but her conclusory statement that the move would be in the best interests of the children had no evidentiary support. Mother offered no evidence on any of the statutory factors. Father established that he was actively involved with the three children, and there was a strong extended family support system in North Florida/South Georgia area.[149]

Child's Relationships with Both Parents and Others

Most courts want to know about the nature, quality, extent of involvement, and duration of the child's relationship with both parents, siblings, and other significant persons in the child's life. This factor allows an analysis of the history of the parents' relationship with the child. If one parent has been the primary caretaker and the other only peripherally involved, the court is likely to grant the relocation request. An Illinois court allowed a primary caretaker mother to move to Arizona with her 11-month-old son where she had more realistic employment opportunities in Arizona and where she could be near family.[150] In a Nebraska case, the court found that the child's strong bond with the mother weighed in favor of allowing her to relocate. While the father had a good relationship with the mother, the relationship between the child and mother was stronger and well established. If the child had to be separated from one parent, he would more easily adapt to not seeing the father regularly than not seeing the mother regularly.[151] In another case, a mother was named the domiciliary parent of a ten-month-old and allowed to move in state where she had been the primary caretaker, and had a flexible work schedule that gave her more time to spend with the child.[152]

A Montana court found allowing the child to relocate with her mother to Nevada was in the child's best interests where mother had been the primary caregiver during the early years; the move would allow the mother to pursue employment in her field of study; and the mother was engaged to marry a man who lived and was employed in Nevada. While the child would be leaving friends, changing schools, and have less parenting time with her father, she was a social child who made friends easily and would be able to maintain a strong relationship with her father, despite the distance.[153]

A Virginia court allowed a primary caregiver mother to relocate to Wisconsin, which would reduce her commute and allow her to have more time with the four- and six-year-old children. The children had visited mother's extended family residing in Wisconsin and had not developed ties to friends and places in Virginia.[154] On the other hand, a mother's requested modification of custody was not in the child's best interests where the child was clearly well-established in her community in Brooklyn, where she had attended school since second grade, had friends and family, and had a stable home life with the father and paternal grandmother.[155]

In an Indiana case, the court allowed the mother to move the children to Texas because father did not establish that relocation was not in the children's best interests. The mother was moving into a specific location where she had strong family ties, was able to purchase a home, had specific plans to teach, and the children had already established friendships in the new neighborhood. Additionally, the children would have ties to both mother and father's families in Texas. Father did not show that there would be any hardship in exercising parenting time and the children's therapist stated that children appeared to accept the move and were looking forward to it. The court noted that having a happier custodial parent should promote their emotional health, and they were young enough to make friends.[156]

A lower court did not err in denying mother's request to relocate to her native Australia. Evidence showed the judge properly weighed the father's former alcohol abuse and the acrimony between the parents with the facts that the children were bonded to the state and that mother's economic standing would improve if she relocated.[157] On the other hand, if there has been ongoing post-dissolution hostility, the lawyer may be able to make a case that removing the child or one parent to another geographic area may reduce the number of opportunities for the child to be in the middle of the parents' constant conflicts.

Siblings and Half Siblings

If the child has a close relationship to siblings who are being allowed to move or who will not move, the court may consider the impact. It may not matter if the siblings were whole or half.[158] While sibling separation should not be encouraged, it may not a sufficiently strong consideration to trump all the other statutory factors. The financial and family considerations favored allowed the mother to relocate to Maine with the three youngest children.[159] While sibling relationships are important, where siblings are not close, separation may actually help relationship.[160]

The Child's Age, Developmental Stage, Needs and Preference

The best-interests-of-the-child statutory custody factor considers the child's developmental needs and the likely impact that relocation would have upon their physical, educational, and emotional development. The authors of an Australian study suggested that the court needs to analyze the closeness and developmental importance of the child's relationship with the nonmoving parent and the viability of proposals for contact between the child and nonmoving parent if the relocation is permitted. If the child's relationship with the nonmoving parent is developmentally important and will be diminished if the move is permitted, the court should examine whether a viable alternative exists to the parents living a long distance from each other and whether the child's move away from a parent is the least detrimental alternative.[161]

The court denied a mother's relocation out of state with child who had been diagnosed with a pervasive development disorder. Stability and routine were paramount to the child's continued development. If the child relocated with the mother, he would go to a new school, have new physicians, and have to make new friends. If the child stayed with the father, he could continue with his private karate instruction, maintain his current friendships, continue to see the same physicians and therapists, and continue with his involvement in programs at the museum and science center.[162] In another case, a father was not allowed to relocate his child from Nebraska to Texas where the child had autism spectrum disorder with disabilities marked by communication problems, stereotypic behavior, and social difficulties. The child was making good progress at the present school. A move would have a negative impact on him and on the mother's ability to have positive visits with him.[163] Research indicates that many children have problems relocating.[164] Courts have changed custody to the parent remaining in the jurisdiction if the reasons for the move and the quality of the new environment do not outweigh the adverse impact.[165] For example, an Indiana court changed custody of an older child who had many relationships that would end if the child were to be relocated to another state.[166]

If a child is adapting well to a new location, that certainly should be a factor for the court to consider. For example, in one case, the 13-year-old daughter had moved with her mother to Indiana. She was getting all A's, was involved in extracurricular activities, and was generally doing well. When the court forced her to return to North Dakota, she lost all interest in activities and her grades plummeted.[167] Parenting plans are discussed in Chapter 13. The child's preferences are discussed in Chapter 14.

Quality of Life for Child as Well as Moving Parent

The lawyer for the relocating parent will want to highlight all of the advantages of the move for the child. Perhaps the most important thing may be the psychological connection the child has with the moving parent if that parent has been the primary nurturer throughout the child's life. The stability of the parent–child relationship may be most important for the child's well-being.

There are other factors to highlight, however, to show improved quality of life in the new location. This means producing evidence, if available, of things like the child may have a room of his or her own for the first time, a bigger house in a nicer neighborhood with less traffic, and better schools and more possibilities for extracurricular activities. If the child is obtaining a religious education, then the lawyer will want to demonstrate the child's ability to continue with the education in the new location. The client may need to commit to continuing the religious training, especially when the parents have different religious affiliations. It may be that the move would benefit a child in a particular activity or sport that could lead to a college scholarship.

If the trial judge allows the move, finding that the child will benefit economically and emotionally, the appellate court generally will uphold the decision.[168] The child's quality of life will be tied to the residential parent's lifestyle. Therefore, the good reasons for the move that usually benefit the child are the parent getting a higher paying job, moving closer to extended family, or marrying someone who will be supporting them so living expenses are considerably reduced.[169] For example, one mother wanted to move with a three-year-old because she was going to remarry, the new location had a lower cost of living than California, she would be able to stay home to care for the child, and she had family there.[170]

A New York trial court properly determined that mother established that her proposed relocation with parties' two children, both of whom had special needs, to Virginia would serve the children's best interests. Mother had been the children's primary caregiver and was responsible for their significant educational and medical needs. By moving to Virginia, mother would have family support, have increased living space, and be in a better position financially to help support her children.[171]

A North Dakota appellate court upheld a trial judge's findings that the prospective advantages of the custodial mother's proposed move with children to Minnesota north-metro area would improve their quality of life and was in children's best interest. The mother would reside in a single-family home with her current husband, saving money and reducing husband's 70-hour week to support living in two households. The benefits to the children included establishing a relationship with the husband, his children, and the mother's extended family. The relocation sites proposed were safe with good schools and amenities for the children.[172]

A Pennsylvania court denied a mother's petition to relocate to California with her new husband because it found there would be no improvement in the child's quality of life. The child, who had Attention Deficit Disorder, had a close relationship with father and stepsiblings. His school had a Wilson Reading Program that helped with his reading skills, but California schools did not have the program. The housing in California would cost $80,000 more; new husband made $56,000 in Pennsylvania and would only make about $55,000 in California. Mother was a realtor but would have to pass the examination in California to be one there.[173]

An Illinois court denied a mother's relocation to Wisconsin. The record showed no meaningful enhancement in circumstances for the children in terms of school or recreational facilities. The children would have their own rooms in either location.[174] In a Florida case, the court found that the evidence was insufficient to support trial court's grant of mother's request for relocation to Louisiana, where there was no evidence presented about Florida's housing market to show she could not find suitable housing and there was no evidence that mother would be employed. There was evidence she would be living next door to her parents who were drug users and not permitted to visit child without a professional present. In addition, there was no evidence that substitute visitation, videocam, telephone contact, and long drives were workable and would foster a continuing relationship with father.[175]

Realistic Opportunity to Preserve the Relationship with the Nonrelocating Party

If both parents have been actively involved in the child's life, this factor can be one of the most important ones.[176] The parties (and court) must explore what alternative custody and residency possibilities exist, as well as the logistics, which include distance, travel time, and financial circumstances. One factor in allowing a move will be the ability to craft a parenting plan that will allow the nonmoving parent to maintain meaningful contact with the children.

If the relocation will not significantly impact the existing parenting arrangements, courts will allow the move.[177] In a Missouri case, the court noted that the mother's move of five miles, even though it required the child to change schools, was motivated by a desire to find a larger and more permanent home that was actually closer to the father's residence. The move would not impact the current visitation schedule.[178]

Where the relationship with the nonrelocating party will not be affected in a major way even though the distance may be great, courts are more willing to allow the move.[179] In one case, the military father had been living in Washington, D.C., and the mother and children in Alabama. The Alabama court allowed the mother and children to move to Arizona, finding the father's travel time to be only slightly longer to Arizona than from D.C. to the current home in Alabama.[180]

All relocations have the potential to result in a some detriment to the relationship between the child and the nonmoving parent. Courts have found that mere disruption or reduced visits alone cannot control or no relocation would ever be allowed.[181] Relocation is not simply a quantitative, but a qualitative, assessment that involves the question of how the facts and circumstances of this relocation will impact the existing parenting time of the parent who is not moving.[182] The real question may be whether substitute visitation arrangements are adequate to foster a continuing meaningful relationship between the child and the nonrelocating parent, not whether the "same degree" of frequent and continuing contact can be maintained.[183] There may also be a question of whether the nonrelocating parent could relocate.[184]

An Indiana court did not allow the children to relocate even though mother's reasons for her proposed relocation to Tennessee (a six-hour drive away) were legitimate and in good faith. The father, however, currently lives one and a half miles from the children and seven and a half miles from their school, picks the children up daily, stays with them until mother gets home, exercises overnight parenting every other weekend, and is active in the two boys' sporting activities. All of father's family lives close and regularly attends sporting events. The children were doing well in school, had friends, and loved both parents. The mother had unilaterally set limits on the father's relationship with the children and the court felt she might be unlikely to be cooperative if she lived in Tennessee.[185]

A North Dakota court allowed a mother and two children to move to neighboring Minnesota with her new husband. The fact a nonmoving parent will not be able to maintain the same parenting time schedule is not, alone, a basis for denying permission to the parent with residential responsibility to leave the state with the child. Distance alone is not sufficient to deny the relocation. The mother's proposed plan allowed father significant time, but not the same amount. Mother had shown flexibility and allowed communication during deployments. Additionally, father had been able to maintain a relationship with a child from a prior relationship with a similar split parenting time.[186]

In some cases, any quality-of-life advantage realized would not necessarily outweigh the disruption in the children's relationship with the nonmoving parent.[187] When a mother with primary residency proposed to relocate to Florida with a new husband, the court found it was not in their best interests where it would disrupt the relationship with their father who frequently picked the children up from school, which was near his home.[188] In another case, the court found that the mother's proposed move to Georgia, over 1,000 miles away, was not in the children's best interests, where father would no longer be able to attend the children's activities without considerable cost and planning, and weekly Wednesday visits would be reduced to phone calls or Internet.[189]

North Dakota courts consider the likelihood that each parent will comply with an alternate visitation schedule.[190] If the moving party cannot convince the judge that there will be an opportunity for meaningful access and parenting time consistent with the existing parenting plan, the court may find the move is not in the best interest of the child.[191]

In one case, a mother's relocation request was denied where she sought to relocate with seven children, ranging from 2 months to 11, to Canada to marry a man she met on the Internet. In addition to finding no reasonable purpose for the mother to move to Canada, the court found that the move would pose a specific and serious harm to the children. Mother testified that father would be able to communicate with the children as often as he wished over the phone, email, and video chatting. As for summer parenting time, mother stated that she would drive their seven children to Tennessee, a 2,700-mile journey that takes four to five days at seven to ten hours per day to complete, each way. Plane tickets cost approximately $1,000 per person; thus, it would not be economically feasible for the children to fly.[192]

The fact that a move of a considerable distance will increase the cost and logistical problems of maintaining contact between the noncustodial parent and the child will not necessarily preclude relocation when other factors militate in favor of it.[193] A couple of courts have worried about the increased costs of access.[194]

The distance can be determinative. More than an hour creates transportation issues and reduces the opportunity to keep relationships going.

Research shows that children suffer the most harm when parents are in chronic high conflict.[195] To the extent that a relocation can reduce the conflict between the parents, the lawyer might be able to make an argument that the relocation will enhance the child's quality of life by removing the child from the day-to-day drama.[196] As a Nevada court noted, if the parents have such high conflict that the parties are better co-parenting from afar, then the best-interest factors of level of conflict and ability to cooperate could be applicable to best interests.[197]

Sometimes it can be in the child's best interests for the parents to live at a greater distance. For example, high-conflict parents actually may be able to parent from a distance better than in regular contact. Indeed, the California *LaMusga* case, in which the father effectively kept the mother from relocating to Ohio or anywhere else for years, was actually resolved once the mother and children obtained permission to move to "Arizona." A psychologist involved in the case said the children and their father had a better relationship once they were at a distance, and the parents were no longer fighting.

Where the custodial parent's reasons for moving are deemed valid and sound, the court in a proper case might consider the possibility and feasibility of a parallel move by an involved and committed noncustodial parent as an alternative to restricting a custodial parent's mobility.[198] Seven states that consider whether the noncustodial parent can relocate are Hawaii, Louisiana, Nebraska, New Jersey, New York, Texas, and Washington.

Importance of Prior Conduct

If the nonrelocating parent does not have much of a relationship with the child, the court may be more willing to allow the move. In a New York case, the father's reasons for the move to South Carolina were that he was no longer able to rent his grandmother's house in New York. He was able to find a job in his field with at least the same salary with lower living expenses, and he and the children would be near extended family. The mother was not involved with the children's lives on a day-to-day basis and only paid $25 in child support. The court allowed the move.[199]

A parent who has chosen not to live close to the children for most of the post-divorce years did not succeed in obtaining a modification to grant him primary custody, when the mother announced her intention to move out of state. Father working in New Jersey asked for divorce and sent mother and children back to Utah. He had voluntarily chosen not to live close to the children for over a year and had declined to move within 15 miles of the mother and children because he remarried. He rented a place near mother's residence only after she planned to move to Washington with her new husband. By the time of trial, the children had lived with mother in Washington for two and a half years and by all accounts were settled and thriving.[200]

Endnotes

1. Stonham v. Widiastuti a/k/a Stonham, 79 P.3d 1188, 1194 (Wyo. 2003).

2. *In re* Marriage of Levites, 185 N.E.3d 263 (Ill. App. Ct. 2021) (denying mother's petition to relocate because she did not meet burden of proving relocation in child's best interests).

3. Linda D. Elrod & Milfred D. Dale, *Paradigm Shifts and Pendulum Swings in Child Custody: The Interests of Children in the Balance*, 42 Fam. L.Q. 381 (2008).

4. *Id.* at 390–403. *See* Utah Code § 81-9-204 (2025).

5. *See* Arulkumar v. Arulkumar, 521 P.3d 131 (Okla. 2022) (trial court is not required to consider each statutory factor in isolation); Vanderhoof v. Armstrong, 383 So. 3d 868 (Fla. Dist. Ct. App. 2024).

6. Merriweather v. Chacon, 639 S.W.3d 494 (Mo. Ct. App. 2021) (judge only needs to make sufficient findings on the factors relevant to the case).

7. Allbright v. Allbright, 215 P.3d 472, 474–76 (Idaho 2009).

8. Lessard v. Johnson, 970 N.W.2d 160 (N.D. 2022)

9. Aragon v. Aragon, 513 S.W.3d 447 (Tenn. 2017); Ianelli v. Camino, 444 P.3d 61 (Wyo. 2019) (noting trial court made no findings on two of the three relocation factors).

10. *In re* Marriage of La Musga, 88 P.3d 81 (Cal. 2004).

11. *In re* Marriage of Burgess, 913 P.2d 473 (Cal. 1996) (mother allowed to move 40 miles away).

12. *See* Hollandsworth v. Knyzewski, 79 S.W.3d 856, 873 (Ark. App. 2002). *In re* Marriage of Abbess, 5165 P.3d 443 (Wash. Ct. App. 2022) (Child Relocation Act governs relocation and presumes relocation should be allowed unless nonresidential parent proves the detrimental effect of relocation outweighs the benefit to the relocating parent.).

13. *In re* Marriage of Abbess, 516 P.3d 443 (Wash. Ct. App. 2022).

14. TENN. CODE ANN. § 36-6-108(d): The parent spending the greater amount of time with the child shall be permitted to relocate with the child unless the court finds: (1) the relocation does not have a reasonable purpose; (2) the relocation would pose a threat of specific and serious harm to the child that outweighs the threat of harm to the child of a change of custody; or (3) the parent's motive for relocating with the child is vindictive in that it is intended to defeat or deter visitation rights of the noncustodial parent.

15. AMERICAN LAW INSTITUTE, PRINCIPLES OF THE LAW OF FAMILY DISSOLUTION: ANALYSIS AND RECOMMENDATIONS § 2.17(1), (4)(a), (c) (2002) [hereinafter ALI PRINCIPLES].

16. Alabama's Parent-Child Relationship Protection Act, ALA. CODE. § 30-3-169.4.

17. *See* Marshall v. Marshall, 346 So. 3d 1008 (Ala. Civ. App. 2021) (mother failed to rebut the presumption that her proposed in-state relocation was not in the children's best interests).

18. Rollie Thompson, *Presumptions, Burdens, and Best Interests in Relocation Law*, 53 FAM. CT. REV. 41 (2015) (discussing proposal by Nicolas Bala & Andrea Wheeler, *Canadian Relocation Cases: Heading Towards Guidelines*, 30 CAN. FAM. L.Q. 1 (2012) and noting it would put too much parental pressure on the child's shoulders).

19. Tropea v. Tropea, 665 N.E.2d 145, 151 (N.Y. 1996).

20. Bodne v. Bodne, 588 S.E.2d 728 (Ga. 2003) (reversing the presumption in favor of allowing custodial parent to move); *In re* Marriage of Ciesluk, 113 P.3d 135, 147 (Colo. 2005) (each parent is on equal footing; a court may not presume either that a child is better off or disadvantaged by relocating with the majority time parent).

21. Markwood v. Markwood, 274 P.3d 1271 (Idaho 2012).

22. *See* Baird v. Baird, 654 S.W.3d 367 (Ark. Ct. App. 2022) (citing Cooper v. Kalkwarf, 532 S.W.3d 58, 67 (Ark. 2017) (the *Hollandsworth* presumption applies only when the parent seeking to relocate is not just labeled the "primary custodian" but also spends significantly more time with the child than the noncustodial parent).

23. *In re* Marriage of Snider and Stroud, 430 P.3d 726 (Wash. Ct. App. 2018) (major modification of parenting plan standard applied).

24. *In re* Marriage of Hauk & Wuesthoff, P.3d, 2025 WL 838208 (Wash. Ct. App. 2025) (Child Relocation Act does not apply when parents share equal time, citing *In re* Marriage of Worthley, 393 P.3d 859 (Wash. Ct. App. 2017).

25. Hull v. Hull, 273 So. 3d 1135 (Fla. Dist. Ct. App. 2019).

26. Bisbing v. Bisbing, 166 A.3d 1155 (N.J. 2017) (discussing the trend toward best interests).

27. Robert George, *Reviewing Relocation*? 24 CHILD & FAM. L.Q. 110 (2012) (English research study showed relocation was less likely to be allowed in shared care for both domestic and international moves.).

28. Hawkes v. Spence, 878 A.2d 273 (Vt. 2005) (using ALI factors—primary caregiver, distance, feasibility of alternate visitation schedule). ALI PRINCIPLES, *supra* note 15.

29. Linda D. Elrod & Milfred D. Dale, *Paradigm Shifts and Pendulum Swings in Child Custody: The Interests of Children in the Balance*, 42 FAM. L.Q. 381 (2008).

30. *See* Cloutier v. Queen, 545 S.E.2d 574, 581, 582–83 (Va. Ct. App. 2001) (the interests to be assessed are solely the child's and do not include the custodial parent's interests).

31. *See* Fleisher v. Fleisher, 56 N.Y.S.3d 406 (App. Div. 2017) (predominant emphasis is on what is most likely to serve the best interests of the child); Harris v. Harris, 379 S.W.3d 8 (Ark. App. 2010) (polestar consideration is the best interest of the child).

32. Vanderhoof v. Armstrong, 383 So. 3d 868 (Fla. Dist. Ct. App. 2024) (reversing temporary order allowing move; no evidence of how six-hour drive from father and other family was in child's best interests); *In re* Marriage of Prusak, 156 N.E.3d 529 (Ill. App. Ct. 2020) (mother failed to show that a move to Indiana five and a half hours away was necessary to improve her and the children's standard of living); Defilippis v. Defilippis, 45 N.Y.S.3d 175 (App. Div. 2017) (mother failed to show that relocating would enhance her and children's lives); *In re* Marriage of Fedorov, 206 P.3d 1124 (Or. Ct. App. 2009) (mother failed to show evidence of benefit of relocation to the child, as opposed to her). *See also* Sanabria v. Sanabria, 271 So. 3d 1101 (Fla. Dist. Ct. App. 2019); Norby v. Hinesley, 946 N.W.2d 494 (N.D. 2020).

33. FLA. STAT. ANN. § 61.13001(8). Other states with the split burden of proof are Alabama, Indiana, Nevada, New Hampshire, Oklahoma, and Pennsylvania. *See* IND. CODE § 31-17-2.2-5(c)(d); OKLA. STAT. § 112.3(K). *See* Nicole L. v. Steven W., 825 S.E.2d 794 (W. Va. 2019) (nonmoving parent can show that that the purpose of the move is achievable without moving or moving to a location that is substantially less disruptive to the opposing parent's ongoing relationship with the child).

34. Cooper v. Chamberlain, 266 So. 3d 316 (La. Ct. App. 2018) (upholding court allowing mother to move to Nashville for postdoctoral fellowship at Vanderbilt University).

35. *See* Chalmers v. Chalmers, 259 So. 3d 878, 879 (Fla. Dist. Ct. App. 2018) (requiring an evaluation of the relocation factors as well as "any other factor" set forth in the general custody factors); A.V. v. S.T., 87 A.3d 818 (Pa. Super. Ct. 2014) (trial court must review not only the ten relocation factors but also the 16 custody factors).

36. COLO. REV. STAT. § 14-10-129; *id.* § 14-10-124. *See In re* Marriage of Ciesluk, 113 P.3d 135 (Colo. 2005).

37. FLA. STAT. § 61.13001(7)(k) incorporates FLA. STAT § 61-13(3)(a)–(t). Hull v. Hull, 273 So. 3d 1135 (Fla. Dist. Ct. App. 2019) (court used all relocation factors and the 20 factors in the general child custody statute).

38. E.C.S. v. M.C.S., 256 A.3d 449 (Pa. Super. Ct. 2021) (remanding for court to interview seven- and six-year-old children as to relocation preference).

39. T.L. v. J.L. 950 N.E.2d 779 (Ind. Ct. App. 2011).

40. Lacour v. Lacour, 231 So. 3d 875 (La. Ct. App. 2017) (denying father's relocation of child from Louisiana to California as not in child's best interests where child was already adjusted and comfortable in military base community, her school, and her church).

41. Mathes v. Faucheuz, 226 So. 3d 503 (La. Ct. App. 2017) (mother's move with child from Louisiana to Texas required court to consider factors in the relocation statute).

42. Rush v. Golkowski, 480 P.3d 1174 (Wyo. 2021) (changing primary custody to father after mother moved from Caspar, Wyoming, to Billings, Montana, five months after the divorce, diminishing father's visitation and attendance at extracurricular activities).

43. *In re* Marriage of Pennamen, 146 P.3d 466 (Wash. Ct. App. 2006) (court did consider parties' agreement with geographical restrictions and properly considered mother's use of methamphetamine as relevant as to why mother lost her job, lost her residence resulting in moves for her and children and failure to get treatment).

44. Wright v. Farris, 563 P.3d 165 (Ariz. Ct. App. 2025).

45. *In re* Paternity of V.D., 226 N.E.2d 816 (Ind. Ct. App. 2024) (denial of relocation was affirmed but reversed for new physical custody determination).

46. Fleisher v. Fleisher, 56 N.Y.S.3d 406 (App. Div. 2017). *See* Chalmers v. Chalmers, 259 So. 3d 878 (Fla. Dist. Ct. App. 2018) (allowing father to relocate with child).

47. Boatman v. Boatman, 404 P.3d 822 (Okla. 2017).

48. Prenaveau v. Prenaveau, 964 N.E.2d 353 (Mass. App. Ct. 2012).

49. Rollie Thompson, *Presumptions, Burdens and Best Interests in Relocation Law*, 53(1) FAM. CT. REV. 40 (2015) (arguing for presumptions, special relocation provisions or use of prior patterns of decisions).

50. *Proposed Model Relocation Act*, 15 J. AM. ACAD. OF MATRIMONIAL L. 1 (1998) [hereinafter AAML Relocation Act].

51. FLA. STAT. § 61.13001(7) (g)–(i).

52. OKLA. STAT. 43 § 112.3 (J).

53. 23 PA. CONSOL. STAT. § 5337(h) (giving weighted consideration to those factors that affect the safety of the child). *See* Allen Bailey, *Prioritizing Child Safety as the Prime Best-Interest Factor*, 47 FAM. L.Q. 35 (2013). *See also* Lynne Hecht Schafran, *Domestic Violence, Developing Brains, and the Lifespan: New Knowledge from Neuroscience*, 53(3) JUDGES' J. 32 (2014); Jeske & Klas, *Adverse Childhood Experiences: Implications for Family Law Practice and the Family Court System*, 50 FAM. L.Q. 123 (2016).

54. Matter of Eddington v. McCabe, 949 N.Y.S.2d 734 (App. Div. 2012); *In re* Marriage of Dorfman, 956 N.E.2d 1040 (Ill. App. Ct. 2011) (mother allowed to relocate to Georgia partly based on father's threatening behavior and improved quality of life for her and the child).

55. *See* Fla. Stat. § 61.130001(7); *see* Conners v. Mullins, 27 So. 3d 199, 200 (Fla. Dist. Ct. App. 2010) (explaining that the statutory factors reveal whether relocation is in the child's best interest).

56. Bartosz v. Jones, 197 P.3d 310, 317 (Idaho 2008).

57. *See* 750 Ill. Comp. Stat. 5/609.2(g) (codifying *In re* Marriage of Eckert, 518 N.E.2d 1041 (Ill. 1988).

58. Estopina v. O'Brian, 68 A.3d 790 (D.C. Ct. App. 2013) (allowing mother to relocate to Virginia Beach where child had close relationship with her family there and mother had employment opportunities; father traveled frequently for his job).

59. Prenaveau v. Prenaveau, 964 N.E.2d 353 (Mass. App. Ct. 2012).

60. W. Dennis Duggan, *Rock-Paper-Scissors: Playing the Odds with the Law of Child Relocation*, 45 Fam. Ct. Rev. 193, 209–10 (2007).

61. La. Rev. Stat. 9:355.12(B).

62. *See In re* Marriage of Adams, 92 N.E.3d 962 (Ill. App. Ct. 2017).

63. Cox v. Cox, 574 S.W.3d 711 (Ark. Ct. App. 2019) (father failed to rebut the presumption in favor of mother's relocation).

64. *See* Schechter v. Schechter, 37 N.E.3d 632 (Mass. App. Ct. 2015); Boyer v. Boyer, 889 N.W.2d 832 (Neb. Ct. App. 2017); Leach v. Santiago, 798 N.Y.S.2d 242, 244 (App. Div. 2005).

65. ALI Principles § 2.17(4)(a). *See* Abbott v. Virusso, 862 N.E.2d 52 (Mass. 2007) (if mother establishes good reason for the move, court then looks at best interest of child); Woodside v. Woodside, 949 N.E.2d 447 (Mass. App. Ct. 2009).

66. *Id.* at § 2.17(4)(a)(ii). *See also* cmt. D.

67. Okla. Stat. 43 § 112.3(K); Mahmoodjanloo v. Mahmoodjanloo, 160 P.3d 951 (Okla. 2007). *See also* Graham v. Graham, 794 A.2d 91 (Pa. Super. Ct. 2002) (denying relocation where mother's desire was called a "momentary whim" to pursue a love interest).

68. Willams v. Cardona-Feliciano, 245 N.E.3d 626 (Ind. Ct. App. 2024) (mother had left Alabama to reside with the father in Indiana; he allegedly was violent and kept her there and she wanted to move back to family).

69. Gold v. Weather, 14 N.E.3d 836, 841–42 (Ind. Ct. App. 2014).

70. Judd v. Burns, 397 P.3d 331 (Alaska 2017) (allowing mother to move for economic reasons, children's education, and increased family stability with new husband); Barblock v. Barblock, 890 A.2d 1005 (N.J. Super. Ct. App. Div. 2006) (allowing mother to relocate to Buffalo where mother's good faith reasons included higher education, long-term job prospects, proximity to extended family, reduced living costs; father never asserted a willingness to take on role of primary caretaker if mother relocated without the children); Scotto v. Alexander, 222 N.Y.S.3d 98 (App. Div. 2024) (among the many reasons, father who had been primary caregiver could no longer rent grandmother's house, mother was only paying $25 in child support and not involved in children's day-to-day lives, and father had opportunity for employment in his field with the same salary but less expensive cost of living in South Carolina).

71. Rebecca HH v. Gerald HH., 12 N.Y.S.3d 666 (App. Div. 2015).

72. Daniels v. Maldonado-Mori, 847 N.W.2d 79 (Neb. 2014) (custodial parent's new spouse's deportation is a legitimate reason for the move); Dawson v. Ojeda, 303 A.3d 569 (R.I. 2023) (mother was primary caregiver of 19-month-old, moving to Rhode Island would be close to her parents who could provide day care at no cost and she would have a better job with fewer hours that would improve child's quality of life); Plica v. Almonte, 222 N.Y.S.3d 620 (App. Div. 2024) (allowing mother to move to Wisconsin where she was primary caregiver, had better understanding of child's medical and educational needs, and move would enhance lives of mother and child economically, emotionally, and educationally).

73. Fohey v. Knickerbocker, 130 S.W.3d 730 (Mo. Ct. App. 2004) (denying mother's relocation in spite of increased salary where no showing of benefit to the child). *See also In re* Marriage of Federov, 206 P.3d 1124 (Or. Ct. App. 2009), *rev. denied*.

74. Scocos v. Scocos, 369 P.3d 1068 (Okla. 2016).

75. State *ex rel.* Ryley G. v. Ryan G., 943 N.W.2d 709 (Neb. 2020).

76. Burmood v. Anderson, 228 N.E.3d 348 (Ill. App. Ct. 2023); Vyhidal v. Vyhidal, 973 N.W.2d 171 (Neb. 2022) (father was $40,000 in arrears in child support and mother was struggling economically so court approved move to Chicago for better job and family support).

77. Hiller v. Hiller, 876 N.W.2d 685 (Neb. Ct. App. 2016) (mother allowed to relocate where father had interfered with her work opportunities in Nebraska).

78. Ulises R. v. Elizabeth H.T., 192 N.Y.S.3d 124 (App. Div. 2023) (court allowed move where mother had been primary caregiver since birth, found a stable job with benefits in another state, and father had never supported child financially).

79. *See* Hass v. Hass, 44 S.W.3d 773 (Ark. App. 2001) (allowing custodial parent to relocate for clerkship with federal judge); Botterbusch v. Botterbusch, 851 So. 2d 903, 905 (Fla. Dist. Ct. App. 2003) (allowing mother to relocate in state where new job offered more money and fewer hours); *In re* S.E.P., 35 S.W.3d 862 (Mo. App. 2001) (allowing move to Florida for promotion where no career potential in Missouri); Keller v. Keller, 584 N.W.2d 509 (N.D. 1998) (allowing move where mother had 14 percent increase in pay with prospect of more); Perrott v. Perrott, 713 A.2d 666 (Pa. Super.1998). *But see* Tremain v. Tremain, 646 N.W.2d 661 (Neb. 2002) (father's job offer of higher paid position not sufficient to justify relocation of children).

80. Boatman v. Boatman, 404 P.3d 822 (Okla. 2017).

81. Lamont v. Lamont, 347 P.3d 645 (Idaho 2015) (allowing relocation).

82. Winn v. Cutting, 835 N.Y.S.2d 467 (App. Div. 2007) (mother was earning $200 a week and $600 working weekends in Pennsylvania; moving to Pennsylvania she could earn $1,200 a week without working weekends).

83. Brett M. v. Amanda M., 445 P.3d 1005 (Alaska 2019) (mother had job offer in Oregon as pediatrician after eight years staying at home; doctors testified no similar jobs were available in Juneau and market was saturated).

84. *See* Levine v. Bacon, 687 A.2d. 1057 (N.J. Super. App. Div. 1997) (denying custodial father's move to Florida with child where he had sold his business with a noncompete clause but had not made a search for a job at the current location; had not cooperated with the mother; and child's relationship with mother and half sibling would be harmed); Baldwin v. Baldwin, 710 A.2d 610 (Pa. Super. 1998) (denying move where mother had not looked for job in the area but was willing to take one in South Carolina for $4,000 less a year).

85. Dickson v. Dickson, 634 N.W.2d 76 (N.D. 2001) (allowing move to California for teaching job that paid more than she could get if she had been able to get a job at any of the places she applied); Boatman v. Boatman, 404 P.3d 822 (Okla. 2017) (allowing mother, who had joint custody but not primary physical residency, to relocate to Georgia for a new job where there was no intent to harm father or deprive him of visitation; father had the burden to show that the proposed relocation was not in the best interest of the child).

86. Dragon v. Dragon, 838 N.W.2d 56 (Neb. Ct. App. 2013).

87. Defilippis v. Defilippis, 45 N.Y.S.3d 175 (App. Div. 2017) (reversing trial court allowing mother to move to East Hampton when it would disrupt father's parenting time).

88. *In re* G.M.N., 433 P.3d 715 (Mont. 2019) (not allowing mother to take child to relocate to Boston).

89. Muller v. Muller, 964 So. 2d 732 (Fla. Dist. Ct. App. 2007) (parties had moved to Miami, Florida, on one-year trial, but wife found out she was pregnant; dissolution proceedings started after birth of child—dissent would have allowed move since mother's support network there and father could get a job).

90. ALI Principles, supra note 15, at § 2.17 (4)(a)(iii).

91. Ness v. Martinez, 249 So. 3d 754 (Fla. Dist. Ct. App. 2018).

92. Geiger v. Yaeger, 846 A.2d 691 (Pa. Super. Ct. 2004) (allowing mother to relocate to North Carolina where the move offered her increased educational opportunities).

93. Cooper v. Chamberlain, 266 So. 3d 316 (La. Ct. App. 2018) (mother was more involved in child's education while father did not attend school activities and had a history of substance abuse). *See also* Veselsky v. Veselsky, 113 P.3d 629 (Alaska 2005) (mother allowed to move to pursue a graduate degree not available in the state); Shafer v. Shafer, 898 So. 2d 1053 (Fla. Dist. Ct. App. 2005) (mother's relocation to attend law school allowed where no law school closer).

94. Sonbuchner v. Sonbuchner, 947 N.Y.S.2d 80 (App. Div. 2012).

95. *In re* Marriage of Kim, 317 P.3d 555 (Wash. Ct. App. 2014) (mother was primary caretaker, attending to all the children's physical and emotional needs and day to day affairs and they had a stronger attachment with her while father worked many hours and was estranged from one child).

96. Potter v. Branson, 877 A.2d 52 (Del. 2005) (denying mother's request to move in state from Dagsboro to Newark, Delaware, to attend the

University of Delaware); Ex Parte Roberts, 796 So. 2d 349 (Ala. 2001) (modifying custody to father when mother wanted to move daughter for college).

97. Flynn v. Flynn, 92 P.3d 1224 (Nev. 2004) (denying mother's relocation to California to enroll in a two-year associate's degree program in theology when degree would not enhance earning ability and educational opportunities existed in area).

98. *See* Rosenthal v. Maney, 745 N.E.2d 350 (Mass. App. 2001) (allowing mother to relocate to Rhode Island to be with new husband); State *ex rel.* Ryley G. v. Ryan G. 943 N.W.2d 709 (Neb. 2020) (allowing mother to move to D.C. for new spouse's job); Caudill v. Foley, 21 S.W.3d 203 (Tenn. Ct. App. 1999) (allowing mother to relocate to Florida after marriage to a man who owned business there).

99. Boyer v. Boyer, 889 N.W.2d 832 (Neb. App. 2017) (mother did not show how relocating to Alaska would enhance her income; housing conditions favored removal; bond with mother favored removal; strength of child's ties to present community and extended family did not weigh in favor or against removal; impact on father's visitation time weighed against removal; evidence was sufficient to support conclusion it was in BIOC to stay in mother's care and move).

100. Webster v. Webster, S.W.3d (Tenn. Ct. App. 2007).

101. Daniels v. Maldonado-Morin, 847 N.W.2d 70 (Neb. 2014).

102. Nelson v. Nelson, 3 N.W.3d 133 (N.D. 2024).

103. *See* Reed v. Reed, 379 P.3d 1042 (Idaho 2016) (allowing move where husband's new job allowed mother to stay home with children who had lived with her for ten years); McLaughlin v. McLaughlin, 647 N.W.2d 577 (Neb. 2002) (allowing mother to move because of new husband's acceptance of out-of-state job).

104. Hogrelius v. Martin, 950 A.2d 345 (Pa. Super. Ct. 2008).

105. Dye v. Fowler, 2007 WL 1515140 (Tenn. Ct. App.) (reversing trial court and finding that it was a good reason for the primary residential parent to seek to relocate the 11-year-old daughter; father had previously agreed to mother and child's move to Owensboro, Kentucky, for her husband's job).

106. Abbott v. Virusso, 862 N.E.2d 52 (Mass. App. Ct. 2007).

107. Smith v. Hoover, 805 N.Y.S.2d 715 (App. Div. 2005).

108. Murray v. Super, 26 N.E.3d 1116 (Mass. App. Ct. 2015).

109. *See* Redman v. Redman, 960 So. 2d 52, 61 (Fla. 2007) (mom would have 3,000 square foot house rather than apartment but schools were comparable; children involved with activities, shared passion for bowling with father and were near father's family; no one but mom and stepdad in Texas); Colling v. Colling, 818 N.W.2d 637 (Neb. Ct. App. 2012) (mother's marriage and desire to live with new spouse was a legitimate reason to want to move to Georgia with children ages 12, 10, and 8, she did not have a job there, was giving up a $51,000 a year job, and new husband earned less than $40,000).

110. *See In re* Marriage of Sale, 808 N.E.2d 1125, 1129 (Ill. App. 2004) (not allowing move because custodial parent did not show how the child's best interests would be served).

111. *See* Paul v. Pagnillo, 786 N.Y.S.2d 662 (App. Div. 2004) (denying mother's request to move to Mississippi where her new husband lived because she did not have any firm job prospects there, had not planned for child's educational needs, and move would deprive child of frequent and regular contact with father); Jones v. Tarnawa, 809 N.Y.S.2d 742 (App. Div. 2006) (affirming denial of move as not in child's best interest).

112. *In re* Paternity of B.R.H., N.E.3d (Ind. Ct. App. 2021).

113. Morrill v. Morrill, 2006 WL 278925 (N.C. Ct. App. 2006).

114. Vanderhoof v. Armstrong, 383 So. 3d 868 (Fla. Dist. Ct. App. 2024).

115. *In re* Marriage of Collingbourne, 791 N.E.2d 532 (Ill. 2003) (allowing mother to relocate to Massachusetts with fiancé where she would work fewer hours and not pay rent).

116. Curtis v. Curtis, 759 N.W.2d 269 (Neb. Ct. App. 2008).

117. Robertson v. Robertson, 370 P.3d 569 (Utah Ct. App. 2016) (allowing mother to relocate with children to Colorado finding greater risk to the children from not living with the mother than the risk associated with the relocation).

118. State *ex rel.* Dep't of Soc. Servs. v. Whittington, 193 So. 3d 1234 (La. Ct. App. 2016) (mother allowed to move with ten-year-old to Texas where starting pay as nurse would be higher).

119. *See* Reel v. Harrison, 60 P.3d 480 (Nev. 2002) (allowing mother to relocate to New Jersey to be near family where she had none in Nevada); Aziz v. Aziz, 779 N.Y.S.2d 539 (App. Div. 2004).

120. Miller v. Miller, 88 N.E.3d 843 (Mass. Sup. Jud. Ct. 2018).

121. Aragon v. Aragon, 513 S.W.3d 447 (Tenn. 2017) (mother put on no evidence showing that father's purpose was not reasonable).

122. Weickert v. Weickert, 602 S.E.2d 337 (Ga. Ct. App. 2004).

123. Masiello v. Milano, 118 N.Y.S. 3d 739 (App. Div. 2020).

124. Brennan v. Brennan, 857 A.2d 927 (Conn. Ct. App. 2004), *app. denied*.

125. Reel v. Harrison, 60 P.3d 480 (Nev. 2002).

126. Nev. Rev. Stat. 125C.200. *See* Potter v. Potter, 119 P.3d 1246, 1248, 1250 (Nev. 2005) (the issue is whether it is in the best interest of the child to live with Parent A in a different state or Parent B in Nevada).

127. Mantonya v. Mantonya, 311 S.W.3d 392 (Mo. Ct. App. 2010).

128. Ovide v. Rivers, 398 So. 3d 1184 (La. Ct. App. 2024) (denying mother's relocation where she had not allowed father to communicate with the child after she relocated six hours away). Murray v. Murray, 318 S.W.3d 149 (Mo. Ct. App. 2010) (allowing mother to move with child where no attempt to deprive nonrelocating parent of contact).

129. Colston v. Williams, 556 S.W.3d 548 (Ark. Ct. App. 2018) (no other family members lived in new location, and guardian ad litem recommended against it). *See also* Green v. Swiers, 920 N.W.2d 471 (N.D. 2018) (mother's motive was to defeat or deter father's visitation with the child).

130. Wild v. Wild, 737 N.W.2d 882 (Neb. App. 2007).

131. *See In re* Martin, 8 A.3d 60 (N.H. 2010) (mother's major purpose was to avoid ongoing interaction with the father so not a legitimate purpose for

relocating, noting she was employed in state and had no prospects out of state).

132. *See* Bodne v. Bodne, 588 S.E.2d 728 (Ga. 2003) (changing custody to mother where physician father's main motive was to distance himself from his predivorce life).

133. Cassady v. Signorelli, 56 Cal. Rptr. 2d 545 (App. 1996).

134. Tuel v. Tuel, 840 S.E.2d 917 (N.C. Ct. App. 2020).

135. *See* Delgado v. Nazario, 677 N.Y.S.2d 336 (App. Div. 1998).

136. Colston v. Williams, 556 S.W.3d 548 (Ark. Ct. App. 2018) (denying the move where mother interfered with telephone visitation, had previously been held in contempt for failure to communicate, and no other family members lived near place of relocation, among other things). *See also* Ganaway v. Ganaway, 238 So. 3d 540 (La. Ct. App. 2018) (denying mother's relocation with children to Texas where parties had litigated continuously since divorce, neither mother nor new husband had a job lined up and mother and her family had coached children to reject father).

137. Lacour v. Lacour, 231 So. 3d 875 (La. Ct. App. 2017) (denying father's relocation of child from Louisiana to California as not in child's best interests where child was already adjusted and comfortable in military base community, her school, and her church).

138. D.K.D. v. A.L.C., 141 A.3d 566 (Pa. Super. Ct. 2016) (finding mother's job search in state was primarily symbolic and her primary concern was a desire to return to her native state; her concern for child's development condition and his need for stability was secondary).

139. Schwartz v. Schwartz, 132 N.Y.S.3d 34 (App. Div. 2020) (parties' agreement had specified mother would live in Scarsdale where father lived until youngest reached 18 unless intolerable conditions).

140. Tibor v. Tibor, 598 N.W.2d 480 (N.D. 1999) (allowing mother to move where father's conduct showed his desire to control and manipulate her; he entered house to check messages and rummage through her trash).

141. Jack v. Clinton, 609 N.W.2d 328 (Neb. 2000).

142. Smith v. Hoover, 805 N.Y.S.2d 715 (App. Div. 2005) (finding parents' tumultuous relationship had endangered mother).

143. For cases where the reasons for the move were found to be inadequate, *see* Cassady v. Signorelli, 56 Cal. Rptr. 2d 545 (Cal. Ct. App. 1996); Levine v. Bacon, 687 A.2d. 1057 (N.J. Super. Ct. App. Div. 1997); Voit v. Voit, 721 A.2d 317 (N.J. Super. Ct. Ch. Div. 1999); *In re* Marriage of Krivi, 670 N.E.2d 1162 (Ill. App. Ct. 1996); *In re* Marriage of Lange, 717 N.E.2d 507 (Ill. App. Ct. 1999).

144. Schultz v. Schultz, 187 P.3d 1234, 1238 (Idaho 2008) (abuse of discretion for court to only consider one factor—the distance between father and child when mother move to Oregon); *In re* Marriage of Kavchak, 107 N.E.3d 287 (Ill. App. Ct. 2018); Lessard v. Johnson, 970 N.W.2d 160 N.D. 2022) (no one factor determinative and allowing mother to relocate to Nebraska).

145. Armstrong v. Draper, 624 S.W.3d 345 (Ark. Ct. App. 2021) (testimony showed no reasonable prospect for meaningful visitation with the father if

she moved to Colorado which would be harmful to the child; in the past, mother had denied father holiday visitation).

146. *In re* LaMusga, 88 P.3d 81, 94 (Cal. 2004).

147. Brett M. v. Amanda M., 445 P.3d 1005 (Alaska 2019) (granting pediatrician mother custody and allowing her to move with children to Oregon).

148. Stacey J. v. Henry A., 842 S.E.2d 703 (W. Va. Ct. App. 2020).

149. Vanderhoof v. Armstrong, 383 So. 3d 868 (Fla. Dist. Ct. App. 2024).

150. *In re* Marriage of Guthrie, 915 N.E.2d 43 (Ill. App. Ct. 2009).

151. Boyer v. Boyer, 889 N.W.2d 832 (Neb. Ct. App. 2017).

152. Murray v. Murray, 398 So. 3d 688 (La. Ct. App. 2024).

153. *In re* S.E.L., 354 P.3d 1237 (Mont. 2015).

154. Judd v. Judd, 563 S.E.2d 913 (Va. Ct. App. 2009).

155. Newton v. McFarlane, 103 N.Y.S.3d 445 (App. Div. 2019).

156. Rogers v. Rogers, 876 N.E.2d 1121 (Ind. Ct. App. 2007), *transfer denied* 891 N.E.2d 37.

157. Ainsworth v. Ainsworth, 186 A.3d 1074 (R.I. 2018) (judge did not overlook or misconceive evidence).

158. Rego v. Rego, 259 P.3d 447 (Alaska 2011) (awarding custody of five-year-old to the mother if father moved to New Jersey partly because of his close relationship with three older half-sisters).

159. Emrich v. Emrich, 15 A.3d 1104 (Conn. Ct. App. 2011).

160. Abbott v. Virusso, 862 N.E.2d 52 (Mass. App. Ct. 2007) (testimony of GAL relationship between brother and sister might improve or be beneficial); Emrich v. Emrich, 15 A.3d 1104 (Conn. Ct. App. 2011) (trial court did not err in crediting and relying to a degree on testimony of children's guardian ad litem regarding whether to permit mother and children to relocate).

161. Patrick Parkinson & Judith Cashmore, *Reforming Relocation Law: An Evidence Based Approach*, 53 Fam. Ct. Rev. 23, 34 (2015).

162. D.K.D. v. A.L.C., 141 A.3d 566 (Pa. Super. Ct. 2016) (trial court erred in granting mother's relocation with child to Florida).

163. Steffy v. Steffy, 843 N.W.2d 655 (Neb. 2014).

164. Roger T. Webb, Carsten B. Pedersen & Pearl L.H. Mok, *Adverse Outcomes to Early Middle Age Linked with Childhood Residential Mobility*, Am. J. of Preventive Med. (2016).

165. Dale v. Pearson, 555 N.W.2d 243 (Iowa App. 1996) (changing custody to father where mother did not have good reason and father was good influence). *See also In re* Marriage of Tade, 938 P.2d 673 (Mont. 1997) (awarding primary custody to father when mother relocated to attend college).

166. Hanks v. Arnold, 674 N.E.2d 1005 (Ind. App. 1996).

167. Keller v. Keller, 584 N.W.2d 509 (N.D. 1998).

168. Alicea v. Fernandez, 102 N.Y.S.3d 639 (App. Div. 2019) (allowing mother to move with child to Florida). *But see* Follini v. Currie, 113 N.Y.S.3d 260 (App. Div. 2019) (finding mother's move to Florida was not in the children's best interests economically or educationally, ordering her to enroll children in school in New York, and changing custody to joint legal).

169. Judd v. Burns, 397 P.3d 331 (Alaska 2017) (allowed mother to move for economic reasons, children's education, and increased family stability with new husband); State *ex rel.* Dep't Soc. Servs. v. Whittington, 193 So. 3d 1234 (La. Ct. App. 2016) (allowed move where mother had extended family, enrolled in nurse anesthetist program, and her fiancé live there).

170. Hales v. Edlund, 78 Cal. Rptr. 2d 671 (App. 1998) (allowing move and increasing the length of visitation but decreasing the frequency where father had never played more than a minimal role in the child's day-to-day care). *See also In re* Marriage of Collingbourne, 791 N.E.2d 532 (Ill. 2003) (allowing mother to relocate to Massachusetts with fiancé where she would work fewer hours and not pay rent); Rosenthal v. Maney, 745 N.E.2d 350 (Mass. App. 2001) (allowing mother to relocate to Rhode Island with new husband); Caudill v. Foley, 21 S.W.3d 203 (Tenn. Ct. App. 1999) (allowing mother to relocate to Florida after marriage).

171. Morelli v. Morelli, 226 N.Y.S.3d 559 (App. Div. 2025). *See also* Taylor v. Taylor, 990 A.2d 882 (Conn. Ct. App. 2010) (allowing mother to move with nine-year-old son to New York for job and family support where father had engaged in seven years of litigation that resulted in the child needing therapy due to the constant conflict).

172. Nelson v. Nelson, 3 N.W.3d 133 (N.D. 2024).

173. Ketterer v. Seifert, 902 A.2d 533 (Pa. Super. Ct. 2006).

174. *In re* Marriage of Matchen, 866 N.E.2d 683 (Ill. App. Ct. 2007).

175. Cecemski v. Cecemski, 954 So. 2d 1227 (Fla. Dist. Ct. App. 2007).

176. *In re* LaMusga, 88 P.3d 81, 94 (Cal. 2004).

177. Fleisher v. Fleisher, 56 N.Y.S.3d 406 (App. Div. 2017) (allowing mother to move from Monroe County to Orleans County where the relocation will not negatively impact father's visitation time and his reasons for opposing the move were unfounded and arbitrary).

178. Merriweather v. Chacon, 639 S.W.3d 494 (Mo. Ct. App. 2021).

179. *In re* Marriage of Williams, 220 S.W.3d 858 (Mo. App. 2007) (allowing mother to relocate with child to Kansas City 55 miles away was in best interest of child; mother encouraged father and his family to visit even though father did not pay any court ordered child support and move would not reduce father's visitation).

180. Bates v. Bates, 103 So. 3d 836 (Ala. Civ. App. 2012).

181. Cartledge v. Evans, 855 N.E.2d 429 (Mass. App. Ct. 2006).

182. Pennington v. Marcum, 266 S.W.3d 758 (Ky. 2008).

183. *In re* B.T.G., 993 So. 2d 1140, 1143 (Fla. Dist. Ct. App. 2008).

184. Quainoo v. Quainoo, 87 So. 3d 364 (La. Ct. App. 2012) (trial court erred in not allowing mother to move with children to Georgia for job with increased salary and advancement opportunities; court erroneously focused on the father's opposition, which was based on fear of losing his social contacts and unreasonable unwillingness to relocate).

185. T.L. v. J.L., 950 N.E.2d 779 (Ind. Ct. App. 2011), *rev. denied* (mother's parents and grandmother lived in Tennessee, she could provide help for her

ill grandmother, live rent-free in a house, and have the opportunity for a new career with an education paid for by her family).

186. Nelson v. Nelson, 3 N.W.3d 133 (N.D. 2024).

187. Matter of Angel D. v. Nieza S., 16 N.Y.S.3d 724 (App. Div. 2015).

188. Yamilly M.S. v. Ricardo A.S., 26 N.Y.S.3d 278 (App. Div. 2016) (even though mother's new husband had bigger house in Florida, liberal visitation would not be enough to maintain quality and amount of father's relationship where he exercised visitation, frequently picked up children from school).

189. Colling v. Colling, 818 N.W.2d 63 (Neb. Ct. App. 2012).

190. Stout v. Stout, 560 N.W.2d 903 (N.D. 1997).

191. Norby v. Hinesley, 946 N.W.2d 494 (N.D. 2020) (evidence showed that relocation to Missouri would defeat or deter father's visitation and have a negative impact on his relationship with the child); Newell v. Rammage, 7 S.W.3d 517, 523–24 (Mo. Ct. App. 1999) (difficulty involved in traveling, such as expenses, child fatigue, or inability of the child to travel alone, and the difficulty in maintaining the same level of activity involvement enjoyed by both parents).

192. Carman v. Carman, 2012 WL 1048600 (Tenn. Ct. App. Mar. 26, 2012) (unpublished).

193. Speck v. Spadafore, 895 A.2d 606, 610 (Pa. Super. Ct. 2006).

194. Fla. Stat. § 61.10003 (considering cost of travel); Kan. Stat. Ann. § 23-2222(c) (requiring consideration of the effect of the move on the best interests of the child and on any party having rights and the increased cost the move will impose on any party seeking to exercise those rights).

195. *See High Conflict Custody Cases: Reforming the System for Children—Conference Report and Action Plan*, 34 Fam. L.Q. 589 (2001); Linda D. Elrod, *Reforming the System to Protect Children in High Conflict Custody Cases*, 28 Wm. Mitchell L. Rev. 495, 515 (2001).

196. Taylor v. Taylor, 990 A.2d 882 (Conn. Ct. App. 2010) (allowing mother to move with nine-year-old son to New York, partly because father had engaged in seven years of litigation and the conflict distressed the child).

197. Monahan v. Hogan, 507 P.3d 588, 595 (Nev. Ct. App. 2022). *See also* Pasternak v. Pasternak, 467 S.W.3d 264, 272 (Mo. 2015) (greater physical distance would reduce stress for children).

198. *See* Merle H. Weiner, *Inertia and Inequality: Reconceptualizing Disputes over Parental Relocation*, 40 U.C. Davis L. Rev. 1747, 1783 (2007) (arguing that failure to consider noncustodial parent's ability to move rests on old notions of women following husbands—to not consider today, gendered expectations of accommodation, perpetuates stereotypes, and sustains different degrees of mobility for custodial and noncustodial parents).

199. Scotto v. Alexander, 222 N.Y.S.3d 98 (App. Div. 2024).

200. Lobendahn v. Lobendahn, 540 P.3d 727 (Utah Ct. App. 2023) (bonding and continuity factors favored allowing primary caregiver mother and children to remain in Washington state).

CHAPTER 10

ADR and Relocation Cases

[A]lternative dispute resolution has become a substantial part of the civil justice system.[1]

Relocation cases are high-conflict cases; emotions run high and judicial outcomes are unpredictable. Judges' views of the best interest of the child are even more unpredictable in relocation and modification cases than the initial custody order. Trials, besides the enormous costs involved, can escalate hostilities, make compromises unlikely, drag on for months or years, and potentially harm the children's relationships with one or both parents. If the parents are in high conflict, the children may suffer long-term consequences of conflict and may be angry at their parents, themselves, and others.[2] Children adjust better if their parents can work together to develop a parenting plan, as well as healthy ways of communicating and resolving problems. The more amicably and quickly the parties can resolve their conflicts, the better for the children.

Alternative dispute resolution (ADR), rather than litigation, may be the better way to help parties resolve their case, or at least some of their issues.[3] ADR allows the parties to retain agency and stability by either making the decisions themselves or selecting the person who is making the decision. Mediation, conciliation, and parent coordination involve the parties directly in the decision-making process with a third-party neutral. Collaborative law uses direct participation between the parties and lawyers in open discovery and four-way meetings.[4] Arbitration and private judging involve a third-party decision-maker the parties choose to resolve their dispute.[5] Most ADR processes are confidential, result in lower costs to the parties, are tailored to the parties' schedules, and are faster than traditional litigation. Perhaps most importantly, the parties know their child, their child's schedules, and more details about their child's and family's needs than usually come out in litigation. To the extent that the parties maintain control of the process, there is more self-determination, less formality, and more privacy.

When the client comes for the first interview (Chapter 2), the lawyer can advise the client about the options available in the jurisdiction. In fact, the ethical rules indicate that lawyers should consult with the client about ADR options.[6] Some states require it.[7] The American Academy of Matrimonial Lawyers' Bounds of Advocacy Rule 1.4 indicates that a lawyer should be knowledgeable about different ways to resolve marital disputes. Clients have the best chance for ADR to succeed if the lawyer participates on behalf of their client.[8] ADR may be particularly well-suited for some relocation cases, but compromises are often difficult because the core issue is one parent trying to move the child some distance from the other parent. The parent hoping to move highlights the advantages while the parent staying in the existing location sees all the disadvantages. Which ADR option fits the relocation conflict depends on numerous factors: statute and case law, the nature of the conflict (relocation), safety issues for the parties, need for speedy resolution, privacy concerns, costs concerns, the need for closure, and the competency of the parties.

A lawyer may be involved in the mediation process in a number of roles:

- The neutral mediator who represents neither party and helps the parties reach agreement
- The lawyer who is representing one of the parties who is in the mediation process
- The lawyer who is appointed to represent the child whose parents are in mediation
- A consultant who is asked to review a mediated agreement for one of the parties

Mediation

Mediation, the most popular and commonly used means of settling cases, other than negotiation, offers the best hope for an amicable, or at least workable, parenting agreement in a relocation case.[9] The confidential process uses the skills of a neutral third party, with no decision-making authority, to help the parties define the issues, communicate more effectively, and brainstorm possible creative solutions that may work for the particular family. Mediation offers the possibility of lower cost, faster time, increased party participation, simplified procedures, and expanded options. Early mediation of relocation can serve many interests of the parties, and especially their children. The Texas Supreme Court has noted that encouragement of mediation as a form of alternative dispute resolution is of critical importance to the emotional and psychological well-being of children involved in high-conflict custody cases.[10]

Ideally, before entering mediation, each party will have consulted with a lawyer to determine what their options and rights would be without an agreement. The ABA *Model Standards of Practice for Family and Divorce Mediation* Overview and Definitions and Standard III provide that mediation is not a substitute for the need for parents to obtain independent legal advice. The 2025 Association for Family and Conciliation Courts (AFCC) draft Family Mediation Standards indicates the mediator should allow time for the parties to consult with appropriate experts and supports persons, including lawyers.

The mediator, even if a lawyer, does not provide legal advice to the parties. Mediation can resolve issues more fairly, completely, and quickly when each party understands their legal rights.[11] If the client chooses, or is ordered, to mediate, the lawyer can guide the client by helping the client determine goals, prepare for the mediation, advise during the mediation process, draft and review the agreements, and finalize the parenting agreement by incorporating the agreement into the judgment.

Mediation works the best for parties who voluntarily chose to mediate because they are usually willing and able to settle;

80 percent reach agreement on all or some of the issues. Court-ordered mediation that is imposed on the parties does not always work as well. Some lawyers call it "hoop" mediation—the parties have to jump through the hoop of going to mediation before going to court. The Maine Supreme Court found that a decree provision mandating parties mediate disputes about parental rights before either could initiate a court action "materially frustrated" a party's right to free and timely access to the courts. The mandate caused a prefiling delay that may impact the best interests of children.[12] On the other hand, the Missouri Court of Appeals found that mandatory mediation did not violate the constitution because either spouse could terminate it and proceed to court. Mediation only delayed court consideration.[13] The Indiana Supreme Court rejected a father's challenge to court-mandated mediation, finding that it was an appropriate procedure and compared it to rules governing discovery and other pretrial procedures. The court found the requirement did not prevent either party from obtaining a judicial resolution of a case or obstruct a party's access to the courts.[14] Theoretically, the party that was compelled to appear could sit down and decline to speak and have fulfilled the mandate to appear. Some states, however, authorize the court to consider bad faith participation in mediation as a custody factor.[15]

All states have either statutes or court rules regulating mediation, and there are numerous books and publications available.[16] In 2001, the American Bar Association (ABA) House of Delegates approved Model Standards of Practice for Family and Divorce Mediation with 13 general principles to guide family law mediators. In March 2025, the AFCC, in collaboration with the ABA Family Law and Dispute Law sections, the Academy of Professional Family Mediators, and the Association for Conflict Resolution sent out a draft of revised standards for comment. These standards reflect current needs and concerns such as more attention to domestic violence, use of technology, and online dispute resolution (ODR). The proposed standards are for the neutral mediator and have 14 headings:

1. Self-Determination
2. Informed Decision-Making
3. Education of Parties
4. Barriers to Participation and Process Modification
5. Domestic Abuse
6. Child Maltreatment
7. Impartiality and Conflict of Interest
8. Confidentiality
9. Technology
10. Child-Centered Process
11. Termination
12. Training and Professional Competence
13. Mediation Fees, Compensation, and Timing
14. Advertisement, Solicitation, and Marketing

Basic Mediation Process

Mediation is a form of negotiation that uses a neutral third party who facilitates communication between the parties but has no power to impose a settlement. Mediation can be facilitative, where the mediator helps parties communicate, brainstorm ideas, and relays proposals. Mediation can be evaluative, where the mediator offers options and suggest solutions. Most custody and relocation cases use a facilitative mediator who helps the parties communicate in order to better understand each other's perspectives and work toward mutually acceptable solutions.

Before the mediation begins, the mediator should provide the parties with an overview of the mediation process, discuss the format, the obligations of the mediator, confidentiality, and the need for independent legal advice. Prior to the first session, the mediator may want to meet individually with each party to examine the parties' ability to make informed decisions and determine if the process will be appropriate and safe. The mediator should screen for domestic violence. If there has been domestic violence, the mediator can assess what types of safeguards, if any, could protect the victim and address any power imbalances, or whether the parties should choose another process. If the mediation can proceed, the mediator should have the parties sign a written agreement to mediate.

The mediator attempts to set a positive tone to create an atmosphere conducive for discussion of the options for parenting arrangements if one of the parties relocates. The 2025 mediation Standard X Child-Centered Process makes it clear that the mediator should help the parties create an age-appropriate parenting plan, addressing the time-sharing schedule with appropriate detail and parental decision-making responsibilities.

The mediator tries to keep the conversation going and focused on the major issues. A family mediator is aware that the emotions the parties are feeling can pose an obstacle to settlement. The mediator may ask each party to describe the issues as they see them. The mediator tries to probe for underlying interests and unspoken issues and to prevent the parties from competitive posturing. While a position is a party's want or demand, the party's interest is why the party is taking the position. A position may be "I want 182.5 days of physical custody." The interest may be the fear of losing their relationship with the child. If the question becomes how best to maintain a strong relationship with the child, there are more options than just 182.5 days. The parents can explore options, assess their merit, and negotiate to accept one or more. If the underlying interest is to pay less child support, there may be ways of arranging transportation costs or other expenses, such as extracurricular activities and uniforms, that may meet the need. By keeping the parties focused on the child, the mediator can try to minimize the harmful effects of the parental conflict. The mediator will help the parties draft a parenting plan that takes into consideration the child's needs. The 2025 proposed Standard X, C & D specifically mentions the possibility of including the child and/or the child's representative in the mediation process with permission of the parents and child's representative if the child's input would be appropriate or helpful.

At the end of each session that results in tentative points of agreement, the mediator drafts a memorandum of understanding that identifies the points of agreement and provides it to the parties for review. When the mediation concludes, the mediator sends the parties the completed terms of the agreement. The parties can consult with their attorneys if they wish. Once the parties execute the agreement, it is submitted to the court as a binding order or for incorporation into the decree.[17] If the parties cannot agree, the parties can litigate or choose some other form of dispute resolution such as arbitration. Because the mediation is confidential, the mediator cannot be called in a trial to testify as to what was discussed in mediation.[18]

Lawyer's Checklist for Client's Mediation[19]

Before Mediation

Before the client commits to mediation, the lawyer needs to determine if the case is appropriate for mediation and if the timing is right. For example, parties go through various emotional stages of separating from their partner. A person who is extremely angry or sad may not be able to make rational decisions without help. The lawyer needs to help the client select the right mediator for the case and prepare the client for the mediation process. There are numerous decisions at each stage.

Decide If the Case Is Ready for Mediation

Although many cases have a good chance of settlement in mediation, relocation cases are among the most difficult. The benefits and burden of a future outcome generally cannot be divided in a way that is acceptable to both parents. The parent desiring relocation may be faced with the choice of staying or converting residential parent status to joint custodian or nonresidential parent. The parent who may live away from the child will suffer disproportionate losses of daily contact and inability to attend parent–teacher conferences, sports, or other school activities, which the parent may not be willing to accept easily and which that parent believes are not in the best interest of the child. The key is whether the parties could come up with an alternative parenting plan that can meet one party's needs without endangering the other parent's needs and rights. Mediation may help the parties see that there is more than one solution. A skilled, interest-based mediator can "transform a 'yes-no' relocation case into a negotiation that substantially satisfies the special circumstances, needs, and wants of the parties."[20] Mediation is even being used with some degree of success in highly contentious international child abduction cases.[21]

Uncovering and understanding the client's goals are essential first steps in the pre-mediation assessment. The lawyer should consider the following questions:

- How will the client's needs and interests impact a settlement?
- If the client is the one relocating, does the client have a good faith, legitimate reason that the court would likely accept? If so, the main issue will be the parenting plan.
- If the client is the nonrelocating parent, has the parent exercised parenting time faithfully and paid child support, if ordered?
- Is the case being driven solely on emotions by one or both parties?
- Does the client's past relationship with the other parent indicate the motive of the move is to remove the other parent from the child's life?
- Is one seeking revenge or being vindictive?
- Does the other side want to reach an agreement?
- What reasons would the client have for agreeing to a parenting plan?
- What are the emotional or personal burdens that the child may face in relocation?
- Is the child in favor of or oppose the proposed relocation?
- What are the incentives promoting agreement of the other parent?
- What will each side win or lose if the case is concluded with mediation instead of going to trial?

As the lawyer is preparing the client for negotiations (Chapter 2), the lawyer should:

- Explain the mediation process to the client.
- Review the strengths and weaknesses of the case.
- Discuss advantages and a plan for mediation versus the risks of litigation.

- Discuss and compare the estimates of costs and expenses of continued negotiations, mediation, and trial.

It Is All in the Timing

The lawyer should consider the time restrictions. Time can drive the case to a mediated agreement or to trial. The timing of a court date can work both ways in prompting mediation or deterring it. In some cases, scheduling mediation close to the trial date drives the parties to an agreement because of the fear of a looming judicial decision over which they will have no control. At other times, if the trial is in the far distant future, the parties may mediate because they realize they both save money (legal fees, experts, and court costs), time, and a long period of uncertainty. The facts may dictate. For example, if one party needs to have a new or modified custody order by August so she can move back to her family in Wisconsin with the children before the start of the next school year, that party may want to push for mediation to start early, especially if the trial date is in November.

Another part of the timing issue is the emotional climate. The lawyer should see if the client is in the right mental space to mediate. If the client is extremely angry, vengeful, or otherwise not able to rationally consider alternatives, mediation might be better after the parent has time to digest the inevitability that one party will not live close to the child.

Choose the Right Mediator with the Right Skills

There are different forms of mediation and different types of mediation. Does the client need a facilitative or evaluative mediator? One estimate is that 80 percent of cases will settle with the right mediator. All mediators should have substantial mediation training and family law experience so as to understand family dynamics. Ideally, the mediator should have effective listening skills, be patient and empathetic, and enjoy working with people. Additionally, the mediator should have the ability to

- reframe contentious issues to set and maintain the right tone;
- distinguish between domestic violence and high conflict;
- be effective at power balancing;

- effectively communicate with both parties in a constructive manner; and
- have appropriate accommodations for meeting face to face with breakout rooms available or have adequate technology for good zoom mediation.

The mediator's background and experience can be key factors in selecting a mediator, especially in a relocation case. Consider whether the need is for an experienced certified mediator, a local attorney, a retired judge who has heard numerous relocation cases, a family law certified specialist, or a fellow of the American Academy of Matrimonial Lawyers. In some instances, a mediator who is a social worker or a clinical psychologist might suffice if the main issue is drafting a child-friendly, long-distance parenting plan. A Montana court found that the guardian ad litem for the child should not be the mediator because the duty to represent the child's interest means that the guardian cannot also be a "neutral mediator."[22]

The lawyer should spend some time analyzing the case and the client to determine what kind of mediator and mediation style is right. One way to "vet" a mediator is for the lawyer to talk to other lawyers who have used mediators who might possess the skills the client needs for the case.

Prepare for Mediation

The time for intensive review of both sides of the case is before the mediation begins. The lawyer, with input from the client, can make an outline of what issues must be resolved in the mediation. The outline will include substantive issues such as relocation; custody; decision making on major issues; visitation for weekends, summer, holidays; and travel logistics. Additionally, there are administrative issues such as how to handle future needed changes in the parenting plan or disagreements, mediation, or arbitration or attorney's fees for breach. Once the lawyer knows what is needed from the client, the lawyer can ask the other side for relevant information by phone, mail, or email. The goal is to have discovery substantially completed before mediation starts.

Clients need to go to the mediation with advice including best- and worst-case scenarios. The lawyer needs to clarify what the client considers to be the best outcome, whether it is the relocating parent wanting to move with the child or the nonmoving parent wanting the child to remain in the same location. The lawyer should ask a lot of "what-if" questions that allow the client to think about them in advance. Does the client want to maintain joint legal custody in any event? Does the client want a change of primary residency for the child? What does the client's idea of a good (fair) parenting plan for the child look like? Most clients want quality time with their children but still have some time for themselves. What is the client's ultimate goal? What is client's "Plan B" if the ultimate goal is not achievable? For example, the client may have 50/50 or 60/40 percent of parenting time. Will this still be possible if one parent relocates? Can the client take a larger percentage of the time based on work schedules and lifestyle? What would happen with a lesser amount of parenting time? Is there a way to restructure parenting time to satisfy both parents and benefit the child? Can either parent afford the travel costs?

The lawyer can suggest that there may be some issues that the parties may agree on without agreeing on the ultimate issue of relocation. For example, can the parents agree at what age the child is old enough to travel on an airplane or a train as an unaccompanied minor? Can parents agree on how many school days it is acceptable to miss to create a new parenting plan to allow for a longer period of access with the nonmoving or the moving parent, depending on which parent has primary residence? Can the parents develop an entire parenting plan based on the best interests of the child without agreeing on whether the parent should be allowed to move or not?[23]

The lawyer can try to assemble the materials needed for the client to try to convince the other parent of the strength of their plan. The lawyer can make a checklist of tasks and deadlines for the client to provide additional information. For example, in a relocation case, the information needed may be school progress reports and report cards, plus a copy of the last two years' medical and dental records. If the quality of the school in the proposed new location is at issue, the test scores, college entrance numbers, and other relevant data may need to be obtained. If the child currently rides a bus to school for an hour, the child's ability to walk to the school in the new location in ten minutes may be significant information. Additionally, what is the plan to cover the current, and potential, travel costs for getting the child to the other parent (car, trains, or planes) and child support.

What information might the other side produce that might convince the client of the merits of the other parent's plan? The client needs to have information on the factors that will affect the child's everyday life. If the child does not move away but in with the nonmoving parent, who has remarried, how well does the child get along with the stepparent? Will the child be sharing a bedroom with step or half siblings? How does the child get along with them? The lawyer can request, by phone, mail, text, or email, additional information from the other side.

The lawyer can review where and how the mediation will take place. This includes such information as where to sit, how to dress, what to bring (e.g., documents or pictures), when to speak, and when to remain silent. The client needs to know how to signal the need for a break. The client should go prepared with a picture of the child and proposals for legal custody and time-sharing plans whether a relocation is allowed or not. The client should have a calendar with the child's current school days, holidays, and activities, as well as the parents' work schedules. The lawyer needs to prepare the client for what to say and what not to say. The lawyer's main emphasis will be trying to keep the emotional element out as much as possible. If the client takes a businesslike approach to the issues, principles will rule, rather than passions and emotions. If emotions rule, the client's venting may unnecessarily inflame the other side to the point that agreement becomes impossible.

Many lawyers schedule a pre-mediation conference with the mediator. The lawyer may conduct a candid confidential case discussion at which the lawyer can disclose and discuss problems, including domestic violence, mental health, alcohol/drug abuse, and child abuse (if any). There may be a discussion of whether the attorney will attend the mediation. This may depend on if mediation is court-mandated or private, voluntary mediation. It may also depend on local custom or whether there is an applicable court order, statute, or rule. A lawyer may want to attend if the lawyer feels the client is at a bargaining disadvantage and needs support. While some feel that lawyers will "spoil" participation by the parties and interfere with the settlement process, a Maine study found that actually the prospects for fairness improve when lawyers assume a protective role.[24] If so, does the mediator want an opening statement? Will position papers be exchanged?

The keys to a successful mediation are preparation, patience, persistence, trust, and respect. Clients can be nervous about the mediation process. If possible, the lawyer might want to meet with the client a few minutes before the starting time to calm the client's fears and answer any last-minute questions or concerns. There may be time for a short rehearsal as to what questions may come up and the need for "give-and-take." The lawyer can help the client trust the mediator and the process. The lawyer can remind the client that neither side can demand results or force a settlement. There will be no agreement unless both parties agree.

Child-Inclusive Mediation

There needs to be a discussion about whether, and if so, how, to include the child in the parents' mediation. Mediation is supposed to be child- focused. The former Standard VIII of the Model Standards required mediators to "assist participants in determining how to promote the best interests of children . . ." but then cautioned against allowing participation except in extraordinary circumstances without the consent of both parents and the children's court-appointed representative. These standards were written 25 years ago. Since then, there has been a substantial body of research showing that children do not want to be kept in the dark about family proceedings that impact their lives. Teenagers often feel marginalized, confused, and angry about being excluded from the family decision-making process.[25] Additionally, children of parents who mediate adjust better to their parents' divorce than children whose parents litigate. The 2025

Proposed Standard X has more emphasis on the process being child centered and mentions participation, but in the commentary retains the language of old Standard VIII.

A growing number of nations, family law scholars, and child advocates recognize children as having a "right" to be heard. Indeed, Article 12 of the United Nations Convention on the Rights of the Child states:

> States Parties shall assure to the child who is capable of forming his or her own views, the right to express those views freely in all matters affecting the child, the views of the child being given due weight in accordance with the age and maturity of the child.
>
> . . . the child shall . . . be provided with the opportunity to be heard in any judicial and administrative proceedings affecting the child, either directly or through a representative . . . .

Although the United States has not ratified the Convention (the only country in the world not to do so), courts (including the U.S. Supreme Court) and policymakers in the United States routinely cite the Convention. Courts in a number of states have allowed for children's participation in the judicial process, including allowing for representation or for the judicial interview of children. While mediation is not a judicial or administrative proceeding, if the mediation does not result in agreement, the parties may go to litigation, which would mean the child's views should be heard.

In England and Wales, the government has a policy that a child is to be involved in family mediation, presumptively from ten years of age, or at a younger age, if of sufficient maturity. This is a rights-based policy. The child's participation is to occur regardless of whether the parents consent.[26] Child-inclusive mediation is better than mediation models that deny the child's input into custody matters.[27]

Having the child involved keeps the focus of the parents on the child. In addition to expressing their views on the parenting arrangements, the child can offer insights into the household dynamics. There are several ways to involve the child in mediation.

- The parents could agree to allow the child to meet with the mediator or therapist confidentially.
- The child could attend a mediation session that deals with the parenting arrangements at which the child could share their views directly.
- The child's lawyer or guardian ad litem could attend a mediation session and present the child's views. See Chapter 14.

The child may benefit from participating in the mediation process. Being allowed to express their feelings openly can empower a child and enhance a child's self-esteem. It gives the child a voice; affords the child status; and provides a forum for asserting their personal and individual rights.[28] Having a child participate can help the child heal and can shorten the length and intensity of family disputes.[29] One study found that child-inclusive mediation agreements had the lowest rates of re-litigation a year later.[30]

The lawyer should consider including children when:

(1) A child consistently expresses a preference for a particular type of time-sharing arrangement and one parent or both parents disagree;
(2) A child has specifically requested to speak to the mediator, therapist, or court official;
(3) Both parents need to hear from their child about the negative impact that their dispute is having;
(4) The child has the cognitive ability to relate their views and wishes;
(5) The information shared will be potentially useful;
(6) The child will benefit;
(7) The parents have the ability to talk with and hear their child (state of mind and level of conflict); and
(8) The parents are fully engaged and want to include the child.

Before speaking with a child, the mediator should get a written agreement from the parents regarding the purpose of gathering information, ensuring the parents understand the child's need for safety and comfort, and helping the parents to be sensitive to divided loyalty and dependency issues.

If the child is going to be included in the mediation process, the mediator should find out from the parents' perspectives what the child is like. The mediator should meet with the parents and child together to explain what the mediator does, go over ground rules, if any, and explain the need for, and limits of, confidentiality. Many mediators get permission from the parents—in front of the child—for the child to talk candidly with the mediator. If the mediator is going to talk with the child alone, the mediator should have parties arrange for neutral transportation. The mediator will set the stage by explaining why the child is meeting with the mediator to get a picture of the child's everyday life. After establishing rapport, the mediator may ask the child to explain what the child likes best and least at each parent's house. What could the parents do to make the child's life easier? What is the child's favorite holiday tradition? What are the child's favorite hobbies?

If the mediator determines that speaking with the child would compromise the child, some will seek permission from the parents to refer the child to a counselor or mutually acceptable child development specialist who will offer an opinion in the child's best interests. Another option would be to have a guardian ad litem or attorney for the child attend who could present the child's views.

There are some arguments against including the child in mediation. First, there are competing goals between protecting a child from emotional harm and protecting the litigants' due process rights. Second, a parent may manipulate a child to take sides, which can create anxiety and loyalty conflicts. A child probably should not be included if

(1) the parties cannot agree on the merits of their child's involvement in the parenting plan;
(2) the child is too young and does not possess the cognitive ability to reliably communicate their wishes;
(3) the child exhibits emotional and behavioral complaints about meeting with the mediator to express their views;

(4) the child is being manipulated by one parent or the other;
(5) one or both parties have unsuitable parental characteristics that include narrow and rigid positions, excessive emotional tension or hypersensitivity, insufficient cognitive and problem-solving capabilities, or high conflict personality.

During Mediation

Most mediators will explain the process to the parties at the outset and describe how mediation will proceed. This will include information about when breaks for refreshments and lunch will occur and if there are time limits on the duration of the mediation. For example, if one of the parties has to leave to pick up a child after school or attend another meeting, that needs to be determined at the outset. Additionally, some mediators like to keep all the parties in the same room for most of the mediation; others like to shuttle mediation, moving back and forth between the clients and their lawyers in different rooms. If the mediator is going between rooms, the standard statement is that whatever is said to the mediator is fair game to repeat to the other side unless the party instructs them otherwise.

If the lawyer is in the mediation session, the lawyer should listen, and the client should be doing the talking. This does not mean that the lawyer cannot bring exhibits that might be used at trial, a spreadsheet, or even a PowerPoint to show the mediator and other side on a particular issue. For example, one of reasons the parent wants to relocate it because there is a job offer in the new city paying twice as much as the current job, the hours are better, and the cost of living is less. A diagram showing jobs using the parent's skills and rate of pay within the geographical area may be a good visual. If representing the parent who wants the child to remain, pictures showing the child and friends or grandparents may emphasize the child's close ties here that would be disrupted.

All parties should listen carefully to the mediator's questions and answer honestly. The issues bothering both parties need to be brought out into the session. Even if the parties cannot agree that the child should relocate with a parent, the parties may be able to determine at what age a child should be able to fly or travel by train alone. The parties need to understand each other's goals, worries, and motivations. Only by exploring these issues in depth can the mediator and parties hope to come up with some creative problem solving. The client may want to take a break to talk to the lawyer privately, or the lawyer may want to talk to the client before the client agrees, even tentatively, to anything.

Sometimes there will be ready agreement on one or two issues. Mediators like to get early agreements to set the pattern for cooperation and agreeing. There are other issues, however, where there may be an impasse—one or the other will not budge. If the mediator is going back and forth with a client who is not "giving" on a particular issue, the lawyer in front of the client might ask the mediator for an opinion on how the issue might be resolved if they went to court. The neutral mediator with experience who is objective may be able to persuade the reluctant client that the issue is a loser. Another way of trying to break an impasse may be to have the mediator explain the problems or issues that are holding back the other side from agreeing.

A three-way meeting with the opposing counsel and mediator may be another way to try to get an impasse resolved. The mediator may be able to see, explain, and articulate the issues or views that are preventing agreement. The mediator can get the attorneys to agree to work with their clients on solving the problems and move them from dealing with personality issues. Another way to move the mediation along may be for the lawyer to ask the mediator how to keep it moving. The experienced mediator might have a suggestion for something the lawyer can say to the client that might make a difference.

Make sure all issues are covered that the parties can agree on. Leave nothing for later resolution unless necessary. If the parties have agreed upon a parenting plan that is fair, but cannot agree on which parent will have custody, that should be stated. The judge will determine at trial, but the parties have agreed on what the parenting plan should look like regardless of the move.

After Mediation

When a session is nearing the end, the lawyer can start drafting an agreement if present, or check the mediator's preliminary agreement. One advantage of having the lawyer present is that if there is an error in the agreement, the lawyer can catch it early. If there is a mathematical error in child support or counting days, the lawyer can, and should, point it out. Factual and data errors should be caught as early as possible.

The document should be the written mediated settlement agreement that will be presented to the court as a formal order. The attorney drafting the formal order must not change the agreement reached without a compelling reason (mathematical error). Once the parties have signed the agreement, it is a contract.[31]

Arbitration

Arbitration is an out-of-court process that closely resembles a court hearing or trial, but is private, confidential, and conducted in a manner that is best-suited for the parties. Arbitration may be the fastest and most efficient way to resolve the relocation issue, depending on the time to get to trial in the state. Arbitration is more closely tied to court proceedings than to negotiation and mediation because the parties submit their dispute to a decision-maker. The difference is that the parties choose that decision-maker. The parties can also select the basic rules to be applied and the procedure to use. Once the arbitrator makes an award, it is confirmed. There are very few grounds to overturn an arbitrator's award. The parties can, and often do, provide within their written arbitration agreement that private financial and personal information is confidential. In addition, within their written arbitration agreement, the parties can structure the arbitration procedure to meet the needs of the participants by streamlining and simplifying the process.

Arbitration has long been used to resolve disputes in labor and commercial law. At one time 49 states had enacted the Uniform Arbitration Act. Since 2000, 23 states have enacted the Revised Uniform Arbitration Act. In 1990, the AAML drafted a set of model rules for family law arbitration and started training family law arbitrators.[32] In 1992, the American Bar Association Family Law Section supported family arbitration through articles in the *Family Law Quarterly* and the *Family Advocate*. The last three decades have seen a slow, but steady, move toward not only allowing but also encouraging arbitration of family law disputes. Colorado added arbitration of family law issues in 1997; North Carolina adopted a comprehensive statute to allow family arbitration in 1999; the AAML adopted a Model Arbitration Act in 2005.

In many states, parties submit property issues to arbitration, using the state's basic commercial arbitration law, which is not particularly suited to family law issues. A few states have specific family law arbitration statutes or court rules.[33] Although a few states have excluded child custody and support from the permissible scope of arbitration,[34] others allow it as long as there is judicial review of the arbitration award to protect the child's best interests.[35] The New Jersey Supreme Court found that

> Parental autonomy includes the right to submit any family controversy, including child-custody and parenting-time issues, to a decision maker of chosen by the parents. . . . *Just as parents choose to decide those issues among themselves, they may opt to sidestep the judicial process and submit their dispute to an arbitrator whom they have chosen.* The right to arbitrate serves an important family value by allowing parents the opportunity to choose an arbitrator based on her familiarity with the family or her understanding of the values that the parents hold dear and have tried to follow in raising their child.[36]

In 2016, the Uniform Family Law Arbitration Act (UFLAA) set out a statutory framework for arbitrating all family law issues.[37] The UFLAA offers parties a choice of a simpler, faster, more convenient, and confidential process with a seasoned "expert" decision-maker of their own choosing. Eight states currently have enacted the UFLAA. The Utah Supreme Court recently found that submitting child custody issues to arbitration is not contrary to public policy.[38] Indeed, the parents' decision to arbitrate is not a delegation of court authority but rather a choice of the proper forum for the dispute. The UFLAA incorporates by reference a state's arbitration law (either the Revised Uniform Arbitration Act or the Uniform Arbitration Act) for procedural requirements that do not implicate family law concerns. Theoretically, under the UFLAA, the parents could choose anyone as arbitrator. For example, if the sticking issue is a valuation of a particular object, someone who deals in buying and selling or collecting that type of object might be used. If relocation is an issue, the parties might choose an experienced clinical psychologist who has dealt with many children who have relocated or a retired trial judge who has decided scores of relocation cases. If the court is doing the appointing by default or because the parties did not select someone, however, the arbitrator must be a lawyer or retired judge with training as required under state law for dealing with domestic violence. States may have or create their own qualifications. The American Academy of Matrimonial Lawyers (AAML) provides comprehensive arbitration training and has endorsed the UFLAA. The AAML urges that lawyers serving as arbitrators comply with all relevant rules relating to judges, including the ABA Code of Judicial Conduct and the AAML Bounds of Advocacy for Family Lawyers section 9.2 (2000).

The UFLAA deals with the issue of domestic violence. Section 12 provides that if a party is subject to an order of protection or if the arbitrator otherwise finds that a party's safety or ability to participate effectively in the arbitration is at risk, the arbitration is suspended unless the party who is at risk reaffirms the desire to arbitrate and a court allows it. Additionally, section 10 provides that a party may be represented by an attorney (and in arbitration most will be) and a party may also bring a support person to the arbitration. If an arbitrator finds during the arbitration that a child is abused or neglected, the arbitrator must report it, and the arbitration is terminated. The UFLAA presumptively applies to child-related issues of parenting time and support. An agreement to arbitrate child-related disputes must be made contemporaneously with the dispute or a prior agreement reaffirmed at the time of the dispute. So the arbitration of a relocation case involving a child would require a contemporaneous agreement of the parties. There are other safeguards built into the arbitration if child-related issues are involved. While a recording is not necessary for most arbitrations, UFLAA section 14(b) requires the arbitrator to cause a verbatim record, that is, Zoom, phone, or other recording, to be made of any part of an arbitration hearing concerning a child-related dispute. Section 13 provides a nonexclusive list of arbitrator powers, including the power to interview a child and appoint a representative for a child. UFLAA requires an award determining a child-related dispute to state the reasons on which it is based as required by the law of the state in family law cases. In most states with extensive factors for child custody, this means the arbitrator will include findings of fact and conclusions of law. Under UFLAA sections 16 and 19, a court cannot confirm an award determining child custody or child support unless it finds that the award complies with applicable law and is in the child's best interests. Vacation of the award is allowed under section 19(b)(1) if the award did not comply with section 15 or law of the state dealing the best interests of the child.

The UFLAA allows an arbitrator to do anything a family court judge could do unless otherwise agreed by the parties or limited by a statute. UFLAA section13(a) allows the arbitrator to conduct arbitration in a manner the arbitrator considers appropriate for a fair and expeditious disposition of the dispute. Section 13(b) mandates that the arbitrator shall provide each party the right to be heard, to present evidence, and to cross-examine witnesses. Section 13(c)(1-15) provides a nonexclusive list of arbitrator powers. The arbitration has the power to interview children and appoint a representative for a child.

Section 11 allows arbitrators to enter temporary awards as needed under the state's law regarding temporary orders, and resort to court is authorized for urgent matters. These orders typically involve maintaining the status quo—who stays in the house, spousal or child support, custody and parenting time issues.

UFLAA section 15 requires the arbitrator to make an award in a record, dated and signed by the arbitrator, and give notice to the parties as the parties agreed or as provided in other arbitration law. Unless otherwise agreed to by the parties, UFLAA defaults to a reasoned award. The parties, however, cannot waive the reasoned award for a child-related award, which must comply with state family law. Section 15 requires a verbatim record to be made. An award can be vacated if there is not a verbatim record or it does not comply with the law of the state dealing with the best interests of the child.

As a general rule, a court may overturn an arbitral award only where the arbitrator engaged in fraud, corruption, or other serious misconduct (or, in some jurisdictions, also where the arbitrator "manifestly disregarded" the applicable law).

As one family practitioner noted in a recent article:

> There are many states, including mine, that constantly see backlogged court dockets for family law cases. The ability of parties to have an expedited final decision pertaining to the most precious things in their lives—their children—would give litigants, among other things, (1) the ability to reduce the stress of lengthy litigation, (2) finality, and (3) the ability to begin to move on with their lives.[39]

Endnotes

1. Model Rules of Pro. Conduct r. 2.4, cmt. 1 (Am. Bar Ass'n 2025).

2. *See* Milfred D. Dale, *Don't Forget the Children: Court Protection from Parental Conflict Is in the Best Interests of Children*, 52 Fam. Ct. Rev. 648 (2014) (helping parents resolve disputes reduces the turmoil for children). *See also* Solangel Maldonado, *Taking Account of Children's Emotions: Anger and Forgiveness in "Renegotiated Families,"* 16 Va. J. Soc. Pol'y & L. 445 (2009).

3. Nancy Ver Steegh, *Family Court Reform and ADR: Shifting Values and Expectations Transform the Divorce Process*, 42 Fam. L. Q. 659 (2008); John Lande & Gregg Herman, *Fitting the Forum to the Family Fuss: Choosing Mediation, Collaborative Law or Cooperative Law for Negotiating Divorce Cases*, 42 Fam. Ct. Rev. 280 (2004).

4. John Lande & Forrest S. Mosten, *Collaborative Lawyers' Duties to Screen the Appropriateness of Collaborative Law and Obtain Clients' Informed Consent to Use Collaborative Law*, 25 Ohio St. J. Disp. Resol. 347 (2010); Pauline H. Tesler, Collaborative Law: Achieving Effective Resolution in Divorce Without Litigation (ABA 2d ed. 2008); Kate Scharff & Lisa Herrick, Navigating Emotional Currents in Collaborative Divorce (ABA 2010).

5. *See* Carolyn Moran Zack, Family Law Arbitration: Practice, Procedure, and Forms (ABA 2022).

6. *See* Model Rules of Pro. Conduct r. 1.1, 1.4, 1.2a, and 2.4, cmt. 1 (Am. Bar Ass'n 2025). *See also* Andrew Schepard, Kramer v. Kramer *Revisited: A Comment on the Miller Commission Report and the Obligation of Divorce Lawyers for Parents to Discuss Alternative Dispute Resolution with Their Clients*, 27 Pace L. Rev. 577 (2007).

7. Connecticut, Georgia, Massachusetts, Minnesota, Missouri, Texas, and Virginia require the lawyer to counsel clients about alternatives. Alaska, Arkansas, Colorado, Delaware, Hawaii, Louisiana, and New Jersey encourage lawyers to counsel clients. The courts advise clients in California and Oregon.

8. Kelly Browe Olson, *The Importance of Using Alternative Dispute Resolution Techniques and Processes in the Ethical and Informed Representation of Children*, 6 Nev. L. Rev. 1333, 1346 (2006).

9. *See* Brian S. Kennedy, *Moving Away from Certainty: Using Mediation to Avoid Unpredictable Outcomes in Relocation Disputes Involving Joint Physical Custody*, 53 B.C. L. Rev. 265 (2012).

10. *In re* Lee, 411 S.W.3d 445 (Tex. 2013) (noting encouragement of mediation as a form of alternative dispute resolution is of critical importance to the emotional and psychological well-being of children involved in high-conflict custody cases).

11. Linda D. Elrod, Child Custody Practice and Procedure § 16.9 (Thomson Reuters 2024).

12. Karamanoglu v. Gourlaouen, 140 A.3d 1249 (Me. 2016).

13. Bauer v. Bauer, 28 S.W.3d 877, 886–87 (Mo. Ct. App. 2000).

14. Fuchs v. Martin, 845 N.E.2d 1038, 1041 (Ind. 2006).

15. Utah Code Ann. § 30-3-38(7). *See* John Lande, *Using Dispute Resolution System Design Methods to Promote Good-Faith Participation in Court-Connected Mediation Programs*, 50 UCLA L. Rev. 69 (2002).

16. Forrest S. Mosten, The Complete Guide to Mediation (ABA 2d Ed. 2015); Forrest S. Mosten, Lara Traum & Elizabeth Potter Scully, Effectively Representing Clients in Family Mediation (ABA 2023).

17. Welch v. Welch, 294 Cal. Rptr. 3d 626 (Ct. App. 2022).

18. Sarah R. Cole, et al., Mediation: Law, Policy & Practice § 8.1, at 295–96 (2018).

19. *See* Mark E. Sullivan, *Family Law Mediation: The Master Checklist*, 30(1) Amer. J. Fam. L. 58 (2016).

20. Carol Gersten, *Mediate the Move: Quelling Clients' Fears and Clarifying Options*, 28(4) Fam. Advoc. 30, 32–33 (2006) (includes lists of pre-mediation questions for both the relocating and nonrelocating party as well as sample clauses for mediated relocation agreements).

21. Sarah Vigers, Mediating International Child Abduction Cases—The Hague Convention (Studies in Private International Law) (2011).

22. *In re* Marriage of Brockington & Brown, 400 P.3d 205 (Mont. 2017).

23. Rebecca N. Morrow, *Mediating Parental Relocation Cases Behind a Veil of Ignorance*, 49 Wake Forest Rev. 771, 780–82 (2014).

24. Craig A. McEwen, Nancy H. Rogers & Richard J. Maiman, *Bring in the Lawyers: Challenging the Dominant Approaches to Ensuring Fairness in Divorce Mediation*, 79 Minn. L. Rev. 1317 (1994–95).

25. Janet Walker & Gabriela Misca, *Why Listening to Children and Young People Is Important in Family Justice*, 57 Fam. Ct. Rev. 375 (2019).

26. Rachel Birnbaum & Nick Bala, Child Inclusive Mediation (2017).

27. Pauline Muto, *A Family Affair: Acknowledging Children's Voices in Custody Mediation*, 71 Disp. Resol. J. 171 (2017) (discussing difference between child-focused mediation and child-inclusive mediation). L.A. Yasenik & J.M. Graham, *The Continuum of Including Children in ADR Processes: A Child-Centered Continuum Model*, 54(2) Fam. Ct. Rev. 186 (2016).

28. Ernest Sanchez & Sherrie Kibler-Sanchez, *Empowering Children in Mediation: An Intervention Model*, 42 Fam. Ct. Rev. 554, 555 (2004).

29. Stacey Platt, *Set Another Place at the Table: Child Participation in Family Separation Cases*, 17 Cardozo J. of Conflict Resol. 749 (2016); Jennifer E. McIntosh, et al., *Child-Focused and Child-Inclusive Divorce Mediation: Comparative Outcomes from a Prospective Study of Postseparation Adjustment*, 46 Fam. Ct. Rev. 105 (2008).

30. B.N. Rudd, et al., *Child Informed Mediation Study Follow Up: Comparing the Frequency of Relitigation Following Different Types of Mediation*, *in* Psychology, Public Policy and Law (2015).

31. Welch v. Welch, 294 Cal. Rptr. 3d 626 (Ct. App. 2022) (parties had entered into mediated property settlement agreement but wife died before divorce; court upheld agreement and children, rather than husband, inherited).

32. *American Academy of Matrimonial Lawyers, Rules for Arbitration of Financial Issues*, adopted by Board of Governors, 1990.

33. Del. Fam. Ct. R. of C.P.R. 16.1(a) (permitting binding arbitration of property division, spousal support, alimony, counsel fees, but excluding proceedings involving protection from abuse, child custody, or visitation); Mo. Rev. Stat. § 435.405(5) (arbitration awards regarding a child shall be subject to de novo judicial review). *But see* Vanderborgh v. Krauth, 370 P.3d 661 (Colo. Ct. App. 2016) (de novo review is discretionary).

34. *See* Conn. Gen. Stat. § 46b-66(c); Fla. Stat. Ann. § 44-104(14). *See* Kelm v. Kelm, 749 N.E.2d 299 (Ohio 2001).

35. Ga. Code Ann. § 19-9-1. *See* Brazzel v. Brazzel, 789 S.E.2d 626 (Ga. Ct. App. 2016) (confirming arbitrator's decision to modify custody as in children's best interests). *See* Linda D. Elrod, *Arbitration of Child-Related Issues and the Uniform Family Law Arbitration Act*, 46(2) Fam. Advoc. 14 (2023).

36. Fawzy v. Fawzy, 973 A.2d 347, 360–61 (N.J. 2009).

37. For a discussion of UFLAA, *see* Linda D. Elrod, *Uniform Family Law Arbitration Act: Adding Another ADR Option: Part I of II*, 34(2) Am. J. Fam. L. 47 (Summer 2020); Linda D. Elrod, *The Case for Arbitration in Family Cases—and for the Uniform Act*, 23(2) Disp. Resol. Mag. 18 (Winter 2017).

38. Taylor v. Taylor, 517 P.3d 380 (Utah 2022).

39. Audrey J. Beeson, *Aribitration: A Promising Avenue for Resolving Family Law Cases?*, 18 Pepper. Disp. Res. L.J. 211, 229 (2018).

CHAPTER 11

Experts and Custody Evaluations

The weight to be given to expert testimony depends on the facts on which it is based as well as the professional qualifications and expertise of the expert.[1]

Experts for Relocation

Relocation trials use experts more than most custody cases. While the most common experts are custody evaluators and mental health consultants, some cases may need vocational, financial, or educational experts. An expert is one who is qualified by knowledge, skill, experience, training, or education. A person can become an expert because of qualifications, expertise relevant to the dispute at hand, publications, and forensic or testifying experience.[2] A witness who qualifies as an expert may testify in the form of an opinion if the expert's specialized knowledge will help the judge understand the evidence or determine a fact in issue. In a relocation case, the court often wants, and needs, expert opinion on the best interests of the child.

An expert may not be needed in every relocation case, but the stakes are high when a child may move a long distance away. The major factors are whether specialized knowledge is needed; the availability of funds to pay an expert; the prospects for settlement; and the availability of an alternative to an expert. Social science data shows that relocation poses risks for the child.[3] A psychological evaluation may be helpful in assessing and minimizing the potential negative consequences for the child by looking at the family's situation, the child's resilience, and protective factors that may exist.[4]

The judge is the gatekeeper of the evidence at trial determining whether to admit expert evidence and the weight to be given it. In most states, experts can be selected and challenged on whether they meet the standard set in the landmark *Daubert* case.[5] For some types of evidence to be admitted at trial, the court must first determine whether (1) a theory or technique can be or has been tested; (2) a theory or technique has been subjected to peer review and publication; (3) this particular technique has a high known or potential rate of error; and (4) the theory or technique enjoys general acceptance within a relevant scientific community. In some states, however, the report of a court-ordered custody investigator may be admitted without meeting the *Daubert* test because of a statute and court discretion.[6] In addition, lay witnesses can testify about their firsthand knowledge: what they heard, saw, said, or did. They may provide an opinion that is rationally based on the witness's perception; helpful to clearly understand the witness's testimony or to determine the fact in issue; and not based on scientific, technical, or specialized knowledge. It may be possible to use neighbors, friends, and family members to testify regarding knowledge they have concerning a party's parenting or specific acts. With either expert or lay witnesses, a foundation must be laid.

Questions

The lawyer needs to answer some preliminary questions, such as:

1. What can the expert do for the client (or me)?
2. What role will the expert play?
   a. Custody evaluation? Parenting assessment? Court-ordered investigation of parents' abilities to co-parent?
   b. Information about the risks/benefits of the child adapting to relocation?[7]
   c. School evaluations in two cities?
   d. Analyze the quality of life in two cities?
3. Where do I find the best expert?
   a. Will a local or a nationally known expert be needed?
   b. Have other lawyers in the area used experts in relocation cases?

   c. Are there recognized experts in reported cases in the state?
   d. Who is writing in the area?
4. How much will an expert cost? Is the cost prohibitive? Is there another way to get similar information?
5. Do I need more than one expert—one expert to prepare the case and another one for trial?
6. Can the expert help negotiate the case?
7. Can the expert help with dealing with the opposing expert?
8. What can the expert do for the client at trial?
9. Should the client agree to a neutral expert?
10. Can an expert help the client after the relocation decision?

The facts of the particular case will dictate the type of expert needed and the role the expert will play. A good expert is a good teacher who is able to educate the lawyer, the client, and most importantly the judge. An expert can be an advisor, evaluator, information provider, negotiator, or coach, as well as a testifying witness at a trial. Mental health professionals can be consultants, therapists, forensic experts, or custody evaluators. Medical doctors, treating physicians, clinical or forensic psychologists, and psychiatrists may also be of help if the mental or physical health of a parent or child is at issue.

Selecting the Expert

Once the lawyer has decided the type of expert needed, the next step is locating the right one. There may be some in the area that are well known and used by other lawyers. Various professional associations maintain data banks of experts. Local colleges and universities may be trusted sources. A referring attorney can offer valuable information about the strengths and weaknesses of a prospective expert as well as the fees.

The lawyer will want an expert with as impressive credentials as possible and prior experience. A psychologist should be a member of the American Psychological Association's Law Society or a fellow of the APA Division or of the American Academy of Forensic Psychology. The lawyer can find out if the psychologist reads or publishes in psychology–law journals or has continuing education training in psychology applied to legal issues.

Qualifications, while important, are not enough. The expert needs to make a credible and persuasive witness. Prior experience in court and reputation are important. The lawyer should interview the potential expert in person. The expert needs to appear confident, honest, and competent, but not condescending. Good eye contact, communication skills, and a personable style can enhance credibility with the judge. The expert must be able to explain their opinions in simple, clear terms.

The lawyer should be familiar with the methodology appropriate for the expert's field and make sure the expert follows it. There should be literature that supports the expert's theory, and the expert should have read it. The expert should be able, and willing, to explain the basis for their opinion. The other side's experts may be helpful if there are agreements, concessions, or stipulations about methodologies.[8] The expert can also help prepare for examining or cross-examining an expert on the other side.

Custody and Parenting Evaluations

Psychological experts may be necessary when a child exhibits emotional and behavioral problems, or refuses contact with a parent; there is sharply conflicting testimony regarding the conduct of the parties; or a party's mental health is an issue. The court has discretion, on its own or on recommendation of one of the parties, to order an evaluation of the parents, whether it is a custody evaluation or an examination about the mother and father's abilities to co-parent.[9] The purpose of the forensic mental health examination is to obtain information about the child's best interests from a neutral source to assist the judge's determination of the child's best interests in the custody and relocation dispute.[10] The evaluator is responsible to the appointing court, even if the parties have to pay for the evaluation. The court may deny a request to appoint an evaluator if there have already been relatively recent evaluations of the parties and child.[11]

Child Custody Evaluation or Forensic Mental Health Evaluation

Because the best interests of the child standard is amorphous, especially in the relocation context, the trial court may rely heavily on the expertise of a neutral mental health professional who performs a forensic mental health evaluation, sometimes called a "custody evaluation."[12] The lawyer should advise the client of the possibility that the court may order an evaluation.

Many states have no statutory authorization for "custody evaluations." Some have a general provision allowing the court to order an investigation or "home study" and make a report concerning legal custody, residency, and parenting time.[13] Colorado has one of the most extensive regulations of the custody evaluation process.

> In all proceedings concerning the allocation of parental responsibilities . . . the court may, upon motion of either party or upon its own motion, order . . . a licensed mental health professional qualified . . . to perform an evaluation and file a written report . . . relating to the allocation of parental responsibilities for the child . . . Colo. Rev. Stat. § 14-10-127(1)(a)(I).

Model standards of practice recommend that a mental health professional with specialized knowledge and formal training in the legal, societal, familial, and cultural issues that arise in custody contests perform the evaluation.[14] Colorado has a statute that prescribes training requirements. Colo. Rev. Stat. § 14-10-127(1)(a) requires:

> (4) A person shall not be allowed to testify regarding a parental responsibilities or parenting time evaluation that the person has performed . . . unless the court finds that the person is qualified as competent, by training and experience, in the areas of:
>
> > (a) The effects of divorce and remarriage on children, adults, and families;
> > (b) Appropriate parenting techniques;
> > (c) Child development, including cognitive, personality, emotional, and psychological development;
> > (d) Child and adult psychopathology;

(e) Applicable clinical assessment techniques; and
(f) Applicable legal and ethical requirements of parental responsibilities evaluation.

If the court is going to seek an evaluation, the lawyer should encourage the client to agree on a neutral evaluation, which may be comprehensive and less expensive. If each party hires their own expert, the case can become a battle of the experts, often without much new or helpful information for the judge. If the parents agree, the sample language could be:

> Both parents agree that [name of mental health professional] shall evaluate [name of the child] and the parents to determine the current adjustment of the child to the parents, school and community and the potential impact of the [name of relocating parent's] proposed relocation. The evaluation may explore the need for any modification of parenting time, decision-making responsibility, or conduct of the parents. The parents agree to cooperate fully in the evaluation and to consider seriously any recommendations that come out of the evaluation.

In 2022, the American Psychological Association published Guidelines for Child Custody Evaluations in Family Law Proceedings.[15] The Association of Family and Conciliation Courts also has developed aspirational guidelines for child custody evaluations. The primary focus of the guidelines is the psychological needs of the child, rather than the educational, medical, social, or physical needs. In the best circumstances, judges, lawyers, and the parties collaboratively develop psycho-legal questions for the evaluator to investigate and on which to provide opinions. Lawyers who are familiar with social science studies and ethical rules are better able to evaluate, examine, and critique the quality of mental health reports and testimony.[16]

Even if the parties agree to a custody evaluation or the court appointed a neutral evaluator, a party may disagree with the evaluation. The lawyer may feel that the research was unreliable or not relevant to the facts of the particular case.[17] Predictions are difficult to make in the best of circumstances with known variables. They are even harder in the midst of the numerous unknowns of a relocation case. One of the parties (or their lawyer) may want to retain privately an expert who can conduct an additional custody evaluation, review the custody evaluation that was done to ensure it meets scientific standards for admissibility, or be a litigation support person.[18] The fact that one parent did not consent to a custody evaluation does not preclude the court from considering the expert's report.[19]

Conducting Custody Evaluations

The custody evaluation is basically an assessment of the parents' parenting abilities and fit with the child, which may assist the judge in determining the parenting plan that is in the child's best interests.[20] In a relocation case, the evaluation may indicate the risks and benefits to the child of the move. There are only national guidelines for custody evaluations,[21] not professional "standards."[22] Some state statutes and court rules reflect methodologies to be used and what constitutes a complete custody evaluation. In conducting comprehensive child custody evaluations, evaluators apply theory, research, and scientific methodology. Evaluators seek information from five types of independent data sources: (1) document or record review; (2) interviews, including individual interviews of the parties and, when appropriate, the children, as well as joint and group interviews, when appropriate; (3) psychological testing; (4) direct observations of parent–child relationships via home or office visits; and (5) contacts with collateral sources or witnesses.

Most custody evaluations are conducted in person. There is evidence, however, that evaluations can be conducted via videoconferencing using modern technology.[23] This makes it possible to do evaluations if one parent is already living in another location with less expense and time than being in person.

Typically, the evaluator reviews the court pleadings and obtains information from the parties' lawyers to set the ground rules and a timeline. The lawyers can provide much relevant information, such as the facts, issues, legal standards, and deadlines or important dates. If there are relevant records, the lawyer should make them available to the evaluator or figure out how to allow access. The custody evaluator generally will interview the parents, the child, and other persons who are living in the child's home, such as a stepparent or partner. The evaluator may also gather information from teachers, coaches, and maybe the pediatrician.[24] The interviews reveal how each parent views the relocation dispute, their skills as a parent, and their knowledge and understanding of each child. The evaluator will get a developmental history of the child, if the parents think the child is exhibiting symptoms of stress (bedwetting, fears, separation anxiety, acting out) and parenting philosophy and practices. The evaluator may ask each parent to describe a day in the life of the child.

The evaluator will want to assess the past and current relationship between the parents. Some evaluators obtain the history of the parent from birth to the present—academic, employment, health issues, mental status, and relationship with their family of origin. At the least, the evaluator will delve into the history of the marriage or relationship, how each has handled the separation, and the current situation of each parent—financial, religious, employment, health, and living situation.

If one parent has had primary physical custody, the evaluator can see how each parent thinks that has worked. Have the parents been able to cooperate and encourage the child's relationship with the other parent? If the parties share joint legal and physical custody or shared parenting either with or without a court order, the evaluator can assess how the parties think co-parenting is working. The evaluator could discover if the parties chose the parenting plan through mediation or negotiation or a judge mandated it. What problems have the parties had? How have they worked them out? The parents may be currently fighting because of the proposed relocation. How have the parents resolved any disputes in the past? If the parents have an unworkable shared parenting arrangement (as evidenced by repetitive litigation, the appointment of a parenting coordinator, or other inability to resolve issues), that information may be important for the court making the decision to allow or disallow a move.

The evaluator will see if the parent seeking to relocate is a stable parent. Relative stability of the parents may become a factor. A series of moves, say four in three years, may show some instability on the part of the moving parent. Divorce is stressful to both parents and child. Moves are also stressful. A move out of state might represent more instability. On the other hand, the present move may be the one that will lead to more permanent stability for both parent and child.

Parents who regularly communicate, have been cooperative in co-parenting, and who support the child's positive relationship with the other parent can ameliorate the risks to the child's development that come from the divorce.[25] Relatively healthy parents who have encouraged and fostered a strong relationship with the other parent are likely to continue that pattern after a move. On the other hand, a parent who has repeatedly interfered with the other parent's relationship with the child may be trying to relocate to put an additional wedge—distance—between the child and parent. The evaluator will investigate any medical pathology, the level of conflict, and the extent to which the move is motivated by a desire to thwart the other parent's access to the child. The evaluator's report may reveal that there are some hidden reasons for the move other than those stated by a party in the petition. For example, a parent may state that they want to move for a new job or to be near relatives. It may turn out that the new job is not as good as the old one or that there are more relatives in the current location.

The evaluator will probe whether the move is a spur of the moment decision or one that has been well thought out. Relocations are more expensive than most people envision. The logistics of changing homes, jobs, schools, and caregivers can be daunting. Transportation costs can increase as gas prices, pandemics, and other unforeseen factors occur.

Psychological Testing

Psychological testing, which can include a range of instruments that include personality measures, projective measures, or parenting inventories, may be used in child custody evaluations.[26] Most of the tests, however, are not designed for custody or relocation evaluations and are not tests of parenting ability. The testing findings need to be integrated with the other information, such as interviews of the parties, child, collateral contacts, firsthand observations, collateral records and documents, and so on. As one psychologist noted, "there is a great risk of . . . misapplication of test data to support a particular conclusion in a relocation case."[27]

The mental health of the parents can be relevant as to whether they will facilitate a positive relationship with the other parent over time. The evaluator will be looking at the level of pathology in the adults, the level of conflict, and the extent to which the move may be to put distance between the parents. Psychologists conducting custody evaluations may give psychological tests to identify mental illness or personality traits that may be relevant, or just to clarify the psychological state of one or both parents.[28] Psychological testing is basically a quick way of getting a lot of information under relatively standardized conditions. If the tests are standardized, they can be an efficient means of comparing the individual's response with responses on other tests. One looks for internal consistency or the individual's responses compared with national norms and with the other parent. While testing may provide helpful information, some believe there is too much reliance on them. As some psychologists have opined, "Tests of intellectual capacity, achievement, personality style, and psychopathology assess constructs that are linked only indirectly, at best, to the key issues concerning custody and visitation."[29]

If tests are to be given, the evaluator should consider tests that are developmentally, culturally, and linguistically appropriate to use in a given situation. The evaluator should determine what the court needs to know in a particular case and which tests can provide valid data about those relevant issues. Some of the usual tests are the Rorschach (Exner), MMPI-2, MMPI-2RX, MMPI-3, and possibly the Wechsler. No single psychological test or battery of tests can replace the court's consideration of custody factors.[30] The evaluator should fully disclose the test's limitations when giving the results.

Evaluation of Child

The evaluator is looking at the gender, temperament and fit between each parent and child, the developmental stage of the child, as well as if the child has special physical or emotional needs. The evaluator will explore what the child knows about the reason for the evaluation and if the child has the ability to express their opinion and wishes about the potential relocation.

The custody evaluator will try to discover the actual relationship between each parent and the child during the parents' relationship, the separation, and the post-separation situation. This is the starting point to look at the potential for harm or benefit from the move. The evaluator will explore how much the child relies on each parent to meet day-to-day needs, such as breakfast, bedtime rituals, transportation to school, appointments, and activities. If one parent does most of the caretaking, why is that happening? Is it work related or is there another reason? Does the child turn to one parent when the child is hurt, angry, happy, afraid, or excited? Does the child feel closer to one parent? Why is that?

If one parent has been the primary resource for the child, the stability and continuity of that relationship may be one of the most important factors in crafting a parenting plan.[31] In a New York case, most of the expert's testimony turned on his recollection of his numerous interviews with the parties and his opinion as to the parties' parental fitness. The court relied more on the expert's testimony than the report. The testimony showed the mother had a strong bond and her parenting history with the child was substantial.[32]

Sometimes one parent was the primary caregiver during the marriage, but roles shifted during and after the separation, and now both parents are equally involved. The evaluator needs to discover the qualitative and quantitative aspects of the parent–child relationship. Does the child still rely on both parents to the same or similar degree as before the separation?

If there is a custody order, the label does not matter as much as the child's actual living arrangement. If the parties think they have joint legal and physical custody, but the child only sees one parent every other weekend, the arrangement is actually one with a primary physical residence. If the parties share joint legal and physical custody, the evaluator can investigate how that has been working.

As with testing for the parents, psychologists can also use a variety of psychological tests for children, including Rorschach,

Roberts Apperception Test for Children (RAT-C), Wide Range Achievement Test-3 (WRAT-3), Personality Inventory for Children or Child Behavior Checklist, Personality Inventory for Youth (PIY), MMPI-A for 14 and up, and Kinetic Family Drawing.

The child's gender, age, and temperament are relevant as well as the psychological fit between a parent and child. Gender cannot be the sole deciding issue but may be relevant depending on the child. At different ages and stages, children need same sex or opposite sex parent role modeling. A child's temperament may affect the child's ability to adjust to a move either to the other parent's house or to a new location. While children are adaptable, some are more temperamental than others. Some children have great difficulty adapting to any change in their lives. A child who had, or is having, great difficulty adjusting to the divorce or separation of the parents may also have difficulty adjusting to a move out of state.

If the child is allowed to move with the moving parent, the child will lose contact with the nonmoving parent. The evaluator will examine the potential meaning of loss to the child if the proposed move does or does not take place. The predictable loss will vary. If the child only saw the nonmoving parent one weekend a month, the loss may be minimal, especially if the proposed relocation can allow for that type of continued visitation. If, however, the child is more bonded and relies more on the nonmoving parent who is the better fit, and who has been actively involved in the child's day to day life, the loss may be great. An athletic child might miss the parent who is involved as coach of the team or attends every game or is also athletic. An artistic child might miss the parent who shares the love of the arts. A nervous child may do better with the calmer parent. The evaluator will want to check for any emotional problems with the child or any pathology due to the parents' high conflict. The child might benefit from a reduction in the conflict rather than a change in relationships.

The evaluator will need to look at other relationships the child has that might be worth protecting. If the child is involved in activities (soccer, dance, softball) or has siblings, stepsiblings, or other friends, the child may lose other things. Some children have particular medical needs or other special needs and may have developed relationships with key medical personnel, including doctors, psychologists, or others. The evaluator may need to assess the availability of comparable services at the new location.

The evaluator will explore whether there are realistic arrangements for visitation if the parent is allowed to move with the child or if the parent moves without the child. The question requires an evaluation of the parties' financial ability to pay for long-distance visitation; the distance to be traveled; whether it is my car, train, or plane; and the costs involved. Some cities are harder to get to than others. Some may only be accessible by car; others may require two or more means of transportation. How easy will it be to arrange flights and pay for them. Some cities are relatively inexpensive because of the volume of planes, but others are always expensive to reach. For a young child who cannot travel alone, what arrangements can be made? Flexibility of the parents is important in trying to navigate airports, airplanes, trains, and other public transportation.

The evaluation will contain an extensive practical analysis as to whether a long-distance parenting plan is workable. If, for example, the child only sees one parent every other weekend, the move may have minimal impact on the relationship if that schedule can still be maintained after the relocation. Sometimes the evaluator will recommend an alternative parenting plan. A parent who wants to move with a three-year-old might be convinced to wait until the child is six to facilitate a stronger bond for the nonmoving parent and child.

Custody Evaluation Report

The evaluator's findings and recommendations, if they are offered, are generally summarized in a written report that is sent to the lawyers for the parties and the court. State law[33] or local practice determines if the report is shared in whole or in part with the parents or summarized for them by their lawyers. The evaluator can be called as a witness at trial and be subject to cross-examination by the parties. If the court has appointed the evaluator, most parties believe that the judge has confidence in the person and is likely to accept the recommendations.

Custody evaluations can be lengthy and generally include:

1. Demographics;
2. Referral information;
3. The procedures used;
4. Materials reviewed and collateral contacts made;
5. Statement of the problem from the point of view of each parent;
6. Current situation of each parent;
7. Section reporting the evaluation of each party;
8. The views of the child, if old enough to express them;
9. Formulation of opinions with direct reference to the law; and
10. Conclusions and recommendations.

Some judges do not want a recommendation on the ultimate issue but do want one from the psychological point of view of what appears to be in the child's best interest or the least detrimental alternative. The evaluator may make predictions about the risks and benefits of living with Parent A in one state or Parent B in another state or of how to rearrange a shared custody arrangement if a move occurs or not.[34] The evaluator also may have an opinion on whether parents will follow the revised plan.

There may be some concern about court-ordered child custody evaluations, including issues of confidentiality, hearsay, and bias.[35] Sometimes the custody evaluation may not be too helpful. In one case, the doctor who prepared the custodial evaluation report criticized both parties' behavior, noting that their divorce was "the most adversarial, chaotic, and destructive process between a couple that [he had] participated in as an examiner in the last 43 years."[36] In another case, the family court found it was not in the child's best interests to remain in Kentucky and granted mother's request to relocate to Washington state. A court-appointed social worker had performed an evaluation where both parents were bipolar and had had substance abuse issues. There was no indication that her report was the sole reason the family court granted the mother's request. The court had also heard from family and friends regarding the ties to the community the child and the parties had.[37]

The Mental Health Consultant

A lawyer may decide to hire a mental health consultant who is usually an experienced evaluator. The three main purposes are (1) to educate and provide support to a party who is being evaluated; (2) to provide case analysis and evaluation for the lawyer's better understanding the quality of the report; and (3) testimony at trial.[38]

The litigant pays the cost of the mental health consultant. The mental health consultant does not have a psychotherapist–patient relationship with the litigant and does not provide psychotherapy. A mental health consultant can provide education and support for a litigant who is participating in a forensic mental health evaluation. Another purpose may be to consult with the lawyer about the forensic mental health evaluation, including review of the quality of the evaluation. The consultant can also help the lawyer prepare for cross-examination of the evaluator. The mental health consultant may be an expert who testifies at the trial.

The lawyer's work product doctrine generally protects the consultant's communications with the litigant from discovery and admission into evidence at trial unless the consultant is called as a witness at trial. A testifying consultant may have to disclose discussions with the lawyer and litigant to the court.[39] The lawyer should prepare the expert to testify if it is the client's expert. It is more difficult if the expert is court-appointed or jointly retained. Ideally there would be some opportunity to meet with the expert to prepare for actual testimony.

Experts in Court

Generally, the expert should be able to testify at the hearing on relocation to allow for direct and cross-examination. The trial court's refusal in divorce proceedings to allow two of wife's expert witnesses to testify via telephone was not an abuse of discretion because the wife failed to comply with the deadlines for disclosure of witnesses, failed to provide expert witness information for one witness, provided the expert witness information for second witness one week before trial, and failed to notify the court or husband of the need for the witnesses to appear via telephone until a few days before trial. The husband was deprived of any opportunity to question witnesses in person.[40] (See generally Chapter 12.) A New York court found the trial court's error in not allowing the pro se father pretrial access to the forensic expert's report was harmless because he had an opportunity to review the report when he had earlier been represented and later with the court-appointed social worker. He had questioned the expert on a number of issues. The court cited to expert's testimony rather than the report in granting the mother's relocation request.[41]

While cross-examination of an expert is discussed in Chapter 12, there are some specific factors to look at in reviewing evaluators and evaluations. A recent article describes the several approaches to reviewing evaluators and evaluations and how to cross-examine each of them.[42]

The Forensic Model

This approach encourages evaluators to use scientific principles in conducting custody evaluations.[43] The court defines the evaluator's role, purpose, and focus of the evaluation. The forensic model emphasizes the standards and guidelines of state regulatory boards and various professional groups.

PLAN: Psychology-Law Analysis

The four-step PLAN approach includes (1) determination of the expert's qualifications; (2) determination of whether the expert's methods conform to relevant professional practice standards (methods reliability); (3) determination of the empirical and logical connections between the data obtained from the use of reliable methods and the expert's social-science based conclusions (reasoning reliability); and (4) determination of the connection between the expert's conclusions and the proffered expert opinions.[44]

The Custody Assessment Analysis System (CAAS)

The CAAS system organizes examination of a child custody evaluation around four general dimensions, each of which consists of three to five variables. The four dimensions are (1) management of professional relationships, (2) data adequacy, (3) technique adequacy, and (4) reasoning adequacy. Each of the general dimensions is broken down into more specific factors.[45]

Weight Given to Expert

Studies suggest that custody evaluation reports exert considerable influence on judges. The quality of reports, however, varies widely.[46] While the extent to which judges rely upon child custody evaluations varies, all agree that a trial judge cannot delegate the obligation to independently weigh evidence in determining the children's best interests to the evaluator.[47]

The trial court has the discretion in determining the weight to be given the expert's report and testimony.[48] The judge, however, is not bound to accept the testimony of an expert. A judge may weigh the expert's testimony as to its credibility and its persuasive influence in light of all of the other evidence in the case. The judge as the fact finder is in the best position to assess the credibility of witnesses and is free to disbelieve their testimony even if that testimony comes from an expert witness, including opinions offered by a child custody evaluator. The court, however, should consider the results of a psychological examination, especially if the court ordered it.[49]

If a court chooses to reject the evaluator's opinion, it is expected to articulate some reason for doing so. Sufficient evidence supported a trial court's determination that the child custody evaluator's recommendation that the parties should continue to share joint physical and legal custody but evidence that the children should relocate back to Utah after moving out of state with mother was outdated at the time of trial. Therefore, it did not weigh in favor of granting change of custody to father. The evidence presented at trial was "virtually unanimous" in establishing that children were happy, well-adjusted, and thriving under their current arrangement. The trial court rejected evaluator's contention that relocating the children back to Utah would not have been that big of a deal.[50]

Mother petitioned to move out of state with the children. The trial court's rejection of the conclusion of father's expert witness that physical proximity was "essential to the fundamental ambitions of a co-parenting model" did not indicate that court had failed or refused to weigh the expert's opinion in determining that relocation was in children's best interests.[51]

Endnotes

1. Fuqua v. Fuqua, 57 So. 3d 534, 540 (La. Ct. App. 2011).

2. Katare v. Katare, 283 P.3d 546 (Wash. 2012) (attorney with 17 years of experience in the field of child abduction could testify as to risk factors for abduction). *See also* Shady v. Shady, 858 N.E.2d 128 (Ind. Ct. App. 2006), *transfer denied* Mar. 8, 2007 (qualifying as an expert in international child abduction was proper where witness was proprietor of counseling firm that provided services for clients of international recovery of abducted children and assessment of the risk of future abduction).

3. *See* William G. Austin & Sol Rappaport, *Parental Gatekeeping Forensic Model and Child Custody Evaluation: Social Capital and Application to Relocation Disputes*, 15 J. Child Custody 55 (2018) (relocation adds to the general risks associated with children of divorce); Matthew M. Stevenson et al., *Associations Between Parental Relocation Following Separation in Childhood and Maladjustment in Adolescence and Young Adulthood*, 24 Psych. Pub. Pol'y & L. 365 (2018) (finding several risks).

4. *See* Philip M. Stahl, *Emerging Issues in Relocation Cases*, 25 J. Am. Acad. Matrim. Lawyers 425 (2013).

5. Daubert v. Merrell Dow Pharmaceuticals, Inc., 509 U.S. 579 (1993). *See also* Kumho Tire Co. v. Carmichael, 526 U.S. 137, 152 (1999). *See also* Sarah H. Ramsey & Robert F. Kelly, *Social Science Knowledge in Family Law Cases: Judicial Gatekeeping in the* Daubert *Era*, 59 U. Miami L. Rev. 1, 4 (2004).

6. *Id.*

7. Sheridan v. Sheridan, 12 N.Y.S.3d 434 (App. Div. 2015) (not modifying custody where court-appointed expert noted that a potential move from the mother's residence in Syracuse to the father's residence in Buffalo would put the child "at risk of experiencing a tremendous sense of loss and disruption" because of his connections to school, community, friends, and activities in Syracuse).

8. *See* Rick Friedman & Patrick Malone, Rules of the Road: A Plaintiff Lawyer's Guide to Proving Liability (2d ed. 2010).

9. *In re* Marriage of L.F. & M.F., 562 P.3d 1014 (Kan. Ct. App. 2025) (statute allowing court-ordered investigations in child custody proceedings does not limit investigator's report to a custody evaluation).

10. Milfred D. Dale & Jonathan W. Gould, *Science, Mental Health Consultants, and Attorney-Expert Relationships in Child Custody*, 48(1) Fam. L.Q. 1 (2014).

11. Bares v. Bares, 40 So. 3d 1153 (La. Ct. App. 2010) (denying mother's motion for mental health professional where both parents and the child had been evaluated by a clinical psychologist twice within the past few years and denying relocation to Texas).

12. For a discussion of the history and role of custody evaluations, *see* Linda D. Elrod & Milfred D. Dale, *Paradigm Shifts and Pendulum Swings in Child Custody: The Interests of Children in the Balance*, 42(3) FAM. L.Q. 381, 410–17 (2008).

13. KAN. STAT. ANN. § 23-3210.

14. Association of Family and Conciliation Courts, *Model Standards of Practice for Child Custody Evaluation* r. 1.1, 1.2, & 1.3, 45 FAM. CT. REV. 70 (2007). *See also* AMERICAN ACADEMY OF MATRIMONIAL LAWYERS, CHILD CUSTODY EVALUATION STANDARDS (2011).

15. *Guidelines for Child Custody Evaluations in Family Law Proceedings*, 65(9) AM. PSYCH. ASS'N 863 (2021).

16. Dale & Gould, *supra* note 10, at 2–3.

17. AFCC Task Force, *Guidelines for the Use of Social Science Research on Family Law*, 57(2) FAM. CT. REV. 193 (2019) provides guidance for how to identify reliable research, how to determine the relevance of the research to the question before the court, and how to generalize from research findings while also noting the limitations of these efforts.

18. Dale & Gould, *supra* note 10.

19. D.J. v. C.J., 464 P.3d 790 (Haw. 2020).

20. Kinsella v. Kinsella, 696 A.2d 556 (N.J. 1997). *See generally* LINDA D. ELROD, CHILD CUSTODY PRACTICE AND PROCEDURE ch. 11 (Thomson Reuters 2024).

21. *Guidelines for Child Custody Evaluations in Family Law Proceedings*, 65(9) AM. PSYCH. ASS'N 863 (2022).

22. Milfred D. Dale, Jonathan Gould & Allyssa Levine, *Cross-Examining Experts in Child Custody: The Necessary Theories and Models . . . with Instructions*, 33(2) J. AM. ACAD. MATRIM. LAWYERS 328 (2021).

23. Milfred D. Dale & Desiree Smith, *Making the Case for Videoconferencing and Remote Child Custody Evaluations (RCCEs): The Empirical, Ethical, and Evidentiary Arguments for Accepting a New Technology*, 27(1) PSYCH. PUB. POL'Y & L. 30 (2021).

24. Barbara Jo Fidler & Rachel Birnbaum, *Child Custody Disputes: Private and Public Assessments*, 25 C.F.L.Q. 137, 150 (2006).

25. Austin & Rappaport, *supra* note 3, at 67.

26. Sol R. Rappaport, Jonathon Gould & Mildred D. Dale, *Psychological Testing Can Be of Significant Value in Child Custody Evaluations: Don't Buy the Anti-Testing, Anti-Individual, Pro-Family Systems Woozle*, 30 J. AM. ACAD. MATRIM. LAWYERS 405 (2018). *See also* Cassandra Valerio & Connie J. Beck, *Testing in Child Custody Evaluations: An Overview of Issues and Uses*, 14 J. CHILD CUSTODY 260 (2017).

27. Philip M. Stahl, *Avoiding Bias in Relocation Cases*, 3 J. Child Custody 109, 117 (2006).

28. Shady v. Shady, 858 N.E.2d 128 (Ind. Ct. App. 2007) (describing test results).

29. Gary B. Melton et al., Psychological Evaluations for the Courts: A Handbook for Mental Health Professionals and Lawyers 559–60 (3d ed. 2007).

30. Rappaport, Gould & Dale, *supra* note 26.

31. *See generally see* Michael E. Lamb, *Critical Analysis of Research on Parenting Plans and Children's Well-Being, in* Parenting Plan Evaluations: Applied Research for the Family Court 170, 192 (Leslie Drozd et al. eds., 2d ed. 2016).

32. Sonbuchner v. Sonbuchner, 947 N.Y.S.2d 80, 568 (App. Div. 2012).

33. Fuge v. Uitrtwyk, 653 So. 2d 7097, 712 (La. Ct. App. 1995) (court's refusal to allow parties access to the psychiatrist's report in a relocation case violated Louisiana statute); Barker v. Barker, 167 So. 3d 703 (La. Ct. App. 2014) (reliance on court appointed mental health professional's report without allowing parties to review it denied them due process).

34. William G. Austin & Jonathan W. Gould, *Exploring Three Functions in Child Custody Evaluation for the Relocation Case: Prediction, Investigation, and Making Recommendations for a Long Distance Parenting Plan*, 3 J. Child Custody 63 (2006).

35. *See* Stahl, *supra* note 27.

36. Albanese v. Albanese, 135 So. 3d 532 (Fla. Dist. Ct. App. 2014) (reversing temporary order allowing father to take children to New York; there was no evidence to support it was in their best interests; neither parent demonstrated the disposition to honor a time-sharing schedule, environments in both households were "chaotic," and both parents lacked veracity).

37. Samson v. Samson, 377 S.W.3d 571 (Ky. Ct. App. 2012).

38. Andrew Schepard, *AFCC Task Force Report on Mental Health Consultants and Child Custody Evaluations: A Discussion Paper*, 49(4) Fam. Ct. Rev. 723 (2011).

39. Fed. R. Civ. P. 26(b)(4).

40. Malenko v. Handrahan, 979 A.2d 1269 (Me. 2009) (citing Fed. R. Evid. 611(a); Fed. R. Civ. P. 43(a)).

41. Sonbuchner v. Sonbuchner, 947 N.Y.S.2d 80 (App. Div. 2012).

42. Dale, Gould & Levine, *supra* note 22.

43. *Id.* at 356–57. *See* Jonathan W. Gould & David A. Martindale, The Art and Science of Child Custody Evaluations 101 (2007).

44. Dale, Gould & Levine, *supra* note 22, at 367. *See* John Zervopolous, Confronting Mental Health Evidence: A Practical Plan to Examine Reliability and Experts in Family Law (2d ed. 2015); How to Examine Mental Health Experts: A Family Lawyer's Handbook of Issues and Strategies (ABA 2d ed. 2020).

45. Dale, Gould & Levine, *supra* note 22, at 373. *See* JEFFREY WITTMAN, EVALUATING EVALUATIONS: AN ATTORNEY'S HANDBOOK FOR ANALYZING CHILD CUSTODY REPORTS (2013).

46. Mary Johanna McCurley et al., *Protecting Children from Incompetent Forensic Evaluations and Expert Testimony*, 19 J. AM. ACAD. MATRIM. LAWYERS 277 (2005).

47. *In re* Nold, 304 P.3d 1093 (Ariz. Ct. App. 2013).

48. Perez v. Perez, 85 So. 3d 273 (La. Ct. App. 2012) (discounting expert's testimony where expert did not have all relevant facts and had not interviewed parties for five months before the hearing and was not in the courtroom when the witnesses testified). *See also* Morgan v. Morgan, 12 A.3d 192 (N.J. 2011).

49. Pontillo v. Johnson Kosiorek, 152 N.Y.S.3d 204 (App. Div. 2021).

50. Lobendahn v. Lobendahn, 540 P.3d 727 (Utah Ct. App. 2023).

51. Wheeler v. Wheeler, 591 S.E.2d 698 (Va. Ct. App. 2004).

CHAPTER 12

Trial of a Relocation Case

> *A child custody determination is much more difficult than an arithmetical computation of factors; it is one of the most demanding undertakings of a trial judge, one in which he must not only listen to what is said to him and observe all that happens before him, but a task requiring him to discern and feel climate and chemistry of relationships between children and parents.*[1]

The trial of a relocation case is similar to that of any other contested custody case.[2] The relocation case feels significantly different in that if the child is allowed to move or if custody is changed, there may be lasting, unforeseen repercussions. There is little way to salvage a "win/win." One parent will move, with or without the child, to another location. The child will be separated geographically from one of the parents. Judges agonize over whether to allow the parent to move with the child, and, if so, what substitute parenting arrangement will best preserve the nonmoving parent's relationship with the child. The stakes are incredibly high. A relocation trial may have more impact than the initial custody decision. The child's relationship with all of the parties, but especially the nonmoving parent, will be forever changed, and possibly harmed, by whatever decision the judge makes.

Counsel must clarify the burden of proof, the applicable standards and procedures, and relate a clear and compelling story as to why the relocation should or should not happen. Counsel must also determine how long the trial judge is going to give parties to put on their evidence. Because of overcrowded court dockets, judges have tried to cut down on the length of trial by imposing time limits for the presentation of evidence. The parties have a right to present all of relevant, non-cumulative evidence, provided the probative value is not outweighed by undue delay and wasting the court's time. Louisiana courts use five factors to consider whether a court denied due process by limiting the hearing time. First, before imposing time limitations, the court is familiar with pretrial proceedings, the claims of the parties, the proposed testimony, and number of witnesses and documentary evidence to be presented. Second, time limits should be imposed on all parties well in advance of trial, so parties have time to prepare for trial within the limits. Third, reasonable extensions should be granted for good cause shown. Fourth, the trial judge should develop an equitable method of charging time against each litigant's time limits; and, fifth, the trial judge should put all rulings regarding time limits on the record.[3] Appellate courts have generally upheld even relatively short time periods. For example, a Louisiana appellate court upheld a trial judge who imposed a two-hour trial limit on each side in a case in which a mother wanted to move her children to Dubai when the parties had a month notice and no party objected.[4]

Preparation is key for any trial. A lawyer prepares for trial from the moment the client enters the office. From the first information intake sheet, through the use of discovery, pretrial conferences, and research, the lawyer prepares for the possibility of trial. Preparation requires not only the thorough knowledge of the applicable law and procedures but also preparing the client to make a good impression at trial. This includes considerations of appropriate dress (no crocs, low cut blouses, jeans, etc.), makeup, and often covering tattoos or anything that might distract from the client's case. If the client is prone to using expletives or comes across as judgmental, racist, or crass, the lawyer can educate the client of how the behavior would come across in court. If the client has said or done some things in the past that show poor decision-making (drugs, excessive alcohol with posts on social media, affairs, trying to poison the child against the other parent), the lawyer can encourage the client to take positive steps to rehabilitate and do better. While the past cannot be changed, the future can. The ultimate goal is to make the parent client look as good as possible.

The parent who wants to move with the child needs to have thoroughly thought out all of the reasons, advantages, and foreseeable ramifications of the move as well as ways to mitigate the other party's strongest objections.[5] The party attempting to keep the child from relocating needs to present as much evidence as possible as to how the move will negatively impact the parent's current integration into the child's daily life. The logistics and ramifications of a change of the child's existing residence, school, and activities can cause irreparable harm to the relationship with the nonmoving parent.

Relocation cases with a child require more preparation and organization than other types of litigation to be successful. The lawyer and client must work as a team to present a convincing case for or against the relocation. The theory of the case is applying the facts to the law and giving the judge the legal basis for the requested relief. The lawyer and client must craft a convincing theme—the reason why allowing the move (or not) is the right thing for the judge to do. The theme is the moral hook that appeals to the judge's sentiments, not just logic. The lawyer will want to develop a trial outline or trial notebook, which can be done on an iPad. The outline will include the order of witnesses, the subject matter about which each of the witnesses will testify, anticipated witnesses for the other party, the evidence to be presented, ideas for cross examination of opposing witnesses, and the development of a list of exhibits.[6]

While jurisdictions differ as to who has the burden of proof (the relocating parent to show either a good faith reason for the move or the benefit to the child or the nonrelocating parent to show the harm, or both), the relocating parent should have thoroughly researched the proposed location. The relocating parent should be able to articulate the advantages to the parent and child in the new location—excellent schools with strong programs in the arts, music, debate, college prep classes, safer community, larger house, less traffic, closer proximity to medical providers, the presence of extended family members, more premium sporting leagues, and the like. By the time the relocating parent is finished, hopefully the judge will be thinking that everyone should move to the new location or, at the least, how could one oppose a move to such a great place.

Know Judge's Philosophy

As in any case, the lawyer must try to get an understanding of the judge's philosophy. The old adage "Know your judge" means to anticipate where the judge is likely to want to go and either drive that direction if it is the client's position or try to get the judge to deviate from their usually preferred path. For example, if the judge has always allowed a mother who has primary residency to move with her child to a new location, then representing the nonmoving father will require a greater amount of evidence showing how the child will be harmed from the lack of a relationship with the concerned, actively involved father. Likewise, if the judge has never allowed a residential parent to move with a child, the lawyer representing the moving parent will need an exceptional evidence to overcome the judge's reluctance to allow a move. The lawyer needs to keep the possibility of settlement on the table. The lawyer should offer a mitigating, second fallback, last fallback, or settlement proposal throughout the proceeding, even if things seem to be going well. The trial judge who hates to allow a parent to move away can find enough evidence of harm to the child to change custody, even if the lawyer and client feel the case is convincing.

As a general rule, judges respect and respond more favorably to a constructive approach. Judges want to protect the child and also to do the "right" thing. The lawyer's job is to guide the judge toward that end by showing the client is the parent with whom the child has the strongest bond and the parent most likely to foster a continuing positive relationship with the other parent.

"Knowing the judge" also requires the lawyer to know the judge's pet peeves. If the judge hates it when someone refers to children as "kids," the lawyer does not want to antagonize the judge over something relatively minor.

Themes or Theories of the Case

Every relocation case needs a theme or a theory to persuade the judge that what the client is requesting is in the best interests of the child. The theory of the case is the basic underlying idea that explains the legal theory and factual background and ties the evidence into a coherent whole.[7] Artful themes encapsulate the core principles of the case, hopefully with a phrase or parable that resonates with the judge. Fairy tales, fables, and classic literature offer many themes. Tying the facts of the case to a familiar theme can make the case become vibrant and more memorable. The theme will be tied to the facts of the specific case. The lawyer paints the picture with the facts and tells a story. The law provides the framework.

The relocating parent needs to convince the judge of the solid and bona fide reason for the move. One theme is that of sacrifice. The mother left her family, friends, and prior job to follow her husband and keep the family together. When he divorced her, she has been left without a job and without her family and friends. She wants to move back to family and friends and a location with better job prospects.[8] The move would improve both her and the child's quality of life as the mother would have a better paying job (often with better hours), more family support, and the child would have access to more extended family.

One way to find the theme is to review all of the relevant factors in state law for relocation of the child. Upon listing the factors, the lawyer can go through them one by one with the client and develop the relevant facts that support each factor. A theme may appear. For example, a common factor is the importance of continuity in the child's life and the length of time the child has lived in a stable, satisfactory environment. The facts may show that mother has been the primary caregiver throughout the marriage (favors mother). Father moved out of the house three months ago, so the mother has been primary parent (favors mother). Father plans to move into marital home if the mother moves to be with family in another state (favors father).

The client should have a good reason for the move. Inability of the parents to cooperate or be in the same room together is generally not a sufficient reason to move (see Chapter 9). A client who cannot articulate a convincing argument to their lawyer about the benefits of relocation or maintaining the status quo is likely to meet the same difficulty when attempting to persuade an impartial observer like the judge.

Common Themes for Relocating Parent

The common themes for a relocating parent involve the necessity of the relocation for financial reasons or to return to family, the improvement in the quality of life for the parent and child, and the ability to maintain a strong relationship with the nonrelocating parent.

1. Relocating parent has always been cooperative and encouraging with parenting arrangements and will continue to create a workable plan to maintain a relationship with the other parent. The primary reason for the move is not to thwart the other parent's access to the child.
2. The relocating parent has made good faith attempts to negotiate or mediate changes to the parenting plan to reach an agreement for the move.
3. There are significant advantages to the relocating parent and child in the new location, such as proximity to extended family and friend support systems.[9]
4. There is a compelling reason for the move. Relocating parent has been transferred or has a new job opportunity that will enhance the parent and child's quality of life.
5. Relocating parent has remarried and new spouse has job in another location. There may also be half-siblings with whom the child is close.
6. There are numerous advantages for the child that will arise from the move to the new location, such as excellent education opportunities, necessary medical facilities, or removing the child from bullying or a negative peer group.
7. The moving parent has been the primary caretaker of the child.

8. The child is of sufficient age and maturity to have a preference and wishes to move to the new location.
9. Relocation will reduce the conflict and improve the relationship between the parents, which will benefit the child.
10. There are well thought out proposed alternative parenting time arrangements after the prospective relocation that are possible both financially and logistically.
11. The parent wishing to move is willing to assist the other parent in moving to the same location.
12. The nonrelocating parent has been an uninvolved parent, has not regularly exercised parenting time, and does not participate in the child's life in current location.
13. The nonmoving parent is violent and there are protective orders in place for the moving parent and/or the child.
14. The nonmoving parent's nonpayment of child support has created economic hardship necessitating a move to a less-expensive area of the country or place where relatives can help support or relocating parent can get work to better support the child.

Common Themes for the Nonmoving Parent

When representing the parent resisting relocation, the themes should emphasize the close relationship between the nonrelocating parent and the child and the motives of the parties. The motives of the nonmoving parent should show desire to maintain an already close relationship. The themes can revolve around the risk factors for children who live a long distance away from one of the parents. The themes may also show improper motives of the relocating parent.

1. The nonrelocating parent has an extremely close relationship with the child as evidenced by active participation in child's life and activities that will be irreparably harmed by relocation. Studies show a move of more than 75 miles reduces the ability of parent to maintain contact.[10]

2. There are more advantages for the child in the current location, extended family, half-siblings, school, sports, and so on, that will not be available after the move.
3. The relocating parent has been uncooperative and there is a history of interfering with the nonrelocating parent's relationship with the child.
4. The relocating parent has inadequate reasons for the move. The parent did not try to find a job or alternative housing in the existing locale.
5. The relocating parent did not give sufficient notice or attempt to negotiate a new parenting plan.
6. Proposed relocation city is not as good a place to live due to poor schools or schools that require long commutes for the child, crime, air or water quality, and so on.
7. Proposed relocation city is too far away to maintain meaningful contact either because the drive is too far, the costs are too burdensome, or both.
8. Studies have shown harm to a child from divorce; that harm can be exacerbated from relocating a distance (actually more than an hour away) from one of the parents.[11]

Burden of Proof

Relocation cases can be tricky as to who bears the burden of proof. The lawyer must consult the statutes and cases in the specific jurisdiction to ascertain the requirements in relocation cases. As a general rule the petitioning party always has the initial burden of proof. So the parent who petitions for the court to allow relocation has the burden. If the parent opposing the move files to prevent the move or to change custody, that parent has the burden.[12] The Florida statute is clear and provides that: The parent or other person wishing to relocate has the burden of proving by a preponderance of the evidence that relocation is in the best interest of the child. If that burden of proof is met, the burden shifts to the nonrelocating parent or other person to show by a preponderance of the evidence that the proposed relocation is not in the best interest of the child.[13] Many courts use a shifting burden. In Indiana, if a person receiving notice of the other parent's intent to move objects within 60 days of the notice, the moving party must prove legitimate purpose for the move. Then the burden shifts to the nonmoving party to prove a move is "not" in the children's best interests. A few states, like Washington, still contain a rebuttable statutory presumption in favor of a primary residential parent's decision to relocate, but it only requires a preponderance of evidence to rebut the presumption.[14]

General Thoughts Preparing for Trial

The judge is the ultimate decision-maker and must make factual findings to support the decision. The judge's decision will rarely be overturned except for an abuse of discretion or using wrong law (see Chapter 16). Therefore, the lawyer needs to make sure that the client makes the best possible impression on the trial judge. Even if the law is on the client's side, if the client comes across as a jerk, uncompromising, overly rigid, selfish, unstable, or disrespectful, the judge may take a dislike to the client. A good judge can word decisions to make them virtually unappealable on the fact issues. Therefore, the lawyer should do the following:

1. Be on time and make sure that the client and any witnesses are also on time.
2. Dress the part and make sure the client and witnesses know proper courtroom attire. Usually at a minimum this means wear a shirt, pants or skirt, and no bare feet.
3. Reread both the pleadings and those filed by opposing counsel. Do not argue for something that was not pled or waste the court's time.
4. Be prepared to show the judge that the client parent has been and will continue to be cooperative and foster a positive relationship with the other parent.

5. Educate the client on proper courtroom decorum—no eye rolling or nasty looks at other parent or the parent's lawyer. Control the entourage—new partners, parents, siblings who may also be in the courtroom can distract from the client's case.
6. Consider preparing a trial brief that narrows the legal issues, the burden of proof, and what must be proved on best interest of the child. The trial brief will present reasons for (or against) the move, the evidence to be presented, issues of compliance with statutory provisions, the burden of proof, and factors found in the statute or cases of the jurisdiction.
7. Have a detailed, working knowledge of the rules of evidence. This is important for introducing exhibits, examining and cross-examining witnesses, and making relevant objections in a timely manner.
8. Make effective use of timely evidentiary objections.
    a. When in doubt, always object to preserve the record for appeal and to keep the flow of evidence straight.
    b. The exclusion of evidence that is harmful to the client's position is important.
    c. Objections can be used to interrupt and break an uncomfortable sequence of questions and answers.
    d. Making an objection will break a series of questions that are going too fast to give the witness time to think before answering. For example, a compound question may create confusion. An objection on the ground that the question is vague or ambiguous should alert the witness that the question is not clear. Other objections that can alert the witness to problems in the question—assumes fact not in evidence, call for speculation, calls for state of mind, or even leading.
9. Make offers of proof.
10. Know the rules of evidentiary foundation of documents and properly admit testimony and evidence.

Opening Statement

The opening statement is one of the most critical stages in a custody trial. It sets the tone and makes the important first impression to the finder of fact. This is where the lawyer starts telling the client's story. The opening statement offers the first opportunity to introduce and personalize the client, and sets the overall structure for the relocation case. The theme should be referenced in the first few lines of the opening statement. Once the theme is set, the lawyer will tailor the trial to persuade the judge to the client's position.

The opening explains a little about the background that led to the trial, informs the judge of the nature of the case, and tells the judge what the client wants. The opening argument should fit into a 15- to 20-minute time frame. It should be organized and succinct as well as supply the basic information.

1. Ages of parties, number and ages of children.
2. Outline the plan for the children. Explain why it is in the child's best interest that your client remain (or become) primary parent.
3. Brief employment or homemaker history.
4. Where the parties live and how long they have lived there.
5. Description of marital situation of each party.
6. Schools and attendance records.
7. Health issues of children or parents.
8. Which parent has been primary residential custodian.
9. Recognition of the importance of maintaining continuity of attachments with both parents (unless abuse or harm).

The opening statement creates a roadmap of what the lawyer is going to prove. It should be strong and express the theme clearly and consistently. It may refer to the type of evidence that will be presented such as witnesses and exhibits. The lawyer should avoid arguing inconsistent themes or making inconsistent statements. A typical opening statement for the moving parent in a relocation case might begin:

> Your Honor, Amanda Long Adams requests that she and her eight-year-old daughter Anna be allowed to move to St. Louis where Amanda grew up. Her parents, the Longs, and most of her close friends still live there. Amanda has been Anna's primary caregiver since birth and has few friends here. Amanda has been unable to find work in her field [list field] here. She has been offered a high paying job in her field that will not only pay her more money but also allow her to spend more time at home with Anna. Dr. Jeffrey Adams is a dentist who has worked 12-hour days, five days a week throughout the marriage and after the divorce. He sees Anna every other weekend. Even though he has not asked and does not want to be the primary caretaker, he does not want Amanda to go on with her life.

Direct Examination

Direct examination is the opportunity to present evidence in support of the client's case. Most cases are won or lost through direct examination. To begin, the lawyer needs to have the goal in mind—what is the direct examination going to show the judge? This means knowing the legal factors at play and evidentiary standards. In most states, the judge is charged with determining the best interests of the child. To present the evidence, the lawyer needs to know how the testimony of the client and witnesses can best be presented in a logical and coherent way to satisfy the relevant burdens of proof. The lawyer can review the statute and case law for the relevant factors and outline what testimony and evidence can show the client's meeting of those factors.

Among the evidence will be testimony of the parties and witnesses and reports of professionals such as a guardian ad litem, social worker, or custody evaluator. A party needs witnesses to testify as to the most important information necessary to prove their case. Determining which witnesses to present and in what order is part of case planning. Courts exercise considerable discretion regarding the mode of interrogation and presentation of witnesses. That discretion includes permitting the "presentation of testimony in open court by contemporaneous transmission from a different location" upon a showing of good cause. When courts are not meeting in person because of a pandemic or when witnesses live in different locations, most courts are now familiar with Zoom and other platforms to allow remote testimony in person.

Live witnesses are best at a hearing or trial. The parties are the primary witnesses. The client or witness is the center of attention during direct examination and is telling a story. The lawyer should encourage a narrative because the witness needs to tell the story in a cohesive, organized manner that will be persuasive to the judge. Preparation and practice can prepare the client for the type of questions that they are likely to get on direct (and cross) examination. The witness needs to sound prepared, but not "over rehearsed" or canned. The witness tells the story.

There may be other witnesses, such as a custody evaluator, a therapist, or someone else who can testify about the environment in the new location. For example, if the child is of school age, both parents may be concerned about the relative quality of the schools in both locations. If the child is in a high school in which 85 percent of the students graduate and go to college, it will be difficult to sell the move of the child to a school in which less than 50 percent of students graduate. If the difference is between a rural or urban school, there may be good explanations for the differences. The National Center for Education Statistics keeps information on schools and includes teacher/student ratios which may be relevant.[15] An organization called Schoolmatch collects comparison information and provides expert witness services for relocation cases.[16] A live expert witness who is in the business of doing school comparisons may be the most reliable from an evidentiary standpoint. Other relevance may be the distance from home to school, whether the child will have to ride a bus one place or the other, crime statistics, and bullying in the schools.

There are a few reminders for direct examination:

1. Be prepared. Have an outline or bullet points so the judge gets the important information the witness has to share.
2. Be brief. Some say, one question, one fact.
3. Use plain English, especially if using an expert.

4. Do not lead the witness. The witness needs to testify as to the evidence. It is the witness's credibility that persuades the judge that the witness is telling the truth and perceived events correctly. The questions on direct should start with "who," "what," "where," "why," "when," and "how."
5. Break up the narrative with occasional questions.
6. Listen to the witness's answers.
7. Ask the witness to explain if something is unclear or not fully developed.
8. Keep in mind the rules for present recollection refreshed and past recollection recorded and use them if necessary.
9. Know how to make an offer of proof.
10. Anticipate negative facts to prepare your client for cross-examination. Clients are rarely perfect. If there is a negative, sometimes the lawyer can bring it out in such a way to minimize the impact. For example, if your client made derogatory remarks about the other parent on social media or in the presence of other persons, sometimes admitting the "error" and discussing what steps the client has taken to shield the child from hearing further negative comments can boost credibility.

Exhibits

Tangible exhibits or "real" evidence are generally in the form of documents, videos, photographs, charts, and diagrams. There may be photographs or videos of the child with siblings, parents, extended family, or others that may help show relationships. Photo albums can be illustrative of activities of the children and lifestyle. Photos of the client parent with the children, coaching the team, fishing, or whatever can show relationships and parenting activity. There may be letters, grade cards, and other documents that may help show how the child is doing in the current location. The parties may want to stipulate to exhibits to save time.

If the parties do not stipulate, the lawyer should have copies of the exhibit for the court clerk, opposing counsel, the judge, one for the client, and a file copy. The first step is to mark the exhibit. Some judges like to have exhibits pre-marked. After the exhibit is marked by the courtroom clerk, the document must be shown to opposing counsel. Then the exhibit is shown to the witness who is asked to identify it. The lawyer will lay the foundation for the document's admissibility, demonstrate the document's relevance to the issues in dispute, and authenticate the document, determine that it is what it says it is. An example of using a picture of the child with grandparents and opposing counsel does not object would be:

Counsel: May I have this picture marked as Exhibit A-3?

Judge: Please show to counsel.

Counsel: Counsel has a copy, your honor. With my colleague's permission, may I provide a bench copy to the court?

Judge: Hearing no objection, I will accept a bench copy.

If there is an objection, the lawyer will ask to approach the witness and say:

Witness, I show you what has now been marked as Exhibit A-3. Can you identify this picture for the court, please?

Counsel: Did you take this picture?

Witness: No.

Counsel: Can you identify the people in this photograph?

Witness: Yes.

Counsel: Who are they?

Witness: This is my daughter. This is my father holding her in his arms.

Counsel: Do you know who took the photo?

Witness: Yes. My wife took the photo, and I was standing next to her.

Counsel: Is this an accurate picture of what it purports to show?

Witness: Yes, it is.

After the witness has identified and authenticated the document, counsel may now ask the court to accept the document by saying: Your honor, I move Exhibit A-3 into evidence. The opposing counsel may object on the grounds of hearsay, relevance, or if the evidence is a copy, it is not the best evidence. Children's report cards may be accepted as business records kept in the ordinary course of business. A psychologist's report, which may be hearsay, may come in by stipulation of the parties or if the psychologist is in court and able to testify. A Hawaii court found that its trial court could consider a custody evaluation and report prepared by the family court's Custody Investigations Unit, even if the parent did not consent to the evaluation.[17] Other states may have a statute allowing some reports to come in.

Experts

In most jurisdictions, the rules of evidence allow an expert witness to offer opinions in court if the expert is qualified and those opinions "will assist the trier of fact to understand the evidence or to determine a fact in issue." Federal Rule of Evidence 702 provides that an expert is one who is qualified by "knowledge, skill, experience, training or education." A person can become an expert because of qualifications, expertise relevant to the dispute at hand, publications, forensic experience, or testifying experience.[18] If using expert testimony, the lawyer can send the resume to the opposing attorney or party and try to get a stipulation in advance to the person being an expert. Sometimes the judge will take judicial notice that someone is an expert if they appear regularly in the courtroom or have a national or state reputation.

The trial judge must ensure that any and all scientific testimony or evidence admitted is not only relevant but also reliable, based on trustworthy methodology.[19] The trial judge is the evidence gatekeeper who must assess whether the reasoning or methodology underlying the testimony is scientifically valid and whether it can properly be applied to the facts at issue.[20] The purpose is to protect opponents from having to expend resources to counter untrustworthy testimony; to keep the courts from wasting time and resources; and to guard the integrity of the system from seeming reliance on bad science.[21] The analysis of whether the expert testimony is reliable looks to

1. Is the witness qualified as an expert by knowledge, skill, experience, training, or education?
2. Did the expert's methods follow applicable professional standards of the relevant professional specialty?
3. Evaluate the empirical and logical connections between the data arising from the expert's methods and the expert's conclusions.
4. Gauge the connection between the expert's conclusions and the proffered expert opinion.

Even if the court appoints an expert, the court makes the final decision as to the weight to be given their opinion. Expert testimony can make the difference in a relocation case. A Tennessee mother wanted to move with 11-year-old daughter 2,000 miles away to Anaheim, California, to study marine biology and marry a man she had been dating. The 17-year-old son was in his last semester of high school and planned to live with dad when he went to college. The court denied the relocation partly on the basis of expert testimony that he had met with the daughter nine times and that moving away from her father, brother, family, and other school friends would cause her to suffer substantial emotional harm.[22] In another case, the court upheld in not modifying custody to the father because it was in the best interests of the children to remain in the custody of the mother. The court-appointed expert noted that a potential move from the mother's residence in Syracuse to the father's residence in Buffalo would put the child "at risk of experiencing a tremendous sense of loss and disruption" because of his connections to school, community, friends, and activities in Syracuse.[23]

Courts have the ultimate discretion as to the weight to give the expert's testimony. Even though the expert witness opined that the children should stay in Louisiana, the court allowed both boys to relocate to Texas with their father.[24] In another Louisiana case, the court granted the mother's relocation petition, putting more credence on the mother's expert than father's. The mother's expert had interviewed all the involved persons and had been in the case for three years. Father's expert did not interview the mother, and his view of many disputed incidents was clearly informed only by the father and his parents. Father did not show that mother's expert's risk assessment model[25] deviated in any material way from governing statutes. In addition, the trial court had previously appointed mother's expert, by parties' agreement, to perform an evaluation.[26] In another case, the court found the mother's doctor's testimony to be more comprehensive than the other doctor who disapproved of relocation. Father had evicted the mother and child.[27]

Objections

The rules of evidence are important. Some states have modified the objections allowable and added additional rules for family court procedure. The lawyer may object to the introduction of evidence if there is an appropriate basis for doing so. Among the most common trial objections to testimony are the following:

- Asked and answered
- Ambiguous
- Argumentative
- Assumes facts not in evidence
- Best evidence
- Unintelligible
- Compound question
- Cumulative
- Vague
- Relevance
- Leading
- Question misstates the evidence

- Calls for a narrative answer
- Speculation
- Evidence is more prejudicial than probative
- Lack of foundation
- Improper opinion testimony
- Experts—lack of qualification
- Hearsay

A question calls for hearsay if it invites the witness to offer an out-of-court statement to prove the truth of some matter in court. There are four types of statements: declarative, imperative, exclamatory, and interrogatory. When a hearsay objection is made, the burden shifts to the proponent of the evidence to state the exception and persuade the court that the proffered evidence comes within the scope of an exception. There are many exceptions to the hearsay rule, including

(1) admission by a party—adoptive, vicarious, or by silence;
(2) declarations against interest—an out-of-court statement by a nonparty that is against that person's interest;
(3) prior consistent or inconsistent out-of-court statement made by a witness;
(4) former testimony of a witness at deposition, trial, or other proceeding;
(5) spontaneous statement of a witness that describes or explains an act, condition, or event perceived by the person making the statement;
(6) statement of the person's then-existing physical state or state of mind which is at issue at trial; and
(7) business record to prove the existence or nonexistence of an act, condition, or event recorded or not recorded in a business record.

In child custody cases, courts are sometimes more willing to allow evidence that might be considered hearsay.[28] For example, a parenting time coordinator's recommendation about children was admissible, even though it was based on hearsay. The court reasoned that the parenting time coordinator served a role similar to that of an expert witness, who reviews information relevant to the case and develops an opinion the trial court can accept or reject. Therefore, the rule that permitted experts to testify to opinions based on inadmissible evidence, provided that it was of the type reasonably relied upon by experts in the field, applied to the parenting time coordinator's recommendation. Therefore, the coordinator's recommendation about children was admissible even though it was based on hearsay.[29]

To preserve an issue for appeal, there must be a timely objection. A husband waived his appellate argument that the trial court abused its discretion by admitting into evidence the wife's exhibit by not objecting to admission of the exhibit and not claiming that the admission was fundamental error.[30]

Admissibility of Online and Electronic Evidence

The process of laying a foundation for electronic evidence requires the lawyer to answer five questions:

(1) Is the evidence relevant?
(2) Is the evidence authentic?
(3) If the evidence is offered for its substantive truth, is it hearsay?
(4) Is the form of the evidence in compliance with the best evidence rule?
(5) Is the probative value of the evidence substantially outweighed by the danger of unfair prejudice, such that it should be excluded?[31]

Federal Rule of Evidence 401 requires the evidence to be relevant. Relevant evidence means evidence having any tendency to make the existence of any fact that is of consequence to be determination of the action more probable or less probable than it would be without the evidence. Relevance is usually broadly interpreted. If the relocating parent indicates that there is no girl or boyfriend motivating the desire to move, a Facebook post of the parent passionately kissing a person in the new location may cause some doubts about motive being parent's wants rather than child's best interests.

A basic requirement for admissibility is authentication. Federal Rule of Evidence 901 covers authentication. For evidence produced by a computer, "evidence describing the process or system used to produce a result and showing that the process or system produces an accurate result," should suffice.[32] One main problem is establishing the identity of the sender—who created the material on the Internet? The second question is ensuring that the document/data has not been altered. The Uniform Electronic Transactions Act, enacted in nearly all jurisdictions now, generally requires courts to treat electronic records the same way as "writings" and allow authentication in the same manner. Emails are authenticated the same way as letters. The easiest way is to offer the testimony of the person with personal knowledge.

The most used way to authenticate electronic evidence is by refence to its "appearance, contents, substance, internal patterns or other distinctive characteristics taken in conjunction with the circumstances."[33] An email address may be authenticated by the presence of both the sender's screen name and real name, its contents, and corroboration linking the contents to the sender and/or to the events. If distinctive characteristics are not available, it may be authenticated under Federal Rule of Evidence 901(b)(3) permitting comparison with specimens that had already been authenticated. An electronic record can be authenticated using metadata. The metadata includes a file's name, a file's location, file format, date, file permissions, etc. Courts differ on what is required to authenticate a website, although testimony of a witness with knowledge works. There is a federal case on authentication of chat room conversations.[34]

As with other forms of evidence, hearsay rules and exceptions apply. Hearsay is a statement "offered in evidence to prove the truth of the matter asserted." A lot of Internet information, including Facebook postings, will be classified as hearsay. The statements, however, are often not to prove the truth of the matter but rather to show state of mind or something else, like the existence of a relationship. The state of mind exception is particularly helpful in evaluating emails. If a website contains hearsay, the lawyer must lay a foundation. While some judges hearing custody disputes will allow a lot of hearsay to get all information in front of the court, many adhere strictly to the rules of evidence.

As to the best evidence rule, the printout of an email would be considered an "original" under Federal Rule of Evidence 1001(3). Whether the probative value outweighs the potential prejudice does not arise too much, because most states favor the admission of relevant evidence, no matter how slight its probative value.

There are several ways to get the evidence admitted; some of them are described in the following sections.

Stipulations

If the lawyer obtains the information early on, the lawyer should have done a set of requests to admit the genuineness of the facts adduced and/or the genuineness of the documents. Submit everything to opposing counsel several weeks before and see if they will stipulate to the exhibits.

Judicial Notice

The lawyer may be able to convince the judge to take judicial notice if the information is the type that people ordinarily rely on in the conduct of their lives and bears an indicia of reliability. Evidence regarding the legal practices and procedures of a foreign country are legislative facts.[35] The Texas Court of Appeals held that facts regarding another country's compliance with the Hague Convention on the Civil Aspects of International Child Abduction is legislative fact. Whether the country poses obstacles to the prompt return of a child taken there or poses risks to the child's safety are legislative facts about which the trial court or appellate court can take judicial notice without prompting of the parties.[36]

Catchall Hearsay Exception—Federal Rule 807 (or State Statute)

The client should (and probably has) traveled to the target city. The client should check out the specific facts about the relevant subjects in the target neighborhood. Much of the information collected in this way is also hearsay, for example, what a teacher or principal told the client about the school. The court may let the rule slide depending on objections from opponent and judicial exercise of discretion.

Video or Pictures

A video recording or a photo album containing pictures of the target neighborhood, school, and city can be helpful. The photos are easily authenticated so will be easy to get into evidence. Photographs taken by a witness and official [paper] publications of an agency. The only testimony allowed had to be firsthand experience, or information from personal conversations with school personnel. A picture from a website may be challenged if

(1) the person allegedly in the picture denies that it is him or her;
(2) the witness identifies one of the parties but cannot identify the location, other individuals, or other identifying characteristics;
(3) no information exists regarding the date the photo was taken; and
(4) photo appears to be altered or manipulated.

AI is creating some new issues with photos.

Cross-Examination

Cross-examination does not prove the case but can bolster it and diminish the strength of the opponent's arguments, especially if a party witness admits to something that is potentially damaging to the party's credibility or the case. There should be a theme, and the lawyer should know the main points the judge should hear, at the beginning and the end. Cross-examination extends to all matters within the knowledge of the witness, the disclosure of which is material to the controversy.[37] Federal Rule of Evidence 611(b) limits cross-examination to the subject matter of the direct examination and matters affecting the credibility of the witness. Relevance is the key.

The lawyer should know what is to be accomplished with each witness, what the endgame looks like. In preparation for cross examination, the lawyer will review all pleadings, all discovery materials, and any prior statements the party or witness may have made. The lawyer should prepare a roadmap and outline by topic or issue. The lawyer will listen attentively to the direct examination and write down exact statements, then pick up where their lawyer left off. Get to the basic points through the questioning of each witness. If there was a deposition, pick the portions of it that serve the purpose. Be prepared to ask the same question as was asked in the deposition if the testimony is helpful to the case factually or to attack credibility. If using a deposition, reference the page number and line of deposition.

A witness's credibility can be impeached if evidence (Facebook posts, texts, etc.) is presented contrary to a statement the person made under oath. Some witnesses destroy their own credibility by evasive or nonresponsive answers. The lawyer can also point out if a witness's testimony contradicts the testimony of others. The lawyer should lock them into the parts of their testimony that help their client's case.

Silence can be golden. The lawyer should ignore useless witnesses. That can send a message that that testimony is irrelevant. Sometimes not cross-examining a relative or best friend who has testified in favor of the other parent is a better strategy if testimony is unlikely to change.

What is asked will depend on the pretrial discovery, if there were depositions, stipulations of documents, and what was presented in the direct examination. For example, on direct examination, a relocating parent claims that they will make more money in the new city. The lawyer will have investigated the cost of living in the current location and the new city and be able to ask questions directed at whether the increase in pay will compensate for the additional housing and living costs in the new city. If the party has testified that the schools are better in the new city, the lawyer should have researched the academic programs, percentage of children who do well on standardized tests, and if there is a bullying problem at the new school. In one case, the lawyer was able to show that a child who now walks a few blocks to school would have a one-hour bus ride to the school in the new location.

With cross-examination, the focus is on the lawyer and the lawyer's leading questions. Tight leading questions become factual assertions that the lawyer tries to make the witness adopt by agreeing with them. This allows the lawyer to tell the story the way the lawyer wants the judge to understand it. So the lawyer is giving the answer desired in the question. The questioning should be done in a friendly tone to keep the cooperation of the witness. The lawyer should also avoid the "why" or "what" questions that call for a narrative answer. The lawyer can also control the witness by moving to strike a nonresponsive answer.

The lawyer should save argument for their closing summary. Destructive cross-examination can create sympathy for the witness and animosity toward the lawyer. Lawyers should not ask argumentative questions that challenge a witness about an answer that has been given. Questions such as "How can you expect . . . ?" And "do you really . . . ?" are argumentative.

Rules for Cross-Examination

The basic rules for cross-examination were set out by Irving Younger years ago. With some variations, the rules are:

1. Be brief.
2. Use plain words and short questions.
3. Use only leading questions to make narrative louder, especially in bench trials.
4. Do not ask questions to which you do not know the answer.
5. Listen to the witness's answers.
6. Loop the next question with the previous answer.
7. Do not argue or quarrel with the witness.
8. Know the theory and theme of the case and try to fit it into the questions so as to direct the witness's responses to support the theme and theory.
9. Avoid repetition to avoid losing the judge's attention.
10. Try to keep the witness from explaining more than the "yes" or "no." Point out a bias. "Is it safe to say you would do anything to help your sister?"
11. Limit questioning—the one question too many problem.

12. Save some things for summation. Summation can point out when a witness's testimony contradicts that of other witnesses.
13. End on a high note. Make sure the last question is a good one to which the witness can only respond with a "yes" or "no."

Cross-Examining an Expert Witness

If the lawyer is cross-examining an expert witness, there are additional considerations.[38] The following topics may be covered:

- The expert's qualifications; interest or bias;
- Status as a professional witness, if appropriate;
- Contents of the expert's file;
- Facts on which expert bases their opinion, and how that opinion would differ if certain assumed facts were changed;
- Any admissions or impeaching statements from the expert's testimony in the case or other cases or from the expert's writings or authoritative treatises.

The lawyer can also cross-examine on violations of professional guidelines or ethical codes as well as errors in psychological testing or errors in clinical decision-making. If the expert is proffering testimony that is speculative, rather than "scientific, technical, or other specialized knowledge, the testimony may not meet the *Daubert* standard, which uses these factors:

(1) Whether the knowledge can and has been tested;
(2) Whether the theory of technique has been subjected to peer review and publication;
(3) The known or potential rate of error; and
(4) Whether the practice is generally accepted.[39]

If the expert is well-known and respected and gave strong, unbiased testimony, sometimes the best thing to do is ask no questions.

Closing Argument

The lawyer can begin to craft a compelling closing argument at the beginning of the case. Keeping the client's theme in mind, the lawyer needs to listen to the case carefully as the evidence is presented. The opposing counsel may make a "big mistake" that favors the client's position or may have put on a witness whose testimony can be used to support the client's position. The lawyer can highlight supporting information for future reference—either with a regular highlighter on paper or using the highlighter font on the computer. By highlighting as the case is progressing, the lawyer can return to important supporting points and find them easily later. For example, one lawyer reports that the custody expert stated that the father was "consistently inconsistent." That phrase could be used effectively in a closing argument. If an exhibit is particularly persuasive, identify it and reference it to testimony. The court can only process so much, so the closing should identify two or three main points the judge needs to hear again. For example, if the testimony shows that in the new location, the child will have to ride for over an hour on a bus where now the child walks to school, that needs to be repeated. If possible, the lawyer should create a catchy introduction that summarizes the case and reminds the judge what should be done. The closing argument gives the lawyer a last chance to get the client's request across.

Findings of Fact, Conclusions of Law

Trial court findings are important. In most states, either statutes or court rules require findings of fact. It makes sure the court does not miss any facts or issues.

Award of Attorneys' Fees

Most states give judges the authority to award attorneys' fees as justice and equity require. In some states, the prevailing party may be awarded fees. In other states, the court may award fees because of the bad conduct of the other party. For example, father could recover reasonable legal fees incurred in undoing mother's unilateral relocation of their daughter to Colorado after she relocated despite a court order denying permission to move.[40]

Post-Trial Motions

The main post-trial motions are a motion to reconsider, a motion to reargue, or a motion for a new trial and an application for a stay of enforcement pending appeal.

Motion to Reconsider or Motion for Rehearing

A motion to reconsider or for rehearing gives the judge one more chance to correct an error. The motion is not a "second bite at the apple" where movant merely wants to reassert the same arguments to persuade the court to rule differently. Because it is treated as a motion to alter or amend the judgment, in most states it must be filed within ten days after the entry of judgment. The content of the motion, rather than its title, determines the statute under which relief is requested. After filing the journal entry and the other party is provided a copy by mail, the recipient has an additional three days to file any post-trial motion. A motion for reconsideration or rehearing may be granted if there has been an intervening change in the law; new evidence has become available; an error in law or fact was made; or there is a need to prevent manifest injustice.

Courts limit consideration to matters that were before the court when it entered its original judgment. A motion to reconsider will generally not be granted when the relief requested was not in the original motion or merely provides additional support that was available at the time of the original hearing.[41] The Florida appellate court found that the mother's motion for rehearing should have been granted as she sought to present new evidence of a diagnostic report generated after the original hearing showing the child was well below grade level in reading and mathematics, which impacted the best interest determination (father had said child was doing well in school). There were also inconsistencies between the final judgment and the parenting plan.[42] An Illinois trial court after a hearing denied mother's petition to relocate the children to Indiana, five and a half hours away by car. The mother filed for a motion to reconsider claiming the trial court misapplied most of the statutory factors that the trial court allowed. The appellate court reversed, finding that no reasonable person would have agreed with the trial court that reconsideration of the denial was warranted. The court reviewed de novo. There was no evidence presented at the hearing on the motion to reconsider, only arguments. Mother's counsel twice argued facts not put into evidence. The fact that there were direct flights between the cities could have been presented at the original hearing.[43]

Appellate courts generally treat motions to reconsider as motions to alter or amend under the state's version of civil procedure federal Rule 59(f). The purpose is to allow the judge to correct previous trial errors. A motion to reconsider is treated as a motion to alter or amend the judgment, which tolls the time to appeal the final order. If a motion offers some identifiable reason for reconsidering the judgment, it is properly construed as a motion to reconsider.

Motion for a New Trial

Rule 59(f) requires a motion for a new trial to be made within ten days after the date of entry of judgment. The grounds for a new trial motion are:

(1) the trial court made an erroneous ruling;
(2) newly discovered evidence has been located that could not be produced at the trial with reasonable diligence; and
(3) the decision is contrary to the evidence.

There usually is not a motion for a new trial filed with respect to custody because custody provisions are modifiable in the best interests of the child throughout the child's minority.

Endnotes

1. Foskett v. Foskett, 634 N.W.2d 363 (Mich. Ct. App. 2001).
2. *See* Linda D. Elrod, Child Custody Practice and Procedure, ch. 14 (Thomson Reuters 2024).
3. Bridges v. Bridges, 316 So. 3d 17 (La. Ct. App. 2020) (trial court denied mother's request to relocate children to Dubai based on children's health care needs and did not err in imposing a two-hour time limit per side on motion to modify custody arrangement to accommodate relocation, only one rebuttal witness was denied because of time limit).
4. *Id.*

5. For a discussion of trial preparation generally, *see* STEVEN N. PESKIND, 100 DAYS BEFORE TRIAL: A LAWYER'S GUIDE TO PREPARATION AND STRATEGY (ABA 2015); for a relocation case specifically, *see* Barbara Ellen Handschu, *Trial Preparation of a Relocation Case,* 2 AM. J. FAM. L. 377 (Winter 1988); Bradley Grundy, *The Trial: Proposing Relocation,* 20(2) FAM. ADVOC. 36 (Fall 1997).

6. STEVEN N. PESKIND, THE FAMILY LAW EVIDENCE HANDBOOK: RULES AND PROCEDURES FOR EFFECTIVE ADVOCACY (ABA 2013). *See also* LYNNE Z. GOLD-BIKIN & STEPHEN KOLODNY, THE DIVORCE TRIAL MANUAL: FROM INITIAL INTERVIEW TO CLOSING ARGUMENTS (ABA 2006).

7. Mildred D. Dale, Jonathan Gould & Allyssa Levine, *Cross-Examining Experts in Child Custody: The Necessary Theories and Models . . . with Instructions,* 33 J. AM. ACAD. MATRIM. LAWYERS 328, 332–37 (2021).

8. Theresa Glennon, *Still Partner? Examining the Consequences of Post-Dissolution Parenting,* 41 FAM. L.Q. 105 (2007).

9. *In re* Marriage of Fatkin, 129 N.E.3d 1230 (Ill. 2019) (father's relocation was to give children better quality of life; father and children would be living with paternal grandparents, father and children had exceptional relationship, son preferred living with father and children would benefit "undoubtedly" from greater ethnic and cultural diversity).

10. E. MAVIS HETHERINGTON & JOHN KELLY, FOR BETTER OR WORSE: DIVORCE RECONSIDERED 134 (2002).

11. *See* William G. Austin & Sol Rappaport, *Parental Gatekeeping Forensic Model and Child Custody Evaluation: Social Capital and Application to Relocation Disputes,* 15 J. CHILD CUSTODY 55 (2018) (relocation adds to the general risks associated with children of divorce); Matthew M. Stevenson et al., *Associations Between Parental Relocation Following Separation in Childhood and Maladjustment in Adolescence and Young Adulthood,* 24 PSYCH. PUB. POL'Y & L. 365 (2018) (finding several risks); Philip M. Stahl, *Emerging Issues in Relocation Cases,* 25 J. AM. ACAD. MATRIM. LAWYERS 425 (2013).

12. *In re* Marriage of Grippin, 186 P.3d 852 (Kan. Ct. App. 2008) (finding that father who filed to prevent relocation had the burden of proving that relocation was not in the best interests of the child).

13. FLA. STAT. ANN. § 61.13001(8). *See* Orta v. Suarez, 66 So. 3d 988 (Fla. Dist. Ct. App. 2011) (mother sustained burden of showing relocation was in child's best interests; father did not show by preponderance of evidence that relocation was not in child's interest). *See also* Petroski v. Petroski, 808 N.Y.S.2d 852 (App. Div. 2005) (parent must prove relocation is in the child's best interest by a preponderance of the evidence).

14. *In re* Marriage of Wehr, 267 P.3d 1045 (Wash. Ct. App. 2011).

15. CDC, National Center for Education Statistics, http://nces.ed.gov.

16. www.schoolmatch.com.

17. DJ v. CJ, 464 P.3d 790 (Hawaii 2020) (finding court should have granted father's motion for a continuance since he could not speak English

to hire a lawyer before allowing mother and children to move to North Carolina).

18. Katare v. Katare, 283 P.3d 546 (Wash. 2012) (attorney who had 17 years of experience in the field of child abduction allowed to testify as to risk factors for abduction). *See also* Shady v. Shady, 858 N.E.2d 128 (Ind. Ct. App. 2006), *transfer denied* Mar. 8, 2007 (witness was proprietor of counseling firm that provided services for clients of international recovery of abducted children and assessment of the risk of future abduction qualified as an expert in international child abduction).

19. Daubert v. Merrell Dow Pharm., Inc. 509 U.S. 579, 589–90, n.9, 11 (1993).

20. *Id.* at 593.

21. John A. Zervopoulos, Confronting Mental Health Evidence: A Practical Guide to Reliability and Experts in Family Law 33 (ABA 2d ed. 2015).

22. Johnson v. Johnson, 2013 WL 411467 (Tenn. Ct. App. 2013) (denying mother's move and distinguishing from earlier case with similar facts but no expert witness).

23. Sheridan v. Sheridan, 12 N.Y.S.3d 434 (App. Div. 2015).

24. Perez v. Perez, 85 So. 3d 273 (La. Ct. App. 2012).

25. William G. Austin, *Relocation, Research, and Forensic Evaluation, Part I: Effects of Residential Mobility on Children of Divorce*, 46 Fam. Ct. Rev. 137 (2008); *Part II: Research in Support of the Relocation Risk Assessment Model*, 46 Fam. Ct. Rev. 347 (Apr. 2008).

26. Fuqua v. Fuqua, 57 So. 3d 534 (La. Ct. App. 2011).

27. *Id.*

28. Linda D. Elrod, *Hearsay and Child Custody: The Twice-Told Story*, 21 Fam. L.Q. 169 (1987).

29. Fed. R. Evid. 703. *See* Gomez v. Gomez, 887 N.E.2d 977 (Ind. Ct. App. 2008) (denying father's petition to modify parenting time finding there was substantial evidence that mother did not willingly acquiesce to father's decision to keep the children overnight on midweek visits).

30. Shady v. Shady, 858 N.E.2d 128 (Ind. Ct. App. 2006) (the exhibit was the American Bar Association's Jurisdiction in Child Custody and Abduction Cases: A Judge's Guide to the UCCJA, PKPA, and the Hague Child Abduction Convention).

31. Lorraine v. Markel Am. Ins. Co., 241 F.R.D. 534 (D. Md. 2007).

32. Fed. R. Evid. 901(b).

33. Fed. R. Evid. 901(b)(4).

34. United States v. Tank, 200 F.3d 627 (9th Cir. 2000).

35. Rodriguez v. State, 90 S.W.3d 340, 360 (Tex. App. 2001) (the ability or inability to subpoena witness or documents from Mexico is a legislative fact regarding the content of law and policy).

36. *In re* Sigmar, 270 S.W.3d 289 (Tex. App. 2008).
37. Simmons v. Williams, 660 S.E.2d 435 (Ga. Ct. App. 2008).
38. Dale, Gould & Levine, *supra* note 7, at 328. *See also* John A. Zervopoulos, How to Examine Mental Health Experts: A Family Lawyer's Handbook of Issues and Strategies (ABA 2d ed. 2020).
39. Daubert v. Merrill Dow Pharm., Inc., 509 U.S. 579, 587–88 (1993). *See also* General Electric Co. v. Joinder, 522 U.S. 136 (1997); Kumho Tire Co. v. Carmichael, 526 U.S. 137 (1999).
40. Papasoff v. Cockrell, 786 N.Y.S.2d 2 (App. Div. 2004) (awarding full amount of attorneys' fees).
41. Horlacher v. Cohen, 96 N.E.3d 438 (Ill. App. Ct. 2017).
42. Dowers v. Johnson, 392 So. 3d 140 (Fla. Dist. Ct. App. 2024).
43. *In re* Marriage of Prusak, 156 N.E.3d 529 (Ill. App. Ct. 2020).

CHAPTER 13

Preparing Parenting Plans

The . . . most successful [cases] in allowing a move have been those where the moving parent has carefully considered and drafted plans that will minimize the adverse effect . . . the move will have on . . . nonmoving parent.[1]

A good parenting plan is one that facilitates healthy child development and family functioning.[2]

Relocation cases need a carefully crafted, child-centered, written parenting plan. The plan, ideally agreed to by the parties, should be incorporated into the court order at a final hearing (or the court will put the plan in a decree if there is no agreement) that contains legal custody, residency, parenting time schedules, decision-making protocols, parenting rules, mechanisms for dispute resolution, and financial arrangements for the child. The law has long presumed that the parents' custody and visitation agreement is in the best interest of their child because parents are in the best position to know their child's needs, desires, and schedules.[3] Today, a parenting plan, if agreed to by the parents, is presumed to be in the child's best interest. What has changed is (1) terms now describe timesharing, parenting time, shared or co-parenting rather than custody and visitation; and (2) statutes and court rules in most states require parents to file a parenting plan at the time of filing an initial or modification of a custody action. If the parents cannot agree on one plan, each files one and the judge will choose.[4] If the parties cannot create their own, the court may order mediation (Chapter 10), unless mediation is inappropriate because of domestic violence, power imbalances, or child abuse.

Although many states now have guidelines for parenting plans, there is no one size fits all model of a parenting plan. A child gets older, parents change partners, jobs, and sometimes cities or states. The parenting plan that met the needs of their child at one time will need "tweaking" if one parent wants to relocate with the child. The best interests of the child requires a plan that is developmentally appropriate, flexible enough to provide for the present and future well-being of the child and provides an enforceable allocation of parental responsibilities.

Even parents who have had common child-care practices, an ongoing ability to communicate, and focus on the needs of their child can run into difficulties if one parent wants to relocate with the child. The potential relocation of a parent should be considered a fundamental part of an initial parenting time determination.[5] (See Chapter 4.) If the parents set out in advance what they consider to be the definition of a relocation (certain number of miles, driving time, school district), the notice required and what the parties consider would be good reasons for the move, the relocation issue may be easier to resolve. If the parents have not set out what happens if one parent wants to move, state law will apply. Generally, if the relocation significantly alters or reduces a parent's time with the child, the court will consider the move a relocation. In most situations, the judge will favor plans with opportunities to maintain frequent and meaningful contact between the child and both parents.

Relocation impacts not only the residential custody of the nonrelocating parent but also that parent's ability to be involved in day-to-day school and medical decisions. The practical reality is that most children need one home base school district for a majority of the year. For example, a 5-2-2-5 parenting plan is not an option when the parents live a long distance apart or sometimes, even in different school districts.[6] If the move is not too distant, the modification may be relatively simple, such as changing the pick-up or exchange location. For example, when a father and his new wife moved an hour away, the mother's travel time quadrupled for exchanges of the children. The plan had worked for four years. The court modified the parenting plan to designate a new custodial exchange location.[7] If the distance is great, the plan needs to be totally redone.

The lawyer for the relocating parent should help with proposing a well-conceived, feasible, and practical plan with details that prioritize the child's needs and clearly recognizes the value of the child maintaining a relationship with the other parent. The plan should set out how the relocating parent will keep the other informed and communicate all important information about the child in a timely manner. The plan should provide for flexibility and how parents will adapt as the child grows and matures. Teenagers may have sports activities, jobs, and dates, and want to spend more time with peers than parents. The specifics of transportation should be as detailed as much as possible to show the parent has considered the feasibility and costs of the relocation. One indicator of a good plan is whether the relocating parent would be willing to accept the plan if the court does not allow the child to relocate.

The lawyer for the nonrelocating parent will help draft a plan that emphasizes the stability and continuity of the existing location, even if there is a change in the child's primary residence. The plan should provide the relocating parent with a generous and reasonable parenting time schedule during summer and school holidays and specify the numerous ways of maintaining contact with the child on a regular basis.

If the parents cannot agree on a parenting plan, the court must decide between the competing plans and select the one that meets the child's best interests. In a Missouri case, the judge selected the mother's proposed parenting plan because after the relocation, she could provide care for the child and his half-brother in the home, and the father would have approximately the same number of days as he enjoyed while they lived in the same state. The father's plan required the child to be in day care a few days per week, he did not know when he would marry his girlfriend, where they would live, or what the child's day care situation would be like if the child resided with him.[8]

What Children Need: Research on Relocation

Parenting plans should be child-centered and further the best interests of the child, not just the desires of the parents. Decades of social science research has identified the essential requirements for a child's healthy development. Children need a relationship with at least one parent who is consistently nurturing, loving, and coping; the perception of opportunity; stability or predictability about adult environment; easy access to the extended family or ethnic or other group; and the availability of adequate economic, social, and physical resources.[9] Beneficial parental behaviors include positive reinforcement, sensitivity to the child's distress, clear communication, appropriate limit setting, and being able to provide for the child's basic needs.

Most children want to have meaningful relationships with both parents. The support and involvement of both parents generally leads to positive outcomes, such as academic achievement, good behavior, psychological adjustment, positive self-concept, and social competence. Therefore, in the absence of domestic violence, child abuse, or alienating behaviors, a child generally benefits from supportive relationships with both parents whether the parents live together or not.[10]

Divorce or parental separation is a negative life event for a child.[11] The negativity is ameliorated if the child has two highly involved and supportive parents, who have consistent, frequent, and predictable contact, relatively low conflict, and an ability to cooperate reasonably.[12] The main protective factor for children of divorce is to have at least one consistent relationship with a stable, competent caregiver who can provide warmth and an effective parenting style.[13] How the child does depends on the individual child's adaptability and resilience and the child's ability to maintain relationships with both parents, if they had a close relationship with the absent parent.[14] The negative impact of divorce is exacerbated by parental conflict,[15] parental maladjustment that affects parenting behavior, the absence of the father before age 12,[16] financial insecurity, stress, loss of contact with a parent, and relocation.[17] Conflict is frightening to a child. Most high-conflict families display a multitude of problems; some have personality disorders.[18] High conflict parents fail to focus on their child's needs while continuing their emotional disputes each other.[19] These parents create tension-filled exchanges for the child and involve the child in the parental conflict by their acrimony and often denigration of the other parent.[20] When the conflict is deep and endemic, the child may not benefit from continued contact with both parents, in which case the child should have more time with the more competent, committed parent.[21]

Contested relocation cases are "high conflict" because they are "no win."[22] If a long-distance move is allowed, the child is exposed to four risk factors: residential mobility, the separation of the parents, a high level of conflict, and loss of regular personal contact with at least one parent.[23] The child may suffer harm to the relationship with the nonmoving parent and may suffer developmental harm due to the diminished parent–child relationship.[24]

Research on relocation itself, without parental conflict, has been relatively scarce. Most of the research has had small sample sizes. A short-distance relocation in the same town seldom creates negative effects, if the child can stay in the same school and maintain the same friends. One early study showed that once a child lives more than 20 minutes away from the nonresidential parent, sustaining the relationship necessitates fragmenting the child's life and activities.[25] Another study indicated that about 75 miles, the maximum radius of a comfortable day trip, seems to be the point at which inconvenience overcomes parental guilt.[26] Two studies have found that the relocation of either parent that resulted in separating the child and father by more than an hour's drive appeared to pose long-term risks to the children's mental and behavioral adjustment.[27] This is because a move that results in a new town, a new school, and an hour or more of travel time produces a qualitative shift in the impact of the move. Brief visits are no longer possible. The child has a different life with new friends, new routines, and new care and medical providers. The nonresidential parent becomes an outsider. Additionally, there may be less financial and emotional support for the child without both parents in relatively close proximity.

Social science data in the United States seems to show that a relocation poses additional risks for a child and may be harmful.[28] One study in the United States found that frequent moves are tough on children and disrupt important friendships, especially for children going through puberty and school changes, those who are introverted, or those who have a tendency toward anxiety and inflexibility. Children who moved frequently did not get involved in activities and friendships they could soon lose.[29] A ten-year longitudinal study in the United States by the American Psychological Association reported in 2018 that relocation post-divorce was associated with (1) heightened risks to adolescents and young adults of being involved with delinquent peers and the juvenile justice system; (2) illicit drug use; (3) symptoms of aggression, depression, and anxiety; and (4) disturbed relationships with mothers, fathers, and stepfathers.[30] The findings indicate that the children not only felt like they mattered less to their fathers, but also to their mothers and stepfathers with whom they lived.[31] Likewise, a Danish study of 1.5 million Danish children born between 1971 and 1997 found that any move could have a negative impact on children. The group most likely to suffer the most negative impact of moving were middle school children aged between 12 and 14.[32]

Research studies on relocation and its effect on children in Australia, New Zealand, and the United Kingdom, however, do not support that relocation is inherently harmful to children. When both parents remained child focused and supported the relationship with the absent parent, relocation was not harmful, and in some instances was a positive experience for the child.[33] The negatives were mainly the burdens of travel, which fell primarily on the children, and communication. Many children wanted more contact with the distant parent and were not satisfied with the electronic means of communication. The New Zealand study found that the children who did the best were those who moved closer to extended family and who were able to maintain their friendships in both locations. The children who did the worst were a small group where the mother was denied relocation and the children were left with fathers who had limited prior involvement in their care.[34] The Australian study noted that courts need to be open to the particular facts within each family, such as the child's age and attitudes of the parents, that will help determine the risks and protective factors, rather than looking at bright line rules.[35]

In summary, children of divorce who relocated generally adjusted well to relocation if the custodial/residential parent had an effective parenting style and did not exclude the parent who did not move. How well the child does depends largely on how the moving parent adjusts to the move; copes with the stress involved in new housing, job, and finding a school; and the extent of social and emotional support in the new location. A primary protective factor is the child's healthy relationship with the moving parent and the moving parent's attitude toward the nonmoving parent. Other factors that lead to positive outcomes for the child include a history of parental cooperation, both parents being effective parents, and a lack of parental conflict or domestic violence.

Drafting Parenting Plans

The parenting plan is the foundation for the parents' post-relocation relationship with the child and relationship between the parents. Parenting plan considerations require foundations based on scientific evidence, relevant legal factors, and most importantly the facts and circumstances of the family and child involved.[36]

The parenting plan should be tailored to the needs of the individual child and the various risks and protective factors that may be involved in the relocation.[37] Therefore, the parenting plan should be developmentally and age appropriate—based on the age and stage of the child and on child development research rather than on preconceptions.[38] The plan should be tailored to meet the needs and abilities of the child with safety being a first priority. High-conflict parents need detailed parenting plans that can reduce conflict by being specific and concrete as to times, dates, places of exchange, who pays costs of transportation, and how parents will communicate with each other and the child.[39]

Custody and Residence

The two main parts of any parenting plan are the designation of legal custody and the child's residential schedule with each parent. The legal custodial relationship of the child can be sole or joint legal custody and primary or joint/shared physical residency with allocation of parental rights and responsibilities. There are questions whether high-conflict parents should have joint legal and physical custody generally. In 2017, several evaluators reached a consensus that shared parenting may be the norm except in situations that post a risk to the child of abuse, neglect, or abduction; where substance abuse or violence exists; and where one parent actively undermines the child's relationship with the other parent.[40] There are others who argue, however, that high-conflict parents probably should not have shared parenting and that the parenting plan should depend on each child.[41] Shared parenting may be risky for children if one or both parents lack a history of competent and safe caregiving, there is unduly high interparental conflict, or a history of poor parental cooperating.[42]

While many states have presumptions for joint legal and physical custody, that can be difficult if the parents are living in different cities, states, or countries. The court may designate joint legal custody but designate one parent the primary residential parent. If the high-conflict parents cannot cooperate as co-parents, the court may designate one parent with sole legal custody or create divided decision-making so one parent may decide medical or religious issues and the other educational issues. Parallel parenting may be appropriate for relocation cases.

The plan should be child centered. One article summarized what children need and want, especially when the parents are separating.[43] The list includes:

- Feeling safe, secure, and loved
- Spending quality time with their parents
- Knowing what to expect day to day
- Being seen and heard
- Feeling like they matter to the adults in their lives
- Being with their siblings and stepsiblings
- Being with their pets

- Staying in touch with extended family
- Spending time with their friends
- Living close to school
- Continuing their hobbies, such as sports, church, and camps
- Having access to special possessions, such as toys, mementos, electronics and school supplies[44]

Schedule

One of the main parts of the parenting plan is the schedule for the child's time with each parent, including holidays, birthdays, vacations, school in-service days, and preceding or following weekends. The plan should be as specific as possible about everything that can be anticipated, especially times for pick up and drop offs. Identify which parent is considered the caretaking parent for each day, in particular the rotating Fridays. For example, typically Friday is considered part of the rotating weekend. The plan should designate a start time for parenting days. In general, a morning start time provides clarity to the school regarding which parent is responsible for the child that day. This is particularly important for early school day dismissals, including planned days and going home sick days. If the parents live in the same town, the parties need to know if the town allows two different school bus routes for the child for drop off/pick up at each parent's residence. If the parents reside in different towns, which town will be considered the child's primary residence for school-related purposes? In which town will the child participate in extracurricular activities?

The plan should protect the important things in the child's life, whether that is piano, soccer, baseball, scouts, dance, or hunting. The plan should designate which parent(s) will transport, pay, and decide on instructors, participation in tournaments, and other camps and activities. In addition to the proper allocation of parental rights and responsibility, the plan should also include:

(1) a plan for parent communication so they can establish an appropriate working relationship to decide matters regarding their child's health, education, and welfare;

(2) provision for the child's physical care at all times;
(3) ways to minimize the child's exposure to harmful parental conflict, which may mean limiting the amount of interchange between parents, including the number of transitions and amount, type, and times of communication (email or text can be helpful and create a record);
(4) provisions for sharing of and access to information regarding the child, but do not make one parent responsible for information easily available to both parents as with online school calendars;
(5) specify and make arrangements for the child's communication with absent parent through telephone, computers, etc.;
(6) detail the transportation, including pick-ups and drop-offs, costs, and other potential problem areas;
(7) provisions for another potential relocation, including how far is considered a relocation, how much notice should be given, and any relevant factors;
(8) indicate parties' choice of methods of resolving disputes, such mediation, arbitration, or parent coordination before going to court;
(9) a provision for review and change of residential time as the child grows and matures to minimize the need for future modifications to the parenting plan;
(10) if the parents are high conflict, omit provisions for a right of first refusal or make up visitation due to illness or holiday visits because high-conflict parents cannot handle these reasonably; and
(11) build in sanctions (such as make-up time) for violations.

In many states, there are sample parenting plans on the Internet on court websites. A google search will find dozens of sample parenting plans with fill-in-the-blank features.

Developmental Age and Stage of Child

The parenting plan will differ depending on the age, maturity, adaptability, and resilience of the particular child. Additional considerations are required for creating parenting plans for a child who has a disorder that requires specialized parenting. The plans will differ for a child with a chronic medical condition, neurodevelopmental disorder, Attention-Deficit/Hyperactivity (ADHD) disorder, or disruptive behavior disorder.[45] Plans will also differ if domestic violence has been a factor in the parents' relationship[46] or if there is parental alienation.[47]

As one appellate court noted:

> [A] child's development is not something with which courts should experiment and risk disruption. Although ideally a child would develop a close relationship with his loving and caring parents through an equal division of parenting time, the ideal is difficult to achieve when, as in this case, the child's parents elect to establish their homes in different communities. This problem is further compounded by the friction that often develops between ex-spouses as they move on with their lives after their divorce. . . . In ordering this change in custody the *trial court forgot that the paramount consideration in a child custody decision is the child's best interests, not those of his parents.*[48]

There are numerous books and articles about attachment and child development that are beyond the scope of this chapter.[49] In addition, states such as Arizona and Michigan have model parenting plans and sample calendars on their court websites. A brief summary of some basic child development may help parents in determining the risk factors and adaptability of their child in the relocation context. There are generally two types of issues to consider: those that relate to the child and family and those that relate to the move itself.

Relocation can be a greater risk factor for a child under five and for teenagers. The child under age five will have more difficulty maintaining a relationship with a distant parent because the child is less able to use means other than personal contact to interact with the parent. The first few years of a child's life are a time of growth, which sets the stage for future social, emotional, and cognitive development. Infants and toddlers are totally dependent on adults and need touching, nurturing, security, and stability. Bonding and attachment occur at about six months when the child begins to distinguish himself from others.[50] The child can bond with more than one caregiver. As the infant ages, the attachment intensifies, and the infant may cry when separated from the primary attachment figure. By 18 months to three years, brief separations are tolerated better. There have been disputes about overnights with infants and young children because of the child's limited perceptions of time and memory, but researchers agree there should not be a presumption against overnights.[51]

Children younger than three may have more difficulty maintaining an attachment with an absent parent if the distance is too great and contact infrequent. While generally the primary residence may be with the parent who has historically provided primary nurturing, three times a week contact may be necessary to develop the bond with the nonresidential parent. If a child under four lives a great distance from the other parent, generally over 100 miles or a two-hour drive, there are substantial obstacles to establishing, maintaining, and strengthening healthy attachment relationships.[52] Researchers suggest that relocation with a very young child be delayed if possible until the child is two or three to prevent long-term adverse consequences as a result of the attenuation, deterioration, and termination of parent-child relationships.[53] By age three, a child can feel secure with other attachment figures and memory is sufficiently well developed for longer periods—seven to ten days away from the primary caregiver.

The school-age child has interests outside of the family and has friends. The child has a unique relationship with each parent. Separating from one of the parents by relocating may cause the child anxiety and fear. The parenting plan needs to consider any educational needs as well as physical and emotional needs. How the child is doing at school and with peers will be relevant. The plan for the school-age child often includes parenting time with one parent during the school year and blocks of time, such as holidays and summers with nonresidential or nonmoving. A school-age child may be able to use phones and computers to stay in contact with the absent parent. If possible, holidays should be kept as stress-free as possible for the child.

The adolescent has a greater capacity to understand the separation, can adapt to predictable schedules, and can maintain relationships over a long distance. The adolescent, however, may express a strong preference for staying close to peers or want to stay with the parent who has the least restrictions. It may be more difficult to justify moving an honor student who is a class officer, captain of whatever sports or math team, surrounded by positive, high-achieving friends than a child who has few friends and is struggling in the current environment. If the child has expressed a preference for a living situation, it is important to understand the children's feelings. As children get older, their ideas and wishes become more important, sometimes determinative (see Chapter 14). Some children express a clear position without hesitation, even if it means a change in primary residence. Others appear to be mouthing what one of the parents wants. Still others may not want to say for fear of hurting one parent's feelings or because it does not matter. If the move is allowed or denied without the child's voice being heard, the child may be angry, feeling disenfranchised. Adolescence is a difficult time for many children. The relocation can exacerbate feelings of isolation, not fitting in, and other issues.

While frequent moves take a toll on children's social-emotional well-being and cause a small decline in social skills and emotional and behavioral problems, the child's age at the time of the move can be important for cognitive skills. Residential moves between birth and kindergarten impede social-emotional but not cognitive functioning in kindergarten. Moves in elementary school affect both cognitive and social-emotional function in fifth grade. Moves in middle school undermine eighth grade cognitive skills.[54] Relocation cases add additional stress factors such as diminished contact with familiar sources of psychosocial support, familiar living settings, and remarriage of a parent.[55]

Parenting Plans and Domestic Violence

While there may not be causal empirical evidence about the benefits or risks of specific parenting plans,[56] there is evidence about the impact of domestic violence on a child. Even if the child is not abused physically, the child suffers emotionally or psychologically from witnessing domestic violence.[57] Children whose mothers are battered are twice as likely as children from nonviolent homes to be abuse victims.[58] The perpetration of child abuse or domestic violence in a household where a child resides is detrimental to a child. At least one scholar has suggested that there should be a presumption in favor of relocation if the moving parent is escaping violence.[59]

The lawyer needs to screen for and identify if there is violence and be able to recognize both a victim and an abuser. Separation, divorce, and contested custody and relocation litigation can cause increased violence. The presence of domestic violence will impact the type of parenting plan that the parties will have.[60] When a judge finds that domestic violence has occurred, the judge must consider additional factors.[61] In some states, there is a presumption against a physical custody award to the abuser. In many instances, the victim parent may be trying to relocate because of the abuse. The lawyer may have to educate the judge who does not understand the extent of the harm to the child from contact with the abuser. Whether a child has witnessed abuse of a parent or been abused themselves are adverse childhood experiences that can impact a child's health throughout life.[62]

> The effects of intimate partner violence on children's adjustment have also been well documented . . . . Violence has an independent effect on children's adjustment and is significantly more potent than high levels of marital conflict . . . . Behavioral, cognitive, and emotional problems include aggression, conduct disorders, delinquency, truancy, school failure, anger, depression, anxiety, and low self-esteem. Interpersonal problems include poor social skills, peer rejection, problems with authority figures and parents, and an inability to empathize with others. Preschool children traumatized by the earlier battering of their mothers had pervasive negative effects on their development, including significant delays and insecure or disorganized attachments. School-age children repeatedly exposed to violence are more likely to develop post-traumatic stress disorders, particularly when combined with other risk factors of child abuse, poverty, and the psychiatric illness of one or both parents.[63]

A Wingspread Conference on Domestic Violence found that not all violence is the same—there may be the serious, pathological violence (coercive controlling) or a situational, one-time type because of the separation.[64] Some researchers have suggested models of parenting time for high-conflict parents depending on the type and severity of the violence. The lawyer may need experts. Joint legal or physical custody is almost always inappropriate when coercive controlling violence or chronic conflict is present. Mediation may also be inappropriate. Co-parenting may still be appropriate for parents where the violence is situational and the parent are sufficiently able to communicate, have some measure of trust and respect for one another, and can focus on the child's needs.

Parallel parenting may be appropriate where each parent has a positive contribution to make in time spent with the children, but direct parent-parent contact provokes acrimony. While parallel parenting can work for school-age children, it is not appropriate for infants, toddlers, and special needs children who require consistency and closely coordinated care between homes.

Supervised exchanges may be appropriate for moderate domestic violence cases, which include moderate ratings on potency, attempt and primary perpetrator of violence where risk or fear of renewed violence occurs only when parents meet. Supervised exchanges are not appropriate for any current threat of violence or ongoing concerns about safety and well-being of the child with either parent alone. A Wyoming court noted that household abuse is always improper and contrary to the best interests of the children.[65]

If the client is the victim, the lawyer should have facts and enough evidence to support, similar to that for obtaining a protection order. Other evidence in addition to the client's testimony might be police reports, or neighbors or other witnesses to the violence. Some abusers try to accuse the victim of not being a friendly parent to maintain control. In no event should the allegation be made if it is not true. If the lawyer is representing the parent who is being accused of domestic violence who claims innocence, the lawyer needs to try to prove the allegations are a strategic or gatekeeping posture.[66]

Child Resisting Contact (aka Parental Alienation Allegations)

The majority of children are eager for contact with both parents.[67] If a child refuses contact with a parent, the judge needs to explore the reasons for the child's opposition. Is the child going through a normal developmental stage or having a predictable reaction to the separation or relocation? Is there something deeper, such as violence in the family or one parent interfering with the other's relationship? If a child has witnessed intimate partner violence or has suffered physical or emotional abuse, the child may rationally resist contact with the abusive parent. The child may exhibit symptoms of "post-traumatic stress disorder."[68] An abusive parent should not be able to argue that the other parent is alienating the child to gain rights to a child who has good reason to refuse contact.[69]

Sometimes a child who refuses contact is justifiably estranged from a parent. An estranged child has a reasonable cause to have negative attitudes and beliefs about a parent based on the child's experience with that parent.[70] A child may have a preference for one parent and an estrangement from the other because the parent has neglected the child or has poor parenting skills. If, however, one parent is interfering with custody, has been thwarting the other parent's parenting time, and undermining the child's bond with the other parent, and the child is actually alienated, the judge should act to create a plan to allow for continuity of contact with the rejected parent if it can be done safely. Therapeutic intervention can help if problems are identified early.[71] Shared parenting is almost always not appropriate.[72] These parents are high-conflict parents that may require a team to help the child reestablish a relationship with the rejected parent. Members of the team may be the family court judge, the lawyers for the parties (and maybe the child), one or more mental health professionals (custody evaluator, therapist for the child, therapist for each parent, coach for one or both parents), court service officers, and possibly neutral site coordinators or visitation supervisors.

Long-Distance Communication

If the child moves, or if the child stays but lives with the nonmoving parent, the next step is to figure out how the away parent can maintain meaningful contact with the child. It is important that the child knows that the nonresidential parent loves them and is there for support. The key is the emotional bond. Courts have become more open to realizing that the children can maintain contact with parents by means other than a traditional, alternating-weekends visitation schedule using modern technology.[73] As the New Jersey court noted:

> Every time a custodial parent moves to a distant location, the ability of the noncustodial parent to exercise visitation rights is adversely affected, but that fact alone may not be contrary to the best interest of the child, so long as an alternate visitation schedule can be created that continues and preserves the relationship between the child and the noncustodial parent. . . . In addition, plaintiff proposed building a web site, which would include the use of camera-computer technology to give defendant, his family and friends, the ability to communicate directly with Katherine on a daily basis and review her school work and records. Defendant would be afforded daily face-to-face communication with Katherine, albeit through an electronic medium.[74]

The lawyer can provide the client with information on how to maintain a long-distance relationship. If the child does move, the next step is to figure out a way to maintain meaningful contact with the child. The key is that the child knows that the nonresidential parent loves them and is there for support. The key is the emotional bond, not the number of days. The nonmoving parent must find a way of keeping in contact with the child after the move.[75]

Today, with the computer technology, there are a variety of unique ways to maintain contact through Zoom, email, voicemail, webpages, and apps.[76] The relocating parent may consent to get a separate phone for the child. A parent can write letters or make audio messages, videos, or send weekly "thinking of you" postcards.

Virtual Visitation

In 2004, Utah became the first state to enact a law expressly authorizing virtual visitation by court order.[77] Today, computers and cell phones make daily communication easy.

The advantages of virtual visitation are that it can bring communication that is intense, regular, and meaningful enough to allow for continuation of a child's contact with a parent. But virtual visitation is not the same as in person.

The Tennessee Court of Appeals approved a parenting plan involving Internet visitation with webcams and email where the parents lived only 70 miles apart. The father agreed to pay for the mother's computer equipment and training, and would contact the children via the Internet three times per week. The children would contact the father whenever they wished. In particular, the court stated:

> We agree with the trial court that Mr. Burke's proposal of internet-based communications is a "unique, forward thinking and viable communication alternative." Furthermore, this . . . alternative will give both parents the opportunity not only to speak to the children, but see them as well.[78]

Internet visitation agreements can be general or very detailed, depending on the issues addressed. At a minimum, the agreement should:

1. Specify who pays for the necessary technology, including computer, computer access to the Internet, web camera, email, and necessary software. For example:

    > By not later than [date], [mother/father's name] shall purchase or lease a separate, state of the art computer system together with appropriate computer furniture for the child's sole and exclusive use in [his/her] [bedroom or other designated room], which shall feature videoconferencing equipment and software, including a video camera with audio capabilities, for child to privately contact her [father/mother] via Internet and email systems. [Ring light might be added.]
    >
    > [Father/mother] shall also obtain and pay for Internet access service for the child, which can be utilized by the child at either residence.

2. Specify the required level of quality of the Internet access. A DSL line or greater quality bandwidth should be required.
3. State that the custodial parent will ensure that any information transmitted between the noncustodial

parent and the child remains private between the noncustodial parent and child.

> Each parent shall allow the other parent reasonable contact with the child by use of the Internet. Reasonable contact shall include sending and receiving emails, sending and receiving "instant messages," and sending and receiving photographs. Parents agree to respect the child's privacy in communications with the other parent.

4. State that the parties agree that they will not use the child to communicate any issues related to the divorce of the parties themselves.
5. Contain sanctions for noncompliance. Remedies, sanctions, or the contempt power of the court should be spelled out. For example:

> If the agreed-upon electronic communications are not in place for a certain period of time, then the caretaker parent of the child will send the child for an extra weekend at his or her expense to visit with the parent remaining behind.

6. Sample language. In a case in which the court allowed the father and child to move to Spain, the language specified:

> Each party may make reasonable telephone, email, or videoconferencing contact with the child while the child is at the home of the other party, during reasonable hours (determined by the location where the child is then located), for so long as such contact is not disruptive to the child's schedule.
>
> To facilitate such contact with the child, each party agrees to keep the other advised of all current home addresses and telephone numbers, including each party's cellular number(s), email addresses, and other addresses at which electronic contact may be made, and to advise the other within forty-eight (48) hours of whenever a change in the same may occur.

> Each party agrees that it is in the best interests of the child for the parents to share information concerning the child.
>
> The petitioner shall provide an appropriate computer and service plan to be delivered to respondent's residence prior to the child's leaving for Spain with petitioner. Thereafter, the petitioner shall be fully and completely responsible for payment of all costs and expenses for necessary and desirable upgrades or replacements to the same, and shall provide ongoing payment to the respondent for monthly DSL or greater quality bandwidth and Internet service for two years.
>
> The petitioner shall, at all times, maintain a website for the child, with the same to include all current schedules, activities, pictures, and information regarding the child, and shall, at all times, ensure that the respondent, and respondent's family have complete access to the same.
>
> Respondent's privacy shall be deemed of paramount concern, and the petitioner hereby agrees that neither he, nor any third person or entity acting by his direction or on his behalf shall, in any way, monitor computer or electronic communication activities or communications of the respondent, either as the same occur with the child, or with any other person or entity.[79]

Parents can keep in touch with children in ways other than the Internet. Some old school ways of connecting still work. For example, one is reading stories; another is sending letters and postcards. Another is using Marco Polo. Marco Polo works well for a parent and child in different time zones. The parent can send a Polo to the child when they get up or are doing something. The child can pick it up whenever the child gets up or has free time. A parent can also create a YouTube video for the child, reading a story or a book in their own voice. The parent can read age-appropriate literature. The child can hear the parent reading a story. The parent can also send the child the book with the story.

Even in the age of computer technology, it is still fun to receive mail. The parent can send postcards to the child. Instead of long letters, sometimes just a little note on a postcard lets the child know the parent is thinking of the child. The parent can find cards from the parent's hometown, a business trip, some vacation place, or from an art museum. The parent might find humorous cards or create some of their own.

Reviewing the Parenting Plan

Once the plan is finished, the parties need to review it to ensure that it is a feasible plan. Among the relevant questions to ask:

1. Is the plan age appropriate for the child's age and stage?
2. Does the plan account for the child's unique needs and desires?
3. If the child has special needs or medical concerns, are they specifically treated?
4. Is the plan sufficiently detailed that the parents will not be constantly fighting over ambiguities?
5. Does the plan provide sufficient contact between the child and the nonrelocating parent to foster and maintain an existing relationship?
6. Does the child have adequate time to develop friends and relationships in the nonrelocating parent's community?
7. Does the plan adequately cover any differences in school and holiday schedules in the different locations? How much school will the child miss with the parenting plan? Can the child afford to miss days of school without impacting academic achievement?
8. Are the travel plans realistic? Are the number of trips adequate to maintain the relationship but not overly burdensome to the child? Are the costs manageable? How much travel time does the plan require of the child, as opposed to the adults?
9. Does the child have adequate vacation time with friends in the new location as well as maintaining connections in the old location?
10. Are the parents' work schedules flexible enough to accommodate numerous trips?

Endnotes

1. Linda D. Elrod, *A Move in the Right Direction? Best Interests of the Child Emerging as the Standard in Relocation Cases*, 3 J. Child Custody 29, 47 (2006).

2. Daniel J. Hynan, PhD, Parenting Plans: Meeting the Challenges with Facts and Analysis 11 (ABA 2019).

3. *See* Linda D. Elrod, Child Custody Practice and Procedure ch. 4 (Thomson Reuters 2024).

4. *See, e.g.*, K.S.A. § 23-3211.

5. *In re* Marriage of Hall, 241 P.3d 540, 543 (Colo. 2010).

6. Jacob A. v. C.H., 127 Cal. Rptr. 3d 611, 617, 620 (Ct. App. 2011). *See also In re* Marriage of Morgan, 428 P.3d 550 (Colo. Ct. App. 2018).

7. Jeffrey P. v. Alyssa P., 164 N.Y.S.3d 265 (App. Div. 2022). *See also* Bergerson v. Zurbano, 432 P.3d 850 (Wash. Ct. App. 2018) (Washington's Child Relocation Act could not be applied to parties agreed upon 50–50 parenting plan when father moved to relocate across the country with parties' child).

8. Murray v. Murray, 318 S.W.3d 149 (Mo. Ct. App. 2010).

9. Michael Lamb, *Mothers, Fathers, Families, and Circumstances: Factors Affecting Children's Development*, 16 Applied Dev. Sci. 98 (2012).

10. Michael E. Lamb, *Critical Analysis of Research on Parenting Plans and Children's Well-Being*, *in* Parenting Plan Evaluations: Applied Research for the Family Court 170 (Leslie Drozd, Michael Saini & Nancy Olesen eds., 2d ed. 2016).

11. *See* Jan Jeske & Mary Louis Klas, *Adverse Childhood Experiences: Implications for Family Law Practice and the Family Court System*, 50(1) Fam. L.Q. 123 (2016) (parental separation is one of the adverse experiences that can harm a child). *See also* Paul R. Amato, *The Consequences of Divorce for Adults and Children*, 62 J. Marriage & Fam. 1269, 1277–78 (2001); Mavis Hetherington & John Kelly, For Better or For Worse: Divorce Reconsidered (2002).

12. Lamb, *supra* note 10. *See also* Judith S. Wallerstein & Tony J. Tanke, *To Move or Not to Move: Psychological and Legal Considerations in the Relocation of Children Following Divorce*, 30 Fam. L.Q. 305, 310–311 (1996).

13. Lamb, *supra* note 10, at 176. *See also* Joan B. Kelley & Robert Emery, *Children's Adjustment Following Divorce: Risk and Resilience Perspectives*, 52 Fam. Relations 352 (2003).

14. Patrick Parkinson & Judith Cashmore, *Reforming Relocation Law: An Evidence Based Approach*, 53 Fam. Ct. Rev. 23 (2015); Patrick Parkinson & Judith Cashmore, *Relocation and the Indissolubility of Parenthood*, 15 J. Child Custody 76 (2018).

15. Sol Rappaport, *Deconstructing the Impact of Divorce on Children*, 47(3) Fam. L.Q. 353 (2013). *See also* Linda D. Elrod, *Reforming the System to Protect Children in High Conflict Custody Cases*, 28(2) Wm. Mitchell L. Rev. 496 (2001) (suggestions from experts at a Wingspread Conference on reducing conflict for children).

16. *See* Matthew M. Stevenson et al., *Associations Between Parental Relocation Following Separation in Childhood and Maladjustment in Adolescence and Young Adulthood*, 24 PSYCH. PUB. POL'Y & L. 365 (2018).

17. HETHERINGTON & KELLY, *supra* note 11, at 88 (noting that poor women moved to cheaper housing seven times in first six post-divorce years to cheaper housing). *See also* Stevenson et al., *supra* note 16.

18. JANET JOHNSTON & L. CAMPBELL, IMPASSES OF DIVORCE: THE DYNAMICS AND RESOLUTION OF FAMILY CONFLICT (1988); WILLIAM A. EDDY, HIGH CONFLICT PERSONALITIES: UNDERSTANDING AND RESOLVING THEIR CUSTODY DISPUTES (2003).

19. *See* E.B. v. D.B., 209 A.3d 451 (Pa. Super. Ct. 2019) (parents divorced in 2005 and had been continually litigating since child was two years old; most recent trial was in 2018).

20. JANET JOHNSTON & VIVIENNE ROSEBY, IN THE NAME OF THE CHILD: A DEVELOPMENTAL APPROACH TO UNDERSTANDING AND HELPING CHILDREN OF CONFLICTED AND VIOLENT DIVORCE (1997).

21. Lamb, *supra* note 10, at 192–193 (noting a child benefits from a joint/shared physical custody (35 percent of child's time with each parent) unless the parent poses a credible risk of abuse, neglect, abduction of the child, or has committed domestic violence, engages in high conflict behaviors, or fails to support the child).

22. Linda D. Elrod, *National and International Momentum Builds for More Child Focus in Relocation Disputes*, 44(3) FAM. L.Q. 341 (2010).

23. William G. Austin, *Relocation, Research, and Forensic Evaluation, Part I: Effects of Residential Mobility on Children of Divorce*, 46 FAM. CT. REV. 137 (2008) (increased risks with multiple moves); William G. Austin, *Relocation, Research, and Forensic Evaluation, Part II: Research Support for Relocation Risk-Assessment Model*, 46 FAM. CT. REV. 347 (2008) (discussing harm if the moving parent engages restrictive gate-keeping behaviors).

24. Patrick Parkinson et al., *Relocation, Research, and Child Custody Disputes, in* PARENTING PLAN EVALUATIONS, 2d ed., *supra* note 10, at 431, 432 (citing studies).

25. Leslie Ellen Shear, *Life Stories, Doctrines and Decision-Making: Three High Courts Confront the Move-Away Dilemma*, 34 FAM. & CONCILIATION CTS. REV. 439 (1996).

26. HETHERINGTON & KELLY, *supra* note 11, at 134.

27. Stevenson et al., *supra* note 16 (citing earlier study).

28. *See* Kenneth Waldron, *A Review of Social Science Research on Post Divorce Relocation*, 19 J. AM. ACAD. MATRIM. LAW. 337, 371 (2005). *See also* William G. Austin & Sol Rappaport, *Parental Gatekeeping Forensic Model and Child Custody Evaluation: Social Capital and Application to Relocation Disputes*, 15 J. CHILD CUSTODY 55 (2018) (relocation adds to the general risks associated with children of divorce); Stevenson et al., *supra* note 16 (noting several risks).

29. Nancy Darling, *Moving Is Tough for Kids*, PSYCH. TODAY (July 22, 2010) (citing study in *Journal of Social Personality Psychology* (2010)).

30. Stevenson et al., *supra* note 16 (study collected data five times starting at age 12 for children who lived with mothers and stepfathers and more than an hour's drive from biological fathers).

31. *Id.* at 376. *See also* Barbara A. Atwood, *Child Relocation: Case Law, Social Science, and Practice Implications*, 32 J. AM. ACAM. MATRIM. LAW. 383 (2022).

32. Roger T. Webb, Carsten B. Pedersen & Pearl L.H. Mok, *Adverse Outcomes to Early Middle Age Linked with Childhood Residential Mobility*, AM. J. PREVENTIVE MED. (2016) (finding higher rate of attempted suicides, substance abuse, mental illness, criminality, and violence among those who moved during childhood; the more frequent the moves, the greater the risk).

33. Nicola Taylor & Marilyn Freeman, *International Research Evidence on Relocation: Past, Present and Future*, 44 FAM. L.Q. 317 (2010); Nicola Taylor, M. Gollop & R. Mark Henaghan, *Relocation Following Parental Separation in New Zealand: Complexity and Diversity*, 97 INT'L FAM. L. (2010); Patrick Parkinson, Judy Cashmore & Judi Single, *The Need for Reality Testing in Relocation Cases*, 44 FAM. L.Q. 1 (2010).

34. Taylor & Freeman, *supra* note 33.

35. Parkinson et al., *supra* note 33.

36. *See* DANIEL J. HYMAN, PARENTING PLANS: MEETING THE CHALLENGES WITH FACTS AND ANALYSIS 42 (ABA 2018).

37. Philip M. Stahl, *Emerging Issues in Relocation Cases*, 25 J. AM. ACAD. MATRIM. LAW. 425, 441 (2013). *See also* Philip M. Stahl, *Avoiding Bias in Relocation Cases*, 3 J. CHILD CUSTODY 111 (2006).

38. *See* HYMAN, *supra* note 36; JOHN HARTSON & BRENDA PAYNE, CREATING EFFECTIVE PARENTING PLANS: A DEVELOPMENTAL APPROACH FOR LAWYERS AND DIVORCE PROFESSIONALS (ABA 2006). *See also* Risa J. Garon et al., *From Infants to Adolescents: A Developmental Approach to Parenting Plans*, 38 FAM. & CONCIL. CTS. REV. 68 (2000).

39. Linda D. Elrod, *Reforming the System to Protect Children in High Conflict Custody Cases*, 28(2) WM. MITCHELL L. REV. 495, 515–17 (2001) (discussing the ABA Wingspread Conference in September 2000, which suggested parents be required to develop parenting plans).

40. Sanford L. Braver & Michael E. Lamb, *Shared Parenting After Parental Separation: The Views of 12 Experts*, 69 J. DIVORCE & REMARRIAGE 372 (2018).

41. *See* Mildred Dale, "Still the One": *Defending the Individualized Best Interests of the Child Standard from Equal Parenting Time Presumptions*, 34(2) J. AM. ACAD. MATRIM. LAW 307 (2022) (presents rationale for individualized best interests standard as based on the circumstances of each family instead of relying on presumptions). *See* Lamb, *supra* note 10, at 192 (if parents manifest long standing conflict without a history of successful cooperation in parenting, children are unlikely to benefit from shared parenting).

42. HYMAN, *supra* note 36, at 44.

43. Rebecca Stahl, *Keeping in Mind the Child's Perspective in Your Parenting Plan*, 47(1) FAM. ADVOC. 15 (Summer 2024) (noting children do not care whether a parent has equal time, they want quality).

44. *Id.* at 17 (noting children do not care whether a parent has equal time).

45. *See generally Section IV. Children's Disorders That Require Specialized Parenting, in* PARENTING PLAN EVALUATIONS: APPLIED RESEARCH FOR THE FAMILY COURT 247–366 (Kathryn Kuehnle & Leslie Drozd, eds. 2012); *see also* Section 4. *Children's Disorders That Require Specialized Parenting in* PARENTING PLAN EVALUATIONS 2d ed., *supra* note 10, at 205–76.

46. *See* Jennifer L. Hardesty et al., *Domestic Violence and Child Custody, in* PARENTING PLAN EVALUATIONS, *supra* note 45, at 442–75. *See also* Dana Harrington Connor, *Back to the Drawing Board: Barriers to Joint Decision-Making in Custody Cases Involving Intimate Partner Violence*, 18 DUKE J. GENDER L. & POL'Y 223, 228 (2011).

47. *See* Michael Saini et al., *Empirical Studies of Alienation, in* PARENTING PLAN EVALUATIONS, *supra* note 45, at 399–441.

48. Winn v. Winn, 593 N.W.2d 662, 669 (Mich. Ct. App. 2000) (emphasis added).

49. *See* Lamb, *supra* note 10; Gwynneth Smith et al., *Attachment and Child Custody: The Importance of Available Parents, in* PARENTING PLAN EVALUATIONS, *supra* note 45, at 5.

50. Pamela S. Ludolph & Milfred D. Dale, *Attachment and Child Custody: An Additive Factor, Not a Determinative One*, 46(1) FAM. L.Q. 1 (2012) (summarizing attachment theory and reviewing the research relevant to the debate about overnight care of infants following divorce or parental separation).

51. *Id. See also* Marsha K. Pruett et al., *Parental Separation and Overnight Care of Young Children, Part I: Consensus Through Theoretical and Empirical Integration*, 52 FAM. CT. REV. 240 (2014). Jennifer E. McIntosh et al., *Parental Separation and Overnight Care of Young Children, Part II: Putting Theory into Practice*, 52 FAM. CT. REV. 256 (2014).

52. Ludolph & Dale, *supra* note 50.

53. Joan B. Kelly & Michael E. Lamb, *Developmental Issues in Relocation Cases Involving Young Children: When, Whether, and How?*, 17 J. FAM. PSYCH. 193 (2003).

54. Rebekah Levin Coley & Melissa Kull, *Cumulative, Timing-Specific, and Interactive Models of Residential Mobility and Children's Cognitive and Psychosocial Skills*, CHILD DEV. 1 (2016).

55. Lucy S. McGough, *Starting Over: The Heuristics of Family Relocation Decision Making*, 77 ST. JOHN'S L. REV. 291, 322–23 (2003).

56. Lamb, *supra note* 10.

57. SARAH BUEL, THE IMPACT OF DOMESTIC VIOLENCE ON CHILDREN: TEN PRACTICAL RECOMMENDATIONS FOR LAWYERS, JUDGES, AND COURT PERSONNEL (1997).

58. *See* Allen Bailey, *Prioritizing Child Safety as the Prime Best Interest Factor*, 47 FAM. L.Q. 35 (2013); Janet Johnston & Nancy VerSteegh, *Historical Trends in Family Court Response to Intimate Partner Violence: Perspectives of Critics and Proponents of Current Practices*, 51 FAM. CT. REV. 63 (2013).

59. Janet Bowermaster, *Relocation Disputes Involving Domestic Violence*, 46 U. KAN. L. REV. 433 (1998).

60. Hardesty et al., *supra* note 46; Peter Jaffe et al., *Custody Disputes Involving Allegations of Domestic Violence: Toward a Differentiated Approach to Parenting Plans*, 46(3) FAM. CT. REV. 500 (2008).

61. *See also In re* Marriage of Morgan, 428 P.3d 550 (Colo. Ct. App. 2018) (magistrate erred in not considering additional statutory factors when it found father had committed domestic violence and a permanent protective order had been issued).

62. Jan Jeske & Mary Louis Klas, *Adverse Childhood Experiences: Implications for Family Law and the Family Court*, 50(1) FAM. L.Q. 126 (2016).

63. *See* Lynne Hecht Schafran, *Domestic Violence, Developing Brains, and the Lifespan: New Knowledge from Neuroscience*, 53(3) JUDGES' J. 32 (2014); Moffatt & Smith, *Childhood Exposure to Conjugal Violence: Consequences for Behavioral and Neural Development*, 56 DEPAUL L. REV. 879 (2007) (exposure to domestic violence during childhood may have lifelong impact on children's developing brains).

64. Peter Jaffe et al., *Custody Disputes Involving Allegations of Domestic Violence: Toward a Differentiated Approach to Parenting Plans*, 46 FAM. CT. REV. 500 (2008).

65. Gjertsen v. Haar, 347 P.3d 1117 (Wyo. 2015).

66. Michael Saini, Taina Laajasalo & Stacey Platt, *Gatekeeping by Allegations: An Examination of Verified, Unfounded, and Fabricated Allegations of Child Maltreatment Within the Context of Resist and Refusal Dynamics*, 58(2) FAM. CT. REV. 417 (2020).

67. Mary E. v. Usher E., 967 N.Y.S.2d 868, 880 (Sup. Ct. 2013) (evaluator testified that hatred of a parent is not a natural emotion for a child).

68. BARBARA JO FIDLER ET AL., CHALLENGING ISSUES IN CHILD CUSTODY DISPUTES: A GUIDE FOR LEGAL AND MENTAL HEALTH PROFESSIONALS 221 (2008).

69. Joan S. Meier, *Getting Real About Abuse and Alienation: A Critique of Drozd and Olesen's Decision Tree*, 7 (4) J. CHILD CUSTODY 219, 237 (2010).

70. Leslie M. Drozd & Nancy W. Oleson, *Is It Abuse, Alienation, and/or Estrangement? A Decision Tree*, 1(3) J. CHILD CUSTODY 65 (2004).

71. Lyn R. Greenberg et al., *Catching Them Before Too Much Damage Is Done: Early Intervention with Resistance-Refusal Dynamics*, 54 FAM. CT. REV. 548 (2016).

72. Marsha Kline Pruett & Herbie DiFonzo, *Closing the Gap: Research Policy Practice and Shared Parenting*, 52(2) FAM. CT. REV. 152, 162 (2014) (courts should not award shared parenting for parents who do not attempt to remove themselves or their child from the conflict and do not support the other parent's presence in the child's life).

73. *In re* Marriage of Thielges, 623 N.W.2d 232 (Iowa App. 2000) (mother was allowed to move from Iowa to North Dakota)).

74. *See* McCoy v. McCoy, 764 A.2d 449 (N.J. Super. App. Div. 2001).

75. Elizabeth Bach-Van Horn, *Comment: Virtual Visitation: Are Webcams Being Used as An Excuse to Allow Relocation?*, 21 J. Am. Acad. Matrim. L. 171 (2008). *See* Joanna Grossman, The Virtues of Virtual Parenting: Can the Internet Replace Visitation When a Custodial Parent Relocates?, www.longdistancefamilies.com.

76. *See In re* S.M., 938 S.W.2d 910 (Mo. Ct. App. 1997) (trial court order directed guardians to permit contact with the natural family by allowing reasonable contact through letters, telephone calls, Internet messages, if reasonably available, video recorded communication).

77. Utah Code Ann. § 30-3-35.

78. Burke v. Burke, 2001 WL 921770 (Tenn. Ct. App. Aug. 7, 2001).

79. Hernandez-Mora v. Jex, No. 01-WY1009-CB (U.S. Dist. Ct., D. Colo., July 12, 2001).

CHAPTER 14

Hearing Children's Voices in Relocation

A move is tough on a kid. . . . Through the end of high school, I attended seven different schools in four different cities in two different states. . . . But whatever the city or neighborhood, however large or small the house or the school or the town, I suffered in ways that my parents often missed. . . . [T]hey forgot what it was like to be a kid unable to express yourself—or even understand why you feel as bad as you do.[1]

A child's voice, however honest and true . . . is meaningless to those who've forgotten how to listen.[2]

A child should be able to express their views, wishes, and preferences when a parent is relocating a distance from the other parent. The child's perspective of a potential move to another school, city, or state may differ from one or both of the parents. An older child who has lots of friends and activities may be adamantly opposed to moving away from their friends. A child in grade school with few friends and activities in the current location may not care either way. A very young child may be unable to articulate any opinion although some studies indicate the younger child needs continual, predictable contact with both parents more than older children who have an established relationship. The child should have a voice, not necessarily a choice.

The parents should know or find out their child's views for several reasons. First, if the child is an older child who wants to move, the parent's case for the move will be stronger. On the other hand, if the older child does not want to move, the other parent is likely to contest the child's move vigorously. A parent who knows the child does not want to move may be able to develop some compelling reasons as to why the child would benefit—better science programs, more sports, or creative arts opportunities. The client parent who assumes the child will be fine because the move is good for the parent needs to know this may not be true. The lawyer can give the client information about how their jurisdiction has handled cases when children do not want to move or studies showing how children can be harmed by a move.

If the parents cannot agree, the judge makes the ultimate best interest determination, usually based on statutory factors. The 1973 Uniform Marriage and Divorce Act listed the child's wishes as one of five factors to consider in determining the child's best interests. Today, all states include the child's wishes or preferences as a statutory or case law factor.[3] The growing consensus is no longer *if* the child's voice should be heard but when, how, where, and what weight to give to the child's voice in custody proceedings.[4] Therefore, the judge needs information about the child's wishes, either from a lawyer or guardian ad litem, a mental health professional, or a custody evaluation report. Another option is to have the judge interview the child in camera. In any case, the child's views should be sought and factored into the custody decision. While the court wants to protect the child from the parents' conflict, the child is already in it. The child can provide the trial judge with insights from the child's perspective into the dynamics of family relationships. Additionally, hearing the child's voice helps ensure the international enforcement of U.S. custody orders.

State statutes list the child's preference or wishes as a factor, not only in child custody cases generally but also in relocation cases specifically. For example, Massachusetts has a specific statute that addresses the issue of the child's choice in relocation disputes:

> Section 30. A minor child of divorced parents who is a native of or has resided five years within this commonwealth and over whose custody and maintenance a probate court has jurisdiction shall not, if of suitable age to signify his consent, be

> removed out of this commonwealth without such consent, or, if under that age, without the consent of both parents, unless the court upon cause shown otherwise orders[.][5]

Colorado is also one of several states that require courts to look at custody factors and additional statutory relocation factors.

Judges vary widely as to whether and how to hear that preference and the weight it is to be given.[6] Only a few courts require family court judges to interview the child,[7] and sometimes, only if a parent requests.[8] States differ considerably on:

- when it is reasonable, appropriate, or necessary to hear a child's voice;
- whether the child's voice should be included in mediation and other forms of dispute resolution;
- the age at which a child may express a preference;
- how the judge assesses age and maturity;
- the best methods to use in determining the child's views;
- the weight to be given a preference; and
- the protection of parents' due process rights when the courts do consider the child's wishes.

Why Listening to a Child Is Important

Relocation issues may impact the child's future more than the initial custody decision if both parents have been residing in the same general vicinity and sharing legal and physical custody. The child will either move with one parent, changing cities, schools, and friends, or the child will stay in same general area but still may be moving homes and schools. In either case, the child will have less access to one of the parents. If that parent was the primary caregiver, the child may suffer significant trauma. If the distance between the parents' homes is great, the child most likely will bear the burden of travel, losing time with friends and others, and possibly straining the relationship with the other parent.

Generally, children do not have many rights.[9] In custody cases, most courts find that a child is not a party to the parents' action.[10] The U.S. Supreme Court has held that constitutional due process requires procedural protection of a parent's interest in the care, custody, and control of their children.[11] Children, however, have not yet been given a comparable right. Justice Stevens, in his dissent in *Troxel v. Granville*, noted, "[T]o the extent parents and families have fundamental liberty interests in preserving such intimate relationships, so too, do children have these interests, and so, too, must their interests be balanced in the equation."[12]

In a child custody proceeding, the child is a subject of the proceeding, not a party. A child does not need to be a part or a participant, however, to have a voice in the proceedings. The Michigan Court of Appeals held that the trial court plainly erred in failing to take into consideration the preference of a seven-year-old child with respect to custody, stating:

> Regardless, we will not ignore the substantial rights of the child whose custody is being decided. To do so would be pedantic and, more importantly, would defeat the very reason why we apply plain-error review in this kind of case, i.e., to ensure that the child's best interests are protected[13]

There was nothing in the record that suggested that the child could not express a reasonable preference. The statute listing the child's preference as a factor in a custody case affords a child the "right and opportunity to have his or her own voice heard" in a child custody proceeding whether the parent wants the court to consider it. The court will evaluate the child's preference along with other relevant evidence. While the court may not follow it, there is independent value in knowing on some level that one's voice has been heard.[14]

A comprehensive 2021 review of 45 studies from seven countries concluded that parental separation can be distressing, traumatic, and confusing to children who are often not informed of what is happening. Children overwhelmingly felt unheard in court proceedings, which added to their distress. They feel a loss of control over the decisions being made and the situation. Many children want to be more involved and be heard but also understand the difference between having input and making decisions.[15]

Studies indicate that children want to be heard, benefit from having their voices heard, and have better outcomes because they have been able to express their views.[16] Studies show that children's voices are particularly important in relocation cases:

- Children generally have better outcomes if they feel that they have a voice in the family dispute resolution process but often report feeling ignored.
- Even if children have a lawyer or there is a custody evaluator involved, a significant portion of children would also like to meet with the judge or decision-maker.
- Children are often traumatized by being involved in high-conflict separations, but meeting the judge is no more stressful than meeting a lawyer or custody evaluator.
- Even though children often report feeling anxious before they meet the judge, they usually feel positively after the meeting, and there is no evidence that they are traumatized.
- Judges report that often they find it helpful to meet children.[17]

Capacity Issue

Many statutes make hearing the child depend upon the child's age and maturity or capacity. Capacity includes the mental ability to comprehend the nature and effect of one's actions, and a person's ability to act or experience an event or occasion. The capacity discussion includes the individual child's cognitive development and experience, personality and emotional state, parental influence, cultural background, and other factors. There are some legal tests for determining if the child has the competency to testify in open court, such as whether the child knows right from wrong.[18] The medical community has developed standards and assessment tools, such as the MacCAT-CR or the Aid to Capacity Evaluation (ACE) clinical interview, for medical decision-making capacity. These tests look at the ability to communicate verbally, understand information provided, balance risks and benefits, and appreciate the nature of what the person is facing.[19] There are studies that can provide useful information about children's abilities generally. But the studies cannot determine if a particular child can understand or decide a certain issue. For example, studies may indicate that 14-year-olds can perform some decision-making tasks similar to adults, while most 11-year-olds are less capable than an adult. But a particular 14-year-old may not be able to understand the situation or the implications of expressing their wishes in a relocation case, while a particular 11-year-old might.

Capacity is not an all-or-nothing proposition nor is it present at a certain age, say 10 or 12 or 14. Age, however, should not be a basis for arbitrarily refusing to hear a child's perspective. It could be considered in determining the weight to be given the child's views. Capacity should be assessed in relation to the issue being considered. Capacity to express views on the current living situation versus moving to a future location are not the same. To ensure the child's voice is heard, the judge should presume the child has capacity.[20] As a general rule, the older the child, the more likely the court will find the child has capacity.[21] As a child matures, that child will likely have reasonable preferences on matters of healthcare, religious practices, education, and athletic activities.[22]

The Pennsylvania Child Custody Act makes clear that a child's preference is per se relevant to the substantive questions of custody and relocation. The appellate court found that the trial court should not have presumed that a six- and seven-year-old were too young to have preferences, when their mother sought to relocate after the father had moved to the place where the mother lived. The appellate court noted that the children were presumably capable of expressing whether they had enjoyed having their father living close by for nearly the first time in their memory. The interview was an opportunity for the court to learn what, in the children's view, was the most important aspect of the custody award. The court noted that even young children are able to express their likes, dislikes, apprehensions, and other relevant information insofar as it relates to custody and relocation; that is, whether they like their school and their routines, whether they have friends, or whether they partake in extracurricular or community activities.[23] On the other hand, an Illinois appellate court found that a trial judge did not err in not interviewing a six-year-old.[24]

Ascertaining the Child's Preference

Fifty states have nearly 50 different ways of viewing child participation. There are numerous ways to get the child's preferences and perspectives into the relocation case. The judge can ascertain a child's perspective through the child's testimony in court, through an interview with the child in chambers, from testimony of the parents, from evidence presented by the child's attorney or guardian ad litem, or from mental health professionals. The court may also obtain the preference indirectly from reports of psychologists, court services officers, or testimony of other witnesses. The method used depends upon the state and the discretion of the individual judges.

Child's Testimony in Court

Theoretically, either party may call the child as a witness, even over the objections of the child's guardian or attorney. For example, Virginia law allows the court to call a child as a witness in a custody proceeding if it finds after a hearing that the child's testimony is necessary, the probative value outweighs the potential detriment, and the evidence is not otherwise available. An attorney must be appointed for the child witness.[25] Note while there is a constitutional right to confront witnesses in a criminal case, there is no such right in a civil case.

Most judges try to avoid having a child testify in open court because it puts the child in the middle of the parents' conflict in a public way. A New York court summed up the reasons, noting that "a child, already suffering from the trauma of a broken home, should not be placed in the position of having [his or her] relationship with either parent further jeopardized by having to publicly relate [his or her] difficulties with them or be required to openly choose between them[.]"[26] While the 14-year-old's preferences were entitled to great weight, the court felt that an interview in the judge's chambers would have limited the harm and would have been "far more informative and worthwhile than the traditional procedures of the adversary system—an examination of the child under oath in open court."[27] The AAML Bounds of Advocacy 6.4 states that an attorney should not bring a child to court or call a child as a witness without full discussion with the client and a reasonable belief that it is in the best interests of the child.

The Uniform (now Model) Child Witness Testimony by Alternative Methods Act (MCWTAMA), only enacted in four states, excludes a child from testifying in person in an open forum in the presence of the fact-finder or parties. The judge can permit testimony by alternative methods. Even without the MCWTAMA, the judge may decline to allow the child to testify if the child might be harmed by testifying or if there is evidence the child has been coached.[28] If the judge decides to allow the child to testify, the judge may make special accommodations to make the child more comfortable, such as rearranging the courtroom, using more informal dress, or using procedures to make the child more at ease. Some judges may have only the attorneys for the parents, not the parents themselves, in the courtroom when the child testifies. Others may choose to have the child testify via a live video feed. Another way is for the judge to record the child's testimony before the trial and play it at the trial.

Nevada has a detailed court rule that specifies alternative methods to testifying in court. Unless the parents waive the requirements by stipulation, the rule applies. If the parties are represented by counsel, the court may interview the child witness outside the presence of the parties, either with the parties' counsel present or with them simultaneously viewing via an electronic method; or allow the parties' counsel to question the child witness in the presence of the court without the parties. Regardless of whether the parties are represented by counsel, the court may interview the child witness with no parties present but allow them to simultaneously view the interview by electronic method as long as not contrary to child's best interest. A record is made.[29]

Most courts will allow an older child to testify if the child requests to. A California statute allows a 14-year-old to address the court. A 15-year-old sought to testify as to why she wanted to reduce the time spent with her father. Her attempts to talk to him and her written letter were unsuccessful in making him understand her needs.[30]

A blanket prohibition on all children having standing to appear in court, regardless of age and competence, is unjustified and violates constitutional due process. While parents have constitutionally protected liberty interests in the care, companionship, and custody of their child that require procedural protection, the court also has a parens patriae obligation to protect the child. At least one commentator has suggested that if a child wishes to testify, allow a child standing to be in court; listen to what the child has to say; weigh what the child says in light of all circumstances, including the child's age and maturity; and determine if the child's wishes are reasonable and justified.[31]

Judicial Interview with Child

The most widely used means of discovering a child's preference is for the trial judge to conduct an in camera interview with a child. The 1973 Uniform Marriage and Divorce Act section 404(a) provided that a judge could interview the child in chambers to ascertain the child's wishes as to his custodian and as to visitation. Several states adopted a similar provision. Other states find that the right to interview a child is implied because of consideration of the child's preference as a factor in divorce.[32]

In most states, as part of the custody hearing, the court may on its own motion, or at the request of a litigant, conduct an in camera interview with the child.[33] If a parent requests the judge interview the child, it may be reversible error to not do so if the child is of sufficient age and maturity.[34] The judge should also interview a child, especially a teenager, who asks to talk to the judge.[35] The child is not a fact witness and is not put under oath.

Judges have broad discretion on whether to interview the child, who can be present for the interview, whether to record the interview, and to whom to disclose the recording. A judge may decline to interview a child if the child is too young,[36] the child's wishes have been clearly presented by others, such as the child's attorney or a custody evaluator, or the child does not have a preference.[37] A judge may decline if the child does not want to talk to the judge.[38]

A judge may decide not to interview a child if the judge thinks the child will be put in the middle of the parents' disputes and feel pressure to choose sides.[39] For example, in Illinois, the appellate court upheld a judge who declined to interview a ten-year-old boy in camera stating in dicta that among the good reasons not to interview a child were the "tremendous amount of pressure" on the child, the enticement for parental manipulation and intimidation, and the child's stated preferences may not coincide with the child's best interests.[40]

Typically, a trial judge will state on the record its preliminary determinations that it is in the child's best interest to conduct an in camera interview and that the child is of a sufficient age to form an intelligent preference. Louisiana has found that only after the judge has determined the competency of a child should the judge continue with an in camera interview of the child in a child custody case. Attorneys may not participate in a judge's determination of a child's competency by questioning, cross-examining, or registering objections to the judge's questions for the child at an in-camera interview.[41]

A Rhode Island trial judge who denied a mother's request to relocate with the parties' four minor children to her home country of Australia was not required to sua sponte seek testimony regarding the children's reasonable preferences. If the mother felt the preferences were important, the mother's attorneys had the responsibility to submit evidence of the preferences.[42]

A growing number of courts, however, not only allow, but also encourage, judges to talk to children.[43]

The purpose of the interview is for the child to express the child's views and obtain the child's wishes regarding parenting time. The child may go beyond stating a preference. The child may explain the reasons why, which may include relevant facts about parental involvement. For example, the child may say she wants to be at her mother's house because her mother helps her with her homework while her father watches television or plays on his computer all evening. The American Bar Association has a book on interviewing children as well as a free video.[44]

One of the best articles on judicial interviewing of children includes *Guidelines for Judges Meeting Children in Family Cases*.[45]

The purpose of the guidelines is to help judges encourage children to be more involved and connected; to give them the opportunity to make the judge aware of their wishes, feelings, and perceptions; and to help them understand the judge's role. The guidelines include the purpose of the interview and suggest interview structure and questions.[46]

Uniform Act on Judicial Interviewing of Children

In 2023, the Uniform Law Commission (ULC) appointed a drafting committee to work on an act on the judicial interviewing of children, encouraging measures to protect children while safeguarding parental concerns.[47] The Judicial Interviewing of Children Act (JICA) will be up for a final reading at the Uniform Law Commission in July 2025. JICA prescribes standards for judicial officers. While most ULC acts are adopted as statutes, this one may be more appropriate for court rule. The JICA draft uses the term "covered proceeding" which includes child custody, visitation, relocation, guardianship, private adoption, and the International Child Abduction Remedies Act.

JICA makes it clear that the child is not considered a "party." JICA recognizes that some states have statutes requiring children of a certain age to be interviewed in court on request so does not displace other law of a state. If not required by law, the judicial officer (a judge in most states) must consider if it is in the child's best interests to conduct an interview. One of the factors to consider is whether the child has expressed a desire to talk to the judicial officer. Parties and their counsel may not attend the interview in person, but the judicial officer may allow them to observe remotely in real time. The child's attorney and/or Guardian ad litem have the right to attend the interview. JICA requires a record of the judicial interview but the parties may stipulate that they will not have access to the record. The judicial officer retains discretion as to how much weight to give the child's preference.

The post interview procedure provides due process protections. The draft brackets two alternatives regarding the parties' access to the interview record in the absence of stipulations. Alternative A gives the parties a right of access to the interview record in the trial court and the right to submit evidence and legal argument. Alternative B gives the parties the right to access the record if an appeal is filed which allows a challenge to the weight the judicial officer gave the child's views.

Presence of Counsel

The court may question a child privately if the parties consent, and sometimes even if they do not.[48] Several states permit the trial judge to interview the child without counsel or the parties.[49] Failure to make a timely objection to a private interview may waive any objections for an appeal.[50] Some states require certain procedures be followed to safeguard the parents' right to rebut any statements made by the child.[51] Custody and relocation cases are civil and do not mandate cross-examination.[52]

In most states, there is no bright-line requirement that counsel be present or permitted to be part of in camera proceedings. Some states do require counsel for the parents to be present during the interview.[53] Others may give the trial judge the discretion to permit counsel to be present.[54] If the lawyers are present, in most states they are observers and do not participate or question the child.[55] In some states, the lawyers can submit questions they would like the judge to ask or not to ask.[56] If the child has an attorney, the court may allow the child's attorney to be present. A Pennsylvania court found that both the child's attorney and the child's best interest attorney, as well as the parties' counsel, were entitled to attend the in camera interview.[57]

An Oklahoma case found that if one or both parents object to being excluded from the interview, the trial court has discretion to allow parents' counsel to be present, allow counsel to question the child, or allow counsel to submit questions to be asked.[58] If a party claims the trial court erred in conducting or relying on an in camera interview, the party should have requested a copy of the transcript or they waive that issue.[59]

Record Made

Many states require a record, such as a transcript, video, or other reliable means of recording, of the judicial interview, either automatically[60] or upon a request of the parties.[61] The Texas statute provides that "on the motion of a party . . . or on the court's own motion, the court shall cause a record of the interview to be made when the child is 12 years of age or older. A record of the interview shall be part of the record in the case.[62] A judge should provide information to the child at the beginning of the interview as to who will have access to the record.[63]

If the parties did not consent to the interview, the judge should make a record. Failure to record may be prejudicial if a statute requires recording, even if the parties do not object.[64] On the other hand, if the court's findings are made solely on the basis of other evidence received in open court, an appellate court may find no prejudice.[65] The child's testimony must be disclosed to the extent necessary for the judge to make a decision based on written findings. In some states, the judge must state the preference of the child and the weight the judge gave it.[66] Because the trial judge can use the child's statements in making decisions in a case, it follows that the child's statements are competent evidence. In a Florida case, the appellate court found that the trial court's failure to record the interview or to provide an appraisal or summary of the children's testimony during the interview violated the mother's due process rights.[67]

In some jurisdictions, the record can be viewed by the parties and becomes part of the record on appeal. Some states give the judge discretion whether to make a record and to seal it, unless there is an appeal.[68] While the parties in some jurisdictions are not entitled to a transcript,[69] the child's attorney should have access to the record.[70]

In a New York case, the court emphasized that the right to confidentiality during the *Lincoln* hearing (interview with the judge) belongs to the child. Only the child's attorney should be present for the interview. The trial judge erred both in allowing the attorneys for the parents in the room during the interview with children ages 10 and 7 and in not sealing the record. The right to confidentiality during a *Lincoln* hearing belongs to the child and is superior to the rights or preferences of the parents. The appellate court stated:

> The child who is explaining the reasons for his or her preference in custody and visitation proceedings "should not be placed in the position of having [his or her] relationship with either parent further jeopardized by having to publicly relate [his or her] difficulties with them or be required to openly choose between them."[71]

Child's Attorney or Guardian Ad Litem

Some judges regularly appoint either an attorney or a guardian ad litem for the child, while other judges rarely use either. The 1973 Uniform Marriage and Divorce Act section 310 authorized the court to appoint an attorney for a child involved in a custody or visitation dispute. Only a few states, however, enacted the UMDA provision or currently require appointment in custody cases.[72] Several states have statutes or court rules allowing the appointment of a lawyer, a best interest attorney, or a guardian ad litem (usually a lawyer) in contested divorce or high-conflict cases, like relocation.[73] Even without a statute or court rule, the court has inherent power to appoint a lawyer or GAL. When and how to give children a voice has generated substantial controversy and resulted in numerous sets of standards and principles.[74] Nine states can appoint a child's attorney with a best interest representative optional.[75] Another dozen jurisdictions appoint a child's attorney and a best interest representative.[76]

The American Bar Association's Standards of Practice for Lawyers Representing Children in Custody Cases (2003) allow the judge discretion to appoint a child's attorney or a best interest attorney.[77] The best interests attorney model, however, has been criticized.[78]

The American Academy of Matrimonial Lawyers 2009 Guidelines say lawyers for children should be the exception, and generally not be appointed for younger children.[79] Some states presume capacity at a certain age so that children over that age are given a client-directed lawyer; below a best interests lawyer.[80] Although the first set of AAML Standards set the age of 12 as the age of capacity for client-directed lawyering,[81] an Indiana court found that an 11-year-old child's desire to remain with her father and not move was entitled to consideration.[82] One scholar argues that lawyers should presumptively function as client-directed attorneys for children age seven and above and best interest lawyers below that.[83]

Most child advocates favor the traditional client-based representation of a child's attorney.[84] The child's attorney for a very young child may be only representing the child's legal interests; but the attorney for an older child will be representing the child as other attorneys. The child's attorney provides advice and helps the child articulate their perspectives, positions, and wishes to the court.[85] The child's lawyer represents the child as any other client by meeting with the child client, investigating, and preparing the case. The child's attorney can appear and participate in the litigation, including the right to call, examine, and cross-examine witnesses, the right to advance arguments on behalf of the child, and the right to appeal.[86] The lawyer owes the child client the same duty of communication under MRPC 1.4. The lawyer needs to consult with the client about the means by which the client's objectives are to be accomplished (how does the child want views expressed?). The lawyer should keep the child client reasonably informed about the status of the case; promptly comply with reasonable requests for information; and explain a matter to the extent reasonably necessary to permit the client to make informed decisions regarding the representation. If the child is represented by counsel, the parent's lawyer cannot contact the child without seeking the permission of the child's counsel.[87]

The most common practice, however, is for a judge to appoint a lawyer as guardian ad litem (GAL) to advocate for the child's "best interests," regardless of the child's wishes. Many states now call a guardian ad litem, a "best interests" attorney (BIA). The GAL or BIA has a duty to present recommendations to the judge as to the best interests of the child.[88] The attorney GAL is considered an officer of the court and does not owe the same duty of confidentiality to the child client.[89] In a few hybrid states, the GAL or BIA must not only present evidence on the child's best interest but also on the child's views and preferences.[90] This can present a conflict between the duty to report to the court and the duty to maintain the child client's confidences.[91] If there is a conflict, some courts can also appoint an attorney for the child. In a

Pennsylvania case, a 16-year-old had an attorney who was serving both as a GAL and the child's counsel. When the child's views and best interests were different, the court should have appointed a separate guardian ad litem.[92]

The Oklahoma Supreme Court found that a guardian ad litem did not have to provide the position the guardian intended to recommend to the parents in mother's request to relocate to New York. The guardian had submitted a comprehensive report prior to trial and the GAL indicated that she wanted to hear testimony of the witnesses before making final recommendations.[93]

Representing Child in Relocation Case

A relocation case is a high-conflict case that warrants appointment of a lawyer for the child just like other high-conflict cases involving a risk of abduction, substance abuse, past or present family violence, parental alienation, or overt hostility between parents.[94] The *ABA Custody Standards* specify that a lawyer appointed to represent a child as a child's attorney should act like a lawyer regardless of the age of the client.[95] Children's attorneys should take their direction from the client to the extent possible, advocating the decision the child would make if they were capable. The lawyer's responsibilities with respect to the child client will depend on the child, the issue, and the situation.[96] At the least, the lawyer should meet with the child. In Pennsylvania, a child's attorney did not properly represent the six-year-old child's legal interest when he did not interview the child or put the child's preferred outcome on the record.[97]

If a child's attorney is involved, most agree that a child who has the capacity to direct the attorney should be able to do so.[98] The ABA Model Rules of Professional Conduct 1.14 requires lawyers to represent clients in the traditional attorney-client relationship unless the client has "diminished capacity." The commentary to Model Rule 1.14 indicates that "even a child as young as five or six and certainly those of ten or twelve will have often have the ability to understand, deliberate upon, and reach conclusions about matters affecting his own well-being."[99] Even if a client has diminished capacity, Rule 1.14 requires a lawyer to intrude on a client's decision-making capacity to the least extent possible,[100] but allows the lawyer to take reasonably necessary protective action to protect a client from physical harm.[101] Capacity is an evolving process and is contextual. Capacity to direct representation may be different from capacity to have views heard on preferences for parents and location.

A lawyer appointed as a "best interests" attorney or a guardian ad litem advocates the child's best interests, is not bound by the child's wishes, and can use confidential information in performing those duties. The best interests attorney, however, acts as an attorney at all times, establishing and maintaining a relationship with the child, conducting an investigation, interviewing witnesses, presenting evidence, and advocating for the child.

Although a Pennsylvania court found that the trial court did not abuse its discretion in denying mother's petition to relocate, the court should not have transferred custody to the father without assessing the benefits of stability on the custodial relationship and considering the child's expressed preference to live with his mother.[102]

Weight Given Preference: A Voice, Not a Choice

The mantra often recited is that a child has a right to a voice, not to a choice.[103] There is a difference between allowing a child to express their wishes and allowing them to chart the course of litigation.[104] One judge noted that the whims, wants, and desires of a minor child are one factor but not the criteria for determining which parent should be granted custody.[105] Therefore, the judge determines the weight to be given the child's preference. Some states require courts to pay attention to the preference of a child over a certain age. The California family code requires that a judge must hear a 14-year-old who wants to be heard and may hear a younger child.[106] Tennessee's statute provides that the court should consider the reasonable preference of the child if twelve (12) years of age or older. The court may hear the preference of a younger child upon request. The Oklahoma Court of Appeals upheld a modification of custody from the mother to the father where the child who was over age 12 had a strong preference to live with the father. The mother had moved to Texas and the daughter wanted to be close to her sibling and extended family.[107] The older the child, the more likely the judge will either interview the child or get evidence as to the child's wishes.[108] The preferences of older children are normally given greater weight than those of younger children.[109]

An older child's expressed preference for relocation is one factor to be considered, but it is not determinative.[110] New York has often noted that a 15-year-old child's expressed preference is a relevant factor in determining the child's best interests in a relocation case.[111] The court considers the age and maturity of the child, as well as the potential for influence having been exerted on the child.[112] A New York court found that the Family Court erred in failing to give due consideration to the expressed preference of the almost 15-year-old child who communicated a clear desire to remain in the father's custody.[113] Although a child's wishes are not controlling, they may be an important factor that must be carefully considered in determining the child's best interests, especially when based upon good reasons.

A West Virginia court erred in not modifying a parenting plan where a 15-year-old stated a reasonable and firm preference to reside with his father.[114] The Montana Supreme Court refused to make a blanket age at which children's wishes could have heavy weight. It found a 14-year-old's desire to live with his mother not to be a change of circumstances justifying a hearing on transfer of custody.[115] In an Illinois case, the court found the preference of a 13-year-old persuasive: "[T]he parties' son clearly stated his preference for the granting of the petition for relocation and did so as an extremely articulate, mature 13-year-old who expressed reasoned and independent preferences as to relocation."[116]

Indiana found that a child's desire to remain with her father was entitled to some consideration when deciding mother's request to relocate to Texas, even though the child was only 11. The guardian ad litem and the child's therapist also thought it was in the child's best interests.[117]

The child's preference standing alone may not be a sufficient change in circumstances.[118] The 12-year-old child's wish to move to Nashville to attend a private school was not a material and substantial change of circumstances to warrant the drastic action of changing custody.[119] A court may not give much weight if there is no showing that the child's quality of life would be improved, the present custody arrangement had been working, and the new place does not have equal educational opportunities.[120] An appellate court was upheld in not modifying custody to the father because it was in the best interests of the children to remain in the custody of the mother. The court-appointed expert noted that a potential move from the mother's residence in Syracuse to the father's residence in Buffalo would put the child "at risk of experiencing a tremendous sense of loss and disruption" because of his connections to school, community, friends and activities in Syracuse.[121] On the other hand, a court did not follow a 14-year-old child's desire to remain with her mother where the court found her home highly dysfunctional, the mother had some mental health issues, and placing the child with her could harm the child's relationship with the father.[122]

If the child's preference is accompanied by other factors, for example, the child has been accepted in a special ballet program and the new location would also cut down on the mother's commute time, there may be a sufficient change. Additionally, the passage of time and the desires of a child to not move may constitute a change of circumstances sufficient for the court to hold a hearing. The trial court relied heavily on the preference of teenage children who wanted to stay in Arkansas with extended family and friends. They did not want to move to Wisconsin partly because they were Catholic and their mother required them to go to Lutheran church where the stepfather was clergy.[123]

When a mother moved 70 miles from Des Moines to a rural area, the teenage daughter was adamant about remaining in the same school district. Her younger brother missed his friends but had no desire to move back. The court indicated that the teenager's preference was less significant in a modification than in the initial custody determination because the objection was to the location, not to living with the parent.[124]

Where mother had been the primary caregiver, had a new job and family in South Carolina, and two children, ages nine and ten, expressed the preference to move with her, the trial court erred in changing custody to the New York father.[125] On the other hand, an 11-year-old's preference to live with his father, rather than move with his mother and sister, was a factor in an Alabama judge changing physical custody to the father.[126]

Appellate courts have found an abuse of discretion when the trial court allows a child, even a teenager, authority to decide when and if to visit the nonresidential parent.[127] A judge erred in granting a 17-year-old authority over decisions regarding parenting time, healthcare, and participation in school, extracurricular, and religious activities. The court found the child was not emancipated until 19 in Indiana and could still benefit from parental guidance.[128] In a New York case, the trial court erred in ordering that the father "have visitation as agreed between the parties in consultation with the children." This was an impermissible delegation of authority to the mother and child, which could cause the father to have no visitation at all.[129]

International Law and Hearing Child's Voice

International law recognizes the child as an independent individual with legal interests separate from those of the parents. Three international treaties require a child's voice to be heard: the UN Convention on the Rights of the Child,[130] the Hague Convention on the Civil Aspects of International Child Abduction (Hague Abduction Convention),[131] and the Hague Convention of October 19, 1996, on Jurisdiction, Applicable Law, Recognition, Enforcement and Co-operation in Respect of Parental Responsibility and Measures for the Protection of Children (1996 Protection of Children Convention).[132] Although the United States has only ratified the Hague Abduction Convention, the other two Conventions are important for ensuring the custody orders from the United States are enforceable in other countries.

The U.N. Convention on the Rights of the Child (UNCRC), adopted by every country except the United States, Article 12 states:

1. States Parties shall assure to the child who is capable of forming his or her own views the right to express those

views freely in all matters affecting the child, the views of the child being given due weight in accordance with the age and maturity of the child.

2. For this purpose, the child shall in particular be provided the opportunity to be heard in any judicial and administrative proceedings affecting the child, either directly, or through a representative or an appropriate body, in a manner consistent with the procedural rules of national law.

The UNCRC reflects the view that children should have a say in the outcome of their own lives. Child advocates around the world have argued that the child's voice should be a part of any custody determination. Therefore, especially in cases involving international relocation, it is imperative that the judge hear the child's voice in some manner so that other countries will honor orders from the United States. The UNCRC does not require that the child testify in court, but only that the child, "either directly, or through a representative" have a say.

The Hague Abduction Convention makes the child's desire to stay in the country to which he or she was abducted a defense to the return.[133] The judge hearing the case determines if the child is of sufficient age and degree of maturity to express an opinion. A Florida appellate court reversed a trial court's denial of return of a child to Mexico based on the exception. The ten-year-old was not sufficiently mature for purposes of the exception and had been unduly influenced by the mother who wrongfully retained him.[134] The age and maturity exception has been narrowly applied.[135] The burden is on the person alleging the defense to establish that the child objects to being returned. The wrongfully removed, sufficiently mature child has agency to interpret their own interests. The drafters of the Convention deemed it inappropriate to return a child against their will regardless of the reason for the child's objection. A mere preference, however, is not an objection.[136]

In March 2010, the International Judicial Conference on Cross-Border Family Relocation produced the Washington Declaration, which requires that judicial discretion be guided by factors that include the views of the child having regard to the child's age and maturity.[137]

Hearing the child's voice in relocation cases is crucial to enforcement in other countries. The 1996 Protection of Children Convention is in effect in 54 countries. The United States signed it in 2010, but it has not been ratified nor is it in force in the United States. The Uniform Law Commission in 2013 created amendments to the UCCJEA in anticipation of ratification which has not yet happened. The 1996 Protection of Children provides for the "recognition and enforcement of . . . measures of protection."[138] "Measures of protection" are custody orders. If ratified, this treaty will enable U.S. custody orders to be recognized more easily by other treaty partners. A foreign country, however, may refuse to recognize a U.S. custody order if that custody order was made "without the child having been provided the opportunity to be heard, in violation of the fundamental principles of procedure of the requested state."[139] Therefore, the lawyer will want to ensure that the record reflects how the child's voice was heard in any state custody proceeding in a manner that comports with the enforcing country's methods of hearing the child. The Hague Conference on Private International Law, at its Seventh Special Commission meeting in October 2017, concluded that a court "should incorporate into the order for measures a record of the way the child was heard, or if a decision is made not to hear the child, an indication that consideration was given to doing so and the reasons for the decision not to hear the child."[140]

International law establishes that a child must be treated with respect, humanity, and dignity. The United States has ratified some international covenants that mandate treating children with respect and dignity. Even when international law is not binding authority in the United States, like the UNCRC, it has a growing influence in courtrooms in the United States. The United States Supreme Court has twice stated that international authority and foreign laws are "instructive" and embody the "opinion of the world community" and, therefore, serve as a source of "respected and significant confirmation for the court's own conclusions.[141]

Endnotes

1. Jeff D. Opdyke, *Time of Transition: A Child's Perspective*, Wall St. J. (Feb. 13, 2005), https://www.wsj.com/articles/SB110826008022953229 (discussing eight-year-old son's transition to move with family). *See also* Nick Sheff, *My Turn: My Long-Distance Life*, Newsweek (Feb. 15, 1999) (describing always missing a parent and never spending vacation time with friends).

2. Albus Dumbledore, *in* J.K. Rowling, Harry Potter and the Prisoner of Azkaban (1997).

3. *See* Linda D. Elrod, *Child's Preference*, Child Custody Practice and Procedure § 4:11, app. 4A (2024 ed). *See* Alaska Stat. §§ 25.24.150(c), 25.24.310.

4. Judith Cashmore & Patrick Parkinson, *Children's "Wishes and Feelings" in Relocation Disputes*, 28(2) Child & Fam. L.Q. 151 (2016); Janet Walker & Gabriela Misca, *Why Listening to Children and Young People Is Important in Family Justice*, 57 Fam. Ct. Rev. 375 (2019).

5. Mass Gen. Laws Ann. ch. 208 § 30.

6. Barbara A. Atwood, *The Child's Voice in Custody Litigation: An Empirical Survey and Suggestions for Reform*, 45 Ariz. L. Rev. 629, 634–35 (2003) (80 percent of judges considered the preferences of teenagers to be important; 40 percent gave weight to 11- to 13-year-olds; 33 percent gave no significance to preferences of children under ten).

7. Duguma v. Ayalew, 145 A.3d 517 (D.C. Ct. App. 2016) (court received no evidence relating to the children's wishes and should have interviewed the children, ages 16, 9, and 7, about their custody choices).

8. Ohio Rev. Code § 3109.04(B) (1).

9. *See* Linda D. Elrod, *Client-Directed Lawyers for Children: It Is the "Right" Thing to Do,* 27 Pace L. Rev. 869, 876–80 (2007) (children lack rights because (1) there is no express grant of positive rights in the Constitution; (2) the United States has failed to ratify the UN Convention on the Rights of the Child; (3) it is difficult to define "rights"; (4) the perceived incapacity of some children to exercise rights; and (5) the fear that children's rights will come at the expense of parental rights).

10. Oscar M. v. Marilyn P., 555 P.3d 40 (Alaska 2024) (not allowing a 13-year-old to intervene in parents' custody dispute); *In re* Marriage of Osborn, 135 P.3d 199 (Kan. Ct. App. 2006).

11. Stanley v. Illinois, 405 U.S. 645, 651 (1972).

12. Troxel v. Granville, 530 U.S. 57, 88–89 (2000).

13. Quint v. Quint, _ N.W.3d, 2024 WL 1470200, at *7 (Mich. Ct. App. 2024).

14. *Id.*

15. Nuffield Family Justice Observatory, Children's Experience of Private Law Proceedings: Six Key Messages from Research (Oct. 2021).

16. Nicolas Bala et al., *Children's Voices in Family Court: Guidelines for Judges Meeting Children*, 47 Fam. L.Q. 379, 381–81 (2013).

17. *Id.* at 382. *See also* Cashmore & Parkinson, *supra* note 4. *See also* Patrick Parkinson & Judith Cashmore, *Children's Participation in Decisions About Parenting Arrangements, in* The Oxford Handbook of Children and the Law 1 (James G. Dwyer ed., 2019).

18. *See* Coulon v. Coulon, 351 So. 3d 823 (La. Ct. App. 2022) (court declined to hold a hearing to inquire as to competency of child to testify as to custody in mother's request to relocate because the majority of factors favored the relocation and testimony not necessary).

19. Petronella Grootens-Wiegers et al., *Medical Decision-Making in Children & Adolescents: Developmental & Neuroscientific Aspects,* BMC Pediatrics (2017).

20. *UNLV Recommendations* IV.A.2a, 6 Nev. L.J. 571, 609 (2006).

21. *See* Samantha WW v. Malek XX, 190 N.Y.S.3d 203 (App. Div. 2023) (judge erred in not interviewing 16-year-old); Oscar M. v. Marilyn P., 555 P.3d 40 (Alaska 2024).

22. Bofysil v. Bofysil, 956 N.W.2d 544 (Mich. Ct. App. 2020).

23. E.C.S. v. M.C.S., 256 A.3d 449, 459 (Pa. Super. Ct. 2021).

24. Burmood v. Anderson, 228 N.E.3d 348 (Ill. App. Ct. 2023). *See also* Cortes v. Byant, 188 N.Y.S.3d 186 (App. Div. 2023) (no error in not interviewing three- and five-year-old).

25. Va. Stat. Ann. ch. 15 § 594(b).

26. Lincoln v. Lincoln, 247 N.E.2d 659, 660 (N.Y. 1969).

27. McGovern v. McGovern, 870 N.Y.S.2d 618, 622 (App. Div. 2009) (giving great weight to the wishes of almost 14-year-old given the legitimate academic, medical, and other bases for his view). *See also* Jacqueline Clarke, *Do I Have a Voice: An Empirical Analysis of Children's Voices in Michigan Custody Litigation*, 47 (3) Fam. L.Q. 457 (2013) (citing study showing 90 percent of judges felt a child should not be called to the stand).

28. *In re* Allen, 97 P.3d 1060 (Kan. Ct. App. 2004) (refusing mother's request to call child to stand where court found it would harm the child); Sheridan v. Cassidy, 273 So. 3d 783 (Miss. Ct. App. 2019) (declining to let child testify where there was evidence of mother's coaching).

29. Nev. R. Civ. P. 16.215.

30. Wright v. Kemp, 207 A.3d 1021 (Vt. 2019).

31. Jerry A. Bahnke, *Pawns or People? Protecting the Best Interests of Children in Interstate Custody Disputes*, 28 Loyola L. Rev. 699, 727 (1995).

32. Karanikas v. Cartwright, 61 A.3d 69 (Md. Spec. App. 2013) (court did not err in interviewing nine-year-old in chambers); Donscheski v. Donscheski, 771 N.W.2d 213 (Nev. App. 2009) (trial court was required to conduct in camera interview with 12-year-old).

33. Bisbing v. Bisbing, 166 A.3d 1155 (N.J. 2017).

34. Badal v. Wilkinson, 183 N.Y.S.3d 567 (App. Div. 2023) (trial court improvidently exercised its discretion in not interviewing the child where mother alleged the child's fear of visiting her in Trinidad and Tobago was based on outside influence); Interest of J.N., 670 S.W.3d 614 (Tex. 2023) (harmful error for judge to reject mother's request for interview of child who was over age 12 to assess child's wishes).

35. Samantha WW. v. Malek XX., 190 N.Y.S.3d 203 (App. Div. 2023).

36. Cortes v. Bryant, 188 N.Y.S.3d 186 (App. Div. 2023) (no interview with children three and five); Pacheco v. Maldonado, 199 N.Y.S.3d 670 (App. Div. 2023) (no interview needed with child age five where neither parents nor child's attorney requested one).

37. *In re* Bunita B. v. Mark P., 89 N.Y.S.3d 55 (App. Div. 2018) (child's attorney stipulated child was neutral on residence so judge was not required to interview the child); Addison v. Addison, 463 S.W.3d 755 (Ky. 2015) (court had multiple reports addressing the young children's wishes and best interests so court could decline to interview them).

38. Interest of C.R.D., 2021 WL 3779224 (Tex. Ct. App. 2021) (unpublished) (trial judge did not err in not interviewing a 12-year-old who opposed the interview and would likely have suffered trauma).

39. Stacey Platt, *Set Another Place at the Table: Child Participation in Family Separation Cases*, 17 Cardozo J. Conflict Resol. 749 (2016).

40. *In re* Marriage of Jessica F. & Justin H., 241 N.E.3d 1068 (Ill. App. Ct. 2024).

41. State v. Titus, 274 So. 3d 591 (La. Ct. App. 2019) (children were nine and ten).

42. Ainsworth v. Ainsworth, 186 A.3d 1074 (R.I. 2018) (judge properly weighed the evidence of father's former alcohol abuse, the acrimony between the parents, the children's friends and family in the state, and the benefit to mother's economic standing if she relocated).

43. Bala et al., *supra* note 16.

44. Dr. Anne Graffam Walker, Handbook on Questioning Children: A Linguistic Perspective (3d ed. ABA Center on Children and the Law, 2013).

45. Bala et al., *supra* note 16, at 394–408.

46. *Id.*

47. *See* Uniform Law Comm'n, Draft of Judicial Interview of Children Act, uniformlaws.org.

48. Cox v. Cox, 515 S.E.2d 61 (N.C. Ct. App. 1999) (no error in conducting a private examination with children in chambers with both parties' counsel present over the mother's objection); Helen S.K. v. Samuel M.K., 288 P.3d 463 (Alaska 2012) (in camera interview did not violate mother's rights); T.E.G. v. G.T.G., 986 N.Y.S.2d 313 (Misc. 2014) (in camera interview did not warrant recusal nor did it violate mother's rights).

49. J.L. v. M.M., 194 N.E.3d 152 (Ind. Ct. App. 2022) (trial court did not abuse its discretion in allowing in camera interview about father's alleged emotional and physical abuse and not letting him cross-examine the children). *See also* Matter of George A. v. Josephine D., 85 N.Y.S.3d 29 (App. Div. 2018) (children's in camera statements about mother's emotional and physical mistreatment with only children's attorney present did not violate mother's due process rights).

50. Dunlap v. Dunlap, 455 P.3d 1 (Okla. Ct. App. 2019). *See also* Fr Wilson v. Wilson, 170 So. 3d 340 (La. App. 2015); Frueh v. Frueh, 771 N.W.2d 593, 600 (N.D. 2009).

51. The American Law Institute's Principles of the Law of Family Dissolution § 2.14 (judges have "discretion to interview the child, or direct another person to interview the child. . . . Counsel for a parent or for a child should be permitted to propose questions to the court that may be asked of the child.").

52. May v. Harrison, 559 S.W.3d 789 (Ky. 2018) (mother's rights were not violated when judge held in camera interview with child regarding mother's sexual abuse and allowed counsel to submit questions). *See also* C.M. v. J.M., 295 A.3d 193 (Md. Ct. App. 2023) (father did not have right to cross-examine where court revealed the overall substance of the interview with the child and the parties could respond to what was said); Glinyanay v. Tobias, 871 S.E.2d 193 (S.C. Ct. App. 2022) (family court did not violate father's due process rights in interviewing child off the record about father's inappropriate touching and not allowing cross examination).

53. *See, e.g.*, Conn. Gen. Stat. § 46-45; 750 Ill. Comp. Stat. 5/604(a); Minn. Stat. § 518.166; Mo. Rev. Stat. § 452.385. *See In re* Marriage of Doe, 250 N.E.3d 283 (Ill. App. Ct. 2024) (trial court erred in conducting in camera interview with daughter about father's sexual abuse without counsel and allowing father to cross-examine).

54. Baxendale v. Raich, 878 N.E.2d 1252, 1255 (Ind. 2008) (judge may interview child with or without counsel present).

55. Woods v. Woods, 987 So. 2d 339, 348 (La. App. 2008), *writ denied*, 996 So. 2d 1110 (La. 2008) (attorney's questioning is limited to the determination of child's competency); Ottolini v. Barrett, 954 A.2d 610, 613 (Pa. Super. 2008) (counsel must be present and allowed to interrogate the child).

56. Ottolini v. Barrett, 954 A.2d 610 (Pa. Super. Ct. 2008) (trial court erred on relying on statements made during in camera interview where parties' attorneys were not permitted question or to submit questions).

57. Interest of J.F., 308 A.3d 1252 (Pa. Super. Ct. 2024).

58. Ynclan v. Woodward, 237 P.3d 145 (Okla. 2010), *as corrected*, (Mar. 25, 2010). *See also* Holiday v. Holiday, 247 P.3d 29, 32 (Wyo. 2011) (where parent objects to private interview with child, the judge or the parties must fashion suitable alternative procedure for obtaining the child's preference).

59. *See* Covell v. Covell, 2018 WL 4203532 (Ohio. Ct. App. 2018) (unpublished) (father alleged error in trial court's in camera interview with daughters who claimed he abused them but never requested a transcript of the interviews or put them in the record).

60. Denham v. Denham, 361 So. 3d 954 (Miss. 2022) (trial court's failure to record in camera interviews of children in parents' divorce deprived appellate court of a complete appellate record). *See also* ND McN v. RJH Sr, 979 A.2d 1195 (D.C. Ct. App. 2009).

61. *See, e.g.*, Del. Code Ann. tit. 13, § 724(a); Ill. Comp. Stat. Ann. 5/604.10(a); Kan. Stat. Ann. § 23-3209; Ohio Rev. Code Ann. § 3019.04.

62. Tex. Fam. Code Ann. § 153.009(f). *See* Interest of C.J., 689 S.W.3d 417 (Tex. Ct. App. 2024) (interviews of children ages 15 and 14 could have been recorded).

63. Helen SK v. Samuel MK, 288 P.3d 463 (Alaska 2013).

64. Couch v. Couch, 146 S.W.3d 923, 925 (Ky. 2004) (unless waived . . . it is manifestly unfair not to record and disclose the contents of the interview to provide an opportunity for rebuttal). *But see* N.D. McN. v. R.J.H., Sr., 979 A.2d 1195 (D.C. Ct. App. 2009) (no reversal where judge failed to record the interview but provided a detailed description of the children's conversation).

65. Schneider v. Schneider, 258 P.3d 350 (Idaho 2011).

66. Holiday v. Holiday, 247 P.3d 29 (Wyo. 2011). *But see* Rivera v. LaSalle, 923 N.Y.S.2d 254 (App. Div. 2011) (finding judge breached children's right to confidentiality by revealing their custodial preference and erred in not considering the older child's preference).

67. Talarico v. Talarico, 305 So. 3d 601 (Fla. Dist. Ct. App. 2020).

68. *See* MONT. CODE ANN. § 40-4-216(5). *See also* Dickison v. Dickison, 874 P.2d 695 (Kan. App. 1994).

69. *See, e.g.*, Myers v. Myers, 867 N.E.2d 848 (Ohio Ct. App. 2007) (parent not entitled to transcript of the recording of interview with child).

70. *In re* A.M.R., 101 N.E.3d 1194 (Ohio Ct. App. 2017).

71. Julie E. v. David E., 1 N.Y.S.3d 431, 434 (App. Div. 2015) (citing Lincoln v. Lincoln, 299 N.Y.S.2d 842 (1969)).

72. *See* LINDA D. ELROD, CHILD CUSTODY PRACTICE AND PROCEDURE § 12:4 (Thomson Reuters, 2024).

73. *See* FLA. STAT. ANN. § 61.401 (judge has the discretion to appoint legal counsel or a guardian ad litem, or both, for the child); 750 ILL. COMP. STAT. 5/506 (allows court to appoint an attorney; guardian ad litem who can testify or submit a written report; or a child representative who has same authority to participate in litigation and to investigate as GAL advocates for best interests).

74. *See* Elrod, *supra* note 9, at 869; Barbara Ann Atwood, *The Uniform Representation of Children in Abuse, Neglect and Custody Proceedings Act: Bridging the Divide Between Pragmatism and Idealism*, 42 FAM. L.Q. 63 (2008).

75. Louisiana, Maryland, Massachusetts, New Jersey, New Mexico (over age 14), Oklahoma, Pennsylvania, West Virginia, and Wisconsin (over age 12).

76. Alaska, Arizona, Connecticut, Georgia, Minnesota (over age ten), Mississippi, Montana, North Dakota, New York, Puerto Rico, Tennessee, Texas, and Virgin Islands.

77. American Bar Association Section of Family Law, *Standards of Practice for Lawyers Representing Children in Custody Cases*, 37 FAM. L.Q. 129 (2003) (ABA Custody Standards); *see also* Linda D. Elrod, *Raising the Bar for Lawyers Who Represent Children: ABA Standards of Practice for Custody Cases*, 37 FAM. L.Q. 105 (2003).

78. MARTIN GUGGENHEIM, WHAT'S WRONG WITH CHILDREN'S RIGHTS 95 (2005) (courts often adopt attorney's views of best interest believing it is child's position). *See also* Mark Henaghan, *What Does a Child's Right to Be Heard in Legal Proceedings Really Mean? ABA Custody Standards Do Not Go*

Far Enough, 42 Fam. L.Q. 117 (2008). *See* Lisa Kelly & Alicia LeVezu, *Until the Client Speaks: Reviving the Legal Interest Model for Preverbal Children*, 50 Fam. L.Q. 383, 395 (2016).

79. *American Academy of Matrimonial Lawyers Representing Children: Standards for Attorneys for Children in Custody or Visitation Proceedings with Commentary*, 22 J. Am. Acad. Matrim. Lawyers 227 (2009) (AAML Standards).

80. *See* N.M. Stat. § 32A-4-10(C)(E) (children over age 14 get lawyers; under 14 get guardians ad litem). *See also* Idaho Code Ann. § 16-1614 (12-year-old, attorney can be either guardian ad litem or client-directed); Minn. Stat. Ann. § 260C.163 (2005) (child over ten gets client-directed attorney); Wis. Stat. Ann. § 48.23 (child over 12 gets lawyer; child under 12 gets guardian ad litem).

81. AAML Standards, *supra* note 79, at 2.2, cmt. (rebuttable presumption that children 12 and older are unimpaired).

82. Milcherska v. Hoerstman, 56 N.E.3d 634 (Ind. Ct. App. 2016).

83. Donald N. Duquette, *Two Distinct Roles/Bright Line Test*, 6 Nevada L.J. 1240 (2006). *See also* Sarah H. Ramsey, *Representation of the Child in Protective Proceedings: The Determination of Decision-Making Capacity*, 17 Fam. L.Q. 287, 311 (1983) (indicating that seven is the age by which children are capable of making decisions).

84. Elrod, *supra* note 9.

85. NYSBA Committee on Children and the Law, *Standards for Attorneys Representing Children in Custody, Visitation and Guardianship Proceedings* (Jan. 2015), https://nysba.org/wp-content/uploads/2020/02/Custody-Standards-April-2015.pdf?srsltid=AfmBOoqZW4LEXx0PLTwQ_PObc9Ancm0qlLUaxq-VyhQOYZadqewWphtu.

86. Newton v. McFarlane, 103 N.Y.S.3d 445 (App. Div. 2019).

87. Model Rules of Pro. Conduct r. 4.2 (Am. Bar Ass'n 2025).

88. Delaware, Florida, Guam, Hawaii, Iowa, Kansas, Kentucky, Maine, Maryland, Mississippi, Nevada, New Mexico (under 14), South Carolina, Vermont, Virginia, Wisconsin (under age 12).

89. Clark v. Alexander, 953 P.2d 145, 154 (Wyo. 1998).

90. Kan. Sup. Ct. Adm. Order 110A. Other states with hybrid duty are Arizona, California, Missouri, North Carolina, and Utah.

91. Morgan v. Getter, 441 S.W.3d 94, 116 (Ky. 2014).

92. *In re* J.K.M., 191 A.3d 907 (Pa. Super. Ct. 2018).

93. Arulkumar v. Arulkumar, 521 P.3d 131 (Okla. 2022) (finding move to New York not to be in child's best interest due to relationships with father and other family and logistics of travel).

94. Melissa A. Kucinski, A Practical Handbook for the Child's Attorney: Effectively Representing Children in Custody Cases (ABA 2018). Rebecca M. Stahl & Philip M. Stahl, Representing Children in Dependency and Family Court: Beyond the Law (ABA 2018).

95. ABA Custody Standards, *supra* note 77; AAML Standards, *supra* note 79.

96. Linda D. Elrod, *Reforming the System to Protect Children in High Conflict Custody Cases*, 28 Wm. Mitchell L. Rev. 495, 525–26 (2001).

97. *In re* Adoption of T.M.LM, 184 A.3d 585 (Pa. Super. Ct. 2018).

98. *See AAML Bounds of Advocacy* section 2.2 (attorney should discuss with a child of 12 or older the objectives of representation).

99. Model Rules of Pro. Conduct r. 1.14, cmt. 1.

100. *Id.* at cmt. 3. Some have suggested that either Rule 1.14 should be amended, or a separate model rule for representing children should be adopted.

101. *Id.* at Rule 1.14(b). *See In re* Christina W., 639 S.E.2d 770 (W. Va. 2006) (guardian ad litem should have disclosed inappropriate touching by mother's boyfriend so child would not be unsupervised).

102. Johns v. Cioci, 865 A.2d 931 (Pa. Super. Ct. 2004) (child had lived primarily with mother since age two; had developed into articulate, intelligent, academically successful child who liked his school; and wanted to live with this mother).

103. *See generally* Bala et al., *supra* note 16, at 394.

104. Mason v. Mason, 193 N.Y.S.3d 803 (App. Div. 2023) (children wanted to stay in New York but mother wanted to move to North Carolina and father to Georgia).

105. Dunlap v. Dunlap, 455 P.3d 1 (Okla. Ct. App. 2019) (custody had been changed to father because mother withheld children from him; older child, age 15, wanted to live with mother who had fewer rules).

106. Cal. Fam. Code § 3042 ((a) If a child is of sufficient age and capacity to reason so as to form an intelligent preference . . . , the court shall consider, and give due weight to, the wishes of the child . . . ; (c) If the child is 14 years of age or older and wishes to address the court regarding custody or visitation, the child shall be permitted to do so, unless the court determines that doing so is not in the child's best interests).

107. Lowry v. Lewis. 317 P.3d 230 (Okla. Ct. App. 2013) (mature child's preference was a sufficient change of circumstances).

108. *In re* Marriage of Mahmoodjanloo, 160 P.3d 951 (Okla. 2007) (interviewing children ages 13 and 14 in camera).

109. Gensmer v. Gensmer, 2017 WL 5952918 (Tenn. Ct. App. 2017) (unpublished) (denying relocation, declining to interview a nine-and-a-half-year-old child over father's objection and naming father as primary residential parent because mother was relocating anyway).

110. Yamilly M.S. v. Ricardo A.S., 26 N.Y.S.3d 278 (App. Div. 2016).

111. Matter of Turvin v. D'Agostino, 58 N.Y.S.3d 155 (App. Div. 2017).

112. Matter of Nevarez v. Pina, 62 N.Y.S.3d 175 (App. Div. 2017).

113. Newton v. McFarlane, 103 N.Y.S.3d 445 (App. Div. 2019). *See also* Matter of Turvin v. D'Agostino, 58 N.Y.S.3d 155 (App. Div. 2017) (15-year-old's expressed preference is relevant factor).

114. Jonpaul C. v. Heather C., 889 S.E.2d 769 (W.Va. Ct. App. 2023).

115. *In re* R.J.N., 403 P.3d 675 (Mont. 2017) (primary residency had been changed to the father when the mother sought to move children to California a few years before).

116. *In re* Marriage of Fatkin, 129 N.E.3d 1230 (Ill. 2019).

117. Milcherska v. Hoerstman, 56 N.E.3d 634 (Ind. Ct. App. 2016).

118. *See* Melvin v. Miller, 181 So. 3d 826 (La. Ct. App. 2015).

119. Pippin v. Pippin, 277 S.W.3d 398 (Tenn. Ct. App. 2008).

120. Ketterer v. Seifert, 902 A.2d 533 (Pa. Super. Ct. 2006).

121. Sheridan v. Sheridan, 12 N.Y.S.3d 434 (App. Div. 2015).

122. Hilfiger v. Hilfiger, 550 P.3d 879 (Okla. Ct. App. 2023).

123. Myers v. McCall, 334 S.W.3d 878 (Ark. Ct. App. 2009) (passage of ten years, mother's remarriage, relocation to Missouri, and intended move to Wisconsin coupled with children's religious preferences and wishes not to move were sufficient change of circumstances justifying change of custody to father).

124. *In re* Marriage of Hoffman, 867 N.W.2d 26 (Iowa 2015).

125. Masiello v. Milano, 118 N.Y.S. 3d 739 (App. Div. 2020).

126. Russell v. Self, 334 So. 3d 229, 235 (Ala. Civ. App. 2021) (father not required to show compelling reason for separating siblings where 16-year-old wanted to move with the mother).

127. *In re* Marriage of Kimbrell, 119 P.3d 684 (Kan. Ct. App. 2007).

128. Moell v. Moell, 84 N.E.3d 741 (Ind. Ct. App. 2017).

129. Michael B. v. Patricia S., 223 N.Y.S.3d 44 (App. Div. 2024).

130. United Nations Convention on the Rights of the Child, 28 I.L.M. 1448 (Nov. 20, 1989) (UN CRC).

131. Hague Convention on the Civil Aspects of International Child Abduction, Oct. 25, 1980, T.I.A.S. No. 11,670, 1343 U.N.T.S. 89 (Hague Abduction Convention).

132. Hague Convention of October 19, 1996, on Jurisdiction, Applicable Law, Recognition, Enforcement and Co-operation in Respect of Parental Responsibility and Measures for the Protection of Children, https://www.hcch.net/en/instruments/conventions/full-text/?cid=70 [Hague Protection of Children Convention].

133. The International Child Abduction Remedies Act (ICARA), 22 U.S.C. §§ 9001 *et seq*. (formerly 42 U.S.C. §§ 11603 *et seq*.). *See* Linda D. Elrod, "Please Let Me Stay": Hearing the Voice of the Child in Hague Abduction Cases, 63 Okla. L. Rev. 663 (2011).

134. De La Cruz v. Garcia, 398 So. 3d 429 (Fla. Dist. Ct. App. 2024) (child desire to not be separated from mother was a custodial preference, not affirmative objection to return to Mexico).

135. England v. England, 234 F.3d 268, 272 (5th Cir. 2000); Tsai Yang v. Fu-Chiang Tsui, 499 F.3d 259, 278 (3d Cir. 2007).

136. Rodriguez v. Yanez, 817 F.3d 466 (5th Cir. 2016) (remanding to see if child actually objected to being returned to Mexico or just preferred to stay in Texas). *See also* Garcia v. Pinelo, 808 F.3d 1158, 1169 (7th Cir. 2015) (finding preference for staying in Chicago was not an "objection" to return).

137. International Centre for Missing and Exploited Children and the Hague Conference on Private International Law, Washington Declaration (2010), https://www.hcch.net/en/news-archive/details/?varevent=188 (outlining 13 factors judges should consider in an international relocation case, including the child's views).

138. Hague Protection of Children Convention, *supra* note 132.

139. *Id.* at Chapter IV, Art. 23(2)(b) (Recognition may however be refused . . . *b)* if the measure was taken, except in a case of urgency, in the context of a judicial or administrative proceeding, without the child having been provided the opportunity to be heard, in violation of fundamental principles of procedure of the requested State;. . . .

140. *See* Conclusions and Recommendations of the 7th Special Commission, ¶ 50, https://www.hcch.net/de/publications-and-studies/details4/?pid=6545.

141. Roper v. Simmons, 543 U.S. 551, 578 (2005); Lawrence v. Texas, 539 U.S. 558, 573 (2003).

CHAPTER 15

International Relocation: Preventing Abduction, Securing Return

> *[T]he best interest of the child is paramount in any award of custody and visitation, and the trial court has a large measure of discretion. . . . Whether one parent is moving with the children across town or across the world, the analysis remains the same.*[1]

> *In matters concerning international relocation the best interests of the child should be the paramount (primary) consideration and determinations should be made without any presumption for or against relocation.*[2]

> *International relocation cases are the "hardest of dilemmas."*[3]

International families present unique challenges when relationships end. One parent, usually the one who has lived in the other parent's country, requests to relocate with a child, often back home. The relative ease of travel for work and leisure; the increasing ability to communicate via satellite, computer, and phones anywhere; the large numbers of students studying in foreign countries; and military operations all over the world provide greater opportunities for people to meet and mingle. These relocation cases are among the most contentious and challenging because they may involve international treaties and another country's law as well as national and state laws. One has only to look at a few international custody battles to know that they are different and more complicated. A California mother took her five-month-old baby to Pakistan and refused to return to California. The court noted,

> [This case] involves an acrimonious six-year international custody battle, in which lawyers on two continents seemingly have left no stone unturned, while the parties themselves have left no rock unhurled. The accusations and counteraccusations include kidnapping, fraud, and domestic violence, all set against a backdrop of INTERPOL, warrants, armed gunmen, and flights from justice. In both California and Pakistan, mud has been slung, court orders flouted, and reputations challenged.[4]

Most American courts use the same basic analysis for an international relocation.[5] While the best interests of the child remains the paramount consideration, there are a number of other relevant factors when the relocation is international. While there is arguably a right to travel within the United States (Chapter 5), there is not a comparable right to travel internationally.[6] Additionally, the logistics of parental interaction with the child who lives a continent away can be formidable.

The reasons for the relocation internationally are often similar to those for interstate relocations: a new job or promotion, a new spouse or partner in the country, a move closer to family members for support or care, and to pursue educational goals. All move-away cases involve some geographical and psychological challenges. But international relocation cases pose greater challenges and more risks than most domestic relocations and require severe alterations of the parenting plan. It is also less likely that a nonmoving parent will be able, or want, to move to a foreign country as opposed to another state.

The lawyer for the nonrelocating parent must demonstrate to the judge why international cases require a substantially different best-interest analysis. In addition to the factors relevant to interstate custody cases discussed in Chapter 9, international relocation involves other concerns: language, distance, culture, and unique jurisdictional problems.[7] While interstate and intrastate moves pose some logistical problems, relocation to a foreign country may involve parents and children with dual citizenships, differences in language, increased travel costs (planes, trains, and ferries instead of cars), and a variety of cultural considerations. The worldwide COVID-19 pandemic emphasized the importance of careful scrutiny of international relocations. To move a child from the United States to a country with a different language, culture, as well as political, educational, and healthcare system may deprive the child of important protections and advantages that may not be available in that country.[8]

The distance to most foreign countries makes travel more difficult, which results in fewer opportunities to visit and spend time with the nonmoving parent. The distance impacts the feasibility of schedules as well as the location and amount of in-person time. There are changes in the logistics of communication by telephone, video calls (Zoom, FaceTime), text, email, and social media. The child may lose not only a positive relationship with the nonmoving parent but also the roots in the extended family and community in a given location that have provided a source of nurture and support.[9]

If the parental relationship is hostile, the distance may magnify the moving parent's ability to exclude the nonmoving parent from the child's life.[10] There may be fears, substantiated or not, that the moving parent will attempt to keep the child in the foreign country, deny the other parent access, and use the foreign court system to change the parenting arrangement. Some Australian research shows that many relocations led to many fathers experiencing difficulty arranging and exercising contacts.[11]

The sole jurisdictional law in the United States for custody is the Uniform Child Custody Jurisdiction and Enforcement Act (UCCJEA). Its home-state basis for jurisdiction and its concept of continuing exclusive jurisdiction (Chapter 3) to modify a decree have not been adopted in the international context. Jurisdictional rules in foreign countries can make the ability to enforce custody and visitation orders in other countries problematic. Just because an American order states that the order will be registered in the foreign country and that continuing exclusive jurisdiction will remain in the United States does not mean that it will happen.

Lawyers dealing with international relocation must be familiar with the Washington Declaration on International Relocation, which was drafted at an international judicial conference on cross-border family relocation in March 2010. The conference was organized by the Hague Conference on Private International Law and the International Centre for Missing and Exploited Children with the support of the U.S. Department of State. There were 50 judges and other experts from numerous countries who agreed on numerous principles. In April 2025, a reconvening to review the prior declaration resulted in a reaffirmation of the 2010 principles. Therefore, lawyers in the United States should be aware of the international consensus on principles with the basic one being that relocation cases should be decided on the basis of a child's best interests with no presumption for or against a relocation request. The Declaration sets out a list of factors summarized as: (1) the right of a child to maintain contact with both parents on a regular basis unless contrary to the child's best interests; (2) the views of the child, depending on age and maturity; (3) the parties' proposals for the practical arrangements for relocation, home, school, and job; (4) the reasons for seeking or opposing the relocation; (5) any history of family violence; (6) the continuity and quality of past and current care arrangements; (7) preexisting custody and access determinations; (8) the impact of grant or refusal on the child, extended family, and the parties; (9) the nature of the parents' relationship and the commitment to support the child's relationship with the absent parent; (10) realistic proposals for post relocation contact in light of cost and burden of travel to child; (11) the enforceability of contact provisions in the state of destination; (12) issues of mobility for family members; and (13) any other circumstances the judge deems relevant.

The Washington Declaration states that the Hague Conventions of 1980 on International Child Abduction and 1996 on International Child Protection provide a global framework for international cooperation in respect of cross-border family relocations. The 1980 Convention on the Civil Aspects of International Child Abduction (Hague Abduction Convention) provides for return of the child to the country of habitual residence—the principal remedy for unlawful relocations. The 1996 Hague Convention on Jurisdiction, Applicable Law, Recognition, Enforcement and Co-operation in Respect of Parental Responsibility and Measures of Protection for Children (1996 Children's Convention) allows for the establishment and advance recognition and enforcement of relocation orders and the conditions attached to them.[12] It facilitates direct cooperation and exchange of information between the judicial or administrative authorities of the two countries involved. There are at least 57 treaty partners, but the United States is not one, even though one Washington case thought so.[13] The 1996 Children's Convention uses the term "habitual residence" of the child. It also does not recognize the concept of exclusive, continuing jurisdiction in the state (country) that made the original order. Thus, any time the child moves to another country, that country can claim, with varying degrees of justification depending on the circumstances of the move, that the foreign nation has become the child's new habitual residence.

A recent case illustrates the problem. Mother, a German citizen doing graduate work in the United States, petitioned to relocate when her visa expired. The parties entered an agreement for joint custody of their then-five-year-old son who would attend school in Germany but spend summer and school breaks with the father in Illinois. The Illinois court entered an Allocation Judgment with agreement that purported to determine the child's habitual residence as the United States and that neither party consented to permanent residence anywhere else. Mother and child moved to Germany. Father exercised parenting time regularly. When father did not return the child's passport after a visit in 2023, the mother sought sole custody in Germany. The parties entered a settlement agreement that retained joint parental care, the Illinois judgment still applied, and neither would file additional actions. The parties, however, continued the dispute. Mother did not send child to father in June 2023. Father filed for sole custody and picked child up in Germany and brought him to Illinois. Mother filed for return of the child in federal court under the Hague Abduction Convention. The court granted the return because the child's habitual residence was Germany—the Illinois agreement and judgment could not change that.[14]

The attorney cannot assume the American custody order will be enforced, and not modified, by a foreign court, even if there is a prior agreement that the parent will return the child.[15] Even though a foreign country order may be registered for enforcement in some countries, the foreign order is not treated as binding because of the principle that the welfare of the child is the court's paramount consideration.[16] The foreign country may find it is the child's habitual residence and enter new orders. Agreements, even mirror-image orders, have not always been successful in preventing the shift of the child's habitual residence from the United States to another nation. The lawyer may need to have counsel in the foreign country advise about the standards for modifying custody in the other country.

If the parent does retain the child, international retentions and abductions pose more obstacles to return than abductions in the United States.[17] The Hague Convention on the Civil Aspects of International Child Abduction (Abduction Convention) offers an important tool for the 103 countries that have ratified or acceded to the Abduction Convention. But not all countries are treaty partners, and not all treaty partners are compliant.[18] In the much-publicized Daniel Goldman case a few years ago, the mother took her son to Brazil to visit her family, refused to come back, obtained a divorce, remarried, and then died. The maternal grandparents and stepfather refused to return the child. The father petitioned for return under the Hague Abduction Convention, but it took five years, several expert Hague attorneys, and political intervention for the father to get his son back to the United States.[19] Even when the parties' agreement and court order states that the United States remains the habitual residence and the decree state has continuing exclusive jurisdiction to modify, if the child has been living in another country, it may claim to be the child's habitual residence and deny a return under the Hague Abduction Convention.[20]

Lawyer's Role

The parent who wants to relocate needs to seek court permission if the other parent does not consent. The Washington Declaration provides that a person who intends to apply for international relocation with the child should provide reasonable notice of their intention before commencing proceedings, or where proceedings are unnecessary, before relocation occurs.[21] Parties are encouraged to use legal procedures and not act unilaterally.

Representing the Relocating Parent

The lawyer representing a client who wants to travel internationally or relocate will need to investigate and answer several questions about the moving parent and the destination country.

1. The history of the parents' relationship with each other and the child.
2. The relocating parent has legitimate reasons for the move. The most common reasons are for a new job or promotion; to be closer to family; to follow a new spouse or partner; and to pursue educational opportunities. The relocating parent should be able to explain how the child will benefit, not just the parent.
3. The relocating parent needs to be aware of how adaptable the child is. Some children are outgoing, make friends easily, and are flexible. Other children require specific schedules and routines.
4. The past parenting relationship of the relocating parent and the nonmoving parent. If the parents have a strong cooperative parenting relationship, the court may be more likely to allow a relocation. If the nonmoving parent has not exercised visitation, not paid child support, and not participated in the child's life, the court may be willing to allow a relocation.
5. The extent that one parent is trying to put distance between the child and the parent. If there have been numerous conflicts between the parents, especially ones that require court intervention, the lawyer may explore if the main reason is the parent's desire to get away.
6. If the nonrelocating parent is violent, threatening, abusive, and a negative influence on the child, this may support a relocation.
7. Whether the parent proposing international travel or an international relocation respects the role of the other parent.
8. The relocating parent's suggestions for travel and contact with the other parent are feasible in light of the age of the child and the parties' finances and employment.

9. The impact of grant or refusal of permission to relocate on the child, in the context of his or her extended family, education and social life, and on the parties.
10. The destination country's child custody laws, practices, and customs.
11. Whether the child custody law climate is favorable or hostile to the left-behind parent having access as in the child's best interest.
12. Whether courts in the country have recognized the intentions of the court that entered the original order.
13. The likelihood that the foreign court will modify or vacate the U.S. order, especially if the child becomes a habitual resident.
14. The possibility that the relocating parent, if allowed to move, can choose to relocate from that country to another that would be less hospitable to the U.S. order.
15. The country's track record for being a good partner in the Hague Child Abduction Convention. Compliance record? Problems?

Representing the Nonrelocating Parent

The lawyer representing the parent who is not relocating will look for factors to maintain the status quo or change physical residency. In addition to some of the preceding questions for the relocating parent, which can be applicable to both, there are some additional questions for the parent trying to block the move.

1. The lawyer must determine if the nonrelocating parent is prepared to take physical residency of the child. A parent who merely wants to block the other parent's move but not assume the primary parenting responsibility is not in as good a position as one who is ready and able to take over.
2. The nonrelocating parent can try to show that the relocating parent's reasons for the move are either inadequate or not legitimate. Just because the relocating parent will benefit from the relocation does not mean that the child will benefit. If the relocating parent is

remarrying or moving into a new relationship, the lawyer must explore how that might impact the child. The addition, or disruption, of sibling relationships can be important.

3. The nonrelocating parent needs to show a close and loving relationship with the child. Disruption of the parent–child relationship is one of the most important factors in courts denying an international relocation.[22] The stronger the relationship, the more likely the court will deny the move. The lawyer can show the parent has paid child support; has exercised parenting time on a regular basis; participates in school, extracurricular, and community activities; and so on. The lawyer can use evidence of pictures, movies, letters, witnesses, coaches, scout leaders, and others to testify to the strength of the relationship.
4. If the relocating parent has been uncooperative and constantly frustrated parenting time while living in close proximity, the relocation will make it easier for a parent to try to alienate the child and deny parenting time.
5. The parent can try to show that the new country is not a safe place to live or has not adopted the Hague Abduction Convention. The distance in miles and time zones makes a visitation or parenting time schedule almost unworkable to maintain the relationship with the nonrelocating parent.

Discovery in an international case may be more difficult to get depending on the country (see Chapter 7). If the parent is moving for employment, the lawyer may need to discover details about the new job and why it is better than what the parent has in the United States. If there is not enough time for regular discovery, the lawyer can send a Subpoena Duces Tecum (SDT) to take a deposition, so the moving parent has to bring documents regarding new employment, address, school system, and whatever the lawyer needs to learn. The lawyer needs enough information to request an Emergency Temporary Order. Depending on how close the parent is with the child, the lawyer may be able to meet the state's burden of showing harm to the child if that relationship is severed. In the alternative, the lawyer can argue that the child cannot go until the court has a hearing to determine if the child will be protected, safe, have a place to live, and find out about new stepparent and siblings.

Relevant documents located in the foreign country may have to be subpoenaed to trial unless witnesses can be flown to the United States to testify (e.g., concerning school programs) or the court will allow testimony to be taken by video conference. The issues need to be analyzed well in advance of trial so that the lawyer may prepare effectively.

Modifying Existing Custody Order and Parenting Plan

If there is an existing order, notice to the parent must be given according to state law (see Chapter 6). If one parent intends an international relocation, the lawyer for the nonmoving parent needs to file a Motion to Modify Custody or Parenting Time, not just an objection to the move. Some courts find a relocation a sufficient change of circumstances; others do not.[23] (See Chapter 8.) Most courts, however, do consider an international relocation a change of circumstances. If the relocation is not a sufficient change of circumstances by itself, the lawyer will want to include information about the close relationship between the left-behind parent and child; other family members, friends, and activities; quality of the current school system; the child's success in the current environment; any medical issues the child needs specific doctors to address that are already in place. If the moving parent has shown a pattern of not including the other parent in decisions, activities, or contact, those allegations should be raised to lay the foundation that the move is not in good faith.

When the nonmoving parent files the motion, they should include a contact schedule for the moving parent that is as liberal as they will want if the child is allowed to move. The plan should include language that states the contact schedule should be implemented only upon verification of the facts surrounding the new location and that it is in the child's best interest to have contact there.

In Oregon, a statute requires the development and filing of a parenting plan, which expressly includes provisions relating to parental relocation, by the parties or, in absence of agreement, the court, and the dispositive question is whether the relocation is in the best interests of the child. The party seeking modification of the parenting plan does not have the obligation to demonstrate a substantial change of circumstances since the entry of the original dissolution judgment.[24]

Preventing Abduction—Uniform Child Abduction Prevention Act (UCAPA) and UCCJEA

There is a link between relocation and abduction. In some cases of international parental abduction, the child traveled to the foreign country with the approval of both parents, but one parent chose to stay and did not return the child to the United States. Some abductions are failed relocations. After a parent is denied relocation, the parent may unilaterally depart with the child during their parenting time.

Many other abductions occur before a court has had the opportunity to enter a child custody determination. Some parents have high levels of anger and distrust, cannot cooperate, have elevated levels of psychological distress, and may be violent. These highly conflicted parents have strong disagreements about parenting generally and dismiss the other parent's value to the child. Afraid that the parent might "lose" in the court system, the parent may try to take the child before any legal proceeding has been filed to what is perceived to be a more friendly forum in another country.

Preventing an abduction is always best. The first step in preventing abduction is to get travel restrictions in place and a custody decree from the child's home state.[25] See Chapters 3 and 4. Most courts allow for temporary or interlocutory orders that could prohibit a parent from removing a child once a divorce or custody action has been filed. A lawyer can obtain a Temporary Restraining Order (TRO) to prohibit travel and compel the surrender of all passports for parents and children from any country as a condition of access to the court. A temporary order can also compel the parent who holds a foreign passport to surrender any passports in the child's name to the embassy that issued them with the request to the consul general that no passports be issued without a court order. The lawyer can send a copy of the TRO prohibiting travel to the counsel for the national airline of the country in question, as well as the counsel for any airline frequently used by the parties. The order should contain "Do not board" language, which, depending on the airport, directs or alerts airport police to not allow the child to board the plane.

If the state has enacted the Uniform Child Abduction Prevention Act (UCAPA), the lawyer can bring an action under UCAPA to prevent the parent from taking the child out of the state if the lawyer fears the child is vulnerable to abduction. If the client's state has jurisdiction under the UCCJEA (Chapter 3), the parent in the home state should file a petition for custody to get a valid, enforceable custody order in the home state.[26] The parenting plan should include restrictions on relocation, both domestic and international. If the agreement or order contains no restrictions on relocation, the parent's move will not violate the agreement or order.[27] Failure to have the child available for designated parenting time probably will be a violation.

The lawyer will want to ask the court to prohibit either party from obtaining a passport for the child or, if a passport already exists, for an order to have the court or lawyers hold the passport. The lawyer must be prepared to present evidence regarding the client's concerns about abduction. The key is to keep the child from leaving the United States, because even though the United States is a party to the Hague Abduction Convention, applications for the return of children to the United States from other countries often do not have satisfactory outcomes.[28]

Generally Accepted Risk Factors for Abduction

One parent's fears alone will not be enough to warrant the imposition of travel or other restrictions. Research over the past 35 years, however, has shown that there are a number of red flags for abduction. The number one predictor of a future abduction is that a parent has made credible threats to abduct a child or has a history of abduction or attempted abduction. Another key risk factor is parents who engage in "abduction planning activities." These include such things as quitting a job, terminating a lease, selling the family house, and moving or removing assets.[29] Research also shows that abducting parents dismiss the value of the other parent in the child's life, have a young child or a child vulnerable to influence, and often have the support of their family and others in another country. The greater the number of these factors that are present, the more likely the chance of an abduction. The mere presence of one or more of these factors, however, does not mean that an abduction will happen, just as the absence of these factors does not guarantee that no abduction will occur. The lawyer must evaluate the entire situation, including the relationship between the parents, whether one parent has more connections to the foreign country than the United States, and the resources of the parents.

A few states list abduction risk factors.[30] The Uniform Child Abduction Prevention Act (UCAPA)[31] Article 7 sets out a comprehensive list of risk factors.[32]

(1) has previously abducted or attempted to abduct the child;

(2) has threatened to abduct the child;

(3) has recently engaged in activities that may indicate a planned abduction, including:

(A) abandoning employment;

(B) selling a primary residence;

(C) terminating a lease;

(D) closing bank or other financial management accounts, liquidating assets, hiding or destroying financial documents, or conducting any unusual financial activities;

(E) applying for a passport or visa or obtaining travel documents for the respondent, a family member, or the child; or

(F) seeking to obtain the child's birth certificate or school or medical records;

(4) has engaged in domestic violence, stalking, or child abuse or neglect;

(5) has refused to follow a child-custody determination;

(6) lacks strong familial, financial, emotional, or cultural ties to the state or the United States;

(7) has strong familial, financial, emotional, or cultural ties to another state or country;

(8) is likely to take the child to a country that:

(A) is not a party to the Hague Convention on the Civil Aspects of International Child Abduction and does not provide for the extradition of an abducting parent or for the return of an abducted child;

(B) is a party to the Hague Convention on the Civil Aspects of International Child Abduction but:

(i) the Hague Convention on the Civil Aspects of International Child Abduction is not in force between the United States and that country;

(ii) is noncompliant according to the most recent compliance report issued by the United States Department of State; or

(iii) lacks legal mechanisms for immediately and effectively enforcing a return order under the Hague Convention on the Civil Aspects of International Child Abduction;

(C) poses a risk that the child's physical or emotional health or safety would be endangered in the country because of specific circumstances relating to the child or because of human rights violations committed against children;

(D) has laws or practices that would:

(i) enable the respondent, without due cause, to prevent the petitioner from contacting the child;

(ii) restrict the petitioner from freely traveling to or exiting from the country because of the petitioner's gender, nationality, marital status, or religion; or

(iii) restrict the child's ability legally to leave the country after the child reaches the age of majority because of a child's gender, nationality, or religion;

(E) is included by the United States Department of State on a current list of state sponsors of terrorism;

(F) does not have an official United States diplomatic presence in the country; or

(G) is engaged in active military action or war, including a civil war, to which the child may be exposed;

(9) is undergoing a change in immigration or citizenship status that would adversely affect the respondent's ability to remain in the United States legally;

(10) has had an application for United States citizenship denied;

(11) has forged or presented misleading or false evidence on government forms or supporting documents to obtain or attempt to obtain a passport, a visa, travel documents, a Social Security card, a driver's license, or other government-issued identification card or has made a misrepresentation to the United States government;

(12) has used multiple names to attempt to mislead or defraud; or

(13) has engaged in any other conduct the court considers relevant to the risk of abduction.

If these risks exist, especially when the relocation could be to another country, the lawyer will want to seek abduction prevention measures as early as possible, because both parents have equal custody rights by operation of law. Either parent may seek prevention measures before custody has been adjudicated when there is a credible risk of abduction. Petitioner (usually the parent who fears the other parent intends to wrongfully remove or retain the child) should file a verified petition with information about the parties, previous proceedings for custody, protection orders, and so on, and supply detailed supporting evidence showing a credible threat to abduct. Unless it is an emergency situation, the filing will generally be in the child's home state with notice given under state law. A court sua sponte may order abduction prevention measures if the court finds that the evidence establishes a credible risk of abduction. If there is an existing court order, the lawyer should file the UCAPA petition in the court having exclusive continuing jurisdiction to modify, unless all parties have left the decree state, or the state has declined to exercise jurisdiction. Then the child's new home state may issue the order. If there is no credible risk of abduction, the judge does not need to order any prevention measure. Where a Michigan mother wanted to take her child to Poland for a funeral, the court found no credible risk of abduction and ordered the release of the child's passport.[33]

When an initial child custody proceeding is pending, the petitioner may seek a custody order with appropriate prevention provisions from the court with jurisdiction to make a child custody determination under the UCCJEA, usually the home state. UCAPA complements UCCJEA by using the same jurisdictional requirements and adds the "threat of abduction" as another basis for temporary emergency jurisdiction (see Chapter 3).

UCAPA allows a court to exercise emergency jurisdiction to enter a temporary abduction prevention order if the child is present in the state and it is necessary to protect the child because of a credible risk of abduction. This could be the case where one parent has not returned the child and is at the airport with the child preparing for an international flight. Emergency jurisdiction is only temporary. The petitioner may have to file with the court having proper UCCJEA jurisdiction for prevention measures after courts communicate with each other. Note, however, a court does not need to use emergency jurisdiction to issue abduction prevention orders when it has either initial or modification jurisdiction.

Abduction Prevention Measures

Section 8 provides a variety of measures the judge may order to prevent a potential abduction. If the judge finds there is a credible risk of abduction, the judge is required to issue some type of abduction prevention order. There are many abduction prevention measures, starting with the initial custody order. Every abduction prevention order must include mandatory provisions found in UCAPA section 8(a)(1)–(5):

> (1) the basis for the court's exercise of jurisdiction (whether it is home state, emergency or other);
>
> (2) the manner in which notice and opportunity to be heard were given to the persons entitled to notice of the proceeding;[34]
>
> (3) a detailed description of each party's custody and visitation rights and residential arrangements for the child;
>
> (4) a provision stating that a violation of the order may subject the party in violation to civil and criminal penalties; and
>
> (5) identification of the child's country of habitual residence at the time of the issuance of the order.[35]

The custody order should be clearly enforceable, not only in the United States but also, if possible, in other countries. It should be apparent on the face of the document that the issuing court has proper jurisdiction so courts in other states and countries will recognize it as valid. There should be a statement that both parties were properly served, given adequate notice to be heard, and their due process rights were protected.

The parenting time arrangements should be as specific as possible. Vague orders are difficult to enforce without additional litigation. The term "reasonable visitation" often leads to conflicts between the parents and makes it difficult for law enforcement officers to know if the order is being violated. The parties or the court should specify the dates and times for each parent's parenting time, including holidays, birthdays, and telephone or Internet contact. Because joint physical or shared custody arrangements create special enforcement problems, the court should specify, or encourage the parents to agree to, specific details about a child's residential placement at all times.[36]

To determine what is reasonably calculated to prevent abduction, the court must consider petitioner's evidence as to the potential harm to the child and obstacles to securing the child's return if an abduction were to occur, as well as respondent's evidence in explanation and/or justification for the alleged conduct. In international cases, this is often easy to show because the obstacles can be many. For example, until relatively recently when Japan amended its custody laws, the mother who took the child to Japan rarely was prosecuted and the child rarely returned.[37]

Types of Restrictions to Prevent Abduction and Ensure Continuing Jurisdiction

The Uniform Child Abduction Prevention Act (UCAPA) provides a list of preventive measures. Section 8 offers the following list:

> (b)(1) an imposition of travel restrictions that require that a party traveling with the child outside a designated geographical area provide the other party with the following:
>
> > (A) the travel itinerary of the child;
> >
> > (B) a list of physical addresses and telephone numbers at which the child can be reached at specified times; and
> >
> > (C) copies of all travel documents;
>
> (2) a prohibition of the respondent directly or indirectly:
>
> > (A) removing the child from this state, the United States, or another geographic area without permission of the court or the petitioner's written consent;
> >
> > (B) removing or retaining the child in violation of a child-custody determination;
> >
> > (C) removing the child from school or a child-care or similar facility; or
> >
> > (D) approaching the child at any location other than a site designated for supervised visitation;
>
> (3) a requirement that a party to register the order in another state as a prerequisite to allowing the child to travel to that state;
>
> (4) with regard to the child's passport:
>
> > (A) a direction that the petitioner to place the child's name in the United States Department of State's Child Passport Issuance Alert Program;

(B) a requirement that the respondent surrender to the court or the petitioner's attorney any United States or foreign passport issued in the child's name, including a passport issued in the name of both the parent and the child; and

(C) a prohibition upon the respondent from applying on behalf of the child for a new or replacement passport or visa;

(5) as a prerequisite to exercising custody or visitation, a requirement that the respondent provide:

(A) to the United States Department of State Office of Children's Issues and the relevant foreign consulate or embassy, an authenticated copy of the order detailing passport and travel restrictions for the child;

(B) to the court:

(i) proof that the respondent has provided the information in subparagraph (A); and

(ii) an acknowledgment in a record from the relevant foreign consulate or embassy that no passport application has been made, or passport issued, on behalf of the child;

(C) to the petitioner, proof of registration with the United States Embassy or other United States diplomatic presence in the destination country and with the Central Authority for the Hague Convention on the Civil Aspects of International Child Abduction, if that Convention is in effect between the United States and the destination country, unless one of the parties objects; and

(D) a written waiver under the Privacy Act, 5 U.S.C. Section 552a [as amended], with respect to any document, application, or other information pertaining to the child authorizing its disclosure to the court and the petitioner; and

(6) upon the petitioner's request, a requirement that the respondent obtain an order from the relevant foreign country containing terms identical to the child-custody determination issued in the United States.

(d) In an abduction prevention order, the court may impose conditions on the exercise of custody or visitation that:

(1) limit visitation or require that visitation with the child by the respondent be supervised until the court finds that supervision is no longer necessary and order the respondent to pay the costs of supervision;

(2) require the respondent to post a bond or provide other security in an amount sufficient to serve as a financial deterrent to abduction, the proceeds of which may be used to pay for the reasonable expenses of recovery of the child, including reasonable attorneys fees and costs if there is an abduction; and

(3) require the respondent to obtain education on the potentially harmful effects to the child from abduction.

UCAPA provides a complete laundry list of remedies, which is not exclusive. UCAPA applies to pre-decree and post-decree cases, intrastate or interstate or international. It can be used in emergency situations as well as where the existing child custody determination lacks abduction prevention measures.[38]

Passport Restrictions

If the child is to leave the country, the child must have their own passport.[39] When there are risk factors for abduction, several states have upheld restrictions on the issuance of passports.[40] Evidence of a mother's irrational and threatening behavior and anger issues sufficiently supported the court's determination that it was in the children's best interest for the father to be in control of any international travel by the children. The mother could not retain or obtain passports for the children.[41] Courts are often willing to make a mutual prohibition on obtaining a passport. If the passport has already been issued, the court may designate one parent to control the children's passports.[42]

A typical order of restraint might be:

It is further ordered and decreed by the court that neither the petitioner mother nor the respondent father shall apply for, nor have the authority to apply for, either a passport or visa within the United States or through any Consulate or Embassy abroad for [full legal name of child] without an express order of this Court authorizing said act.

Another way to prevent the issuance of a passport for a minor child is to control the necessary documents required to be presented with the passport application. The client may be able to secure exclusive control of all documents relating to the child's evidence of citizenship in the United States. If the client cannot secure exclusive control, the lawyer can ask the court to limit the foreign national parent from obtaining any documents relating to the child's evidence of citizenship.

Passports Procedure for Minor

The State Department requires both parents to execute the passport application on behalf of a minor under age 16 and attach documentary evidence showing the minor's name, date and place of birth, and the names of the parent or parents.[43] One parent may execute the passport application if that person provides evidence that they are the sole parent, have sole custody of the child, there is a written statement of consent from the non-applying parent, or the court order allows one parent to apply. There are exceptions for emergency or health or safety reasons, such as a medical evacuation or emergency evacuation of U.S. citizens from a foreign country.

The custody order may state that the mother and father agree that either parent may apply for a passport on behalf of the child(ren), without the written consent of the other parent, provided that a copy of each child's passport application is sent to the other parent, by certified mail, return receipt requested, at the same time that it is submitted to the Department of State.

Passport Issuance Alert Program and Prevention Departure Program

The U.S. State Department Office of Children's Issues has numerous ways to prevent child abduction. There is a Prevention Team, phone number 888-40704747. Two key programs are: the Passport Issuance Alert Program, which is to prevent one parent from obtaining a passport for the child without the knowledge or valid permission of the other parent, and the Prevent Departure

Program. A person applying for a passport for a child under 16 must show that both parents consent to the issuance or that the applying parent has sole authority to obtain a passport. The Department of State Children's Passport Issuance Alert Program can be used to inform a parent or a court when an application for a U.S. passport is executed on behalf of a child.[44]

The Prevent Departure Program allows both children with foreign passports, as well as children traveling on U.S. passports, to be placed in the Prevent Departure Program.[45] Any parent who believes that the child is at risk for international abduction (whether the country is a Hague Convention signatory or not) should enroll the child in the Prevent Departure Program. The program operates through the Department of Homeland Security in collaboration with the transportation industry. It provides a single, comprehensive prevent departure lookout database of subjects whose imminent departure can be flagged. "Imminent departure" means that a parent needs to alert Children's Issues at the State Department. If a named abductor and/or child seek to leave the country by means of a public carrier, the transportation company is required to prevent the departure. To enroll a child in the program, the lawyer (or parent) should send a court order to the Children's Issues Office that states in very simple terms something like this:

> Neither Petitioner/Mother nor Respondent/Father, nor any agent acting on either parent's behalf, shall remove the parties' minor children: Jane Elizabeth Doe, DOB 01/12/2016 and John Robert Doe, DOB 06/01/2013 from the United States until further order of this Court. A parent may apply to the Court by motion seeking relocation or a travel order, and by showing proof of service of that motion, a proposed order and notice of hearing on the motion upon the other parent or his/her legal representative. This order remains in effect unless modified by this Court.

If the children are in the lookout database, the adult might be able to travel (depending upon a criminal check), but the children are prevented from departing the United States. The details are found on the State Department website.

Other Travel Restrictions

Several courts, however, have upheld travel restrictions on vacations or visits outside of the United States if in the best interests of the child.[46] Courts are willing to impose restrictions when a parent has a history of abducting the children or where a parent has withheld the child in a foreign country whose laws favor one of the parents and which makes it difficult for the other parent to enforce orders. American courts have been protective of the American parent's rights and imposed severe restrictions.[47]

Travel restrictions, however, should be clear. In one case, the parents had agreed to allow either parent to travel out of the United States, so long as they always visited countries that were signatories to the Hague Convention of 1980 on the Civil Aspects of International Child Abduction and the children could not be taken to countries where the U.S. government had issued travel restrictions or warnings. The parties could not agree on whether Jamaica was included because it was not a signatory to the treaty and there had been previous travel warnings.[48]

Recognizing the complexities of international removals, the court could look at other factors. In a case involving visitation in Lebanon, the New Jersey court looked at:

1. the domicile and roots of the parent seeking such visitation;
2. the reason for the visit, the safety and security of the child;
3. the age and attitude of the child to the visit, the relationship between the parents;
4. the propriety and practicality of a bond or other security; and
5. the character and integrity of the parent seeking out-of-country visitation as gleaned from past comments and conduct.

The court noted that the "danger of retention of a child in a country where prospects of retrieving the child and extraditing the wrongful parent are difficult, if not impossible, is a major factor for a court to weigh," a bright-line rule prohibiting visitation to a country not a signatory to the Hague Convention would "unnecessarily penalize a law-abiding parent and could conflict with a child's best interest."[49] A Michigan court, however, did not abuse its discretion in not allowing a mother to relocate with the child to Pakistan, even though Pakistan had acceded to the Hague Abduction Convention.[50]

A typical travel restriction might read:

> It is ordered, adjudged and decreed that neither petitioner/mother nor respondent/father shall travel outside the United States with [child's full legal name] without an expressed order of this Court authorizing such travel.

A Washington appellate court upheld a travel restriction in a parenting plan which read:

> [N]either parent shall take the child out of the country, except to Canada and Mexico, until she reaches the age of 13 years unless otherwise agreed by the parties in writing[.]

The restriction was based on daughter's sensory impairment and limited food tolerance. She needed routine, stability, and structure. The travel restriction was not imposed based on conduct of parents but because the daughter had special needs and the restriction was in the child's best interest.[51]

The parent who wants the restrictions should provide enough evidence for the trial court to impose them.[52] If there is no credible risk of abduction, the court may decline to impose restrictions.[53] A judge erred in relying on extraneous documents in denying the father's petition to take children to Syria as provided by the agreement.[54] Even though the Unified Arab Emirates is not a party to the Hague Abduction Convention, an Illinois court allowed mother to have visitation there, noting that the UAE had enforced United States custody orders.[55]

Factors in International Relocation Cases

The best interest or welfare of the child is the major consideration in all custody cases, including international. As with domestic cases, the trial judge gets to determine based on the evidence presented whether it is in the best interests of the child to relocate with the relocating parent or to remain in the current location and the other parent have primary residency.[56]

Judges have broad discretion. There has been considerable social science research in the past thirty years on the risks and benefits of relocation.[57]

Some of the factors for relocation remain the same, that is, good faith reason for the relocation, and which parent is more stable, better able to manage and nurture the child and to encourage a continuing positive relationship with the other parent.[58] Good faith reasons may be a return to home country and family, new spouse in another country, military deployment, corporate job transfer, or educational opportunities. Sometimes the parent or child has special health needs best met in another country. There may be educational or athletic opportunities more available in one place or the other.

As in other custody cases, there may be a combination of factors that influence the decision. In a Pennsylvania case, the court awarded primary physical residential custody to the father who had been living in Germany because he was the parent most likely to permit contact with mother and could better address the child's stability and attend to the child's daily needs. When the child was in the mother's care, the child spent large amounts of time on the computer and YouTube, fell behind in kindergarten, and had to repeat.[59]

The Washington Declaration provides there should be no presumption for or against the relocation.[60] To promote a more uniform approach internationally, the Declaration suggests that that the exercise of judicial discretion should be guided in particular, but not exclusively, by the following factors listed in no order of priority:[61]

1. The right of the child separated from one parent to maintain personal relations and direct contact with both parents on a regular basis in a manner consistent with the child's development, except if the contact is contrary to the child's best interest;
2. Views of the child having regard to child's age and maturity;

3. The parties' proposals for the practical arrangements for relocation, including accommodation, schooling, and employment;
4. where relevant to the determination of the outcome, the reasons for seeking or opposing the relocation;
5. any history of family violence or abuse, whether physical or psychological;
6. the history of the family and particularly the continuity and quality of past and current care and contact arrangements;
7. preexisting custody and access determinations;
8. the impact of grant or refusal on the child, in the context of their extended family, education, and social life, and on the parties;
9. the nature of the inter-parental relationship and the commitment of the applicant to support and facilitate the relationship between the child and the respondent after the relocation;
10. whether the parties' proposals for contact after relocation are realistic, having particular regard to the cost to the family and the burden to the child;
11. the enforceability of contact provisions ordered as a condition of relocation in the state of destination;
12. issues of mobility for family members; and
13. any other circumstances deemed to be relevant by the judge.

The Washington Declaration notes that the factors support research findings concerning children's needs and development in the context of relocation. The weight to be given to any one factor will vary from case to case.

Hearing the Voice of the Child

The child's preference, listed second on the list of the Washington Declaration, can be particularly important in an international relocation case depending on the child's age and maturity level. (See Chapter 14.) Every country except the United States has enacted the UN Convention on the Rights of the Child. The CRC requires hearing the voice of the child in *all* matters relating to the child's custody.[62] In addition, 103 countries have adopted the Hague Abduction Convention which includes at article 13b, paragraph 2, the objections of a mature child as an affirmative exception to return.[63]

Additionally, 57 countries have adopted the 1996 Hague Protection of Children Convention, which requires custody orders to state how the child's voice was heard. The court in those countries can refuse to enforce an order that does not show how the child's voice was heard (or that there was an opportunity for the child to be heard). Therefore, it is imperative in an international relocation to make the order enforceable that the lawyers ensure that the custody order states how the child was given an opportunity to be heard or how the child's voice was heard.

The Washington Declaration encourages voluntary agreements of the parties and suggests mediation and similar facilities outside of court proceedings. The views of the child should be considered, having regard to the child's age and maturity, within the various processes.

The child's age and wishes, temperament, and relationships with siblings and extended family may be important factors. Some children make friends easily and are able to adapt to new situations; others are less likely to have an easy adjustment to a new location. Most children want to spend time with both parents, which is usually best achieved if the parents live relatively close to each other. Many children are reluctant to move far away from the other parent and friends. If the child wants to stay in the existing location, it may be important to find out if the major concern is loyalty to the nonmoving parent, friends, school, or activities. In some jurisdictions, the preference of a child over a certain age, 12 or 14, may be determinative.

Whether the child wants to go or stay, the preference may have been influenced by one of the parents. That may be important information. If the child wants to move, it may be the child is being loyal to the moving parent who may have been the primary caregiver. The moving parent may have convinced the child the move is necessary or important or will be a great adventure. On the other hand, if the child has been to the country before, speaks the language if different than English, and has relatives or friends there, the decision to move may be based on the child's knowledge of the new location. Sometimes school or extracurricular activities may be a key consideration. If the child expresses irrational negative attitudes about the nonmoving parent's value and character, the lawyer for the nonmoving parent may need to discuss possible alienating behaviors. It is possible that the move could alleviate the negativity, but it is also possible that it may entrench it.

If the parent wants to move a preverbal child, there are concerns that the child will not learn the language of the left-behind parent who may not know the foreign language. The left-behind parent may not be able to talk to teachers, doctors, or law enforcement officers.

Reasons for Relocation

Courts have been sympathetic to a parent's desire to return to their home country.[64] A California court allowed a mother, who had some questionable conduct in the past, to relocate to her native Israel with her son because her visa was expiring, and she had better job prospects and family there. The child was more bonded to the mother, was familiar with Israel, spoke the language and had family there.[65] In another case, a Massachusetts court found that under the real advantage test, the German citizen mother's request to move the daughter to Germany was in her best interests. The current shared parenting schedule was financially untenable for the mother who had applied for 400 jobs but was living in poverty. She had been offered a well-paying job in Germany with benefits and an opportunity to work from home. Because she also had family near, she would benefit financially, emotionally, and socially. The daughter would benefit because she would be attending better schools, would again be treated by her long-time pediatrician, spoke German, retained friends from attending school in Germany before, and had frequent and extensive contact with the maternal extended family since birth. The father traveled for work frequently, had missed allotted parenting time that he had not tried to make up, and was not seeking sole physical custody.[66]

A Rhode Island judge, however, denied an Australian mother's request to relocate the parties' four children to Australia to improve her economic situation. The parties and children had lived in Rhode Island for years and both parents were engaged in meaningful relationships with the children. Even though the mother's economic prospects were better in Australia, the father was an offshore fisherman who was often gone and the mother was allegedly trying to alienate the children and had planted a recording device in one of the children's clothing. The guardian ad litem noted that the relocation would benefit the mother, but not necessarily the children who would have minimal contact with the father.[67] The guardian ad litem, noting the practical difficulties that an international relocation would occasion for the parties due to the complex nature of international travel and the parties' limited financial means, recommended that relocation was not in the best interests of the children.[68]

As in all cases, the best interests of the child are paramount. A mother who shared joint legal and physical custody was allowed to relocate two children to England where the relocation was economically necessary for her and would enhance the children's lives economically and educationally. Both children expressed a preference to go and the attorney for the children supported the move. The court noted that a liberal visitation schedule, including extended visits during the summer and school vacations, would allow for the continuation of a meaningful relationship between the father and the children.[69] On the other hand, a Connecticut appellate court found a mother's motion to relocate her 12-year-old son to France to marry a former classmate was not a legitimate reason when she could not legally work there. Although she argued moving to France would be an incredible cultural opportunity for the child who could have a speed skating coach, the court found that Connecticut also had speed skating coaches.[70]

Nature, Quality, Extent of Involvement and Duration of the Child's Relationship with Each Parent

The generally accepted consensus is that children benefit from spending at least 35% of their time with each parent except situations in which the parent is a credible risk to abuse, neglect or abduct the child; or where the parent suffers from substance abuse issues or has committed domestic violence.[71] If both parents are fit and competent, and share physical residency of the child or are actively involved with the child, the relocation decision will essentially remove the child from daily or weekly contact with one of the parents. Where the move would harm the relationship with the left-behind parent, the court will deny the relocation. A mother wanted to move the children to Vancouver. The court found that the father had never missed a child support payment, had never missed an hour of visitation available to him, and had built a home designed around the needs of his children. He regularly took the children skiing, crabbing, and camping. The disruption of contact between the father and his children would have a damaging impact on them.[72] In an initial custody dispute, a court in New York found it in the children's best interests to grant the mother and father joint custody and denied mother's request to relocate the children to the Netherlands.[73]

If one parent has primary residency and the other parent has failed to exercise their parenting time, has a poor relationship with the child, has substance abuse issues, or has committed domestic violence, the court may be more inclined to allow a relocation.

If the parents have had a good co-parenting relationship where each parent respects and supports the child's relationship with the other parent, the parties may continue to do that even if the distance is greater. Both parents need to remain involved in setting and enforcing limits and reacting to normal conflict. It is important that the moving parent be willing to comply with the visitation times in the parenting plan.

If, however, the parties have not been able to cooperate, the distance may make it easier for one parent to reduce substantially the role of the other parent. If, however, the distance reduces the conflict or contact of the child and parent with extreme conflict and negativity, the move may be allowed. In one case, an Idaho court allowed a mother to relocate to her native Australia. The trial court included 15 pages of factual findings that father had serious boundary issues, controlling conduct, and an unhealthy parental relationship. Even if the mother had not been allowed to move, the father would have been denied overnight visits.[74]

Feasibility of the Long-Distance Parenting Plan

International relocation cases differ fundamentally from domestic relocations.[75] The plan should provide for sufficient contact between the child and the nonmoving parent to continue to foster the development of a strong and meaningful relationship. There should be adequate time in the nonmoving parent's home and community for normal parent–child interaction, not just vacation and fun times. An international relocation removes the nonmoving parent as a fully involved parent during the school year. Many plans provide for the child to spend blocks of time with the nonmoving parent during some holidays and school vacation periods.

There are additional considerations for an international parenting plan. For example, if a parent relocates to another state, generally, there are usually a maximum of three time zones to navigate. If a parent moves from Los Angeles to South Africa, however, there may be eight time zone differences. The parenting plan should try to minimize the disruption of contact by providing longer periods of visitation during school breaks as compensation for the loss of more frequent visitation. While extended school breaks are a way to make up time, it may not be possible to get a child to another country for four or five days. The plan also must take into account the child's activities and the destination country's school and holiday schedule. The other parent is less likely to follow a parent to the foreign country as they might be if the relocation were to another state.

International travel is more difficult than interstate travel. A viable parenting plan will usually involve less frequent, but longer, parenting periods both in the United States and in the foreign country. The logistics need to take into account the child's age, temperament, maturity, and comfort with air travel. The plan must be feasible in terms of time involved in the travel, the distance to airports, and the cost involved. The lawyer should propose the number of trips that are realistic and affordable for this family. The parenting plan often needs complete alterations to allow time for international travel, jet lag, and so on. An additional consideration is the physical burden of international travel, which may require multiple stops and several hours of airplane travel with airport transfers in foreign cities. The lawyer for the relocating party can introduce evidence concerning telephone rates, airfares, and hotel rates.

Flight time is only a portion of the travel time between two homes. There may be transportation by car, train, bus, or other going to and from the airport both at home and in the other country. International flights generally require passengers to be at the airport three hours in advance of an overseas flight. There can be delays going through airport security. There can also be weather and other cancellations. Usually baggage retrieval takes additional time, as does waiting in line for customs.

Language differences can make international travel more difficult. Airport signs, announcements, and unfamiliar signage can create anxiety for adults, let alone a child. Jet lag is more than just being tired from traveling, especially if moving more than three or four time zones. For example, there are nine time zones between Los Angeles and Paris. If the child is only there for one week, the body and mind may be out of sync the whole time.

The ability of the parties to finance overseas visitation and parenting time is important. Depending on the age of the child, the need for a parent or another adult to accompany the child will also increase the costs. For parents with average income, an order allowing the child to relocate to a foreign country may be tantamount to terminating that parent's in-person relationship with the child because the parent cannot afford to travel. Additionally, one parent may have family responsibilities that constrain the ability to travel—other children, inflexible job, or aging parents. The plan should include the type of parenting the nonmoving parent is capable of executing and maintaining.

Cultural factors also need to be considered. The child may be taken to a country with cultural conditions and practices different from those in the United States. If an American Christian married an Iraqi Muslim, the parents need to be able to help the child navigate the potential clash in cultural, religious, and social norms. It may help if the child has been to the country before and has some familiarity with it. Additionally, the legal systems will be different. The child may not have the same protections and advantages in a foreign country that would be available in the United States. Some foreign governments do not protect human rights. Extreme examples would be the practice of genital mutilation or the nonavailability of education for girls, which would argue against the move of a girl to those countries.

Communication

The lawyer for the relocating parent should be prepared to offer evidence of the different modes of communication available to the parties as well as their cost. A viable plan will include opportunities for frequent contact between the child and the absent parent. Young children who have not yet developed a sense of time need frequent communication with the nonmoving parent. Low-cost technological solutions include the use of videoconferencing, Zoom, and FaceTime, as well as email. The relocating party can arrange for the use of technological services such as the Internet and can purchase identical videoconferencing systems so that the parties will have compatible equipment and be able to begin communicating immediately upon the move. The plan should provide for the various means of communication available and who bears the costs. Time differences may also create challenges for phone and video communications. The child's excitement at winning a game, getting a good grade, or making the choir, for example, may result in a call to the other parent who is asleep or at work.

Enforcing Court Orders

The lawyer for the nonmoving parent needs to be aware of the problem with enforceability.[76] Courts are reluctant to grant an international relocation if the court orders cannot be enforced in the new country.[77] After a relocation, however, it is unlikely that the United States will retain exclusive continuing jurisdiction over its custody and visitation orders under the laws of the foreign nation, even if the parties had an agreement.[78] If continuing U.S. jurisdiction cannot be guaranteed by law, the trial court can enforce its order by imposing a financial sanction in the form of a bond or forfeiture of spousal or child support on the moving parent that would be forfeited in the event they fail to comply with the custody order. The linking of the enforcement of a support order to the support obligor's access to the children can be waived in the context of an international move. The lawyer for the moving parent should investigate the mechanism for funding a bond if one is required. The bond company may require the yearly payment of a percentage of the face value of the bond and may not accept all kinds of collateral. The moving parent may or may not be able to afford the yearly cash expenditure. In securing a bond, the moving parent will need to make full disclosure of their assets.

When a court allows an international relocation, the court will often impose some restrictions on the relocating parent. For example, a California court conditioned relocation of the child to Israel on the mother's fulfilment of six conditions:

1. Post a substantial financial bond in a specific amount sufficient to ensure her compliance with the court's judgment and orders;
2. Consent to California's continuing jurisdiction over the child;
3. Agree to a prohibition against attempting to modify the judgment except upon application to a California state court;
4. Agree that any attempt by such parent to modify the judgment by application to any non-California court could be deemed a violation of the court's judgment and grounds for forfeiture of the bond and other appropriate sanctions;
5. Register the trial court's judgment with the proper Israeli authorities; and
6. Refrain from taking the child to Israel until the judgment was registered and until the trial court made a further determination that she had fully complied with the court's judgment.[79]

Another California case included some additional provisions:

- Require the relocating parent to annually register the custody order under the Hague Convention;
- Require the relocating parent to waive extradition if an arrest warrant is issued for parental kidnapping under the federal international child kidnapping statute;
- Provide that support payments will be forfeited in the event of noncompliance; and
- Require the moving parent to deposit support payments in a trust fund to finance travel for visitation.[80]

The Washington Declaration provides that orders for relocation and the conditions attached to the relocation should be able to be enforced in the destination state (country). The destination state should consider making orders that reflect the state of origin (mirror orders). The lawyer for either parent should research the effect of the law of the country of the proposed relocation on the proposed or existing U.S. custody order.

1. One issue is whether the U.S. judgment can be made enforceable in the foreign country. If so, how?
2. If the judgment can be made enforceable in the foreign country, the lawyer must explore the legal consequences. Can the foreign court system impose any penalties on the relocating parent for failure to comply with the terms of the U.S. judgment? If the moving parent repeatedly violates the judgment, what is the foreign court likely to do?
3. Is it against the public policy of the foreign nation for the relocating parent to waive the jurisdiction of its court system? If not, what is the procedure for waiving the jurisdiction of the foreign court?
4. Will the foreign nation respect the moving parent's stipulation to this state's jurisdiction over the issues of custody and visitation?
5. Generally, what is the foreign country's public policy with regard to issues of custody and visitation? Is joint

legal and/or physical custody favored? Are mothers favored? Fathers?

6. Will the foreign nation at some point in time obtain jurisdiction over the issues of custody and visitation of the relocated children? If so, how and when?
7. If the foreign nation obtains jurisdiction, can it modify the U.S. judgment? Can it create a new order for the parents? Under what circumstances?

The relocating party has a better chance of getting approval if the country to which the child is to be relocated is a signatory to the Hague Convention on the Civil Aspects of International Child Abduction. If the country is a party, then it will be easier to get the child returned if the child is wrongfully retained or removed. The parent can seek return of the child pursuant to Article 3 of the Uniform Child Custody Jurisdiction and Enforcement Act (UCCJEA) and the Parental Kidnapping Prevention Act (PKPA). If there is a court order, the party can sue in tort[81] or seek sanctions for contempt. There are state criminal kidnapping statutes and interference with custody.[82] There is also a criminal action under the International Parental Kidnapping Crime Act of 1993, 18 U.S.C. § 1204.

The Hague Convention on the Civil Aspects of International Child Abduction

If the country is a party to the 1980 Hague Convention on the Civil Aspects of International Child Abduction Convention, the parent may choose to use it to try to get return of a wrongfully retained or removed child. The Convention recognizes "custody" rights and "access" rights.[83] The Convention is international law and is applicable whether or not a U.S. judgment has been made enforceable in the foreign nation. The Hague Abduction Convention operates to promptly return a wrongfully removed or retained child under age 16 to their habitual residence.[84] The purposes are (1) to secure the prompt return of children who have been wrongfully removed to or retained in any contracting state; (2) to ensure that rights of custody and visitation are effectively respected in other contracting states and countries; (3) to preserve the status quo custody arrangement of the parties; and (4) to deter a parent from crossing international boundaries in search of a more sympathetic court.[85] The Convention empowers courts to determine only rights under the Convention and not the merits of any underlying child custody claims.[86]

The Hague Abduction Convention is implemented by the International Child Abduction Remedies Act (ICARA), 22 U.S.C.A. § 9001-9011.[87] The treaty and statute must be read together.[88] Article 6 requires each contracting state to designate a central authority that can cooperate with other central authorities. Executive Order 12648 designated the Department of State. The Abduction Convention applies to countries that have ratified or acceded to it and between countries that have accepted the accession of the other as a treaty partner. One hundred and three countries have ratified or acceded. The Department of State is required to make an annual report on countries that are noncompliant. The lawyer for the nonmoving parent will want to make sure the court knows if a parent wants to relocate to a country that has not ratified, whose accession the United States has not accepted, or that is noncompliant with the Hague Abduction Convention. Three valuable resources are the Hague Conference website, www.hcch.net, the U.S. State Department website, and Jeremy Morley's *The Hague Abduction Convention: Practical Issues and Procedures for Family Lawyers*, published by the ABA in 2025.

ICARA section 4(a) grants federal and state courts have concurrent original jurisdiction over all actions arising under the Convention. The choice of court belongs to the petitioner abroad who is seeking return of the child from the United States or access rights. Whether to file in the state or federal system depends on the speed of getting to hearing, known judicial biases, home turf attitudes, and precedential cases in state or federal system.

The person may commence civil action by filing a petition in the jurisdiction in which the child is located.[89] ICARA requires notice and hearing to the abducting parent. Notice of an action shall be given in accordance with laws governing notice in interstate custody proceedings, that is, the UCCJEA, PKPA. Failure to give notice and opportunity to be heard violates due process.[90]

The Hague Abduction Convention did not preempt a noncustodial father's conviction under a felony child abduction law for failing to return his eight-year-old daughter to her mother in the United Kingdom. The mother was allowed to testify remotely via two-way audio/video communication technology.[91]

The Convention requires the return of a child "wrongfully abducted" from a parent exercising "rights of custody" to the state of the child's "habitual residence." The petitioner has the burden of proving by a preponderance of evidence that the child was wrongfully removed or retained. Article 12 of the Convention states that if the proceeding is brought within one year after the wrongful removal or retention, the child must be returned forthwith unless a defense exists.

Habitual Residence

The Abduction Convention does not define "habitual residence." Before 2020, there was a split in court definitions—settled parental intent, agreement or child's acclimation. The U.S. Supreme Court held that "a child's habitual residence depends on the totality of circumstances specific to the case."[92] This means that the trial judge retains much discretion. If the facts could have been decided either way, the judge will be affirmed.[93] If the child is too young to acclimate, the intentions and circumstances of the caregiving parents are relevant.[94] Where evidence of the parties' intentions conflicted, as is often the case, the court looked at the fact the family lived together in Japan for three years but had never lived together in the United States.[95] There can be only one habitual residence. If a child has acquired a new habitual residence, a retention in that jurisdiction is not wrongful.

Rights of Custody

The Convention protects a parent who has a right of custody under the law of the habitual residence and was actually exercising that right, or would have but for the removal. Biological and legal parents of a child have "rights of custody," so return proceedings are not contingent upon the existence of a court order. An unwed father may have rights of custody under a foreign country's law.[96] A ne exeat right, one that provides a parent cannot remove a child from the country without the consent of the other parent, is a right of custody.[97]

Failure to exercise rights of custody is a defense. The respondent can show by a preponderance of the evidence that the petitioner failed to exercise their rights of custody, but the test is stringent.[98] In applying the "failure to exercise" defense, the facts will be liberally construed to find an exercise of custody rights whenever a parent keeps, or seeks to keep, any sort of regular contact with their child, provides financial support, or otherwise demonstrates they have not abandoned their custodial role.[99]

Wrongful Retention or Removal

Article 3 of the Convention defines a wrongful removal and does not require that an actual custody order has been entered. A removal or retention is wrongful where: (1) it is in breach of rights of custody attributed to a person . . . either jointly or alone, under the law of the state in which the child was habitually resident immediately before the removal or retention; and (2) at the time of removal or retention those rights were actually exercised, either jointly or alone, or would have been so exercised but for the removal or retention.[100]

Defenses to Return

Once the petitioner establishes a prima facie case for return because the child was wrongfully removed or retained from the place of habitual residence, the court must order return unless the respondent establishes one of the affirmative defenses stated in the Convention. The burden of proof varies with the defense. The exceptions are intended to be construed and applied very narrowly to effectuate the objectives of the Convention.[101] Even if an exception is established, the court has the discretion to order the return of a child if return would further the aims of the Hague Convention.[102]

Acquiescence

Article 13a of the Convention and ICARA provide that the court is not bound to order the return of the child if the respondent establishes by a preponderance of the evidence that the petitioner "consented to or subsequently acquiesced in the removal or retention" of the child. Acquiescence requires "either an act or statement with the requisite formality, such as testimony in a judicial proceeding; a convincing written renunciation of rights; or a consistent attitude of acquiescence over a significant period of time."[103]

Child Is Settled in New Environment

Article 12 provides that if a Hague proceeding is commenced within one year after the wrongful retention, the child will be returned "forthwith." If the proceeding is commenced after one year, the judicial or administrative authority shall also order return unless it is demonstrated that the child is settled in the new environment.[104] The one-year period runs from the date of the wrongful retention or removal. That is the date that the parent's actions were so unequivocal that the left-behind parent knew or should have known the other parent was not going to return the child.[105] The respondent has the burden of proving that the child is settled. The court looks at the age of the child, the stability of the child's new residence, whether the child attends school of day care consistently, whether child attends church regularly, the stability of the parent's employment, whether the child has friends of relatives in the area, the extent that the child has maintained ties to the habitual residence, active measures to conceal the child, and immigration status of the child and parent.[106]

If a party fails to file within the one-year period, the court may choose not to return the child.[107] On the other hand, the Supreme Court found that Article 12 is not a statute of limitations.[108] The return remedy, however, remains available after the one year; if the child is not "well settled" in the new place. This can happen when the child is young, not in school, and lacks ties to the community.[109]

Grave Risk of Harm

Article 13(b) allows a court to not return a child if there is a "grave risk that his or her return would expose the child to physical or psychological harm or otherwise place the child in an intolerable situation." At the evidentiary hearing, the respondent has the burden of proving by clear and convincing evidence that an Article 13b defense applies.[110] One federal court distinguished the 13b defenses as follows:

> [A]t one end of the spectrum are those situations where repatriation might cause inconvenience or hardship, eliminate certain educational or economic opportunities, or not comport with the child's preferences; at the other end of the spectrum are those situations in which the child faces a real risk of being hurt, physically or psychologically, as a result of repatriation. The former do not constitute a grave risk of harm under Article 13(b); the latter do.[111]

As stated in Friedrich v. Friedrich, 78 F.3d 1060 (1996):

> First, there is a grave risk of harm when return of the child puts the child in imminent danger prior to the resolution of the custody dispute—e.g., returning the child to a zone of war, famine, or disease. Second, there is a grave risk of harm in cases of serious abuse or neglect, or extraordinary emotional dependence, when the court in the country of habitual residence . . . may be incapable or unwilling to give the child adequate protection.

Most courts have rejected psychological harm alone as a basis for not returning a wrongfully retained child.[112] A court did find the child's psychological well-being was threatened by evidence of petitioner's escalating violence, including choking the mother who had the child in her arms at the time.[113] Courts have recognized that the Article 13(b) defense poses a mixed question of law and fact.[114] The parent alleging the offense must produce credible evidence that the petitioning parent has subjected the child to grave risk of abuse or the child will be returned.[115]

Serious concerns have arisen because large numbers of abductors have turned out to be women victims of domestic violence fleeing abusive situations. The courts have considered whether the child was abused or only the spouse, the nature and frequency of abuse, and the likelihood of its recurrence.[116] Courts also looked to see if there were ameliorative measures that could be undertaken to protect the child if the child were returned. The Hague Conference on Private International Law in 2020 issued an *HCCH: Guide to Good Practice on Article 13(1)(b).* The Guide aims to "promote . . . the proper and consistent application of the grave risk exception in accordance with the terms and purpose of the 1980 Convention." The Guide provides advice for good practices for parties, practitioners, courts, and central authorities to offer more uniform responses to allegations of domestic violence.[117]

The U.S. Supreme Court answered a question about the presence of domestic violence, the "grave risk" defense, and whether a court has to look at all ameliorative measures before denying return of the child. An Italian father had successfully petitioned for return of his child to Italy, the child's habitual residence. The mother presented undisputed evidence of the father's abusive conduct that could expose the child to a grave risk of harm. The Supreme Court noted that the Hague Convention is premised on the idea that it is in the best interests to have custody determined by the habitual residence of a child. Where abuse takes place in front of the child, it may not be the case. The lower court has broad discretion to deny a child's return to a foreign country if the return could pose a grave risk of harm without exploring ameliorative measures. The court may decline to consider ameliorative measures not raised by the parties that are unworkable, draw the court into the merits of the custody proceeding, or risk overly prolonging return proceedings.[118]

Mature Child Objection

A court is not bound to order the return of the child if the respondent demonstrates by a preponderance of the evidence that the child objects to being returned and has reached an age or maturity where it is appropriate to take the child's views into account.[119] A preference to stay with a parent in a country is not the same as an objection to being returned.[120] The court has wide discretion as to whether the child's age and maturity qualify. Teenagers have better luck than younger children.[121] Many courts, however, have found that 11- and 12-year-old children may be old and mature enough to object to their return.[122] Courts also have great discretion as to what weight to give the preference even if the child is of sufficient age and maturity.[123]

Human Rights and Fundamental Freedoms

A court is not bound to return the child if respondent demonstrates by clear and convincing evidence that the return of the child would not be permitted by U.S. fundamental principles regarding protection of human rights and fundamental freedoms. Article 20.[124] This defense is seldom used. The Fifth Circuit reviewed the history of Article 20 in the Elisa Perez-Vera Report, which states that it is concerned only with the principles accepted by the law of the requested state, either through general international law and treaty law, or through internal legislation. It is not to be used to litigate custody on the merits or passing judgment on the political system of the country from which the child was removed.[125] A mother brought an action against the father seeking return of her children to Mexico. The lower court found that the mother's inability to go with her two special needs children to school because of work led to them not getting an education. This violated the Universal Declaration of Human Rights, the Individuals with Disabilities Education Act, and the Texas Constitution. On appeal, the Fifth Circuit found the father did not establish either an Article 20 or a grave risk of harm by clear and convincing evidence and ordered the children returned to Mexico.[126]

Costs and Fees

No costs and fees may be imposed on an applicant in relation to administrative processing of applications. Petitioners may be required to pay the costs of legal counsel, court costs, and transportation costs related to return of the child, unless covered by legal aid or ordered by the court to be paid by respondent. Under ICARA, attorney fees and costs are to be awarded to the prevailing petitioner unless the respondent can show that the award could be "clearly inappropriate."[127] The petitioner's costs can include court costs, legal costs, costs of foster or other care during proceedings, and transportation costs related to the child's return. The district courts have broad discretion to determine when an award of attorney fees is appropriate.[128] The court can consider whether a fee award would impose such financial hardship that it would significantly impair the ability to care for the child and whether the respondent had a good faith belief that her actions in removing the child were justified.[129] A court does have the authority to order fees and costs even if the child turns 16 after the return order was given.[130]

Endnotes

1. Stonham v. Widiastuti a/k/a Stonham, 79 P.3d 1188, 1194 (Wyo. 2003).

2. Washington Declaration on International Family Relocation, Mar. 23–25 2010, reaffirmed Apr. 2025.

3. S v. Z Leave to Remove [2012] EWHC 846 (fam), [2012] 2 FLR 581.

4. *In re* Marriage of Nurie, 98 Cal. Rptr. 3d 200 (Ct. App. 2009).

5. MacKinnon v. MacKinnon, 922 A.2d 1252 (N.J. 2007) (Japan); *In re* Marriage of Condon, 62 Cal. Rptr. 2d 33 (Ct. App. 1998) (Australia); Hayes v. Gallacher, 972 P.2d 1138 (Nev. 1999) (Japan); Arnold v. Arnold, 847 A.2d 674 (Pa. Super. Ct. 2004).

6. Haig v. Agee, 453 U.S. 280, 306 (1981) (distinguishing the right to interstate travel from the freedom to travel internationally).

7. Janet Leach Richards, *Children's Rights v. Parents' Rights: A Proposed Solution to the Custodial Relocation Conundrum*, 29 N.M. L. Rev. 245, 265 (1999).

8. Political and cultural considerations are important. Thirty countries in Africa, Asia, and the Middle East still practice female genital mutilation as of 2024. Others allow violence against women, have laws favoring fathers, or do not allow women to get an education or pursue careers. A dictator may deny its citizens the freedoms and rights guaranteed in the United States Constitution.

9. Linda D. Elrod, *National and International Momentum Builds for More Child Focus in Relocation Disputes*, 44 Fam. L.Q. 341 (Fall 2010) (discussing trends in both national and international relocation standards).

10. *See* Patrick Parkinson, Judy Cashmore & Judi Single, *The Need for Reality Testing in Relocation Cases*, 44(1) Fam. L.Q. 1 (2010).

11. *Id.*

12. *See* Ann Laquer Estin, International Family Law Desk Book, Ch. 5 (ABA 2d ed. 2016). The Protection of Children Convention applies to children from birth to 18 and to proceedings concerning attribution and restriction of parental responsibility; rights of custody, including rights to care and determine the child's place of residence; rights of access to take child to place other than habitual residence; guardianship; designation of functions for person having charge of child's property or representing child; placement of child in a foster family or institutional care; and supervision by public authority.

13. *In re* Marriage of Long & Borrello, 421 P.3d 989 (Wash. Ct. App. 2018).

14. *See* Baz v. Patterson, 100 F.4th 854 (7th Cir. 2024).

15. *See* Johnson v. Johnson, 493 S.E.2d 668 (Va. Ct. App. 1997).

16. Estin, *supra* note 12. *See also* David Hodson, A Practical Guide to International Family Law (2008); Jeremy D. Morely, International Family Law Practice (2009); Stephen Cullen, *International Families and Litigation*, 43(2) Fam. Advoc. 26 (2020).

17. *See* Maryl Sattler, Note, *The Problem of Parental Relocation: Closing the Loophole on the Law of International Child Abduction*, 67 Wash. & Lee L. Rev. 1709 (2010).

18. Even signatory countries vary in their record, speed of compliance, and enforcement. The Abduction Convention has no mechanism for enforcing custody orders abroad. Compliance reports with the Convention are available on the U.S. Dep't of State website.

19. Jeffrey Kofman, Christine Brouwer & Sonia Gallego, *David Goldman Is Reunited with Son Sean in Brazil: The Five-Year Custody Battle over a 9-Year-Old Boy Ends*, ABC News, Dec. 22, 2009, https://abcnews.go.com/GMA/david-goldman-reunited-son-sean-brazil/story?id=9414986.

20. The concept of exclusive, continuing jurisdiction may conflict with the jurisdictional rules in another country. Under the UCCJEA, a state in the United States may retain jurisdiction to modify its child-custody determination as long as one contestant remains in the state and the child has some ties there. It only loses jurisdiction when all parties have left the state, even if the child and a parent have a new "home state." A court in another country, however, that is the child's habitual residence will also have jurisdiction to modify the order issued in the United States.

21. Int'l Judicial Conference on Cross-Border Family Relocation, *Washington Declaration on International Family Relocation*, Mar. 25, 2010, http://www.hcch.net/upload/decl_washington2010e.pdf (*Washington Declaration*). *See also* Elrod, *supra* note 9 (includes discussion of the Washington Declaration).

22. *See In re* Marriage of Fedorov, 206 P.3d 1124 (Or. Ct. App. 2009) (denying mother's proposed relocation with child to Australia because father-daughter relationship would be significantly harmed).

23. Martinez v. Kurt, 9 So. 3d 54 (Fla. Dist. Ct. App. 2009) (mother's desire to relocate from Istanbul to Antalya, which did not have English-speaking schools, was not a substantial change in circumstances where parties' agreement provided that children will attend full-time English-speaking private school in Turkey).

24. Or. Rev. Stat. § 107.102. *See In re* Marriage of Fedorov, 206 P.3d 1124 (Or. Ct. App. 2009).

25. *See* Estin, *supra* note 12, at chs. 5 & 6.

26. Robert G. Spector, *International Abduction of Children: Why the UCCJEA Is Usually a Better Remedy Than the Abduction Convention*, 49(3) Fam. L.Q. 385 (2015).

27. Dickson v. Dickson, 169 So. 3d 287 (Fla. Dist. Ct. App. 2015).

28. *See* Michael R. Walsh & Susan W. Savard, *International Child Abduction and the Hague Convention*, 6 Barry L. Rev. 29, 59 (2006).

29. *See* Patricia Hoff, *"UU" UCAPA: Understanding and Using UCAPA to Prevent Child Abduction,"* 41 Fam. L.Q. 1 (2007). *See also* Janet Johnston & Linda Girdner, *Family Abductors: Descriptive Profiles and Preventative Interventions* (U.S. Dep't of Justice, OJJDP 2001 NCJ 182788); ABA, Early Identification of Risk Factors for Parental Abduction (NCJ185026).

30. *See* Ark. Stat. Ann. § 9-13-401-407; Cal. Fam. Code § 3408. Fla. Stat. § 61.45; Or. Rev. Stat. § 109.035; Tex. Fam. Code §153.501–153.503.

31. *Uniform Child Abduction Prevention Act (Statutory Text, Comments and Unofficial Annotations by Linda D. Elrod, Reporter*)*, 41 Fam. L.Q. 23 (2007) [UCAPA article]. Twenty states have enacted UCAPA, and other states have cited it in opinions.

32. *Id. See also* Hoff, *supra* note 29.

33. Kostreva v. Kostreva, 976 N.W.2d 889 (Mich. Ct. App. 2021).

34. *See* Uniform Child Custody Jurisdiction and Enforcement Act § 108 and § 205. States do not require personal jurisdiction of the parents to make a child-custody determination.

35. Cal. Fam. Code. § 3408.

36. *See* UCAPA article, *supra* note 31, at 47–48.

37. *See* Wiencko v. Takayama, 745 S.E.2d 168 (Va. Ct. App. 2013) (court awarded the mother custody of four boys, prohibited her from traveling to her native Japan with the children, but did not impose other international travel restrictions because she had become a citizen and resided here for over 20 years). *See also* Linda D. Elrod, *Japan Joins Hague Abduction Convention*, 48 Fam L.Q. 351 (2014).

38. *See* Lehn v. Al-Thanayyan, 438 P.3d 646 (Ariz. Ct. App. 2019) (using UCAPA). *See also* Linda D. Elrod, Child Custody Practice and Procedure § 15:17 (2024).

39. 8 U.S.C. § 1185(b). *See* http://travel.state.gov/passport/get/minors/minors_834.html.

40. Mitchell v. Mitchell, 311 S.E.2d 456, 457–59 (Ga. 1984) (trial court had discretion to prohibit obtaining passports; father would have no legal recourse if mother took children back to United Arab Emirates).

41. Messier v. Messier, 389 S.W.3d 904 (Tex. App.-Houston 2012) (mother wanted to return to Hong Kong, allegedly killed the family's pet bird, and psychiatrists found her to be self-centered, narcissistic, and manipulative).

42. Gopalan v. Marsh, 706 S.W.3d 650 (Tex. Ct. App. 2025) (father from India was required to post a $250,000 bond before traveling internationally with the child because he had threatened to take the child to India and had emotional and family connections there).

43. 22 C.F.R. § 51.27(b).

44. 8 U.S.C. § 1101(3). https://travel.state.gov/content/childabduction/en/preventing/passport-issuance-alert-program.html.

45. Sean and David Goldman International Child Abduction Prevention and Return Act of 2014, Pub. L. No. 113-150. tit. III.

46. Kamal v. Imroz, 759 N.W.2d 914, 919 (Neb. 2009) (trial court did not abuse its discretion in restricting child's travel out of country, when prohibition was not absolute and father once took child out of state without informing mother); Katare v. Katare, 283 P.3d 546 (Wash. 2012) (because father presented serious risk of absconding to India with children, trial court had statutory ground for imposing travel and passport access restrictions).

47. Ahmad v. Naviwala, 762 N.Y.S.2d 125 (App. Div. 2003) (father took the children to Saudi Arabia for a three-month visit, then refused to return them and denied the mother all contact).

48. Morrisey v. Morrisey, 45 A.3d 102 (Del. Sup. 2012) (father wanted approval to take children to Jamaica).

49. Abouzahr v. Matera-Abouzahr, 824 A.2d 268 (N.J. Super. Ct. App. Div. 2003).

50. Safdar v. Aziz, 992 N.W.2d 913 (Mich. Ct. App. 2022) (finding child had an established custodial environment with the father that would be altered and move was not in child's best interests).

51. *In re* Marriage of Condie, 475 P.3d 993 (Wash. Ct. App. 2020).

52. Hale v. Hale, 2025 WL 271165 (Tex. Ct. App. 2025) (fact that mother had emigrated from Russia did not show any risk of abduction justifying imposing prevention measures where she had not denied father access and was employed in the United States).

53. *See In re* Marriage of Badawiyeh, 528 P.3d 194 (Colo. Ct. App. 2023) (even though the father was traveling to a non-Hague country, the court did not find a credible risk of abduction based on mother's fear alone); *In re* Rix, 20 A.3d 326, 329 (N.H. 2011) (trial court did not abuse discretion in permitting father to vacation with child in India, a non-Hague Convention country, in part, when mother's evidence gave no indication father intended to flee with child and not return); Puran v. Murray, 829 N.Y.S.2d 227, 228 (App. Div. 2007) (family court permitted father to take child to home country of Guyana when mother offered no proof father threatened to abscond with the child).

54. Waliagha v. Kaiser, 989 So. 2d 660 (Fla. Dist. Ct. App. 2008) (reversing travel restrictions and holding trial court erred in relying on facts gleaned from Consular Information Sheet and State Department Travel Warning not in evidence).

55. *In re* Marriage of Saheb v. Khazal, 880 N.E.2d 537 (Ill. App. Ct. 2007).

56. Richard A. Warshak, *In a Land Far Away: Assessing Children's Best Interests in International Relocation Cases,* 10 J. Child Custody 295 (2013).

57. *See* Nicola Taylor and Marilyn Freeman, *International Research Evidence on Relocation, Past, Present and Future,* 44 Fam. L.Q. 317 (2010); Matheu D. Nunn & Jeralyn L. Lawrence, *Child Relocation: Case Law, Social Science, and Practice Implications,* 32 J. Am. Acad. Matrimonial L. 383

(2022) (summarizing the recent research on shared parenting and on risks of relocation generally). Two California cases sparked the increase in social science research: *In re Marriage of Burgess*, 913 P.2d 473 (Cal. 1996) (importance of continuing bond with the custodial parent) and *In re Marriage of LaMusga*, 88 P.3d 81 (Cal. 2004) (custodial parent did not have to prove move was necessary but court could consider impact on nonmoving parent and child relationship).

58. *In re* Marriage of Rostrom, 339 P.3d 185 (Wash. Ct. App. 2014) (allowing mother who was more stable parent to relocate to Australia with children ages 11 and 6 to marry father of unborn child where children's father had alcohol problem).

59. White v. Malecki, 296 A.3d 1210 (Pa. Super. Ct. 2023).

60. *See also* Philip M. Stahl, *Emerging Issues in Relocation Cases*, 25 J. Am. Acad. Matrim. Law. 425, 441 (2013) (noting that courts need to be open to the particular facts within each family that will help determine the risk and protective factors for the child).

61. *Washington Declaration*, *supra* note 21.

62. U.N. Convention on the Rights of the Child, art. 12, G.A. Res. 44/25, U.N. GAOR, 44th Sess., U.N. Doc. A/Res/44/25 (1989) [CRC], 28 I.L.M. 1448, 1461 (1989).

63. Art. 13b, para. 2 of Hague Convention on the Civil Aspects of International Child Abduction (Oct. 25, 1980), T.I.A.S. No. 11,670, 1343 U.N.T.S. 89 [Hague Abduction Convention]; International Child Abduction Remedies Act (ICARA), 22 U.S.C. §§ 9001 *et seq. See* Linda D. Elrod, *"Please Let me Stay:" Hearing the Voice of the Child in Hague Abduction Cases*, 63 Okla. L. Rev. 663 (2011).

64. Lenz. v. Lenz, 79 S.W.3d 10 (Tex. 2002) (allowing mother to move to native Germany where both children had strong ethnic and cultural ties to Germany, maintained strong relationships with extended family on both sides, would benefit from their mother's increased well-being, and could still maintain frequent contact with their father). *See* Abargil v. Abargil, 131 Cal. Rptr. 2d 429 (Ct. App. 2003) (upholding order allowing a custodial mother to relocate to Israel with her five-year-old son where she had returned to care for dying mother and was unable to return to the United States for ten years; father was applying for permanent residency and could not leave).

65. J.M. v. G. H., 175 Cal. Rptr. 3d 371 (Ct. App. 2014).

66. Miller v. Miller, 88 N.E.3d 843 (Mass. 2018).

67. Ainsworth v. Ainsworth, 186 A.3d 1074 (R.I. 2018).

68. *Id.* at 1080.

69. Lecaros v. Lecaros, 7 N.Y.S.3d 490 (App. Div. 2015) (remitting case for post relocation visitation schedule).

70. Tow v. Tow, 64 A.3d 128, 132 (Conn. App. Ct. 2013).

71. Matthew M. Stevenson et al., *Associations Between Parental Relocation Following Separation in Childhood and Maladjustment in Adolescence and Young Adulthood*, 24 Psychol. Pub. Pol'y & L. 365 (2018).

72. *In re* Marriage of Wehr, 267 P.3d 1045 (Wash. Ct. App. 2011).

73. Forrestel v. Forrestel, 3 N.Y.S.3d 483 (App. Div. 2015).

74. Wilson v. Wilson, 560 P.3d 1126 (Idaho 2024).

75. Leslie Ellen Shear & Leslie M. Drozd, *To Speak of All Kinds of Things: Child Custody Evaluations and the Unique Characteristics of Relocations to Foreign Countries*, 10 J. Child Custody 325 (2013) (in depth discussion of differences that need to be recognized).

76. *See* Osmanagic v. Osmanagic, 872 A. 2d 897 (Vt. 2005) (allowing mother to relocate with child to Bosnia over father's objections, noting trial court was not required to consider the jurisdictional problems); MacKinnon v. MacKinnon, 922 A.2d 1252 (N.J. 2007) (allowing mother to relocate with child to Japan and assumed the mother would follow the court's visitation order).

77. *See also* Jeremy D. Morley, *The Impact of Foreign Law on Child Custody Determinations*, 10 J. Child Custody 209 (2013).

78. *See* Baz v. Patterson, 100 F.4th 854 (7th Cir. 2024), *cert. denied*.

79. Abargil v Abargil, 131 Cal. Rptr. 2d 429 (Ct. App. 2003). *See also In re* Marriage of Condon, 73 Cal. Rptr. 2d 33 (Ct. App. 1998) (listing the numerous problems posed by international relocation cases). *See* Sattler, *supra* note 17, at 1726–28 (discussing *Condon* and restrictions).

80. *In re* Marriage of Lasich, 121 Cal. Rptr. 2d 356 (Ct. App. 2002) (allowing move from California to Spain).

81. Haines v. Vogel, 249 A.3d 151 (Md. Ct. Spec. App. 2021) (father failed to allege he experienced emotional distress as result of mother's conduct). *But see* Khalifa v. Shannon, 945 A.2d 1244 (Md. Ct. App. 2008) (punitive damages where mother intentionally interfered with father's custody and visitation); Stewart v. Walker, 5 So. 3d 746 (Fla. Dist. Ct. App. 2009) (unwed father had standing to claim intentional infliction of emotional distress).

82. New Jersey v. Froland, 874 A.2d 568 (N.J. Super. Ct. App. Div. 2005), *aff'd in part, rev'd in part*, 936 A.2d 947 (N.J. 2008); State v. Adler, 1743783 (Minn. Ct. App. 2011) (unpublished) (mother convicted of interfering the father's custody rights).

83. *See* Anne-Marie Hutchinson et al., International Parental Child Abduction 3–5 (1998).

84. Hague Abduction Convention, art. 4. *See* Bourdelais v. Bourdelais, 844 F. App'x 910 (7th Cir. 2021) (Convention no longer applied where child over 16).

85. Acosta v. Acosta, 725 F.3d 868 (8th Cir. 2013). *See also* Linda D. Elrod, *The Global Effort to Deter Parental Kidnapping: A History of the Hague Abduction Convention*, *in* Research Handbook on International Child Abduction (Marilyn Freeman & Nicola Taylor eds., 2023).

86. *See* Linda Silberman, *Hague Convention on International Child Abduction: A Brief Overview and Case Law Analysis*, 28 Fam. L.Q. 9 (1994).

87. Chafin v. Chafin, 568 U.S. 165, 168 (2013).

88. Fed. Reg. 10494 (Mar. 26, 1986) contains a detailed legal analysis of the Child Abduction Convention by the State Department.

89. Section 4(b). 22 U.S.C. § 9003(b).

90. *See* Egervary v. Rooney, 80 F. Supp. 2d 491 (E.D. Pa. 2000).

91. People v. Coulthard, 307 Cal. Rptr. 3d 383 (Ct. App. 2023).

92. *See* Monaksy v. Taglieri, 589 U.S. 68 (2020).

93. Harm v. Lake-Harm, 16 F.4th 450 (5th Cir. 2021) (many conflicting facts but no clear error in district judge's findings and young child's habitual residence was United States, not Ireland).

94. *See* Smith v. Smith, 976 F.3d 558 (5th Cir. 2020) (habitual residence in the United States); Rishmawy v. Vergara, 540 F. Supp. 3d 1246 (S.D. Ga. 2021) (child's habitual residence was still in Honduras); Babcock v. Babcock, 503 F. Supp. 3d 862 (S.D. Iowa 2022) (Canada remained habitual residence where parties had no clear intent to abandon it).

95. Tsuruta v. Tsuruta, 620 F. Supp. 3d 942 (E.D. Mo. 2022).

96. Palencia v. Perez, 921 F.3d 1333 (11th Cir. 2019). *See also* Ann Laquer Estin, *Where Is the Child at Home? Determining Habitual Residence After* Monasky, 54 FAM. L.Q. 127 (2020).

97. *See* Abbott v. Abbott, 560 U.S. 1, 10 (2010); Harm v. Lake-Harm, 16 F.4th 450 (5th Cir. 2021).

98. Lopez v. Bamaca, 455 F. Supp. 3d 76 (D. Del. 2020) (father had not clearly and unequivocally abandoned the child); Baxter v. Baxter, 423 F.3d 363 (3d Cir. 2005).

99. Sampson v. Sampson, 975 P.2d 1211 (Kan. 1999).

100. Mozes v. Mozes, 239 F.3d 1067, 1070 (9th Cir. 2001).

101. *See* Rydder v. Rydder, 49 F.3d 369, 372 (8th Cir. 1995).

102. *See* Miller v. Miller, 240 F.3d 392, 402 (4th Cir. 2001); England v. England, 234 F.3d 268, 270–71 (5th Cir. 2000).

103. *See* Friedrich v. Friedrich, 78 F.3d at 1070 (6th Cir. 1996). *See* Fernandez v. Yeager, 121 F. Supp. 2d 1118 (W.D. Mich. 2000); Bromley v. Bromley, 30 F. Supp. 2d 857 (E.D. Pa. 1998).

104. *See* Lops v. Lops, 140 F.3d 927 (11th Cir. 1998).

105. Lopez Moreno v. Zank, 456 F.3d 904 (W.D. Mich. 2020).

106. Monzon v. De La Roca, 910 F.3d 92, 105 (3d Cir. 2018).

107. Luis Alfonso V.H. v. Banessa Cristina A.Z., 512 F. Supp. 3d 633 (W.D. Va. 2021) (not returning child where father did not file within a year); de Jesus Joya Rubio v. Alvarez, 526 F. Supp. 3d 1186 (S.D. Fla. 2021) (child was well settled where father did not file until 15 months).

108. Lozano vs. Montoya Alvarez, 572 U.S. 1 (2014).

109. De Carvalho v. Carvalho Pereira, 308 So. 3d 1078 (Fla. Dist. Ct. App. 2020).

110. Hague Abduction Convention, art. 13 b.

111. Mendez Lynch v. Mendez Lynch, 220 F. Supp. 2d 1347, 1365 (M.D. Fla. 2002).

112. *See* England v. England, 234 F.3d 268 (5th Cir. 2000) (mother argued unsuccessfully that the children would be subject to psychological harm if returned to Australia).

113. *In re* M.U., 178 N.E.3d 754, 764 (Ill. App. Ct. 2020).

114. *See, e.g.*, da Silva v. de Aredes, 953 F.3d 67, 72 (1st Cir. 2020); Salame v. Tescari, 29 F.4th 763, 767 (6th Cir. 2022); Acosta v. Acosta, 725 F.3d 868, 874 (8th Cir. 2013); Silva v. Dos Santos, 68 F.4th 1247, 1253 (11th Cir. 2023).

115. Nowlan v. Nowlan, 543 F. Supp. 3d 324 (W.D. Va. 2021) (mother failed to show father had subjected child to abuse).

116. *See* Tabacchi v. Harrison, 2000 WL 190576 (N.D. Ill. 2000) (father's abusive conduct toward the mother was not a sufficient reason to deny return of the daughter). *See* Merle Weiner, *International Child Abduction and the Escape from Domestic Violence*, 69 Fordham L. Rev. 593 (2000).

117. *See* Kevin Puckett, *Hague Convention on International Child Abduction: Can Domestic Violence Establish the Grave Risk Defense Under Article 13?*, 30 J. Acad. Matrim. L. 259 (2017); Brian Quillen, *The New Face of International Child Abduction: Domestic-Violence Victims and Their Treatment Under the Hague Convention on the Civil Aspects of International Child Abduction*, 49 Tex. Int'l L.J. 621 (2014); Shani M. King, *The Hague Convention and Domestic Violence: Proposals for Balancing the Policies of Discouraging Child Abduction and Protecting Children from Domestic Violence*, 47 Fam. L.Q. 299 (2013).

118. Golan v. Saada, 596 U.S. 666, 142 S. Ct. 1880, 1888–92 (2022). *See* Molshree "Molly" A. Sharma, Golan v. Saada*: Protecting Domestic Abuse Survivors in International Child Custody Disputes*, 56 Fam. L.Q. 251 (2022–23).

119. *See* Linda D. Elrod, *"Please Let Me Stay": Hearing the Voice of the Child in Hague Abduction Cases*, 63 Okla. L. Rev. 663 (2011).

120. *See* Custodio v. Samillan, 842 F.3d 1084 (8th Cir. 2016); Rodriguez v. Yanez, 817 F.3d 466 (5th Cir. 2016) (a preference is not an objection); Vite-Cruz v. Sanchez, 360 F. Supp. 3d 346 (D.S.C. 2018); Hazbun Escaf v. Rodriguez, 200 F. Supp. 2d 603 (E.D. Va. 2002).

121. De Silva v. Pitts, 481 F.3d 1279 (10th Cir. 2007) (finding teenage boy's "considered decision" to stay with father in Oklahoma was appropriate basis to deny mother's Hague return request).

122. Rodriguez v. Yanez, 817 F.3d 466 (5th Cir. 2016) (11-year-old mature, remanded to see if objection or preference); Avendano v. Balza, 958 F.3d 8 (1st Cir. 2021) (12-year-old sufficiently mature); de Jesus Joya Rubio v. Alvarez, 526 F. Supp. 3d 1186 (S.D. Fla. 2021) (12-year-old objected to being returned to Mexico); Swett v. Bowe, 733 F. Supp. 3d 225 (S.D.N.Y. 2024) (11-year-old mature enough to object to return to Chile); Davis v. Lake, 647 F. Supp. 3d 482 (W.D. Va. 2022) (11-year-old daughter objected to return to Anguilla where she was doing well in school, was involved in church and school activities and she found her life superior in the United States).

123. Nicholson v. Nicholson, No. 97-1273-JTM, 1997 WL 446432 (D. Kan. July 7, 1997); *In re* Robinson, 983 F. Supp. 1339 (D. Colo. 1997).

124. *See* Tahan v. Duquette, 613 A.2d 486 (N.J. Super. Ct. App. Div. 1992). *See* Merle H. Weiner, *Strengthening Article 20*, 38 U.S.F. L. Rev. 701 (2004); *Using Article 20*, 38 Fam. L. Rev. 583 (2004).

125. Galaviz v. Reyes, 95 F.4th 246, 252–54 (5th Cir. 2024).

126. *Id.* at 262–63.

127. 22 U.S.C. 9007(b)(3). *See* Distler v. Distler, 26 F. Supp. 2d 723 (D.N.J. 1998) (father ordered to pay mother's expenses including the fees charged by Israeli counsel).

128. *See* West v. Dobrev, 735 F.3d 921 (10th Cir. 2013); Whallon v. Lynn, 356 F.3d 138 (1st Cir. 2004).

129. *See* Mendoza v. Silva, 987 F. Supp. 2d 910, 914 (S.D. Iowa 2014) (citing cases). *See* Forcelli v. Smith, 2021 WL 638040 (D. Minn. Feb. 18, 2021) (reducing award of petitioner's attorney fees to $32,000 because they greatly exceeded the other attorney's in same legal market, question of habitual residence was close, and both parties had some bad conduct).

130. Noergaard v. Noergaard, 271 Cal. Rptr. 3d 905, 915 (Ct. App. 2020) *rev. denied; cert. denied.*

CHAPTER 16

Appeal of the Relocation Case

The authority to exercise the judicial discretion [about best interests of the child] is conferred . . . upon the trial court, and . . . we are not privileged to usurp that authority or to substitute ourselves for the trial court.[1]

[A]ppellate courts are in a poor position to look at a cold transcript of the record, and conclude that the trial judge, who saw the witnesses, observed their demeanor, and scrutinized their testimony as it came from the witness stand, did not properly understand the significance of the evidence.[2]

Appeals in relocation cases present unique challenges. Appellate courts rarely reverse a trial judge's decision of a child custody determination, whether in an initial or modification/relocation case. Winning at the trial court level gives the lawyer and client two advantages—not having to contemplate an appeal and a presumption in favor of the trial judge's decision, if the other side chooses to appeal.

As in other family law cases, managing client expectations is crucial. Clients with unrealistic expectations may automatically assume the lawyer will appeal the case. They see the appeal as a chance to relitigate the entire case before the appellate court. The lawyer must explain the appellate rules and procedures, which limit what can be presented on the record as presented at the trial court level. Appellate procedure limits all arguments to what already is reflected in the transcripts and exhibits in the court file. Neither party can call new witnesses or present any new exhibits or evidence.

The appellate judges review the case on the record presented and use formal standards for review. Those standards for judicial review make it difficult to prevail on appeal. Appellate courts give broad discretion to the trial judge to determine a child's best interests. The appellate court will overturn a fact decision only if the trial court abused its discretion.[3] Because the trial judge heard the witnesses and evidence, the appellate courts are only reviewing the record and tend to affirm. A "losing" party may appeal a relocation decision, if he or she believes the trial judge has made substantial errors of fact or law or has abused their discretion.[4] Appellate courts have reversed trial court decisions when the court used the wrong burden of proof,[5] abused its discretion, or failed to consider the statutory (or case) factors. The lawyer must advise the party, however, of the risks of substantial attorney's fees, long delays, and long odds of success before undertaking an appeal.

The lawyer should consider whether the appeal has a reasonable chance of success before encouraging the client to appeal. Effectively presenting an appeal requires as much skill as the initial trial preparation. The lawyer will use research and writing skills, as well as oral advocacy skills. The right to appeal is statutory. Each state has its own statutes and court rules for appellate practice. Usually, the procedural rules governing civil appeals apply to child custody decrees, but lawyers must check local practice. The audience on appeal is usually a panel of appellate judges.

Preparing for a possible appeal requires the lawyer to make a proper record at every stage of the proceedings. Because the appellate court does not hear live testimony, the written record is vital. The lawyer must object at appropriate stages to preserve issues for appeal. Once the trial is over, there is a relatively short window of time in which to file a notice of appeal. Therefore, the lawyer should discuss the possibility of an appeal with the client long before trial.

Deciding Whether to Appeal

Relocation disputes generate extremely strong emotions. An upset client may want to take the case to the highest court and be unrealistic about the chances for success on appeal. Some clients automatically want to appeal any adverse ruling. The lawyer must advise the client about the costs of an appeal and the chances for success. Whether to take an appeal depends on the basis of the appeal—an alleged error of law or a judge's weighing of the facts.

One estimate is that only 16 percent of all reported custody cases are reversed because of two things. First, there is a presumption of correctness in the trial court's judgment. Second, because the "best interests" of the child standard used for custody disputes is vague, the appellate courts give trial judges wide latitude. Most appellate courts refuse to substitute their judgment for that of the trial judge, who saw the witnesses and was able to evaluate credibility, temperament, personalities, and parenting capacities. The usual standard for review for an original decree has been an abuse of the trial court's discretion.[6] As the Indiana Court of Appeals stated:

> In family law matters, appellate courts are in a poor position to look at a cold transcript of the record, and conclude that the trial judge, who saw the witnesses, observed their demeanor, and scrutinized their testimony as it came from the witness stand, did not properly understand the significance of the evidence.[7]

Another court noted that the appellate court would not review the trial court's credibility determinations or weigh conflicting evidence when reviewing a relocation decision.[8] The odds favor upholding the trial judge. One study found close to 90 percent of cases were affirmed on appeal. If there is less than a 50 percent chance for success, the lawyer should probably discourage the client from appealing. In the few states in which the appellate court makes a de novo review of the record, the chances for reversal may be greater.[9]

The client's dissatisfaction with the judgment alone is not a sufficient basis for an appeal. Among the factors to be considered in deciding whether to take or hear the appeal are:

1. The court or panel that will hear the appeal;
2. Precedent in the jurisdiction;
3. Whether the major arguments are based on claims of errors of law or fact;

4. Whether there is a new statute or case in the jurisdiction justifying a change in prior decisions;
5. Any national trends in relocation law;
6. Financial costs of appeal in terms of filing fees, attorney fees, and other costs;
7. Emotional stress of continued litigation on the client and child; and
8. Whether there is a fast-track appeal process.[10]

If the client decides not to appeal, the lawyer should confirm the decision in a written letter. The letter should confirm the discussion between the lawyer and client, that the lawyer advised the client of the right to appeal, and that the client is aware that if a notice of appeal is not filed within the required time period following the order, the right to appeal is lost. The letter should also reflect that the lawyer has advised the client to file a notice of appeal to preserve the right, but the client has decided not to file. This letter should help protect the lawyer from the client changing their mind on the 35th day and "forgetting" that the lawyer mentioned a 30-day appeal time.

Appealable Orders

Appealable orders generally are either final orders or specified nonfinal orders. Each state has its own rules as to when a judgment is final and what orders are appealable. A premature appeal may result in dismissal of the appeal. Generally, if all that remains is implementation of the court's order, the judgment is final. In most civil cases, there must be a journal entry or judgment form filed with the court.

A final order granting or denying a relocation or modification of a custody or visitation order is appealable.[11] If one of the orders allows for relocation, the court may find that it is a final and appealable order, even if there are some remaining divorce issues to be resolved. In one Illinois case, the court found that the order granting father's petition to relocate from Illinois to Virginia was an "allocation of parental responsibilities judgment or modification of such judgment" so it was a final appealable order.[12]

Sometimes the order allowing a relocation is made in conjunction with other orders. An order awarding custody, which is part of a court order resolving all issues in the divorce, is appealable. An order denying a motion to relocate may not be final, however, if there is a counterclaim for a change of custody pending.[13] Some states allow an appeal if the custody order has been made even if there are other issues, such as the property division, pending.

In some states, temporary orders are appealable if certain conditions are met.[14] In other states they are not. If the temporary order is made but the rest of the issues are reserved, the order may not be appealable. A strong argument that temporary custody orders should be appealable, especially in relocation cases, is that if an error has been made, the child's best interests will be furthered by correcting the error as soon as possible. The Connecticut court noted that an otherwise interlocutory order is appealable (1) where the order or action to terminate is a separate and distinct proceeding, or (2) where the order or action so concludes the rights of the parties that further proceedings cannot affect them. The relocating mother should have appealed the temporary order rather than collaterally attacking it by appealing it as part of her appeal of the permanent custody order. The collateral attack was procedurally an impermissible substitute for appeal of a temporary order giving the father primary physical custody.[15] In a Texas case, the court noted that because temporary orders in child custody cases are not subject to interlocutory appeal, mandamus relief would be appropriate if the relator could establish a clear abuse of discretion.[16]

In most states, an order entered by agreement or stipulation is not appealable because the party consented to the order. In addition, judgments entered on a default of the party are not appealable. The appropriate action is to file a motion to open the default judgment or have it set aside. If the application is denied, the lawyer can appeal the denial. Appeals from awards of relocation are taken like appeals in other civil and custody cases.

Waiver of Right of Appeal

As a general rule, the party must raise issues in the trial court before being allowed to appeal a ruling on the issue. By not making the argument in the trial court, a father waived his claim that the trial court, in making its best interests finding in favor of relocation, improperly relied on evidence obtained when mother had relocated the children to the Czech Republic without his consent.[17] Where a father never raised the issue of his constitutional right to travel in the trial court, the appellate court found that he had waived the issue for appellate review.[18] A party may also waive the right to appeal through failure to file a timely notice of appeal, through failure to object at relevant times during the trial, failure to require findings of fact or by acquiescence. The party may lose the right to appeal by not protecting the right or by accepting the benefits of the judgment.

Contemporaneous Objection

The party may lose the right to appeal certain points, if the attorney fails to timely object to the admission of evidence or statements of witnesses.[19] To preserve a point for appeal, the attorney is required to make a contemporaneous objection.[20] Not objecting at the right time can result in denial of the right to appeal on that issue. A father waived his appellate argument that the trial court abused its discretion by admitting into evidence the mother's exhibit, the American Bar Association's (ABA) *Jurisdiction in Child Custody and Abduction Cases: A Judge's Guide to the UCCJA, PKPA, and the Hague Child Abduction Convention*, because he did not object to admission of the exhibit and did not claim the admission of the exhibit was a fundamental error in his brief. In order to preserve the issue of whether the trial court erroneously admitted evidence, he had to make a specific and timely objection.[21]

If the lawyer fails to object to the appointment of a guardian ad litem, the admission of evidence, the credentials of an expert witness, or the admission of hearsay testimony, that issue cannot be raised on appeal. Because the mother did not object to the trial judge having the appellant and her daughters testify by telephone in a relocation custody modification case, the appellate court declined to entertain the issue. The appellate court will not consider an issue raised for the first time on appeal.[22] Additionally, if the lawyer made the objection on the wrong basis, the party may waive the objection on appeal.[23] Facial constitutionality of a statute, however, may be raised for the first time on appeal if the error is fundamental.[24] Additionally, the lack of jurisdiction can be raised for the first time on appeal (see Chapter 3).

Acquiescence

If a party accepts the benefits of a judgment, the party may lose the right to appeal. Acquiescence in the judgment can indicate a waiver of appeal. Acquiescence usually does not arise in the custody context because an appellant's acceptance of spousal support, child support payments, or a distribution of property generally would not be considered an acquiescence in the custody decision. The custody issues can be separated. A court may refuse an appeal because of other conduct of the appellant. In one case, the appellant violated a court decree by hiding the children. The court refused to allow an appeal because of the appellant's reprehensible conduct.[25]

Timeliness

An appeal must be taken within a specified time after the judgment is rendered or the court lacks jurisdiction to hear the case. Statutes or court rules set out the time for appeal, usually 20 to 30 days.[26] If the appeal is not filed within the required days from the entry of an appealable order, it will be dismissed. Therefore, if the client is indecisive, the lawyer may want to file the notice of appeal to preserve the right to appeal should the client so decide. If the client decides not to appeal, the appeal can be withdrawn.

The date of the judgment depends upon local law. Some confusion may arise in ascertaining the date of the entry of judgment. In some jurisdictions, the date of judgment may be the date it is reduced to writing and signed by the judge. In other jurisdictions, the date of entry of judgment is the date of filing a journal entry or a judgment form. In yet others, the relevant date is that of service on the appellant of the copy of the judgment. Failure to comply with the statutory requirements may prevent the time for appeal from running.

The filing of a post-trial motion may extend the time to file a notice of appeal. For example, filing a petition to vacate within 30 days of the judgment of dissolution may extend the normal period for appealing. There may be some confusion if the rules do not specify how much additional time is given to file. An Alabama court found that the mother's appeal was timely where it was filed 35 days after the denial of the later of two post-judgment motions.[27]

A motion to alter or amend a judgment can be made in most states under the state's version of Federal Civil Procedure Rule 59(f). This tolls the time within which an appeal may be taken. A motion to reconsider is treated as a motion to alter or amend the judgment and also tolls the time to appeal the final order. If a motion offers some identifiable reason for reconsidering the judgment, it is properly construed as a motion to reconsider.[28] In other states, filing a motion to reconsider will not stay the 30-day period for filing the notice of appeal. Therefore, the party should file a motion to reconsider and a notice of appeal at the same time. The court, however, may not strictly enforce the time requirements on one party if the other party also has been delinquent or if the party was not aware of the entry of judgment.

Notice of Appeal

Jurisdiction of an appellate court rests upon the law. It cannot be conferred by consent, waiver, or estoppel. Appellate courts obtain jurisdiction only over the rulings specifically designated in the notice of appeal as the ones from which the appeal is being taken. Without proper notice of appeal, the appellate court lacks jurisdiction.[29]

To perfect an appeal, the appellant must file a notice of appeal within the time prescribed by statute or court rule with the clerk of the trial court. The notice invokes the jurisdiction of the appellate court. Some states also require a copy of the notice to be sent to the court from which the appeal was taken. A court may require strict adherence to the procedure, such that mailing a copy of the notice to the clerk of the trial court, instead of filing it, may result in dismissal of the appeal.

The notice of appeal must identify the parties taking the appeal, the court to which the appeal is taken, the orders and judgments being appealed, and the relief sought. If only part of an order is being appealed, it is crucial to specify which part. For example, the client may want to appeal only the post-relocation visitation schedule. Failure to specify that only the visitation schedule is being appealed could result in other issues also being reconsidered on appeal. Some states require the notice to contain the statutory authorization for appeal, counsel's phone number, or other information.

If a bill of exceptions is required, it should specify the decision from which the appeal was taken and the alleged error. If local rule requires other papers to be submitted, such as the documents submitted by the parties and used by the trial court in making its decisions, failure to include those papers may make it impossible for the appellate court to fully review the issues.

Notice of the appeal must be served, as required, on the opposing party. Failure to serve the notice within the allowed time period may result in dismissal of the appeal. In one case, however, where a father was found in contempt, the appellate court reviewed the judgment even though the father's notice of appeal was not timely filed because the filing time constraints were not made clear to him.[30] In some jurisdictions, the appellant may need to file a docketing statement, which sets out the nature of the case, the issues that will be raised, the parties involved, and whether or not the parties anticipate oral arguments. State appellate practice rules dictate whether a docketing statement is required. The docketing statement, unlike the notice of appeal, is not jurisdictional. A court, however, may dismiss an appeal for failure to file the statement if filing is required. In addition, a parent cannot appeal the failure of the trial judge to do something, if the parent did not ask for the relief.

Record on Appeal

The record on appeal must be adequate and without defects for the appellate court to review. The appellant bears the burden to ensure that a sufficient appellate record is presented to show reversible error. If an appellate fails to present a complete record, the appellate court must presume the omitted portions are relevant and support the trial court's judgment. Points of error dependent on the state of the evidence will be deemed to have been waived.

In a Texas case, the mother failed to include the judicial in chamber interviews of the two older children (15 and 14) in the appellate record. The statute provides that the parties are entitled to have a child interview recorded on request if the child is at least 12 years old. The court found the interviews to be evidence and used the missing-record presumption that the interviews contained sufficient evidence to support the trial judge's findings. Father's failure to request record of interviews did not result in a waiver of his argument that mother's appeal should be overruled.[31]

If there was no record made or if the record presented to the appellate court is inadequate, the trial judge's decision may be upheld. On the other hand, a trial court's denial of a mother's petition to relocate for two years without any evidence of a ten-year-old child's preference or allowing the mother to introduce evidence and changing custody to the father required a de novo hearing.[32]

Stay of Execution Pending Appeal

Jurisdictions differ as to whether the trial court's judgment is stayed pending the appeal. Some jurisdictions enforce orders immediately, while others may be stayed until final resolution of an appeal. For example, in some states, property orders are stayed automatically, while orders pertaining to custody and child support are not. In other states, the lawyer may have to ask or move for a stay.

Appellate Brief

As in other civil cases, the appellant must file a brief. Legal briefs are the first, last, and sometimes only impression the lawyer can make with the judges who will decide the appeal.[33] Appellate rules in all jurisdictions set out the technical requirements of the contents and form of a brief. In some states, there may be page limits on appellate briefs.

All briefs must include the facts, procedure, and law. The typical brief has:

- a cover page (different colors depending on if appellant, appellee, or amicus);
- a table of contents;
- a statement of the issues on appeal;
- a table of authorities;
- a statement of the proceedings and facts;
- a statement of the proper standard of review;
- the argument;
- scope of remand;
- conclusions; and sometimes
- an appendix.

The brief should be persuasive, accurate, clear, concise, and forceful. This means it should be well argued and well supported. The statement of facts should be long enough to get the story across yet short enough to hold the reader's attention. There should be a compelling framing of the issues. The points on appeal should be persuasively argumentative. There should be convincing and sound legal argument, supported with correct citations to the record and to authority. The brief should be understandable and interesting, as well as written in plain English. If possible, the lawyer may attach a useful supporting appendix.

Statement of Issues

Many judges read the statement of the issues before reading the rest of the brief. The reader should grasp the issues immediately and feel compelled to answer the question in the client's favor. For example, some use a conventional: "Did the trial court abuse its discretion in allowing mother to relocate to Maine with the child?" A stronger, more dynamic statement of the issue on appeal would be a more specific: "When the father and his ten-year-old son have a loving and supportive relationship with the father being involved in the child's day-to-day activities, did the trial court abuse its discretion in allowing the mother to move the child 500 miles away?"

If possible, the lawyer should try to limit the statement of issues to three questions. Otherwise, the appellate court may think the lawyer is using the "throw everything at the wall and hope something sticks" approach. Too many issues may obscure the strongest ones. The lawyer, however, should pick the main issues. Any issues not covered in the brief may be deemed abandoned. A party abandons a claim on appeal by failing to make a meaningful argument in support of its position.[34] An appellate court can regard an appellee's failure to file an answering brief as a confession of error.[35]

Statement of Facts

The statement of facts should read like an objective presentation of the record, but subtly encourage the reader to decide in the advocate's favor. The brief should present the facts in such an order and with such emphasis that the reader gets the conclusion intended without the brief editorializing or proclaiming what it should be. An introductory summary tells the reader how the statement of facts is organized, usually by topic or chronologically. The statement of facts should avoid overly descriptive adjectives and adverbs such as "clearly," "blatantly," or "incredibly." It should also avoid inflammatory, or emotional, irrelevant information that is not germane to the issues being appealed.

The statement of facts should include details supported by precise and accurate references. Important exhibits and transcript excerpts should be in the appendix. Summary statements that are unsupported by a reference to the record are liable to lack substance and lose credibility if the other side cites conflicting facts with support. The lawyer should present unfavorable facts in a manner that is accurate but understated. If there is a conflict in the evidence, admit it. If the lawyer identifies unfavorable facts and conflicting evidence, the lawyer may gain credibility and control the narrative.

Argument

The argument section is limited by the boundaries of the law, specific procedural requirements (page length, etc.), the record, and decorum. A simple structure works best. The argument starts by explaining what the brief intends to show. It explores relevant law, identifies the evidence in the record that supports or contradicts the position, and concludes by summarizing what has been shown.

If the appeal will be resolved based primarily upon how the appellate court interprets a statute and applies a leading case, then the statute and case should appear in the summary of the argument. Section headings should be argumentative and briefly summarize the client's positions. For example, if the argument is that the trial court lacked jurisdiction under the Uniform Child Custody Jurisdiction and Enforcement Act (UCCJEA) to modify the custody order because another state had continuing, exclusive jurisdiction, then the section heading would be "Jurisdiction under the UCCJEA." The wording can be important if there is a table of contents.

The topic headings should flow together as a persuasive summary. The argument should start with the most compelling legal arguments, not necessarily those selected by the opponent's brief. Within the subheadings, the legal analysis should include the relevant statute and legislative history, if relevant, or the case being applied. The lawyer must apply the existing law to the unique facts of the case. Before turning in the brief, the lawyer should proofread and make sure all of the citations are correct and stand for the proposition the brief says. The Indiana Court of Appeals noted that a brief should not only present the issues to be decided but also be of material assistance to the court in deciding those issues. The brief was not helpful where the appendix did not include the mother's two notices of intent to relocate, contained improper self-serving statements and argument and inappropriate editorializing, and relied on statutory language that had been amended or removed at least three years before the brief was filed.[36] The lawyer should not rely on AI to cite check. Finally, the lawyer should delete the weaker points; they will detract from the strong ones.

Oral Argument

Oral argument is the opportunity to use persuasion either to convince the court that an error has been made or that the trial judge decided the case correctly. The lawyer may need to explain to the client the difference between the trial presentation and an oral argument. The appeal is not a retrial of the initial case. The lawyer is trying to show that the trial judge erred in applying the law or abused its discretion in weighing the facts. If there is applicable adverse authority that is precedent, the lawyer will present it and try to distinguish it. Every case has two sides. Courts are unlikely to overrule, ignore, or modify binding precedent absent extraordinary circumstances. The lawyer is attacking the trial court's rationale, not the judge personally.

Appellate practice rules provide a limited amount of time for the argument, usually 30 minutes, with no breaks. The argument is to a panel. The argument should be structured to win the appeal, not make an impassioned plea. Most appellate judges think the purpose of oral argument is to answer their questions so they can render a decision. In most instances, the panel will have read the brief and come loaded with questions.

The lawyer must be flexible and respond immediately to difficult questions, often without any references to notes. That means the lawyer must know the facts, the record, and both parties' briefs inside and out before starting the argument. Lawyers should carefully select the points from the brief that should be argued. These will be the strongest points and the ones that can be expressed simply. A two-minute opening statement should tell the whole story and move toward the discussion of the points on appeal. The lawyer should also prepare a 30-second closing statement. While flexibility is required throughout, lawyers should rehearse the argument and refine the points so that it flows. Sometimes, the lawyer can actually present the rehearsed argument; other times the lawyer does little but answer questions from the panel.

The actual argument requires the lawyer to use the tools of public speaking—dress appropriately, stand up straight, maintain eye contact with the judges, not read the argument, and speak in a loud and clear voice. Strategic pauses can be used, or heightened volume, if one of the judges appears to be losing interest. The lawyer should be respectful, listening carefully to the questions posed. It is fine to engage in a give and take of ideas if the position taken is different from that of the appellate judge.

Standard of Review

The standard of appellate review depends on the state and the issue involved. For example, in Michigan, a trial court's findings regarding the existence of an established custodial environment and regarding each custody factor will be affirmed unless the evidence clearly preponderates in the opposite direction. An abuse of discretion standard applies to the trial court's discretionary rulings such as custody decisions. Questions of law are reviewed for clear legal error. A trial court commits clear legal error when it incorrectly chooses, interprets, or applies the law.[37]

Appellate courts review most family law decisions using an abuse of discretion standard, which is highly deferential to the trial judge's findings. Appellate courts do not retry the facts, reweigh the evidence, nor substitute their judgment for that of the trial judge.[38] Generally, the appellate courts defer to trial court's factual findings and credibility determinations that are supported by the record. If the court considered the statutory factors in making the factual relocation decision, the abuse of discretion standard applies.[39] The appellate court may not be bound by the court's deductions or inferences, nor is it required to adopt a finding that cannot be sustained with competent evidence.[40] Granting or denying a relocation of a child based on findings that are not supported by competent, substantial evidence constitutes reversible error.[41]

When the motion to reconsider is based on new evidence, the review is abuse of discretion, which occurs when "no reasonable person could agree with the position taken by the trial court." Whether the trial judge erred in denying a motion for a new trial or in making a decision to allow or deny relocation is reviewed for an abuse of discretion.[42]

Generally, review of jurisdictional issues is de novo[43] as is whether the trial court properly applied a statute or court rule.[44] If the question is whether the trial court properly applied the correct legal standard, the review is de novo.[45] A grant of a motion to dismiss is a question of law that the appellate court may review de novo.[46] If the issue is a question of law or question of statutory construction, the standard is less deferential. In some jurisdictions, like New York, the appellate court's authority is as broad as that of the hearing court, and a relocation will not be permitted to stand unless it is supported by a sound and substantial basis in the record.[47]

Sometimes a mixed standard of review applies, for example, the relocation determination may be reviewed on an abuse of discretion standard, but whether the court properly applied the relocation statute is a matter of law, reviewed de novo.[48] Where the trial court has considered the statutory factors in determining if relocation is in the best interest of the child, the appellate court reviews for abuse of discretion. If the trial court failed to consider the statutory factors, that is legal error, and the appellate court makes an independent de novo review.[49]

Abuse of Discretion

Appellate courts review a judge's decision to grant or deny relocation for an abuse of discretion, with a preference for granting latitude and deference to trial judges in family law matters.[50] A child custody determination that does not comport with statutory requisites is an abuse of discretion.[51] In New York, it was an abuse of discretion for a judge to determine whether an out-of-state relocation was in the child's best interests without a full evidentiary hearing.[52] The Washington Court of Appeals found a court abuses its discretion when its decision is manifestly unreasonable, or exercised on untenable grounds or for untenable reasons.[53] A Pennsylvania appellate court found the trial court's custody order making mother responsible for costs of the child's travel between mother's residence in the United States and father's residence in Germany was manifestly unreasonable, especially where mother was receiving social security disability benefits and could not afford the price of international flights.[54]

The trial court's opportunity to observe witnesses is especially important in child custody cases. A mere difference of opinion or judgment cannot justify an appellate court's intervention in child custody proceedings, only a clear abuse of discretion.[55] The presumption of correctness is based in part on the trial court's unique ability to observe the parties and the witnesses and to evaluate their credibility and demeanor.[56] In general, the appellate court does not readily second-guess a trial court's child custody determination because it is the function of the trial court to judge witnesses' credibility and weigh conflicting evidence.[57] The appellate court accepts each factual finding unless a particular finding is manifestly erroneous.[58] A Pennsylvania appellate court summed up the standard of review:

> Our . . . standard is abuse of discretion. We must accept findings of the trial court that are supported by competent evidence of record . . . with regard to issues of credibility and weight of the evidence, we must defer to the presiding trial judge who viewed and assessed the witnesses first-hand. However, we are not bound by the trial court's deductions or inferences from its factual findings. Ultimately, the test is whether the trial court's conclusions are unreasonable as shown by the evidence of record. We may reject the conclusions of the trial court only if they involve an error of law, or are unreasonable in light of the sustainable findings of the trial court.[59]

A judicial abuse of discretion requires that the reasons or rulings of a trial judge be clearly untenable, unfairly depriving a litigant of a substantial right and a just result.[60] Other states defer to the trial court's ultimate ruling unless it is manifestly unreasonable or based on untenable grounds or reasons.[61] A judge will not be found to have abused discretion, if the record contains evidence that the guardian ad litem's recommendations, witness testimony, and a number of exhibits support the judge's decision.[62]

Abuse of discretion is established if the trial court considered improper factors in making its determination, failed to consider statutorily mandated factors,[63] or assigned disproportionate weight to particular factors while ignoring others.[64] If there are several factors to be considered, an appellate court may find that the judge abused its discretion by only considering one—the distance between the parents' homes.[65] Where a father had a history of domestic violence, it was plain error for the court not to address the domestic violence statutory provisions stating that there is rebuttable presumption that a parent who has a history of perpetrating domestic violence against the other parent may not be awarded sole or joint physical custody of the child.[66]

Texas found that public policy provisions in the family code, to assure that children will have frequent and continuing contact with parents and a safe, stable, and nonviolent environment for child, did not support an order permanently enjoining the divorced mother from having the ability to travel outside the continental United States without the father's permission. The injunction went far beyond public policy considerations by permanently restricting the mother's right to travel even to Hawaii, as well as internationally, whether or not she intended to have her child travel with her. The order did not even mention the child.[67] A trial court did not abuse its discretion in permitting the father to vacation with his child in India, a non-Hague Convention country. The mother's evidence gave no indication that the father intended to flee with the child and not return.[68] In another case, the trial court did abuse its discretion in requiring supervised visitation when the father had engaged in planning activities to facilitate the child's removal from the country.[69]

A mother appealed, arguing that the judge did not hear testimony as to the children's preferences, but the appellate court found that if the mother believed that the children's reasonable preferences should have been made known during the hearing, it was her attorney's responsibility to submit evidence of those preferences if the guardian ad litem had not. The court did not have to sua sponte call the children as witnesses.[70] Failure to allow the father to depose children was harmless error where the children testified at trial in father's favor, indicating they wanted to go live with him and attend the private school.[71] On the other hand, the trial court's complete sealing of the child's therapy records and denying father an opportunity to offer proof pertaining to the child's potential testimony in a custody modification was reversible error.[72] In another case where the mother sought a protective order for the daughter based on father's past sexual abuse, the appellate court found a violation of the father's due process rights when trial court conducted an in camera examination but did not allow father to cross-examine the daughter.[73]

Supported by Substantial Evidence

New Jersey and New York require a sound and substantial basis in the record to support the trial judge's decision.[74] An appellate court affirmed a modification of sole legal and primary custody to the father when mother had relocated to Maryland, 250 miles away, with new boyfriend by whom she was pregnant and who had strained relationship with children who wanted to return to New York.[75] In another case, there was substantial evidence to deny mother's relocation request to West Virginia, as the mother showed no improved financial circumstances, child had been attending same school, and mother had given little thought to the impact of the relocation on father's (and extended family's) relationship with the child.[76] A decision lacked substantial evidence where the trial court denied the mother's request to modify the parenting plan and relocate to North Carolina, without resolving the cross-petition of the father to modify and move to Georgia.[77]

A Washington case found that substantial evidence supported the conclusion that the Child Relocation Act factor of children's age, developmental stage, and needs weighed against allowing mother's relocation. The children were eight and ten, one had special needs but was thriving with assistance of professionals, and both children's educational needs were being met.[78]

Missouri appellate courts must affirm the trial court's ruling if it is supported by substantial evidence, is not against the weight of evidence, and does not erroneously declare or apply the law.[79] The court views the evidence in the light most favorable to the circuit court's judgment and defers to the court's credibility determinations.[80] Where the factual findings supported the trial court's determination that mother's relocation was in the son's best interest, the decision was upheld.[81]

Florida appellate courts reviewing an order on a petition to relocate are limited to an abuse of discretion review based on whether the trial court's statutory findings are supported by substantial competent evidence.[82] Where the trial court applied the proper legal standard of best interests of the child, the appellate court found substantial competent evidence to support the denial because of the father's relationship with the children.[83] If there is no transcript of a relocation hearing such that the appellate court is unable to see if there is competent, substantial evidence to support the trial court's finding, the order must be upheld unless it is erroneous as a matter of law.[84]

An Illinois appellate court found that a trial court's decision to deny a mother's removal petition was "against the manifest weight of evidence." The mother was changing a bad job for a good one and the move was in good faith.[85] In another case, however, Illinois found a trial court's decision to allow a father to relocate to Virginia with two children was not against the manifest weight.[86]

The Idaho Supreme Court found that the court had substantial evidence to support its conclusions to allow mother and children to move to Utah, where the mother had family in the Salt Lake area; the children had attended church in Utah and have cousins and acquaintances there; parties had previously discussed a move to Utah; and, the mother would be on welfare if she remained in Idaho.[87] Where, however, the court's findings are contrary to the clear weight of the evidence, the trial court will be reversed.[88]

Clearly Erroneous

Some states may do a de novo review but will only reverse a trial court's decision on a motion to relocate if it is clearly erroneous.[89] In West Virgina, the court of appeals reviews findings of fact under the clearly erroneous standard and the application of law to the facts under an abuse of discretion standard.[90] The North Dakota Supreme Court noted that "a finding is clearly erroneous if it is induced by an erroneous view of the law, there is no evidence to support it, or the Supreme Court is convinced, based on the entire record, that a mistake has been made."[91] The court will not reweigh the evidence, reassess party credibility, retry a custody case, or substitute its judgment for the trial judge.[92] The appellate court weighs the evidence in the light most favorable to the finding. A decision is not clearly erroneous if it is based either on physical or documentary evidence, or an inference from other facts, or on credibility determinations.[93] A conclusion of law that presents mixed questions of fact and law is reviewed under the clearly erroneous standard because the court's conclusions are dependent upon the facts and circumstances of each individual case.[94]

A trial court's findings that the oldest son did not have Asperger's syndrome or other form of autism, that many of his emotional and behavioral problems stemmed primarily from the parties' divorce and custody dispute, and that mother's care of her sons was not endangering their emotional or physical health, were not clearly erroneous. Doctor determined that the oldest son did have some emotional and behavioral problems, but they stemmed primarily from the divorce and the continued struggle over custody. The oldest son's school records showed good grades, and only minor disciplinary concerns.[95]

De Novo

When the appellate court is presented with an issue of law, the court reviews the judgment of the trial court de novo, without affording it any presumption of correctness.[96] In Florida, the appellate court's review of a trial court's interpretation and application of the statute governing parental relocation with a child is de novo.[97] Interpretation of a parenting plan is a question of law that is reviewed de novo in Washington.[98] In Tennessee, the review of the trial court's findings of fact is de novo with a presumption of correctness, unless the evidence preponderates otherwise.[99] For the evidence to preponderate against a trial court's finding of fact, it must support another finding of fact more convincingly.[100] Louisiana evaluates relocation factors de novo, often affirming the trial court.[101]

Whether a decision by the trial court conforms to the law is by definition a question of law. A Louisiana trial judge was reversed for failure to consider any of the statutory factors for determining whether a relocation out of state was in the best interests of the child. There was legal error involved.[102] A court errs as a matter of law when it misapplies the correct legal standard set out in statute.[103] If the statute does not set out the quantum of proof standard for relocation, the standard should be preponderance of the evidence.[104] The trial court improperly applied the clear and convincing standard to a petitioner's request for removal.[105]

Endnotes

1. Noonan v. Noonan, 998 A.2d 231 (Conn. App. Ct. 2010).
2. D.C. v. J.A.C., 977 N.E.2d 951, 956–57 (Ind. 2012).
3. *In re* Salenu S. v. Ahmad G., 58 N.Y.S.3d 35 (App. Div. 2017) (defer to fact finder unless lacks sound and substantial basis in the record).
4. *In re* Marriage of Rostrom, 339 P.3d 185 (Wash. Ct. App. 2014).
5. Aragon v. Aragon, 513 S.W.3d 447 (Tenn. 2017) (reversing trial court for improperly placing the burden of proof on father to show that there was a reasonable purpose for the relocation).
6. Markwood v. Markwood, 274 P.3d 271 (Idaho Ct. App. 2012) (upholding judge allowing mom and two daughters to move to Oregon where mother was to be married); LaGraize v. Filson, 171 So. 3d 1047 (La. Ct. App. 2015).
7. Jarrell v. Jarrell, 5 N.E.3d 1186 (Ind. Ct. App. 2014).
8. *In re* Marriage of Rostrom, 339 P.3d 185 (Wash. Ct. App. 2014). *See also* Julie E. v. David E., 1 N.Y.S.3d 431 (App. Div. 2015) (upholding trial court's denial of mother's move with children from New York to Texas).
9. *In re* Marriage of Hoffman, 867 N.W.2d 26 (Iowa 2015) (petition to modify custody lie in equity and review is de novo). *But see* Smith v. Smith, 661 S.W.3d 273 (Ark. App. 2023) (court did de novo review and upheld the trial court allowing mother to move).
10. Brokaski v Brokaski, No. 70865, 2017 WL 946325 (Nev. Ct. App. Mar. 6, 2017) (unpublished) (fast track appeal affirming trial court order modifying order to joint physical custody and denying mother's motion to relocate to Denver).
11. Zihala v. Staley, 689 S.W.3d 82 (Ark. Ct. App. 2024) (court's order denying mother's motion to relocate was intermediate order that could be raised on appeal of final divorce decree); Wardell v. Hincka, 822 N.W.2d 278 (Mich. Ct. App. 2012) (once a trial court issues an order denying a motion to change custody, the order is final and triggers the right to an appeal).
12. *In re* Marriage of Fatkin, 129 N.E.3d 1230 (Ill. 2019) (mother would not see the children for one-third of the year instead of every day).
13. Kines v. McBride, 511 S.W.3d 352 (Ark. Ct. App. 2017).
14. Surman v. Surman, 745 N.W.2d 802 (Mich. Ct. App. 2007) (finding ex parte order awarding mother temporary legal possessory custody of the children was a "final order," for purposes of appeal).
15. Brennan v. Brennan, 857 A.2d 927 (Conn. App. 2004).

16. *In re* Sigmar, 270 S.W.3d 289 (Tex. App. 2008).
17. K.S. v. R.S., 326 A.3d 187 (Conn. 2024).
18. Hull v. Hull, 273 So. 3d 1135 (Fla. Dist. Ct. App. 2019).
19. Fed. R. Evid. 103.
20. *See* Vanderzon v. Vanderzon, 402 P.3d 219 (Utah Ct. App. 2017) (mother failed to preserve issue of whether court order violated her constitutional right to travel); Powell v. Powell, 976 So. 2d 358 (Miss. Ct. App. 2008) (father failed to preserve for appellate review his argument that chancellor erred in considering testimony regarding the family's pre-divorce relocations, where he failed to object at trial to questions).
21. Shady v. Shady, 858 N.E.2d 128 (Ind. Ct. App. 2006).
22. Myers v. McCall, 334 S.W.3d 878 (Ark. Ct. App. 2009) (trial court changed custody to father where mother remarried and moved children to Missouri without notice required by agreement and was planning to move to Wisconsin). *See also* Kulstad v. Maniaci, 244 P.3d 722 (Mont. 2010); *In re* Marriage of Cooksey, 125 P.3d 57 (Or. Ct. App. 2005).
23. Harbin v. Harbin, 495 So. 2d 72 (Ala. Civ. App. 1986).
24. Fredman v. Fredman, 960 So. 2d 52 (Fla. Dist. Ct. App. 2007).
25. *See, e.g.*, Hemenway v. Hemenway, 339 A.2d 247 (R.I. 1975).
26. Kan. Stat. Ann. § 60-2103(a).
27. Boyd v. Boyd, 291 So. 3d 488 (Ala. Civ. App. 2019).
28. *In re* Marriage of Lentz, 312 Kan. 490, 476 P.3d 1151 (2021).
29. Warner v. Brickhouse, 658 S.E.2d 313 (N.C. Ct. App. 2008).
30. Bruzzi v. Bruzzi, 481 A.2d 648 (Pa. Super. Ct. 1984).
31. Interest of C.J., 689 S.W.3d 417 (Tex. Ct. App. 2024).
32. David v. LoPresti, 111 N.Y.S.3d 356 (App. Div. 2019) (mother was the child's primary caregiver since birth, the relocation was temporary, the child's preferences were not elicited and record is insufficient to enable this court to make its own determination of the petition).
33. Sam V. Schoonmaker IV & Kenneth J. Bartschi, *Effective Family Law Appeals*, 28(4) Fam. Advoc. 6 (2006).
34. Johnson v. Spurlock, 986 So. 2d 724 (La. Ct. App. 2008) (finding mother abandoned for appellate review claim that trial judge's failure to take child's preference into consideration in child relocation dispute was error, where she did not brief these assignments on appeal); Berger v. Berger, 747 N.W.2d 336 (Mich. Ct. App. 2008).
35. Thompson v. Thompson, 176 P.3d 722 (Ariz. Ct. App. Div. 1 2008).
36. Pilkington v. Pilkington, 277 N.E.3d 885 (Ind. Ct. App. 2024) (awarding joint legal custody and denying mother's request to move to Utah where she minimized father's importance and court did not feel she would facilitate relationship with father).
37. Quint v. Quint, N.W.3d , 2024 WL 1470200 (Mich. Ct. App. 2024).
38. Solomon v. Solomon, 221 So. 3d 652, 655 (Fla. Dist. Ct. App. 2017); Green v. Swiers, 920 N.W.2d 471 (N.D. 2018); Salenu S. v. Ahmad G., 58 N.Y.S.3d 35 (App. Div. 2017).
39. Bailey v. Bailey, 196 So. 3d 96 (La. Ct. App. 2016), *reh'g denied*.

40. D.K.D. v. A.L.C., 141 A.3d 566 (Pa. Super. Ct. 2016) (reversing trial court decision allowing mother to move).

41. Buschor v. Buschor, 252 So. 3d 833 (Fla. Dist. Ct. App. 2018) (reversing trial court for not considering best interest of child in relocation and denying mother due process by giving no notice it would award more than the equal time share father requested).

42. Mingott v. Mingott, 337 So. 3d. 408, 410 (Fla. Dist. Ct. App. 2021); State v. Titus, 274 So. 3d 591 (La. Ct. App. 2019); Lobendahn v. Lobendahn, 540 P.3d 727 (Utah Ct. App. 2023).

43. *See* Kogel v. Kogel, 786 S.E.2d 518 (Ga. Ct. App. 2016); *In re* K.U.-S.G., 702 S.E.2d 1103, 105 (N.C. Ct. App. 2010).

44. *In re* Marriage of Fatkin, 129 N.E.3d 1230 (Ill. 2019); Hull v. Hull, 273 So. 3d 1135 (Fla. Dist. Ct. App. 2019).

45. Brett M. v. Amanda M., 445 P.3d 1005 (Alaska 2019) (upholding trial court finding mother's superior emotional stability favored the move even though geographical stability would be to retain); Chalmers v. Chalmers, 259 So. 3d 878 (Fla. Dist. Ct. App. 2018); Horlacher v. Cohen, 96 N.E.3d 438 (Ill. App. Ct. 2017) (on a motion to reconsider, court may review allegation that trial court misapplied existing law de novo).

46. Ashton v. Ashton, 511 S.W.3d 473 (Mo. Ct. App. 2017).

47. Defilippis v. Defilippis, 46 N.Y.S.3d 175 (App. Div. 2017) (reversing trial court finding that relocation was not in child's best interests).

48. Milton v. Milton, 113 So. 3d 1040, 1041 (Fla. Dist. Ct. App. 2013).

49. Bailey v. Bailey, 196 So. 3d 96 (La. Ct. App. 2016), *reh'g denied*. *See also* Havis-Carbone v. Carbone, 112 A.3d 779 (Conn. App. Ct. 2015) (where trial court did not consider all required statutory factors, trial court abused its discretion in granting mother permission to relocate with the child).

50. Taylor-Couchman v. Dewitt-Couchman, 964 N.W.2d 320 (Neb. Ct. App. 2021) (abuse of discretion if reasons untenable or clearly against justice or conscience, reason, and evidence). *See also In re* Marriage of Grippin, 186 P.3d 852 (Kan. Ct. App. 2008); Dixon v. Dixon, 982 N.E.2d 24 (Ind. Ct. App. 2013); *In re* Marriage of Laidlaw, 409 P.3d 1184 (Wash. Ct. App. 2018).

51. Zahl v. Zahl, 736 N.W.2d 365 (Neb. 2007).

52. Michael B. v. Latasha T.-M., 89 N.Y.S.3d 83 (App. Div. 2018). *See also* Havis-Carbone v. Carbone, 112 A.3d 779 (Conn. App. Ct. 2015) (abuse of discretion to allow relocation before holding a hearing on the petition to relocate and not considering all of the statutory factors).

53. Cowan v. Cowan, 540 P.3d 158 (Wash. Ct. App. 2023) (finding abuse of discretion where court ordered restrictions in parenting plan based on the adverse effects of its own temporary orders).

54. White v. Malecki, 296 A.3d 1210 (Pa. Super. Ct. 2023). *See also* Carrero v. Lopez, 300 A.3d 494 (Pa. Super. Ct. 2023) (appellate court found it unreasonable for trial court to deny mother's petition to relocate two children to Florida where father already lived out of state, had not fully exercised his periods of partial custody, and had not attended reunification therapy with oldest child).

55. *See* Brown v. Brown, 84 A.3d 905 (Conn. App. Ct. 2013) (upholding decision allowing mother to relocate with 12-year-old son and his 17-year-old brother). *See also* Ness v. Martinez, 249 So. 3d 754 (Fla. Dist. Ct. App. 2018) (upholding denial of mother's relocation where negative impacts outweighed benefits); Scocos v. Scocos, 369 P.3d 1068 (Okla. 2016) (trial court abused its discretion in not allowing mother to move with child to Louisiana for job and family).

56. *See* Bates v. Bates, 103 So. 3d 836 (Ala. Civ. App. 2012) (allowing mother to move); Waldron v. Dussek, 851 N.Y.S.2d 630 (App. Div. 2008) (noting that custody and visitation determinations depend to a great extent upon court's assessment of credibility of witnesses, as well as parties' character, temperament, and sincerity); Klos v. Klos, 934 A.2d 724 (Pa. Super. Ct. 2007) (with regard to issues of credibility and weight of the evidence, appellate court reviewing a custody order must defer to the presiding trial judge who viewed and assessed the witnesses first-hand).

57. Solomon v. Solomon, 221 So. 3d 652, 655 (Fla. Dist. Ct. App. 2017) (appellate court does not reweigh the evidence). *See also* Dawson v. Ojeda, 303 A.3d 569 (R.I. 2023) (finding trial court did not abuse its discretion in allowing primary caregiver mother to move with 19-month-old one hour away to Massachusetts for better job and family support; mother was willing to work around father's work schedule).

58. Wingate v. Wingate, 333 So. 3d 848 (La. Ct. App. 2022) (allowing mother to relocate).

59. C.R.F. v. S.E.F., 45 A.3d 441, 443 (Pa. Super. Ct. 2012); R.L.P. v. R.F.M., 110 A.3d 201, 207–08 (Pa. Super. Ct. 2015).

60. Maska v. Maska, 742 N.W.2d 492 (Neb. 2007). Emrich v. Emrich, 15 A.3d 1104 (Conn. App. Ct. 2011) (noting appellate court cannot usurp authority of trial court or substitute its judgment for the trial court).

61. Lynn v. Freeman, 157 N.E.3d 17 (Ind. Ct. App. 2020); V.B. v. J.E.B., 55 A.3d 1193 (Pa. Super. 2012) (scope is of broadest kind looking to see if trial court's decision was unreasonable); *In re* Marriage of Fahey, 262 P.3d 128 (Wash. Ct. App. 2011) (finding no abuse of discretion in imposing geographical limitations on father's post-relocation parenting time because father did not take into consideration his daughters' needs and desire to not spend hours commuting in a car).

62. Bentley v. Harper, No. 18CA3858, 2019 WL 7369247 (Ohio Ct. App. Dec. 19, 2019) (mother not allowed to move child to Wyoming).

63. *See* Mata v. Mata, 75 So. 3d 341 (Fla. Dist. Ct. App. 2011) (failure to comply with statutory requirements to receive and consider evidence on the factors listed in the statute was abuse of discretion); Johns v. Ciocci, 865 A.2d 931 (Pa. Super. Ct. 2004) (finding abuse of discretion to change custody without analyzing best interest factors).

64. Schrauner v. Olsen, 483 P.3d 815 (Wash. Ct. App. 2020) (abuse of discretion for court to consider irrelevant information regarding mother's lifestyle and disregarding fact that mother had been the primary caregiver); McLane v. Paul, 189 P.3d 1039 (Alaska 2008).

65. Schultz v. Schultz, 187 P.3d 1234, 1238 (Idaho 2008) (in addition to distance, the court should have considered the mother's wishes for the child, history of domestic violence in the presence of the child, father's lack of attempts to visit the child in Oregon, and the stability and community offered the child in Oregon).

66. Michele M. v. Richard R., 177 P.3d 830 (Alaska 2008).

67. Arredondo v. Betancourt, 383 S.W.3d 730 (Tex. App. 2012).

68. *In re* Rix, 20 A.3d 326, 329 (N.H. 2011).

69. *In re* Sigmar, 270 S.W.3d 289 (Tex. App. 2008) (father had ties to Mexico and had sold office building without evidence as to why and done several other things indicating he was planning to leave with the child).

70. Ainsworth v. Ainsworth, 186 A.3d 1074 (R.I. 2018).

71. Pippin v. Pippin, 277 S.W.3d 398 (Tenn. Ct. App. 2008).

72. Daly v. Kelly, 846 S.E.2d 830 (N.C. Ct. App. 2020).

73. *In re* Marriage of Doe, 250 N.E.3d 283 (Ill. App. Ct. 2024).

74. *See* Sonbuchner v. Sonbuchner, 947 N.Y.S.2d 80 (App. Div. 2012) (finding mother was primary caregiver, her decisions centered around the child, and she would continue to foster a relationship between father and child; expert testimony supported); Barblock v. Barblock, 890 A.2d 1005 (N.J. Super. Ct. App. Div. 2006) (allowing mother to relocate in a de facto shared parenting arrangement in which parents perform equal caretaking roles).

75. Anwar RR. v. Robin RR., 151 N.Y.S.3d 214 (App. Div. 2021).

76. Holly F. v. Daniel G., 147 N.Y.S.3d 703 (App. Div. 2021).

77. Mason v. Mason, 193 N.Y.S.3d 803 (App. Div. 2023).

78. *In re* Marriage of Weaver, 505 P.3d 560 (Wash. Ct. App. 2021).

79. Allen *ex rel.* Allen v. Gatewood, 390 S.W.3d 245, 249 (Mo. Ct. App. 2013) (trial court's findings that mother's parenting plan and her move out of state were in child's best interest were supported by substantial evidence that mother had been the primary caretaker for child since birth, was more likely to allow child contact with the father than vice versa and relocation would benefit child economically and emotionally).

80. Henry v. Henry, 353 S.W.3d 368, 371 (Mo. Ct. App. 2011) (trial court's determination in a child custody matter is given more deference than in any other type of case).

81. Merriweather v. Chacon, 639 S.W.3d 494 (Mo. Ct. App. 2021) (schools were comparable, there were children in new neighborhood with whom child could ride the bus, the guardian ad litem recommended the relocation and change of schools, residence would actually be closer to father's).

82. Cruz v. Morales, 400 So. 3d 716 (Fla. Dist. Ct. App. 2024) (affirming denial of relocation after four-day evidentiary hearing). *See also* Vanderhoof v. Armstrong, 383 So. 3d 868 (Fla. Dist. Ct. App. 2024) (substantial evidence did not support trial court's temporary order granting mother's petition to relocate with the parties' three children three hours away); Albanese v. Albanese, 135 So. 3d 532 (Fla. Dist. Ct. App. 2014) (reversing a decision allowing

father's request to relocate to New York where there was a lack of competent evidence to support the finding that relocation was in the best interests of the child).

83. Pun v. Pun, 363 So. 3d 1113 (Fla. Dist. Ct. App. 2023).

84. Tillotson v. Tillotson, 32 So. 3d 191, 191–92 (Fla. Dist. Ct. App. 2010).

85. *In re* Marriage of Tedrick, 25 N.E.3d 1233 (Ill. App. Ct. 2015).

86. *In re* Marriage of Fatkin, 129 N.E.3d 1230 (Ill. 2019).

87. Peterson v. Peterson, 281 P.3d 1096 (Idaho 2013) (no abuse in not following evaluator recommendation for joint legal and physical custody, awarding mother primary residential custody and allowing mother and five children to move to Utah after three-day trial; family had lived numerous places in last 15 years).

88. Harrison v. Morgan, 191 P.3d 617 (Okla. Civ. App. 2008) (reversing denial of father's relocation request).

89. Wells v. Wells, 691 S.W.3d 269 (Ark. Ct. App. 2024) (mother had been primary caregiver even though decree said "joint physical custody" so mother was entitled to a presumption in favor of relocation); Cox v. Cox, 574 S.W.3d 711 (Ark. Ct. App. 2019); Green v. Swiers, 920 N.W.2d 471 (N.D. 2018) (upholding denial of mother's motion to relocate with out of wedlock child to Seattle where reasons appeared to be to put distance between her and father).

90. Katherine A. v. Jerry A., 889 S.E.2d 754 (W. Va. Ct. App. 2023) (remanding because of trial court's inadequate analysis and evaluation of children's best interests in denying mother's request to relocate).

91. McCay v. McCay, 9 N.W.3d 687 (N.D. 2024). *See also* Dunn v. Dunn, 775 N.W.2d 486 (N.D. 2009) (evidence supported trial judge's decision to allow father to have primary residency of all three children and move to Wyoming for work).

92. *See* B.L. v. J.S., 59 N.E.3d 253 (Ind. Ct. App. 2016).

93. *McCay*, 9 N.W.3d at 687.

94. Inoue v. Inoue, 185 P.3d 834 (Hawai'i Ct. App. 2008).

95. Stanhope v. Phillips-Stanhope, 747 N.W.2d 79 (N.D. 2008).

96. Feria v. Soto, 990 So. 2d 418 (Ala. Civ. App. 2008).

97. Hull v. Hull, 273 So. 3d 1135 (Fla. Dist. Ct. App. 2019) (decision denying the father's relocation was supported by substantial competent evidence); Chalmers v. Chalmers, 259 So. 3d 878 (Fla. Dist. Ct. App. 2018); Clark v. Meizlik, 289 So. 3d 983 (Fla. Dist. Ct. App. 2020) (inclusion of erroneous language in the parenting plan that did not comply with relocation statute did not require reversal of entire parenting plan).

98. Bergerson v. Zurbano, 432 P.3d 850 (Wash. Ct. App. 2018).

99. Blair v. Brownson, 197 S.W.3d 681, 684 (Tenn. 2006); Bogan v. Bogan, 60 S.W.3d 721, 727 (Tenn. 2001).

100. Mann v. Mann, 299 S.W.3d 69, 71 (Tenn. Ct. App. 2009); Whaley v. Perkins, 197 S.W.3d 665, 670 (Tenn. 2006).

101. *See* State v. Titus, 274 So. 3d 591 (La. Ct. App. 2019); H.S.C. v. C.E.C., 944 So. 2d 738 (La. Ct. App. 2006) (affirming mother's relocation to Oregon with five-year-old for work, educational opportunities).

102. Bailey v. Bailey, 196 So. 3d 96 (La. Ct. App. 2016) (best interests of children to not relocate with mother to Mississippi; father could not move and mother's economic situation would not improve).

103. Mata v. Mata, 75 So. 3d 341 (Fla. Dist. Ct. App. 2011).

104. *See* Ward v. Waters, 389 So. 3d 652 (Fla. Dist. Ct. App. 2024).

105. *In re* Rogan, 19 N.E.3d 140 (Ill. App. Ct. 2014).

APPENDIX A

State Statutes on Relocation*

State	Notice	Presumption Used	Child's Preference	Recent Case
Ala. Code § 30-3-160-169.10	45 days or 10 after knows	Against	§ 30-3-163	Crenshaw v. Crenshaw, 386 So. 3d 42 (Ala. Civ. App. 2023)
Alaska Stat. § 25.24.150, 25.24.110		No—if good reason—BIOC	§ 25.24.150	J.M. v. S.C., 552 P.3d 475 (Alaska 2024)
Ariz. Rev. Stat. Ann. §§ 25-408, 25-403(A)(B)	45 days	Burden on moving party	§ 25-403	Wright v. Farris, 563 P.3d 165 (Ariz. App. 2025)
Ark. Code Ann. § 25.24.150, § 9-13-101(a)(5)		For if sole; BIOC if equal parenting	§ 9-13-101	Wells v. Wells, 691 S.W.3d 269 (Ark. App. 2024).
Cal. Fam. Code § 3024	45 days	For	§ 3024	*In re* Marriage of LaMusga, 88 P.3d 81 (Cal. 2004)
Colo. Rev. Stat. Ann. § 14-10-129, § 14-10-124	As soon as practicable	Both parents must show BIOC	X	*In re* Marriage of Ciesluk, 113 P.3d 135 (Colo. 2005)
Conn. Gen. Stat. § 46b-56d		Initial burden on moving party	X	N.R. V. M.P., 323 A.3d 1142 (Conn. App. 2024)
13 Del. Code §§ 722, 734		BIOC	13 Del. Code § 734(4)	Ravin v. Spears, 2019 WL 7369432 (Del. 2019) (unpublished)

State	Notice	Presumption Used	Child's Preference	Recent Case
D.C. Code § 16-914		Burden on party moving	D.C. Code § 16-914(a)(3)(A)	Estopina v. O'Brian, 68 A.3d 790 (D.C. Ct. App.2016)
Fla. Stat. § 61.13001		Burden on relocating party	Fla. Stat. § 61.13001(7)(d)	Vanderhoof v. Armstrong, 383 So. 3d 868 (Fla. Dist. Ct. App. 2024)
Ga. Code Ann. § 19-9-3	30 days		X	Hether v. Campbell, 912 S.E.2d 349 (Ga. Ct. App. 2025)
Haw. Rev. Stat. § 571-46			X	Waldecker v. O'Scanlon, 375 P.3d 239 (Haw. 2016)
Idaho Code § 32-717(1), 717B		Initial burden on moving party	§ 32-717(1)(b)	Wilson v. Wilson, 560 P.3d 1126 (Idaho 2024)
750 Ill. Comp. Stat. Ann. § 5/609.2	60 days	Burden on party seeking to relocate	§ 5-609.2(g)(8)	*In re* Marriage of Prusak, 256 N.E.3d 529 (Ill. App. Ct. 2020).
Ind. Code. Ann. § 31-17-2.2-1, 31-17-2-8	90 days	Shifting burden	X	Emslander v. Baine, 247 N.E.3d 1246 (Ind. Ct. App. 2024)
Iowa Code § 598.21D		Burden on party seeking to modify		*In re* Marriage of Theilges, 623 N.W.2d 232 (Iowa Ct. App. 2000)
Kan. Stat. Ann. § 23-3222	30 days		§ 23-3203(a)(3)	*In re* Marriage of Grippin, 186 P.3d 852 (Kan. Ct. App. 2008)

State	Notice	Presumption Used	Child's Preference	Recent Case
Ky. Rev. Stat. Ann. § 403.340		Burden on party seeking modification	X	Pennington v. Marcum, 266 S.W.3d 759 (Ky. 2008)
La. Stat. Ann. § 9.355.1-.17	60 days or 10 days after known	Burden on moving party	X	Coulon v. Coulon, 351 So. 3d 823 (La. App. 2022)
Me. Stat. tit. 19-A § 1653 (3) & 1657	30 days or as soon as possible	Burden on moving party	X	Reiman v. Toland, 269 A.3d 229 (Me. 2022)
Md. Code Ann. Fam. Law § 9-106	90 days	Burden on nonmoving party		Braun v. Headley, 750 A.2d 624 (Md. Ct. Spec. App. 2000); Skiles v. Saia, 2020 WL 6282020 (Md. Ct. Spec. App.).
Mass. Gen. Laws Ch. 208, § 30, 31		Real advantage test if sole custody; BIOC if shared physical	X	E.K. v. S.C., 148 N.E.3d 414 (Mass. App. Ct. 2020)
Mich. Comp. Laws § 722.27, .28		Burden on moving party if objection	X	Safdar v. Aziz, 992 N.W.2d 913 (Mich. Ct. App. 2022)
Minn. Stat. § 518.175, sub. 3		Best interests standard applies	518.175 subdiv. 3(b)(4)	Anh Phuong Le v. Holter, 838 N.W.2d 803 (Minn. App. 2013), rev. denied

State	Notice	Presumption Used	Child's Preference	Recent Case
Miss. Code Ann. § 93-5-23		Burden on party seeking modification	X	Scott v. Boudreau, 375 So. 3d 688 (Miss. Ct. App. 2023)
Mo. Rev. Stat. § 452.377	60 days	Burden on moving party	X	Merriweather v. Chacon, 639 S.W.3d 494 (Mo. App. 2021)
Mont. Code Ann. § 40-4-217	30 days	Burden on party opposing	X	*In re* Marriage of Solem, 464 P.3d 981 (Mont. 2020)
Neb. Rev. Stat. § 42-364, 43-2929	Written notice	Shifting burden	X	Korth v. Korth, 958 N.W.2d 683 (Neb. 2021)
Nev. Rev. Stat. § 125C.006 - .0075		Relocating parent has initial burden	X	Monahan v. Hogan, 507 P.3d 588 (Nev. Ct. App. 2022)
N.H. Rev. Stat. Ann. § 461-A:12	60 days	Shifting burden	X	Matter of Rourke, 320 A.3d 23 (N.H. 2024)
N.J. Stat. Ann. § 9:2-2		Shifting burden	X	Bisbing v. Bisbing, 1166 A.3d 1155 (N.J. 2017)
N.M. Stat. Ann. § 40-4-9.1	30 days	Equal burden, BIOC	X	Hopkins v. Wollaber, 458 P.3d 583 (N.M. Ct. App. 2018)
N.Y. Dom. Rel. Law § 240	90 days		X	Alicia SS v. Andrew RR, 206 N.Y.S.3d 769 (App. Div. 2024)

State	Notice	Presumption Used	Child's Preference	Recent Case
N.C. Gen. Stat. § 50-13.2			X	Munoz v. Munoz, 864 S.E.2d 364 (N.C. Ct. App. 2021)
N.D. Cent. Code § 14-09-07		Burden on moving party	X	Nelson v. Nelson, 3 N.W.3d 133 (N.D. 2024)
Ohio Rev. Code Ann. § 3109.051	Yes	Initial burden on moving party	§ 3109.04(B),(E)	Jourdan v. Jourdan, 216 N.E.3d 42 (Ohio Ct. App. 2023)
Okla. Stat. Ann. tit. 43 § 112.3	60 days or 10 days after info	Shifting, if relocating parent good faith		Boatman v. Boatman, 404 P.3d 822 (Okla. 2017)
Or. Rev. Stat. § 107.159	Reasonable		X	*In re* Marriage of Stancliff, 513 P.3d 20 (Or. Ct. App. 2022)
23 Pa. Cons. Stat. § 5337	60 days or 10 after knows	Burden on relocating parent	X	Carrero v. Lopez, 300 A.3d 494 (Pa. Super. Ct. 2023)
R.I. Gen. Laws § 15-5-16	90 days		X	Dawson v. Ojeda, 303 A.3d 569 (R.I. 2023); Ainsworth v. Ainsworth, 186 A.3d 1074 (R.I. 2018)
S.C. Code Ann. § 63-15-230-240	45 days		X	Gandy v. Gandy, 898 S.E.2d 208 (S.C. Ct. App. 2024), remanded on other grounds
S.D. Codified Laws § 25-5-13; 25-4A-17-19	45 days	For	X	Kolbach v. Kolbach, 877 N.W.2d 822 (S.D. 2016)

State	Notice	Presumption Used	Child's Preference	Recent Case
Tenn. Code Ann. § 36-6-108	60 days if 50 miles away		X	Barrett v. Killings, 700 S.W.3d 399 (Tenn. Ct. App. 2023); Aragon v. Aragon, 513 S.W.3d 447 (Tenn. 2017)
Tex. Fam. Code Ann. § 156.101	Yes, no time	Burden on moving parent	X	Interest of A.C.M., 593 S.W.3d 894 (Tex. App. 2019)
Utah Code Ann. § 30-3-37	60 days			Ross v. Ross, 447 P.3d 104 (Utah Ct. App. 2019)
Vt. Stat. Ann. tit. 15, §§ 665(b), 668(a)	Yes, no time	Burden on noncustodial party	X	Quinones v. Bouffard, 179 A.3d 173 (Vt. 2017)
Va. Code Ann. § 20-124.2, 3, 5	30 days			Brandon v. Coffey, 886 S.E.2d 780 (Va. Ct. App. 2023)
Wash. Rev. Code § 26.09.405-.560	60 days	For, if custodial parent	X	*In re* Marriage of Weaver, 505 P.3d 560 (Wash. Ct. App. 2021)
W. Va. Code § 48-9-403	60 days	For, if legit reason, good faith, and location reasonable	X	Katherine A. v. Jerry A., 889 S.E.2d 754 (W. Va. Ct. App. 2023)
Wis. Stat. § 767.481	60 days	Burden on moving party		Shulka v. Sikraji, 856 N.W.2d 617 (Wis. Ct. App. 2014)
Wyo. Stat. Ann. § 20-2-204(c)	60 days	For	X	Gutierrez v. Bradley, 500 P.3d 984 (Wyo. 2021)

- Always check the current statutes because they are often amended.

APPENDIX B

Bibliography of Relocation Articles

Model Relocation Acts and Principles

American Academy of Matrimonial Lawyers Proposed Model Relocation Act an Act Relating to the Relocation of the Principal Residence of a Child, 15 J. AM. ACAD. MATRIM. LAW. 1 (1998).

Barbara Ellen Handshu, *The Making of a Model Relocation Act: A Committee Member's Perspective*, 15 J. AM. ACAD. MATRIM. LAW. 25 (1998).

American Bar Association Family Law Section, Model Relocation Act (2011).

Jeff Atkinson, *The Law of Relocation of Children*, 28 BEHAV. SCI. LAW 563 (2010).

AMERICAN LAW INSTITUTE, PRINCIPLES OF THE LAW OF FAMILY DISSOLUTION: ANALYSIS AND RECOMMENDATIONS 2.17 (2002).

Washington Declaration on International Family Relocation, 44(3) FAM. L.Q. 369 (Fall 2010), reaffirmed April 2025.

General Relocation

Charles C. Abut, *A Child Removal Checklist*, 28 FAM. ADVOCATE 21 (2006).

Roger M. Baron, *Custody Relocation Restrictions: A Tool for Preventing Conflicts*, 17 FAIR$HARE 5–6 (Apr. 1997).

Roger M. Baron, *Refining Relocation Laws—The Next Step in Attacking the Problem of Parental Kidnaping*, 25 TEX. TECH. L. REV. 11936 (1993).

Lewis Becker, *Ethical Responsibilities of a Lawyer for a Parent in Custody and Relocation Cases: Duties Respecting the Child and Other Conundrums*, 15 J. AM. ACAD. MATRIM. LAW. 33 (1998).

Bridgette M. Bodenheimer, *Equal Rights, Visitation, and the Right to Move*, 1(1) FAM. ADVOCATE 18 (1978).

Carol S. Bruch & Janet M. Bowermaster, *The Relocation of Children and Custodial Parents: Public Policy, Past and Present*, 30 FAM. L.Q. 245 (1996).

David V. Chipman & Mindy M. Rush, *The Necessity of "Right to Travel" Analysis in Custodial Parent Relocation Cases*, 10 WYO. L. REV. 267 (2010).

David M. Cotter, *Oh, The Places You'll (Possibly) Go! Recent Case Law on Relocation of the Custodial Parent*, 16(9) DIVORCE LITIG. 152 (Sept. 2004).

W. Dennis Duggan, *Rock, Paper, Scissors: Playing the Odds with the Law of Child Relocation*, 45 FAM. CT. REV.193 (2007).

Linda D. Elrod, *States Differ on Relocation: A Panorama of Expanding Case Law*, 28 FAM. ADVOC. 8 (2006).

Linda D. Elrod, *A Move in the Right Direction? Best Interest of the Child Emerging as the Standard for Relocation Cases*, 3 J. CHILD CUSTODY 29 (2006).

Linda D. Elrod, *National and International Momentum Builds for More Child Focus in Relocation Disputes*, 44(3) FAM. L.Q. 341 (Fall 2010).

LINDA D. ELROD, CHILD CUSTODY PRACTICE AND PROCEDURE, Chs. 3, 4, 17 (Thomson Reuters 2024).

FAMILY ADVOCATE

Special Issue on Relocation, 11 (3) FAM. ADVOC. (1989); *Rethinking Relocation*, 20(2) FAM. ADVOC. (1997); *Relocation: A Delicate Balance of Competing Interests*, 28(4) FAM. ADVOC. (2006).

Chris Ford, *Untying the Relocation Knot: Recent Developments and a Model for Change*, 7 COLUM. J. GENDER & L. 1 (1997).

Theresa Glennon, *Still Partners? Examining the Consequences of Post-Dissolution Parenting*, 41 FAM. L.Q. 105 (2007).

Sarah Gottfried, *Virtual Visitation: The Wave of the Future in Communication Between Children and Non-Custodial Parents in Relocation Cases*, 36 FAM. L.Q. 3 (2002).

Kimberly K. Holtz, Comment, *Move-Away Custody Disputes: The Implications of Case-by-Case Analysis and the Need for Legislation*, 35 SANTA CLARA L. REV. 319–66 (1994).

Cheryl S. Karner, *Relocation: What Ought to Be*, 20 FAM. ADVOC. 12–14 (Fall 1997).

Charles P. Kindregan, Jr., *Family Interests in Competition: Relocation and Visitation*, 36 SUFFOLK U. L. REV. 31 (2002).

Mary Kay Kisthardt & Nancy Levit, *The Relocation of Children: An Annotated Bibliography 1988–98*, 15 J. Am. Acad. Matrim. Law. 245 (1998).

Arthur B. LaFrance, *Child Custody and Relocation: A Constitutional Perspective*, 34 Louisville J. Fam. L. 1–158 (1995–96).

Christopher C. Melcher & David R. Bass, *Relocation Factors: A Lawyer's Guide*, 43(4) Fam. Advoc. 45 (2021).

J. Thomas Oldham, *Limitations Imposed by Family Law on a Separated Parent's Ability to Make Significant Life Decisions: A Comparison of Relocation and Income Imputation*, 8 Duke J. Gender L. & Pol'y 333 (2001).

Robert E. Oliphant, *Relocation Custody Disputes—A Binuclear Family-Centered Three-Stage Solution*, 25 N. Ill. U. L. Rev. 363 (2005).

Patrick Parkinson & Judy Cashmore, *Reforming Relocation Law—An Evidence-based Approach*, 53(1) Fam. Ct. Rev. 23 (2015).

Patrick Parkinson & Judy Cashmore, *Reforming Relocation Law—A Reply to Prof. Thompson*, 53(1) Fam. Ct. Rev. 56 (2015).

Patrick Parkinson & Judy Cashmore, *When Mothers Stay: Adjusting to Loss After Relocation Disputes*, 47(1) Fam. L.Q. 65 (Spring 2013).

Patrick Parkinson, Judy Cashmore & Judi Single, *The Need for Reality Testing in Relocation Cases*, 44(1) Fam. L.Q. 1 (2010).

Janet Leach Richards, *Resolving Relocation Issues Pursuant to the ALI Family Dissolution Principles: Are Children Better Protected?*, 2001 B.Y.U. L. Rev. 1105 (2001).

Philip M. Stahl, *Avoiding Bias in Relocation Cases*, 3 J. Child Custody 109 (2006).

Edwin J. Terry et al., *Relocation: Moving Forward or Moving Backward?*, 31 Tex. Tech. L. Rev. 983 (2000).

Rollie Thompson, *Presumptions, Burdens and Best Interests in Relocation Law*, 53(1) Fam. Ct. Rev. 40 (2015).

Norma Levine Trusch, *A Panoramic View of Relocation: Where Have We Been? Where Are We Going?*, 20 Fam. Advoc. 18 (Fall 1997).

Norma Levine Trusch, *Relocation of Children After Divorce: The Winds of Change*, 18 Fair$hare 2 (Apr. 1998).

Elizabeth Bach-Van Horn, Comment, *Virtual Visitation: Are Webcams Being Used as an Excuse to Allow Relocation?*, 21 J. Am. Acad. Matrim. Law. 171 (2008).

George K. Walker, *The Hague Child Abduction Convention and the International Child Abduction Remedies Act: Comments for U.S. Practice*, 41(4) N.C. J. Int'l L. 741 (2016).

Merle H. Weiner, *Inertia and Inequality: Reconceptualizing Disputes Over Parental Relocation*, 40 U.C. Davis L. Rev. 1747 (2007).

Children's Rights and Voices

Barbara A. Atwood, *The Child's Voice in Custody Litigation: An Empirical Survey and Suggestions for Reform*, 45 Ariz. L. Rev. 629 (2003).

Gary A. Debele, *A Children's Rights Approach to Relocation: A Meaningful Best Interests Standard*, 15 J. Am. Acad. Matrim. Law. 75 (1998).

Linda D. Elrod, *Reforming the System to Protect Children in High Conflict Custody Cases*, 28(2) Wm. Mitchell L. Rev. 495 (2001).

Linda D. Elrod, *Client-Directed Lawyers for Children: It Is the "Right" Thing to Do?*, 27(4) Pace L. Rev. 869 (2007).

Ursula Kilkelly, *Relocation: A Children's Rights Perspective*, 1(1) J. Fam. L. & Prac. 23 (2010).

Pauline Mato, *A Family Affair: Acknowledging Children's Voices in Custody Mediation*, 71 Disp. Resol. J. 171 (2016).

David D. Meyer, *The Modest Promise of Children's Relationship Rights*, 11(3) Wm. & Mary Bill of Rts. J. 1117 (2003).

Janet Leach Richards, *Children's Rights v. Parents' Rights: A Proposed Solution to the Custodial Relocation Conundrum*, 29 N.M. L. Rev. 245 (1999).

Samuel Roll, *How a Child Views the Move: The Psychology of Attachment, Separation, and Loss*, 20 Fam. Advoc. 26 (Fall 1997).

Hon. Arline S. Rotman, *Reconciling Parents' and Children's Interests in Relocation: In Whose Best Interest?*, 38 Fam. Ct. Rev. 341 (2000).

Ernest Sanchez & Sherrie Kibler-Sanchez, *Empowering Children in Mediation*, 42 Fam. Ct. Rev. 554 (2004).

Nick Sheff, *My Long-Distance Life*, Newsweek 18 (Feb. 15, 1999).

Rebecca Stahl, *Keeping in Mind the Child's Perspective in Your Parenting Plan*, 47(1) Fam. Advoc. 15 (Summer 2024).

Karen Tapp, *In Whose Best Interest? Legal Standards on Relocation of the Custodial Parent*, 3 Ky. Children's Rts. J. 19 (Spring 1993).

Ruth Zafran, *Children's Rights as Relational Rights: The Case of Relocation*, 18 Am. U. J. Gender, Soc. Pol'y & Law 163 (2010).

Domestic Violence Issues and Relocation

National Council of Juvenile and Family Court Judges, Model Code on Domestic and Family Violence (1994). Factors for courts to consider.

Allen S. Bailey, Prioritizing Child Safety as the Prime Best Interest Factor, 47 Fam. L.Q. 35 (2013).

Janet M. Bowermaster, *Relocation Custody Disputes Involving Domestic Violence*, 46 U. Kan. L. Rev. 433–63 (1998).

SARAH BUEL, THE IMPACT OF DOMESTIC VIOLENCE ON CHILDREN: TEN PRACTICAL RECOMMENDATIONS FOR LAWYERS, JUDGES, AND COURT PERSONNEL (1997).

William Fabricius & Sanford Braver, *Relocation, Parental Conflict and Domestic Violence: Independent Risk Factors for Children of Divorce*, 3 J. CHILD CUSTODY 7 (2006).

Jennifer L. Hardesty et al., *Domestic Violence and Child Custody*, *in* PARENTING PLAN EVALUATIONS: APPLIED RESEARCH FOR THE FAMILY COURT 442 (Leslie Drozd & Nancy Olesen eds. 2012).

Dana Harrington Connor, *Back to the Drawing Board: Barriers to Joint Decision-Making in Custody Cases Involving Intimate Partner Violence*, 18 DUKE J. GENDER L. & POL'Y 223, 228 (2011).

Peter Jaffe et al., *Custody Disputes Involving Allegations of Domestic Violence: Toward a Differentiated Approach to Parenting Plans*, 46(3) FAM. CT. REV. 500 (2008).

Fernanda S. Rossi, Amy Holtzworth-Munroe & Brittany N. Rudd, *Intimate Partner Violence and Child Custody*, *in* PARENTING PLAN EVALUATIONS: APPLIED RESEARCH FOR THE FAMILY COURT 346 (Leslie Drozd, Michael Saini & Nancy Olesen eds., 2d ed. 2016).

Lynne Hecht Schafran, *Domestic Violence, Developing Brains, and the Lifespan: New Knowledge from Neuroscience*, 53(3) JUDGES' J. 32 (2014).

Neil Websdale, *Lethality Assessment Tools: A Critical Analysis*, VAWNET APPLIED RESEARCH FORUM (Feb. 2000).

Jennifer White, *Avoiding Custodial Landmines: Arguing Against Relocation Law That Perpetuates Domestic Violence*, The LAPTOP Update, Legal Assistance Providers' Technical Outreach Project (Fall 2005).

International Relocations

Books

ANN LAQUER ESTIN, INTERNATIONAL FAMILY LAW DESK BOOK (2d ed. 2016).

ROBERT GEORGE, RELOCATION DISPUTES: LAW AND PRACTICE IN ENGLAND AND NEW ZEALAND (2014).

DAVID HODSON, THE INTERNATIONAL FAMILY LAW PRACTICE (4th ed. 2015).

INTERNATIONAL HANDBOOK ON CHILD PARTICIPATION IN FAMILY LAW (Wendy Schrama, Marilyn Freeman, Nicola Taylor & Marielle Bruning eds. 2021).

JEREMY D. MORLEY, THE HAGUE ABDUCTION CONVENTION: PRACTICAL ISSUES AND PROCEDURES FOR FAMILY LAWYERS (ABA 3d ed. 2025).

Articles

Nicholas Bala & Andrea Wheeler, *Canadian Relocation Cases: Heading Towards Guidelines*, 30 CAN. FAM. L.Q. 271 (2012).

Timothy Carmody, *Child Relocation: An Intractable International Family Law Problem*, 45 FAM. CT. REV. 214 (2007).

Linda D. Elrod, *The Global Effort to Deter Parental Kidnapping: A History of the Hague Abduction Convention*, *in* RESEARCH HANDBOOK ON INTERNATIONAL CHILD ABDUCTION (Marilyn Freeman & Nicola Taylor eds., 2023).

Linda D. Elrod, *Uniform Child Abduction Prevention Act, A Way to Curb Parental Abductions*, 47(4) FAM. ADVOC. 17 (2025).

Linda D. Elrod, *Uniform Child Abduction Prevention Act (Statutory Text, Comments and Unofficial Annotations by Linda D. Elrod, Reporter*)*, 41 FAM. L.Q. 23 (2007).

Linda D. Elrod, *National and International Momentum Builds for More Child Focus in Relocation Disputes*, 44(3) FAM. L.Q. 341 (Fall 2010).

Marilyn Freeman, *The Effects and Consequences of International Child Custody and Abduction Law*, 32 FAM. L.Q. 603 (1998).

Megan Gollop & Nicola J. Taylor, *New Zealand Children and Young People's Perspectives on Relocation Following Parental Separation*, *in* 14 LAW AND CHILDHOOD STUDIES: CURRENT LEGAL ISSUES 219 (Michael Freeman ed., 2012).

James Grayson, *International Relocation, the Right to Travel, and the Hague Convention: Additional Requirements for Custodial Parents*, 28 FAM. L.Q. 531 (1994).

Mark Henaghan, *Relocation Cases—The Rhetoric and the Reality of a Child's Best Interests—A View from the Bottom of the World*, 23 CHILD & FAM. L. 226 (2011).

Mark Henaghan, *Going, Going . . . Gone—To Relocate or Not to Relocate, That Is the Question*, FAM. L. N.Z. L. SOC. (2009).

Patricia Hoff, *UU UCAPA: Understanding and Using UCAPA to Prevent Child Abduction*, 41 FAM. L.Q. 1 (2007)

Jeremy D. Morley, *The Impact of Foreign Law on Child Custody Determinations*, 10 J. CHILD CUSTODY 209 (2013).

Patrick Parkinson & Judy Cashmore, *Reforming Relocation: An Evidence Based Approach*, 53(1) FAM. CT. REV. 23 (2015).

Patrick Parkinson & Judy Cashmore, *Reforming Relocation Law: A Reply to Prof. Thompson*, 53(1) FAM. CT. REV. 56 (2015).

Maryl Sattler, *The Problem of Parental Relocation: Closing the Loophole in the Law of International Child Abduction*, 67 WASH. & LEE L. REV. 1709 (2010).

Leslie Ellen Shear & Leslie M. Drozd, *To Speak of All Kinds of Things: Child Custody Evaluations and the Unique Characteristics of Relocations to Foreign Countries*, 10 J. CHILD CUSTODY 325 (2013).

Nicola Taylor & Marilyn Freeman, *Relocation: The International Context*, 1 J. FAM. L. & PRAC. 19 (2010).

Nicola Taylor & Marilyn Freeman, *International Research on Relocation: Past, Present, and Future*, 44(3) FAM. L.Q. 317 (Fall 2010).

Nicola Taylor, M. Gollop & R. Mark Henaghan, *Relocation Following Parental Separation in New Zealand: Complexity and Diversity*, 97 INT'L FAM. L. (2010).

Louise Ellen Teitz, *Children Crossing Borders: Internationalizing the Restate of the Conflict of Laws*, 27 DUKE J. COMP. & INT'L LAW 519 (2017).

Richard Warshak, *In a Land Far, Far Away: Assessing Children's Best Interests in International Relocation Cases*, 10 J. CHILD CUSTODY 295 (2013).

Mediation/Arbitration

Linda D. Elrod, *Arbitration of Child-Related Issues and the Uniform Family Law Arbitration Act*, 46(2) FAM. ADVOC. 14 (Fall 2023).

Robert E. Emery et al., *Divorce Mediation: Research and Reflection*, 43 FAM. CT. REV. 22 (2005).

Carol Gersten, *Mediate the Move: Quelling Clients' Fears and Clarifying Options*, 28 FAM. ADVOC. 30 (2006).

Hanley M. Gurwin, Settling Relocation Issues Through Dispute Resolution, 20 FAM. ADVOC. 24–25 (Fall 1997).

Barbara Ellen Handschu, *13 Negotiated Provisions That Anticipate Geographic Relocation*, 14 MATRIM. STRATEGIST 1–5 (Jan. 1997).

Brian S. Kennedy, *Moving Away from Certainty: Using Mediation to Avoid Unpredictable Outcomes in Relocation Disputes Involving Joint Physical Custody*, 53 BOSTON COLL. L. REV. 265 (2012).

Melissa A. Kucinski, *The Delicate Art of Mediating International Parental Child Abduction Cases*, DISPUTE RESOL. MAG. 18 (Winter 2014).

Thomas Luchs, *Is Your Client a Good Candidate for Mediation? Screen Early, Screen Often, and Screen for Domestic Violence*, 28 J. AM. ACAD. MATRIM. LAW. 455 (2016).

Rebecca N. Morrow, *Mediating Parental Relocation Cases Behind a Veil of Ignorance*, 49 WAKE FOREST L. REV. 771 (2014).

JANE C. MURPHY & JANA B. SINGER, DIVORCED FROM REALITY: RETHINKING FAMILY DISPUTE RESOLUTION (2015).

ANDREW I. SCHEPARD, CHILDREN, COURTS, AND CUSTODY: INTERDISCIPLINARY MODELS FOR DIVORCING FAMILIES (2004).

Nancy Ver Steegh, *Family Court Reform and ADR: Shifting Values and Expectations Transform the Divorce Process*, 42 FAM. L.Q. 659 (2008).

SARAH VIGERS, MEDIATING INTERNATIONAL CHILD ABDUCTION CASES—THE HAGUE CONVENTION (2011).

Carolyn Moran Zack, *Family Law Arbitration: An Underutilized Option*, 46(2) FAM. ADVOC. 18 (Fall 2023).

Post-Decree Relocation Issues

Nancy Zalusky Berg & Gary A. Debele, *Post Decree Custody Modification: Moving Out of State and Changes to the Parenting Relationship*, 10 AM. J. FAM. L. 183–95 (1996).

Emanuel A. Bertin, *Relocation: No Common Ground—All States Agree That What's Good for the Child Is What Counts—But That's All They Agree On*, 11 FAM. ADVOC. 6–8 (Winter 1989).

Janet M. Bowermaster, *Sympathizing with Solomon: Choosing Between Parents in a Mobile Society*, 31 U. LOUISVILLE J. FAM. L. 791–884 (1992).

Janet Bulow & Steven G. Gellman, Note, *The Judicial Role in PostDivorce Child Relocation Controversies*, 35 STAN. L. REV. 949–74 (1983).

Mandy S. Cohen, Note, *A Toss of the Dice . . . The Gamble with Post-Divorce Relocation Laws*, 18 HOFSTRA L. REV. 127–56 (1989).

Pamela Coyle, *A Parent's Moving Checklist: Sell and Buy House, Call Mover, Seek Court's Permission*, 84 A.B.A. J. 26–27 (Feb. 1998).

Willard H. DaSilva, *The Relocation Trial: Techniques to Use—Techniques to Avoid*, 11 FAM. ADVOC. 36–42 (Winter 1989).

Kathleen Donelli & Joshua E. Kimerling, *The Drafting of Relocation Clauses and the Challenge It Presents*, 14 MATRIM. STRATEGIST 1–5 (May 1996).

Ellen J. Effron, *Fighting Over a Good Education: Quality of Schools Can Be a Key Factor in the Outcome of Custody Cases*, 82 A.B.A. J. 78 (July 1996).

Linda D. Elrod & Robert G. Spector, *A Review of the Year in Family Law: Of Welfare Reform, Child Support, and Relocation*, 30 FAM. L.Q. 765, 782–83 (1997).

Major Fenton, *Relocation After Initial Custody Determination*, ARMY LAW 58 (July 1998).

John E. Finnerty, *Relocation—How To Do It (Or Stop It)*, 11 FAM. ADVOC. 1315 (Winter 1989).

Lyn R. Greenberg, Dianna J. Could-Saltman & Hon. Robert Schnider, *The Problem with Presumptions: A Review and Commentary*, 3 J. CHILD CUSTODY 139 (2006).

Caroline Ritchie Heil, *Relocation Cases as Change in Custody Proceedings: "Judicial Blackmail" or Competing Interests Reconciled?*, 51 S.C. L. REV. 885 (2000).

Dennis J. Jacobsen, *A Judge Looks at Relocation: What Works in Court?*, 11 FAM. ADVOC. 30 (Winter 1989).

Sandra Morgan Little, *A Move in the Right Direction: How to Sidestep Relocation Troubles Through Cooperation and Coparenting*, 20 FAM. ADVOC. 32 (Fall 1997).

Martha Ann Lott, *Relocation Cases: Analyzing Relevant Evidence*, 3 J. CHILD CUSTODY 125 (2006).

Dorene Marcus & Jeffrey I. Garfinkel, *The Trial Opposing Relocation in a Society in Which Mobility and the Right to a Fresh Start Are Highly Valued, A Lawyer for the Parent Opposing Relocation Must Marshal for Trial Every Fact Likely to Tip the Balance Against Relocation*, 20 FAM. ADVOC. 41 (Fall 1997).

Pamela Markert, *Custody Relocation: More Questions Than Answers Result from High Court Opinions in California and New York*, 38 SANTA CLARA L. REV. 521 (1998).

Enrico A. Mazzoli, *The Court's Role Facilitating an Effective Relationship Between the Noncustodial Parent and Child When the Custodial Parent Relocates with Child*, 37 BRANDEIS L.J. 259 (1998–1999).

Lucy S. McGough, *Starting Over: The Heuristics of Family Relocation Decision Making*, 77 ST. JOHN'S L. REV. 291, 322–23 (2003).

Albert A. Menashe & William E. Hensley, *What About the Parent Left Behind?*, 11 FAM. ADVOC. 16 (Winter 1989).

Tabitha Sample & Teresa Reiger, *Relocation Standards and Constitutional Considerations*, 15 J. AM. ACAD. MATRIM. LAW. 229 (1998).

Leslie Shear, *Life Stories, Doctrines, and Decision Making: Three High Courts Confront the Move-Away Dilemma*, 34 FAM. CT. REV. 439 (1996).

Edwin J. (Ted) Terry et al., *Relocation: Moving Forward, or Moving Backward?* 15 J. AM. ACAD. MATRIM. LAW. 167 (1998).

Edwin J. Terry et al., *Relocation: Moving Forward or Moving Backward?*, 31 TEX. TECH. L. REV. 983 (2000).

Merle H. Weiner, *Inertia and Inequality: Reconceptualizing Disputes Over Parental Relocation*, 40 U.C. DAVIS L. REV. 1747 (2007).

Social Science, Evaluations, Impacts on Children

Paul R. Amato, *The Consequences of Divorce for Adults and Children*, 62 J. Marriage & Fam. 1269 (2001).

L. Anderzen et al., *Stress and Sensitization in Children: A Controlled Prospective Psychophysiological Study of Children Exposed to International Relocation*, 43 J. Psychosomatic Res. 259 (Sept. 1997).

William G. Austin & Sol Rappaport, *Parental Gatekeeping Forensic Model and Child Custody Evaluation: Social Capital and Application to Relocation Disputes*, 15 J. Child Custody 55 (2018).

William G. Austin, James N. Bow, Andrea Knoll & Rebecca Ellens, *Relocation Issues in Child Custody Evaluations: A Survey of Professionals*, 54 Fam. Ct. Rev. 477 (2016).

William G. Austin, *Relocation, Research and Child Custody Disputes*, *in* Parenting Plan Evaluations: Applied Research for the Family Court (K. Kuehnle & L. Drozd eds. 2012).

William G. Austin, *Relocation, Research, and Forensic Evaluation, Part I: Effects of Residential Mobility on Children of Divorce*, 46 Fam. Ct. Rev. 137 (2008).

William G. Austin, *Relocation, Research, and Forensic Evaluation, Part II: Effects of Residential Mobility on Children of Divorce*, 46 Fam. Ct. Rev. 347 (2008).

William G. Austin & Jonathan W. Gould, *Exploring Three Functions in Child Custody Evaluation for the Relocation Case: Prediction, Investigation, and Making Recommendations for a Long Distance Parenting Plan*, 3 J. Child Custody 63 (2006).

William G. Austin, *A Forensic Psychology Model of Risk Assessment for Child Custody Relocation Law*, 38 Fam. & Conciliation Cts. Rev. 192 (2000).

William G. Austin, *Relocation Law and the Threshold of Harm: Integrating Legal and Behavioral Perspectives*, 34 Fam. L.Q. 63 (2000).

Carol S. Bruch, *Sound Research or Wishful Thinking in Child Custody Cases? Lessons from Relocation Law*, 40 Fam. L.Q. 281 (2006).

James Byrne et al., *Practitioner's Review: Contribution of Attachment Theory to Child Custody Assess*, 46 J. Child Psych. & Psychiatry 2 (2005).

Rebekah Levin Coley & Melissa Kull, *Cumulative, Timing-Specific, and Interactive Models of Residential Mobility and Children's Cognitive and Psychosocial Skills*, Child Dev. 1 (2016).

T.A. Cornille, *Support Systems and the Relocation Process for Children and Families*, 19 Marriage & Fam. Rev. 281 (1993).

D.J. DeWit, *Frequent Childhood Geographic Location: Its Impact on Drug Use Initiation and the Development of Alcohol and Other Drug-Related Problems Among Adolescents and Young Adults*, 23 ADDICTIVE BEHAVIORS 623 (1998).

WILLIAM A. EDDY, HIGH CONFLICT PERSONALITIES: UNDERSTANDING AND RESOLVING THEIR CUSTODY DISPUTES (2003).

Frank F. Furstenberg, Jr. et al., *Paternal Participation and Children's Well-Being After Marital Dissolution*, 52 AM. SOC. REV. 695 (1987).

Marion Gindes, The Psychological Effects of Relocation for Children of Divorce, 15 J. AM. ACAD. MATRIM. LAW. 119 (1998).

MAVIS HETHERINGTON & JOHN KELLY, FOR BETTER OR FOR WORSE: DIVORCE RECONSIDERED (2002).

Christiane Humke & Charles Shaefer, *Relocation: A Review of the Effects of Residential Mobility on Children and Adolescents*, 32 J. HUMAN BEHAVIOR 16 (1995).

Jan Jeske & Mary Louis Klas, *Adverse Childhood Experiences: Implications for Family Law Practice and the Family Court System*, 50(1) FAM. L.Q. 123 (2016).

JANET R. JOHNSTON & VIVIENNE ROSEBY, IN THE NAME OF THE CHILD: A DEVELOPMENTAL APPROACH TO UNDERSTANDING AND HELPING CHILDREN OF CONFLICTED AND VIOLENT DIVORCE (1997).

JANET R. JOHNSTON & LINDA E.G. CAMPBELL, IMPASSES OF DIVORCE: THE DYNAMICS AND RESOLUTION OF FAMILY CONFLICT (1988).

Joan B. Kelly, *Current Research on Children's Postdivorce Adjustment: No Simple Answers*, 31 FAM. & CONCILIATION CTS. REV. 29 (1993).

Joan B. Kelly, *Longer-Term Adjustment in Children of Divorce: Converging Findings and Implications for Practice*, 2 J. FAM. PSYCH. 119 (Dec. 1988).

Joan B. Kelly & Michael E. Lamb, *Developmental Issues in Relocation Cases Involving Young Children: When, Whether, and How?*, 17 J. FAM. PSYCH. 193 (2003).

Joan B. Kelly & Michael E. Lamb, Using Child Development Research to Make Appropriate Custody and Access Decisions for Young Children, 38 FAM. & CONCILIATION CTS. REV. 297, 309 (2000).

Robert F. Kelly & Sarah H. Ramsey, *Assessing and Communicating Social Science Information in Family and Child Judicial Settings: Standards for Judges and Allied Professionals*, 45 FAM. CT. REV. 22 (2007).

Michael E. Lamb, *Developmental Issues in Relocation Cases Involving Young Children: When, Whether, and How?*, 17 J. FAM. PSYCH. 193 (2003);

Michael E. Lamb, *Mothers, Fathers, Families, and Circumstances: Factors Affecting Children's Development*, 16 APPLIED DEVELOPMENTAL SCI. 98 (2012).

Michael E. Lamb, *Critical Analysis of Research on Parenting Plans and Children's Well-Being*, *in* PARENTING PLAN EVALUATIONS: APPLIED RESEARCH FOR THE FAMILY COURT 170 (Leslie Drozd, Michael Saini & Nancy Olesen eds., 2d ed. 2016).

Pamela S. Ludolph & Milfred D. Dale, *Attachment and Child Custody: An Additive Factor, Not a Determinative One*, 46(1) FAM. L.Q. 1 (2012).

Matheu D. Nunn & Jeralyn L. Lawrence, *Child Relocation: Case Law, Social Science, and Practice Implications*, 32 J. AM. ACAD. MATRIM. LAW. 383 (2020).

Robert Pasahow, *A Critical Analysis of the First Empirical Research Study on Child Relocation*, 19 J. AM. ACAD. MATRIM. LAW. 321 (2005).

Philip M. Stahl, *Emerging Issues in Relocation Cases*, 25 J. AM. ACAD. MATRIM. LAW. 425 (2013).

Matthew M. Stevenson et al., *Associations Between Parental Relocation Following Separation in Childhood and Maladjustment in Adolescence and Young Adulthood*, 24 PSYCH. PUB. POL'Y & L. 365 (2018).

Kenneth Waldron, *A Review of Social Science Research on Post Divorce Relocation*, 19 J. AM. ACAD. MATRIM. LAW. 337, 371 (2005).

JUDITH S. WALLERSTEIN, JULIA M. LEWIS & SANDERA BLAKESLEE, THE UNEXPECTED LEGACY OF DIVORCE: A 25 YEAR LANDMARK STUDY (2000).

JUDITH S. WALLERSTEIN & SANDERA BLAKESLEE, WHAT ABOUT THE KIDS? RAISING YOUR CHILDREN BEFORE, DURING AND AFTER DIVORCE (2003).

Judith Wallerstein & Julia Lewis, *The Unexpected Legacy of Divorce*, 21 PSYCHOANALYTIC PSYCH. 3, 353–70 (2004).

Judith Wallerstein & Tony J. Tanke, *To Move or Not to Move: Psychological and Legal Considerations in the Relocation of Children Following Divorce*, 30 FAM. L.Q. 305 (1996).

Richard A. Warshak, *Social Science and Children's Best Interests in Relocation Cases: Burgess Revisited*, 34 FAM. L.Q. 83 (2000).

Roger T. Webb, Carsten B. Pedersen & Pearl L.H. Mok, *Adverse Outcomes to Early Middle Age Linked with Childhood Residential Mobility*, AM. J. PREVENTIVE MED. (2016).

D. Wood et al., *Impact of Family Relocation on Children's Growth, Development, School Function, and Behavior*, 270 J. AM. MED. ASS'N 1334 (Sept. 15, 1993).

INDEX

Endnote information is indicated by n and note number following the page number.

A

D

H

I

N

O

P

Q

R

T